SELF PREPARATION GUIDE

PGT

COMPUTER SCIENCE

Recruitment Examination

Highly Useful for

KVS, NVS & other PGT Examinations

Compiled & Edited by
Arihant 'Expert Team'

ARIHANT PUBLICATIONS (INDIA) LIMITED

12. (c) We know that for short dipole,

field at axial point, $E_a = \frac{2p}{d^3}$

and field at equatorial point, $E_q = \frac{p}{d^3}$

So, $E_a = 2E_q$

13. (c)

We know that moment of inertia of a disc about its diameter is $= \frac{1}{4}mr^2$.

In the figure AB is a diameter. Which passes through centre of mass of the disc. CD is another axis which is parallel to AB and about which we shall have to calculate moment of inertia.

Now, from the theory of parallel axis

$$I = I_g + md^2 = \frac{1}{4}mr^2 + mr^2 = \frac{5mr^2}{4}$$

14. (a) Due to the charge inside a sphere of radius r only.

15. (b) $\frac{1}{f} = ({}^m\mu_g - 1)\left(\frac{1}{R_1} - \frac{1}{R_2}\right)$

$$\Rightarrow 1.25 = \left(\frac{1.5}{\mu_m} - 1\right)\left(\frac{1}{0.2} + \frac{1}{0.4}\right)$$

$$\Rightarrow \frac{1.25}{7.5} = \frac{1.5}{\mu_m} - 1 \Rightarrow \frac{7}{6} = \frac{1.5}{\mu_m} \Rightarrow \mu_m = \frac{9}{7}$$

16. (b) Acceleration $= \frac{d^2s}{dt^2} = \frac{2}{3}$ m/s^2

Force acting on the body

$= 3 \times \frac{2}{3} = 2$ newton

Displacement in 2 sec $= \frac{1}{3} \times 2 \times 2 = \frac{4}{3}$ m

Work done $= 2 \times \frac{4}{3} = \frac{8}{3}$ J

17. (d) Torque $= \frac{dL}{dt} = \frac{4A - A}{4} = \frac{3}{4}A$

[dL is change in angular momentum]

18. (a)

We have, $E - ir_1 = 0$ $\quad [\because V_{r_1} = 0]$

$\Rightarrow E = ir_1$

Now, $i = \frac{2E}{r_1 + r_2 + R}$

$$\Rightarrow \frac{E}{r_1} = \frac{2E}{r_1 + r_2 + R} \qquad \left[\because i = \frac{E}{r_1}\right]$$

$$\Rightarrow r_1 + r_2 + R = 2r_1 \Rightarrow R = r_1 - r_2$$

19. (d) We know that $\frac{g'}{g} = \frac{R^2}{(R+h)^2}$

$$\therefore \frac{g/9}{g} = \left[\frac{R}{R+h}\right]^2 \qquad \therefore \frac{R}{R+h} = \frac{1}{3}$$

$\therefore h = 2R$

20. (a) According to conservation of charge, the displacement current must be leftward.

21. (b) From Wien's displacement law,

$\lambda_{max} T =$ constant

$\therefore (\lambda_{max})_1 T_1 = (\lambda_{max})_2 T_2.$

$$\therefore (\lambda_{max})_2 = \frac{4800 \times 6000}{3000} \text{Å} = 9600\text{Å}$$

22. (b) Equation of S.H.M. is given by

$x = A\sin(\omega t + \delta)$

$(\omega t + \delta)$ is called phase.

When $x = \frac{A}{2}$, then

$\sin(\omega t + \delta) = \frac{1}{2}$

$\Rightarrow \omega t + \delta = \frac{\pi}{6}$

or $\phi_1 = \frac{\pi}{6}$

For second particle,

$\phi_2 = \pi - \frac{\pi}{6} = \frac{5\pi}{6}$

$\therefore \phi = \phi_2 - \phi_1 = \frac{4\pi}{6} = \frac{2\pi}{3}$

23. (c) Work done,

$$W = \Delta U = U_f - U_i = 0 - \left[\frac{-GMm}{R}\right]$$

$$W = \frac{6.67 \times 10^{-11} \times 100}{0.1} \times \frac{10}{1000}$$

$= 6.67 \times 10^{-10}$ J

24. (d) Helicopter's horizontal speed,

$u = 360 \times \frac{5}{18} = 100$ m/s

Horizontal displacement,

$x = u \times t = 2 \times 10^3$ m

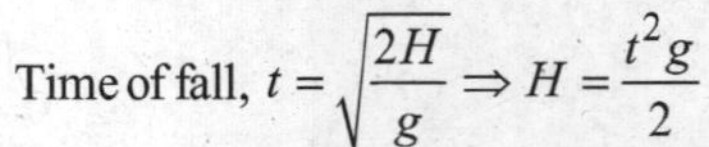

Time of fall, $t = \sqrt{\frac{2H}{g}} \Rightarrow H = \frac{t^2 g}{2}$

Altitude, $H = 2$ km $\Rightarrow H = 2000$ m

$D = \sqrt{x^2 + H^2} \Rightarrow D = 2\sqrt{2}$ km

25. **(b)** As we know, dU = F.dr

$$U = \int_0^r \alpha r^2 dr = \frac{ar^3}{3} \quad ...(i)$$

As, $\frac{mv^2}{r} = \alpha r^2$

$m^2v^2 = m\alpha r^3$

or, $2m(KE) = \frac{1}{2}\alpha r^3 \quad ...(ii)$

Total energy = Potential energy + kinetic energy
Now, from eqn (i) and (ii)
Total energy = K.E. + P.E.

$$= \frac{\alpha r^3}{3} + \frac{\alpha r^3}{2} = \frac{5}{6}\alpha r^3$$

26. **(d)** All the given phenomena are explained by kinetic theory of gases.

27. **(b)** The velocity of a transverse wave in a stretched wire is given by

$$v = \sqrt{\frac{T}{\mu}}$$

Where, T = Tension in the wire
μ = linear density of wire $\quad (\because V \propto T)$

$$\therefore \frac{v_1}{v_2} = \sqrt{\frac{T_1}{T_2}} \Rightarrow \frac{v}{v} \times 2 = \sqrt{\frac{2.06\times10^4}{T_2}}$$

$$\Rightarrow T_2 = \frac{2.06\times10^4}{4} = 0.515\times10^4 N \Rightarrow T_2 = 5.15\times10^3 N$$

28. **(a)** The magnetic field of a plane electromagnetic wave is given by $\vec{B} = 2\times10^{-8}\sin(0.5\times10^3 x + 1.5\times10^{11}t)\hat{j}T$
The amplitude of the electric field would be
$|E| = c|B| = 3\times10^8\times2\times10^{-8}$
$\Rightarrow |E| = 6\ Vm^{-1}$ along x-axis.

29. **(b)** The work done = force × displacement
$\therefore$ unit, $u_1 = Fs$ and $u_2 = 4F\times4s = 16u$.

30. **(b)** $S_1 = \frac{1}{2}g\left(\frac{1}{2}\right)^2, S_1 + S_2 = g(1)^2$

$$\frac{1}{2}g\left(\frac{3}{2}\right)^2 = S + S_2 + S_3$$

31. **(c)**

32. **(b)** Let W newton be the load suspended. Then

$$Y = \frac{(W/A_1)}{(\ell_1/L)} = \frac{WL}{A_1\ell_1} \quad ...(1)$$

and $$Y = \frac{(W/A_2)}{(\ell_2/L)} = \frac{WL}{A_2\ell_2} \quad ....(2)$$

Dividing equation (1) by equation (2), we get

$$1 = \left(\frac{\ell_2}{\ell_1}\right)\left(\frac{A_2}{A_1}\right) = \left(\frac{\ell_2}{\ell_1}\right)\left(\frac{2}{1}\right)$$

$$\therefore \frac{\ell_1}{\ell_2} = \frac{2}{1} \text{ or } \ell_1 : \ell_2 = 2:1$$

33. **(c)** In the uniform magnetic field, radius of the circular path is given by;

$$R = \frac{mv}{qB} = \frac{\sqrt{2m(K.E)}}{qB}$$

$$\Rightarrow R \propto \frac{\sqrt{m}}{q}; \ (\because \text{KE in same})$$

$$\therefore \frac{R_{deutron}}{R_{proton}} = \sqrt{\frac{m_d}{m_p}} \times \frac{q_p}{q_d} \because m_d = 2m_p \text{ and } q_d = q_p$$

$$\therefore \frac{R_d}{R_p} = \sqrt{\frac{2m_p}{m_p}} \times \frac{q_p}{q_p} = \sqrt{2} \therefore R_d : R_p = \sqrt{2}:1$$

34. **(b)** Given,
Angle of contact $\theta = 30°$
Surface tension, $T = 0.05\ Nm^{-1}$
Radius of capillary tube, $r = 0.15$ mm $= 0.15\times10^{-3}$m
Density of methylene iodide, $\rho = 667\ kg\ m^{-3}$

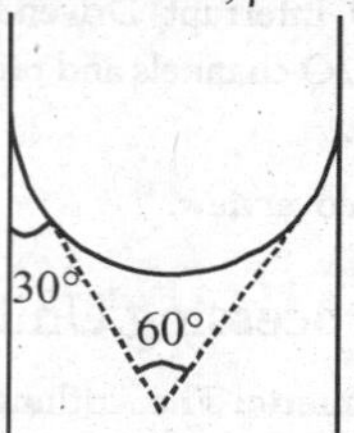

Capillary rise, $h = \frac{2T\cos\theta}{\rho gr}$

$$= \frac{2\times0.05\times\frac{\sqrt{3}}{2}}{667\times10\times0.15\times10^{-3}} = 0.087\ m$$

35. **(b)** Mean free path, $\lambda = \frac{1}{\sqrt{2}\pi nd^2}$
where, d = diameter of the molecule
n = number of molecules per unit volume

But, mean time of collision, $\tau = \frac{\lambda}{v_{rms}}$

But $v_{rms} = \sqrt{\frac{3kT}{R}}$

$$\therefore \tau = \frac{\lambda}{\sqrt{\frac{3kT}{m}}} \Rightarrow t \propto \frac{1}{\sqrt{T}}$$

36. **(b)** Dipole mement, $|\vec{P}| = qd$
$= 0.01\times0.4\times10^{-3} = 4\times10^{-6}$

And torque, $|\vec{\tau}| = PE\sin\theta$

$$= 4\times10^{-6}\times10\times10^{-5}\times\sin30 = 4\times10^{-6+5+1}\times\frac{1}{2}$$

$$\therefore |\vec{\tau}| = 2\times10^{-10}$$

37. **(b)** $L = \mu_0 nI$

$\therefore \quad \frac{L_2}{L_1} = \frac{\mu}{\mu_0}$ ----($\because$ n and I are same)

$\therefore \quad L_2 = \mu_r L_1 = 900\times0.18 = 162$ mH

SYLLABUS

COMPUTER SYSTEM ARCHITECTURE

The Computer System

- **System Buses:** Computer components, Computer function, Interconnection structures, Bus interconnection, PCI.
- **Internal Memory:** Computer memory system overview, Semiconductor main memory, Cache memory, Advanced DRAM organisation.
- **Input/Output:** External devices, I/O modules, programmed I/O, Interrupt- Driven I/O, Direct memory access, I/O channels and producers, The external interface.
- Operating system overview.

The Central Processing Unit

- **Computer Arithmetic:** The Arithmetic and Logic Unit (ALU), Integer arithmetic, Floating-point representation, Floating-point arithmetic.
- **Instruction Sets:** Characteristics and function, Machine instruction characteristics, Types of operands, Types of operation, Addressing modes and formats, Register organisation, The instruction cycle, Instruction pipelining.
- **Assembly Language**
- **The Control Unit:** Micro-operations, control of the CPU, hardwired Implementation, Microprogram Controller, Basic Concepts, Microinstructions, Sequencing, Microinstruction Execution.
- **Reduced Instruction Set Computer:** An Introduction.

OPERATING SYSTEM

- **Introduction:** System software, resource abstraction, OS strategies; multiprogramming, batch, time sharing, personal computers and workstation, process control & real time systems, processes & threads using FORK, JOIN, QUIT.
- **Operating System Organization:** Factors in operating system design, basic OS function, implementation consideration: process modes, kernels, methods of requesting system services, device drivers.
- **Device Management:** Service management approaches, buffering, device drivers, performance tuning.
- **Process Management:** System view of the process and resources, initiating the OS, process address space, process abstraction, resource abstraction, process hierarchy.
- **Scheduling:** Scheduling mechanisms, Strategy selection, non-preemptive and preemptive strategies.
- **Synchronization Principles:** Interactive processes, critical section, deadlock, coordinating processes, semaphores, spread memory, multiprocessors, events, monitors and the inter-process communication.
- **Deadlocks:** System deadlock model, prevention strategies, hold and wait, circular wait, allowing pre-emption, Banker's Algorithm, serially reusable resources, consumable resources, general resources system recovery.
- **Memory Management:** Mapping address space to memory space, memory allocation strategies, fixed partition, variable partition, segmentation.
- **File Management:** Directory structure, basic file operations and their implementation.
- **Protection and Security:** Policy mechanism, authentication, internal access authorization.

DIGITAL ELECTRONICS

- **Fundamental Concepts:** Digital signal, NAND, NOR and Exclusive-OR operation, Boolean algebra, Basic digital circuits.
- **Number System and Codes:** Primary, Octal, Hexadecimal, Signed numbers codes, hamming codes.
- **Combinational Logic Design:** K-map representation of logical functions and simplification using K-map of 4 and 5 variables, Quine- McCluskey's method.
- Multiplexers, Demultiplexers, Adders and subtracters, multipliers, Comparators, Parity generators and checkers, Code converters, Priority encoders, Decoders, Races, hazards and asynchronous behaviour
- **Flip-Flops:** Clocked RS flip flop, D-type flip flop, Excitation table of flip flop, Edge triggered flip flop, Clocked flip flop design.
- **Sequential Logic Designs:** Registers, Shift registers, Asynchronous counters, synchronous counters, RAM, ROM.

PROGRAMMING FUNDAMENTALS

- **Basic Computer Organization:** Functional units, Basic I/O devices and storage devices; Representation of integers, real (fixed and floating point), Characters (ASCII and Unicode); Basic operations of a programming environment.
- **Problem Solving Approaches:** Notion of an algorithm, Problem solving using top-down design and decomposition into sub-problems, Stepwise methodology of developing an algorithm, Methodology of developing an algorithmic solution from a Mathematical specification of the problem, use of recursion for problems with inductive characterization.
- **Programming using a Modern Programming Language such as Java, Emphasizing the following Notions: Building Blocks:** Arithmetic and logical expression, Variables, Assignment; Specifying the input-output interface (type); Control structures including sequencing, Conditionals, Loops, Procedural abstractions (procedures, methods); Basic data structures-integers, Reals, Strings and arrays-and internal representation of scalar and vector data; Data abstraction and encapsulation-objects, Classes and packages; Input/output of data.
- Numerical and non-numerical applications using above concepts.

PROGRAMMING TOOL : VISUAL BASIC

- **Introduction to Programming** : Modular programming, Object oriented programming, Event driven programming:
- About Visual Basic (Object based programming language), Rapid application development using Visual basic;
- Concept of project in visual basic, VB project options- Standard EXE, ActiveX DLL, ActiveX EXE, ActiveX control, ActiveX document EXE, Addin, VB application wizard, IIS application, DHTML application;
- Getting familiar with Visual Basic user interface-Pull-Down menus, Toolbar, Toolbox, Project Explorer, Properties window, Form Layout window, Form, Immediate window;
- Opening and Closing window, Resizing and moving windows, Docking windows; Quitting Visual Basic;
- **Visual Basic tool box** (Standard window controls): Pointer, Picture Box, Lbel, Text Box, Frame, Command Button, Check Box, Option Button, Combo Box, List Box, Horizontal Scrollbar, Vertical Scrollbar, Timer, Drive List box, Directory List box, File List Box, Shape, Line, Image, Data, OLE;
- Object Naming Conventions, Event Procedures;
- **Data Types:** Integer, Long, Single, Double, Currency, String, Byte, Boolean, Date, Object, Variant;
- **Variables:** Need to use variable, Declaring variables, Variable naming convention, Assigning value to variables, Data types of variable, Scope and lifetime of variables (Public and Private);
- **Menu Editor :** Concept of menus, Shortcut menus and Popup menus, Designing menu system, Menu editor dialog box options (Name, Index, Shortcut, Help Context ID, Negotiate Position, Checked, Enabled, Visible, Window List, Right Arrow, Left Arrow, Up Arrow, Down Arrow, Menu List, Next, Insert, Delete, OK, Cancel), To Create Menu Controls in the Menu Editor, Menu Naming Conventions, Setting the Name Property, Creating a Menu Control Array, Creating Sub Menus, Separating Menu Controls, Assigning Access Keys and Shortcut Keys, Controlling Menus at Runtime-Enabling and Disabling Menu Commands, Displaying a Checkmark on a Menu Control, Making a Menu Control Invisible, Adding Menu Control at Runtime, Displaying Pop-Up Menu;
- **General Controls** (Advance)**:** Image list, Common dialog box, ADO DC, DB Combo, Media Player Control, DB Grid;
- **Adding a Toolbar:** Creating an image list, Adding images to the toolbar, To Add Code for the toolbar buttons;
- **Adding Status Bar:** Adding status bar panels, Adding time on the panel.
- **Dialog Boxes:** Pre-defined dialog box, Custom dialog box;

DATA STRUCTURES

- Introduction to the object-based and object-oriental programming paradigms; records, abstract data types and objects, data abstraction and internal representation;
- **Programming-in-the-Large Issues:** Modularity and code re-usability, Classes and packages; Graphical user interfaces; Command-line arguments; Interfacing with libraries and separate compilation;
- **Language Support and OOP:** Sub-typing, Inheritance, Classes and subclasses, Header files, Function templates, overloading.
- **Programming with Data structures:** Stacks, Queues, Lists, Trees and balanced binary trees, Specification of exception conditions and exception handling, Notion of efficient algorithmic solution, Efficient representations of data structures (e.g. sparse arrays), Algorithms for searching and sorting.

75. (d) Acidic strength ∝ –I, –M effect. Due to strong – I, and –M effect of three – $COOCH_3$ groups, it has most acidic Hydrogen.

76. (d) A – IV, B – I, C – II, D – III

77. (c) Gluconic acid is obtained by partial oxidation of glucose by mild oxidising agent e.g. Tollen's reagent, Fehling solution, Br_2 water.

$$\underset{\text{Glucose}}{\begin{matrix} CHO \\ | \\ (CHOH)_4 \\ | \\ CH_2OH \end{matrix}} \xrightarrow{Br_2\text{ water}} \underset{\text{Gluconic acid}}{\begin{matrix} COOH \\ | \\ (CHOH)_4 \\ | \\ CH_2OH \end{matrix}}$$

Gluconic acid can not form hemiacetal or acetal.

78. (a) Aldehydes, other than formaldehyde, when treated with RMgX give 2° alcohols

79. (a)

80. (c) Copper is present in brass, bronze and german silver.

81. (d)

$$\underset{\substack{(C_3H_6Cl_2) \\ (I)}}{H_3C-\overset{Cl}{\underset{Cl}{C}}-CH_3} \xrightarrow[\text{(aq.)}]{KOH} \underset{\text{Unstable}}{CH_3-\overset{OH}{\underset{OH}{C}}-CH_3}$$

$$\xrightarrow{KOH} \underset{(II)}{CH_3-\overset{O}{\overset{\|}{C}}-CH_3} \xrightarrow[\text{(II) } H_2O/H^+]{\text{(I) } CH_3MgBr}$$

$$\underset{3^\circ\text{ alcohol}}{CH_3-\overset{OH}{\underset{CH_3}{C}}-CH_3} \xrightarrow[\text{Lucas Test}]{\text{Anhy. } ZnCl_2 + HCl} \text{Gives turbidity immediately}$$

82. (d) Each anions have particular confirmatory test.

- CO_3^{2-} ion will evolve $CO_2(g)$ which will turns lime water milky.
- S^{2-} ion will give $H_2S(g)$, that turns lead acetate paper black.
- SO_3^{2-} ion will give $SO_2(g)$, which turns acidified potassium dichromate solution green.
- NO_2^- ion will give brown fumes of $NO_2(g)$, which turns KI solution blue.

83. (b) Follow ECS, more the reduction potential, the stronger the oxidising power and vice versa.

84. (d) HVZ reactions = Br_2 / red P
Iodoform reaction = NaOH + I_2
Etard reaction = (i) CrO_2Cl_2, CS_2 (ii) H_2O
Gattermann–Koch Reaction = CO, HCl, Anhydrous, $AlCl_3$

85. (d) $k = \dfrac{2.303}{t}\log\dfrac{a}{a-x}$

$$= \frac{2.303}{24}\log\frac{1}{\frac{1}{8}} = \frac{2.303}{24}\log\frac{8}{1}\,\text{min}^{-1}$$

86. (c)

$$\underset{\substack{(A) \\ C_9H_{10}O}}{C_6H_5-CH_2-O-CH=CH_2} \xrightarrow{HI} \underset{(B)}{C_6H_5-CH_2-I} + \underset{(C)}{CH_2=CH-OH} \xrightleftharpoons{\text{Tauto-merisation}} \underset{(D)}{CH_3-CH=O}$$

(D) → +ve Iodoform test

(B) $\xrightarrow{AgNO_3}$ $\underset{\text{Yellow ppt.}}{AgI\downarrow} + C_6H_5-CH_2-ONO_2$

87. (b) $M = \dfrac{K_b \times w \times 1000}{\Delta T_b \times W}$

$$= \frac{2.16 \times 0.11 \times 1000}{0.1 \times 15} = 158.4$$

88. (d) To calculate the value of K_4 in the given equation we should apply :
eqn. (2) + eqn.(3) × 3 – eqn. (1)

hence $K_4 = \dfrac{K_2K_3^3}{K_1}$

89. (c) Generally, the ionization enthalpies or energy increases from left to right in a period and decreases from top to bottom in a group. Several factor such as atomic radius, nuclear charge, shielding effect are responsible for change of ionization enthalpies.
Here, Ist ionization enthalpy of *A* and *B* is greater than group I (Li 520 kJmol^{-1} to Cs374 kJmol^{-1}), which means element *A* and *B* belong to group –2 and all three given ionization enthalpy values are less for element *B* means *B* will come below *A*.

90. (b) Desired eqn;

$$C_2H_4 + 3O_2 \longrightarrow 2CO_2 + 2H_2O$$

$$\Delta H = 2(-394) + 2(-286) - (52) = -1412\,kJ$$

PART-III: BIOLOGY

91. (b) According to rules of binomial nomenclature, correctly written scientific name of mango is Mangifera indica Linn. This system of nomenclature was given by Carl Linnaeus. The scientific name of mango is given as Mangifera indica Linn. Mangifera indicates the 'genus' while indica represents a particular species or 'specific epithet' and Linn indicates the Biologist Linnaeus who first described the species of mango.

92. (d) Kingdom animalia includes all heterotrophic, multicellular complex eukaryotes. They depend either upon plants or on other animals for their food requirements. Kingdom monera includes prokaryotic organisms lacking membrane bound nucleus. Hence, nuclear membrane cannot be found in Monera. Protista is a eukaryotic kingdom.

93. (a) A – III, B – IV, C – I, D – II

94. (c) All the spores are of similar kinds in majority of the pteridophytes; such plants are called homosporous. Genera like *Selaginella* and *Salvinia* produce two kinds of spores i.e. macro (large) spores and micro (small) spores, hence, are known as heterosporous.

95. (b) Radioactive labelling with Carbon-14 (C-14)

96. (a)

97. (c)

98. (a) Meiosis I is known as reductional division due to reduction in the number of chromosomes. Meiosis II is called equational division because of maintaining the same number of chromosomes.

99. (b)

100. (c) Crossing over leads to recombination between homologous chromosomes. Recombination is the rearrangement of genetic information within and among DNA molecules.

101. (c) In the non-cyclic photophosphorylation pathway the PSI receives electrons from PSII. The PSII receives electrons from photolytic dissociation of water. The formation of NADPH is associated with PSI and not- with the PSII, hence statement (c) is incorrect. The reaction centre of PSI is called P700 and that of PSII is P680 respectively.

102. (b) Repeated or repetitive sequences make up a large portion of human genome. These sequences are nucleotide sequences that are repeated many times, sometimes hundred to thousand times. They have no direct coding function but provide informations as to chromosome structure, dynamics and evolution.

103. (d) 104. (a) 105. (d) 106. (d)

107. (a) Natural auxin are naturally occurring auxin plants hormone which is called phytohormones. Eg. IAA and IBA. These are synthesized in shoot apices, leaf primordial and developing seeds from tryptophan. Some of the important synthetic auxins are 2, 4-D; 2, 4, 5-T (2, 4, 5-trichlorophenoxy acetic acid).

108. (c) Integument & nucellus are diploid develop from sporophytic tissue

109. (b) Awareness and preventive measures

110. (d) Gemmae are a means of asexual reproduction found in many bryophytes (e.g, liverworts). They are 1 to many celled, specially produced clonal plant fragments. They are green asexual buds which develop in small receptacles (called gemma cups) located on the thalli. Gemmae become detached from the parent body and germinate to form new individuals.

111. (a) 112. (b)

113. (d) Order being higher category is the assemblage of families which exhibit a few similar characteristics.
Dog (*Canis familaris*) and Cat (*Felis domesticus*) belong to two different families—Cancideae and Felidae respectively.

114. (b)

115. (b)

116. (b) Diploid cell produces haploid cell by meiosis. It occurs due to synapsis. A chromosome has two chromatids, hence a bivalent has 4 chromatids.

117. (b) Ex-situ conservation is the conservation of selected organism in places outside their natural homes. They include off site collection and gene banks.

118. (d)

119. (b) Protein synthesis takes place in ribosomes, which are attached to surface of endoplasmic reticulum by ribophorin-I and ribophorin-II. About 50 hydrolytic enzymes are found in the lysosome. They include proteases, nucleases, glycosidases, lipases, phospholipases, phosphatases and sulphatases. All lysosomal enzymes are acid hydrolases and optimally active at pH-5.

120. (b) 121. (a)

122. (d) The term 'auxin' is applied to the indole-3-acetic acid (IAA), and to other natural and synthetic compounds having certain growth regulating properties. Cytokinin has specific effects on cytokinesis, & was discovered as kinetin (a modified form of adenine) from the autoclaved herring sperm DNA. Gibberellic acid is a simple gibberellin, a pentacyclic diterpene acid promoting growth and elongation of cells.

123. (b) 124. (b)

125. (c) ***Metaphase chromosome*** is made up of two sister chromatids which are held together by the centromere. Chromosomes are moved to spindle equator and gets aligned along metaphase plate through spindle fibres to both poles.

126. (d) 127. (a) 128. (d)

129. (d)

(a) Chromatids separate but remains in the centre of the cell in metaphase.

(b) Chromatids start moving towards opposite poles in anaphase.

(c) Golgi complex and endoplasmic reticulum are still visible at the end of telophase.

130. (c) C_4 plants are more efficient in picking up CO_2 even when it is found in low concentration because of its high affinity for PEP. They show kranz anatomy i.e. vascular bundle is surrounded by bundle sheath and mesopyll cells.

131. (a) 132. (a)

133. (c) By aiding in the design of cochlear implants and hearing aids.

134. (c)

135. (a) Double fertilisation is a characteristic feature of angiosperms. It involves two fusions in which one male gamete fuses with egg cell to form zygote and other male gamete fuses with the diploid secondary nucleus to produce triploid primary endosperm nucleus.

136. (a) Plasmids are small intranuclear circular DNAs which carry extra chromosomal genes in bacteria.

137. (c)

- **Advance Program Development Methodology:** System Development life cycle, Relational database concept, Relational database, Management system, data models (Entity Relationship Model), Entity and entity set, Attributes (Single, Composite and Multi-Valued), Relationship (One-to-One, One-to-Many and Many-to-Many), Entity relationship modeling conventions, Communicating with an RDBMS using SQL, Relational database management system, SQL statements, About programming language in SQL.
- Data dictionary, Data warehousing, Data mining, Meta data.
- **Object Modeling:** Introduction to object oriented modeling using unified modeling language (Concepts only).
- **Client Server Computing:** Concept of client server computing.

WEB DEVELOPMENT

1. HTML/ DHTML

- Introduction, Objectives, Introduction to Universal Resource Identifier (URI) – Fragment identifiers and relative URI's, History of HTML, SGML, Structure of HTML/ DHTML document, Switching between opened windows and browser (Container tag, Empty tag, Attribute);

- **Basic Tags of HTML :** HTML, HEAD, TITLE, BODY (Setting the Font colour and Background colour, Background Image, Background sound), Heading tag (H1 to H6) and attributes (Align), FONT tag and attributes (Size: 1 to 7 Levels, BASEFONT, SMALL, BIG, COLOR), P, BR, Comment in HTML (<!>), Formatting text (B, I, U, EM, BLOCKQUOTE, PREFORMATTED, SUB, SUP, STRIKE), Ordered list-OL (L1, Type-1, I, A, a; START, VALUE), Unordered list-UL (Bullet type- Disc, Circle, Square, DL, DT, DD), ADDRESS tag.

- **Creating Links:** Link to other HTML documents or data objects, Links to other places in the HTML documents, Links to places in other HTML documents.

- Anchor Tag<A HREF> and <A NAME>, Inserting Inline Images <IMG ALIGN, SRC, WIDTH, HEIGHT, ALT, Image Link, Horizontal Rules <HR ALIGN, WIDTH, SIZE, NOSHADE>.

2. Web Page Authoring Using HTML

- **Tables:** Creating Tables, Border, TH,TR, TD, CELLSPACING, CELLPADDING, WIDTH, COLSPAN, CAPTION, ALIGN, CENTER.

- **Frames:** Percentage dimensions, Relative dimensions, Frame- Src, Frameborder, height and width, Creating two or more rows Frames <FRAMESET ROWS>, Creating two or more Columns Frames <FRAMESET COLS>, <FRAME NAME SRC MARGINHEIGHT MARGINWIDTH SCROLLING AUTO NORESIZE>, <NOFRAMES>, </NOFRAMES>.

- **Forms:** Definition, Use- Written to a file, submitted to a database such as MS-Access or Oracle, E-mailed to someone in particular, Forms involve two way communication.

- **From Tags:** FORM, <SELECT NAME, SIZE, MULTIPLE/ SINGLE> <OPTION>...</SELECT>, <TEXTAREA NAME ROWS COLS>, </TEXTAREA>, METHOD, CHECKBOX, HIDDEN, IMAGE, RADIO, RESET, SUBMIT, INPUT <VALUE, SRC, CHECKED, SIZE, MAXLENGTH, ALIGN>.

3. Document Object Model

- Concept and importance of Document Object Model, Dynamic HTML document and Document Object Model, Cascading Style Sheets.

- Introduction to Cascading Style Sheet (CSS), Three ways of introducing the style sheets to your document, Basic Syntax; Creating and saving cascading style sheets. <STYLE> tag, Examples showing the linking of external style sheet files to a document; Inline and Embed, <DIV>tag; COLOR, BACKGROUND-COLOR, FONT-FAMILY, FONT-STYLE, FONT SIZE and FONT-VARIANT; FONT- WEIGHT, WORD-SPACING, LETTER-SPACING, TEXT DECORATION, VERTICAL-ALIGN, TEXT-TRANSFORM; TEXT-ALIGN, TEXT-INDENT, line height, Introduction to Margin, Padding and Border.

- Margins (all values), MARGIN- PROPERTY, PADDIND (all values), PADDING-PROPERTY; BORDER (all values), BORDER-PROPERTY, BACKGROUND-IMAGE, BACKGROUND-REPEAT; Additional Features, Grouping Style Sheets, Assigning Classes; Introduction to Layers, <LAYER>, </LAYER> tag.

4. eXtensible Markup Language (XML)

- **XML:** Introduction, Features of XML, XML can be used with exiting protocols, Supports a wide variety of applications, Compatible with SGML, XML documents are reasonably clear to the layperson.
- **Structure of XML:** Logical Structure, Physical Structure.
- **XML Markup:** Element markup i.e (<foo>Hello</foo>), Attribute markup i.e. (<!element.name property="value">).
- **Naming Rules:** used for elements and attributes, and for all the descriptors, Comments Entity
- **Declarations:** <! ENTITY name "replacement text">.
- **Element Declarations:** <! ELEMENT name content>.
- **Empty Elements:** <! ELEMENT empty. element EMPTY>.
- **Unrestricted Elements:** <! ELEMENT any. element ANY>.
- **Element Content Models:** Element Sequences i.e. <! ELEMENT counting (first, second, third, fourth)>.
- Element Choices <! ELEMENT choose (this.one/ that.one)>, Combined Sequences and Choices.
- **Element Occurrence Indicators:** Discussion of three occurrence indicators
- ? (Question Mark)
- * (Asterisk Sign)
- + (Plus Sign)
- **Character Content:** PCDATA (Parseable Character data) <! ELEMENT text (#PCDATA), Document Type Declaration (DTD) and validation.
- **Developing a DTD:** Modify and existing SGML DTD, Developing a DTD from XML Code, either automatically or manually.
- **Viewing:** Viewing XML in Internet Explorer, Viewing XML using the XML data source object XSL (Extensible Style Sheet Language) or CSS (Cascading Style Sheet).
- **Browse the records:** Single record at a time (Using buttons), Multiple record at a time (Using an HTML Table).

5. Active Server Pages (ASP)

- **Active Server Pages (ASP):** Concept of ASP, Features of ASP, Other equivalent tools-JSP, PHP.
- **Constants:** String and Numeric.
- **Data Types:** Integer, Floating point (Single, Double), String, Date, Boolean, Currency, Variant, Object.
- **Variables:** Explicit and Implicit Declaration;
- Operators:
- **Arithmetic:** +, - (Unary and Binary), *, /, \(integer division) mod,^.
- **Comparison:** <, >, <=, >=, <>, =.
- **Logical:** AND, OR, NOT, XOR, EQV, IMP.
- **String Operator:** & or + (for Concatenation).
- Functions:
- **Conversion Functions:** Abs (), Cbool (), CByte (), Cint(), CStr (), CSng (), CLng (), Cdate ().
- **String Manipulation Functions:** Ucase (), Lcase (), Len (), Left (), Right (), Mid (), Ltrim (), InStr(), Rtrim (), Ltrim ().
- **Time & Date Functions:** Date (), Day(), Hour (), Left (), Len (), Minute (), Month (), Monthname (), Now ().
- **Arrays:** Declaration and use of 1 dimensional and 2 dimensional arrays.
- **Controls:** OF..THEN, IF..THEN..ELSE..END IF, IF..THEN..ELSEIF..THEN..END IF, SELECT..CASE..END SELECT, FOR ..NEXT, FOR EACH..NEXT, DO WHILE.. LOOP, DO..LOOP WHILE, DO UNTIL. LOOP.
- Procedures and Functions, Passing parameters/ arguments.
- Concept of object model structure (client to server and server to client).
- **Objects:** Properties, Methods, Events, Setting Object properties, Retrieving Object properties, calling objects/ methods.
- **Types of Objects:** Response, Request, Application, Session, Server, ASP Error.
- **Response Object:** Write method, Addheader, Append To Log, Binary Write, Using Shortcuts <%=value/ expr%>.
- **Controlling information:** Buffer, Flush Clear, End.
- **Request Object:** Request object collection: Querystring, Form, ServerVariables, Cookies, Client Certificate.

13. (b) For a diamagnetic material, the value of μ_r is slightly less than one. For any material, the value of $\in_r$ is always greater than 1.

14. (a) We know that
Maximum velocity = ωA
Their velocity are same
$\omega_1 A_1 = \omega_2 A_2 = \omega_3 A_3$

15. (a) $F = 20t - 5t^2$

$\therefore \alpha = \frac{FR}{I} = 4t - t^2 \Rightarrow \frac{d\omega}{dt} = 4t - t^2$

$\Rightarrow \int_0^{\omega} d\omega = \int_0^{t} (4t - t^2) dt$

$\Rightarrow \omega = 2t^2 - \frac{t^3}{3}$ (as $\omega = 0$ at $t = 0$, 6s)

$\int_0^{\theta} d\theta = \int_0^{6} \left(2t^2 - \frac{t^3}{3}\right) dt$

$\Rightarrow \theta = 36 \text{ rad} \Rightarrow n = \frac{36}{2\pi} < 6$

16. (c) $q = 1\mu C = 1 \times 10^{-6} C$
$r = 4 \text{ cm} = 4 \times 10^{-2} \text{ m}$

Potential $V = \frac{kq}{r} = \frac{9 \times 10^9 \times 10^{-6}}{4 \times 10^{-2}} = 2.25 \times 10^5$ V.

Induced electric field $E = -\frac{kq}{r^2}$

$= \frac{9 \times 10^9 \times 1 \times 10^{-6}}{16 \times 10^{-4}} = -5.625 \times 10^6$ V/m

17. (a) By Einstein's equation of photo-electric effect, the maximum kinetic energy of emitted photo-electrons is given by

$E_k = h\nu - W$ or $E_k = \frac{hc}{\lambda} - W$

Where, h = Planck's constant
ν = frequency of incident light
W = work function of metal
λ = wavelength of incident light

$E_k = \frac{6.6 \times 10^{-34} \times 3 \times 10^8}{2000 \times 10^{-10} \times 1.6 \times 10^{-19}}$ eV 4.2eV

So, E_k = 2eV

18. (c) For maximum current, $X_L = X_C$

i.e., $\frac{1}{2\pi f C} = 2\pi f L$

$\Rightarrow \quad C = \frac{1}{4\pi^2 f^2 L} = \frac{1}{4 \times \pi^2 \times 49 \times 10^6 \times 2 \times 10^{-6}}$

$\Rightarrow \quad C = \frac{1}{3872}$ F

x = 3872

19. (b)

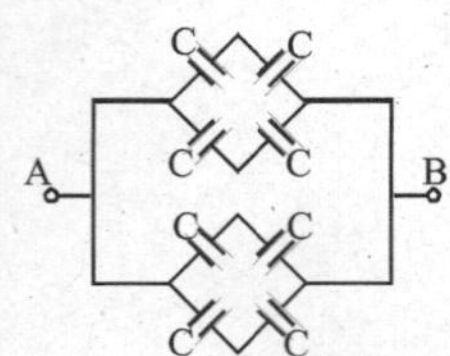

The figure shows two independent balanced wheatstone Brides connected in parallel each having a capacitance C. So, $C_{net} = C_{AB} = 2C$

20. (c) Silicon is an indirect-band gap semi- conductor.

CB
Donar level
VB

21. (c) Given,
Mass of cricket ball, m = 150 g
Speed of cricket ball, V = 20 m/s

Force, $F = \frac{\Delta P}{\Delta t} = \frac{(mv - 0)}{0.1} = \frac{150 \times 20}{1000 \times 0.1} = 30$ N

22. (d) $E = \frac{G \times 1}{1^2} + \frac{G \times 1}{2^2} + \frac{G \times 1}{4^2} + \ldots +$

P 1 kg 1 kg 1 kg
1 m
2 m
4 m

$E = G\left[1 + \frac{1}{4} + \frac{1}{16} + \ldots\right] \Rightarrow E = G \frac{1}{1 - \frac{1}{4}} = \frac{4G}{3}$

23. (c) $W = \frac{\pi r_1 r_2}{2} = \frac{\pi \times 1 \times 1}{2} = \pi/2$ J

24. (a) On comparing the given equation to

$\vec{E} = a_0 \hat{i} \cos(\omega t - kz)$

$\omega = 6 \times 10^8$,

$k = \frac{2\pi}{r} = \frac{\omega}{c}$

$k = \frac{\omega}{c} = \frac{6 \times 10^8}{3 \times 10^8} = 2 \text{ m}^{-1}$

25. (d) As range and maximum height are equal, R = H

$\Rightarrow \frac{2v_x - v_y}{g} = \frac{v_y^2}{2g}$

$\Rightarrow v_x = \frac{v_y}{4} \Rightarrow u\cos\theta = \frac{u \sin\theta}{4} \Rightarrow \tan\theta = 4$

26. (c) Field at Q is E. So, force on Q = QE
This force will be applied on –2Q. Also according to Coulomb's law. So, field at –2Q is $\frac{QE}{-2Q} = -\frac{E}{2}$.

27. (a)

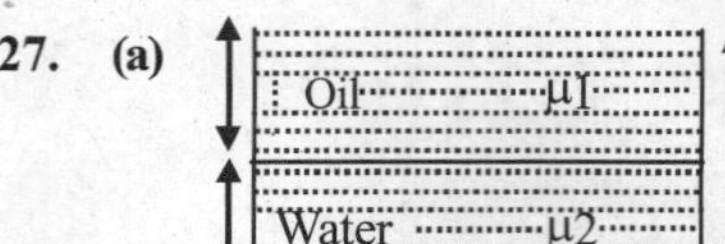

As refractive index, $\mu = \frac{\text{Real depth}}{\text{Apparent depth}}$

$\therefore$ Apparent depth of the vessel when viewed from above is

$$d_{\text{apparent}} = \frac{x}{2\mu_1} + \frac{x}{2\mu_2} = \frac{x}{2}\left(\frac{1}{\mu_1} + \frac{1}{\mu_2}\right)$$

$$= \frac{x}{2}\left(\frac{\mu_2 + \mu_1}{\mu_1\mu_2}\right) = \frac{x(\mu_1 + \mu_2)}{2\mu_1\mu_2}$$

28. **(d)** 1st process is isothermal expansion which is only correct shown in option (d)
2nd process is isobaric compression which is correctly shown in option (d)

29. **(b)** As $R = \frac{mv}{qB} = \frac{\sqrt{2m(K.E)}}{qB} \Rightarrow q \propto \frac{\sqrt{m}}{R}$

$$\Rightarrow \frac{q_1}{q_2} = \sqrt{\frac{m_1}{m_2}} \times \frac{R_2}{R_1} = \sqrt{\frac{9}{4}} \times \frac{5}{6} = \frac{3}{2} \times \frac{5}{6} = \frac{5}{4}$$

30. **(b)** Let the final temperature be T

Heat gained by ice $= mL + m \times s \times (T - 0)$

$= 10 \times 80 + 10 \times 1 \times T$

Heat lost by water $= 55 \times 1 \times (40 - T)$

By using law of calorimetery,

$800 + 10T = 55 \times (40 - T)$

$\Rightarrow T = 21.54°C = 22°C$

31. **(a)** In an isothermal process, the temperature remains constant. So, the internal energy remains same.
If the gas is expanded by adding more molecules to it then the internal energy of the gas increases.

32. **(d)** Given: $Z = \frac{a^2 b^{2/3}}{\sqrt{c d^3}}$

Percentage error in z,

$$\frac{\Delta z}{z} = \frac{2\Delta a}{a} + \frac{2}{3}\frac{\Delta b}{b} + \frac{1}{2}\frac{\Delta c}{c} + \frac{3\Delta d}{d}$$

$$= 2 \times 2 + \frac{2}{3} \times 1.5 + \frac{1}{2} \times 4 + 3 \times 2.5 = 14.5\%.$$

33. **(d)** The fringe width in Young's double slit experiment is

$$\beta = \frac{\lambda D}{d}$$

where λ is the wavelength of light used. D is the distance between slit and screen. d is the distance between the slit.

$$\beta' = \frac{\lambda(2D)}{d/2} = 4\frac{\lambda D}{d} = 4\beta$$

34. **(b)** (A) Surface Tension $= \frac{F}{\ell} = \frac{MLT^{-2}}{L} = MT^{-2}$

$= Kgs^{-2}$

(B) Pressure $= \frac{F}{A} = \frac{MLT^{-2}}{L^2} = Kgm^{-1}s^{-2}$

(C) Viscosity $= \frac{F}{A\left(\frac{dV}{dz}\right)} = \frac{MLT^{-2}}{L^2\left(\frac{LT^{-1}}{L}\right)}$

$= ML^{-1}T^{-1} = Kg\,m^{-1}\,s^{-1}$

(D) Impulse $= \int F dt = MLT^{-2} \times T$

$= MLT^{-1} = Kg\,ms^{-1}$

35. **(a)** Let a be the radius of the wire

Magnetic field at point A (inside)

$$B_A = \frac{\mu_0 i r}{2\pi a^2} = \frac{\mu_0 i \frac{a}{3}}{2\pi a^2} = \frac{\mu_0 i}{\pi a^2}\frac{a}{6} = \frac{\mu_0 i}{6\pi a}$$

Magnetic field at point B (outside)

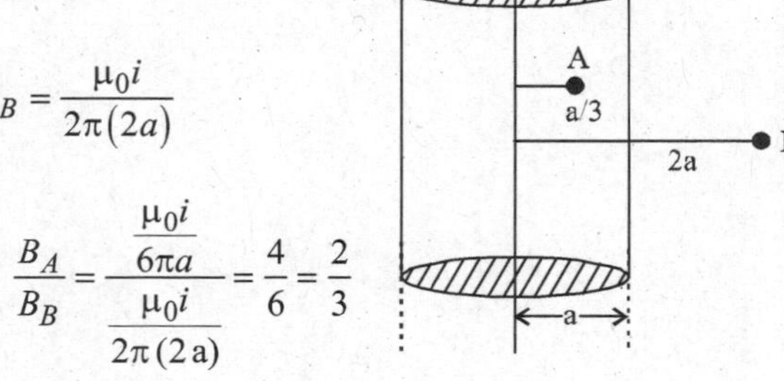

$$B_B = \frac{\mu_0 i}{2\pi(2a)}$$

$$\therefore \frac{B_A}{B_B} = \frac{\frac{\mu_0 i}{6\pi a}}{\frac{\mu_0 i}{2\pi(2a)}} = \frac{4}{6} = \frac{2}{3}$$

36. **(d)** From equation of motion, $s = ut + \frac{1}{2}gt^2$

For first $\frac{h}{2}, \frac{h}{2} = \frac{1}{2}gt_1^2$ ...(i)

For total height h,

$h = \frac{1}{2}g(t_1 + t_2)^2$ ...(ii)

Divide equation (ii) by (i) we have $\frac{1}{2} = \frac{t_1^2}{(t_1 + t_2)^2}$

$$\frac{1}{\sqrt{2}} = \frac{t_1}{t_1 + t_2};\ 1 + \frac{t_2}{t_1} = \sqrt{2}$$

$$\frac{t_1}{t_2} = \frac{1}{\sqrt{2} - 1} \Rightarrow t_2 = (\sqrt{2} - 1)t_1$$

37. **(a)** Work done in rotating dipole from angle 'θ_1' to 'θ_2' is given as

$W = MB(\cos\theta_1 - \cos\theta_2)$

$= 5 \times 0.4\,(\cos 0° - \cos 180°)$

$= 5 \times 0.4 \times 2 = 4J$

38. **(d)** In elastic collision, the velocities get inter changed if the colliding objects have equal masses.

39. **(a)**

40. **(d)** Moment of inertia of disc about its axis

$$= \frac{1}{2}mr^2 = \frac{1}{2} \times 0.4 \times \left(\frac{100}{100}\right)^2$$

$$= \frac{1}{2} \times 0.4 = 0.2\ kgm^2$$

Solved Paper 2017

Instructions

- *There are total 100 questions in this solved paper.*
- *For every correct attempt the students will be awarded 1 mark.*
- *All the questions are in MCOs form.*

1. Anti-aliasing is important to improve readability of text. It deals with the
(1) elimination of "jaggies".
(2) spacing between two individual characters
(3) underlining of letters
(4) spacing of a group of characters

2. Consider a set of n tasks with known runtimes r_1, r_2, r_n, to be run uniprocessor machine. Which of the following processor scheduling algorithm will result in the maximum throughput?
(1) Priority scheduling (2) Round-robin
(3) FCFS (4) Shortest job first

3. Which of the following is the appropriate format for graphics that can be embedded within an Internet document?
(1) HTML (2) BMP
(3) TIFF (4) GIF

4. Which of the following is true to declare variable of ASP?
(1) Var (2) Dim
(3) S (4) Set

5. In the context of Visual Basic, multiple controls of the same type can be grouped into an array, in the same manner as a collection of data items. Such a grouping is known as
(1) control array (2) primary array
(3) secondary array (4) an integer array

6. Consider two database relations R and S having 3 tuples in R and 2 tuples in S. What is the maximum number of tuples that could appear in the natural join of R and S?
(1) 6 (2) 2 (3) 3 (4) 5

7. Which of the following protocol is used for transferring electronic mail messages from one machine to another?
(1) HTTP
(2) FTP
(3) SMTP
(4) SNMP

8. OLE, a Microsoft's Component document technology, means
(1) Overlay Linking and Exchange
(2) Online Linking and Embedding
(3) Open Learning Exchange
(4) Object Linking and Embedding

9. The problem of indefinite blockage of low priority jobs in general priority scheduling algorithm can be solved using
(1) swapping (2) dirty bit
(3) aging (4) compaction

10. What result set is returned from the following SQL query?

```
.SELECT customer_name, telephone
FROM customers
WHERE city IN ('Jaipur', 'Delhi', 'Agra');
```

(1) The customer_name of all customers who are not living in Jaipur, Delhi or Agra.
(2) The customer_name and telephone of all customers
(3) The customer_name and telephone of all customers living in either Jaipur, Delhi or Agra
(4) The customer_name and telephone of all customers living in Jaipur, Delhi and Agra

11. Which of the following data structures is most suitable for evaluating postfix expressions?
(1) Tree (2) Stack (3) Linked list (4) Queue

12. The major goal of object-oriented programming is
(1) top-down program development
(2) speed
(3) user interface
(4) reuse

13. Which of the following is the default scripting language in Active Server Pages (ASP)?
(1) JavaScript (2) PHP (3) HTML (4) VBScript

14. What is the bit-rate for transmitting uncompressed 800×600 pixel color frame with 8 bits / pixel at 40 frames/second?
(1) 1536 Mbps (2) 2.4 Mbps
(3) 15.36 Mbps (4) 153.6 Mbps

66. **(d)** Carbon atoms have the tendency to link with one another through covalent bonds to form chains. This property is called catenation. This is because C – C bonds are very strong. Down the group, the size increases and electronegativity decreases. The order of catenation is C >> Si > Ge ≈ Sn.

Bond	C – C	Si – Si	Ge – Ge	Sn – Sn
Bond Enthalpy (kJ/mol)	348	297	260	240

67. **(c)** K_w depends upon temperature as it is an equilibrium constant.

68. **(a)** $[Co(NH_3)_5CO_3]ClO_4$ Six monodentate ligands are attached to Co hence C. N. of Co = 6;

$$O.N. = x + 5 \times (0) + 1 \times (-2) + 1 \times (-1) = 0$$

$\therefore x = +3$; electronic configuration of Co^{3+}[Ar] $3d^6 4s^0$ hence number of *d* electrons is 6 : All *d* electrons are paired due to strong ligand hence unpaired electrons zero.

69. **(c)** A – III, B – IV, C – I, D – II

70. **(c)** Higher the value of K_a lower will be the value of pK_a i.e. higher will be the acidic nature. Further since CN^-, F^- and NO_2^- are conjugate base of the acids HCN, HF and HNO_2 respectively hence the correct order of base strength will be

$$F^- < NO_2^- < CN^-$$

($\because$ stronger the acid weaker will be its conjugate base)

71. **(a)** Bond energy of F_2 less than Cl_2 due to lone pair-lone pair repulsions and small size of fluorine.

$\therefore$ Bond energy order $Cl_2 > Br_2 > F_2 > I_2$

72. **(a)** Hinsberg reagent is benzene sulphonyl chloride. It is used for the separation of primary, secondary and tertiary amines in a given sample. Use of *p*-toluene sulphonyl-chloride is more effective than Hinsberg reagent.

73. **(d)** A – IV, B – I, C – II, D – III

74. **(b)** Organic compound is heated with fuming nitric acid in the presence of silver nitrate in Carius method.

Lunar caustic ($AgNO_3$) is used as reagent here to distinguish halide ions as follows.

$$Cl^-(aq) \xrightarrow{AgNO_3} AgCl \downarrow \text{ (White)}$$

$$Br^-(aq) \xrightarrow{AgNO_3} AgBr \downarrow \text{ (Pale yellow)}$$

$$I^-(aq) \xrightarrow{AgNO_3} AgI \downarrow \text{ (Dark yellow)}$$

75. **(b)**

76. **(a)** $\lambda = \dfrac{h}{mv} = \dfrac{6.63 \times 10^{-34}}{0.060 \times 10} = 1.1 \times 10^{-33}$ m

77. **(a)** The two structures involve only movement of electrons and not of atoms or groups, hence these are resonating structures.

78. **(c)**

79. **(a)** (a) V^{2+}(Violet), Cr^{3+}(Violet), Mn^{3+}(Violet)
(b) Zn^{2+}(Colourless), V^{3+}(Green), Fe^{3+}(Yellow)
(c) Ti^{4+}(Colourless), V^{4+}(Blue), Mn^{2+}(Pink)
(d) Sc^{3+}(Colourless), Ti^{3+}(Purple), Cr^{2+}(Blue)

80. **(c)** Atomic no. 17 (Cl) and 53 (I) are present in the same group

81. **(d)** $[Co(NH_3)_6]^{3+}$,
$NH_3 \Rightarrow$ SFL, $Co^{+3} = [Ar]3d^6$, $t_{2g}^6 e_g^0$

⇅	⇅	⇅	••	••		••		••	••	••

$\therefore$ Diamagnetic & Low spin complex.

82. **(b)** (A) First law is given by
$\Delta U = Q + W$
If we apply reversible work at constant P.
$\Rightarrow \Delta U = Q - P\Delta V$
(D) $\Delta H = \Delta U + \Delta nRT$

83. **(d)** All statements given above are correct.

84. **(b)** The hydrogen atom that is added to the carbonyl carbon of the aldehyde in the reduction is derived directly from the other aldehyde molecule as a hydride ion. The second hydrogen that is added to the negatively charged oxygen is coming from the solvent (consult mechanism of Cannizzaro reaction). Oxidation of one molecule of the compound at the expense of other molecule of the same compound is known as disproportionation.

85. **(b)** An equilibrium constant does not give any information about the rate at which the equilibrium is reached.

86. **(a)** Solubility of AgI in KI soln. $= \dfrac{k_{sp} \text{ of AgI}}{[I^-]}$

$$= \frac{1.0 \times 10^{-16}}{10^{-4}} = 1.0 \times 10^{-12} \text{ mol}^{-1}$$

87. **(c)** Electron withdrawing substituents like $-NO_2$, –Cl increase the acidity of phenol while electron releasing substituents like $-CH_3$, $-OCH_3$ decreases acidity. hence the correct order of acidity will be

OH / NO_2	>	OH / Cl	>	OH / CH_3	>	OH / OCH_3
III		I		II		IV
(–M, –I)		(–I > +M)		(+I + HC)		(+ M)

88. **(c)** Reaction (c) is endothermic. Electrolysis or decomposition of H_2O endothermic in nature.

89. **(b)**

$N(CH_3)_2$ / OCH_3	$N(CH_3)_2$	$NHCH_3$ / CN	$NHCH_3$ / OH
I	II	III	IV
+R effect and –I effect of $-OCH_3$		(–I effect of –CN group)	(–I effect of –OH group)

$-OCH_3$ group increases electron density of ring at *o*- and *p*- position making (I) most basic. (III) is least basic due to –I effect of –CN group at meta position.

Since, –I effect of –CN > –I effect of –OH group.

Hence, correct basic strength will follow the order

I > II > IV > III

Basic strength $\propto \frac{1}{pK_b \text{ value}}$

Order of K_b value is, I < II < IV < III.

90. (c) A. Lucas reagent - Conc. $HCl/ZnCl_2$
B. Dumas method - CuO/CO_2
C. Kjeldahl's method - H_2SO_4
D. Hinsberg test - $C_6H_5SO_2Cl$/aq. KOH

PART-III : BIOLOGY

91. (c) 92. (a)

93. (c) Photorespiration is the uptake of O_2 and release of CO_2 in light and results from the biosynthesis of glycolate in chloroplasts and subsequent metabolism of glycolate acid in the same leaf cell. During photorespiration loss of carbon takes place in the form of CO_2.

94. (c) Chemiosmotic theory postulated by the British biochemist, Peter Mitchell (1920-22) to explain the formation of ATP in the mitochondrial electron transport chain. As electrons are transferred along the electron carrier system in the inner mitochondrial membrane, hydrogen ions (protons) are actively transported into the space between the inner and outer mitochondrial membranes, which thus contains a higher concentration of protons than the matrix. This creates an electrochemical gradient across the inner membrane, through which protons move back into the matrix.

95. (b)

96. (b) A – III; B – I; C – IV; D – II

97. (d) Symbiotic association is exhibited by mycorrhiza and *Rhizobium*.

98. (b) Meiosis II is known as equational or homotypic division like mitosis. It ensures the maintenance of constant number of chromosomes from generation to generation of a species.

99. (b) The diatom shells accumulating up at the bottom of oceans over millions of years formed deposits called diatomaceous earth. These deposits may be thousand metres thick with as many as five million diatom shells in each cubic centimetre. This diatomaceous earth is used in many small and large scale industries.

100. (b) 101. (b)

102. (d) *Albugo* is the parasitic fungi which is found on mustard. It is the member of phycomycetes that are found in aquatic habitats and on decaying wood in moist and damp places.

103. (a) Asexual reproduction takes place by zoospores (motile) or by aplanospores (non-motile). These spores are endogeneously produced in sporangium.

104. (a) 105. (a) 106. (d) 107. (b)

108. (d)
(a) Gametophyte of bryophytes bears protonemal & leafy stage.
(b) In gymnosperm female gametophyte is not free living.
(c) They are present in *Marchantia* or which is a bryophyte.
(d) Origin of seed habit started in pteridophyte *Selaginella*.

109. (a) An allergen is a harmless substance that triggers an immune overreaction, producing IgE antibodies and causing allergy symptoms.

110. (a) 111. (a) 112. (a)

113. (b) Chargaff's rule states that A = T and G ° C. The molar amount of adenine = molar amount of thymine. The molar amount of guanine = molar amount of cytosine.
Hence, G is 17%, so, C = 17%
A = 33%, so, T = 33%

114. (c)

115. (b) Cytokinin are usually amino purine so they resemble nucleic acids in structural aspects.

116. (c)

117. (a) Yoghurt (yogurt) is produced by curdling milk with the help of *Streptococcus thermophilus* and *Lactobacillus bulgaricus*. The temperature is maintained at about 45°C (40° – 46°C) for four hours. It has a flavour of lactic acid and acetaldehyde.

118. (b) In B–DNA, one turn of the helix has about 10 nucleotides on each strand of DNA. A turn occupies a distance of about 3.4 nm (34Å or 3.4×10^{-9} m) so that adjacent nucleotides or their bases are separated by a space of about 0.34 nm (0.34×10^{-9} m or 3.4 Å).

119. (d)

120. (c) Mosses and ferns belong to bryophtes and pteridophytes respectively. In bryophytes, the dominant phase in the life cycle is the gametophytic plant body. However, in pteridophytes, the main plant body is a sporophyte, which is differentiated into true root, stem and leaves. These organs possess well – differentiated vascular tissues.

121. (d) mRNA provides the template for synthesis of proteins. A segment of DNA coding for polypeptide is called exon. Single DNA dependent-RNA polymerase that catalyses transcription of all types of RNA in bacteria.

122. (c)

123. (c) mRNA has some additional sequences that are not translated and are referred as untranslated regions (UTRs). The UTRs are present at both 5'-end (before start codon) and at 3'-end (after stop codon). They are required for efficient translation process.

124. (c) They can survive without oxygen

125. (d) When the placenta is axial and the ovules are attached to it in a multilocular ovary, the placentation is said to be axile, as in china rose, tomato and lemon. In parietal placentation, the ovules develop on the inner wall of the ovary or on peripheral part.

126. (a) 127. (c) 128. (b) 129. (c)

130. (a)
UUU – Phenylalanine
GGG – Glycine
UCU – Serine
CCC – Proline

131. (b) 132. (c) 133. (c)

134. (a) In case of incomplete linkage, the linked gene shows new combination along with parental combination due to crossing over between chromatids.

135. (d)

52. What do data warehouse support?
(1) Operational databases (2) OLAP
(3) OLTP (4) OLAP and OLTP

53. The term sum-of-product in Boolean algebra means
(1) the AND function of several AND functions
(2) the AND function of several OR functions
(3) the OR function of several AND functions
(4) the OR function of several OR functions

54. What is the correct HTML tag for the largest heading?
(1) <H1> (2) <HEAD>=large
(3) <HEADING> = large (4) <H6>

55. Which of the following techniques allows execution of programs larger than the size of physical memory?
(1) Thrashing (2) DMA
(3) Buffering (4) Demand paging

56. For the following binary tree, inoperate the traversal yields the expression

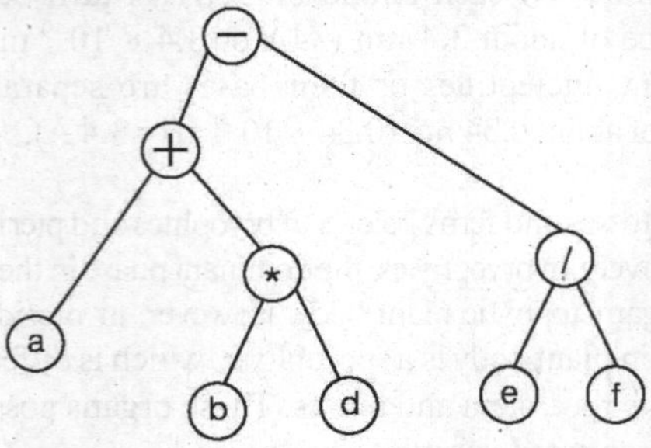

(1) – + * / abdef (2) a + bd * – ef /
(3) abdef * / + – (4) a + b * d – e / f

57. _______ is a special effect in motion pictures and animations that changes one image or shape into another through a seamless transition.
(1) Tweening (2) Inverse kinematics
(3) Morphing (4) Tweaking

58. In which addressing mode, the operand is given explicitly in the instruction (example instruction : ADD R4, #3)?
(1) Based Indexed mode (2) Absolute mode
(3) Immediate mode (4) Register indirect mode

59. Which of the following is not a program instruction?
(1) CMP (2) MOV (3) JMP (4) CALL

60. Based on the current technology, ____ is the fastest logic family.
(1) CMOS (2) TTL (3) MOS (4) ECL

61. Which of the following represents the life cycle of software development?
(1) Design → Analysis → Coding → Operation and maintenance → Testing
(2) Analysis → Design → Coding → Testing → Operation and maintenance
(3) Design → Analysis → Coding → Testing → Operation and maintenance
(4) Analysis → Design → Coding → Operation and maintenance → Testing.

62. Given that a 22 inch monitor with an aspect ratio of 16:9 has a monitor resolution of 1920 × 1080, what is the width of the monitor?
(1) 22 inches (2) 8.53 inches
(3) 10.79 inches (4) 19.17 inches

63. The five items P,Q,R,S and T are pushed in a stack, one after the other starting from P. The stack is popped four times and each element is inserted in a queue. Then two elements are deleted from the queue and pushed back on the stack? Now one item is popped from the stack. The popped item is
(1) S (2) P
(3) Q (4) R

64. How many bits are used in the exponent part of IEEE single precision for the representation of floating point numbers?
(1) 32 bits (2) 8 bits
(3) 16 bits (4) 24 bits

65. Buying and selling goods over the Internet is called:
(1) Euro-conversion (2) Hyper-marketing
(3) Cyber- selling (4) E-commerce

66. Which one of the following most accurately describes "multiple inheritance"?
(1) When a child class has both an "is a" and "has a" relationship with its parent class.
(2) When two classes inherit from each other
(3) When a base class has two or more derived classes
(4) When a child class has two or more parent class

67. When an ASP.NET file is placed on an IIS server and viewed through a browser, the resulting HTML page contains?
(1) a mix of ASP. NET and HTML code
(2) all ASP.NET code
(3) all HTML code
(4) as much ASP. NET code as is in the ASP.NET file.

68. In C++, which of the following statements correctly returns the memory from the dynamic array pointer pp to the free store?
(1) delete pp; (2) delete pp[];
(3) delete [ ] pp; (4) delete * pp;

69. The logic circuit binary adder which is used to add two 4-bits binary numbers, requires ___ half adder (s) and _____ full adder (s).
(1) 4, 0 (2) 1, 3 (3) 2, 2 (4) 3, 1

70. The 10 Base 5 cabling is also known as ____.
(1) fast ethernet (2) thick ethernet
(3) thin ethernet (4) gigabit ethernet

71. In a positive edge triggered JK flip-flop, a low J and a low K produces
(1) no change (2) low state
(3) high state (4) toggle state

72. An entity set that does not have sufficient attributes to form a key is termed as:
(1) primary entity set (2) strong entity set
(3) weak entity set (4) simple entity set

73. Which of the following devices understands the format and contents of the data and translate messages from one format to another?
(1) Gateway (2) Hub (3) Switch (4) Router

74. In which of the following state, the process is waiting for processor?
(1) Running (2) New (3) Ready (4) Waiting

75. The complexity of linear search algorithm is
(1) O (n log n) (2) O (n) (3) O (log n) (4) O (n* n)

76. In relational databases, the natural join of two tables is
(1) cartesian product always
(2) combination of union and filtered cartesian product
(3) combination of selection and filtered cartesian product
(4) combination of projection and filtered cartesian product

77. Java is a ________ language. This means that you must be explicit about what type of data you are working with.
(1) weakly typed (2) strongly typed
(3) dynamically typed (4) loosely typed

78. With SQL, how can you return the number of records in the "Persons" table?
(1) SELECT COUNT (*) FROM Persons
(2) SELECT COUNT ( ) FROM Persons
(3) SELECT COLUMN ( ) FROM Persons
(4) SELECT COLUMN (*) FROM Persons

79. Assume X and Y are non-zero positive integers. Consider the following pseudo-code fragment:

```
while X < > Y do
if X > Y then
      X ← X – Y
else
      Y ← Y – X
end if
end while
print (X)
```

What is the code doing?
(1) It computes the GCD of two numbers
(2) It computes the LCM of two numbers
(3) It finds the smallest of two numbers
(4) It divides the largest number by the smaller

80. The boolean expression

$$(A+C)(A\overline{B}+AC)(A\overline{C}+\overline{B})$$

can be simplified as
(1) $\overline{A}B+BC$ (2) $A\overline{B}$ (3) AB + BC (4) $AB+\overline{A}C$

81. In a relational database model, cardinality of a relation means
(1) the number of constraints (2) the number of tuples
(3) the number of attributes (4) the number of tables

82. Conceptual level, Internal level and External level are three components of the three-level RDBMS architecture.
Which of the following in not a part of the conceptual level?
(1) Storage dependent details
(2) Entities, attributes, relationships
(3) Constraints
(4) Semantic information

83. Which of the following transmission media works on the principle of total internal reflection?
(1) Optical fiber cable
(2) Shielded twisted pair cable
(3) Unshielded twisted pair cable
(4) Coaxial cable

84. The mechanism that brings a page memory only when it is needed in ________.
(1) page replacement (2) segmentation
(3) fragmentation (4) demand paging

85. Which of the following topologies highest reliability?
(1) Mesh topology (2) Bus topology
(3) Star topology (4) Ring topology

86. What is the length of an IP address in (Pre-1PU6)?
(1) 8 (2) 1 (3) 2 (4) 4

87. Consider the following statements respect to JavaScript

(i) A variable is created using the keyword

(ii) JavaScript is untyped language

Which of the above are true?
(1) Neither (i) nor (ii) (2) Only (i)
(3) Only (ii) (4) Both (i) and (ii)

88. A condition that is caused by run-time error in a computer program is known as
(1) exception (2) syntax error
(3) semantic error (4) fault

89. Program counter contents indicate
(1) the time needed to execute a program
(2) the time elapsed since execution begins
(3) the address where next instruction is stored
(4) the count of programs being executed after switching the power ON.

90. Semaphores are used to solve the problem of _____ .
(1) mutual exclusion (2) race condition
(3) process synchronisation (4) the belady problem

91. A multimedia project is said to be _____ and user-interactive when users are given navigational control.
(1) secure (2) hypertext
(3) linear (4) non-linear

92. An analog signal carries 4 bits in each signal unit. If 1000 signal units are sent per second, then baud rate and bit rate of the signal are ____ and ____ .
(1) 1000 bauds / sec, 1000 bps
(2) 1000 bauds / sec, 500 bps
(3) 4000 bauds / sec, 1000 bps
(4) 2000 bauds / sec, 1000 bps

8. (b) [logic circuit: A and B into OR gate giving A + B; A and (A + B) into AND gate giving C = A . (A + B)]

The output of the logic circuit is

$C = A.(A+B) = A.A + A.B = A + AB = A.(1+B) = A.1 = A$

$\therefore$ Output C only depends on input A and independent of input B

9. (c) Here, $\theta = 30°$, $\tau = 0.018$ N-m, $B = 0.06$ T

Torque on a bar magnet :

$\tau = MB\sin\theta \Rightarrow 0.018 = M \times 0.06 \times \sin 30°$

$\Rightarrow 0.018 = M \times 0.06 \times \frac{1}{2} \Rightarrow M = 0.6$ A-m^2

Position of stable equilibrium ($\theta = 0°$)

Position of unstable equilibrium ($\theta = 180°$)

Minimum work required to rotate bar magnet from stable to unstable equilibrium

$\Delta U = U_f - U_i = -MB\cos 180° - (-MB\cos 0°)$

$W = 2MB = 2 \times 0.6 \times 0.06 \Rightarrow W = 7.2 \times 10^{-2}$ J

10. (c) Compairing the given $y = 0.5\sin\left(\frac{2\pi}{\lambda}400t - \frac{2\pi}{\lambda}x\right)$ with standard equation

$\omega = \frac{2\pi}{\lambda}400$ and $k = \frac{2\pi}{\lambda}$

$\therefore$ velocity of the wave $v = \frac{\omega}{k} = \frac{\frac{2\pi}{\lambda}400}{\frac{2\pi}{\lambda}}$

$\therefore$ v = 400 m/s

11. (b) As, $n = \sqrt{\mu_r \varepsilon_r} = \sqrt{\frac{4}{3} \times 3} = 2$

And, $\sin\theta_c = \frac{1}{n} = \frac{1}{2}$ $\quad\therefore$ Critical angle, $\theta_c = 30°$

12. (a) Tension, $F = (Y\alpha\Delta T)A$

$= (2 \times 10^{11}) \times (10^{-5}) \times (25 - 0) \times \pi(0.5 \times 10^{-2})^2$

= 3925 N.

13. (b)

14. (c) The sum of their KE and PE is a constant.

15. (a) Each degree of rotation of diatomic molecule has energy $\frac{RT}{2}$ per mole.

16. (b) For second harmonic of open organ pipe, the length given as $L = \frac{n\lambda}{2}; n = 2$

So frequency of vibration is $f = \frac{v}{\lambda}$

$f = \frac{v}{\lambda} = \frac{v}{L} = \frac{360}{\frac{40}{100}} = 900$Hz

17. (a) A - (ii); B - (i); C - (iv); D - (iii)

18. (a) Path difference, $\Delta P = d\sin\theta = d\theta$

d = distance between slits = 1 mm = 10^{-3} mm

D = distance between the slits and screen = 100 cm = 1 m

y = distance between central bright fringe and observed fringe = 1.27 mm

$\therefore \Delta P = \frac{dy}{D} = \frac{10^{-3} \times 1.270 \times 10^{-3}}{1\text{ m}} = 1.27$ μm

19. (b) For projectile motion,

Range $R = \frac{u^2 \sin 2\theta}{g}$

As range is same for angle of projection θ and $90 - \theta$. So, range is same for 42° and 48°.

Height in projectile motion, $H = \frac{u^2 \sin^2\theta}{2g} \Rightarrow H \propto \sin^2\theta$

So H is higher for 48° than H for 42°.

20. (b) As given that, $y = 3\cos\left(\frac{\pi}{4} - 2\omega t\right)$

Velocity of the particle

$v = \frac{dy}{dt} = \frac{d}{dt}\left[3\cos\left(\frac{\pi}{4} - 2\omega t\right)\right]$

$= 3(-2\omega)\left[-\sin\left(\frac{\pi}{4} - 2\omega t\right)\right]$

$= 6\omega\sin\left(\frac{\pi}{4} - 2\omega t\right)$

So, acceleration,

$a = \frac{dv}{dt} = \frac{d}{dt}\left[6\omega\sin\left(\frac{\pi}{4} - 2\omega t\right)\right]$

$= (6\omega) \times (-2\omega)\cos\left(\frac{\pi}{4} - 2\omega t\right)$

$= -4\omega^2\left[3\cos\left(\frac{\pi}{4} - 2\omega t\right)\right]$

$a = -4\omega^2 y$

In simple harmonic motion acceleration (or force) is directly proportional to the negative of displacement of particle

$\Rightarrow$ as acceleration, $a \propto -y$

Hence, due to negative sign motion is simple harmonic motion (SHM.)

A simple harmonic motion is always periodic. So motion is periodic simple harmonic.

From the given equation,

$$y = 3\cos\left(\frac{\pi}{4} - 2\omega t\right)$$

Compare it by standard equation

$y = a\cos(\omega t + \phi)$

So, $\omega' = 2\omega$

$$\frac{2\pi}{T'} = 2\omega \Rightarrow T' = \frac{2\pi}{2\omega} = \frac{\pi}{\omega}$$

Hence, the motion is SHM with period $\frac{\pi}{\omega}$

21. **(b)** Given wavelength of neon lemp $\lambda_1 = 670.5$nm

Stopping potential $V_1 = 0.48V$.

From the Einstein's photoelectric equation

$$kE_{max} = \frac{hc}{\lambda_1} + \phi \Rightarrow eV_1 = \frac{hc}{\lambda_1} + \phi$$

$$\Rightarrow e(0.48) = \frac{1240}{670.5} + \phi \quad \text{...(i)}$$

For second case wavelength $\lambda_2 = 474.6$ nm stlopping potential = V_2.

$$e(V_2) = \frac{1240}{474.6} + \phi \quad \text{...(ii)}$$

Subtrating equation (i) from (ii) we get

$$e(V_2 - 0.48) = 1240\left(\frac{1}{474.6} - \frac{1}{670.5}\right)eV$$

$$\Rightarrow V_2 = 0.48 + 1240\left(\frac{670.5 - 474.6}{474.6 \times 670.5}\right) \text{ volts}$$

$$\Rightarrow V_2 = 0.48 + 0.76 = 1.25V$$

22. **(b)** Torque = $\tau = \vec{r} \times \vec{F} = rF\sin\theta = rF\sin 0^\circ = 0$

23. **(b)** $\frac{1}{2}kx^2 = Mgx$ or $x = \frac{2Mg}{k}$

24. **(d)** $[E] = ML^2T^{-2}$

$[L] = ML^2T^{-1}$

$[G] = M^{-1}L^{+3}T^{-2}$

$$P = \frac{EL^2}{M^5G^2} \Rightarrow [P] = \frac{(ML^2T^{-2})(M^2L^4T^{-2})}{M^5(M^{-2}L^6T^{-4})} = M^0L^0T^0$$

25. **(d)** Critical angle at the interface of n_1 and n_2 is

$$\sin\theta_{1C} = \frac{n_1}{n_2}$$

Critical angle at the interface of n_1 and n_3 is

$$\sin\theta_{2C} = \frac{n_1}{n_3} \quad \therefore \quad \sin\theta_{2C} - \sin\theta_{1C} = \frac{1}{2}$$

$$\Rightarrow \frac{n_1}{n_3} - \frac{n_1}{n_2} = \frac{1}{2} \Rightarrow \frac{n_1}{n_2}\left(\frac{n_2}{n_3} - 1\right) = \frac{1}{2}$$

$$\Rightarrow \frac{n_1}{n_2}\left(\frac{2}{5} - 1\right) = \frac{1}{2} \quad \frac{n_1}{n_2} = \frac{-5}{6}$$

$$\therefore \theta_{1C} = \sin^{-1}\left(\frac{n_1}{n_2}\right) = \theta_{1C} = \sin^{-1}\left(-\frac{5}{6}\right)$$

26. **(c)** We know that $h = \frac{2T\cos\theta}{r\rho g}$

In a moving lift acceleration becomes

$= (g + a) = (g + 2g) = 3g$

$$\therefore h' = \frac{2T\cos\theta}{r\rho(3g)} = \frac{h}{3}$$

27. **(c)** When the ray suffers minimum deviation, it becomes parallel to the base of prism P. As prisms Q and R are of same material and have identical shape, therefore, the ray continues to be parallel to base of Q and R. Hence final deviation of the ray remains the same as before.

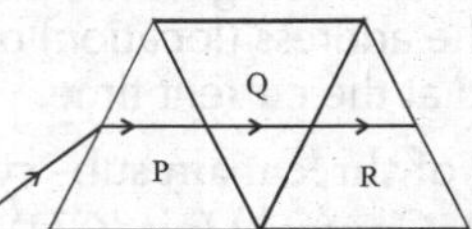

28. **(a)** For balancing, $mg\sin\theta = f = \mu mg\cos\theta$

$$\Rightarrow \tan\theta = \mu = \frac{3}{4} = 0.75$$

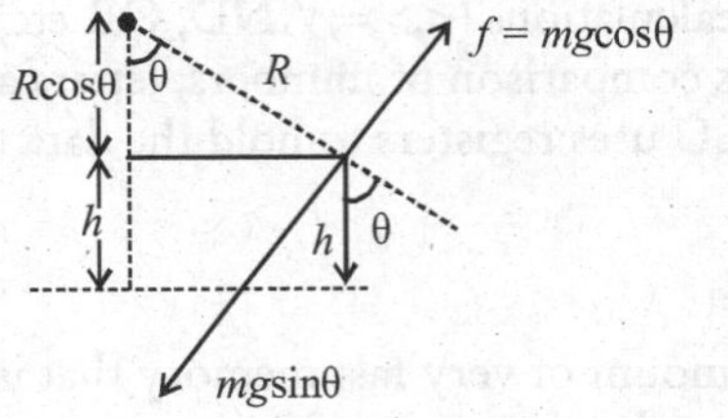

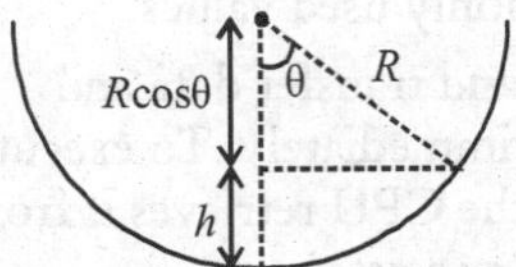

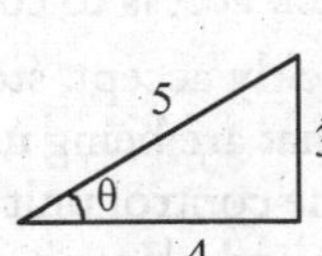

$$h = R - R\cos\theta = R - R\left(\frac{4}{5}\right) = \frac{R}{5}$$

$$\therefore h = \frac{R}{5} = 0.2 \text{ m}$$

[$\because$ radius, $R = 1$m]

1.3.1 Input Unit

The computer accepts coded information through input unit by the user. It is a device that is used to give required information to the computer. e.g. keyboard, mouse etc.

1.3.2 Output Unit

The output unit sends the processed results to the user. It is mainly used to display the desired result to the user as per input instruction. e.g. monitor, printer and plotter etc.

1.3.3 Central Processing Unit (CPU)

The central processing unit consists set of registers, arithmetic and control circuits, which together interpret and execute instructions in assembly language.

Central processing unit is often called the *brain of computer*. The CPU is fabricated as a single Integrated Circuit (IC) chip and is also known as **microprocessor.** A CPU controls all the internal and external devices and performs arithmetic and logic operations.

⚠ A program counter is a register in a computer processor that contains the address (location) of the CPU instruction being executed at the current time.

The CPU consists of three main sub- systems; Arithmetic Logic Unit (ALU), Control Unit (CU) and Registers.

1. Arithmetic Logic Unit (ALU)

The arithmetic logic unit contains the electronic circuitry that executes all arithmetic and logical operations on the available data. It is used to perform all arithmetic calculations (addition, subtraction, multiplication and division) and logical calculations (<,> =, AND, OR etc). Logical unit performs comparison of numbers, letters and special characters. ALU uses registers to hold the data that is being processed.

2. Registers

A register is a small amount of very fast memory that is built into the CPU in order to speed up its operations by providing quick access to commonly used values.

Registers quickly accept, store and transfer data and instructions that are being used immediately. To execute an instruction, the control unit of the CPU retrieves it from main memory and places it into a register.

Some of the registers are as follows:

1. **Program Counter** (PC) It keeps the address of the next instruction.
2. **Memory Address Register** (MAR) It holds the address of memory location.
3. **Memory Data Register** (MDR) It stores the data to be stored in the computer storage (e.g. RAM) or the data after fetch from the computer storage.
4. **Current Instruction Register** (CIR) It stores the instruction that is currently being executed.
5. **Accumulator** (A) It is used for storing data and for carrying out arithmetic and logic manipulations.

3. Control Unit (CU)

It is also known as nerve center. Control unit coordinates with the input and output devices of a computer. It directs the computer to carry out stored program instructions by communicating with the ALU and the registers. It organises the processing of data and instructions. To maintain the proper sequence of processing data, the control unit uses *clock* inputs. The basic function of control unit is to fetch the instruction stored in the main memory, identify the operations and the devices involved in it and accordingly generate control signals.

1.3.4 Memory Unit

This unit is responsible to store programs or data on a temporary or permanent basis. It has primary memory (main memory) and secondary memory (auxiliary memory).

The input data which is to be processed is brought into main memory before processing. The needed instruction for processing and any kind of intermediate results are also stored in primary memory. Together with these, the final output is also stored in primary memory before transferring it to the output unit. Secondary memory is used to permanently store data, programs and output. This unit does not deal directly with CPU.

1.4 Functioning of a Computer System

Computer is responsible for performing four basic functions as follows:

1. **Input** Information or data that is entered into a computer is called input. It sends data and instructions to the Central Processing Unit (CPU).
2. **Processing** It is the sequence of actions taken on data to convert it into information which is meaningful to the user. It can be calculations, comparisons or decisions taken by the computer.
3. **Output** It makes processed data available to the user.
4. **Storage** It stores data and programs permanently.

Interconnection Structures

The collection of paths connecting the various modules of a computer (CPU, memory, I/O) is called the **interconnection structure**. The design of this structure will depend on the exchange that must be made between modules.

1.5 Bus

The term bus refers to a collection of wires through which data is transmitted from one part of a computer to another. You can think of a bus as a highway on which data travels within a computer.

A computer's bus can be divided into two different types as follows:

1.5.1 Internal Bus

When it is used in reference to personal computers, the term bus usually refers to internal bus. This is a bus that connects all the internal computer components to the CPU and main memory. It is also referred to as **system bus.**

1.5.2 External Bus

It connects the different external devices, peripherals, expansion slots, I/O ports and drive connections to the rest of the computer. External bus is also called an **expansion bus.**

Some commonly used buses in microprocessor are given below:

(i) **Data Bus** The data bus is used to transfer actual data.

(ii) **Address Bus** The address bus transfers information about where the data should go.

(iii) **Control Bus** The control bus is used by the CPU to direct and monitor the actions of other functional areas of the computer. It is used to transmit a variety of individual signals (read, write, interrupt, acknowledge and so forth) necessary to control and coordinate the operation of the computer.

1.6 Peripheral Component Interconnect (PCI)

It is high performance bus that is used to integrate chips, processors, memory sub-systems and expansion boards. This bus was designed by Intel in 1992 for integrating chips on a board. This is most popular bus that is mostly used for integrating peripherals. Now, a new version of PCI, known as PCI mini also developed by notebook manufacturers, so that they can reduce the manufacturing costs for notebooks.

PCI bus provides a bus architecture that also supports peripherals and devices like hard disk drives, networks etc. It is the only bus that can carry 64 bits of data in each clock cycle which makes it useful for Pentium processor family.

PCI successfully replaced all other older buses like ISA, EISA and VL.

Advantages of PCI

The PCI technology offers a number of advantages compared to the VL-bus or ISA.

(i) You can have multiple PCI buses on the same computer.

(ii) You can connect a maximum of five components to the PCI and you can also replace each of them by fixed devices on the motherboard.

(iii) The PCI bus will enhance the speed of the transfers from 33 MHz to 133 MHz with a transfer rate of 1 GB per second.

(iv) The PCI can handle devices using a maximum of 5 volts and the pins used can transfer more than one signal through one pin.

1.7 Input and Output

1.7.1 Input Devices

An input device is an external hardware device that sends data into the computer system. These devices are used to input (or enter) data and instructions into the computer system. All instructions are accepted by the CPU through electrical pulses from various kinds of input devices.

Some of the input devices are explained as follows:

1. Keyboard

It is the most commonly used input device which uses an arrangement of keys. Both data and program can be entered into the computer through the keyboard. It is an essential device for interactive processing because the user can easily issue commands to receive the data response immediately on the computer screen.

2. Mouse

The mouse is a pointing device that allows to control the movement of pointer (also known as **mouse pointer**) on screen. Mouse performs various functions by detecting two-dimensional motion relatively to its supporting surface.

A mouse can be of different types like wired mouse, wireless mouse, optical mouse, mechanical mouse etc. Generally a mouse have two buttons – a **right button** and a **left button.**

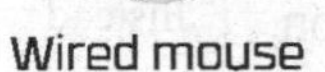
Wired mouse

Wireless mouse

(c) $[CoCl_4]^{2-}$ Co^{2+} d^7 $\sqrt{15}$

(d) $[Mn(H_2O)_6]^{2+}$ Mn^{2+} d^5 $\sqrt{35}$

Since (a) and (b), each has 4 unpaired electron they will have same magnetic moment.

59. **(c)** These two components *A* and *B* follows the condition of Raoult's law if the force of attraction between *A* and *B* is equal to the force of attraction between *A* and *A* or *B* and *B*.

60. **(a)** $Cr(OH)_3(s) \rightleftharpoons Cr^{+3}(aq) + 3OH^-(aq)$

At eq: s 3s

$K_{sp} = (s).(3s)^3 = 27s^4$

$27s^4 = 1.6 \times 10^{-30}$; $s = \left(\frac{1.6}{27} \times 10^{-30}\right)^{1/4}$

61. **(a)** According to the stoichiometry of balanced equation 28 g N_2 react with 6 g H_2

$N_2 + 3H_2 \longrightarrow 2NH_3$

1 mole 3 mole
28 g 6 g

For 56 g of N_2, 12 g of H_2 is required.

62. **(c)** Correct formula for calculation of E_a is

$$\log\frac{k_2}{k_1} = \frac{E_a}{2.303R}\left[\frac{T_2 - T_1}{T_1T_2}\right]$$

63. **(c)** Elements (1), (2) and (4) belong to the same group since each one of them has two electrons in the *s* sub shell. In contrast, element (3) has seven electrons in the valence shell and hence does not lie in the same group in which elements (1), (2) and (4) lie.

64. **(c)** $F < Cl < Br < I$ (Covalent radius)
$Cl > F > Br > I$ (Electron affinity) (Irregularity)
$F^- < Cl^- < Br^- < I^-$ (Ionic radius)
$F > Cl > Br > I$ (Ist ionization energy)

65. **(b)** A – IV, B – III, C – II, D – I

66. **(a)** By sodium fusion extract we can detect sulphur, nitrogen, phosphorus and halogens, because they are converted into their ionic form with sodium metal.

67. **(c)** Rotation around a C-C single bond is not completely free. It is hindered by a small energy barrier of 1-20 kJ mol^{-1} due to weak repulsive interaction between the adjacent bonds. Such a type of repulsive interaction is called **torsional strain**.

68. **(c)** A cation having highest reduction potential will be reduced first and so on. However, Mg^{2+} in aqueous solution will not be reduced.

$\left(E^0_{Mg^{2+}/Mg} < E_{H_2O/\frac{1}{2}H_2+OH^-}\right)$. Instead water would be reduced in preference.

69. **(d)** 1,2-dimethyl... cyclohexanol (CH₃, CH₃, OH) $\xrightarrow{H^+}$ protonated alcohol (OH_2^+) $\xrightarrow{-H_2O}$ carbocation $\xrightarrow{[1,2]\text{ methyl shift}}$ carbocation (CH₃, CH₃) $\xrightarrow{-H^+}$ alkene (CH₃, CH₃)

70. **(b)** A – III; B – I; C – II; D – IV
For spontaneity, $\Delta H - T\Delta S < 0$

71. **(d)** Phenol $\xrightarrow{\text{Zn dust}}$ Benzene, (X) $\xrightarrow[\text{Friedel Craft reaction}]{CH_3Cl,\ \text{anhy. } AlCl_3}$ Toluene, (Y) $\xrightarrow{KMnO_4}$ Benzoic acid, (Z)

72. **(b)** Aniline (NH_2) $\xrightarrow[\text{(0-5°C) (diazotisation reaction)}]{NaNO_2 + HCl}$ $\overset{+}{N_2}Cl^-$ $\xrightarrow[\text{(Sandmeyer reaction)}]{Cu_2Cl_2}$ Chlorobenzene (Cl) $\xrightarrow[\text{623K, 300 atm (Dow's process)}]{NaOH,}$ ONa $\xrightarrow{H^+}$ OH

73. **(a)** A – II; B – I; C – III; D – IV

74. **(c)** The oscillating fields are perpendicular to the direction of propagation.

75. **(c)** Lucas reagent is a mixture of anhydrous $ZnCl_2$ and conc. HCl. It is used for the distinction of monohydric alcohols. Tertiary alcohols on addition produce a precipitate immediately while secondary alcohols produce ppt. after 5 minutes. Primary alcohols do not produce any precipitate.

76. **(c)** $Mg + 2HCl \rightarrow MgCl_2 + H_2$
Volume of H_2 evolved = 220 mL

Moles of H_2 at STP $= \dfrac{\text{Volume}}{\text{Molar Volume at STP}}$

$= \dfrac{220 \times 10^{-3} \text{L}}{22.4 \text{L}} =$ moles of Mg used

$\therefore$ Mass of Mg used $= \dfrac{220 \times 10^{-3}}{22.4} \times 24 \text{ g/mol}$

$= 235.7 \times 10^{-3}$ g

$= 235.7$ mg

≈ 236 mg

77. **(d)** Lone pair present at X can enter in the ring. This gives rise to double bond character in C – X bond attached to the ring.

78. **(a)** According to Henry's law

$p = K_H \chi$

for χ constant : $p \propto K_H$

p has max partial pressures.

So it should have maximum K_H and s have minimum partial pressure, So K_H should be minimum.

79. **(b)** Oxidation takes place at zinc anode.

80. **(c)** Greater the surface area, greater will be the boiling point of a compound. Surface area decreases with increases in branching.

Increasing order of boiling point

$(H_3C)_3—C—Br_3 <$ $(H_3C)_2$>$CHCH_2Br_2$

$< CH_3CH_2CH_2CH_2Br$

81. **(b)** (Cyclohexyl)–$CH_2 - CH = CH_2$ $\xrightarrow[\text{(ii) Zn.}H_2O]{\text{(i) }O_3}$ (Cyclohexyl)–$CH_2 - \overset{\overset{O}{||}}{C} - H$ + $H - \overset{\overset{O}{||}}{C} - H$ (Methanal)

82. **(b)** A, C and D

83. **(c)** Rate = k[A]²[B]

When concentration of A is tripled, [A′] = [3A]

New rate, r′ = k[A′]²[B] = k[3A]²[B] = 9k[A]²[B]

⇒ r′ = 9r, increases by factor of nine.

84. **(b)** (Cyclohexanone)=O + $H_2NCH_2CH_3$ → (Cyclohexylidene)= NCH_2CH_3

$\xrightarrow[\text{reduction}]{H_2/Pt}$ (Cyclohexyl)–$NHCH_2CH_3$

85. **(b)** The delocalised $p\pi - p\pi$ bonding between filled p-orbital of F and vacant p-orbital of B leads to shortening of B–F bond length which results in higher bond dissociation energy of the B–F bond.

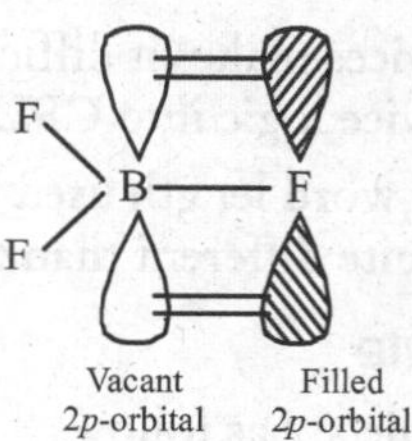

$F_2B{=}F^+ \longleftrightarrow F_2B{-}F$ (with F^+ double bonded) $\longleftrightarrow$ …

$F_2B - F \equiv$ B with three partial bonds to F, each F carrying $+1/3$

86. **(d)** $AB(g) \rightleftharpoons A(g) + B(g)$

$(1-\alpha)P \quad\quad \alpha P \quad\quad \alpha P$

Applying law of mass action,

$K_p = \dfrac{\alpha^2 P}{1-\alpha^2}$ (considering a is the degree of dissociation)

$\dfrac{\alpha^2}{1-\alpha} = 2.56 \times 10^{-2}$

$\Rightarrow \alpha^2 = 2.56 \times 10^{-2}$ $\quad [\approx (1-\alpha) = 1]$

$\Rightarrow \alpha = \sqrt{2.56 \times 10^{-2}} \Rightarrow \alpha = 0.16$

% age dissociation = 16%

87. **(b)** The energy involved in the conversion of $\frac{1}{2}Cl_2(g)$ to $Cl^-(aq)$ is given by

$\Delta H = \frac{1}{2}\Delta_{diss}H_{Cl_2} + \Delta_{eg}H_{Cl} + \Delta_{hyd}H_{Cl}$

Substituting various values from given data, we get

$\Delta H = \left(\frac{1}{2} \times 240\right) + (-349) + (-381) \text{ kJmol}^{-1}$

$= (120 - 349 - 381) \text{ kJ mol}^{-1} = -610 \text{ kJ mol}^{-1}$

88. **(c)** As per Pauli exclusion principle, "no two electrons in an atom can have all the four quantum numbers equal or an orbital cannot contain more than two electrons and it can accommodate two electrons only when their directions of spin are opposite".

An I/O module is needed because of:

(i) Diversity of I/O devices makes it difficult to include all the peripheral device logic into CPU.

(ii) The data format and word length used by the peripheral may be quite different than that of a CPU.

Features of I/O Module

The features of I/O module are as follows:

(i) It is a mediator between the processor and an I/O devices.

(ii) It controls the data exchange between the external devices and the main memory.

(iii) It should not only communicate the information from CPU to I/O device but it should also coordinate these two.

(iv) An I/O module provides an interface internal to the computer which connects it to CPU and main memory and an interface external to the computer connecting it to external device or peripheral.

1.7.4 Programmed I/O

Using this technique, data transfer takes place under the direct control of the processor. The processor must continuously check an I/O device and hence it cannot do another task. This method is hence inefficient (slow).

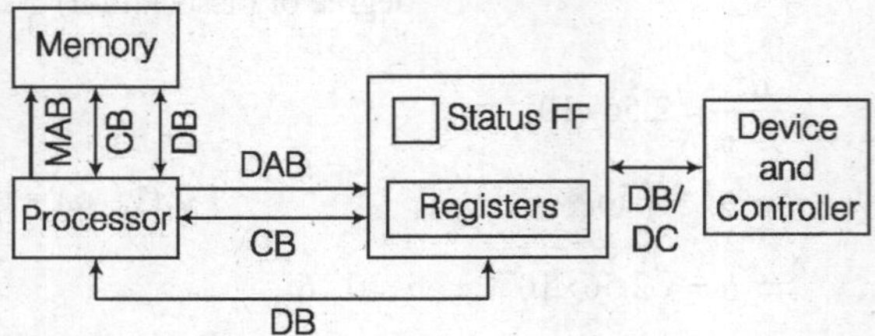

DB - Data Bus,

DAB - Device Address Bus,

DC - Device Control Signals,

MAB - Memory Address Bus,

CB - Control Bus.

Characteristics of Programmed I/O

Characteristics of programmed I/O are as follows:

(i) In programmed I/O, the I/O operations are completely controlled by the CPU.

(ii) Used in real-time and embedded systems.

(iii) Used in CPUs, which have a single input and a single output instruction. Each of these instructions selects one device.

(iv) The disadvantage of this technique is that the CPU spends most of its time waiting for the device to become ready.

1.7.5 Interrupt Driven I/O

The term interrupt is used for any event that causes temporary transfer of control of CPU from one program to the other which is causing the interrupt.

Interrupts are primarily issued on:

(i) Initiation of I/O operation

(ii) Completion of an I/O operation

(iii) Occurrence of hardware or software errors.

Interrupts can be generated by various sources internal or external to the CPU.

In the interrupt driven I/O, the processor issues a READ/WRITE instruction to the device and then continue doing its task. When the interface buffer is full, and it is ready to send data to the processor, the interface sends a signal to the processor informing it that data is ready. This signal is called as **interrupt signal.** When the processor receives the interrupt signal, it knows that the data is ready; it suspends its current job and transfers data from buffer to its own registers.

1.7.6 Direct Memory Access (DMA)

The transfer of data between a fast storage device such as magnetic disk and memory of often limited by the speed of the CPU. An efficient method is that we can facilitate I/O device to directly communicate with memory and keep CPU free for other task. For this purpose, DMA device is used.

The DMA controller is a device that facilitates data between memory and I/O device directly without the interrupt of CPU.

The working of DMA is illustrating in following logic diagram:

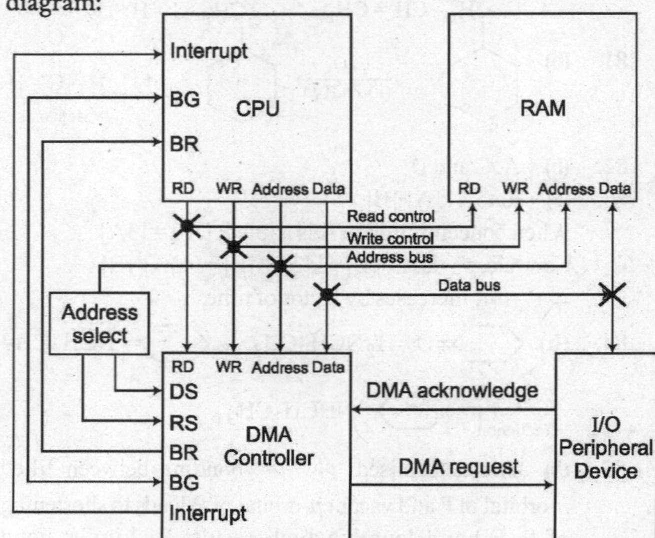

DMA transfer in a computer system

When I/O device wants to access the memory through DMA, it generates DMA request to DMA controller. After receiving the DMA request signal the DMA controller interrupts the CPU and sends the Bus Request (BR) signals to indicate that it is a DMA request. After receiving BR signal CPU responds with its BG (Bus Grand) lines that buss are free for DMA transfer. The DMA then puts the current value of its address register to the address line and sets DMA acknowledge signal high to indicate I/O device that it can now receive/send data from/to memory device. Once the transfer is done the DMA request signal is set to low and BR/BG and interrupt signal is also set to low to indicate that memory is now used by CPU.

There are two methods by which DMA transfer is done:

(i) **Cycle Stealing** In this method, the data transfer is done when CPU is busy in other last.

(ii) **Bulk Transfer** In this method, all data is transferred after DMA acknowledgement.

1.7.7 Input /Output (I/O) Channels

I/O channels provide for communications between the CPU and all peripheral devices. This is accomplished by electrical cables that carry both data and control information to and from the computer and peripheral devices. Signals are transmitted and received through a cable connecting the CPU and its online devices. This cable or line provides a path for the signal to travel and is called a **channel**.

I/O Channel Types

I/O channel may be simplex or duplex:

(i) **Simplex channel** In simplex channel, communications are in one direction only, such as a radio.

(ii) **Duplex channel** This channel simply means that within each cable connection, there are two paths for the transmission of data. One path is for sending and other is for receiving, similar to your telephone.

1.7.8 External Interface

The connections of the core of the processor to the outside world is done by the external interface. It is important that this interface minimizes the overhead required for the processor to do a transaction with the outside world. The goal is to allow the implementation of straight forward external circuits to connect the processor to the external cache, coprocessors and main system bus.

1.8 Computer Memory

The computer memory is one of the most important elements in a computer system. It is the internal or external storage area, which holds the data and instructions during processing in the form of binary numbers.

It also relates to many devices and components that are responsible for storing data and applications on a temporary or a permanent basis.

Computer memory can be classified into two types:

1. Primary memory
2. Secondary memory/Storage device.

1.8.1 Primary Memory

It is also known as **main memory**. It is the internal storage memory used by computer to hold data and instructions. The primary memory has limited storage capacity. Primary memory holds the data and programs needed at that instant by CPU.

There are two types of primary memory as follows:

1. RAM (Random Access Memory)

It is the internal memory that can be read from as well as written to. This memory is often associated with volatile types of memory. It can hold data only on temporary basis because it requires a continuous flow of electrical current. If current is interrupted, data is lost. It is an integrated circuit that enables you to access the stored data in a random order constantly.

⚠ A framebuffer is a portion of RAM containing a bitmap that is used to refresh a video display from a memory buffer containing a complete frame of data.

The two main forms of RAM are as follows:

(i) **Static RAM** It is also written as SRAM. It is a computer memory that requires a constant power flow in order to hold information. SRAM is more expensive and requires more power therefore it is commonly used in cache and video card memory. It is faster than DRAM.

(ii) **Dynamic RAM** It is also written as DRAM. It stores information in a cell containing a capacitor and transistor, these cells must be refreshed with electric impulses in few milliseconds. This process allows memory to keep charge and hold the data as long as needed.

2. ROM (Read Only Memory)

In ROM information once stored remain fixed, i.e. it cannot be changed. So, ROM can only be read and used. Generally, it contains a set of start-up instructions, i.e. what to do when a computer is turned ON. The contents of ROM remain stored even if power is turned OFF. This memory is often associated with non-volatile types of memory. A ROM cannot be altered once the chip has been made.

130. (d) New cells are produced by mitotic divisions of the meristematic cells. These cells have cellulosic cell walls, large nucleus and rich in protoplasm.

131. (d) The symbol [pedigree symbol] shows parents with female child affected with disease.

132. (a) **133. (a)**

134. (c) In a mature pollen grain, the generative cell is smaller and the tube (or vegetative) cell is larger. In the later stages of development of pollen grain, callose dissolves and the naked generative cell comes to lie freely in the cytoplasm of the tube cell. The tube cell has a cytoplasm which is rich in the food reserve (starch, protein, fat with mostly unsaturated fatty acids).

135. (a) Double fertilisation is a characteristic feature of angiosperms. It involves two fusions in which one male gamete fuses with egg cell to form zygote and other male gamete fuses with the diploid secondary nucleus to produce triploid primary endosperm nucleus.

136. (a)

137. (a) Female wasp and fig species is not an example of commensalism. It show mutualism in which each organism benefits from the interaction in some way. While orchid on trees on which it grows, cattle egret and grazing cattle, and sea anemone and clown fish show commensalism. Commensalism is an association between two organisms, in which one benefits and the other derives neither benefit nor harm.

138. (d) Hepatitis B and AIDS are transmitted through infected blood. Hepatitis B, poputarly called serum hepatitis or transfusion hepatitis is caused by hepatitis B virus. It is also called Dane parlicle. Transmission of hepatites B includes blood (blood transfusion), tattoos etc. AIDS is caused by HIV which belongs to retrovirus. It is transmitted through body fluids by sexual contact, infected blood shared needles etc.

139. (c)

140. (d) Glomerulus is a tuft of capillaries formed by ***afferent arteriole*** (a fine branch of renal artery).

141. (a) In the human heart, there is no mixing of deoxygenated and oxygenated blood due to the presence of inter - atrial and inter - ventricular septum. These septa completely divide the atria and ventricles into right and left and thus avoid mixing of blood. As the heart muscle contracts and relaxes, the valves open and shut, letting blood flow into the ventricles and atria at alternate times. This heart valve minimises any obstruction and allows blood to flow smoothly and freely in one direction. It closes completely and quickly, not allowing any blood to flow back through the valve. The heart has 4 valves: the mitral valve and tricuspid valve, which control blood flow from the atria to the ventricles and the aortic valve and pulmonary valve, which control blood flow out of the ventricles.

142. (a) **143. (c)** **144. (d)** **145. (a)** **146. (c)** **147. (b)**

148. (c) *Struthio* (Ostrich) is the largest living flightless bird.

149. (d)

150. (b) Copper-T is copper releasing intra uterine devices (IUD). It increases phagocytosis of sperms within the uterus and suppress sperm motility and fertilising capacity of sperms.

151. (a) Use of contraceptive pills is a widespread form of birth control. Contraceptive pills contain oestrogen and progesterone. The production of the pituitary hormones FSH and LH in the normal sexual cycle of a female is shut down by these hormones. In the absence of FSH, the ovarian follicles do not ripen and ovulation does not occur in the absence of LH.

152. (b) Circulatory system in arthropods is of open type. i.e. blood flows in irregular spaces called lacunae. It does not flow in definite blood vessels.

153. (c) AIDS is caused by HIV. When HIV enters into helper T-cells, it replicates and produces other viruses that kill the helper T-cells. Thus, the number of helper T-cells decreases in the body of the infected person and the person starts suffering from various infections.

154. (c) Roundworms are pseudocoelomate animals. The coelom is not completely lined by mesoderm, there are scattered patches or pouches of mesoderm inbetween ectoderm and endoderm.

155. (a) Frequency of dominant allele (p) = 60% = 0.6

The frequency of recessive allele, according to (p + q) = 1, will be 0.4

The value of pq = 0.6 × 0.4 = 0.24

The frequency of heterozygous individuals, therefore, will be 2pq = 2 × 0.24 = 0.48 or 48%.

156. (c) Human embryo have gills. This shows ontogeny repeats phylogeny. Ontogeny is the life history of an organism while phylogeny is the evolutionary history of the race of that organism. Modern theory of origin of life was propounded by Oparin and Haldane which is based on chemical evolution. Chemical evolution, also called chemogeny, involves the synthesis of simple organic molecules. Miller and Urey experimentally supported Oparin and Haldane theory with the help of stimulation experiment. Analogous organs are those organs which are similar in shape and function but their origin, basic plan and development are dissimilar. Example, wings of butterfly, bird and bat. Such similarities are because of convergent evolution for adaptation to a common condition.

157. (b) Tidal volume is the normal volume of air displaced between normal inhalation and exhalation. It is approximately 500 mL.
The inspiratory reserve volume (IRV) is the additional amount of air that can be inhaled after a normal inspiration (tidal volume). It is between 2500-3000 mL in humans.
The expiratory reserve volume (ERV) is the amount of extra air above a normal breath, exhaled during a forceful breath out. The average ERV volume is about 1100 mL in males and 800 mL in females.
The residual volume is the amount of air remaining in the lungs at the end of a normal exhalation. This averages 1100 mL to 1200 mL.

158. (d) In peroxidase and catalase which catalyse the break down of hydrogen peroxide to water and oxygen, heme is a prosthetic group.

159. (d) Analogy is the example of the eye of the octopus and of mammals or the flippers of Penguins and Dolphins.

160. (a) Both the statements are correct.

161. (b)

162. (c) Autonomic nervous system (ANS) automatically regulates the activities of smooth muscles, cardiac muscles and glands. This coordination is involuntary.

163. (c) Splicing is the removal of introns and joining of exons which is necessary in eukaryotes for functional mRNA.

164. (a) In vertebrates, the lungs, liver & skin are referred as accessory excretory organs because besides the urinary system these organs also participate in the removal of waste products from the body. The liver is the principal organ for the excretion of cholesterol, bile pigments (bilirubin and biliverdin) and inactivated products of steroid hormones, some vitamins and many drugs. It secretes these substances in the bile and indirectly helps in formation of urea through amino acids in ornithine cycle. It has no role in secretion of urine.

165. (d)

166. (b) For a gene with two alleles, A (dominant) and a (recessive), if the frequency of A is p and the frequency of a is q, then the frequencies of the three possible genotypes (AA, Aa, and aa) can be expressed by the Hardy-Weinberg equation:
$p2 + 2pq + q2 = 1$
where, p2 = frequency of AA (homozygous dominant) individuals, 2pq = frequency of Aa (heterozygous) individuals and q2 = frequency of aa (homozygous recessive) individuals. The equation can be used to calculate allele frequencies if the numbers of homozygous recessive individuals in the population is known.
Here, p = 0.7 and q = 0.3 (given)
$\therefore$ 2pq (frequency of heterozygote)
$= 2 \times 0.7 \times 0.3 = 0.42$

167. (a) Lipid droplets are structures that store fat in the form of neutral lipids. Lipid droplets are composed of a core of triglycerides and sterol esters.
Membrane lipids are present in form of phospholipids. They form lipid bilayer because of their amphipathic characters.
Steroid hormones are released by animals such as glucocorticoids (cortisol), mineralocorticoids (aldosterone).
Wax is waterproof coating on the surface of leaves. It reduces transpiration.

168. (c)

169. (b) Morphine is the principle opium alkaloid. It is a strong analgesic. Opium is dried latex of unripe capsular fruits of poppy plant, *Papaver somniferum*. It is eaten or smoked. Morphine depresses respiratory centre, contributes to the fall in BP and cause bradycardia. It causes addiction.

170. (a) *Azolla* and BGA are biofertilizer which increases the fertility of soil.

171. (a) Interstitial cells secrete androgens but not FSH. Cleavage occurs in zygote. In males, spermatogenesis starts at puberty.

172. (c)

173. (d) Bt toxins is harmful to insects like lepidopteron (tobacco budworm, armyworm), coleopterans (beetles) and dipterans (flies and mosquito) because they kill larvae of certain insects by binding the activated toxins on midgut epithelial cells, creating pores which causes swelling and lysis of the cells leading to the death of the insect larva.

174. (a)

175. (d) Every enzyme possesses an optimum pH value, where it is most effective. Most enzymes show maximum activity in a pH range of about 6.0 to 7.5, i.e., near neutral pH. Some digestive enzymes have their optimum pH in the acidic or activity alkaline range. e.g., pepsin of gastric juice has its optimum at pH 2 (acidic), and trypsin of pancreatic juice shows maximum activity at pH 8.8 (alkaline). A rise and fall in pH reduces enzyme activity by changing the degree of ionisation of its side chain.

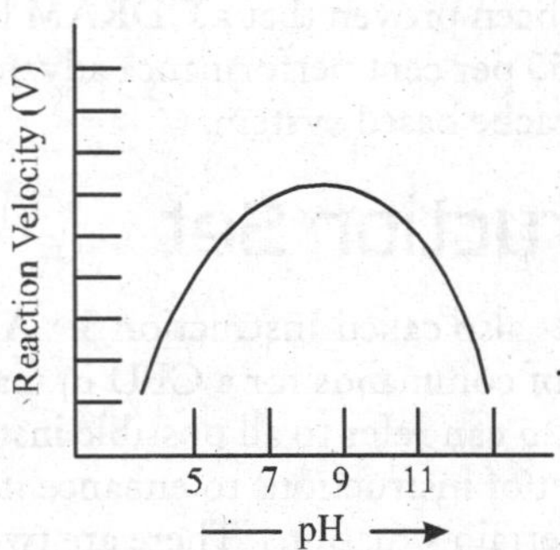

Fig.: Effect of pH on the velocity of enzyme action

(iii) More expensive memory chips.
(iv) Concurrent RDRAMs have been used in video games, while direct RDRAMs have been used in computers.

3. Double Data Rate DRAM (DDR DRAM)

(i) Uses both rising (positive edge) and falling (negative) edge of clock for data transfer. That is DDR SDRAM can send data twice per clock cycle - once on the rising edge of the clock pulse and once on the falling edge.
(ii) There has been improvement in DDR DRAM technology. The later generations (DDR2 and DDR3) increases the data rate by increasing the operational frequency of the RAM chip and by increasing the prefetch buffer from 2 bits to 4 bits per chip.
(iii) DDR can transfer data at a clock rate in the range of 200 MHz to 600 MHz, DDR2 can transfer in the range of 400 MHz to 1066 MHz and DDR3 can transfer in the range of 800 MHz to 1600 MHz.

4. Cache DRAM (CDRAM)

(i) Integrates a small SRAM cache onto a generic DRAM chip.
(ii) The SRAM on CDRAM can be used in two ways
   (a) It can be used as true cache.
   (b) It can be used as buffer to support the serial access of a block of data.
(iii) This architecture achieves concurrent operation of DRAM and SRAM synchronised with an external clock. Separate control and address input terminals of the two portions enable independent control of the DRAM and SRAM, thus the system achieves continuous and concurrent operation of DRAM and SRAM.
(iv) CDRAM can handle CPU, DMA and video refresh at the same time by utilising a high-speed video interface.
(v) CDRAM can replace cache and main memory, and it has already been proven that a CDRAM based system has a 10 to 50 per cent performance advantage over a 256 Kbyte cache based system.

1.10 Instruction Set

An instruction set also called Instruction Set Architecture (ISA) is a group of commands for a CPU in machine language. The term can refer to all possible instructions for a CPU or a subset of instructions to enhance its performance in certain situations. There are two commonly known instruction sets:

(i) CISC (ii) RISC (iii) EPIC

1.10.1 Complex Instruction Set Computing/Computer (CISC)

The CISC architecture contains a large set of computer instructions that range from very simple to very complex and specialised. The primary goal of CISC architecture is to complete a task in as few lines of assembly as possible. This is achieved by building processor hardware that is capable of understanding and executing a series of operations, e.g. we want to find the product of two numbers-one stored in location 2 : 3 and another stored in location 5 : 2 and then store the product back in location 2 : 3.

For this particular task, a CISC processor would come prepared with a specific instruction (i.e. MULT). When executed, this instruction loads the two values into separate registers, multiplies the operands in the execution unit and then stores the product in the appropriate registers.

Thus, the entire task of multiplying two numbers can be completed with one instruction.

MULT 2 : 3, 5 : 2

Some characteristics of CISC are given below:

(i) A large number of instructions- typically from 100 to 250 instructions.
(ii) A large variety of addressing modes- typically 5 to 20 different modes.
(iii) Variable-length instruction formats.
(iv) A small number of general purpose registers.

Examples of CISC processors are Intel 386, Intel 486, Pentium Pro, Pentium III, Motorola's 68040 etc.

1.10.2 Reduced Instruction Set Computing/Computer (RISC)

RISC microprocessor has a relatively limited number of instructions. It is designed to perform a **smaller number of types of computer** instructions, so that it can operate at a higher speed (perform more million of instructions per second). This concept was developed with the belief that a computer uses only 20% of the instructions, making the other 80% unnecessary.

A processor based on this concept would use few instructions. By reducing the number of instructions to only those most frequently used, the computer would get more work done in a shorter amount of time. RISC processors only use simple instructions that can be executed within one clock cycle.

Thus, the MULT command described above could be divided into three separate commands: **LOAD** which moves data from the memory bank to register, **PROD** which finds the product of two operands located within the register and **STORE** which moves data from a register to the memory banks.

In order to perform the exact series of steps described in the CISC approach, a programmer would need to code four lines of assembly:

```
LOAD    A,    2:3
LOAD    B,    5:2
PROD    A,    B
STORE   2:3,  A
```

Some characteristics of RISC are given below:

(i) Relatively few instructions and few addressing modes
(ii) Memory access limited to load and store instructions.
(iii) All operations are done within the register of the CPU.
(iv) Fixed-length and easily-decoded instruction set.
(v) Single cycle instruction execution.

Examples of RISC processors are IBM RS 6000, MC88100, DEC's Alpha 21064, 21164, 21264 processors etc.

1.10.3 Explicitly Parallel Instruction Computing/Computer (EPIC)

EPIC refers to architecture in which features are provided to facilitate compiler enhancements of Instruction Level Parallelism (ILP) in all programs, while keeping hardware complexity relatively low.

Using ILP enhancement techniques such as speculation and prediction, the compiler identifies the operation that can execute in parallel in each cycle and communicates a plan of execution to the hardware.

Some characteristics of EPIC are given below:

(i) Uses parallel instructions.
(ii) Programs must be written using sequential semantics with explicitly laid out parallelism.
(iii) Compiler plays the key role in designing the plan of execution.
(iv) The architecture provides the requisite support to the compiler to design the plan of execution successfully.
(v) The architecture provides the mechanisms to communicate the compiler's plan of execution to the hardware.

Examples of EPIC processors are Intel IA-64, Itanium processors etc.

1.11 Operand

In computing, an operand is the part of a computer instruction which specifies what data is to be manipulated or operated on, while at the same time representing the data itself. A computer instruction describes an operation such as add or multiply x, while operand specify on which x to operate as well as the value of x.

The operand is also called as **data**.

Types of Operands

The most important general categories of data are as follows:

1. Addresses

This is nothing but a form of data. Here, some calculations must be performed on the operand reference in an instruction, which is to determine the physical address of an instruction.

2. Numbers

All machine languages include numeric data types. Even in non-numeric data processing, there is a need for numbers to act as counters, field widths and so forth. Three types of numerical data are common in computers:

(i) Integer or fixed point
(ii) Floating point
(iii) Decimal

3. Characters

A common form of data is text or character strings. While textual data are most convenient for human beings, they cannot in character form, be easily stored or transmitted by data processing and communications systems.

4. Logical data

Normally, each word or other addressable unit (byte, half-word and so on) is treated as a single unit of data. It is sometimes useful, however to consider an n-bit unit as consisting 1-bit terms of data, each item having the value 0 or 1. When data are viewed in this way, they are considered to be logic data.

1.12 Operation

In computing, operation is data processing in which the result is completely specified by a rule (specially the processing that results from a single instruction).

Types of Operations

The number of different opcodes varies widely from machine to machine. However, the same general types of operations are found on all machines.

Arihant Publications (India) Ltd.

Administrative & Production Offices

Regd. Office

'Ramchhaya' 4577/15, Agarwal Road, Darya Ganj, New Delhi -110002

Tele: 011- 47630600, 43518550; Fax: 011- 23280316

Head Office

Kalindi, TP Nagar, Meerut (UP) - 250002

Tele: 0121-2401479, 2512970, 4004199; Fax: 0121-2401648

Sales & Support Offices

Agra, Ahmedabad, Bengaluru, Bhubaneswar, Bareilly, Chennai, Delhi, Guwahati, Hyderabad, Jaipur, Jhansi, Kolkata, Lucknow, Meerut, Nagpur & Pune

ISBN : 978-93-12145-10-4

Printed and bound at Repro Knowledgecast Limited, Thane

For further information about books Published by Arihant log on to www.arihantbooks.com or email to info@arihantbooks.com

CONTENTS

In the above figure, the ALU gets the data from the register and the result is stored back into these registers. The two multiplexers are connected to the output of the register to form two buses A and B. These buses provides the input to the ALU, where the arithmetic, logic, or shift operations are performed depending upon the opcode specified by the instruction. Once the micro-operations are performed, the result is stored back into the registers. Let us consider the following operation:

R1 <- R2 R3

The binary selection variables must be provided by the control unit for the following selector inputs:

1. **MUX A Selector** (SEL A) Places the content of R2 into the bus A.
2. **MUX B Selector** (SEL B) Places the content of R3 into the bus B.
3. **ALU Operation Selector** (OPR) Provides the arithmetic subtraction A B.
4. **Decode Destination Selector** (SEL D) Transfers the content of the result to register R1.

Control unit generates all four selection variable mentioned in above example and these variable must be available before the beginning of the instruction cycle.

1.16 Instruction Cycle

The instruction cycle represents the sequence of events that takes place as an instruction is read from memory and executed. The program is executed in the computer by going through a cycle for each instruction. Each instruction is subdivided into a sequence of subcycles.

Instruction Fetch Execute Cycle

A more complete form of the Instruction Fetch Execute cycle can be broken down into the following steps:

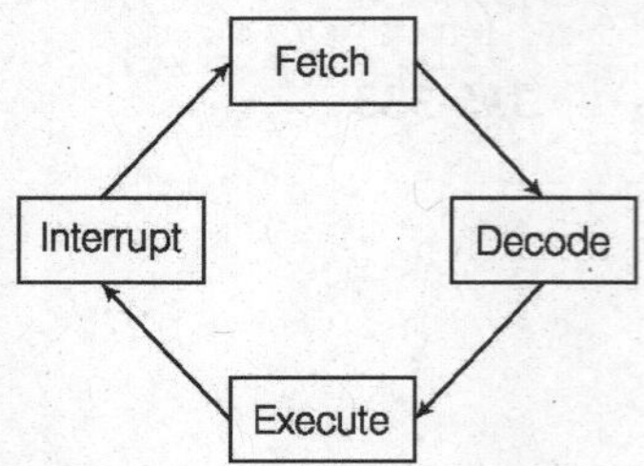

1. **Fecth Cycle** The fetch cycle begins with retrieving the address stored in the Program Counter (PC).
2. **Decode Cycle** The decode cycle is used for interpreting the instruction that was fetched in the fetch cycle. The operands are retrieved from the addresses if the need be.
3. **Execute Cycle** This cycle as the name suggests, simply executes the instruction that was fetched and decoded.
4. **Interrupt Cycle** An interrupt can occur any time during the program execution. Whenever it is caused, a series of events take place so that the instruction fetch execute cycle can again resume after the OS calls the routine to handle the interrupt.

1.17 Instruction Formats

1. Three Address Instructions

Three address instruction requires 3 address spaces to define instructions. 1 address is used to define the operation code and next 2 address space is used to define the address of an operand.

Opcode	Higher byte of address	Lower byte of address

3 address space instructions are direct addressing, 16-bit immediate addressing.

2. Two-Address Instructions

In two-address instructions, 1 address is used to define operation code and 1 address space is used to define the register or operand directly.

Opcode	Operand or register

2-byte address space is required in immediate addressing mode.

3. One-Address Instruction

In one-address instruction, only operation code is required to defined the instruction.

Opcode

One address space is required in all remaining addressing mode.

1.18 Instruction Pipelining

A procedure for processing instructions in a computer program, more rapidly, in which each instruction is divided into numerous small stages and the population of instructions are in various stages at any given time, is called instruction pipelining. Pipelining is a technique of decomposing a sequential process into suboperations, with each subprocess being executed in a special dedicated segment that operates concurrently with the other segments.

For executing an instruction, four phases are required fetching, decoding, executing and storing result. In normal execution of program, four machine cycles are required to execute an instruction. For executing two instructions

$2 \times 4 = 8$ machine cycles are required. Instruction pipeline facilitates that the second instruction can be fetched when the first instruction is being executed. This can be illustrated by following diagram:

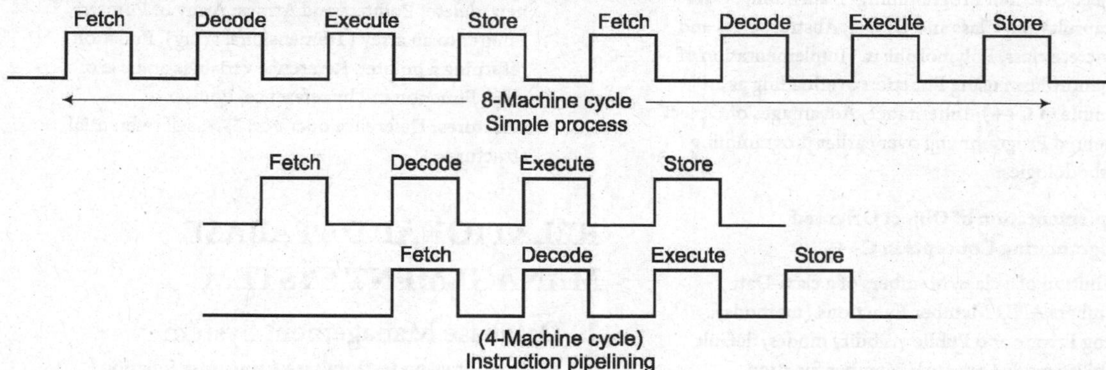

Thus from the above diagram, we can see that time required to execute several instructions in instruction pipelining is much less than simple processor. Thus, instruction pipelining is used to speed up the system.

(i) To complete n tasks using a k-segment pipeline requires $k + (n - 1)$ clock cycles.

(ii) The speed up of a pipeline system over an equivalent non-pipeline processing is defined by the ratio:

$$S = \frac{nt_n}{(k + n - 1)t_p}$$

Where, t_n = time required by non-pipelined process to complete each task,

n = number of tasks,

k = number of pipelines,

t_p = clock cycle time required by pipeline process to execute n tasks

when $n >> k - 1$

$$S = \frac{t_n}{t_p}$$

The maximum speed up that a pipeline can provide is k means the number of segment pipelines.

e.g. the diagram given below shows 4-segments and six tasks. The time required to complete all the operations is $4 + (6 - 1) = 9$ clock cycles.

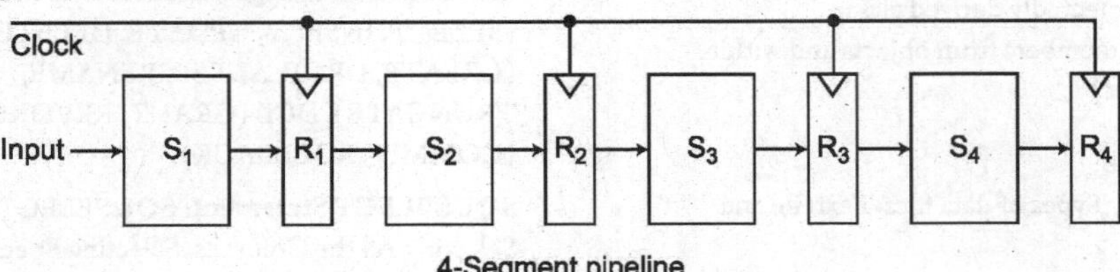

4-Segment pipeline

⚠ Efficiency of K stage pipeline = $\frac{\text{Speed Up factor } (S_K)}{\text{Number of stages } (K)}$

1.19 Control Unit

It is a component of computer's Central Processing Unit (CPU) that directs the operations of the processor. It tells the computer's memory, arithmetic/logic unit and input and output devices how to respond to a program's instructions.

1.19.1 Micro-operations

The programs are executed as a sequence of instructions, each instruction consists of a series of steps that make up the instruction cycle fetch, decode etc. Each of these steps are in turn, made up of a smaller series of step called **micro-operations.** Micro-operations are the fundamental or atomic operations of the processor.

PROGRAMMING IN C++

1. **Object Oriented Programming:** Concept of Object Oriented Programming- Data hiding, Data encapsulation, Class and Object, Abstract class and Concrete class, Polymorphism (Implementation of polymorphism using Function overloading as an example in C++); Inheritance, Advantages of Object Oriented Programming over earlier programming methodologies.

2. **Implementation of Object Oriented Programming Concepts in C++:**
   Definition of a class, Members of a class-Data Members AND Member Functions (methods), Using Private and Public visibility modes, default visibility mode (private); Member function definition: inside class definition and outside class definition using scope resolution operator (::); Declaration of objects as instances of a class; accessing members from object (s), Array of type class, Objects as function arguments-pass by value and pass by reference;

3. **Constructor and Destructor:**
   - **Constructor:** Special Characteristics, Declaration and Definition of a constructor, Default Constructor, Overloaded Constructors, Copy Constructor, Constructor with definition of destructor
   - **Destructor:** Special Characteristics, Declaration and definition of destructor
   - **Inheritance** (Extending Class): Concept of Inheritance, Base class, Derived class, Defining derived classes, Protected visibility mode; Single level inheritance, Multilevel inheritance and Multiple inheritance, Privately derived, Publicly derived and Protectedly derived class, accessibility of members from objects and within derived class (es)

4. **Data File Handling:**
   Need for a data file, Types of data files-Text file and Binary file.
   - **Basic File Operations on Text File:** Creating/ Writing text into file, Reading and manipulation of text from an already existing text file (accessing sequentially).
   - **Binary File:** Creation of file, Writing data into file, Searching for required data from file, Appending data to a file, Insertion of data in sorted filed, Deletion of data from file, Modification of data in a file.
   - Implementation of above mentioned data file handling in C++.
   - Components of C++ to be used with file handling.

5. **Pointers:**
   - **Declaration and Initialization of Pointers:** Dynamic memory allocation/ deallocation operators: new, delete; Pointers and Arrays: Array of Pointers, Pointer to an array (1dimensional array), Function returning a pointer, Reference variables and use of alias; Function call by reference, Pointer to structures: Deference operator: *,->; self referential structures;

RELATIONAL DATABASE MANAGEMENT SYSTEM

1. Database Management System

- **Introduction to Database Concepts:** Relation/ Table, Attribute, Tuple/ Rows, Fields, Data, Concept of String, Number and Date values, Data type and Data Integrity, (Domain and Referential Integrity). Candidate key, Alternate key, Primary key, Foreign keys; Data Normalization-first, second, third, BCNF normal form;
- **Examples of Commercially available Database Management System's** (Back-End): Oracle, MS-SQL Server, DB2, MySQL, Sybase, INGRES.
- **Examples of Front End Software's:** Oracle Developer, Visual Basic, Visual C++, Power Builder, Delphi;

2. RDBMS Tools: Oracle

- **ORACLE:** Introduction, Version, Two Tier and Three Tier support.
- Interface with oracle, Login Screen, Entering Name and Password.
- **Classification of SQL Statements:** DML (SELECT, INSERT, UPDATE, DELETE), DDL (CREATE, DROP, ALTER, RENAME, TRUNCATE), DCL (GRANT, REVOKE), TCL (COMMIT, ROLLBACK).
- **SQL SELECT Statement:** SQL SELECT statement, Selecting All the Columns, Selecting Specific Column, Column Heading Default, Using Arithmetic Operators, Operator Precedence, Significance of NULL value, NULL values in Arithmetic Expressions, Defining and using Column Alias, Concatenation Operator (ll), Duplicate rows and their Elimination (DISTINCT keyword), Role of SQL and SQL*Plus in interacting with RDBMS, Displaying Table Structure (DESC command).
- **SELECT Statement Continued:** Limiting Rows during selection (using WHERE clause), Working with Character Strings and Dates, Using Comparison operators, BETWEEN operator, IN operator, LIKE operator, IS NULL comparison, Logical operators, Use of Logical Operators (AND/OR/NOT

operators), Logical operator Precedence, ORDER BY clause, Sorting in Ascending/Descending order, Sorting By Column Alias Name, Sorting On multiple Columns.

- **Functions:** SQL functions, Types of SQL function (Single Row/ Multiple Row), Single row SQL functions, Character functions (Case Conversion/ Character Manipulation), Case conversion functions [lower (), InitCap (), UPPER ()] Character manipulation function [CONCAT (), INSTR (), LENGTH (), TRIM (), SUBSTR (), LPAD ()], Number functions (ROUND (), TRUNC (), MOD()), Working with Dates [LAST_DAY(), MONTHS_ BETWEEN(), NEXT_DAY(), ADD_MONTHS(), ROUND(), TRUNC()] Arithmetic operation on dates, Date functions and their usage, Data type conversion functions, Implicit and explicit conversion, TO_CHAR function with dates, TO_CHAR function For numbers, TO_NUMBER and TO_DATE functions, NVL function and its usage, DECODE function and its usage.
- **Grouping Records:** Concept of grouping records and nested grouping, Nested grouping of records, Group functions, Types of group functions [MAX (), MIN (), AVG (), SUM (), COUNT ()], Using AVG and SUM functions, Using MIN and MAX functions, Using the COUNT function, Using COUNT(*), DISTINCT clause with Count, Group functions and Null Values, Using NVL function with group functions, Grouping records: Group by Clause, Grouping by more than one column, Illegal Queries with Group By Clause, Excluding group results: Having clause, Nesting group functions.
- **Sub Queries:** Concept of sub-query, Sub-query to solve a problem, Guidelines for using sub queries, Types of sub-queries (Single Row and Multiple Row) and (Single Column and Multiple Column); Single row sub-query and its execution.
- **Displaying Data From Multiple Tables:** Concept of join, Result of join, Cartesian product and generating cartesian production example using Mathematical Set, Types of joins (EQUL, SELF, NON-EQUI, OUTER (LEFT and RIGHT)), Equi-join, Additional search conditions using AND operator, Short naming convention for tables (Table Aliases), Non- Equi join and its implementation, Outer-join and its usage, Self-join (Joining a table to Itself);
- **Manipulating Data of A Table /Relation:** Concept of DML (Data Manipulation Language), INSERT statement, Inserting new rows, Inserting new rows with null values, Inserting date values, Use of substitution Variable to insert values, copying rows from another table, Update statement to change existing data of a Table, Updating Rows In A table, Updating rows Based on another table, Delete statement/ Removing Row/ Rows from a Table, Deleting, rows based on condition from another table; Making data manipulation permanent (COMMIT), Undo data manipulation changes (ROLLBACK)
- **Database Objects:** View, Table, Sequence, Index, and Synonyms, DDL (Data Definition Language), Naming convention, Creating views, Creating synonyms, Simple views and complex views, Retrieving data from a view, Querying a view, Modifying a view.
- **Including Constraints:** Constraints, Concept of using constraints, Constraint guidelines, Defining constraints, NOT NULL, UNIQUE KEY, PRIMARY KEY, FOREIGN KEY, FOREIGN KEY constraint keywords, CHECK, Adding a constraint, Dropping a constraint, Disabling constraints, Enabling constraints, Viewing constraints, Viewing the columns, Associated with constraints;
- **Creation of a Table/ Relation:** CREATE TABLE statement, Data types, The DEFAULT option, Creating tables, Referencing another user's tables, Querying the database dictionary to view all tables in the Oracle database, Creating a table by using a Sub-Query;
- **Managing Existing Tables and other Database Objects:** The ALTER TABLE statement, Adding a new column in a table, Modifying existing column, Dropping a column, renaming an object, Truncating a table, Adding comments to a table, Dropping views, Dropping synonyms, Dropping tables; Giving permission to other users to work on created tables and revoking it (GRANT and REVOKE statement).

BUSINESS COMPUTING

- General concept, User interfaces (front end), Underlying Database (back End), Integration of User Interface and Database;
- **More application areas of Databases:**
- Inventory control, Financial accounting, Pay-accounting system, Invoicing management system, Personal management system/ hard system, Fees management system, Result analysis system, Admission management system, Income tax management system;

28. What is the speed up factor of n-stage pipeline?
(1) $(n+1)$ (2) $(n-1)$
(3) $2n$ (4) n

29. Branch instructions are handled in pipeline using
(1) prefetch target instruction strategy
(2) loop greffer strategy
(3) Both (1) and (2)
(4) None of the above

30. The performance of a pipelined processor suffers if
(1) the pipeline stages have different delays
(2) consecutive instructions are dependent on each other
(3) the pipeline stages share hardware resources
(4) All of the above

31. Which of the following is displacement addressing mode?
(1) Relative (2) Indexed
(3) Base (4) All of these

32. Which of the following may not occur in an instruction cycle?
(1) Fetch (2) Decode
(3) Execute (4) Indirect

33. The device which is used to connect a peripheral to bus is called
(1) control register
(2) communication protocol
(3) interface
(4) None of the above

34. Any instruction should have atleast
(1) 2 operands
(2) 1 operand
(3) 3 operands
(4) None of the above

35. A microprogrammed control unit
(1) as faster than a hard wired control unit.
(2) facilitates easy implementation of new instruction.
(3) is useful when very small program are to be use.
(4) usually refers to the control unit of a microprocessor.

36. Addressing modes are
(1) explicitly specified
(2) implied by the instruction
(3) Both (1) and (2)
(4) Neither (1) nor (2)

37. Microprogram is
(1) the name of source program in micro computers.
(2) the set of instructions indicating the primitive operations in a system.
(3) primitive form of macros used in assembly language programming.
(4) program of very small size.

38. Microprogramming is a technique for
(1) writing small programs effectively
(2) programming output/input routines
(3) programming the microprocessor
(4) programming the control steps of a computer

39. The control signal indicates
(1) whether a data is read into or written out to memory
(2) whether CPU is accessing memory of input/output device
(3) whether input/output device or memory is ready to transfer data
(4) All of the above

40. Linkage between CPU and the user is provided by
(1) peripheral devices
(2) control unit
(3) storage
(4) software

41. Assembly language uses
(1) hex code
(2) binary code
(3) mnemonics
(4) ASCII code

42. An assembler converts
(1) machine code to mnemonics
(2) high level language to assembly level
(3) assembly language to machine language
(4) All of the above

43. An assembly program contains
(1) imperative and declarative statements
(2) imperative statements and assembler directives
(3) imperative and declarative statements as well as assembler directives
(4) Declarative statements and assembler directive

44. Which of the following is a program control instruction?
(1) MOV
(2) MBR
(3) CMJ
(4) DBC

45. A(n) ....device is any device that provides information, which is sent to the CPU.
(1) input
(2) output
(3) CPU
(4) memory

46. This component is required to process data into information and consists of integrated circuits.
(1) Hard disk (2) RAM
(3) CPU (4) ROM

47. Which computer memory is used for storing programs and data currently being processed by the CPU?
(1) Mass memory
(2) Internal memory
(3) Non-volatile memory
(4) PROM

48. When machine instructions are being executed by a computer, the instruction phase followed by the execution phase is referred to as
(1) program cycle
(2) machine instruction
(3) instruction cycle
(4) task cycle

49. A group of bits that tells the computer to perform a specific operation is known as
(1) instruction code
(2) micro-operation
(3) accumulator
(4) register

50. The load instruction is mostly used to designate a transfer from memory to a processor register known as
(1) accumulator
(2) instruction register
(3) program counter
(4) memory address register

51. An input device that transfers information from the punched card to the computer's memory is
(1) cassette tape
(2) card
(3) card reader
(4) magnetic disk

52. Some devices require urgent service normal execution or programs may sometimes be preempted using
(1) an interrupt signal
(2) a request to memory modules
(3) DMA
(4) All of the above

53. The OCR recognises the ...... of the characters with the help of light source.
(1) size
(2) shape
(3) colour
(4) used ink

54. Which key is used in combination with another key to perform a specific task?
(1) Function (2) Space bar
(3) Arrow (4) Control

55. The rate at which scanning is repeated in a CRT is called
(1) refresh rate (2) resolution
(3) pitch (4) bandwidth

56. The transfer of data from a CPU to peripheral devices of computer is achieved through
(1) interfaces (2) buffer memory
(3) modems (4) I/O ports

57. The cache is used because reading external memory is very .... compared to the speed of the processor.
(1) slow (2) fast
(3) equal (4) unpredictable

58. External devices such as printers, keyboards and modems are known as
(1) add on devices
(2) PC expansion slot add-ons
(3) peripherals
(4) special buys

59. Which of the following devices is having a highest priority while assigning interrupts?
(1) Hard disk (2) Printer
(3) Keyboard (4) Floppy

60. The ability to temporarily halt the CPU and use this time to send information on buses is called
(1) direct memory access
(2) vectoring the interrupt
(3) palling
(4) cycle stealing

61. In implementing interrupts, action that is done by the hardware include
(1) souring all the register on stack
(2) souring the interrupt vector into special register
(3) fetching the address of the interrupt handler
(4) Both (2) and (3)

62. The data transfer scheme which prevents the CPU from doing any other task while it is waiting for data transfer is
(1) programmed I/O
(2) interrupt I/O
(3) DMA
(4) None of the above

63. The correct matching for following pair is

(a) DMA I/O	I. High speed DMA
(b) Cache	II. Disk
(c) Interrupt	III. Printer
(d) Condition code register	IV. ALU

(1) a-IV, b. III, c. I, d. II
(2) a-II, b. I, c. III, d. IV
(3) a-IV, b. III, c. II, d. I
(4) a-II, b. III, c. IV, d. I

64. Which output device is used for translating information from a computer into pictorial form on paper?
(1) Mouse (2) Plotter
(3) Touch panel (4) Card punch

65. A disk's content that is recorded at the time of manufacture and that cannot be changed or erased by the user is
(1) memory - only (2) write - only
(3) read - only (4) run - only

66. Which of the following statements is correct about the program counter?
(i) Program counter points to the instruction to be executed
(ii) The program counter contents are used as address and instruction is read from memory.
(1) (i) and (ii) (2) Only (ii)
(3) Only (i) (4) Neither (i) nor (ii)

67. The term .... refers to data storage systems that make it possible for a computer or electronic device to store and retrieve data.
(1) retrival technology
(2) input technology
(3) output technology
(4) storage technology

68. Magnetic tape is not practical for applications where data must be quickly recalled because tape is
(1) a random access medium
(2) a sequential access medium
(3) a read only medium
(4) fragile and easily damaged

69. Which of the following processor register are used for fetch and execute operations?
(i) Program counter
(ii) Instruction register
(iii) Memory Address register
(1) (i), (ii) (2) (ii), (iii)
(3) (i), (iii) (4) None of these

70. The technique that extends storage capacities of main memory beyond the actual size of the main memory is called
(1) multitasking
(2) virtual storage
(3) multiprocessing
(4) multiprogramming

71. The primary device that a computer uses to store information is
(1) TV
(2) storehouse
(3) desk
(4) hard drive

72. .... is the ability of a device to 'jump' directly to the requested data.
(1) Sequential access
(2) Random access
(3) Quick access
(4) All of the above

73. The storage device used to compensate for the difference in rates of flow of data from one device to another is termed as
(1) chip (2) floppy
(3) call (4) buffer

74. In order to reproduce sound, a Compact Disc (CD) audio player uses a
(1) quartz crystal
(2) titanium needle
(3) laser beam
(4) barium titanate ceramic

75. Which of the following are advantages of CD-ROM as a storage media?
(1) CD-ROM is an inexpensive way to store large amount of data and information
(2) CD-ROMs discs retrieve data and information more quickly than magnetic disks do
(3) CD-ROMs make less errors than magnetic media
(4) All of the above

76. ...... acts as temporary high speed holding area between the memory and the CPU thereby improving processing capabilities.
(1) ROM
(2) RAM
(3) Temporary memory
(4) Cache memory

- **Application:** Contents, Lock, Unlock, Remove, Remove ALL.
- **Asp Components:** AD rotator, content rotator, Counter, Page counter, Permission checker.
- **Text Files:** Open and Read content from a text file.
- **Elementary Database Concepts:** Concept of Table/ Relation, Relationship, Candidate key, Primary key, Alternate key, Foreign key
- **Connecting with Databases:** Creation of DSN, using OLEDB.
- **Working on Databases**: Inserting, Retrieving, Modifying/ Updation of records from Tables in Databases using server objects (ADODB. Connection, DODB. Recordset).
- **Server Variables:** HTTP_User_Agent, REMOTE_ADDER, REMOTE_HOST, SERVER_NAME;

WEB SCRIPTING

1. VBScript

- Introduction, Adding VBScript code to HTML page, VBScript Data type-Variant Subtypes, VBScript Variables: (Declaring variable, Naming restrictions, Assigning value to variables, Scalar variables and Arrays), VBScript Constants, VBScript Operators, and Operator precedence.
- **MsgBox:** Functions of message box (Prompt, Buttons, Title, Helpline, Context), Return values of MsgBox function, button argument setting.
- **Conditional Statement:** If..Then..Else, Select case.
- **Loops:** Do loops, While..Wend, For..Next, For..Each..Next.
- **VBScript Variables:** Sub procedures, Function procedures.
- Using VBScript with HTML form controls, Data handling functions, String functions, Date and Times function.

2. JavaScript

- Introduction, History of JavaScript, Using Java Script in an HTML Page, Objectives, Properties Methods and Events.
- Event handling, Adding JavaScript in an HTML page (Using SRC attribute within script with examples), Variable and data types- Data types and type casting, String processing, Arrays, Operators, Control flow with looping- for loop, while loop, using continue and break statement, Adding comments to scripts, The Window object, The Document Object, The Location Object, The Form Object, Working with control Objects (Button, reset and submit objects, Checkbox objects and Radio objects, Select object, Password, text and text area object, The Data object, Performing calculation.

MULTIMEDIA AND AUTHORING TOOLS

1. Graphics Devices

- Monitor display configuration, Basics of Graphics Accelerator Card and its importance.
- **Basic Concepts of Images:** Digital images, digital image representation
- **Image Formats** TIFF, BMP, JPG/ JPEG, GIF, IC, PDF, PSD:
- **Graphic Formats** Theory of design, Form, Line, Space, Texture, Color, Typography, Layout, Color harmony, Unity, Balance, Proportion, Rhythm, Repetition, Variety, Economy, Still life, Light and shade.
- **Poster Design:** Still life, Coloured layout, Poster Design, Designing of Books, Magazines brochures, children's literature, narrative text handling, scripts in Indian Languages, picture books, comics, illustrations with photographs, scientific illustrations, conceptual illustrations, handling of assignment for the market.
- **Image Scanning with the help of Scanner:** Setting up Resolution, Size, File formats of images; image preview, Bitonal, Grey Scale and colour options.
- Significance of PDF-creation, modification.
- Animation, Morphing and Applications

Graphic Tools: Image Editing Software (Photoshop/ CorelDraw)

- **Basic Concepts:** An Introduction, Creating, Opening and saving files, Menus, Toolbox, Colour control icons, Mode control icons, Window controls icons; Creating new images, Image capture (TWAIN) from scanner other files;
- **Image Handling:** Cropping an image, Adjusting image size, Increasing the size of the work canvas, Saving an image.

- **Layers:** Adding layers, Dragging and pasting selections on to layers, Dragging layers between files, Viewing and hiding layers, Editing layers, rotating selections, Scaling an object, Preserving layers transparency, Moving and copying layers, duplicating layers, Deleting layers, Merging layers, Using adjustment layers.
- **Channels and Masks:** Channel palette, Showing and hiding channels, Splitting channels in to separate image, Merging channels, Creating a quick mask, Editing masks using quick mask mode.
- **Painting and Editing:** Brushes palette, Brush shape, Creating and deleting brushes, creating custom brushes, Setting brush options, Saving, loading and appending brushes, Options palette.
- Opacity, pressure, or exposure, Paint fade-out rate, Making selections, Using selection tools, Adjusting selections, Softening the edges of a selection, Hiding a selection border, Moving and copying selections, Extending and reducing selections, Pasting and deleting selections, Image tracing (CorelDraw).
- **Concept of Multimedia:** Picture/ Graphics, Audio, Video.
- **Sound:** Recording Sound using Sound Recorder (Capture), Sound capture through sound editing software (ex: Sound forge), Sound editing, Noise correction, Effect enhancement.
- Voice Recognition Software Philips/ Dragon, MIDI player, Sound recorder, MONO & Stereo.
- **Sound File Format:** AIFF (Audio input file format from Apple Mac), MIDI, WAV, MP3, ASF (Streaming format from Microsoft), Importing audio and saving audio from Audio CD.
- **Sound Quality:** CD Quality, Radio Quality, Telephone Quality, Picture/ Graphics/ Image files.

2. Movie File Formats:

AVI, MPEG, SWF, MOV, DAT;

Movie Frames: Concept of Frame, Frame buffer, and Frame rate, Authoring tools, making Animation, embedding Audio/Video, and Embedding on the web page.

3. Multimedia Authoring Using Macromedia Flash

- Making of simple flash movie, Setting properties, Frame rate, Dimensions, and background colour.
- **Scene:** Concept of scene, Duplicate scene, Add scene, Delete scene, and Navigating between scenes.
- **Layers:** Concept of layer, Layer properties, Layer name, Show/ Hide/ Lock layers, Type of Layer-Normal/Guide/ Mask, Outline Color, Viewing Layer as outline, Layer Height, Adding/ deleting a layer.
- **Frame:** Concept of frame; Creating a key frame, Inserting text Into the frame, Inserting graphical elements into the frame, Converting text/ graphics to symbol, Inserting symbol into the frame, Setting symbol property (Graphics/ Button/ Movie), Inserting blank frame, Inserting blank key frame, inserting Key Frame into the Blank frame, Selecting all/ specific frames of a layer, Copying/ Pasting selected frames.
- **Special Effects:** Motion tweening, Shape tweening, Color effect, Inserting sound layer; Testing a scene and movie.
- Import/ Export (Movie/ Sound and other multimedia objects)
- **Publishing:** Publishing a flash movie; Changing publish settings; Producing SWF (Flash movie), HTML page, GIF image, JPEG image (*. Jpg), PNG image, Windows projector (*. Exe), Macintosh projector (*. Hqx), Quick time (*. Mov), Real player (*.smil). Testing with publish preview.

COMMUNICATION AND NETWORK CONCEPTS

- **Evolution of Networking:** ARPANET, Internet, Interspace; Different ways of sending data across the network with reference to switching techniques.
- **Data Communication Terminologies:** Concept of Channel, Baud, Bandwidth (Hz, KHz, MHz) and Data transfer rate (bps, Kbps, Mbps, Gbps, Tbps).
- **Transmission Media:** Twisted pair cable, Coaxial cable, Optical fiber, Infrared, Radio link, Microwave link and Satellite link.
- **Network Devices:** Modem, RJ45 connector, Ethernet card, Hub, Switch, Router, Gateway.
- **Different Topologies**- Bus, Star, Tree; Concepts of LAN, WAN, MAN.
- **Protocol:** TCP/IP, File Transfer Protocol (FTP), PPP, Level-Remote Login (telnet), Internet, Wireless/ Mobile communication, GSM, CDMA, WLL, 3G, SMS, Voice mail, Electronic mail, Chat, Video Conferencing.
- **Network Security Concepts:** Cyber Law, Firewall, Cookies, Hackers and Crackers.
- WebPages; Hyper Text markup Language (HTML), eXtensible Markup Language (XML); HyperText Transfer Protocol (HTTP); Domain Names; URL; Protocol address; Website, Web browser, Web servers, Web hosting.

CHAPTER 02

Operating System

An operating system is a system software which performs various types of functions in order to manage and organise files.

Software is a conceptual entity which is a set of computer programs, procedures and associated documentation concerned with the operation of a data processing system. Software, commonly known as a **set of programs**, consists of all the required instructions that tell the hardware how to perform a particular task.

Two types of software are as follows:

1. Application Software

It is a computer software designed to help the user to perform single or multiple tasks. They act as a set of instructions which direct the hardware to perform specific functions. e.g. office suites, graphics software, media players etc.

2. System Software

It is a program that manages and supports the computer resources and operations of a computer system while the computer executes its various tasks such as processing data and information, controlling hardware components, and allowing users to use application software, i.e. system software functions as a bridge between computer system hardware and the application software. System software monitors the basic activities of a system. It makes the operation of the computer system more effective and efficient.

2.1 Definition of Operating System

An Operating System (OS) is the core software component of your computer system, that manages the hardware and application softwares (e.g. compiler, linkers, DBMS, utility programs). The OS performs basic tasks, such as controlling and allocating memory, prioritising the processing of instructions, controlling input and output devices, networking, facilitating and managing files, calling the application program whenever needed, translates the specific service programs and manages data needed to produce the output as desired by users. It activates all devices and make them ready for work.

2.2 Functions of Operating System

Operating system provides many functions for ensuring the efficient operation of the system itself. The various functions are listed as under:

1. Resource Allocation

Sometimes multiple jobs are running at the same time and resources must be allocated to each of them. The different resources are managed by the operating system.

2. Accounting

Operating system may also be used to keep track of the various computer resources and how much and which users are using these resources.

3. Protection

Protection ensures that all access to the system resources is controlled. When several processes execute concurrently, it should not be possible for one process to interface with the other or with the operating system itself.

2.3 Operating System Strategies

An operating system may be designed to use different strategies to solve the user's need, which are as follows:

1. Multi-Programming Operating System

In multi-programming OS, more than one program reside in the main memory. When one job is unable to execute because of I/O operation, it switches to another program and allows that program to run.

2. Time Sharing Operating System

In time sharing, a small amount of time is allocated for the processing simultaneously. e.g. Mac OS. The time sharing operating system allows multiple programs to simultaneously share the computer resources. Time sharing operating system provides scheduling to each process to be run on.

3. Batch Processing Operating System

In batch processing operating system, a number of jobs are put together and executed as a group. This operating system is responsible for scheduling the jobs according to priority and the resource required. It is the type of OS which does not interact with the computer directly.

The batch processing system works in two steps as follows:

(i) The first step deals with the storage of processes in the form of a batch (collection) is known as **accumulation of jobs.**

(ii) The jobs are processed in a sequential manner within the batch. This working stage is known as **periodical processing of jobs.**

4. Real Time Operating System (RTOS)

The main objective of real time operating system is their quick and predictable response to events than any other operating system. Real time operating systems are designed to respond to an event within a predetermined time. It must have preemptive kernels to execute a program.

They are often used in applications such as flight reservation system, military applications etc.

Initiating the Operating System (Booting)

It is the process of restarting a computer or its operating system software. It starts with switching ON of the computer and ends when the operating system is loaded in main memory and the computer is ready to take commands from the user. The word 'boot' comes from 'bootstrap', since bootstrap helps you to get your boots on; likewise booting the computer helps it to get its Read Only Memory (ROM) instruction loaded in its main memory.

Types of Booting

The two types of booting which are as follows:

(i) **Cold Booting** When the computer is started after having been switched OFF.

(ii) **Warm Booting** When the operating system alone is restarted (without being switched OFF) after a system crash or freeze.

Both types of booting clear out (for the time being) the bugs, bombs, memory conflicts and other idiosyncrasies of the operating system.

2.4 Operating System Organisation

The below figure illustrate the operating system organisation:

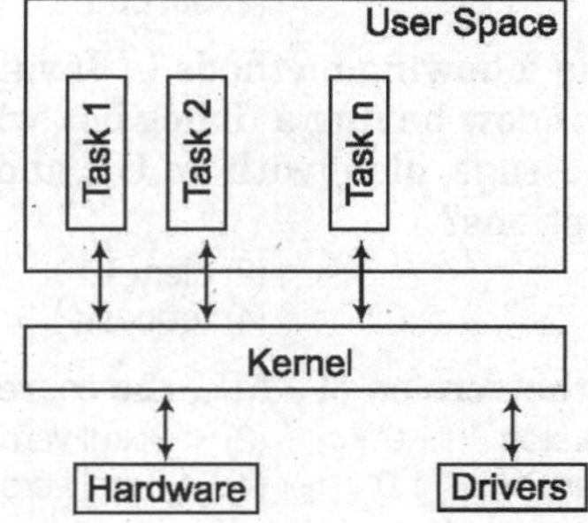

1. Hardware

It provides the basic computing resources for the system. It consists of CPU, memory and I/O devices.

2. Kernel

The kernel is the trusted part of the OS. As given in the fig, the kernel communicates to hardware directly or through drivers.

3. Drivers

Drivers communicate with the kernel. A driver acts like a translator between the device and the program which used by that device.

4. User Space

A place where all programs run by the user is known as user space. Each program runs in user space, talking to the kernel through system calls.

15. Assume the C++ definition: class circle: public point which of the following is false?

(1) 'point' is the base class and 'circle' is the derived class.
(2) The colon (:) in the header of class definition indicates inheritance
(3) The keyword 'public' indicates type of inheritance
(4) All the public and protected members of class 'circle' are inherited as public and protected members respectively into class 'point'.

16. Which of the following Java statement declare and allocate a 2-dimensional array integers with four rows and five columns?

(1) int array [ ] [ ] = new int [5] [4];
(2) int array [4] [5];
(3) int array [5] [4];
(4) int array [ ] [ ] = new int [4] [5];

17. The technology that stores only the essential instructions on a microprocessor chip and thus enhances its speed is referred to as

(1) MIMD (2) CISC (3) RISC (4) SIMD

18. Ten signals, each requiring 3000 H_Z, are multiplexed onto a single channel using FDM. How much minimum bandwidth is required for the multiplexed channel? Assume that the guard bands are 300 H_Z wide.

(1) 33, 700 (2) 30, 000
(3) 32, 700 (4) 33, 000

19. Which of the following methods in JavaScript will display a window having a dialog box with a specified message, alongwith an OK and a CANCEL button as options?

(1) prompt( ) (2) alert( )
(3) confirm( ) (4) request( )

20. To declare the version of XML, the correct syntax is

(1) < / xml version = '1.0' / > (2) < ? xml version = '1.0' / >
(3) < * xml version = '1.0' / > (4) < ? xml version = *1.0* / >

21. Which of the following statements best describes the main reasons for normalising relational database?

(i) To achieve physical data independence.

(ii) To remove data anomalies (insertion, update, deletion, annomalies).

(iii) To save space on disk.

(1) (i), (ii) and (iii) (2) (i) and (ii)
(3) (i) and (iii) (4) (ii) and (iii)

22. A thread is also called

(1) a scheduler (2) a virtual process
(3) a heavyweight process (4) a lightweight process

23. Copying a process from memory to disk to allow space for other processes is called ____.

(1) demand paging (2) deadlock
(3) pagefault (4) swapping

24. When a subroutine is called, the add the instruction following the instruction stored in / on the ____.

(1) program counter (2) stack
(3) stack pointer (4) accumulator

25. Consider the following code segment

```
if (Y < 0)
{X = – X; Y = – Y}; Z = 0;
while (Y > 0)
{Z = Z + X; Y = Y – 1;}
```

Assume that X, Y and Z are inter variables, and that X and Y have be initialised. Which of the following best describes what this code segment does?

(1) Sets Z to be the product X * Y
(2) Sets Z to be the sum X + Y
(3) Sets Z to be the absolute value of Y
(4) Sets Z to be the value of Y.

26. A combinational logic circuit that is used when it is desired to send data from two more source through a single transmission line is known as ____.

(1) demultiplexer (2) encoder
(3) decoder (4) multiplexer

27. What is garbage collection in the context of Java?

(1) The Java Virtual Machine (JVM) checks the output of any Java program and deletes anything that does not make sense at all.
(2) The operating system periodically deletes all of the Java files available on the system.
(3) Any Java package imported in a program and not being used, is automatically deleted.
(4) When all references to an object are going, then the memory used by the object is automatically reclaimed.

28. What is the full form of DTD that is used to describe content in an XHTML document?

(1) Document To Definition
(2) Document Type Definition
(3) Document Towards Definition
(4) Document Text Definition

29. A register in the microprocessor that keeps track of the answer or result of any arithmetic or logic operation is the ____.

(1) accumulator
(2) stack pointer
(3) program counter
(4) instruction pointer

30. If the time quantum size is 2 units of an there is only one job of 14 time unit in a ready queue, the round-robin scheduling algorithm will cause ____ connected switches.

(1) 1 (2) 5
(3) 6 (4) 7

31. The memory which does not loose its content on failure of power supply is known as ___ memory.

(1) main memory (2) volatile
(3) non-volatile (4) RAM

32. The easiest method in flash to draw a heptagon, is to use the ____.

(1) Polystar Tool with the "Polygon" style
(2) Polygon Tool
(3) Lasso Tool with the "create star" option
(4) Polystar Tool with the "star" style

33. **If the period of a signal is 1000 ms, then what is its frequency in kilohertz?**
(1) 10^{-1} KHz (2) 1 KHz (3) 10^{-3} KHz (4) 10^{-2} KHz

34. **Which of the following Visual Basic statements will assign the value "QUICK" from the variable y to the string variable x?**
y = "THE QUICK RED FOX JUMPED OVER THE DOG"
(1) x = middle (y, 5, 5) (2) x = Left (y, 5)
(3) x = mid (y, 5, 5) (4) x = Instr (5, y, "QUICK")

35. **In structured programming, a program is de-composed into modules. Coupling and cohesion describe the characteristics of modules. A good decomposition should attempt to**
(1) Minimize coupling and minimize cohesion
(2) Maximize coupling and minimize cohesion
(3) Minimize coupling and maximize cohesion
(4) Maximize coupling and maximize cohesion

36. **Consider the database table "Persons" having Person_ID as the primary key.**

Person_ID	Name	Age
1000	Rajan	10
–	Jatin	-45
1001	Rajesh	35

What are the constraints violated by the above table?
(1) Relationship integrity
(2) Referential integrity only
(3) Entity and domain integrities
(4) Referential and domain integrities

37. **On which of the following storage media, storage of information is organised as a single continuous spiral groove?**
(1) CD-ROM (2) RAM
(3) Hard disk (4) Floppy disk

38. **The kernel keeps track of the state of each executing program by using a data structure called ____.**
(1) process control block (2) user control block
(3) file control block (4) memory control block

39. **Recursive procedure is implemented using**
(1) string (2) queue
(3) stack (4) linked list

40. **For a tree with just one node, the root node is the height of a binary tree is defined to zero, if there are 2 levels of nodes, the height is 1 and so on.**
A Binary Search Tree is built according to the usual rules with the following six key inserted one at a time as given
B, I, N, A, R, Y. What is the height of the tree?
(1) 5 (2) 2 (3) 3 (4) 4

41. **Which of the following sorting algorithms uses recursion?**
(1) Insertion sort (2) Heap sort
(3) Merge sort (4) Bubble sort

42. **Mechanism that is used to convert domain name into IP address is known ____.**
(1) HTTP (2) URL (3) FTP (4) DNS

43. **The unit receiving the data item response with another control signal to acknowledgement receipt of the data. This type of agreement between two independent units is known as.**
(1) strobe control (2) multitasking
(3) handshaking (4) piggybacking

44. **What correction is required for following Java code snippet to compile?**

```
int [ ] X = new int [10];
for (int P = 0; P< = X. length ( ); P++)
X [P] = 5;
```

(1) X [P] = 5 should be X (P) = 5
(2) P < = X. length () should be P< X. length()
(3) X.length () should be X.length
(4) P++ should be P+1

45. **Which of the following is not a transaction management SQL command?**
(1) Rollback (2) Commit (3) Select (4) Savepoint

46. **Concurrency control in RDBMS is important for which of the following reasons?**
(1) To ensure data integrity when reads occur to the database in a multi-user environment
(2) To ensure data integrity when updates occur to the database in a single user environment
(3) To ensure data integrity when updates occur to the database in a multi-user environment
(4) To ensure data integrity when reads occur to the database in a single user environment

47. **An operating system contains 3 user processes each requiring 2 units of resource R. The minimum number of units of R such that no deadlock will ever occur is**
(1) 5 (2) 2 (3) 3 (4) 4

48. **The number of bits required to represent decimal number 4096 in binary form is ____.**
(1) 16 (2) 10 (3) 12 (4) 13

49. **Which of the following memory improves the speed of execution of a program?**
(1) Virtual memory (2) Primary memory
(3) Secondary memory (4) Cache memory

50. **Which of the following statements is false with respect to relational DBMS?**
(1) A disadvantage of highly normalised tables is that queries may require too many time consuming joins
(2) Foreign key constraints are referential integrity constraints
(3) A primary key uniquely identifies a row in a table
(4) Nulls reduce space requirements in tables

51. **How many gate(s) would be required to implement the following boolean expression after simplification?**
Expression : AC + ABC
(1) 4 (2) 1 (3) 2 (4) 3

3. **Direct Memory Access** It involves designing of hardware to avoid the performance of CPU for transferring the information between the device (controller's data registers) and the memory.

2.11 Process Management

Process is a program in execution. A process needs certain resources e.g. CPU time, memory files and I/O devices to accomplish its task.

Process management is the important part of an operating system which enables the activities of planning, monitoring and performance of a process.

The two crucial issues are as follows:

(i) The operating system must ensure that each running application (or process) is treated fairly in terms of processor time allocated in a multi-tasking environment.

(ii) The processor is maximally and efficiently utilised.

The processor management activities handled by an OS are as follows:

(i) Control access of shared resources like file, memory, I/O and CPU.
(ii) Schedule process.
(iii) Control execution of applications.
(iv) Create, execute and delete a process.
(v) Synchronisation, communication and deadlock handling for processes.
(vi) Abort or resume a process.

2.11.1 Process Control Block (PCB)

Each process is represented in an operating system by its own process control block. A PCB is a data structure containing information regarding a specific process. This includes

(i) Process state may be new, ready, running, waiting or halted.

(ii) Program counter indicates the address of the next instruction to be executed for this process.

(iii) CPU registers include accumulators, index registers, stack pointers and general purpose registers. This information is saved when an interrupt occurs.

(iv) CPU scheduling information include process priority, pointers for scheduling queues etc.

Pointer	Process state
Process number	
Program counter	
Register	
List of open files	
Memory limit	
⋮	

Process control block

2.11.2 Processes and Threads Using Fork, Join, Quit

A process is simply defined as program under execution. And a thread is a single sequence stream within a process because threads have some of the properties of processes, they are sometimes called light weight processes.

Fork/Join/Quit can express arbitrary functional parallelism (any process flow graph). These are used to create multiple threads of control. A brief overview of fork, join and quit are as follows:

(i) **FORK** (Label) Creates another process in the same address space beginning execution at instruction label.

(ii) **QUIT** ( ) Terminates the process.

(iii) **JOINT** (Count) Merges processes into one.

e.g. the sequential (or linear) code on the left, below, executes statement by statement, top to bottom. However, we can observe a number of things about when each statement can execute. The computation of:

(i) a, r, and s can occur in parallel (i.e. at the same time)
(ii) b must wait for r and s to complete
(iii) c must wait on a and b;
(iv) w must wait on the completion of the other statement simply because its purpose to count loop iterations.

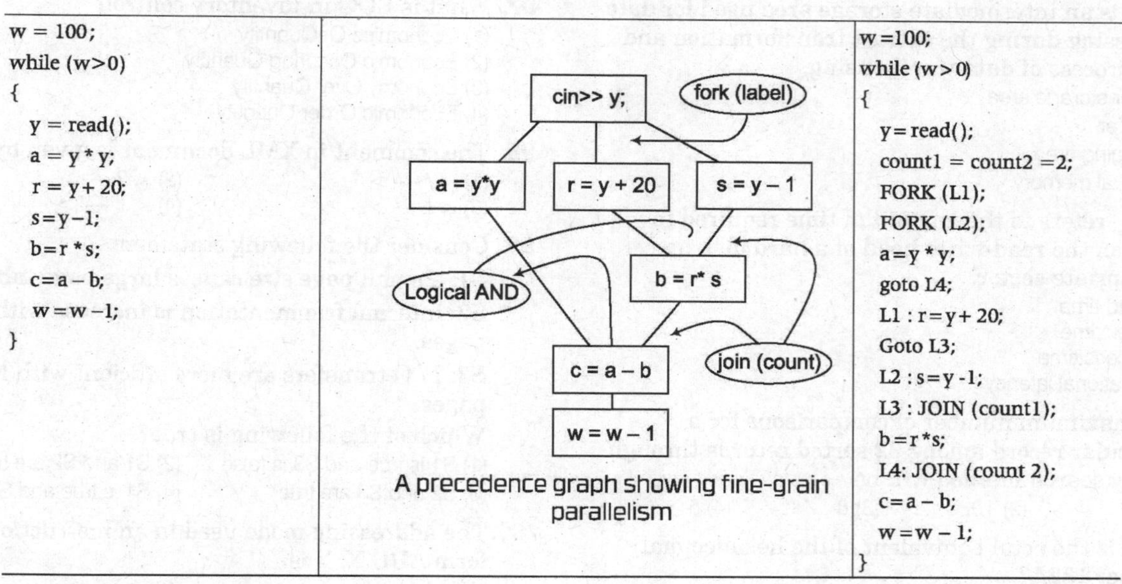

A precedence graph showing fine-grain parallelism

2.11.3 Process Modes

Two modes of process execution are user mode and kernel mode. Normally, a process executes in the user mode. When a process executes a system call, the mode of execution changes from user mode to kernel mode. The bookkeeping operations related to the user process (interrupt handling, process scheduling, memory management) are performed in kernel mode.

1. User Mode

(i) Processes can access their own instructions and data but not kernel instructions and data.

(ii) Cannot execute certain privileged machine instructions.

2. Kernel Mode

(i) Processes can access both kernel as well as user instructions and data.

(ii) No limit to which instructions can be executed.

2.11.4 Process Address Space

All 32-bit applications have a 4 GB process address space (32-bit addresses can map a maximum of 4 GB of memory). Microsoft Windows operating systems provide applications with access to 2GB of process address space (specifically known as **user mode virtual address space**). All threads owned by an application share the same user mode virtual address space. The remaining 2GB are reserved for the operating system (also known as **kernel mode address space**). All operating system editions have a boot.ini switch that can provide applications with access to 3GB of process address space, limiting the kernel mode address space to 1GB.

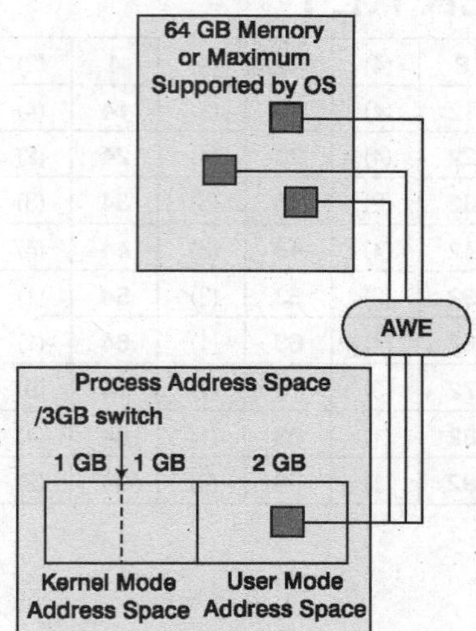

Address Windowing Extensions (AWE) extend the capabilities of 32-bit applications by allowing access to as much physical memory as the operating system supports. AWE accomplishes this by mapping a subset of upto 64 GB into the user address space. Mapping between the application buffer pool and AWE-mapped memory is handled through manipulation of the Windows virtual memory tables.

2.11.5 Process Abstraction

Abstraction allows one to collect instances of entities into groups in which their common attributes need not be considered. The concept of process abstraction is one of the

93. **_____ is an intermediate storage area used for data processing during the extract transformation and load process of data warehousing.**
(1) Inter storage area
(2) Buffer
(3) Staging area
(4) Virtual memory

94. **______ refers to the amount of time required to position the read-write head of a hard disk on appropriate sector.**
(1) Load time
(2) Seek time
(3) Access time
(4) Rotational latency

95. **The maximum number of comparisons for a particular record among 32 sorted records through binary search method will be**
(1) 2 (2) 10 (3) 8 (4) 5

96. **What is the octal equivalent of the hexadecimal number 132A?**
(1) 46252 (2) 11450
(3) 11452 (4) 45250

97. **What is EOQ in inventory control?**
(1) Economics Of Quantity
(2) Economic Occuring Quantity
(3) Economy Over Quantity
(4) Economic Order Quantity

98. **The comment in XML document is given by**
(1) < / --- > (2) < ? --- >
(3) < ! ---- > (4) < ! ----! >

99. **Consider the following statements**
S1: a small page size causes large page tables.
S2: internal fragmentation is increase with small pages.
S3: I / O transfers are more efficient with large pages.
Which of the following is true?
(1) S1 is true and S3 is false (2) S1 and S2 are true
(3) S2 and S3 are true (4) S1 is true and S2 is false

100. **The addressing mode used in an instruction of the form ADD X, Y is:**
(1) index (2) absolute
(3) immediate (4) indirect

ANSWER KEY

1	(2)	2	(4)	3	(4)	4	(2)	5	(1)	6	(4)	7	(3)	8	(4)	9	(3)	10	(3)
11	(2)	12	(4)	13	(3)	14	(4)	15	(4)	16	(4)	17	(3)	18	(3)	19	(3)	20	(4)
21	(4)	22	(4)	23	(4)	24	(2)	25	(3)	26	(4)	27	(4)	28	(2)	29	(1)	30	(3)
31	(3)	32	(2)	33	(3)	34	(3)	35	(3)	36	(3)	37	(1)	38	(1)	39	(3)	40	(2)
41	(3)	42	(4)	43	(3)	44	(4)	45	(3)	46	(3)	47	(4)	48	(3)	49	(4)	50	(4)
51	(4)	52	(2)	53	(3)	54	(1)	55	(4)	56	(4)	57	(3)	58	(3)	59	(1)	60	(4)
61	(2)	62	(4)	63	(1)	64	(1)	65	(4)	66	(4)	67	(3)	68	(1)	69	(1)	70	(2)
71	(1)	72	(3)	73	(1)	74	(3)	75	(2)	76	(4)	77	(2)	78	(1)	79	(3)	80	(2)
81	(2)	82	(1)	83	(1)	84	(4)	85	(1)	86	(4)	87	(4)	88	(1)	89	(3)	90	(3)
91	(3)	92	(1)	93	(3)	94	(2)	95	(4)	96	(3)	97	(4)	98	(3)	99	(4)	100	(1)

CHAPTER

01

Computer System Architecture

A computer is a fast electronic calculating machine that accepts digitised information from the user, processes it according to a sequence of instructions stored in the memory and provides the processed information to the user. In computer science, computer architecture is a set of disciplines that describes the part of computer system and their relations. Computer architecture deals with the functional behaviour of a computer system as viewed by a programmer. It can also be described as the logical structure of the system unit that housed electronic components. The computer architecture forms the backbone for building successful computer systems.

1.1 Personal Computer

Personal computers are the most widely used computers which have applications used in everyday activity of the modern world. The speed and accuracy of processing of the personal systems accounts for their high popularity. These computers are found almost everywhere, in all middle class Indian homes, cyber cafes, shopping malls, business institutions etc.

1.2 Workstations

This is slightly different from the regular PC in respect that it has evolved from the mini computers. Originally used for engineering, graphics and such other non-personal work or technical work, workstation computers were designed for the purpose of singular interaction of computer with one person at a time.

1.3 Components of a Computer

A computer consists of four main components as follows:

(i) Input Unit
(ii) Output Unit
(iii) Central Processing Unit (CPU)
(iv) Memory Unit

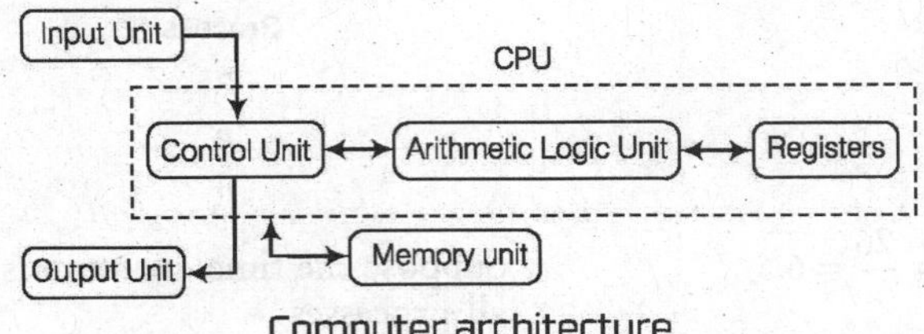

Computer architecture

Suppose that arrival time of all processes is 0. Then

Waiting time of $P_1 = 3 - 0 - 0 = 3$

Waiting time of $P_2 = 16 - 0 - 0 = 16$

Waiting time of $P_3 = 9 - 0 - 0 = 9$

Waiting time of $P_4 = 0 - 0 - 0 = 0$

Average waiting time $= \dfrac{3+16+9+0}{4} = \dfrac{28}{4} = 7$

The shortest job first gives the minimum average waiting time. For this reason, it is an optimal algorithm for CPU scheduling.

When in SJF algorithm processes are preemptive it is called **shortest-remaining time first** scheduling.

3. Shortest Remaining Time First (SRTF) Scheduling

This algorithm works same as SJF except that the process are preemptive.

e.g.

Process	Arrival time	Burst time
P_1	0	8
P_2	1	4
P_3	2	9
P_4	3	5

Processes will executed in following sequence:

P_1	P_2	P_4	P_1	P_3

0, 1, 5 (1+4), 10 (5+5), 17 (10+7), 26 (17+9)

The arrival time of P_1 is 0. At time 0 only P_1 is in ready queue. So at this time, CPU will be alloted to P_1. Process P_2 arrives at time 1.

The remaining time for process P_1 is $8-1=7$ which is larger than the process $P_2[4]$ so the process P_1 is preempted and process P_2 is scheduled. Process P_2 will continue its processing because the burst time of P_3 and P_4 is larger than P_2. At time 5, process P_3, P_4 will also be queued in ready queue. Process P_4 has smallest burst time among all process (i.e. P_1, P_3, P_4)

Thus, CPU will be alloted to P_4.

Waiting time of P_1 = last response time to P_1 − arrival time − amount of time P_1 has been allocated before.

$= 10 - 0 - 1 = 9$

Waiting time of $P_2 = 1 - 1 - 0 = 0$

Waiting time of $P_3 = 17 - 2 - 0 = 15$

Waiting time of $P_4 = 5 - 3 - 0 = 2$

Average waiting time $= \dfrac{(9+0+15+2)}{4} = \dfrac{26}{4} = 6.5$

4. Priority Scheduling

In this scheduling algorithm, a priority is associated with each process and the CPU is allocated to the process with the highest priority.

e.g.

Process	Burst time	Priority
P_1	10	3
P_2	1	1
P_3	2	4
P_4	1	5
P_5	5	2

These processes will be scheduled according to the following Gantt chart. Suppose that arrival time of all processes is 0.

P_2	P_5	P_1	P_3	P_4

0, 1, 6, 16, 18, 19

In above example, the lowest number will be treated as highest priority.

Waiting time of $P_1 = 6 - 0 = 6$

Waiting time of $P_2 = 0$

Waiting time of $P_3 = 16$

Waiting time of $P_4 = 18$

Waiting time of $P_5 = 1$

Average waiting time $= \dfrac{6+0+16+18+1}{5} = \dfrac{41}{5} = 8.2$

Priority scheduling can also be preemptive and non-preemptive. A preemptive priority scheduling will preempt the CPU if the priority of newly arrived process is higher than the priority of the currently running process.

A major problem with priority scheduling is starvation, means the lower priority process will continuously wait for CPU if there is a large number of higher priority process.

5. Round-Robin Scheduling

The round-robin algorithm is designed specially for time-sharing system. It is similar to FCFS scheduling, but preemption is added to switch between processes. A small unit time quantum or time slice is defined. The CPU scheduler goes around the ready queue, allocating CPU to each process for a time interval of upto 1 time quantum. In this, the ready queue behaves as circular FIFO queue.

e.g.

Process	Burst time
P_1	24
P_2	3
P_3	3

Suppose the time quantum is 2 and arrival time is 0 for all processes

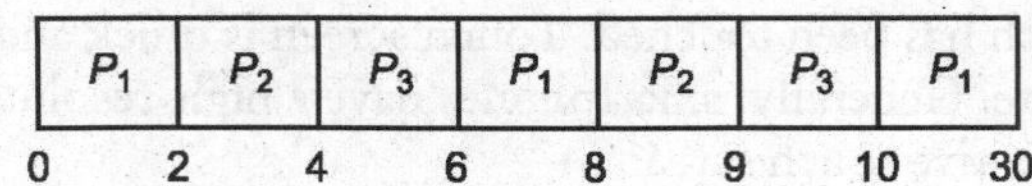

Waiting time of $P_1 = (10) - (0) - (2 + 2) = 10 - 4 = 6$

Waiting time of $P_2 = 8 - 0 - 2 = 6$

Waiting time of $P_3 = 9 - 2 = 7$

Average waiting time $= \frac{6+6+7}{3} = \frac{19}{3} = 6.33$

2.13 Synchronisation

When several processes access and manipulate the same data concurrently and the outcome of the execution depends on the particular order in which the access takes place is called **race condition**, e.g. suppose we have two variables A and B. The operation on A and B are as follows:

Operation 1 $A = \text{Result}$

$A = A + 1$

$\text{Result} = A$

Operation 2 $B = \text{Result}$

$B = B - 1$

$\text{Result} = B$

Now, initially if value of Result = 4 and sequence is operation 1 then operation 2.

Then, $A = 4$

$A = 4 + 1 = 5$

$\text{Result} = A = 5$

$B = \text{Result} = 5$

$B = 5 - 1 = 4$

$\text{Result} = B = 4$

If the sequence of operation is operation 2 then operation 1.

Then, $B = \text{Result} = 4$

$B = B - 1 = 4 - 1 = 3$

$\text{Result} = B = 3$

$A = \text{Result} = 3$

$A = A + 1 = 4$

$\text{Result} = A = 4$

To guard against the race conditions above, we need to ensure that only one process at a time can be manipulating the variable result. To make such a guarantee, we require that the process be synchronised in some way.

2.13.1 Interactive Processes

Interactive process can be defined as a term describing a program whose input and output are interleaved, like a conversation, allowing the user's input to depend on previous output from the same run.

The interaction with the user is usually conducted through either a text-based or a graphical user interface. Other kinds of interface like speech recognition or speech synthesis are also possible.

2.13.2 Critical Section

The segment code of a process where it tries to modify common variables, updating table, writing file and so on. To avoid race around condition, it is necessary that when one process is executing in its critical section, no other process is to be allowed to execute in its critical sections at the same time.

The critical section problem is to design a protocol that the process can use to cooperate. A solution to the critical section problem must satisfy the following three requirements:

1. Mutual Exclusion

If process P_i is executing in its critical section, then no other processes can be executing in their critical sections.

2. Progress

If no process is executing its critical section and some other processes wish to enter their critical section, then only those processes that are not executing in their remainder sections can participate in the decision on which will enter its critical section next.

3. Bounded Waiting

There exists a bound, or limit, on the number of times that other processes are allowed to enter their critical section after a process has made a request to enter into its critical section and before that request is granted.

2.13.3 Process Coordination

Process coordination or concurrency control consists of mutual exclusion and synchronisation.

(i) Mutual exclusion ensures that two concurrent activities do not access shared data (or resource) at the same time.

(ii) Synchronisation means sharing resources by processes.

When considering process coordination, we must keep in mind the following situations:

(i) Deadlock occurs when two activities are waiting each other and neither can proceed.

(ii) Starvation occurs when a blocked activity is consistently passes over and not allowed to run.

Mouse also include **a scroll wheel** between the buttons to scroll down the application window and their contents also.

3. Joystick

It is also a pointing device like the mouse, which consists of a stick that pivots on a spherical ball on its base. A joystick is similar to a mouse excepts that the moment of cursor on screen stops working as soon as user stop moving the mouse. But with a joystick, the pointer continuous moving in the previously pointing direction.

Commonly, joysticks are used for playing computer games like **flight simulators** but occasionally used for CAD/CAM systems and other applications.

Some joysticks also have a third degree of freedom, i.e. the stick can be twisted in clockwise or anti-clockwise direction.

4. Light Pen

It is a pointing device shaped like a pen and is connected to a Visual Display Unit (VDU).

The tip of the light pen contains light-sensitive element which, when placed against the screen, detects the light from the screen enabling the computer to identify the location of the tip of pen on screen.

5. Graphics Tablet

A graphics tablet (or digitisers, digitising tablet, tough tablets or simply tablet) is an input device that consists of an electronic writing area and a special pen that works with it. It allows artists to create hand-made images and graphical images with motion and action, similar to the way a person draws images with pencil and paper.

The pen of the graphics tablet is pressure sensitive, so pressing harder or softer can result in brush strokes of different width.

When user draws anything on the tablet with the special pen, the drawing appears on the screen.

Graphics tablet

6. Touch Screen

It is an electronic visual display that can detect the presence and location of a touch within the display area. The term touch screen generally refers to touching the display of the device with a finger. The touch screen sends a signal to the computer. This signal gives the location on the screen, which has been touched. Touch screen is quick and simple to use. Generally, smartphones have a high-resolution capacitive touch screen.

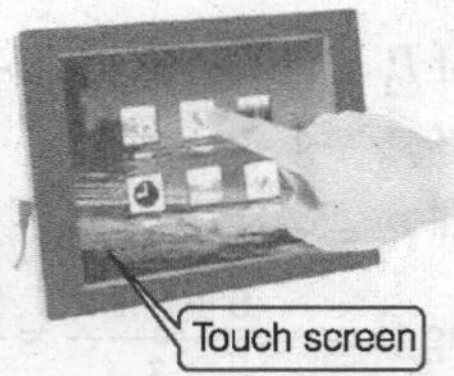

There are different types of touch screens available with electronic devices like capacitive touch screen, resistive touch screen and gorilla glass touch screen etc.

7. Scanner

It is a device that allows a user to take an image or text and converts it into a digital file, allowing the computer to read or display the scanned object. It is mainly used to convert a scanned document in a digital format.

8. MICR (Magnetic Ink Character Recognition)

It is a character recognition technology which is primarily used by the banking industry to facilitate the processing of cheques. This technology allows the computers to read information (such as account numbers) on printed documents. Characters are printed in special typefaces with a magnetic ink (that contains iron oxide).

MICR can read upto 2400 documents/min.

9. OCR (Optical Character Recognition)

It is used to translate scanned images of handwritten, type-written, printed text or special type font printed on conventional paper with conventional ink into machine-encoded text.

It is widely used to convert books and documents into electronic files, to computerise a record keeping system in an office or to publish the text on a website.

An optical reader uses **photoelectric devices** to scan the characters being read and converts the reflected light patterns of the data into binary data suitable for computer input.

10. OMR (Optical Mark Reader)

It is used to capture human marked data from document form such as surveys and tests.

One of the most familiar application of optical mark reader is the checking of optical answer sheets in multiple choice questions. It uses high intensity to read the marks or symbols.

11. Web Camera (Webcam)

Webcam is a digital camera attached to computers and can be used for video conferencing or online chatting etc. It is a video capturing device. Webcams are able to capture full motion videos as well. A webcam connected to a computer allows the user to view either a still picture or motion video of a user or other object.

Now-a-days, webcams are either embedded into the display with laptops or connected *via* USB or firewire port or wi-fi to the computer system. After connecting webcam to a computer, you need to install required software or drivers.

12. Card Reader

A card reader is a data input device that reads data from a card-shaped storage medium. The first were punched card readers, which reads the paper or cardboard punched cards that were used during the first several decades of the computer industry to store information and programs for computer systems. Modern card readers are electronic devices that can read plastic cards embedded with either a barcode, magnetic strip, computer chip or another storage medium.

1.7.2 Output Devices

An output device is a part of computer hardware equipment, used to communicate the results of data processing which are carried out by an information processing system (such as a computer), to the outside world. Output devices carry the results of various operations performed by the user.

Some of the devices, which are used to display the processed result or output are as follows:

1. Monitor

A monitor (called a visual display unit) is an electronic device used to display the output. The rectangular area of the monitor, its refresh rate and dot pitch, all directly affect the resolution of the display.

Resolution refers to the clarity of screen and measured by the number of individual tiny coloured dots (known as pixels), scattered on the screen. Resolution indicates the number of dots per inch. The smaller the dot pitch is, the better the resolution will be.

2. Printer

A printer is an output device, which produces a hard copy of documents that are stored in an electronic form on physical print media such as paper or transparencies. So, printers are the primary output devices used to prepare permanent documents. The speed of a printer is normally rated either by Pages Per Minute (PPM) or by Characters Per Second (CPS).

Printers can be classified into two broad categories:

(i) **Impact Printers** Impact printers rely on a forcible impact to transfer ink to the print media, similar to the action of a typewriter. There is a mechanical contact between the paper and the print head. Line printer, drum printer daisy wheel printer and dot matrix printer are the types of impact printers.

(ii) **Non-impact Printers** Non-impact printers are much quieter than impact printers as their printing heads do not strike the paper. Most non-impact printers produce dot-matrix patterns. There is no mechanical contact between the paper and the print head. These printers are comparatively faster and produce high quality output. They can be used for printing text and graphics both in black and white coloured. Electromagnetic printer, thermal printer, electrostatic printer, laser printer and inkjet printer are the types of non-impact printer.

3. Plotter

It is an output device similar to a printer that uses a pen, pencil, marker or other writing tool to make a design.

Plotters are generally used to generate the map of building and shopping malls. A plotter is a computer printing device for printing vector graphics. In the past, plotters were widely used in applications such as Computer Aided Design (CAD) and other print jobs. Though they have generally been replaced with wide format conventional printers.

4. Speaker

Speaker is an output device that receives the sound in the form of electric current from the sound card and converts it into sound format. Speakers are used for listen to music.

Computer speakers (multimedia speakers) are the speakers, which are attached internally or externally to a computer system.

5. Headphones

Headphones are a pair of small loudspeakers or less commonly a single speaker, held close to a user's ears and connected to a signal source such as an audio amplifier, radio, CD player or portable media player. They are also known as **stereo phones, headsets or cans.**

6. Projector

It is an output device, which is used to project information from a computer onto a large screen, so it can be viewed by a large group of people simultaneously.

Projectors are widely used for classroom training or conference holes with a large audience. It provides a temporary output display.

1.7.3 Input-Output Modules

The input-output module (I/O module) is normally connected to the computer system on one end and one or more input/output devices on the other.

(ii) The preempted resources are added to the list of resources for which the process in waiting. The process will be restarted only, when it can regain its old resources, as well as ones that is in requesting.

Circular Wait

The protocol used to ensure that circular wait condition never hold is to improve a total ordering of all resource types and to require that each process requests resource is an increasing order of enumeration.

3. Deadlock Detection and Recovery Algorithm

In this method of deadlock handling, a detection algorithm is invoked to check whether the system is in deadlock state, if yes then following recovery mechanism are used.

Process Termination

To eliminate deadlock by aborting a process, one of following methods is used:

(i) **Abort all Deadlock Processes** This method clearly will break the deadlock cycle but at great expense. If the deadlock process is about to complete.

(ii) **Abort One Process at a Time** Until deadlock is eliminated.

Resource Preemption

To eliminate deadlock using resource preemption, we successively preempt some resources from processes and given these resources to other processes until the deadlock cycle is broken. This is done by following 3 steps:

(i) **Selecting a Victim** The first step is to identify, which process and resources are to be preempted.

(ii) **Rollback** Once the victim process is selected, we must rollback the process to some safe state and restart it from that state.

(iii) **Starvation** This must be ensured that resources will not always be preempted from the same process.

2.15 Memory Management

Memory management is the act of managing computer memory. The essential requirement of memory management is to provide ways to dynamically allocate portions of memory to programs at their request, and freeing it for reuse when no longer needed.

The primary role of the memory management system is to satisfy requests for memory allocation. Sometimes this is implicit, as when a new process is created. At other times, processes explicitly request memory. Either way, the system must locate enough unallocated memory and assign it to the process.

2.15.1 Logical *v/s* Physical Address Space

1. Logical Address

An address generated by CPU is commonly referred to as a **logical address.** The logical address is also known as **virtual address.** The set of all logical addresses generated by a program is a **logical address space.**

2. Physical Address

The address seen by the memory unit that is one loaded into the memory address register of the memory is commonly referred to as a **physical address.** The set of all physical addresses corresponding to the logical address generated by a program is known as **physical address space.**

2.15.2 Memory Mapping

Memory mapping is the translation between the logical address space and the physical memory. The objectives of memory mapping are to translate from logical to physical address, to aid in memory protection, and to enable better management of memory resources.

Mapping is imporant to computer performance, both locally and globally. In fact, each time a program presents a logical memory address and requests that the corresponding memory will be accessed, the mapping mechanism must translate that address into an appropriate physical memory location. The simpler this translation, the lower the implementation cost and higher the performance of the individual memory reference.

It is also a mechanism that maps a portion of a file, or an entire file, on disk to a range of addresses within an application's address space. The principal benefits of memory mapping are as follows:

1. **Faster File Access** Accessing files *via* memory map is faster than using I/O functions. Data are read and written using the virtual memory capabilities that are built into the operating system rather than having to allocate, copy into, and then deallocate data buffers owned by the process.
2. **Efficiency** Mapping a file into memory allows access to data in the file as if that data has been read into an array in the application's address space.
3. **Efficient Coding Style** Memory mapping enables you to access file data using standard indexing operations. Once you have mapped a file to memory, you can read the contents of that file using the same type of statements that are used to read variables from the workspace. The contents of the mapped file appear as if they were an array in the currently active workspace. You simply index into this array to read or write the desired data from the file.

4. **Sharing Memory between Applications** Memory mapped files also provide a mechanism for sharing data between applications, as shown in the figure below. This is achieved by having each application map sections of the same file.

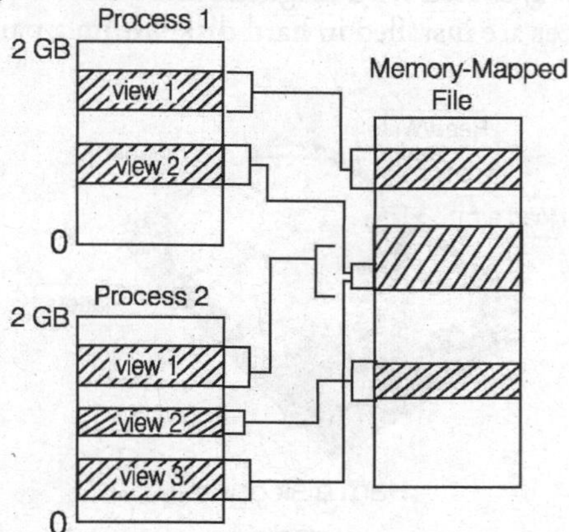

Also, within a single application, you can map the same segment of a file more than once.

2.15.3 Memory Management/ Allocation Techniques

1. Single Partition Allocation

(i) The memory is divided into two parts. One to uses the operating system and the other is for user programs.

(ii) The operating system code and date is protected from being modified by user programs using a base register.

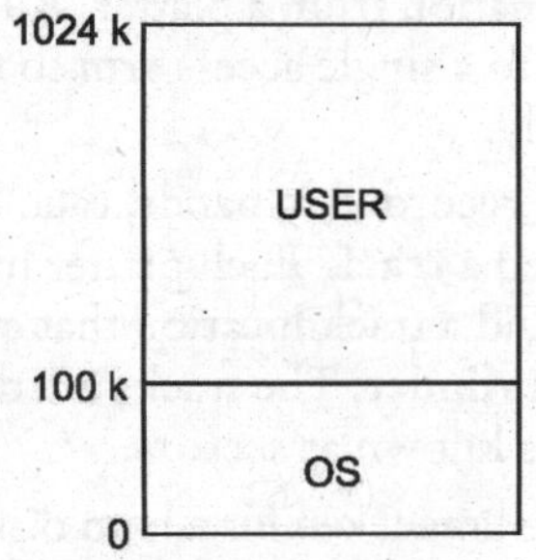

2. Multiple Partition Allocation

(i) Fixed Partition Scheme

(a) Memory is divided into a number of fixed size partitions. Then, each partition holds one process.

(b) This scheme supports multi-programming as a number of processes may now be brought into memory and the CPU can be switched from one process to another.

(c) The degree of multi-programming is however limited by the number of partitions. The size and number of processes in memory is limited by the size and number of partitions.

(d) When a process arrives for execution, it is put into the input queue of the smallest partition which is large enough to hold it.

(ii) Variable Partition Scheme

(a) A block of available memory is designated as a hole at any time, a set of holes exists which consists of holes of various sizes scattered throughout the memory. When a process arrives and needs memory, this set of holes is searched for a hole which is large enough to hold the process. If the hole is too large, it is split into two parts, the unused part is added to the set of holes. All holes which are adjacent to each other are merged.

(b) There are several algorithms which are used to search for the hole in the set.

- **First-Fit** This allocates the first hole in the set which is big enough to hold the process.
- **Next-Fit** This works like the first-fit algorithms except that it keeps track of the position of the hole found in the set. The next time it is called it starts searching from that position.
- **Best-Fit** This allocates the smallest hole which is large enough to hold the process.
- **Worst-Fit** This algorithm simply allocates the largest hole.

2.15.4 Segmentation

Segmentation is one of the most common ways to achieve memory protection. It is a memory management technique in which each job is divided into several segments of different sizes, one for each module that contains pieces that perform related functions.

Each segment is actually a different logical address space of the program. Logical address consists of two things:

```
<segment_number, offset>
```

When a process is to be executed, its corresponding segmentation are loaded into a non-contiguous memory through every segment is loaded into a contiguous block of available memory.

A table stores the information about all segments and is called **Segment Table.** It maps two dimensional logical address into one dimensional physical address. It's each table entry has:

1. **Base Address** It contains the starting physical address where the segments reside in memory.
2. **Limit** It specifies the length of the segment.

ROM is further sub divided into several types as follows:

(i) **PROM** (Programmable ROM) It is a computer memory chip capable of being programmed after it has been created. But once the PROM has been programmed, the information written is permanent and cannot be erased or deleted.

(ii) **EPROM** (Erasable Programmable ROM) It is a computer memory chip on which the written information can be changed by exposing to ultra voilet light. It is just like a small glass circle that expose the chip that can be reprogrammed.

(iii) **EEPROM** (Electrically Erasable Programmable ROM) It is a PROM that can be erased and reprogrammed using an electrical charge.

1.8.2 Storage Devices/Secondary Memory

Secondary memory also known as **secondary storage** or **auxiliary memory**, is the slower and cheaper form of memory. It is a permanent storage device.

CPU does not access the secondary memory directly. The content in it must first be copied into the RAM to be processed. Secondary memory is non-volatile in nature, i.e. the information does not get erased even when power is switched OFF and data will not be destructed until and unless the user erases it.

Secondary Memory devices

Magnetic disks	Optical discs	Solid state
Floppy Disk	CD	Pen/Flash Drive
Hard Disk Drive	DVD	
Magnetic Tape	Blu-ray Disc	

1. Floppy Disk (Diskette)

A Floppy Disk Drive (FDD) is a computer disk drive that enables a user to save data on removable diskettes. This portable storage device is a rewritable media and can be reused a number of times. It is made of plastic with magnetic coating on it. It is round in shape and is covered by square plastic jacket.

Floppy disks are commonly used to move files between different computers. Although 8" disk drives made available in 1971 were the first real disk drives, the first widely used floppy disk drives were the 4", $5\frac{1}{4}$" floppy disk drives, which were later replaced with $3\frac{1}{2}$" floppy disk drives. However, today these drives are being replaced with CD-R and other writable disks drives and flash drives.

2. Hard Disk Drive

A Hard Disk Drive (HDD) is a non-volatile random access digital data storage device. It is a data storage device used for storing and retrieving digital information using rotating disks (platters) coated with magnetic material. All programs of a computer are installed in hard disk within a particular drive.

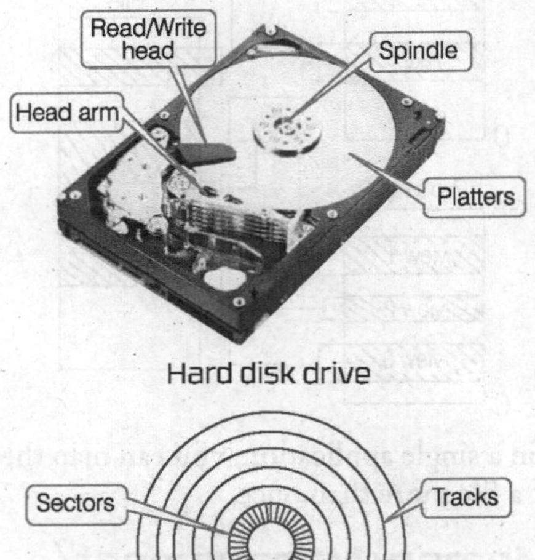

Hard disk drive

Sectors
Tracks

Tracks and sectors

It consists of a **spindle** that holds non–magnetic flat circular disks, called **platters**, which hold the recorded data. Each platter requires two read/write heads, that is used to write and read the information from a platter. All the read/write heads are attached to a single access arm so that they cannot move independently.

The information is recorded in bands, each band of information is called a **track**. Each platter has the same number of tracks and a track location that cuts across all platters is called a **cylinder.** The tracks are divided into pie-shaped sections known as **sectors.**

⚠ Seek time is the time taken for a hard disk controller to locate a specific piece of stored data. When anything is read or written to a disc drive, the read/write head of the disc needs to move to the right position.

3. Magnetic Tape

It is a storage medium on a large open reel or in a smaller cartridge or cassette (like a music cassette) made up of a magnetic material. It is used for those applications that are based on sequential data processing, i.e. it is a sequential data access medium.

Due to this (sequential data access) nature, these tapes are not suitable for data files that need to be revised or updated often. They are generally used to store backup data or that type of data, which is not frequently used or to transfer data from one system to another.

4. **Compact Disc** (CD)

CD is an optical media that is used to store digital data. The compact discs are relatively cheap storage devices. The most common storage capacity of CD is 700 MB.

Compact disc are categorised into three main types as follows:

(i) CD-ROM (Compact Disc-Read Only Memory)
(ii) CD-R (Computer Disc-Recordable)
(iii) CD-RW (Compact Disc-Rewritable)

5. **Digital Video Disc** (DVD)

DVD is also known as Super Density (SD) disc. A DVD is an optical disc storage media manufactured for the first time by Philips, Sony, Toshiba and Panasonic in 1995. DVDs offer higher storage capacity than CDs while having the same dimensions. Depending upon the disk type, DVD can store several gigabytes of data (4.7 GB-17.08 GB).

DVDs are primarily used to store music or movies and can be played back on your television or on the computer too. They are not rewritable media. DVDs come in three varieties as follows:

(i) DVD-ROM (Digital Video Disc-Read Only Memory)
(ii) DVD-R (DVD-Recordable)
(iii) DVD-RW (DVD-Rewritable)

6. **Blu-ray Disc** (BD)

It is an optical disc storage medium designed to recapture the data normally in DVD format. Blu-ray discs contain 25 Gb (23.31 GB) per layer space. The name blu-ray disc refers to the blue laser used to read the disc, which allows information to be stored at a greater density.

Blu-ray can hold almost 5 times more data than a single layer DVD.

The variations in the formats are as follows:

(i) BD-ROM (Read only) for pre-recorded content
(ii) BD-R (Recordable) for PC data storage
(iii) BD-RW (Rewritable) for PC data storage
(iv) BD-RE (Rewritable) for HDTV recording

There is also been the recent roll out of the BDXL format, which increases that capacity to 128 GB.

7. **Pen/Flash/Thumb Drive**

A flash drive is a data storage device that consists of flash memory (USB memory/key memory) with an integrated, **Universal Serial Bus** (USB) interface.

USB flash drives are typically removable, rewritable and physically much smaller than a floppy disk. A USB flash drive, data stick, thumb drive and a pen drive is a portable drive that is same as the size of your thumb that connects to the computer USB port. Today, flash drives are available in various storage capacities as 256 MB, 512 MB, 1 GB, 4 GB, 16 GB and 64 GB, 512 GB etc. Flash drives are widely used as an easy and small medium to transfer and store the information from the computers.

Cache Memory

Cache (pronounced cash) memory is extremely fast memory that is built into a computer's central processing unit, or located next to it on a separate chip. The CPU uses cache memory to store instructions that are repeatedly required to run programs, improving overall system speed.

As the microprocessor processes data, it first looks in the cache memory and if it finds the data there (from a previous reading of data), it does not have to do the time-consuming reading of data from larger memory.

The advantage of cache memory is that if needed data is found in cache then the CPU does not have to use the motherboard's system bus for data transfer and thus processing gets fast.

1.9. Advanced DRAM Organisation

The traditional DRAM is constrained both by its internal architecture and by its interface to processor's memory bus. The new enhancements (most common) on DRAM architecture are as follows :

1. **Synchronous DRAM** (SDRAM)

(i) SDRAM has multiple-bank internal architecture that improves opportunities for on-chip parallelism. Generally it uses dual data banks internally. It starts access in one bank then next, and then receives data from first then second.
(ii) SDRAM performs best when it is transferring large blocks of data serially, such as for applications like Word processing, spreadsheets and multimedia.
(iii) Exchange data with the processor synchronised to an external clock signal and running at the full speed of the processor/memory bus without imposing wait states.
(iv) Typical clock frequencies are 100 and 133 MHz.

2. **Rambus DRAM** (RDRAM)

(i) RDRAM chips are vertical packages with all pins on one side. The chip exchanges data with the processor over 28 wires no more than 12 cm long. The bus can address upto 320 RDRAM chips.
(ii) Entire data blocks are access and transferred out on a high-speed bus-like interface (500 Mbps to 1.6 Gbps).

CHAPTER PRACTICE

1. An operating system is
(1) a collection of hardware components
(2) a collection of input-output devices
(3) a collection of software routines
(4) All of the above

2. Time sharing provides
(1) disk management
(2) file system management
(3) concurrent execution
(4) All of the above

3. Which of the following is/are the objective(s) of operating system?
(1) Scan the system
(2) Provide a connectivity
(3) Managing the system hardware
(4) All of the above

4. The primary job of the operating system of a computer is to
(1) command resources
(2) manage resources
(3) provide utilities
(4) provide connection

5. The term 'time sharing' has been replaced by ....
(1) multi-programming system
(2) multi-processing system
(3) multi-tasking system
(4) multi-execution system

6. The primary function of an operating system is
(1) memory management
(2) process management
(3) disks and I/O device management
(4) All of the above

7. The primary purpose of an operating system is
(1) to make the most efficient use of the computer hardware
(2) to allow people to use the computer
(3) to keep systems programmers employed
(4) to make computers easier to use

8. The term operating system means
(1) a set of programs which controls computer working
(2) the way a computer operating works
(3) conversion of high level into machine level language
(4) the way a floppy disk drive operates.

9. The operating system manages
(1) memory
(2) processes
(3) disks and I/O devices
(4) All of the above

10. What is the function of an operating system?
(1) Manages computer's resources very efficiently
(2) Takes care of scheduling jobs for execution
(3) Manages the flow of data and instructions
(4) All of the above

11. Which is not the function of the operating system?
(1) Memory management
(2) Disk management
(3) Application management
(4) Virus protection

12. Which of the following is system software?
(1) Operating system
(2) Compiler
(3) Utilities
(4) All of the above

13. A process having multiple threads of control, implies
(1) more than one task at a time
(2) only one task at a time, but much faster
(3) only one thread per process to use
(4) All of the above

14. A thread
(1) is a light weight process where the context switching is low
(2) is a light weight process where the context switching is high
(3) is used to speed up paging
(4) None of the above

15. An executed program of computer system is called
(1) trap (2) process
(3) program (4) interrupt

16. Operating system maintains the page table for
(1) each process
(2) each thread
(3) each instruction
(4) each address

17. Device drivers are implemented to interface
(1) character devices
(2) block devices
(3) network devices
(4) All of the above

18. Thread scheduling of operating system programs is done by
(1) input
(2) output
(3) operating system
(4) memory

19. A process of operating system for execution needs
(1) throughput
(2) timers
(3) resources
(4) Both (1) and (2)

20. .... is one of preemptive scheduling algorithm
(1) Shortest job first
(2) Round-robin
(3) Priority based
(4) Shortest job next

21. Semaphore can be used for solving
(1) wait and signal
(2) deadlock
(3) synchronisation
(4) priority

22. Interprocess communication ....
(1) is required for all processes
(2) is usually done *via* disk drives
(3) is never necessary
(4) allows processes to synchronise activity

23. Multi-processor is used because
(1) it saves money compared to multiple single system
(2) it increases reliability
(3) it distributes tasks
(4) All of the above

24. What is interprocess communication?
(1) Communication within the process
(2) Communication between two processes
(3) Communication between two threads of same process
(4) None of the above

25. A semaphore is a shared integer variable
(1) that cannot drop below zero
(2) that cannot more than zero
(3) that cannot drop below one
(4) that cannot more than one

26. Process synchronisation can be done on
(1) hardware level
(2) software level
(3) Both (1) and (2)
(4) None of the above

27. Banker's algorithm is used for ...... purpose.
(1) deadlock avoidance
(2) deadlock removal
(3) deadlock prevention
(4) deadlock continuations

28. Necessary conditions for deadlock are
(1) no preemption and circular wait
(2) mutual exclusion and partial allocation
(3) Both (1) and (2)
(4) None of the above

29. Banker's algorithm for resources allocation deals with
(1) deadlock prevention
(2) deadlock avoidance
(3) deadlock recovery
(4) mutual exclusion

30. Program preemption is
(1) forced deallocation of the CPU from a program which is executing on the CPU
(2) release of CPU by the program after completing its task
(3) forced allotment of CPU by a program to itself
(4) a program terminating itself due to detection of an error.

31. A deadlock in an operating system is
(1) desirable process
(2) undesirable process
(3) definite waiting process
(4) All of the above

32. The Banker's algorithm is used
(1) to prevent deadlock in operating systems
(2) to detect deadlock in operating systems
(3) to rectify a deadlock state
(4) None of the above

33. Which is not the state of the process?
(1) Blocked (2) Running
(3) Ready (4) Privileged

34. A set of processes is deadlock if
(1) each process is blocked and will remain so forever
(2) each process is terminated
(3) all processes are trying to kill each other
(4) None of the above

35. Mutual exclusion can be provided by the
(1) mutex locks
(2) binary semaphores
(3) Both (1) and (2)
(4) None of the above

36. Memory management is
(1) not used in modern operating system
(2) replaced with virtual on current systems
(3) not used on multi-programming systems
(4) critical for even the simplest operating system

37. Main function of shared memory is
(1) to use primary memory efficiently
(2) to do intraprocess communication
(3) to do interprocess communication
(4) None of the above

38. A tree structured file directory system
(1) allows easy storage and retrieval of file names
(2) is a much debated unnecessary features
(3) is not essential when we have millions of files
(4) None of the above

39. What should be the extension to execute files?
(1) EXE (2) BAT
(3) Com (4) All of these

40. In a time sharing operating system, when the time slot given to a process is completed, the process goes from the running state to the
(1) blocked state (2) ready state
(3) suspended state (4) terminated state

41. The operating system of a computer serves as a software interface between the user and the
(1) hardware (2) peripheral
(3) memory (4) screen

42. It refers to the process of managing various devices connected to the computer.
(1) Memory management
(2) File management
(3) Device management
(4) Security management

43. Which one of the following is not the function of operating system?
(1) Resource management
(2) File management
(3) Networking
(4) Processor management

44. It refers to the process of managing files stored in the computer.
(1) Device management
(2) File management
(3) Traffic management
(4) Process management

45. Which of the following error will be handled by the operating system?
(1) Power failure
(2) Lack of paper in printer
(3) Connection failure in the network
(4) All of the above

46. Which is used to keep track of information, its location and status?
(1) Device management
(2) Memory management
(3) Storage management
(4) Both (1) and (2)

47. It is also a layer of a computer system between the hardware and the user program
(1) operating environment
(2) operating system
(3) system environment
(4) application software

48. Which of the following will determine your choice of system software for your computer?
(1) Is the applications software you want to use compatible with it
(2) Is it expensive
(3) Is it compatible with your hardware
(4) Both (1) and (3)

49. Which of the following is not true about deadlock prevention and deadlock avoidance schemes?
(1) In deadlock prevention, the request for resources is always granted if the resulting state is safe.
(2) In deadlock avoidance, the request for resources is always granted if the resulting state is safe
(3) Deadlock avoidance is less restrictive than prevention
(4) Deadlock avoidance requires knowledge of resource requirements

50. In a page segment scheme of memory management, the segment table itself must have a page table because

A useful and typical categorisation is the following:

1. Data Transfer

The most fundamental type of machine instruction is the data transfer instruction.

The data transfer instruction must specify several things. If both source and destination are registers then the CPU simply causes data to be transferred from one register to another.

2. Arithmetic

Most machines provide the basic arithmetic operations of adds, subtract, multiply and divide.

3. Logical

Most machines also provide a variety of operations for manipulating individual bits of a word or other addressable units, often referred to as **bit twiddling**. They are based upon boolean operations. Some of the basic logical operations that can be performed on boolean or binary data are AND, OR, NOT and XOR.

4. Conversion

Conversion instructions are those that change the format or operate on the format of data. An example is converting from decimal to binary.

5. Input/Output

There are a variety of approaches taken, including isolated programmed I/O, memory mapped programmed I/O, DMA and the use of an I/O processor. Many implementations provide only a few I/O instructions with a specific actions specified by parameters, codes or command words.

6. System Control

System control instructions are those that can be executed only while the processor is in a certain privileged state or is executing a program in a special privileged area of memory, typically these instructions are reserved for the use of the operating system.

7. Transfer of Control

The next instruction to be performed is the one that immediately follows in memory, the current instruction. However, a significant fraction of the instructions in any program have as their function changing the sequence of instruction execution.

1.13 Machine Instructions

Machine instruction includes some instruction for various operations in a processor and can be converted into binary code. The translation is done by special program called **assembler.** Machine instructions are also called **assembly language program.**

Machine Instructions

Instruction	Format	Description
ADD	ADD B	Add register B to register A and place result in A.
	ADD M	Add memory M content to A and place result in A.
	ADD A, B	Add A and B and place result in A.
	ADI data	Add immediate data to A and place result in A.
SUB	SUB B	Subtract register B from A and place result in A.
	SUB M	Subtract memory M content from A and place result in A.
	SUB A, B	Subtract B from A and place result in A.
	SBI data	Subtract immediate data from A.
LDA	LDA M	The content of memory M load to A.
STA	STA M	State the content of register A to memory M.
CMA	CMA	Complement A.
MOV	MOV R_1, R_2	Move the content of R_2 in the register R_1.
DCR	DCR R_1	Decrement the content of register R_1 by 1.
INR	INR R_1	Increment the content of register R_1 by 1.
CMP	CMP R_1	Compare R_1 with A.
INP	INP data	Input data and clear flag.
OUT	OUT data	Output data and clear flag.
HLT	HLT	To halt the processor.
LXI	LXI H, 2050	Load immediate data to HL pair.

Here, register A is a special purpose register called **accumulator.** A simple machine language program for addition of two numbers.

LDA NUM1 \\load first number to register A.

ADD NUM2\\load number 2 to A.

HLT

1.14 Addressing Modes

Addressing mode basically describes how operands (data *m* which execution is to be performed) are used in the instruction. Means addressing modes are used to defined the address of data.

1. Immediate Addressing Mode

This addressing mode includes the instruction in which data is directly given in instruction.

e.g. ADD 05

Add immediate data 05 to accumulator.

2. Register Addressing Mode

In this type of addressing mode, data is stored in same register.

e.g. ADD B

Here, the data is stored in register B.

3. Direct (Absolute) Addressing Mode

In this addressing mode, data is stored in same memory location and the address of that memory location is given directly in the instruction.

e.g. LDA 2050

Load the content of memory location 2050 to register *A*. Here, the address is given directly in the instruction that is 2050.

4. Indirect Addressing Mode

When the data is stored in memory location and the memory location is stored in another register which is given in the instruction.

e.g. ADD M [AR]

ADD data whose address is stored in register AR. This is also called **register indirect addressing mode.** Here, the address of data is stored in register AR.

5. Implicit Addressing Mode

In the addressing mode of instruction address of data is not defined in the instruction. But the instruction known on which data it has to perform execution.

e.g. CMA

Complement of A. Here, the address of data is not given in the instruction. But the instruction known that it has to complement the content of register A.

6. Auto Increment or Auto Decrement Mode

This is similar to register indirect mode expect that the value of register is incremented or decremented automatically after its value is used to access memory. This addressing mode can be used in branch type instruction.

7. Relation Addressing Mode

In this mode, content of program counter is added to the address part of instruction in order to obtain the effective address. The address part of instruction is a signed number that could be positive or negative. This addressing mode can also be used in branch type instruction. It results a shorter address field as relative field required less address space.

Effective address = program counter
+ address part of instruction

8. Indexed Addressing Mode

In this mode, content of index register is added to the address part of the instruction to abstain effective address. This type of instruction is used to access array elements. If address field of instruction is not given then this addressing mode will work as register indirect mode.

9. Base Addressing Mode

In this mode, the content of base register is added to the address part of instruction to obtain effective address. This addressing mode is used for relocation of program in memory.

1.15 General Register Organisation

During execution of a program, data values, results, return addresses and partial results are stored in the memory location. Accessing the memory is the most time consuming operation in a computer. The CPU can access a register more quickly than a memory location and the register-to-register operation executes faster than compared to the memory-to-memory or register-to-memory operation. Due to the faster execution in register, the intermediate data is stored in the register so that it is more convenient and more efficient for CPU to access these data and perform operation.

There are large numbers of registers present in the computer, which are connected with the common bus system. Hence, all the arithmetic, logic and shift operation in the CPU are performed by the common unit. In the following figure, a seven register bus organisation is displayed which has a common ALU to perform all the computation.

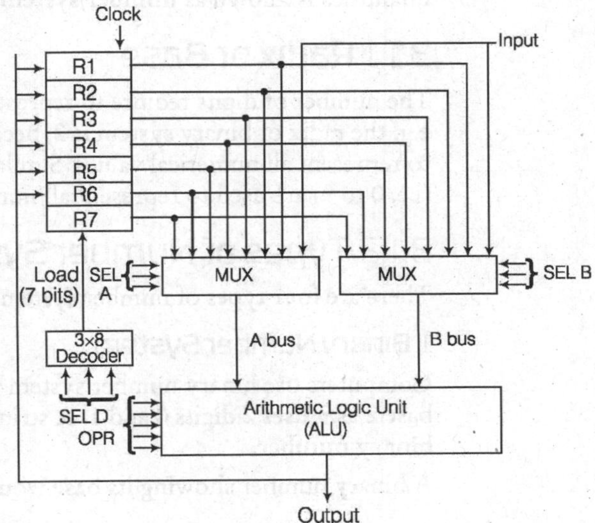

CHAPTER 03

Digital Electronics

Digital electronics are those electronics systems that use a **digital signal** instead of an **analog signal.** Digital electronics are the most common representation of **Boolean algebra** and are the basis of all digital circuits for computers, mobile phones and numerous other consumer products.

The most common fundamental unit of digital electronics is the **logic gate.** By combining numerous logic gates more complex systems can be created. The complex system of digital electronics is collectively referred to as a digital circuit.

1. **Digital Signal** It is a signal that is constructed from a discrete set of waveforms of a physical quantity so as to represent a sequence of discrete values.

2. **Analog Signal** It is any continuous signal for which the time varying feature (variable) of the signal is a representation of some other time varying quantity, i.e. analogous to another time varying signal.

3.1 Number System

Number system basically means the representation of number with limited number of symbols. Like most widely used number system is the positional number system. The position of various digits indicates the significance to be attached to that digit. Thus, a set of values used to represent the different quantities is known as **number system.**

3.1.1 Radix or Base

The number of digits require to represent all the numbers in a particular number system is called **radix.** e.g. the radix of binary system is 2, because in binary number system just two digits (i.e. 0 or 1) are used to represent all numerical values. Similarly, the radix of decimal number system is 10 because 10 digits (i.e. 0 to 9) are used to represent all numerical values.

3.1.2 Types of Number System

There are four types of number system as follows:

1. Binary Number System

Computers use binary number system for counting and arithmetic operations. This number system has base 2 as it uses 2 digits 0 and 1. A string which have any combination of these two digit is called **binary number.**

A binary number showing its base would be written as $(11001)_2$.

2. Octal Number System

The octal number system has a base of 8, meaning that it has eight unique symbols 0, 1, 2, 3, 4, 5, 6 and 7. Thus, each digit of an octal number can have any value from 0 to 7. Any octal number is a string of any combination of these digits. An octal number showing its base would be written as $(2317)_8$, $(7065)_8$, $(1257)_8$, $(6857)_8$ etc.

3. Decimal Number System

The number system that we use in our day-to-day life is the decimal number system. It has base 10 as it uses 10 digits from 0 to 9 (i.e. 0, 1, 2, 3, 4, 5, 6, 7, 8 and 9). Any decimal number is a string of any combination of these digits. A decimal number showing its base would be written as $(257)_{10}$ or $(257)_d$. Where, '10' and the small letter 'd' designate that it is a decimal number.

4. Hexadecimal Number System

In hexadecimal number system, the base or radix is 16. Thus, it has 16 possible digit symbols. It uses the digits 0 to 9 and letters *A*, *B*, *C*, *D*, *E* and *F* (with respect to 10, 11, 12, 13, 14 and 15). Any hexadecimal number is a string of any combination of these digits. This number system is generally used in micro computers.

A hexadecimal number showing its base would be written as $(134BD)_{16}$.

3.1.3 Conversion between the Number Systems

Different types of conversion between the number system are discussed below:

1. Decimal to Binary

***Step* 1** Divide the given number by 2.

***Step* 2** Note the quotient and remainder. Remainder should be 0 or 1.

***Step* 3** If quotient ≠ 0, then divide the quotient by 2 and again back to step 2. If quotient = 0, then stop the process.

***Step* 4** First remainder is called as **Least Significant Bit** (LSB) and last remainder is called as **Most Significant Bit** (MSB). Arrange all remainders from MSB to LSB.

e.g. $(43)_{10} \rightarrow (?)_2$

		Remainder
2	43	1 → LSB
2	21	1
2	10	0
2	5	1
2	2	0
2	1	1 → MSB
	0	

Then, $(43)_{10} \rightarrow (101011)_2$

2. Binary to Decimal

***Step* 1** Multiply the all binary digits by powers of 2.

***Step* 2** The power for integral part will be positive and for fractional part will be negative.

***Step* 3** Add the all multiplying digits.

e.g. $(1101.10)_2 \rightarrow (?)_{10}$

$$(1101.10)_2 = 1\times 2^3 + 1\times 2^2 + 0\times 2^1 + 1\times 2^0 + 1\times 2^{-1} + 0\times 2^{-2}$$
$$= 8+4+0+1+0.5+0 = 13.5$$

Then, $(1101.10)_2 \rightarrow (13.5)_{10}$

3. Binary to Octal

***Step* 1** Make the group of three bits from right to left.

***Step* 2** Now, convert each group to decimal number.

e.g. $(110110100)_2 \rightarrow (?)_8$

110 110 100
↓ ↓ ↓
6 6 4

Then, $(110110100)_2 \rightarrow (664)_8$

4. Octal to Binary

Convert every digit of the number from octal to binary in the group of three bits.

e.g. $(1034.5)_8 \rightarrow (?)_2$

1 0 3 4 5
↓ ↓ ↓ ↓ ↓
001 000 011 100 101

Then, $(1034.5)_8 \rightarrow (001000011100.101)_2$

5. Binary to Hexadecimal

***Step* 1** Start making the group of four bits each from right to left from the given binary number.

***Step* 2** Now, each group will be converted to decimal number.

e.g. $(11110101111011)_2 \rightarrow (?)_{16}$

0011 1101 0111 1011
↓ ↓ ↓ ↓
3 13 *D* 7 11 *B*

Then, $(11110101111011)_2 \rightarrow (3D7B)_{16}$

1.19.2 Hardware Implementation

In a hardware implementation, the control unit is essentially considered as a logic circuit. Its input logic signals are transformed into the set of output logic signals, which are the control signals.

1.19.3 Microprogrammed Controller

An alternative and flexible way of implementing the control subsystem is to use a microprogrammed controller. Such a controller implementation may use a general purpose system or a specially designed one and the algorithm can be modified by changing the microprogram-a sequence of micro-instructions.

Micro-instruction formats vary, but a format system must include a control field for the values of the control signals, and a sequencing field which specifies the address of the next micro-instruction.

Micro-instruction with no sequencing information control unit are as follows:

1. Micro-instruction Sequencing

The microprogrammed control unit get the next micro-instruction from the control memory. Two problems are involved in the design of a micro-instruction sequencing technique is the size of micro-instruction and the address generation time. The first concern is obvious minimizing the size of the control memory.The second concern is simply a desire to execute micro-instruction as fast as possible.

2. Micro-instruction Execution

The micro-instruction cycle is the basic event on a microprogrammed processor. Each cycle is made up the two parts: fetch and execute. This section deals with the execution of micro-instruction. The effect of the execution of a micro-instruction is to generate control signals for both the internal control to processor and the external control to processor.

1.20 Assembly Language

This language is devised where English-like words are used to represent the binary instructions of a machine. This English likes words for each instructions is called as **mnemonic.** These mnemonics suggest the operation to be performed by that instruction.

These mnemonic are used for writing machine language instructions in symbolic form where each machine instructions is represented by one equivalent symbolic instruction given a new language definition known as assembly language.

An assembly language program is written according to a set of rules that defines the instruction set of that machine. Any Word processor can be used for writing the assembly program and then assembler is used to translate the program into machine understandable code. The assembly program written using symbolic notation is known as **source program.** Assembler is a program that translates the source program into machine language is known as **object program.**

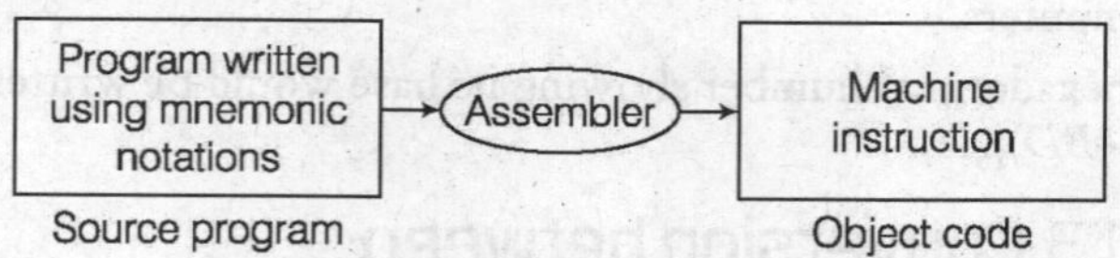

Program Control instruction in Assembly Language

Program control instructions change or modify the flow of a program. The most basic kind of program control is the unconditional branch or unconditional jump.

Some important program control instructions are follows:

(i) JMP	(ii) JSJ
(iii) JOV	(iv) LOOP
(v) CALL	(vi) RET
(vii) RTD	(viii) NOP
(ix) HLT	(x) MOV

CHAPTER PRACTICE

1. Which of the following components is the most essential for the computer system to work?
(1) Input system (2) Output system
(3) Storage system (4) CPU

2. Pick the one that is used for logical operations or comparisons such as less than, equal to or greater than.
(1) ALU (2) CU
(3) Input unit (4) MU

3. The control unit controls other units by generating
(1) control signal (2) timing signal
(3) transfer signal (4) command signal

4. The .... is responsible for performing calculations and contains decision-making mechanisms.
(1) CPU (2) MU
(3) ALU (4) CU

5. The Central Processing Unit (CPU) in a computer consists of
(1) input, output and processing
(2) control unit, primary storage and secondary storage
(3) control unit, arithmetic logic unit, registers
(4) None of the above

6. Internal memory in a CPU is nothing but
(1) a set of registers
(2) a set of ALU
(3) microprocessor
(4) bus

7. The word 'computer' usually refers to the central processing unit plus
(1) external memory
(2) internal memory
(3) input devices
(4) output devices

8. Which of the following is a part of central processing unit?
(1) Printer
(2) Keyboard
(3) Mouse
(4) Arithmetic and Logic Unit

9. Control unit of a digital computer is often called the
(1) clock
(2) nerve centre
(3) Both (1) and (2)
(4) IC

10. Both the ALU and control section have special purpose storage locations, called
(1) address (2) registers
(3) accumulators (4) bus

11. Pipeline strategy is called implement
(1) instruction execution
(2) instruction prefetch
(3) instruction decoding
(4) instruction manipulation

12. The communication line between CPU memory and peripherals is called a
(1) bus (2) line
(3) media (4) All of these

13. Which device of computer operation dispenses with the use of the keyboard?
(1) Joystick (2) Light pen
(3) Mouse (4) Touch

14. Which of the following produces high quality output?
(1) Impact printer
(2) Non-impact printer
(3) Plotter
(4) Both (1) and (2)

15. The pattern of printed lines on most products are called
(1) prices (2) OCR
(3) scanners (4) bar codes

16. The higher the resolution of a monitor, the
(1) larger the pixels
(2) less clear the screen is
(3) further apart the pixels
(4) closer together the pixels

17. What are the units used to count the speed of a printer?
(1) CPM (2) DPR (3) PPM (4) BIT

18. What type of devices are computer speakers or headphones?
(1) Input/Output (2) Software
(3) Storage (4) Output

19. The OCR is used for the preparation of
(1) electricity bills
(2) insurance premium
(3) telephone bills
(4) All of the above

20. Interrupt driven I/O
(1) has its main drawback in the software overhead of interrupts
(2) may be better than busy waiting I/O, since less hardware support is required
(3) is equal or faster than DMA for a signal word register
(4) Both (1) and (3)

21. The data transfer in which data transfer is to be done quickly
(1) programmed I/O
(2) interrupt I/O
(3) DMA
(4) None of the above

22. Which of the following can hold maximum data?
(1) Optical disk
(2) Floppy disk
(3) Magnetic disk inside
(4) Magnetic tape

23. Which storage device is mounted on 'reels'?
(1) Floppy disk
(2) Hard disk
(3) Magnetic tapes
(4) CD-ROM

24. Cache and main memory will not be able to hold their contents when the power is OFF. They are
(1) dynamic (2) static
(3) volatile (4) non-volatile

25. More than one word are put in one cache block to
(1) exploit the temporal locality of reference in a program
(2) exploit the spatial locality of reference in program
(3) reduce the miss penalty
(4) None of the above

26. Which of the following is not a form of main memory?
(1) Instruction cache
(2) Instruction register
(3) Instruction opcode
(4) Translation look-aside buffer

27. The refreshing rate of dynamic RAMs is in the range of
(1) 30 μs (2) 3 μs
(3) 50 μs (4) 500 μs

The 8421 code is predominant BCD code and when we referred to BCD, we always mean 8421 code unless otherwise stated.

3.3.2 BCD to Decimal Conversion

In this conversion, every four bit digit BCD code is replaced by its equivalent decimal number.

e.g. (i) $(10010110)_{BCD} = (?)_{10}$ 1001 → 9, 0110 → 6 $= (96)_{10}$

(ii) 1011 → *, 0001 → 1

This conversion is impossible because 1011 is not a valid binary coded decimal. It is not in the range 0 to 9.

(iii) $(011000100100)_{BCD}$ 0110 → 6, 0010 → 2, 0100 → 4 $= (624)_{10}$

3.4 Hamming Codes

Hamming codes fall under the category of linear block codes of Forward Error Correcting (FEC) codes. To understand how it can be constructed, consider the simplest (7,4) (7,4) hamming code. The notation (7,4) (7,4) indicates that the codewords are of length 7 bits. Out of these 7 bits, 4 bits are the original message and remaining 3 bits are added for detecting and correcting errors. These remaining 3 bits are called **redundant bits.**

The structure can be indicated as follows:

4 message bits + 3 redundant bits ⇒ 7 bit Hamming code.

Hamming code can also be represented in two forms: Systematic and non-systematic form.

Construction of Hamming Codes

Consider transmitting 4 data bits and these data bits are represented by letter *D*. We are going to find the 3 redundant bits (represented by letter *P*) using Hamming code algorithm and form the 7 bit Hamming code. The codewords made in this way is called (7, 4) Hamming code which is a very basic code.

Let the codeword bits be represented by $D_7, D_6, D_5, D_4, D_3, D_2, D_1$. Here D_7, D_6, D_5 and D_3 are the message bits and P_4, P_2, P_1 are the parity or redundant bits.

The parity bits are calculated using the following equations:

$$P_4 = D_7 + D_6 + D_5$$
$$P_2 = D_7 + D_6 + D_3$$
$$P_1 = D_7 + D_5 + D_3$$

Here, + sign indicated modulo-2 addition or XOR operation.

3.5 Computer Arithmetic

3.5.1 Arithmetic Operation

1. **Binary Addition** works in the same way, except that only 0's and 1's can be used, instead of the whole spectrum of 0-9. This actually makes binary addition much simpler than decimal addition, as we only need to remember the following rule:

   0 + 0 = 0; 0 + 1 = 1
   1 + 0 = 1; 1 + 1 = 10 (which is 0 carry 1)

   As an example of binary addition we have,

```
 101
+101
----
1010
```

   (i) To add these two numbers, we first consider the "ones" column and calculate 1 + 1, which (in binary) results in 10. We "carry" the 1 to the "tens" column and the leave the 0 in the "ones" column.
   (ii) Moving on to the "tens" column, we calculate 1 + (0, 0), which gives 1. Nothing "carries" to the "hundreds" column and we leave the 1 in the "tens" column.
   (iii) Moving on the "hundreds" column, we calculate 1 + 1, which gives 10. We "carry" the 1 to the "thousands" column, leaving the 0 in the "hundreds" column.

   Another example of binary addition:

```
 1011
+1011
-----
10110
```

   ⚠ In the "tens" column, we have 1 + (1 + 1), were the first 1 is "carried" from the "ones" column. Recall that in binary, 1 + 1 + 1 = 10 + 1 =11.

2. **Binary Subtraction** is simplifies as well, as long as we remember how subtraction and the base 2 number system. To subtraction as we only need to remember the following

   0 − 0 = 0
   1 − 0 = 1
   1 − 1 = 0
   0 − 1 = 1 (with a borrow of 1)

   ⚠ The difference is the same, if this is a decimal subtraction. Also, similar to decimal subtraction is the concept of "borrowing". "Borrowing" occurs when a larger digit, say 8, is subtracted from a smaller digit, say 5, as shown below in decimal subtraction.

```
 35
 -8
---
 27
```

For 10 minus 1, 1 is borrowed from the "tens" column for use in the "ones" column, leaving the "tens" column with only 2.

The following examples show "borrowing" in binary subtraction:

10	100	1010
-1	-10	- 110
1	10	100

3.5.2 Representation of Numbers

In general, a number can be represented by its magnitude and a sign to show that whether it is a positive number or negative number. For positive number, a plus (+ve) sign is indicated before number and for negative number a minus (– ve) sign is indicated before number. A number with no sign is treated as a positive number. But in case of computer system due to hardware limitation everything has to be represented either by 0's or 1's including the sign of a number.

Thus, in computer system an extra bit is introduced called **sign bit**. When the value of sign bit is 1, it indicated that the number is negative and when sign bit is 0, it indicates that the number is positive. The number that is represented by system can be integer fraction or mixed integer fraction numbers.

There are two representation techniques used to represent a number:

(i) Fixed point representation

(ii) Floating point representation.

1. Fixed Point Representation

In fixed point representation, we assume that the decimal point is fixed. In this representation, left most bit of register is used to store point. This register is used to store fraction number. In second register, right most bit is used to store the decimal point. This is used for integer storage. There are three ways of storing signed number as follows:

(i) **Sign-magnitude Representation** In this representation, MSB is used to represent sign (0 for positive and 1 for negative) and the remaining bits are used to represent the magnitude of the number.

e.g. Binary six bit number 011000 represent a positive number and its value is 24, whereas 111000 represents a negative number –24.

The maximum positive number that can be represent using sign magnitude form is $+(2^{n-1}-1)$ and maximum negative number is $-(2^{n-1}-1)$ where, n is number of bits.

(ii) **One's Complement Notation** The 1's complement of a binary number is found by simply changing all 1's to 0's and all 0's to 1's. e.g. $+9_{10}$ is represented by $(1001)_2$ and its 1's complement.

```
1001  +9
↓
0110  −9
```

$(0110)_2$ represents -9_{10}.

The maximum positive and negative number that can be represented are $(2^{n-1}-1)$ and $-(2^{n-1}-1)$ respectively.

(iii) **2's Complement Notation** The 2's complement of a binary number is found by adding 1 to the 1's complement.

e.g. Binary number 1 0 0 1 1

0 1 1 0 0	1's complement of 1 0 0 1 1
+ 1	Add 1
0 1 1 0 1	2's complement of 1 0 0 1 1

2. Floating Point Number Representation

The floating point number has both an integer part as well as fractional part. Thus, 0.726, 2.3462, 555.55 etc, are all floating point numbers. The floating point number consists of two parts, i.e. they are expressed as a combination of mantissa (the fraction part) and the exponent. e.g. 0.00726 can be written as 7.26×10^{-3}.

Thus, a floating point number can be expressed as

$N = M \times R^e$

Where, M is the mantissa and e represents exponent.

IEEE Standard Floating Point Representation

IEEE standard specifies two formats for representing floating point number. One for 32 bits operand (known as single precision) and another for 64 bits operand (known as double precision).

S	Exponent	Mantissa Fraction
1 bit	8 bit	23 bit

(a) Single precision

S	Exponent	Mantissa Fraction
1 bit	11 bit	52 bit

(b) Double precision

Both formats starts with a sign bit, 0 for positive sign and 1 for negative sign. Next comes the exponent, using excess-127 representation for single precision and excess-1023 representation for double precision.

Finally, we have the mantissa fractions consisting of 23 bits in case of single precision and 52 bits in case of double precision. Thus, a total of 32 bits is needed for single precision and 64 bits is needed for double precision.

77. **Increasing the RAM of a computer typically improves performance because**
(1) virtual memory increases
(2) larger RAMs are faster
(3) fewer segmentation faults occur
(d) fewer page faults occur

78. **Consider a 4-way set associative cache consisting of 128 lines with a line size of 64 words. The CPU generates a 20-bit address of a word in main memory. The number of bits in the TAG, LINE and WORD fields are respectively**
(1) 7, 7, 6 (2) 9, 6, 5
(3) 7, 5, 8 (4) 9, 5, 6

79. **How many $32K \times 1$ RAM chips are needed to provide a memory capacity of 256 KB?**
(1) 8 (2) 32
(3) 64 (4) 128

80. **The total size of address space in a virtual memory system is limited by**
(1) the length of MAR
(2) the available secondary storage
(3) the available main memory
(4) None of the above

81. **The memory which does not loose its content of failure of power supply it known as .... memory.**
(1) main memory (2) volatile
(3) non-volatile (4) RAM

82. **On which of the following, storage media, storage of information is organised as a single continuous spiral groove?**
(1) CD- ROM
(2) RAM
(3) Hard disk
(4) Floppy disk

83. **Which of the following memory improves the speed of execution of a program?**
(1) Virtual memory
(2) Primary memory
(3) Secondary memory
(4) Cache memory

84. **A pipeline is having speed up factor as 10 and operating with efficiency of 80%. What will be the number of stages in the pipeline?**
(1) 10
(2) 8
(3) 13
(4) None of the above

85. **A non-pipeline system takes 50 ns to process a task. The same task can be processed in a 6-segment pipeline with a clock cycle of 10 s. Determine the speed up ratio of the pipeline for 100 tasks.**
(1) 4 : 8 (2) 5 : 1
(3) 4 : 76 (4) None of these

86. **Comparing the time T_1 taken for a single instruction on a pipelined CPU with time T_2 taken on a non-pipelined but identical CPU, we can say that**
(1) $T_1 \le T_2$
(2) $T_1 \ge T_2$
(3) $T_1 < T_2$
(4) T_1 is T_2 plus line taken for one instruction fetch cycle

87. **Match the following**

(a) Immediate address mode	I. Local variables
(b) Direct address demode	II. Relocatable program
(c) Indirect address mode	III. Pointers
(d). Index address mode	IV. Locality of references
(e) Base address mode	V. Arrays
(f) Relative address mode	VI. Constant operands

(1) a-IV, b-I, c-III, d-V, e-II, f-IV
(2) a-V, b-IV, c-VI, d-III, e-I, f-II
(3) a-III, b-V, c-II, d-IV, e-I, f-6
(4) a-VI, b-V, c-II, d-III, e-I, f-IV

88. **Which of the following cycle is used for interpreting the instruction that was fetched in the fetch cycle?**
(1) Fetch cycle
(2) Decode cycle
(3) Execute cycle
(4) Interrupt cycle

89. **Addressing mode facilitates access to an operand whose location is defined in relative to the beginning of the data structure in which it appears?**
(1) Absolute (2) Immediate
(3) Index (4) Indirect

90. **The most relevant addressing mode to write position independent code is**
(1) direct mode (2) indirect mode
(3) relative mode (4) indexed mode

91. **Which of the following instructions is an example of direct addressing mode?**
(1) MOV A, B (2) LDA 2050
(3) 05 (4) HLT

92. **The sequence of events that happens during a typical fetch operation is**
(1) PC→MAR→Memory→MDR→1R
(2) PC→Memory→MDR→1R
(3) PC→Memory→1R
(4) PC→MAR→Memory→1 R

93. **Which of the following are typical characteristics of a RISC algorithm?**
(1) Highly pipelined
(2) Multiple register set
(3) Both (1) and (2)
(4) None of the above

94. **The most appropriate matching for the following pairs:**

(a) Indirect addressing	I. Loop
(b) Immediate addressing	II. Pointers
(c) Auto decrement	III. Constants addressing

(1) a-III, b. II, c. I
(2) a-I, b. III, c. II
(3) a-II, b. III, c. I
(4) a-III, b. I, c. II

95. **Which is the most appropriate match for the items in the first columns with the items in the second column?**

(a) Indirect addressing	I. Array implementation
(b) Indexed addressing	II. Writing relocatable code
(c) Base register addressing	III. Passing array as parameter

(1) a-III, b-I, c-II (2) a-II, b-III, c-I
(3) a-III, b-II, c-I (4) a-I, b-III, c-II

96. **Which of the following addressing modes are suitable for program relocation at run time?**
I. Absolute addressing
II. Based addressing
III. Relative addressing
IV. Indirect addressing
(1) I and IV (2) I and II
(3) I, II and IV (4) II and III

97. **Which of the following units is used to superwise each instruction in the CPU?**
(1) Control logic unit
(2) Accumulator
(3) ALU
(4) Control register

98. **Which of the following units is responsible for coordinating various operations using timing signals?**
(1) ALU (2) Control unit
(3) Memory unit (4) I/O unit

99. **The register which contains the data to be written into or read out of the addressed location is called**
(1) memory addressed register
(2) memory data register
(3) program counter
(4) index register

100. **The CPU of a computer takes instruction from the memory and executes them. This process is called**
(1) load cycle
(2) time sequencing
(3) fetch-execute cycle
(4) clock cycle

101. **An interrupt can be temporarily ignored by the counter is called**
(1) vectored interrupt
(2) non-maskable interrupt
(3) maskable interrupt
(4) low priority interrupt

102. **The number of references required for CPU to execute direct mode address reference is**
(1) 0 (2) 1
(3) 2 (4) 3

103. **The addressing mode in an instruction of the form ADD 05, 06 is**
(1) absolute (2) immediate
(3) indirect (4) index

104. **The addressing mode used in the instruction PUSH B is**
(1) direct
(2) register
(3) register indirect
(4) immediate

105. **In a microprocessor, the address of the next instruction to be executed, is stored in**
(1) stack pointer
(2) address latch
(3) program counter
(4) general purpose register

106. **Programming that actually controls the path of the data within the computer is called**
(1) micro programming
(2) system programming
(3) assembly language
(4) machine language programming

107. **The technology that stores only the essential instructions on a microprocessor chip and thus enhances its speed is referred to as:**
(1) MIMD (2) CISC
(3) RISC (4) SIMD

108. **A register in the microprocessor that keeps track of the answer or result of any arithmetic or logic operation is the ....**
(1) accumulator
(2) stack pointer
(3) program counter
(4) instruction pointer

109. **In which addressing mode, the operand is given explicitly in the instruction (example instruction ADD R4, #3)?**
(1) Based indexed mode
(2) Absolute mode
(3) Immediate mode
(4) Register indirect mode

110. **Which of the following is not a program control instruction?**
(1) CMP (2) MOV
(3) JMP (4) CALL

111. **The addressing mode used in an instruction of the form ADD X,Y is**
(1) index (2) absolute
(3) immediate (4) indirect

112. **........... provides a bus architecture that also supports peripherals and devices like hard disk, drives network etc.**
(1) PCI bus (2) Data bus
(3) Address bus (4) Control bus

ANSWER KEY

1	(4)	2	(1)	3	(1)	4	(3)	5	(3)	6	(1)	7	(1)	8	(4)	9	(2)	10	(2)
11	(2)	12	(1)	13	(3)	14	(2)	15	(4)	16	(4)	17	(3)	18	(4)	19	(4)	20	(4)
21	(3)	22	(4)	23	(3)	24	(3)	25	(2)	26	(3)	27	(2)	28	(4)	29	(1)	30	(4)
31	(4)	32	(4)	33	(3)	34	(2)	35	(2)	36	(2)	37	(2)	38	(4)	39	(4)	40	(1)
41	(3)	42	(3)	43	(3)	44	(1)	45	(1)	46	(3)	47	(2)	48	(3)	49	(1)	50	(1)
51	(3)	52	(1)	53	(2)	54	(4)	55	(1)	56	(4)	57	(1)	58	(3)	59	(3)	60	(4)
61	(4)	62	(1)	63	(2)	64	(2)	65	(3)	66	(1)	67	(4)	68	(2)	69	(3)	70	(2)
71	(4)	72	(2)	73	(4)	74	(3)	75	(4)	76	(4)	77	(4)	78	(4)	79	(3)	80	(2)
81	(3)	82	(1)	83	(4)	84	(3)	85	(3)	86	(2)	87	(1)	88	(2)	89	(3)	90	(3)
91	(2)	92	(1)	93	(3)	94	(3)	95	(1)	96	(4)	97	(1)	98	(2)	99	(2)	100	(3)
101	(3)	102	(3)	103	(2)	104	(2)	105	(3)	106	(1)	107	(3)	108	(1)	109	(3)	110	(1)
111	(2)	112	(2)																

3.8.5 OR Gate

The output Q is true if input A and input B are true, i.e.

$$Q = A \text{ OR } B$$

An OR gate can have two or more inputs, its output is true if atleast one input is true.

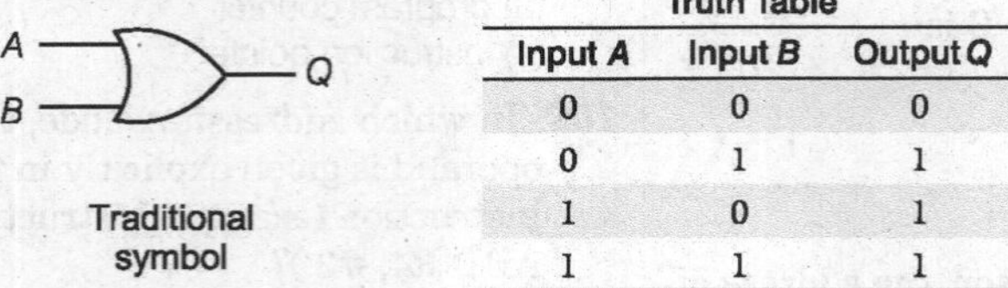

Traditional symbol

Truth Table

Input *A*	Input *B*	Output *Q*
0	0	0
0	1	1
1	0	1
1	1	1

3.8.6 NOR Gate (NOR = Not OR)

This is an OR gate with the inverted output, as shown the '0' on the output. The output Q is true if not inputs A and B are true,

$$Q = \text{NOT } (A \text{ OR } B).$$

A NOR gate can have two or more inputs, its output is true if no inputs are true.

Traditional symbol

Truth Table

Input *A*	Input *B*	Output *Q*
0	0	1
0	1	0
1	0	0
1	1	0

3.8.7 XOR (Exclusive OR) Gate

XOR gate is also termed as anti-coincidence detector or inequality detector.

The output Q is true if either input A is true or input B is true, but not when both of them are true,

$Q = (A \text{ AND NOT } B) \text{ OR } (B \text{ AND NOT } A)$.

This is like an OR gate but exclusing both inputs being true.

The output is true if inputs A and B are different.

XOR gates can only have 2 inputs.

Traditional symbol

Truth Table

Input *A*	Input *B*	Output *Q*
0	0	0
0	1	1
1	0	1
1	1	0

3.8.8 XNOR (Exclusive-NOR) Gate

XNOR gate is also termed as **coincidence detector** or **equivalence detector.**

This is an XOR gate with the inverted output, as shown by the '0' on the output. The output Q is true if input A and B are the same (both true or both false)

$$Q = (A \text{ AND } B) \text{ OR } (\text{NOT } A \text{ AND NOT } B)$$

XNOR gates can only have 2 inputs.

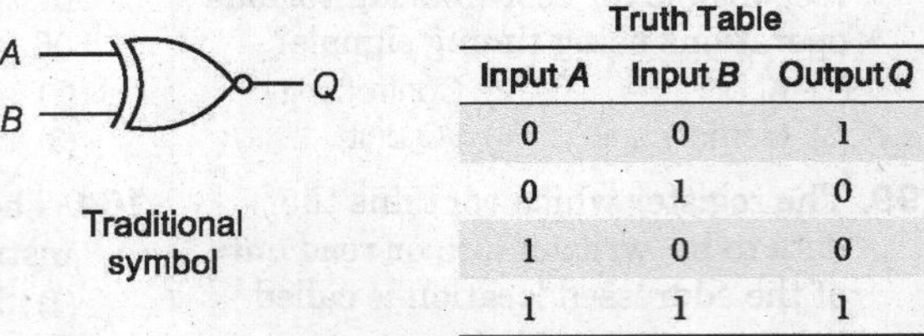

Traditional symbol

Truth Table

Input *A*	Input *B*	Output *Q*
0	0	1
0	1	0
1	0	0
1	1	1

3.8.9 Design of Combinational Circuit Using Logic Gates

Combinational circuits are simply connection of logic gates. This section will describe how to design a combinational circuit for a given boolean expression. Suppose, we have a boolean function,

$$F = \bar{x}yz + xy + x\bar{y}\bar{z}$$

Here, F has 3 variables that are x, y, z so we will have 3-inputs in our combinational circuit that are x, y, z. Logic gates will be used as,

1. **NOT gate** To complement some variables like to complement x.

2. **AND gate** For AND operation between two variables, e.g. xy.

3. **OR gate** OR gate will be used for OR operation between two variables like $x + y$

Now, function $\bar{x}yz + xy + x\bar{y}\bar{z}$ can be divided into three parts $\bar{x}yz$, xy and $x\bar{y}\bar{z}$. So, for $\bar{x}yz$, we have

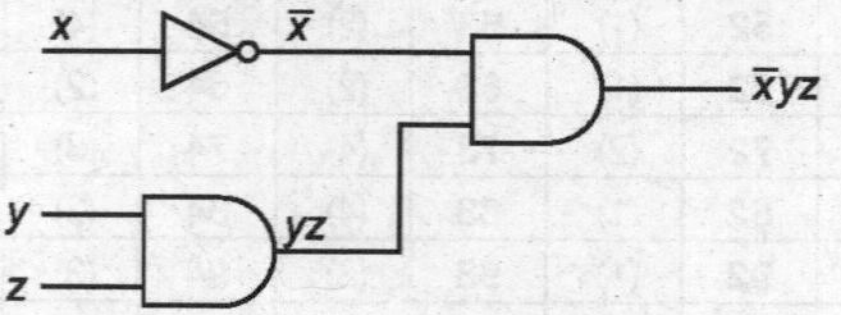

Second for xy, we have

For $x\bar{y}\bar{z}$, we have

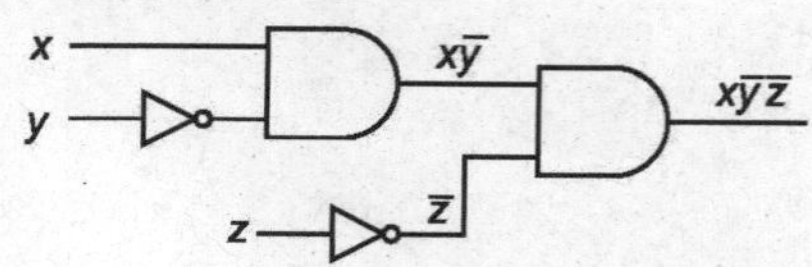

Now, after combining these circuits, we have boolean function $F = \bar{x}yz + xy + x\bar{y}\bar{z}$ will be drawn as

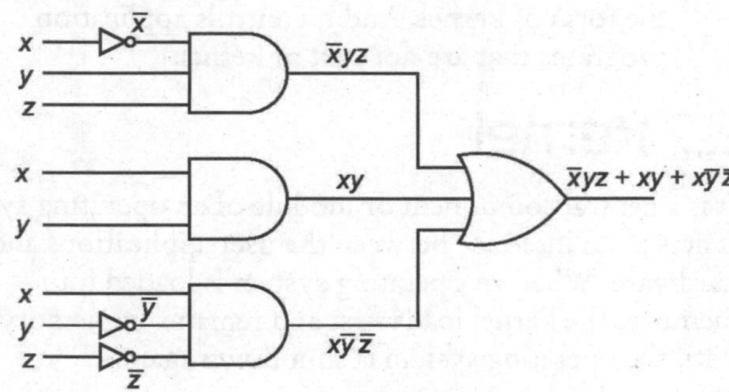

3.9 Logic Family

In computer engineering, a logic family may refer to one of two related concepts. A logic family of monolithic digital integrated circuit devices is a group of electronic logic gates constructed using one of several different designs, usually with compatible logic levels and power supply characteristics within a family.

The main types of logic families are as follows:

1. **TTL Logic** In transistor, transistor logic, logic gates and other digital circuits are made using bipolar junction transistors and resistors.
2. **ECL** Emitter coupled logic, also referred to as **current mode logic families,** is a digital technology with extremely high speed.
3. **CMOS** Complementary metal oxide semiconductor (CMOS) has complementary and symmetrical NMOS and PMOS transistor. Because of high noise immunity and law static power dissipation, now CMOS logic families is most preferred in large scale integrated circuits.

3.10 Standard Form of Boolean Function

The standard form of the boolean function is expressed in two fashion, these are as follows:

1. **Sum of Product** (SOP) It is a boolean expression in which product terms (AND terms) are connected by the OR operator. Each AND term contains one or more variables in complemented or normal form. e.g. $\bar{X}Y + X\bar{Y}$
2. **Product of Sum** (POS) It is a boolean expression in which sum of terms (OR terms) are connected by the AND operators. Each OR term contains one or more variables in complemented or normal form. e.g. $(X + Y).(\bar{X} + \bar{Y})$

3.11. Minimisation of Boolean Expression

The standard forms of boolean expression is usually not a minimised expression. A minimised boolean expression means less number of boolean variables.

The following two methods used for the simplification of boolean expression:

1. Boolean Algebra (Algebraic) Method

The algebraic method is used with the basic postulates and theorems to minimise boolean expression.

e.g. $x.(x + y) = x$

Take LHS,

$\Rightarrow \quad x.(x + y) = (x + 0).(x + y)$ (by identity law)

$\Rightarrow \quad x.(x + y) = x + 0.y$ (by distributive law)

$\Rightarrow \quad x.(x + y) = x + y.0$ (by commutative law)

$\Rightarrow \quad x.(x + y) = x + 0$ (by basic postulates)

$\Rightarrow \quad x.(x + y) = x$ (by identity law)

So, LHS = RHS

2. Karnaugh Map (K-Map)

K-map is a very popular technique used for the simplification of boolean expressions. It is drawn in the form of a diagram divided by rows and columns into squares and the number of square corresponds to a row number in the truth table.

K-map is composed of arrangement of cells each representing one particular combination on variables product form. For a total number of n variables, K-map consists of 2^n cells.

(i) Four Variables K-Map

For four variables (A, B, C and D), K-map have $2^4 = 16$ cells. The four variables K-map with 16 cells as shown below:

AB \ CD	$\bar{C}\bar{D}$ 00	$\bar{C}D$ 01	CD 11	$C\bar{D}$ 10
$\bar{A}\bar{B}$ 00	0	1	3	2
$\bar{A}B$ 01	4	5	7	6
AB 11	12	13	15	14
$A\bar{B}$ 10	8	9	11	10

2.5 Factors in Operating System Design

The main factors of operating system are as follows:

(i) **Performance** The operating system is an overhead function should not use too much of machine's resources. Minimum functionality of OS is to implement abstractions and additional function must be traded off against performance, i.e. DOS : One process and UNIX : Low level file system.

(ii) **Protection and Security** Security policy means sharing strategy chosen by computer's owner, where as protection mechanism is a tool to implement a family of security policies.

(iii) **Correctness and Maintainability** Security depends on correct operation of software, i.e. trusted vs untrusted software. Maintainability relates to ability of software to be changed.

(iv) **Standards and Open Systems**

IEEE POSIX 1. Open System Standard It specifies a set of system calls and their semantics that must be supported by a compliant operating system.

TCP/IP It is a Internet network protocol supported by most operating systems.

2.6 User View and System View

Operating system is designed both by taking user view and system view into consideration.

1. User View

(i) Most of the systems are designed to be operated by single user, however in some systems multiple users can share resources, memory. In these cases, operating system is designed to handle available resources among multiple users and CPU efficiently.

(ii) Operating system must be designed by taking both usability and efficient resource utilisation into view.

(iii) Operating system gives an effect to the user as if the processor is dealing only with the current task, but in background processor is dealing with several processes.

2. System View

(i) From the system point of view, operating system is a program involved with the hardware.

(ii) Operating system is allocator, which allocates memory, resources among various processes. It controls the sharing of resources among programs.

(iii) It prevents improper usage, error and handles deadlock conditions.

(iv) It is a program that runs all the time in the system in the form of kernel. And it controls application programs that are not part of kernel.

2.7 Kernel

It is a central component or module of an operating system. It acts as an interface between the user applications and the hardware. When an operating system is loaded into memory, the kernel loads first and remains in memory until the operating system is shut down again.

The kernel is responsible for:

(i) Process management for application execution.

(ii) Memory management, allocation and I/O.

(iii) Device management through the use of device drivers.

(iv) System call control, which is essential for the execution of kernel services.

Types of Kernel

There are five types of kernel as follows:

1. **Monolithic Kernels** provide rich and powerful abstractions of the underlying hardware.
2. **Micro** (or modular) **Kernels** provide a small set of simple hardware abstractions and use applications called servers to provide more functionality.
3. **Hybrid** (or modular) **Kernels** (modified microkernels) are much like, pure, microkernels, except that they include some additional code in kernel space to increase performance.
4. **Exokernels** provide minimal abstractions allowing low-level hardware access. In exokernel systems, library operating system provides the abstractions typically present in monolithic kernels.
5. **Nano Kernels** simplify the memory requirements by delegating services, including the basic ones like interrupt controllers or timers to device drivers.

2.8 Device Drivers

Device drivers are software modules that can be plugged into an OS to handle a particular device. An operating system takes help from device drivers to handle all I/O devices.

Device driver is generally written by the device's manufacturer and delivered along with the device on a CD-ROM. A device driver performs the following jobs:

(i) To accept request from the device independent software above to it.

(ii) Interact with the device controller to take and give I/O and perform required error handling.

(iii) Making sure that the request is executed successfully.

2.9 System Call

It is the programmatic way in which a computer program requests a service from the kernel of the operating system. This may include hardware related services (e.g. accessing a hard disk drive), creation and execution of new processes, and communication with integral kernel services such as process scheduling. It provides an essential interface between a process and the operating system.

Methods for System Call

For Process Control	CreateProcess( ), ExitProcess( ), WaitForSingleObject( )
For File Manipulation	CreateFile( ), ReadFile( ), WriteFile( ), CloseHandle( )
For Device Manipulation	SetConsoleMode( ), ReadConsole( ), WriteConsole( )
For Information Maintenance	GetCurrentProcessID( ), SetTimer( ), Sleep( )
For Communication	CreatePipe( ), CreateFileMapping( ), MapViewOfFile( )
For Protection	SetFileSecurity( ), InitializeSecurityDescription( ), SetSecurityDescriptorGroup( )

2.10 Device Management

In a computer system, there is a tremendous speed mismatch between the CPU and the I/O devices. The job of an operating system is to maintain a balance between the CPU and I/O devices. Apart from this, it has to maintain a balance between various I/O devices and has to keep the CPU busy in various processing.

Device management includes some features of I/O devices which are as follows:

1. Speed

The speed of different I/O devices are generally different from one another. e.g. The speed of a printer is very fast as compared to keyboard (based on OS processing). So, it is OS's responsibility to maintain a coordination between the speed of various devices.

2. Unit of Transfer

Data can be transferred in the form of units such as characters, words, bytes, blocks or records from one component to another and it is maintained by an operating system.

3. Data Representation

Data can be represented in different forms on different I/O devices. OS manages the data representation of I/O devices. e.g. Some devices use ASCII codes, whereas others use BCD or EBCDIC codes.

4. Sharing

A device can be either a shareable device or non-shareable device. OS works as an interface between the devices and application programs and determines which device can share their task *via* which application program. e.g. Disk drives (floppies, hard disks) and magnetic drums are shareable devices because they can handle successive requests from different programs or processes. Card readers and keyboards are the examples of non-shareable devices.

5. Buffering

It is a technique of storing data in memory area called *buffers* while data is being transferred between two devices or between a device and an application program.

It can be done because of the following three reasons:

(i) It manages the speed mismatch between the sender and the receiver.

(ii) It maintains a balance between the devices.

(iii) It supports copy semantics for an I/O application.

6. Spooling

It is the process of sending data to a spool (or buffers or temporary storage area) of the computer's memory. OS maintains the spooling of data by adding an address location with every element in the memory. This data may contain files or processes. It is useful because different devices access data at different rates.

The most common type of spooling is print spooling, in which print jobs are sent to a print buffer before being transmitted to the printer.

Device Management Approaches

There are three approaches of device management as follows:

1. **Direct I/O** In this approach, computer software explicitly transfer data to and from the controller's data registers. This include:
   - Direct I/O with polling
   - Interrupt driven direct I/O
2. **Memory Mapped I/O** In this approach, device addressing simplifies the interface (device seen as a range of memory locations). This include:
   - Memory mapped I/O with polling
   - Interrupt driven I/O

2. Full Adder

A full adder is a combinational circuit that forms the arithmetic sum of three input bits. It consists of three inputs and two outputs. Two input variables denoted by x and y represent the two significant bits to be added. The third input z represents the carry from previous significant position. Two outputs are necessary for sum and carry, respectively. The two outputs are represented by the symbols S for sum and C for carry. The binary variable S gives the value of least significant bit of sum. The binary variable C gives the output carry.

The truth table of the full adder is as follows:

Input			Output	
x	y	z	S	C
0	0	0	0	0
0	0	1	1	0
0	1	0	1	0
0	1	1	0	1
1	0	0	1	0
1	0	1	0	1
1	1	0	0	1
1	1	1	1	1

The truth table with eight row shows all possible combinations of variables x, y, z. When all input bits are 0 it will result 0 and no carry (i.e. 0). When any one bit is set to one, result of sum will set to 1 with no carry (i.e. 0). In case, if two bits are set to 1, it will result the sum as 10 (in decimal 2) from which 0 will be kept for variable S and 1 for carry C. When all binary digits are set to 1. It will result sum as 11 (in decimal 3) and will set $S = C = 1$.

Thus, in case of sum, sum is 1 only when odd numbers of variables are equal to 1 (i.e. either 1 or 3) for even number of 1's sum is zero or we can say that sum $= x \oplus y \oplus z$ (result is 1 when either 1 variable is set to 1 or all),

We get the carry expression as follows:

$$C = \bar{x}yz + x\bar{y}z + xy\bar{z} + xyz = (\bar{x}y + x\bar{y})\,z + xy\,(\bar{z} + z)$$

$$C = (x \oplus y)\,z + xy \qquad (\because \bar{z} + z = 1)$$

$$S = \bar{x}\,\bar{y}z + \bar{x}y\bar{z} + x\overline{y}\overline{z} + \bar{x}\,\overline{y}\overline{z}$$

$$S = x \oplus y \oplus z$$

Thus, the combination circuit for full adder will be as follows:

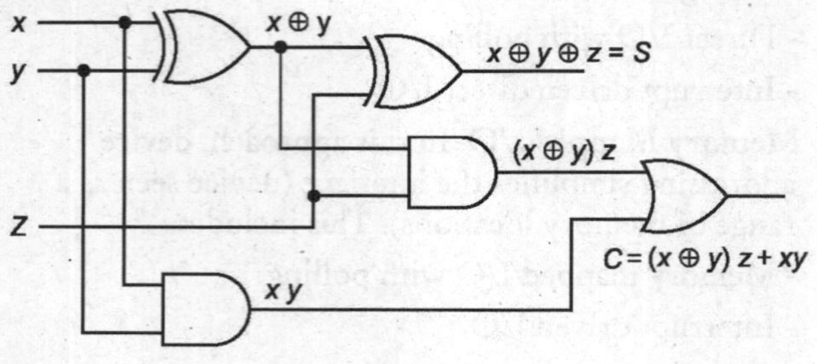

3.12.2 Subtractors

1. Half Subtractor

A half subtractor is a combinational circuit that subtracts two bits and produces their difference. It also has an output to specify if a 1 has been borrowed. The truth table for half subtractor is given below:

x	y	Result	Borrow
0	0	0	0
0	1	1	1
1	0	1	0
1	1	0	0

In case of binary arithmetic 1 borrow contributes 2 in minued thus, $2 - 1 = 1$. Means, when 1 will be deducted from 0 result will be 1 and borrow will also set to 1. The boolean expression for Borrow and Result will be given as:

$\Rightarrow$ Result $= \bar{x}y + x\,\bar{y} = x \oplus y$

and Borrow $= \bar{x}y$

The combination circuit for Result and Borrow will be drawn as follows:

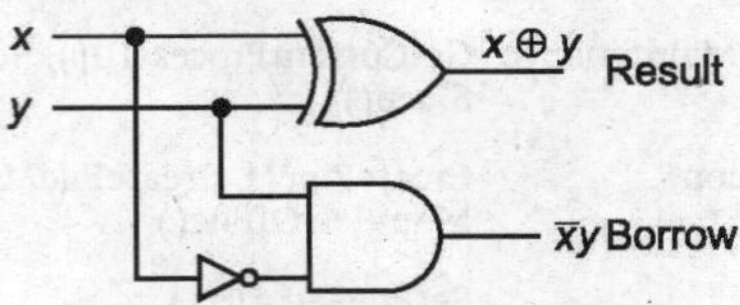

2. Full Subtractor

A full subtractor is a combinational digital circuit that is used to carry out subtraction involving three bits. There are three inputs and two bits that are involved in an nth bit full subtractor circuit.

The truth table for the circuit is as follows:

Truth Table

x	y	z	Difference	Borrow
0	0	0	0	0
0	0	1	1	1
0	1	0	1	1
0	1	1	0	1
1	0	0	1	0
1	0	1	0	0
1	1	0	0	0
1	1	1	1	1

The boolean expression for Difference and Borrow will be given as:

$$\text{Difference} = \bar{x}\,\bar{y}z + \bar{x}y\bar{z} + x\bar{y}\bar{z} + xyz$$

$$= x \oplus y \oplus z$$

$$\text{Borrow} = \bar{x}\,\bar{y}z + \bar{x}y\bar{z} + \bar{x}yz + xyz$$

$$= \bar{x}\bar{y}z + \bar{x}yz + \bar{x}y\bar{z} + \bar{x}yz + xyz + \bar{x}yz \qquad [\because A + A = A]$$

$$= \bar{x}z(\bar{y} + y) + \bar{x}y(\bar{z} + z) + yz(x + \bar{x})$$

$$= \bar{x}z + \bar{x}y + yz$$

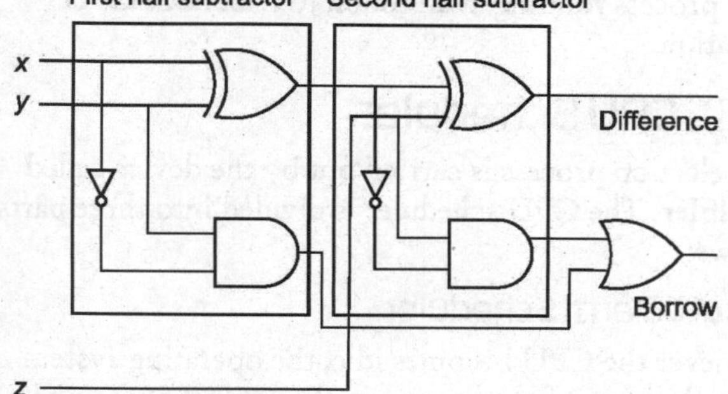

This circuit has three inputs and two outputs. The three inputs *x*, *y* and *z* denote the minuend, subtrahend and previous borrow respectively. The two outputs Difference and Borrow represent the difference and borrow respectively.

3.12.3 Decoders

A decoder is a combinational circuit that converts binary information from n input lines of a maximum of unique output lines. If the n-bit decoded information has unused or don't care combinations, the decoder output will have less than 2^n outputs. A 3-bit binary to decimal decoder is illustrated below:

Truth Table of 3-bit Binary to Decimal Decoder

Input			Output	Minterm
x	y	z		
0	0	0	D_0	$\bar{x}\,\bar{y}\,\bar{z}$
0	0	1	D_1	$\bar{x}\,\bar{y}\,z$
0	1	0	D_2	$\bar{x}\,y\,\bar{z}$
0	1	1	D_3	$\bar{x}\,yz$
1	0	0	D_4	$x\,\bar{y}\,\bar{z}$
1	0	1	D_5	$x\,\bar{y}\,z$
1	1	0	D_6	$xy\,\bar{z}$
1	1	1	D_7	xyz

The 1 as output shows the combination of inputs. Means if D_3 is high it shows the binary combination of 3 that is 011, means $x = 0$, $y = 1$ and $z = 1$. This decoder basically the input binary value to decimal at output means. 101 input combination makes D_5 high at output.

To make D_0 high for input combination 000 we need to AND the negation of all input variables. Means $\bar{x}\,\bar{y}\,\bar{z}$ will make D_0 high when the input combination 000. Similarly, the term $\bar{x}\,\bar{y}\,z$ will make D_1 high for input variable combination 001. At a given time only 1 output will be high for the given combination of input variables.

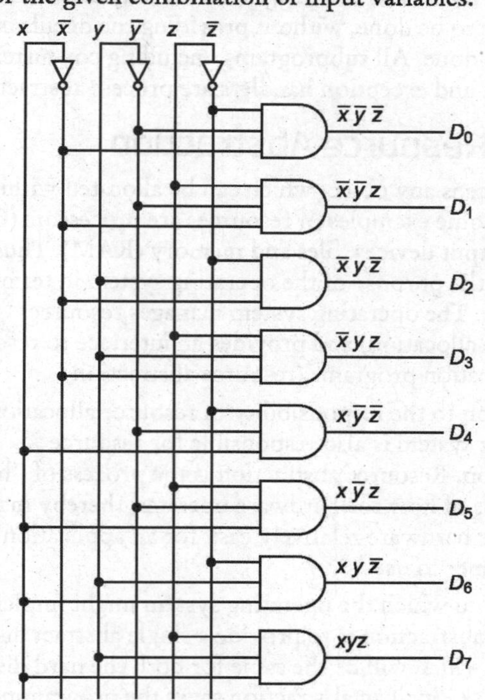

Combination circuit for 3×8 decoder

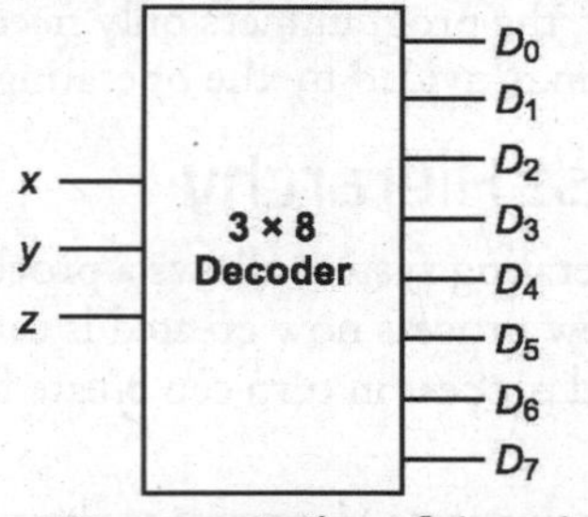

IC-presentation of decoder

3.12.4 Encoders

An encoder is a digital function that produces a reverse operation from that of a decoder. An encoder has 2^n (or less) input lines and n output lines. The output lines generate the binary code for 2^n inputs variable.

An example of 8×3 encoder is given below:

Input								Output		
D_0	D_1	D_2	D_3	D_4	D_5	D_6	D_7	x	y	z
1	0	0	0	0	0	0	0	0	0	0
0	1	0	0	0	0	0	0	0	0	1
0	0	1	0	0	0	0	0	0	1	0
0	0	0	1	0	0	0	0	0	1	1
0	0	0	0	1	0	0	0	1	0	0
0	0	0	0	0	1	0	0	1	0	1
0	0	0	0	0	0	1	0	1	1	0
0	0	0	0	0	0	0	1	1	1	1

oldest. All subprograms are process abstractions because they provide away for a program to specify that some process is to be done, without providing the details of how it is to be done. All subprograms, including concurrent sub programs and exception handlers are process abstractions.

2.11.6 Resource Abstraction

A resource is any object which can be allocated within a system. Some examples of resources are processors (CPUs), input/output devices, files and memory (RAM). Thus, we can state the purpose of the operating system in terms of resources. The operating system manages resources (resource allocation) and provides an interface to resources for application programs (resource abstraction).

In addition to the responsibility of resource allocation, the operating system is also responsible for resource abstraction. Resource abstraction is the process of "hiding the details of how the hardware operates, thereby making computer hardware relatively easy for an application programmer to use".

One way in which the operating system might implement resource abstraction is to provide a single abstract disk interface which will be the same for both the hard disk and floppy disk. Such an abstraction saves the programmers from needing to learn the details of both hardware interfaces. Instead, the programmers only needing to learn the disk abstraction provided by the operating system.

2.11.7 Process Hierarchy

Normally, the operating system allows a process to have offsprings. The new process now created is called a **child process.** This child process in turn can create further child processes.

Hence, creating the process hierarchy as shown in below figure:

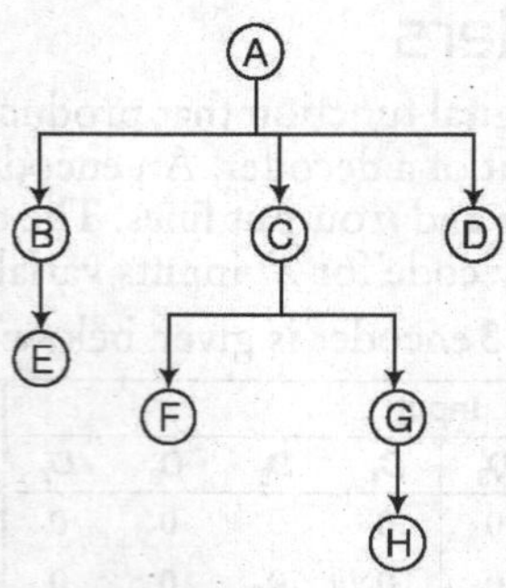

Process hierarchy

Unix calls a process group to this process hierarchy. Windows has no concept of process hierarchy in which all processes are created equally.

2.12 Process Scheduling

In a single processor system, only one process can run at a time, any other must wait until the CPU is free and can be rescheduled. The goal of multi-programming is to have some process running at all times, to maximize CPU utilisation.

2.12.1 CPU Scheduler

The selection process is carried out by the device called **scheduler**. The CPU scheduler is divided into three parts as follows:

1. Short-Term Scheduler

Whenever the CPU becomes idle, the operating system must select one of the process in the ready queue to be executed. The selection process is carried out by the short-term scheduler or CPU scheduler. The scheduler selects a process from the processes in memory that are ready to execute and allocates the CPU to that process.

2. Long-Term Scheduler

The long-term scheduler, or job scheduler, selects processes from the queue and loads them into memory for execution. Processes loads into the memory for CPU scheduling.

3. Medium-Term Scheduler

It is a part of **swapping**. It removes the processes from the memory. It reduces the degree of multiprogramming. This scheduler is in-charge of handling the swapped out-processes.

Scheduling Concepts

(i) As processes enter the system, they are put into a job queue. This consists of all processes residing on mass storage awaiting allocation of main memory.

(ii) The process which are in ready state in main memory are put in a ready queue. The processes waiting for a particular I/O devices are put in a device queue.

(iii) The operating system has to select processes from these queues. The selection is done by appropriate scheduler.

(iv) The long-term scheduler selects from the job queue and allocates main memory.

(v) The short-term scheduler selects process from the ready queue and allocates the CPU to it. The medium term scheduler removes processes from main memory to reduce the degree of multi-programming. This is known as **swapping.** At some later time the process is swapped in memory by the medium term scheduler.

(vi) Scheduler decisions are taken under the following circumstances:
   (a) Process switches from running state to waiting state.
   (b) Process switches from running state to ready state.
   (c) Process switches from waiting state to ready state.
   (d) Process terminates.

Preemptive Scheduling

Preemptive scheduling is one which can be done in the circumstances when a process switches from running state to ready state or from waiting state to ready state. In this scheduling, the resources are allocated to the process for the limited amount of time and then are taken away, and the process is placed back in the ready queue again if it still has CPU burst time remaining. The process stays in ready queue till it gets next chance to execute.

If a process with high priority arrives in the ready queue, it does not have to wait for the current process to complete its burst time. Instead, the current process is interrupted in the middle of execution and is placed in the ready queue till the process with high priority is utilising the CPU cycles.

Non-Preemptive Scheduling

Non-preemptive scheduling is one which can be applied in the circumstances when a process terminates, or a process switches from running to ready state. In this scheduling, once the resources are allocated to a process, the process holds the CPU till it gets terminated or it reaches a waiting state.

Like preemptive scheduling, non-preemptive scheduling does not interrupt a process running CPU in middle of the execution. Instead, it waits for the process to complete its CPU burst time and then it can allocate the CPU to another process.

Scheduling Algorithms Criteria

Criteria used to compare various scheduling algorithm:

1. **CPU Utilisation** Keep the CPU as busy as possible. It range from 0 to 100%.
2. **Throughput** Number of processes completed per unit time.
3. **Turn Around Time** The total time taken by a process to complete.
   Turn around time = Waiting time + Execution time + Time spent in I/O + Time spent to get into memory
4. **Waiting Time** Time spent by a process in ready queue.
5. **Response Time** Amount of time process takes to start responding, i.e. the time from submission of a request until the first response is produced.

2.12.2 Scheduling Algorithm

1. First Come First Served (FCFS) Scheduling

First come first served scheduling is the simplest scheduling algorithm. Under this algorithm, the process that request to the CPU first is allocated to the CPU first.

e.g.

Arrival time	Process	Burst time
0	P_1	24
1	P_2	3
2	P_3	3

P_1	P_2	P_3

0 24 27 30

Waiting time of P_1 = (last response time to P_1 – arrival time–amount of time process P_1 has been executed)

$$= (0 - 0 - 0) = 0$$

Waiting time of P_2 = (last response time to P_2 – arrival time – amount of time process P_1 has been executed)

$$= 24 - 1 - 0 = 23$$

Waiting time of $P_3 = 27 - 2 - 0 = 25$

$$\text{Average waiting time} = \frac{0 + 23 + 25}{3} = \frac{48}{3} = 16$$

In above example, process P_1 has arrived first so the CPU will execute P_1 first, then P_2 and then P_3. The drawback of this scheme is that if process has more I/O burst than CPU burst then CPU utilisation decreases. The FCFS scheduling is non-preemptive.

2. Shortest Job First (SJF) Scheduling

In this algorithm, when the CPU is available, it is assigned to that process which has smallest CPU burst. Means the process that has smallest burst time will be executed first.

e.g.

Process	Burst time
P_1	6
P_2	8
P_3	7
P_4	3

Here, process P_4 has smallest burst time so process P_4 will execute first and then P_1, P_3, P_2 (according to increasing order of their burst time). This can be illustrated by following Gantt chart:

P_4	P_1	P_3	P_2

0 3 (0+3) 9 (3+6) 16 (9+7) 24 (16+8)

3.12.11 Code Converters

The availability of a large variety of codes for the same discrete elements of information results in the use of different codes by different digital systems. It is sometime necessary to use the output of one system as the input to the other. The conversion circuit must be inserted between the two systems if each uses different codes for the same information.

Thus, a code converter is a circuit that makes the two systems compatible even though each uses the different code.

1. Binary to Gray Code

Truth Table

Binary				Gray			
D	*C*	*B*	*A*	*G3*	*G2*	*G1*	*G0*
0	0	0	0	0	0	0	0
0	0	0	1	0	0	0	1
0	0	1	0	0	0	1	1
0	0	1	1	0	0	1	0
0	1	0	0	0	1	1	0
0	1	0	1	0	1	1	1
0	1	1	0	0	1	0	1
0	1	1	1	0	1	1	0
1	0	0	0	1	1	0	0
1	0	0	1	1	1	0	1
1	0	1	0	1	1	1	1
1	0	1	1	1	1	1	0
1	1	0	0	1	0	1	0
1	1	0	1	1	0	1	1
1	1	1	0	1	0	0	1
1	1	1	1	1	0	0	0

Equation $G0 = B \oplus A$

$G1 = C \oplus B$

$G2 = D \oplus C$

$G3 = D$

Logic diagram for Binary to Gray code converter is given below:

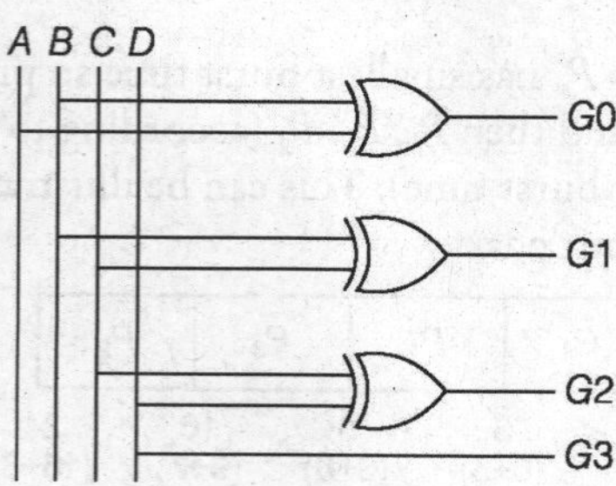

2. Gray to Binary Code

Truth Table

Gray				Binary			
G3	*G2*	*G1*	*G0*	*D*	*C*	*B*	*A*
0	0	0	0	0	0	0	0
0	0	0	1	0	0	0	1
0	0	1	1	0	0	1	0
0	0	1	0	0	0	1	1
0	1	1	0	0	1	0	0
0	1	1	1	0	1	0	1
0	1	0	1	0	1	1	0
0	1	0	0	0	1	1	1
1	1	0	0	1	0	0	0
1	1	0	1	1	0	0	1
1	1	1	1	1	0	1	0
1	1	1	0	1	0	1	1
1	0	1	0	1	1	0	0
1	0	1	1	1	1	0	1
1	0	0	1	1	1	1	0
1	0	0	0	1	1	1	1

Equation $A = (G3 \oplus G2) \oplus (G1 \oplus G0)$

$B = G3 \oplus G2 \oplus G1$

$C = G3 \oplus G2$

$D = G3$

Logic diagram for Gray to Binary code converter is given below:

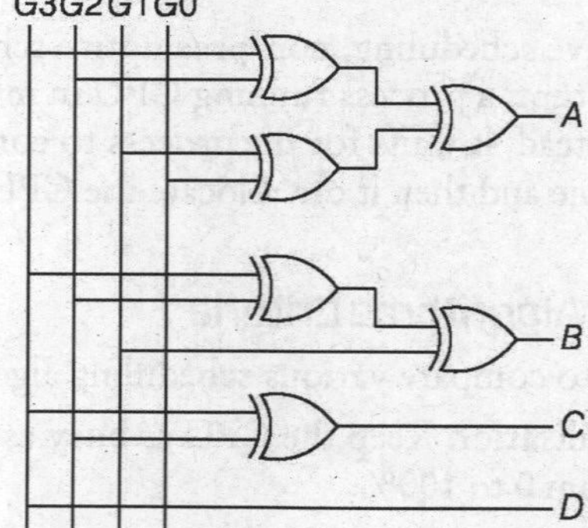

3.12.12 Binary Comparators

Binary comparators, also called **digital comparators** or **logic comparators** are combinational logic circuits that are used for testing whether the value represented by one binary word is greater than, less than or equal to the value represented by another binary word.

Two basic types of comparator can be used as follows:

1. Equality Comparators

An equality comparator is the simplest multi-bit logic comparator and can be used for such circuits as electronic locks and security devices where a binary password consisting of multiple bits is input to the comparator to the compared with another preset word.

The circuit of the equality comparator consists of an exclusive NOR gate (XNOR) per pair of input bits. If the two inputs are identical (both 1's or both 0's) an output of logic 1 is obtained. The outputs of XNOR gates are then combined in an AND gate, the output of which will be 1, only when all the XNOR gates indicate matched inputs.

2. Magnitude Comparator

The magnitude comparator can also be used to indicate equality, but has a further two outputs, one that is logic 1 when word A is greater than word B and another that is logic 1 when word A is less than word B. Magnitude comparators therefore form the basis of decision making in logic circuits. Any logical problem can be reduced to one or more yes/no decisions based on a pair of compared values.

The basis circuit for a magnitude comparator may be extended for any number of bits but the more bits the circuit has the compare, the more complex the circuit becomes.

3.12.13 Hazards

Hazards in any system are obviously an un-desirable effect caused by either a deficiency in the system or external influence. In digital logic, hazards are usually referred to in one of three ways:

1. Static Hazards

When one input variables changes, the output changes at one time when it should not. This particular type of hazard is usually due to a NOT gate within the logic.

The hazard can be dealt within two ways as follows:

(i) Insert another delay to the circuit. This then eliminates the static hazard.

(ii) Eliminate the hazard by inserting more logic to counteract the effects.

2. Dynamic Hazards

A dynamic hazard is the possibility of an output changing more than one as a result of a single input change.

Dynamic hazards often occur in larger logic circuits where there are different routes to the output. If each route has a different delay, then it quickly becomes clear that there is the potential for changing output values that differ from the required/excepted output.

3. Function Hazards

Function hazards are non-solvable hazards which occur when more than one input variable changes at the same time. Hazards such as function hazards cannot be logically eliminated as the problem lies with actual specification of the circuit. The only real way to avoid such problems is to restrict the changing of input variables so that only one input should change at any given time.

3.12.14 Race Condition

In general, race condition refers to a situation in which the result depends upon the sequence in which events happen. In particular, a race condition occurs when a system/device is designed assuming a particular sequence of events without taking steps to ensure it. In logic gates, it happens when the inputs arrive at the gate in a sequence not assumed while deriving the function.

One way to design in a race condition is to use the same signal to perform two functions. In some cases, a race condition could also be a logic hazard. Another case for a race condition could be caused from floating inputs. Multiple floating inputs which perform the same function could rise to a logic one at random times. So, as two floating inputs rise from a logic 0 to a logic 1, they will race against each other.

3.13 Sequential Circuit

A switching circuit whose output depends not only on the present state of its input but also on what its input conditions have been in the past.

Sequential Logic Circuit

Digital electronics are classified into combinational logic and sequential logic. Combinational logic output depends on the inputs, whereas sequential logic output depends on stored levels and also the input levels.

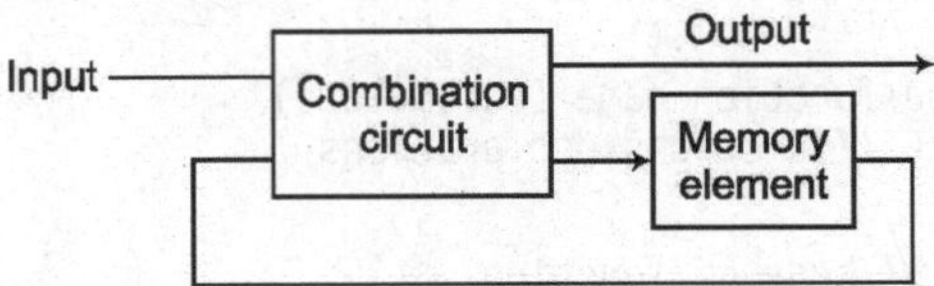

The memory elements are capable of storing binary information. This binary information stored in the memory elements at any given time defines the state of the sequential circuit. The input and the present state of the memory element decides the output. A sequential circuit is specified by a time, sequence of inputs, output and internal states.

There are two types of sequential circuits. This classification depends on the timing of their signals:

1. Asynchronous Sequential Circuits

This is a system whose outputs depend upon the order in which its input variable changes and can be affected at any instant of time.

2.13.4 Semaphores

To overcome the mutual exclusion problem, a synchronisation tool called **semaphore** is used.

(i) A semaphore is a integer variable that apart from initialisation can be accessed only through two standard atomic operations wait and signal.
Wait (s) : while $S \leq 0$ do no-op

$$S = S - 1$$

Signal(s) : $S = S + 1$

(ii) Wait and signal operations are executed individually.

(iii) Semaphores can be used to solve various synchronisation problems. The no-op in wait causes busy waiting. To prevent that a process is made to wait while it finds the value of the semaphore $S \leq 0$.
The blocked process is put in a waiting queue associated with the semaphore. Then, the signal operation wakes up all the process waiting on the semaphore queue.

2.13.5 Monitors

Semaphores can be very useful for solving concurrency problems, but only if programmers use them properly. If even one process fails to abide by the proper use of semaphores, then the whole system breaks down.

For this reason, a higher-level language has been developed called **monitors.**

A monitor is essentially a class which consists of declaration of shared data (or variables), procedures or functions that access these variables and initialisation code. The general syntax of declaring a monitor:

```
monitor <monitor_name>
{
  datatype <variable_name>; //shared data declarations
  ......
  return_type<function_name>(parameters)
           //functions declarations
  {
          //body of function
  }
  ⋮
  monitor_name()
  {
     //initialisation
  }
}
```

2.13.6 Events

In computing, an event is an action or occurrence recognised by software that may be handled by the software. Computer events can be generated or triggered by the system.

The events initially originate from actions on the operating system level, such as interrupts generated by hardware devices, software interrupt instructions or state changes in polling. On this level, interrupt handlers and signal handlers correspond to event handlers.

2.13.7 Interprocess Communication

Processes executing concurrently in the operating system may be either independent processes or cooperating processes. A process is independent if it cannot affect or be affected by the other processes, executing in the system. Any processes, that does not share data with any other processes is independent. A process is known as cooperating if it is affected by or affects any other processes executing in the system.

All cooperating processes require interprocess communication that helps them to exchange data between processes. There are two fundamental models of interprocess communication as follows:

1. Shared Memory

Shared memory systems require communicating process to share their variables. The process share information by the use of shared variables. The responsibility of providing communication resets with the application programmers. The operating system only provides the ways to access and create shared memory.

2. Message System

The message systems allow processes to exchange messages. The responsibility of providing communication rests with the operating system. Two operations are provided send (message), receive (message). Messages send by processes can be fixed size or variable size.

2.14 Deadlock

When a process requests resources and if the resources are not available at that time, the process enters a wait state. Sometimes a wait process is never again able to change state, because the resources, it has requested, are held by other waiting processes. This situation is called a deadlock.

2.14.1 Deadlock System Model

A system model of deadlock consists of a finite number of resources to be distributed among a number of completing processes. Multiple processes utilise resources during execution in a three phase resources request, use and release - if a resource is not immediately available upon request, then the process must wait for its release by another process, where deadlock can happen.

Under the normal mode of operation, a process may utilise a resource in only the following sequence:

1. **Request** If the request cannot be granted immediately then the requesting process must wait until it can acquire the resource.
2. **Use** The process can operate on the resource.
3. **Release** The process release the resource.

2.14.2 Operating System Resources

These are the physical or virtual components of limited availability within a computer system. Every device connected to a computer system and every internal system component is a resource.

CPU time, memory (RAM as well as virtual memory), secondary storage like hard disks, network throughput, battery power, external devices are all resources of a computer which an operating system manages.

There are three kinds of resources as follows:

1. Sharable Resources

These resources can be used by more than one process at a time. Input devices tend to be sharable resources.

2. Serially-Reusable Resources

Also known as **dedicated resources.** These resources can be used by at most one process at a time. Output devices tend to be serially reusable resources.

3. Consumable Resources

These resources can only be used by one process, and the resources gets "used up". A consumable resource disappears after being used. Network packets and IPC messages are consumable resources.

2.14.3 Methods of Handling Deadlock

Deadlock situation can be handled in following three manners:

1. Deadlock Avoidance

Deadlock avoidance ensures that the system will never enter a deadlock state. Deadlock avoidance requires that the operating system be given in advance additional information concerning, which resource a process will request and use during its lifetime.

Banker's Algorithm

Banker's algorithm is used for deadlock avoidance for multiple resources. We meet the following data structure:

(i) **Available** This indicates the number of available resources of each types.

(ii) **Max** This defines the maximum demand of each process.

(iii) **Allocation** This defines the number of resources of each type currently allocated to each process.

(iv) **Need** The remaining need of each process.

Steps of Banker's algorithm are as follows:

(i) Let work and finish be vectors of length m and n, respectively initialise work = available and finish = false for $i = 0, 1 \ldots n-1$.

(ii) Find as i such that both

(a) Finish $[i]$ = false

(b) $\text{need}_i \leq \text{work}$

if no such i exist, go to step 4

(iii) work = work + allocation

finish $[i]$ = true

go to step 2

(iv) if finish $[i]$ == true for all i then the system is in a safe state.

2. Deadlock Prevention

Deadlock prevention provides a set of methods for ensuring that atleast one of the necessary conditions cannot hold.

Mutual Exclusion

The mutual exclusion condition must hold for non-sharable resources. e.g. printer cannot be simultaneously shared by several process. We cannot prevent by denying the mutual exclusion.

Hold and Wait

To ensure that hold and wait never occur in the system following protocol is used:

(i) Whenever a process request a resource occur, it does not hold any other resources, means before requesting for a new resource a process must release all resources that, it is currently allocated.

(ii) Another protocol that can be used requires each process to request and be allocated all its resources before it begin execution, means before starting execution the process must acquire all the resources that will be required in process life time.

No Preemption

The third necessary condition for deadlock is that there is no preemption of resources that have already been allocated. To ensure this condition does not hold following protocol can be used:

(i) If a process is holding some resources and request another resources that can be immediately allocated to it, then all resources currently being held is preempted.

The truth table of clocked SR flip-flop is given below:

Q_n	S	R	Q_{n+1}
0	0	0	0
0	0	1	0
0	1	0	1
0	1	1	indeterminate
1	0	0	1
1	0	1	0
1	1	0	1
1	1	1	indeterminate

6. Edge Triggered Flip-Flop

Another type of flip-flop that synchronises the state changes during a clock pulse transition is the edge triggered flip-flop.

In this type of flip-flop, output transitions occur at a specific level of the clock pulse.

When the clock pulse input exceeds a specific threshold level, the inputs are locked out and the flip-flop is not affected by further changes in the inputs until the clock pulse returns to 0 and another pulse occurs.

Some edge triggered flip-flops cause a transition on the positive edge of the clock pulse (positive edge triggered) and others on the negative edge of the pulse (negative edge triggered).

When using different types of flip-flops in the same circuit, one must ensure that all flip-flop outputs make their transitions at the same time, i.e. during either the negative edge or the positive edge of the clock pulse.

3.15 Register

A register is a group of flip-flop with each flip-flop capable of storing one bit of information.

Shift Registers

A register that is used to assemble and store information arriving from a serial source is called a shift register. Each flip-flop output of a shift register is connected to the input of the following flip-flop and a common clock pulse is applied to all flip-flops, clocking them synchronously. Hence, the shift register is a synchronously sequential circuit. An n-bit shift register consists of n flip-flops and the gates control the shift operation. There are four type of shift registers:

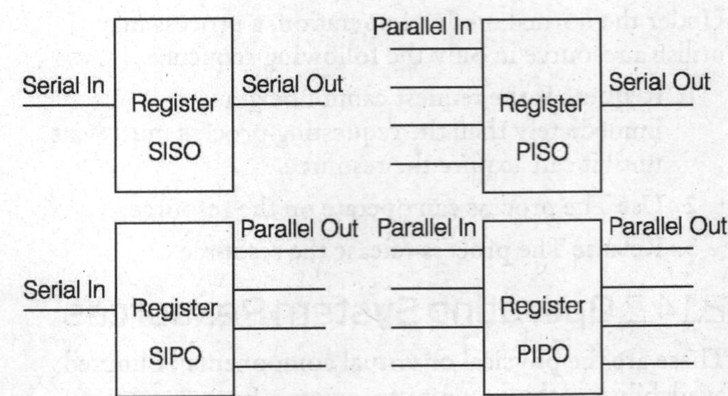

1. Serial-In Serial-Out (SISO)

SISO shift register can be constructed by using D flip-flops. This type of shift register accepts data serially, i.e. one bit at a time and produces stored information on its output serially.

2. Serial-In Parallel Out (SIPO)

SIPO shift register can be constructed by using D flip-flops. This type of shift register accepts data serially, i.e. one bit at a time and produces stored information on its output parallely, i.e all the outputs are available simultaneously.

3. Parallel-In Serial Out (PISO)

PISO shift register can be constructed by using D flip-flops. This type of shift register accepts data parallely, i.e. all the bits are input simultaneously and produces stored information on its output serially.

4. Parallel-In, Parallel Out (PIPO)

PIPO shift register can be constructed by using D flip-flops. This type of shift register accepts data parallely, i.e. all the bits are input simultaneously and produces stored information on its output parallely, i.e. all the outputs are available simultaneously.

3.16 Counters

A counter is a device which stores (displays) the number of times a particular event or process has occurred, after in relationship to a clock signals. In practice, there are two types of counters as follows:

1. Up counters which increase (increment) in value.
2. Down counters which decrease (decrement) in value.

We can say the counter is a device that counts the value from one state to another state. Counters come in two categories ripple counters and synchronous counters.

3.16.1 Asynchronous or Ripple Counters

The logic diagram of a 2-bit ripple up counter is shown in figure. The toggle (*T*) flip-flop are being used. But we can use the JK flip-flop also with *J* and *K* connected permanently to logic 1. External clock is applied to the clock input of flip-flop *A*, i.e. FF-A and Q_A output is applied to the clock input of the next flip-flop, i.e. FF-B.

Logical Diagram

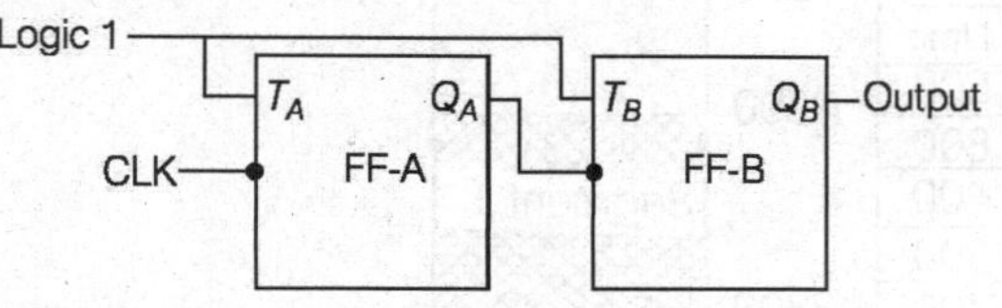

Operation

Condition	Operation
Initially let both the flip-flops be in the reset state	$Q_BQ_A = 00$ initially
After 1st negative clock edge	As soon as the first negative clock edge is applied, FF-A will toggle and Q_A will be equal to 1. Q_A is connected to clock input of FF-B. Since, Q_A has changed from 0 to 1, it is treated as the positive clock edge by FF-B. There is no change in Q_B because FF-B is a negative edge triggered FF. $Q_BQ_A = 01$ after the first clock pulse.
After 2nd negative clock edge	On the arrival of second negative clock edge, FF-A toggles again and $Q_A = 0$. The change in Q_A acts as a negative clock edge for FF-B. So, it will also toggle and Q_B will be 1. $Q_BQ_A = 10$ after the second clock pulse.
After 3rd negative clock edge	On the arrival of 3rd negative clock edge, FF-A toggles again and Q_A become 1 from 0. Since, this is a positive going change, FF-B does not respond to it and remains inactive. So, Q_B does not change and continues to be equal to 1. $Q_BQ_A = 11$ after the third clock pulse.
After 4th negative clock edge	On the arrival of 4th negative clock edge, FF-A toggles again and Q_A becomes 1 from 0. This negative change in Q_A acts as clock pulse for FF-B. Hence, it toggles to change Q_B from 1 to 0. $Q_BQ_A = 00$ after the fourth clock pulse.

3.16.2 Synchronous Counters

If the "clock" pulses are applied to all the flip-flops in a counter simultaneously, then such a counter is called as synchronous counter.

2-bit Synchronous up counter

The J_A and K_A inputs of FF-A are tied to logic 1. So, FF-A will work as a toggle flip-flop.

The J_B and K_B inputs are connected to Q_A.

Logical Diagram

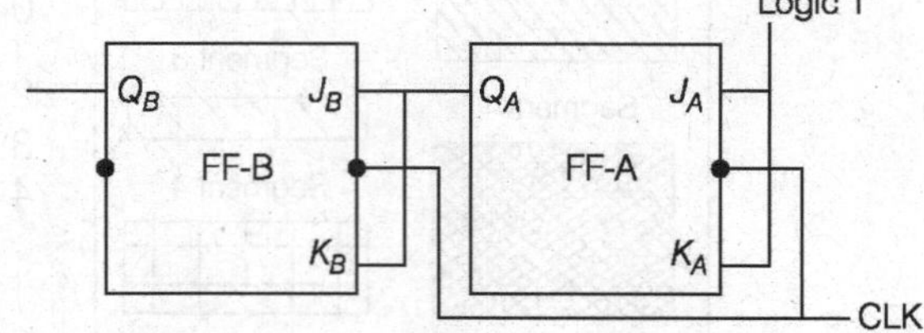

Operation

Condition	Operation
Initially let both the flip-flops be in the reset state	$Q_BQ_A = 00$ initially.
After 1st negative clock edge	As soon as the first negative clock edge is applied, FF-A will toggle and Q_A will change from 0 to 1. But at the instant of application of negative clock edge, Q_A, $J_B = K_B = 0$. Hence, FF-B will not change its state. So, Q_B will remain 0. $Q_BQ_A = 01$ after the first clock pulse.
After 2nd negative clock edge	On the arrival of second negative clock edge, FF-A toggles again and Q_A changes from 1 to 0. But at this instant Q_A was 1. So $J_B = K_B = 1$ and FF-B will toggle. Hence, Q_B changes from 0 to 1. $Q_BQ_A = 10$ after the second clock pulse.
After 3rd negative clock edge	On application of the third falling clock edge, FF-A will toggle from 0 to 1 but there is no change of state for FF-B. $Q_BQ_A = 11$ after the third clock pulse.
After 4th negative clock edge	On application of the next clock pulse, Q_A will change from 1 to 0 as Q_B will also change from 1 to 0. $Q_BQ_A = 00$ after the fourth clock pulse.

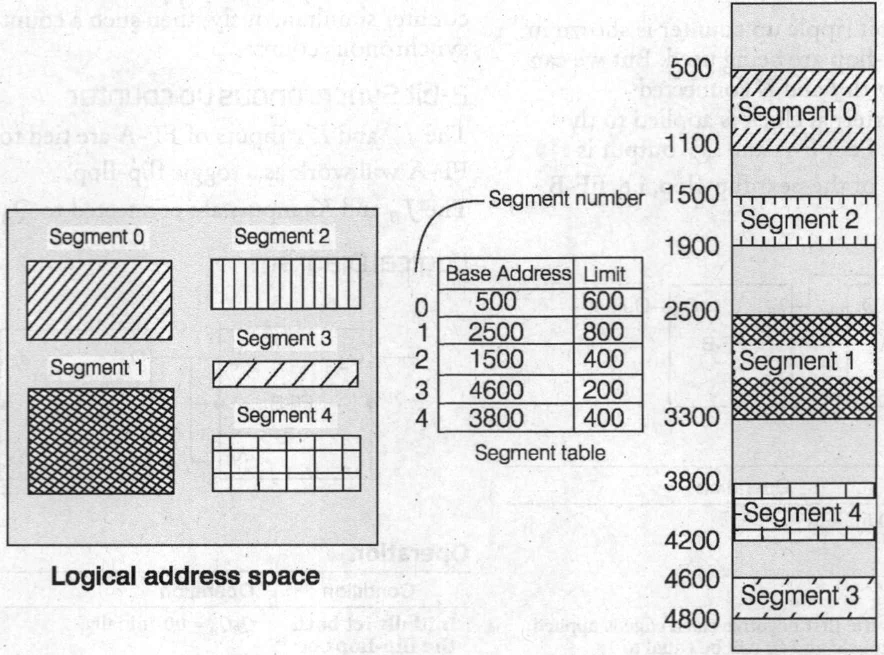

2.16 File Management

Logically related data items on the secondary storage are usually organised into named collections called files. A file may contain a report, an executable program as a set of commands to the operating system. A file often appears to the users as a linear array of characters or record structures.

The file system consists of two parts as follows:

(i) A collection of files

(ii) A directory structure

The file management system can be implemented as one or more layers of the operating system.

The common responsibilities of the file management system includes the following:

(i) Mapping of access requests from logical to physical file address space.

(ii) Transmission of file elements between main and secondary storage.

(iii) Management of the secondary storage such as keeping track of the status, allocation and deallocation of space.

(iv) Support for protection and sharing of files and the recovery and possible restoration of the files after system crashes.

Directory Structure

The names of all the files created in a disk are stored in its directory. Directory is just like a file folder, which contain all the logically related files.

The directory structure is the organisation of files into a hierarchy of folders. It should be stable and scalable, it should not fundamentally change, only be added to computers have used the folder metaphor for decades as a way to help users keep track of where something can be found.

There are following directory structures available for organising all the files:

1. Single Level Directory

It is the simplest directory structure. All files are contained in the same directory. The major disadvantage to a single level directory is the confusion of file names between different users.

2. Two Level Directory

In this, a separate file is created for each user.

3. Tree Structure Directory

This structure allows users to create their own sub-directories and to organise their files accordingly.

File Operations

The OS provides system call to create, read , write, delete and truncate files. The common file operations are as follows:

- **File Creation** For a file to be created firstly, a space must be found for a file, in the file system and secondarily a new entry must be made in the directory for the new file.
- **Writing a File** In order to write a file, a system call is made, which specifies the file name and the information to be written in file.
- **Reading a File** To read from a file, we use a system call that specifies the name of the file and where in the memory. The next block of the file should be put and again for the associated directory entry.
- **Repositioning within a File** Repositioning within a file does not need to invoke any actual I/O. This is also known as **file seek.**
- **File Deletion** The directory for the named file is searched in order to delete a file and when the associated directory entry is found, all the file space is released and the directory entry is removed.
- **Truncating a File** Truncating a file is used when the user wants the attributes of the file to remain the same but wants to erase the contents of the file. There is no use of deleting a file and recreating it rather this function allows all attributes to remain unchanged but for the file to reset the length to zero.

2.17 Protection and Security

Protection can be provided in many ways. For a small single user system, we might provide protection by physically removing the floppy disks or file cabinet. In file protection, replacing or deleting a system file that has no file lock. File system often contains information that is highly valuable to their users. Protecting this information against unauthorised usage.

Security protects the integrity of the information stored in the system (both data and code) as well as the physical resources of the system, from unauthorised access, malicious destruction or alteration, and accidental introduction of inconsistency.

2.17.1 Policy Mechanism

A security policy reflects on organisation's strategy to authorise access to the computer's resources.

Policy decisions are important for all resource allocation. Whenever it is necessary to decide whether or not to allocate a resource, a policy decision must be made.

2.17.2 Authentication

Authentication refers to identifying each user of the system and associating the executing programs with those users. It is the responsibility of the operating system to create a protection system which ensures that a user who is running a particular program is authentic. Operating system generally identifies/authenticates users using following three ways:

- **Username/Password** User needs to enter a registered username and password with operating system to login into the system.
- **User Card/Key** User need to punch card in card slot, or enter key generated by key generator in option provided by operating system to login into the system.
- **User Attribute – fingerprint/eye retina pattern/signature** User need to pass his/her attribute *via* designated input device used to operating system to login into the system.

2.17.3 Authorisation

Authorisation is the process of giving someone permission to do or have something. In multiuser computer system, a system administration defines for the system which users are allowed to the system and what privileges of use.

Assuming that someone has logged into a computer operating system or application, the system or application may want to identify what resources the user can be given during this session.

58. The number of bits require to represent decimal number 4096 in binary form is ....

(1) 16 (2) 10 (3) 12 (4) 13

59. How many gates would be required to implement the following boolean expression after simplification?

Expression : AC + ABC

(1) 4 (2) 1
(3) 2 (4) 3

60. How many bits are used in the exponent part of IEEE single precision format for the representation of floating-point numbers?

(1) 32 bits (2) 8 bits
(3) 16 bits (4) 24 bits

61. When signed numbers are used in binary arithmetic then which one of the following notations would have unique representation for zero?

(1) Sign magnitude (2) 1's complement
(3) 2's complement (4) 9's complement

62. The code where all successive numbers differ from their preceding number by single bit is

(1) binary code (2) BCD
(3) excess-3 (4) gray

63. Which of the following logic circuits accepts two binary digits on its inputs and produces two binary digits, a sum bit and a carry bit on its outputs?

(1) Full adder (2) Half adder
(3) Decoder (4) Multiplexer

64. The number of full and half adders required to add 16-bit numbers are

(1) 8 half adders, 8 full adders
(2) 1 half adder, 15 full adders
(3) 16 half adders, 0 full adder
(4) 4 half adders, 12 full adders

65. The circuit given below is a

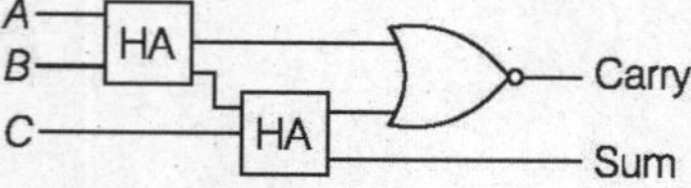

(1) full adder (2) full subtractor
(3) multiplexer (4) parity checker

66. Which of the following combinational circuit converts binary information of n input lines to a maximum of 2^n unique output lines?

(1) Encoder (2) Multiplexer
(3) Decoder (4) Demultiplexer

67. A logic circuit which is used to change a BCD number into an equivalent decimal number is

(1) decoder (2) encoder
(3) multiplexer (4) code converter

68. The following circuit performs the operation of ...... gate.

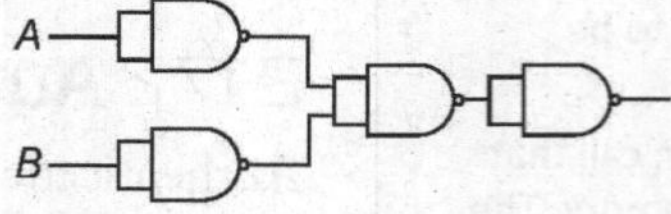

(1) NOT (2) AND (3) OR (4) NOR

69. Without any additional circuitry, an 8:1 MUX can be used to obtain

(1) some but not all boolean functions of 3 variables
(2) all functions of 3 variables and some but not all of 4 variables
(3) all functions of 3 variables but none of 4 variables
(4) all function of 4 variables

70. The minimum number of 2 to 1 (2:1) multiplexers required to realise a 4 to 1 multiplexer is

(1) 4 (2) 3 (3) 2 (4) 1

71. The output F of the below multiplexer circuit can be represented by

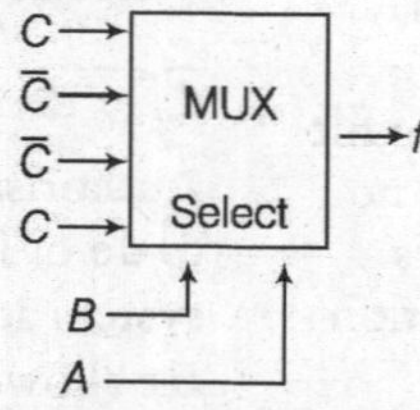

(1) $AB + B\bar{C} + \bar{C}A + \overline{BC}$
(2) $A \oplus B \oplus C$
(3) $A \oplus B$
(4) $\overline{AB}C + \bar{A}B\bar{C} + A\overline{BC}$

72. State whether true or false

The look-ahead carry adder in the parallel carry adder where all sum digits are generated directly from the input digits.

(1) False (2) True
(3) Cannot Say (4) Data insufficient

73. For a 1 binary half subtractor having two inputs A and B, the correct set of logical expression for the output

$D = (A$ minus $B)$ and X (= borrow) are

(1) $D = AB + \bar{A}B$, $X = \bar{A}B$
(2) $D = \bar{A}B + A\bar{B}$, $X = \bar{A}B$
(3) $D = \bar{A}B + A\bar{B}$, $X = A\bar{B}$
(4) $D = AB + \overline{AB}$, $X = A\bar{B}$

74. The number of half adder and full adder required to add m-bit data is

(1) $\frac{m}{2}$ half adder, $\frac{m}{2}$ full adder
(2) 1 half adder, $m-1$ full adder
(3) 16 half adder, 0 full adder
(4) 4 half adder, 12 full adder

75. What are the minimum number of 2 to 1 multiplexers required to generate a 2 input AND gate and a 2 input XOR gate?

(1) 1 and 1 (2) 1 and 2
(3) 1 and 3 (4) 2 and 2

76. The minimum number of NAND gates are required for realised a 4×1 MUX is

(1) 1 (2) 2 (3) 5 (4) 7

77. A logic circuit which is used to change a BCD number into an equivalent decimal number is

(1) decoder (2) MUX
(3) encoder (4) code converter

78. The maximum number of outputs for a decoder with 6-bit word would be

(1) 64 (2) 6 (3) 24 (4) 256

79. Which of the following statements is true?

S_1 : In combinational circuits we require a memory unit to store past output.

S_2 : Parallel adder is a combinational circuit.

(1) S_1 is true
(2) S_2 is true
(3) Both S_1 and S_2 are true
(4) None of the above

80. A $X:Y$ decoder can be constructed using, how many $A:B$ decoders with enable?

(1) $\frac{Y}{B}$ (2) $\frac{X}{A}$ (3) $\frac{X}{B}$ (4) $\frac{y}{A}$

81. A combinational logic circuit that is used when it is desired to send data from two or more source through a single transmission line is known as ....

(1) demultiplexer (2) encoder
(3) decoder (4) multiplexer

82. The logic circuit of binary adder which is used to add two 4-bits binary numbers, requires ...... half adder(s) and .... full adder(s).

(1) 4, 0 (2) 1, 3
(3) 2, 2 (4) 3, 1

83. For an input pulse train of clock period T, the delay produced by an n stage shift register is
(1) $(n-1)T$
(2) $(n+1)T$
(3) nT
(4) $2nT$

84. In modern digital computer, a subtractor is normally not used because
(1) subtractors are very expensive
(2) the design of a subtractor is very complex
(3) the adder geared for doing subtraction also
(4) most of the programs do not require subtraction

85. Karnaugh map is used for the purpose of
(1) reducing the electronic circuits used
(2) map the given boolean logic function
(3) minimizing the terms in a boolean expression
(4) maximizing the terms of a given boolean expression

86. A switching circuit, whose output depends not only on the present state of its input but also on its previous state, is called ……… .
(1) combinational circuit
(2) sequential circuit
(3) multiplexer
(4) counter

87. SR flip-flop can be converted to T-type flip-flop if
(1) S is connected to Q
(2) R is connected to Q
(3) Both S and R are shortened
(4) S and R are connected to Q and $\overline{Q}$ respectively.

88. A ……… is a device which displays the number of times a particular event has occurred.
(1) counter
(2) multiplexer
(3) demultiplexer
(4) shift register

89. In ………, the flip-flop transition serve as a source for triggering other flip-flop.
(1) ripple counter
(2) synchronous counter
(3) shift register
(4) All of the above

90. In which of the following, a common pulse triggers all the flip-flops simultaneously?
(1) Ripple counter
(2) Synchronous counter
(3) Shift register
(4) All of the above

91. A flip-flop is a ……… element that stores a binary digit as a low or high voltage.
(1) chip
(2) bus
(3) I/O
(4) memory

92. A sequential circuit using D flip-flop and logic gates is shown in figure, where X and Y are the inputs and z is the output. The circuit is

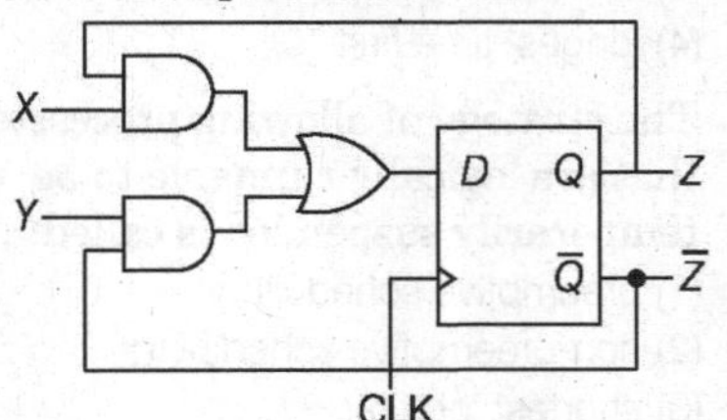

(1) SR flip-flop with input $X=S$ and $Y=R$
(2) SR flip-flop with input $X=R$ and $Y=S$
(3) JK flip-flop with input $X=K$ and $Y=J$
(4) JK flip-flop with input $X=J$ and $Y=K$

93. A pulse train can be delayed by a finite number of clock periods by using
(1) a serial-in-serial out shift register
(2) a serial-in-parallel out shift register
(3) a parallel-in-serial out shift register
(4) a parallel-in-parallel out shift register

94. The present output Q_n of an edge triggered JK flip-flop is logic 0. If $J=1$ then Q_{n+1}
(1) will be logic 0
(2) will be logic 1
(3) cannot be determined
(4) will race around

95. When the load input of a buffer register is active, then input word is stored on the next positive ……… edge.
(1) clock (2) pulse
(3) register (4) transistor

96. Computers use thousands of flip-flops. To coordinates the overall action, a common signal called the ……… is sent to each flip-flop.
(1) latch (2) master
(3) clock (4) slave

97. Advantage of synchronous sequential circuits over asynchronous ones is
(1) faster operation
(2) lower hardware requirement
(3) case of avoiding problems due to hazards
(4) better noise immunity

ANSWER KEY

1	(1)	**2**	(2)	**3**	(2)	**4**	(4)	**5**	(1)	**6**	(2)	**7**	(2)	**8**	(3)	**9**	(1)	**10**	(4)
11	(3)	**12**	(1)	**13**	(2)	**14**	(1)	**15**	(3)	**16**	(1)	**17**	(1)	**18**	(2)	**19**	(4)	**20**	(3)
21	(2)	**22**	(1)	**23**	(2)	**24**	(1)	**25**	(3)	**26**	(4)	**27**	(1)	**28**	(2)	**29**	(4)	**30**	(4)
31	(3)	**32**	(4)	**33**	(4)	**34**	(4)	**35**	(2)	**36**	(1)	**37**	(2)	**38**	(3)	**39**	(1)	**40**	(1)
41	(4)	**42**	(3)	**43**	(1)	**44**	(4)	**45**	(4)	**46**	(1)	**47**	(2)	**48**	(1)	**49**	(3)	**50**	(1)
51	(2)	**52**	(3)	**53**	(3)	**54**	(1)	**55**	(4)	**56**	(4)	**57**	(1)	**58**	(3)	**59**	(4)	**60**	(2)
61	(1)	**62**	(4)	**63**	(2)	**64**	(2)	**65**	(1)	**66**	(3)	**67**	(1)	**68**	(3)	**69**	(2)	**70**	(2)
71	(2)	**72**	(2)	**73**	(2)	**74**	(2)	**75**	(2)	**76**	(4)	**77**	(1)	**78**	(4)	**79**	(2)	**80**	(1)
81	(4)	**82**	(2)	**83**	(1)	**84**	(1)	**85**	(3)	**86**	(2)	**87**	(4)	**88**	(1)	**89**	(1)	**90**	(2)
91	(4)	**92.**	(3)	**93.**	(1)	**94.**	(2)	**95.**	(1)	**96**	(3)	**97**	(4)						

(1) the segment is spread over a number to hit in one page
(2) each segment is spread over a number of pages
(3) segment tables point to page tables and not to the physical location of the segments
(4) the processor's description base register points to a page table

51. Match List I with List II and select the correct answer using the codes given below the lists:

List I	List II
P. Disk scheduling	1. Round Robin
Q. Batch processing	2. SCAN
R. Time sharing	3. LIFO
S. Interrupt processing	4. FIFO

Codes

	P	Q	R	S
(1)	3	4	2	1
(2)	4	3	2	1
(3)	2	4	1	3
(4)	1	4	3	2

52. The kernel keeps track of the state of each executing program by using a data structure called
(1) process control block
(2) user control block
(3) file control block
(4) memory control block

53. A single threaded process of operating system program has
(1) one program counter
(2) two program counters
(3) three program counters
(4) four program counters

54. An operating system uses SRTF process scheduling algorithm. Consider the arrival times execution times for the following processes.

Process	Execution Time	Arrival Time
P_1	20	0
P_2	25	15
P_3	10	30
P_4	15	45

What is the total waiting time for process p_2?
(1) 5 (2) 15 (3) 40 (4) 55

55. What is the process by which the operating system is loaded into the memory?
(1) Booting (2) Processing
(3) Loading (4) Multi-tasking

56. The major number identifies the ..... associated with the device.
(1) driver (2) protocol
(3) port (4) None of these

57. If we use a driver for various device files, then
(1) minor number will be different for every device file
(2) minor number will be same for every device file
(3) minor number cannot be allocated for any device file
(4) None of the above

58. The connection between the device file and device driver is based on the
(1) name of device file
(2) number of device file
(3) Both (1) and (2)
(4) None of the above

59. Which scheduling policy is most suitable for a time-shared operating system?
(1) Shortest job first
(2) Round-robin
(3) First come first serve
(4) Elevator

60. Round-robin scheduling is essentially the preemptive version of ....
(1) FIFO
(2) shortest job first
(3) shortest remaining
(4) longest time first

61. The strategy of allowing processes that are logically runnable to be temporarily suspended is called
(1) preemptive scheduling
(2) non-preemptive scheduling
(3) shortest job first
(4) None of the above

62. Preemptive scheduling is the strategy of temporarily suspending a running process
(1) before the CPU time slice expires
(2) to allow starving process to run
(3) when it requests I/O
(4) None of the above

63. In round-robin CPU scheduling, as the time quantum is increased, the average turn around time
(1) increases (2) decreases
(3) remains constant (4) varies irregularly

64. Consider the following set of processes with the arrival times and the CPU burst time in milliseconds.

Process	Arrival Time	Burst Time
P_1	0	5
P_2	1	3
P_3	2	3
P_4	4	1

What is the average turn around time for these processes with the preemptive shortest remaining time first scheduling algorithm?
(1) 5.50 (2) 5.75 (3) 6.00 (4) 6.25

65. Consider a set of n tasks with runtimes $r_1, r_2, \ldots, r_n$, to be run in uniprocessor machine. Which of the following processor scheduling algorithm will result in the maximum throughput?
(1) Priority scheduling
(2) Round-robin
(3) FCFS
(4) Shortest job first

66. Which of the following statements is true?
(i) Shortest remaining time first scheduling may cause starvation
(ii) Preemptive scheduling may cause starvation
(iii) Round-robin is better than FCFS in terms of response time
(1) Only (i) (2) (i) and (iii)
(3) (ii) and (iii) (4) (i), (ii) and (iii)

67. Which of the following is a criterion to evaluate a scheduling algorithm?
(1) CPU Utilisation : Keep CPU utilisation as high as possible.
(2) Throughput : number of processes completed per unit time.
(3) Waiting Time : Amount of time spent ready to run but not running.
(4) All of the above

68. The initial value of the semaphore that allows only one of the many processes to enter their critical sections is
(1) 8 (2) 1 (3) 16 (4) 0

69. Which one of the following is a synchronisation tool?
(1) Thread (2) Pipe
(3) Semaphore (4) Socket

70. A monitor is a module that encapsulates
(1) shared data structures
(2) procedures that operate on shared data structure
(3) synchronisation between concurrent procedure invocation
(4) All of the above

71. To enable a process to wait within the monitor
(1) a condition variable must be declared as condition
(2) condition variable must be used as boolean objects
(3) semaphores must be used
(4) All of the above

72. ...... is the situation in which a process is waiting on together process, which is also waiting on process. None of the processes involved in this circular wait are making progress.
(1) Deadlock (2) Stravation
(3) Dormant (4) All of these

73. A system has 3 processes sharing 4 resources. If each process need a maximum of 2 units, then
(1) deadlock can never occur
(2) deadlock may occur
(3) deadlock has to occur
(4) None of the above

74. Mutual exclusion is a problem occurs between
(1) two disjoint process that do not interact
(2) processes that share resources
(3) processes that do not use the some resources
(4) None of the above

75. An operating system contains 3 user processes each requiring 2 units of resource R. The minimum number of units of R such that no deadlock will ever occur is:
(1) 5 (2) 2
(3) 3 (4) 4

76. The necessary conditions needed before deadlock can occur?
(1) No mutual exclusion, hold and wait preemption, circular wait
(2) Mutual exclusion, no hold and wait, preemption, circular wait
(3) Mutual exclusion, hold and wait, no preemption, circular wait
(4) Mutual exclusion, hold and wait, preemption, no circular wait

77. Resources are allocated to the process on non-sharable basis is
(1) mutual exclusion
(2) hold and wait
(3) no preemption
(4) circular wait

78. Which of the following is not true about the memory management?
(1) Virtual memory is used only in multi-user systems
(2) Segmentation suffers from external fragmentation
(3) Paging suffers from internal fragmentation
(4) Segmented memory can be paged

79. The first fit, best fit and worst fit algorithm can be used for
(1) contiguous memory location
(2) linked allocation memory
(3) index allocation memory
(4) All of the above

80. CPU fetches the instruction from memory according to the value of
(1) program counter
(2) status register
(3) instruction register
(4) program status word

81. If there are 32 segments, each of size 1 Kb, then the logical address should have
(1) 13 bits
(2) 14 bits
(3) 15 bits
(4) 16 bits

82. If the offset is legal:
(1) it is used as physical memory address itself
(2) it is subtracted from the segment base to produce the physical memory address
(3) it is added to the segment base to produce the physical memory address
(4) None of the above

83. When the entries in the segment tables of two different processes point to the same physical location:
(1) the segments are invalid
(2) the processes get blocked
(3) segments are shared
(4) All of the above

84. In which type of allocation method each file occupy a set of contiguous block on the disk?
(1) contiguous allocation
(2) dynamic-storage allocation
(3) linked allocation
(4) indexed allocation

85. An optimal scheduling algorithm in term of minimizing the average waiting time of a given set of processes is ....
(1) FCFS scheduling algorithm
(2) Round robin scheduling algorithm
(3) Shortest job-first scheduling algorithm
(4) None of the above

86. A .... is a software that manages the time of a microprocessor to ensure that all time critical events are processed as efficiently as possible. This software allows the system activities to be divided into multiple independent elements called tasks.
(1) Kernel (2) Shell
(3) Processor (4) Device Driver

ANSWER KEY

1	(3)	2	(4)	3	(3)	4	(2)	5	(3)	6	(4)	7	(1)	8	(2)	9	(4)	10	(4)
11	(4)	12	(1)	13	(1)	14	(2)	15	(2)	16	(1)	17	(4)	18	(3)	19	(3)	20	(1)
21	(3)	22	(4)	23	(4)	24	(2)	25	(1)	26	(3)	27	(1)	28	(3)	29	(4)	30	(1)
31	(2)	32	(1)	33	(4)	34	(1)	35	(3)	36	(4)	37	(3)	38	(1)	39	(1)	40	(2)
41	(1)	42	(3)	43	(3)	44	(2)	45	(4)	46	(3)	47	(2)	48	(4)	49	(3)	50	(2)
51	(3)	52	(1)	53	(1)	54	(2)	55	(1)	56	(1)	57	(1)	58	(2)	59	(2)	60	(1)
61	(1)	62	(1)	63	(4)	64	(1)	65	(4)	66	(4)	67	(4)	68	(2)	69	(3)	70	(4)
71	(1)	72	(1)	73	(2)	74	(2)	75	(4)	76	(3)	77	(1)	78	(1)	79	(1)	80	(1)
81	(1)	82	(1)	83	(3)	84	(1)	85	(3)	86	(1)								

4.3 Pseudocode

It is a simple way of writing programming code in English. Pseudocode is not actual programming language. It uses short phrases to write code for programs before you actually create it in a specific language.

e.g. To display the average of four numbers which will be input by user and also write its pseudocode.

Pseudocode

1. Accept four numbers M, N, O, P
2. Add M, N, O, P and giving to A
3. Divide A by 4 and giving to Average
4. Print Average

4.4 Introduction to Java Programming

Java is a general purpose, and third generation programming language like C++, FORTRAN, COBOL etc.

Java is also a high level and object oriented programming language developed by James Gosling, Patrik Naughton, Ed Frank, Mike Sheridan at Sun Microsystems company in the year 1991.

The original implementation of Java was not for Internet, the primary motivation for Java was the need of a platform independent language for the widely emerging web, i.e. WWW (World Wide Web).

Java programming language is strongly typed, which means that all variables must first be declared before they can be used.

4.4.1 Data Types

Data types specify the size and types of values that can be stored. Java language is rich in its data types. In Java, two categories of data types are given below:

1. Primitive Data Types

Primitive data types are the basic building blocks of any programming language. A primitive data type can have only one value at a time and is the simplest built-in form of data within Java.

Java supports following four categories of primitive data types:

Category	Data type	Size	Range
Integer Type	byte	1 byte	−128 to + 127
	short	2 bytes	− 32768 to + 32767
	int	4 bytes	-2^{31} to $+(2^{31}-1)$
	long	8 bytes	-2^{63} to $+(2^{63}-1)$
Floating Point	float	4 bytes	1.4e – 045 to 3.4e + 0.38
	double	8 bytes	4.9e – 324 to 1.8e + 308
Character Type	char	2 bytes	0 to 65535
Boolean Type	boolean	Java reserves 8 bits but only uses 1 bit.	True or False

2. Non-Primitive (Reference) Data Types

In Java, a reference data type is a variable that can contain the reference or an address of dynamically created object. These data types are not predefined like primitive data type. The reference data types are arrays, classes and interfaces that are made and handled according to a programmer in a Java program.

e.g. A class is an example of reference data type.

Consider the following class definition

```
class TypeDemo
{
  byte a;
            //a, b and c are defined manually
 int b;
 float c;
}
```

The primitive data types of above class are int b, byte a, float c.

4.4.2 Identifiers

These are names assigned to variables, constants, methods, classes, packages and interfaces. An identifier may be any descriptive sequence of uppercase and lowercase letters, numbers, the underscore and dollar sign characters.

Java identifiers follow the following rules:

1. They can have alphabets, digits, the underscore or dollar sign characters.
2. They must not begin with a digit.
3. Uppercase and lowercase letters are distinct because Java is case sensitive.
4. They can be of any length.
5. The whitespaces are not allowed within identifiers.

e.g.

Legal Identifiers	Illegal Identifiers
MyClass	My Class
Samount	23amount
_total$Pay	num^2
total_Commission	total@Commission

4.4.3 Variables

A variable is an identifier that holds values that are used in a Java program. e.g. Average, Height, Total_strength etc.

Variable names may consists of alphabets, digits, underscore (_) and dollar characters subject to the rules for naming identifiers.

1. Declaration of Variables

A variable must be declared before it is used in the program. Declaration specified two things as follows:

(i) It tells the compiler what the variable will hold.

(ii) It specifies size of the memory required for variable.

The general form of declaration of a variable is as follows:

```
Data_Type variable1, variable2, ........ variableN;
```

Variables are separated by commas. A declaration statement must end with a semicolon, some valid declarations are as follows:

```
int     count;
float   x, y;
double  p1;
char    C1, C2, C3;
```

2. Initialising the Variables

In a simple declaration, the initial value of the variable is undefined. We can combine a declaration with an assignment statement to provide an initial value for the variable.

e.g. `int val = 10;`

Here, variable **val** is initialised with the value 10.

If the variable is not initialised, then a default value is assigned to that variable according to its data type.

For the default values, consider the following table:

Type	Initial/Default Value
byte	0 (Zero) of byte type
short	0 (Zero) of short type
int	0
long	0 L
float	0.0 f
double	0.0 d
char	Null character i.e. '\u0000'
boolean	False
All reference types	Null

4.4.4 Constants

In Java, constants refer to fixed values that do not change during the execution of a program. The keyword **final** makes a variable as constant, i.e. whose value cannot be changed during program execution.

e.g. `int hours = 24;`

Here, we know this value will remain unchanged as a day always has 24 hours so the final keyword can be used.

```
final int hours = 24;
```

4.4.5 Operators

An operator is a symbol that takes one or more arguments and operates on them to produce a result.

Following is the list of various operators available in Java:

Unary Operators	Increment operator (++)	Takes one argument and increments the value by one, i.e. a + + ⇒ a = a + 1
	Decrement operator (– –)	Takes one argument and decrements the value by one, i.e. a – – ⇒ a = a – 1
Binary Operators	Arithmetic operators (+, –, *, /, %)	Takes two operands and operates on them to generate the desired result.
	Relational operators (>,<,>=,==,<=,!=)	Takes two operands, compares them and returns True or False, i.e. the results of comparison.
	Assignment operator (=)	Assign right hand side value on left hand side.
	Shift operators (>>, <<, >>>)	Performs right shift or left shift on the binary equivalent of the operand and returns the resultant value.
Ternary Operator	Conditional operator (?:)	Works as a shorthand for if else construct.

4.4.6 Expression

An expression is a combination of operators and/or operands. Java expressions are used to create objects, arrays, pass values to methods and call them, assigning value to variables and so on. Broadly, Java's expressions can be categorised into following two categories:

1. **Arithmetic Expression** An arithmetic expression is a combination of variables, constants and arithmetic operators arranged as per the syntax of the language.

   e.g.

Algebraic Expression	Java Expression
$ab - c$	$a*b - c$
$(m + n)(x + y)$	$(m + n)*(x + y)$
$\frac{ab}{c}$	$a*b/c$
$3x^2 + 2x + 1$	$3*x*x + 2*x + 1$
$\frac{x}{y} + c$	$x/y + c$

2. **Logical** (Boolean) **Expression** The boolean expression is a combination of constants, variables, logical and relational operators. The expressions that result into true or false are called **boolean** or **logical expression**. The

6. Hexadecimal to Binary

For this type of conversion, convert each hexadecimal digit to 4 bit binary equivalent.

e.g. $(BA81)_{16} \rightarrow (?)_2$

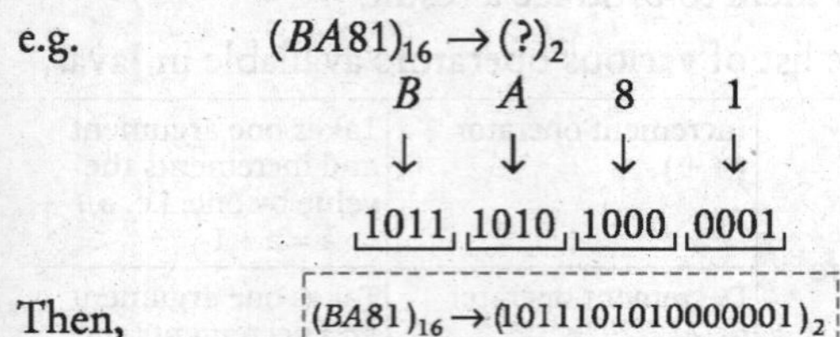

Then, $(BA81)_{16} \rightarrow (1011101010000001)_2$

7. Decimal to Octal

***Step* 1** Divide the given number by 8.

***Step* 2** Note the quotient and remainder. Digits of remainder will be 0 to 7.

***Step* 3** If quotient $\neq 0$, then again divide the quotient by 8 and go back to step 2.

***Step* 4** If quotient $= 0$, then stop the process.

***Step* 5** Write each remainder from MSD to LSD.

e.g. $(97647)_{10} \rightarrow (?)_8$

8	97647	7 LSD
8	12205	5 ↑
8	1525	5
8	190	6
8	23	7
8	2	2 MSD
	0	

Then, $(97647)_{10} \rightarrow (276557)_8$

8. Octal to Decimal

***Step* 1** Multiply each digit of octal number with power of 8.

***Step* 2** These powers should be positive for integral part and negative for fractional part.

***Step* 3** Add the all multiplying digits.

e.g. $(327.4)_8 \rightarrow (?)_{10}$

$$(327.4)_8 = 3\times 8^2 + 2\times 8^1 + 7\times 8^0 + 4\times 8^{-1}$$

$$= 3\times 64 + 2\times 8 + 7\times 1 + \frac{4}{8}$$

$$= 192 + 16 + 7 + 0.5 = 215.5$$

Then, $(327.4)_8 \rightarrow (215.5)_{10}$

9. Decimal to Hexadecimal

***Step* 1** Divide the given number by 16.

***Step* 2** Note the quotient and remainder. Digits of remainder will be 0 to 9 or *A* to *F*.

***Step* 3** If quotient $\neq 0$, then again divide the quotient by 16 and go back to step 2.

***Step* 4** If quotient $= 0$ or less than 16, then stop the process.

***Step* 5** Write each remainder from MSD to LSD.

e.g. $(929987)_{10} \rightarrow (?)_{16}$

16	929987	3 LSD
16	58124	12 → *C* ↑
16	3632	0
16	227	3
16	14	14 → *E* MSD
	0	

Then, $(929987)_{10} \rightarrow (E30C3)_{16}$

10. Hexadecimal to Decimal

***Step* 1** Multiply each digit of hexadecimal number with power of 16.

***Step* 2** These power should be positive for integral part and negative for fractional part.

***Step* 3** Add the all multiplying digits.

e.g. $(BC9.8)_{16} \rightarrow (?)_{10}$

$$(BC9.8)_{16} = B\times 16^2 + C\times 16^1 + 9\times 16^0 + 8\times 16^{-1}$$

$$= 11\times 256 + 12\times 16 + 9\times 1 + \frac{8}{16}$$

$$= 2816 + 192 + 9 + 0.5$$

$$= 3017.5$$

Then, $(BC9.8)_{16} \rightarrow (3017.5)_{10}$

11. Octal to Hexadecimal

***Step* 1** Convert the each digit of octal number to binary number.

***Step* 2** Again, convert each binary digit to hexadecimal number.

e.g. $(7632)_8 \rightarrow (?)_{16}$

7 6 3 2

Now, ↓ ↓ ↓ ↓

111 110 011 010

$(7632)_8 \rightarrow (111110011010)_2$

1111 1001 1010

↓ ↓ ↓

15 9 10

F 9 *A*

Then, $(7632)_8 \rightarrow (F9A)_{16}$

12. Hexadecimal to Octal

***Step* 1** Convert the each digit of hexadecimal number to binary number.

***Step* 2** Again, convert each binary digit to octal number.

e.g. $(AC2D)_{16} \rightarrow (?)_8$

$$\begin{array}{cccc} A & C & 2 & D \\ \downarrow & \downarrow & \downarrow & \downarrow \\ 1010 & 1100 & 0010 & 1101 \end{array}$$

Now, $(AC2D)_{16} \rightarrow (1010110000101101)_2$

$$\begin{array}{cccccc} 001 & 010 & 110 & 000 & 101 & 101 \\ \downarrow & \downarrow & \downarrow & \downarrow & \downarrow & \downarrow \\ 1 & 2 & 6 & 0 & 5 & 5 \end{array}$$

Then, $(AC2D)_{16} \rightarrow (126055)_8$

3.2 Computer Codes

In computer, any characters like alphabet, digit or any special character is represented by collection of '1' and '0' in a unique coded pattern. In computers, the code is made up of fixed size groups of binary positions.

The binary coding schemes that are most commonly used are as follows:

1. Binary Coded Decimal (BCD)

Binary coded decimal is a number system where four bits are used to represent each decimal digits. BCD is a method of using binary digits to represent the decimal digits (0-9). In BCD system, there is no limit on size of a number.

2. American Standard Code for Information Interchange (ASCII)

ASCII characters are represented by seven bits. There are standard character codes used to store data so that it may be used by other software programs. The standard ASCII codes defines 128 character codes (from 0 to 127). Basically, ASCII codes are of two types:

1. ASCII-7 is a 7-bit standard ASCII code. It allows $2^7 = 128$ unique symbols.
2. ASCII-8 is a extended version of ASCII-7. It is an 8-bit code, allows $2^8 = 256$ unique symbols or character.

3. Extended Binary Coded Decimal Interchange Code (EBCDIC)

In EBCDIC, characters are represented by eight bits. These codes store information which is readable by other computers. It allows $2^8 = 256$ combinations of bits.

4. Excess-3 code

The Excess-3 code is also called as XS-3 code. It is used to express decimal numbers. The Excess-3 code words are derived from the 8421 BCD code words adding $(0011)_2$ or $(3)_{10}$ to each code word in 8421. The Excess-3 codes are obtained as follows:

$$\text{Decimal Number} \longrightarrow \text{8421 BCD} \xrightarrow[0011]{\text{Add}} \text{Excess-3}$$

5. Gray Code

It is not arithmetic code that means there are no specific weights assigned to the bit position. It has a very special feature that, only one bit will change each time the decimal number is incremented as shown in table. As only one bit changes at a time, the gray code is called as a unit distance code. The gray code is a cyclic code.

Decimal	BCD 8421	Excess-3 BCD+0011	Gray
0	0000	0011	0000
1	0001	0100	0001
2	0010	0101	0011
3	0011	0110	0010
4	0100	0111	0110
5	0101	1000	0111
6	0110	1001	0101
7	0111	1010	0100
8	1000	1011	1100
9	1001	1100	1101

⚠ **Unicode** is an international encoding standard for use with different languages and scripts, by which each letter, digit on symbol is assigned a unique numeric value that applies across different platforms and programs.

3.3 Binary Coded Decimal System

The binary coded decimal (BCD) system used each of the 10 decimal digits as a 4-bit binary code. Binary coded decimal is useful for outputting to display that are always numeric (0 to 9).

3.3.1 Decimal to BCD Conversion

To express any decimal number in BCD, simply replace each decimal digit by the appropriate four bit code.

e.g.

(i) $(151)_{10} = (?)$

1 5 1

0001 0101 0001 ⇒ 000101010001

(ii) 3 4 . 8

0011 0100 1000 = $(00110100.1000)_{BCD}$

Syntax

```
if(condition)
{
     statement1; //if condition is true
}
else
{
     statement2; //if condition is false
}
```

Here,

- condition is a boolean expression.
- if condition is true, then statement1 or if block will execute.
- if condition is false, then statement2 or else block will execute.

Nested if Statement

The if statement can be nested in Java, which means one if or if else statement inside another if or if else statement can be used.

Syntax

```
if(condition1)
{
     if(condition2)
     {
          statement1;
     }
     else
     {
          statement2;
     }
}
else
{
     if(condition3)
     {
          statement3;
     }
     else
     {
          statement4;
     }
}
```

Here,

- if condition1 is true, then condition2 will execute.
- if condition2 is true, then statement1 will execute.
- if condition2 is false, then statement2 will execute.
- if condition1 is false, then in else block condition3 will be evaluated.
- if condition3 is true, then statement3 will execute.
- if condition3 is false, then statement4 will execute.

if else if Ladder

When a series of decisions are involved, we have to use more than one if else statement.

An if statement can be followed by an optional else if...... else statement, which is very useful to test various conditions.

Syntax

```
if(condition1)
     statement1;
else if(condition2)
     statement2;
else if(condition3)
     statement3;
:
else
     statementn+1;
```

Here,

- The if statements are executed from the top.
- As one of the conditions controlling the if, is true, the statement will be executed.
- If none of the conditions is true, the final else statement will be executed. The final else acts as a default condition, if all the conditions become false, then it will be executed.

switch Statement

In Java, the switch statement is another selection statement that defines different paths of execution for a program. It can be used in place of chain of if-else statements.

Syntax

```
switch(expression)
{
  case value1:    //statement sequence
    break;
  case value2:    //statement sequence
    break;
  :
  case valueN:    //statement sequence
    break;
  default:        //default statement sequence
}
```

Here,

- The expression must be of type byte, short, int or char.
- Each case value must be a unique literal (that is, it must be a constant, not a variable).
- The break statement is used inside the switch to terminate a statement sequence.
- If none of the constants matches with the value of the expression, then the default statement will be executed.

Conditional Operator (?:)

Conditional operator is a substitute of normal if else statement, i.e. the shorthand form of if else statement is the conditional operator (?:). It is also known as **ternary operator**.

e.g.
```
if(condition1)
        expression1;
else
        expression2;
```

It can be written as,

```
condition1 ? expression1 : expression2
```

2. Iteration Statements

The most basic method of looping in Java is iteration. The repetition of a block of statements either a fixed number of times or until a specific condition occurs is called **iteration** or **looping.**

A looping process includes the following four steps:

- Initialisation of expression.
- Evaluation of the loop condition.
- Execution of the loop when the specified loop condition is true.
- Incrementing/Decrementing the expression.

Java provides three kinds of loops as follows:

for Loop

When fixed number of iterations are to be performed, for loop is used.

Syntax

```
for(initialisation; condition; increment/decrement)
{
    //body of for loop
}
```

Here,

for loop grouped the following three common parts together into one statement:

(i) **Initialisation** The control variables is initialise first, using assignment statement such as i = 1 and count = 0. The variables i and count are known as **loop-control variables.**

Initialisation expression is executed only once.

(ii) **Condition** The value of the control variable is tested using test condition. If the condition is true, then the body of the loop is executed, otherwise the for loop is terminated and the execution continues with the statement that immediately follows the for loop.

(iii) **Increment or Decrement** When the body of the loop is executed, the control is transferred back to the for statement after evaluating the last statement in the loop. Now, the control variable is incremented/decremented using an assignment statement and the new value of the control variable is again tested to see whether it satisfies the loop condition or not. If the condition is satisfied, the body of the loop is again executed. This process continues till the value of the control variable fails to satisfy the test condition.

while Loop

The while loop is used to repeatedly execute a block of statements based on a condition. The condition is evaluated before the iteration starts.

Syntax

```
while(condition)
{
    :    //while loop body
}
```

Here,

- The condition is evaluated and if the condition is true, then the body of the while loop is executed.
- When the condition becomes false, the program control passes to the statement written immediately after the while loop body.

do-while Loop

The do-while loop always executes its body at least once, because its conditional expression is at the bottom of the loop.

Syntax

```
do
{
    //body of do-while loop
}while(condition);
```

Here,

- Each iteration of the do-while loop first executes the body of the loop and then evaluates the conditional expression.
- If this expression is true, the loop will repeat.
- Otherwise, the loop will terminate.

3. Jump Statements

Java supports three jump statements, i.e. break, continue and return. These statements transfer control to another part of the program.

break Statement

This statement is generally used to break the loop of while do-while, for or switch statement.

It has three uses as follows:

- It terminates a statement sequence in a switch statement.
- It can be used to exit a loop.
- It can be used as a 'civilised' form of goto statement.

By using break, you can force immediate termination of a loop, by passing the conditional expression and any remaining code in the body of the loop. The break statement should be used to cancel a loop only when some sort of special situation occurs.

continue Statement

In Java, continue statement is used to skip the part of loop. Unlike break statement, it does not terminate the loop,

3.6 Floating Point Arithmetic

The four possible floating-point arithmetic operations are as follow:

(i) Floating point addition
(ii) Floating point subtraction
(iii) Floating point multiplication
(iv) Floating point division

Floating point arithmetic operations are more complicated as compared to fixed point operations.

3.6.1 Floating Point Addition and Subtraction

The floating point addition/subtraction algorithm can be stated as:

(i) Check whether any of two number is 0; if so, the result is the another number.
(ii) Align the mantissas by finding difference between the exponents, so that both numbers have same exponent.
(iii) Perform addition or subtraction operation on two mantissas and determine the sign of the result.
(iv) Normalise the result value, if necessary.

3.6.2 Floating Point Multiplication

Multiplication of two floating point numbers requires to multiply the two mantissas and add the two exponents. The algorithm can be explained by the flour parts as follow:

(i) Check for zeros (ii) Add the exponents
(iii) Multiply the mantissas (iv) Normalise the product

3.6.3 Floating Point Division

Floating point division is an important operation in scientific computing and multimedia applications. The algorithm for floating point division can be explained by following steps:

(i) Check for zeros.
(ii) Initialise register and evaluate the sign.
(iii) Align the dividend
(iv) Subtract the exponents
(v) Divide the mantissas.

3.7 Boolean Algebra

Boolean algebra like any other deductive mathematical system, may be defined with a set of elements, a set of operators and a number of proved axiom or postulates. A set of elements is any collection of objects having a common property. If k is a set and a, b are objects then the notation $a, b \in k$ is used to indicate that a and b are elements of k.

A binary operator defined over a set k is a rule that assign to each pair of elements taken from k. e.g. if $a = b = c$ then '=' is a binary operator if and only if a, b and $c \in k$. The postulates of a mathematical system from the basic of assumptions from which it is possible to deduce the rules, theorems and properties of the system.

The common postulates are as follows:

Boolean Laws

Theorem	Name
$A + B = B + A$ $A \cdot B = B \cdot A$	Commutative law
$(A + B) + C = A + (B + C)$ $(A \cdot B) \cdot C = A \cdot (B \cdot C)$	Associative law
$A \cdot (B + C) = A \cdot B + A \cdot C$ $A + (B \cdot C) = (A + B) \cdot (A + C)$	Distributive law
$A + A = A$ $A \cdot A = A$	Idempotent law
$\bar{\bar{A}} = A$	Involution (Negation) law
$A + A \cdot B = A$ $A \cdot (A + B) = A$	Absorption law
$0 + A = A$ $1 \cdot A = A$	Identity law
$1 + A = 1$ $0 \cdot A = 0$	Dominant law
$\bar{A} + A = 1$ $\bar{A} \cdot A = 0$	Complement law
$\overline{A + B} = \bar{A} \cdot \bar{B}$ $\overline{A \cdot B} = \bar{A} + \bar{B}$	Demorgan's law

3.7.1 Boolean Values

The value of boolean variable can be either 1 or 0. Means if A is a boolean variable then the value of A is either 1 or 0.

3.7.2 Boolean Operators

There are four boolean operators that are used in boolean algebra which are as follows:

1. AND (.) Operator

AND operator between two boolean elements 1 and 0 can be defined as follows:

$0 \cdot 0 = 0$; $0 \cdot 1 = 0$
$1 \cdot 0 = 0$; $1 \cdot 1 = 1$

AND operator is also known as $(\cdot)$ operator. The value of AND operation is 1 if and only if all operands (elements) are 1. You can write $A \cdot B$ as AB (Meaning of both are same).

2. OR (+) Operator

The function of OR operator is given below:

$0+0=0;\quad 0+1=1$
$1+0=1;\quad 1+1=1$

You can easily see that the result of OR operation is 0 if and only if all elements are 0.

3. NOT Operator

NOT operator is also known as **compliment operator** and is denoted as $\overline{A}$ or A'.

$\overline{1}=0;\quad \overline{0}=1$

4. XOR Operator

XOR operator is represented as ($\oplus$) and is defined as follows:

$$A\oplus B=\overline{A}\cdot B+A\cdot\overline{B}$$

$0\oplus 0=0$ means $(\overline{0}\cdot 0+0\cdot\overline{0})=1\cdot 0+0\cdot 1=0+0=0$

$0\oplus 1=1$ means $(\overline{0}\cdot 1+0\cdot\overline{1})=1\cdot 1+0\cdot 0=1+0=1$

$1\oplus 0=1$ means $(\overline{1}\cdot 0+1\cdot\overline{0})=0\cdot 0+1\cdot 1=0+1=1$

$1\oplus 1=0$ means $(\overline{1}\cdot 1+1\cdot\overline{1})=0\cdot 1+0\cdot 1=0+0=0$

We can say that the value of XOR operation is 0 if $A=B$ and 1 if $A\neq B$ for $A\oplus B$.

3.7.3 Operator Precedence

The operator precedence for evaluating boolean expression is (1) parentheses (2) NOT (3) AND (4) OR,

e.g. for a boolean expression $(\overline{A}\cdot B+B\cdot C)+AC$, the operations will be as follows:

(i) Complement A means calculate $\overline{A}$
(ii) AND $\overline{A}$ with B (calculate $\overline{A}\cdot B$)
(iii) AND B and C (calculate $B\cdot C$)
(iv) OR $\overline{A}.B$ and $B\cdot C$ (calculate $\overline{A}.B+B\cdot C$)
(v) AND A and C (calculate $A\cdot C$)
(vi) OR $(\overline{A}\cdot B+B\cdot C)$ with $A\cdot C$ (calculate $(\overline{A}\cdot B+B\cdot C)+A\cdot C$)

Remember, operator precedence is very important concept for solving boolean expression like algebraic expression.

3.8 Logic Gates

Logic gates are the basic building block of any digital system. It is an electronic circuit having one or more than one input and only one output. The relationship between the input and the output is based on a **certain logic**. Based on this, logic gates are named as AND gate, OR gate, NOT gate etc.

3.8.1 Truth Tables

A truth table is a good way to show the functions of a logic gate. It shows the output states for every possible combination of input states. The symbols 0 (false) and 1 (true) are usually used in the truth tables.

The example of truth table shows the inputs and output of an AND gate.

Input *A*	Input *B*	Output *Q*
0	0	0
0	1	0
1	0	0
1	1	1

3.8.2 NOT Gate (Inverter)

The output Q is true when the input A is not true, i.e. the output is the inverse of the input

$$Q=\text{NOT } A$$

A NOT gate can only have one input.

A — B

Traditional symbol

Truth Table

Input *A*	Output *B*
0	1
1	0

3.8.3 AND Gate

The output Q is true if input A and input B are both true

$$Q=A \text{ AND } B$$

An AND gate can have two or more inputs, its output is true if all inputs are true.

A, B — Q

Traditional symbol

Truth Table

Input *A*	Input *B*	Output *Q*
0	0	0
0	1	0
1	0	0
1	1	1

3.8.4 NAND Gate (NAND = Not AND)

This is an AND gate with the inverted output, as shown by the '0' on the output. The output is true if input A AND input B are both not true.

$$Q=\text{NOT }(A \text{ AND } B)$$

A NAND gate can have two or more inputs, its output is true if all inputs are not true.

A, B — Q

Traditional symbol

Truth Table

Input *A*	Input *B*	Output *Q*
0	0	1
0	1	1
1	0	1
1	1	0

Interface	Description
DataOutput	This provides for converting data from any of the Java primitive types to a series of bytes and writing these bytes to a binary stream.
Externalizable	This provides only the identity of the class of an Externalizable instance is written in the serialization stream and it is the responsibility of the class to save and restore the contents of its instances.
FileFilter	This is a filter for abstract pathnames.
FilenameFilter	This is instances of classes that implement this interface are used to filter filenames.
Flushable	This is a destination of data that can be flushed.
ObjectInput	This extends the DataInput interface to include the reading of objects.
ObjectInputValidation	This is the callback interface to allow validation of objects within a graph.
ObjectOutput	This is the ObjectOutput extends the DataOutput interface to include writing of objects.
ObjectStream Constants	The constants written into the Object Serialization Stream.
Serializable	This is enabled by the class implementing the java.io.Serializable interface.

4.4.14 Input/Output of Data

A stream can be defined as a sequence of data. The java.io package contains nearly every class you might ever need to perform input and output in Java. All these streams represent an input source and an output destination. A stream represent different kinds of data, including small bytes, primitive data type, localised characters and objects.

InputStream

It is used to read data from a source. If you are writing a component that needs to read input from command prompt then you should use this class in your Java program. The class **java.io.InputStream** is the base class for all Java input streams.

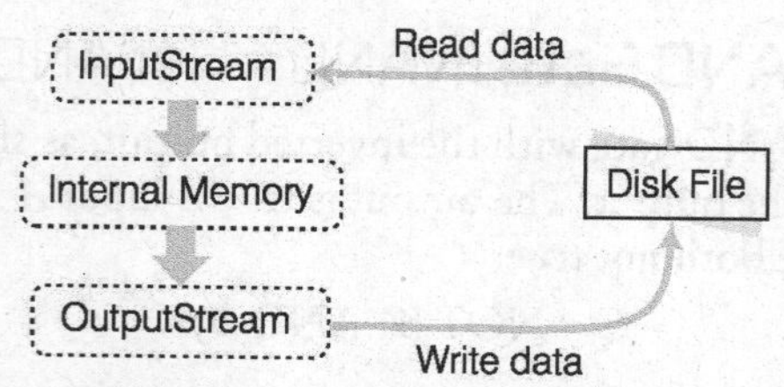

Flow of input and output stream

OutputStream

It is used for writing data to a destination. The class **java.io.OutputStream** is the base class for all Java output streams.

⚠ **import java.io.***, is first Java library package, which holds all other package inside it.

Buffer

Buffer can be very useful in Java, since they can speed up I/O operation considerably. Basically, a buffer is a space allocated into memory for bytes, char and other data types to be entered.

1. Activating Buffer in Java

Using the following statements, you can activate input buffer:

Syntax

```
InputStreamReader <object name 1>
                 = new InputStreamReader(System.in);
BufferedReader <object name 2>
              = new BufferedReader(<object name 1>);
                        or
DataInputStream <object name>
                  = new DataInputStream(System.in);
```

e.g.

```
InputStreamReader read
               = new InputStreamReader(System.in);
BufferedReader br = new BufferedReader(read);
                        or
DataInputStream ds = new DataInputStream(System.in);
```

2. BufferedReader Class

The **java.io.BufferedReader** class reads text from a character-input stream, buffering characters so as to provide for the efficient reading of characters, arrays and lines.

Following are the most useful methods of java.io.BufferedReader class:

- **int read( )** This method reads a single character from this buffered reader.
- **String readLine( )** This method read a line of text. A line is considered to be terminated by any one of a line feed ('\n'), a carriage return ('\r'), or a carriage return followed immediately by a line feed.

Printer Class

Printer classes are required when we need to create a formatted output stream.

There are two kinds of print statements as follows:

- **System.out.print** (argument) prints its argument.
- **System.out.println** (argument) prints its argument and ends the line.

e.g.

```
import java.io.BufferedReader;
import java.io.IOException;
import java.io.InputStreamReader;
public class BufferedReaderDemo
{
    public static void main(String args[])
                                 throws IOException
```

```
  {
      InputStreamReader IR=new
                      InputStreamReader(System.in);
      BufferedReader br=new BufferedReader(IR);
      System.out.println("Enter any line");
      String str = br.readLine();
      System.out.println("Enter a character");
      char ch=(char)br.read();
      System.out.println("Entered line is:
                                          "+str);
      System.out.println("Entered character is:
                                           "+ch);
  }
}
```

Output Enter any line

This is a BufferedReader class program.

Enter a character

C

Entered line is: This is a BufferedReader class program.

Entered character is: C

4.4.15 Abstract Class and Methods

An abstract class is designed only to act as a base class, i.e. we cannot create object of an abstract class. Abstract classes cannot be instantiated. It contains one or more abstract methods that is declared but contains no implementation (i.e. no method body). Methods that are declared without any body within an abstract class is known as abstract method. The method body will be defined by its subclass.

Syntax `abstract class classname{}`

e.g.

```
abstract class Animal    //name of abstract class
{
    String name;
    String species;
    void init(String n, String s)
                            // method with argument
    {
        name = n;
        species = s;
    }
    void eat(String fooditem)
                            // method with argument
    {
        System.out.println(species+"
                "+name+"likes to have"+fooditem);
    }
    abstract void sound();
                // declaration of abstract method
}
class Lion extends Animal
                    // subclass of abstract class
{
    Lion() // default constructor
    {
        init("Lion","Asiatic");
    }
    void sound()
              // implementation of abstract method
    {
        System.out.println("Lions Roar! Roar!");
    }
    public static void main(String args[])
    {
        Lion l = new Lion();      //object reaction
        l.eat("flesh");
        l.sound();
    }
}
```

Output

Asiatic Lion likes to have flesh

Lions Roar! Roar!

4.4.16 Data Encapsulation

Encapsulation is the mechanism that binds code and the data together that it manipulates. Data encapsulation is

(i) the wrapping up of data and methods into a single unit (called class).

(ii) provides the interface between the objects's data and the program.

(iii) makes it possible for objects to be treated like "black boxes" each performing a specific task without any concern about internal implementation.

e.g.

```
public class Student
{
    private String name;
    public String getName()
    {
        return name;
    }
    public void setName(String name)
    {
        this.name=name;
    }
}
class Test
{
  public static void main(String[] args)
  {
      Student s=new Student();
      s.setName("Devyansh");
      System.out.println(s.getName());
  }
}
```

(ii) Five Variables K-Map

A 5-variables K-map will have $2^5 = 32$ cells. A function F which has maximum decimal value of 31, can be defined and simplified by a 5-variable K-map.

A 5-variables K-map is shown below:

$\overline{A}$

BC \ DE	$\overline{D}\overline{E}$ 00	$\overline{D}E$ 01	DE 11	$D\overline{E}$ 10
$\overline{B}\overline{C}$ 00	0	1	3	2
$\overline{B}C$ 01	4	5	7	6
BC 11	12	13	15	14
$B\overline{C}$ 10	8	9	11	10

A

BC \ DE	$\overline{D}\overline{E}$ 00	$\overline{D}E$ 01	DE 11	$D\overline{E}$ 10
$\overline{B}\overline{C}$ 00	16	17	19	18
$\overline{B}C$ 01	20	21	23	22
BC 11	28	29	31	30
$B\overline{C}$ 10	24	25	27	26

K-Map Simplification Rules

The K-map uses the following rules for the simplification of expressions by grouping together adjacent cells containing ones.

- **Groups may not include any cell containing a zero**

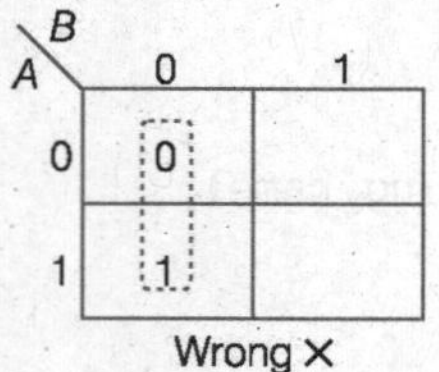

Wrong ×

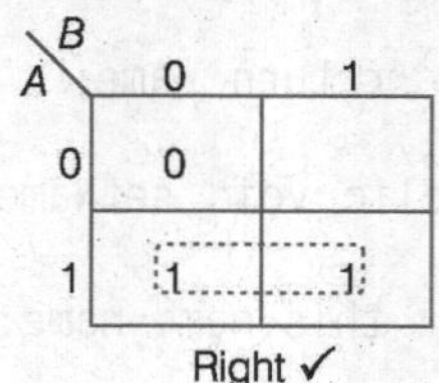

Right ✓

- **Groups may be horizontal or vertical, but not diagonal**

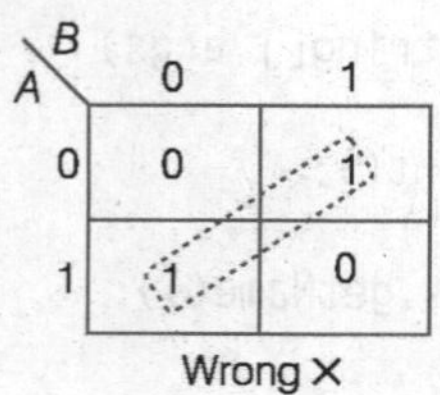

Wrong ×

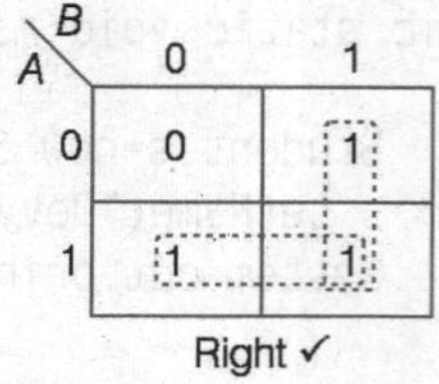

Right ✓

- **Groups must contain 2, 4, 8 or in general 2^n cells, i.e.** if n = 1, a group will contain two 1's since $2^1 = 2$, i.e. pair. If n = 2, a group will contain four 1's since $2^2 = 4$, i.e. quad. If n = 3, a group will contain eight 1's since $2^3 = 8$, i.e. octet.

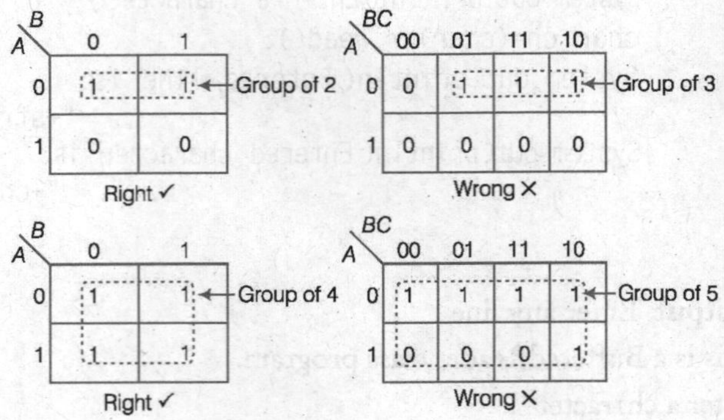

- **Each group should be as large as possible**

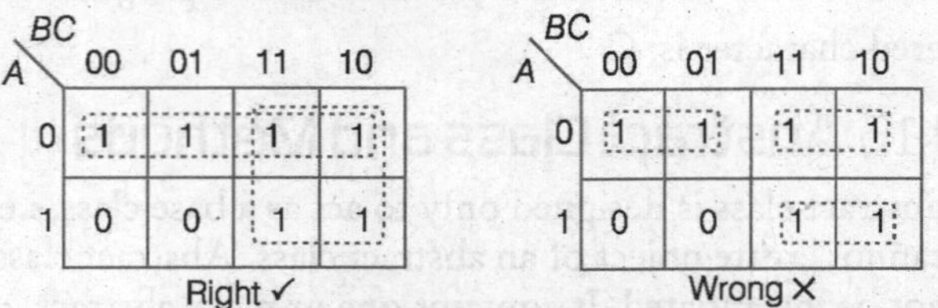

(Note that no boolean laws broken, but not sufficiently minimal)

- **Each cell containing a one(1) must be in atleast one group**

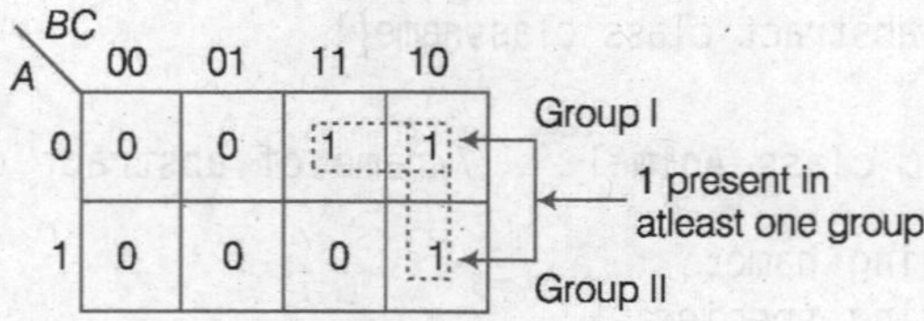

- **Groups may overlap**

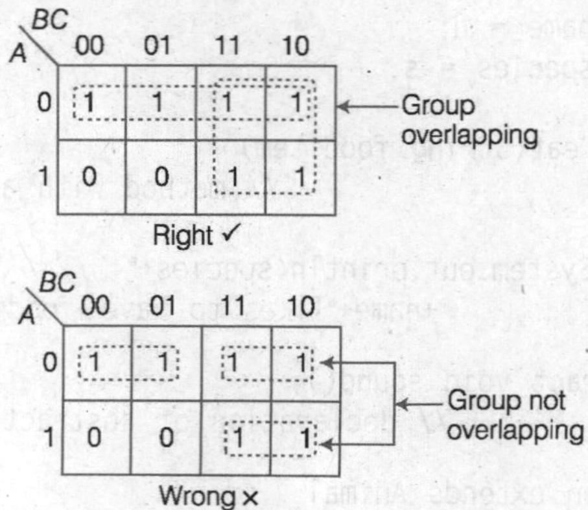

- **Groups may wrap around the table**
The leftmost cell in a row may be grouped with the rightmost cell and the top cell in a column may be grouped with the bottom cell.

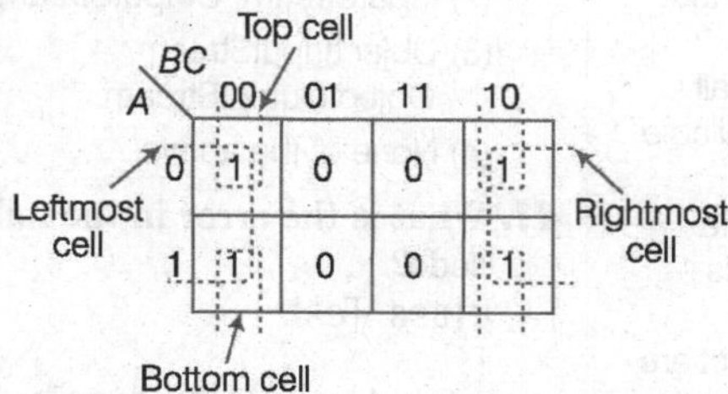

- **There should be as few groups as possible as long as this does not contradict any of the previous rules**

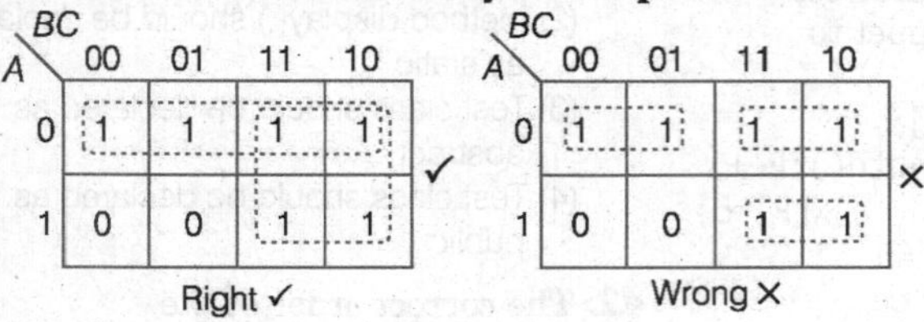

How to Reduce Boolean Expression in SOP form Using K-Map

For reducing the expression, first we have to mark pairs, quads and octets.

While encircling groups of 1's, firstly search for octets and mark them, then for quads and mark them and lastly go for pairs. This is because a bigger group removes more variables thereby making the resultant expressions simpler.

- **Octet Reduction Rule** Removes the variables which change their state from complemented to uncomplemented (normal) or *vice-versa*. An octet removes three variables.
- **Quad Reduction Rule** Removes the variables which change their states. A quad removes two variables.
- **Pair Reduction Rule** Remove the variables which change its state pair removes only one variable.
Thus, reduced expression for entire K-map is sum of all the groups (i.e. pair, quad and octet).

⚠ Sum of Product (SOP) reduction each square of K-map represents a minterm while Product of Sum (POS) reduction each square of K-map represents maxterm. SOP and POS reduction follow same rules but the only difference is that in SOP expression adjacent 1's are encircled in the form of pairs, quads and octets and in POS expression adjacent '0's are encircled in the form of pairs, quads and octets.

Quine-McCluskey's Method

The Quine-McCluskey method is an exact algorithm which finds a minimum cost sum of products implementation of a boolean function. It is functionally identical to Karnaugh mapping, but the tabular form makes it more efficient for use in computer algorithms and it also gives a deterministic way to check that the minimal form of a boolean function has been reached. It is sometimes referred to as the **tabulation** method.

There are 4 main steps in the Quine-McCluskey algorithm:

(i) Generate Prime Implicants
(ii) Construct Prime Implicant Table
(iii) Reduce Prime Implicant Table
  (a) Remove essential Prime Implicants
  (b) Row Dominance
  (c) Column Dominance
(iv) Solve Prime Implicant Table

3.12 Combinational Circuits

Combinational circuit is a circuit in which we combine the different gates in the circuit, e.g. encoder, decoder, multiplexer and demultiplexer etc.

We are going to elaborate few important combinational circuits as follows:

3.12.1 Adders

1. Half Adder

Addition of two binary digits requires two inputs and two outputs, one for result and one for carry.

The value of result and carry can be illustrated by following truth table:

Input		Output	
x	y	Result	Carry
0	0	0	0
0	1	1	0
1	0	1	0
1	1	0	1

	Result	Carry
0 + 0 = 0	0	0
0 + 1 = 1	1	0
1 + 0 = 1	1	0
1 + 1 = 10	0	1

From above truth table, we get

$$\text{Result} = \bar{x}y + x\bar{y} = x \oplus y; \quad \text{Carry} = xy$$

Thus, combinational circuit for result is,

and for carry

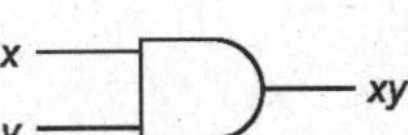

Combining both, we get

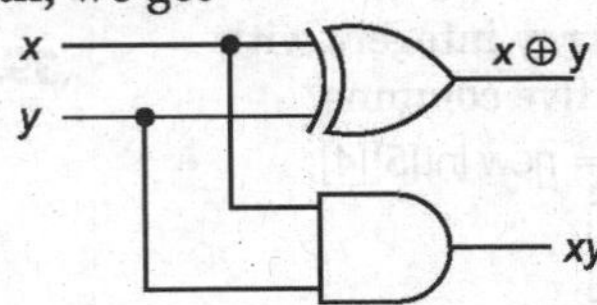

27. Which of the following statement is true about an interface?
(1) Methods inside Interface can be static, final, native or strictfp.
(2) Interface cannot extend one or more other interface.
(3) Interface cannot implement a class.
(4) Interface cannot be nested inside another interface.

28. Which of the following is true regarding the continue statement in a for loop?
(1) continue transfers the control flow to the initialisation statement of the for loop.
(2) continue transfers the control flow to the conditional statement of the for loop.
(3) continue transfers the control flow to the update statement of the for loop.
(4) continue transfers the control flow to the statement just after the for loop.

29. Which of the following statements is true?
(1) The JAVA compiler produces a code for JVM, which is executed by a JAVA interpreter.
(2) The JAVA compiler produces a code directly for JAVA interpreter.
(3) The JAVA compiler directly executes code in JVM.
(4) The JAVA compiler helps in directly executing a code on different operating systems.

30. Which of the following is not a valid declaration of a top level class?
(1) final public class Test {}
(2) class $ Test {}
(3) static class Test {}
(4) public abstract class Test {}

31. Java is a .... language. This means that you must be explicit about what type of data you are working with.
(1) weakly typed
(2) strongly typed
(3) dynamically typed
(4) loosely typed

32. Which of the following Java statement declares and allocates a 2-dimensional array integers with four rows and five columns?
(1) int array[ ][ ]= new int[5][4];
(2) int array[4][5];
(3) int array[5][4];
(4) int array[ ][ ]= new int[4][5];

33. What is garbage collection in the context of Java?
(1) The Java Virtual Machine (JVM) checks the output of any Java program and deletes anything that does not make sense at all.
(2) The operating system periodically deletes all of the Java files available on the system.
(3) Any Java package imported in a program and not being used, is automatically deleted.
(4) When all references to an object are gone, then the memory used by the object is automatically reclaimed.

34. What correction is required for following Java code snippet to compile?
```
int[] x = new int[10];
for(int P=0; P<=x.length();P++)
                          x[P]=5;
```
(1) x [P]=5 should be x(P)=5
(2) P<=x.length ( ) should be P<x. length( )
(3) x.length ( ) should be x.length
(4) P++ should be P+1

35. When the operators are having the same priority, they are evaluated from .... in the order they appear in the expression.
(1) right to left
(2) left to right
(3) any of the order
(4) depends on compiler

36. In Java, ... can only test for equality, where as .... can evaluate any type of the Boolean expression.
(1) switch, if (2) if, switch
(3) if, break (4) continue, if

37. The .... looks only for a match between the value of the expression and one of its case constants.
(1) if (2) match
(3) switch (4) None of these

38. By using ...., you can force immediate terminate of a loop, by passing the conditional expression and any remaining code in the body of the loop.
(1) break (2) continue
(3) terminate (4) loop close

39. The compiled Java program can run on any .... plateform having Java Virtual Machine (JVM) installed on it.
(1) program (2) Java
(3) hardware (4) non java

40. The .... and .... classes are abstract classes that support reading and writing of byte streams.
(1) Reader, Writer
(2) InputStream, OutputStream
(3) ObjectInputStream, ObjectOutputStream
(4) None of the above

41. What is the error in the following code?
```
class Test
{
    abstract void display();
}
```
(1) No error
(2) Method display( ) should be declared as static
(3) Test class should be declared as abstract
(4) Test class should be declared as public

42. The correct order of the declarations in a Java program is
(1) package declaration, import statement, class declaration
(2) import statement, package declaration, class declaration
(3) import statement, class declaration, package declaration
(4) class declaration, import statement, package declaration

43. What will be the output of the following code?
```
byte x=64,y;
y= (byte)(x<<2);
System.out.println(y);
```
(1) 0 (2) 1
(3) 2 (4) 64

44. If m and n are int type variables, what will be the result of the expression m%n when m=5 and n=2?
(1) 0 (2) 1
(3) 2 (4) None of these

45. Which of the following do not represent legal flow control statements?
(1) break; (2) return;
(3) exit( ); (4) continue outer;

46. What is the type and value of the following expression? (Notice the integer division)

$-4 + 1/2 + 2 * -3 + 5.0$

(1) int – 5 (2) double 4.5
(3) int – 4 (4) double – 5.0

47. **Which is used as an internal buffer and adds more efficiency than to write data directly into a stream. So, as it makes the performance fast?**
(1) BufferedOutputStream
(2) ByteArrayOutputStream
(3) BufferedInputStream
(4) ByteArrayInputStream

48. **If m and n are int type variables, what will be the result of the expression m%n when m=–14 and n=–3?**
(1) 4 (2) 2
(3) –2 (4)–4

49. **Which of the following statements are valid array declaration?**
(i) int number( );
(ii) float average[ ];
(iii) double[ ] marks;
(iv) counter int[ ];
(1) i and ii
(2) ii and iii
(3) iii and iv
(4) i, ii, iii and iv

50. **Given the following code fragment**
```
int A[];
int i = 0;
A= new int A[4];
while(i<4)
{
  A[i]= 10;
  i= i+1;
}
```
What is the value of A[3]?
(1) 0 (2) 3
(3) 10 (4) Unknown

51. **Which of these literals can be contained in a data type float variable?**
(1) 1.7 e–308 (2) 3.4e–0.38
(3) 1.7e+ 308 (4) 3.4e–050

52. **Which of these is an incorrect array declarations?**
(1) int arr[ ]= new int [5]
(2) int[ ]arr= new int [5]
(3) int arr[ ] arr= new int [5]
(4) int[ ] arr= new int [5]

53. **What will this code print?**
```
int arr[]= new int[5];
System.out.print(arr);
```
(1) 0
(2) value stored in arr [0]
(3) 00000
(4) Garbage value

54. **Which options describe the correct default values for array elements of the types indicated?**
(i) int → 0
(ii) String → "null"
(iii) char → '\u0000'
(iv) float → 0. 0f
(v) boolean → true
(1) (i), (ii), (iv) (2) (i), (iii), (iv)
(3) (ii), (iv), (v), (vi) (4) (iv), (v), (vi)

55. **Which will legally declare, construct and initialise an array?**
(1) int [ ] myList= {"1", "2", "3"};
(2) int [ ] myList= (5,8,2);
(3) int myList[ ] [ ]= {4,9,7,0};
(4) int myList [ ]= {4,3,7};

56. **Which of the following are legal array declarations?**
(i) int [ ] myScores [ ];
(ii) char[ ] myChars;
(iii) int [6] myScores;
(1) (i), (ii) (2) (ii), (iii)
(3) (i), (iii) (4) All of these

57. **Which one of the following will declared an array and initialise it with five numbers?**
(1) Array a= new Array (5);
(2) int [ ]a = {23,22,21,20,19};
(3) int a [ ]= new int [5];
(4) int [5] array;

58. **Which of the given statement is not true about a Java package?**
(1) A package can be defined as a group of similar types of classes and interfaces.
(2) Packages are used in order to avoid name conflicts and to control access of classes and interfaces.
(3) A package cannot have another package inside it.
(4) Java uses file system directory to store package.

59. **Given two files, what will be the output?**
```
package pck1;
public class A
{
  int x=10;
  public int y= 20;
}
package pck2;
import pck1.*;
class Test
{
    public static void main
                    (String []args)
    {
      A a= new A(); //line 7
      System.out.println(a.x);
                           //line 8
      System.out.println(a.y);
                           //line 9
    }
}
```
(1) 10 20
(2) Compilation error at line 7
(3) Compilation error at line 8
(4) Compilation error at line 9

60. **Which of the statement is false about an abstract class?**
(1) An abstract class is a class that contains one or more abstract methods.
(2) An abstract class cannot have normal method.
(3) An abstract class cannot be instantiated.
(4) An abstract class can be extended.

61. **Fill in the blank to compile the code successfully.**
```
abstract class A
{
  int a = 100;
  public abstract void showA();
}
public class B extends A
{
--------------------------------
                    //Fill the
                        blank
  public static void main(String
                       []args)
  {
     A objA = new A();
     objA.showA();
  }
}
```
(1) public abstract void showA( ){}
(2) public void showA( ) {}
(3) void showA( ) {}
(4) public B showA( ) {}

62. **Consider**
```
int a = 6;
int b = 12;
while(a<b)
{
  System.out.println("In the
                    loop");
  a+=2;
  b-=2;
}
```
How many times is the phrase "In the loop" printed?
(1) 1 (2) 2
(3) 3 (4) 4

Here, from above truth table, we get

$$x = D_4 + D_5 + D_6 + D_7$$
$$y = D_2 + D_3 + D_6 + D_7$$
$$z = D_1 + D_3 + D_5 + D_7$$

Thus, the obtained combinational circuit for x, y, z is given in following figure:

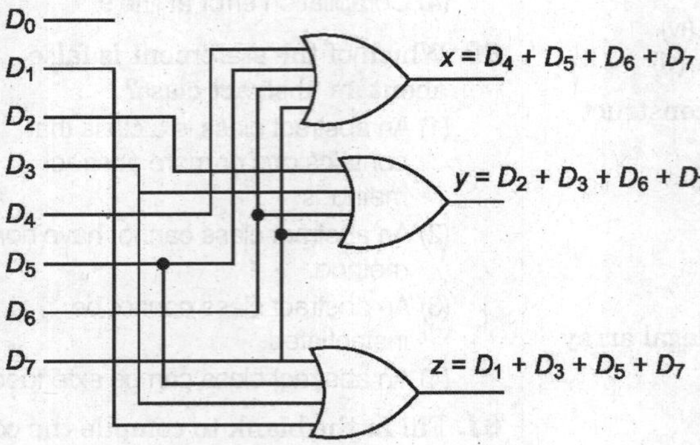

3.12.5 Priority Encoder

This is a special type of encoder. Priority is given to the input lines. If two or more lines are 1 at the same time, then the input line with highest priority will be considered. There are four inputs D_0, D_1, D_2, D_3 and two outputs Y_0, Y_1. Out of the four inputs D_3 has the highest priority and D_0 has the lowest priority.

Block diagram of priority encoder is as follows:

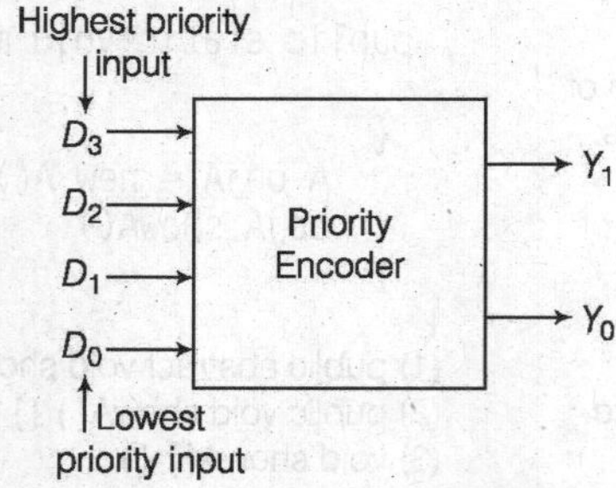

Truth table of priority encoder is as follows:

Highest	Inputs		Lowest	Outputs	
D_3	D_2	D_1	D_0	Y_0	Y_1
0	0	0	0	×	×
0	0	0	1	0	0
0	0	1	×	0	1
0	1	×	×	1	0
1	×	×	×	1	1

3.12.6 Multiplexer

Multiplexing means transmitting a large number of information units over a smaller number of channels or lines. A digital multiplexer is a combinational circuit that selects binary information from one of many input lines and directs it to the output line. The selection of a particular input line is controlled by a set of selection line. Normally, there are 2^n lines and n selection lines whose bit combinations determine which input is selected.

A 4-line to 1-line multiplexer is shown in the following block diagram:

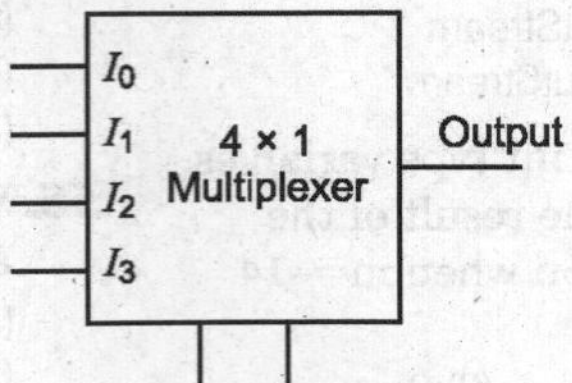

The selection of inputs will be as follows:

S_1	S_0	Output
0	0	I_0
0	1	I_1
1	0	I_2
1	1	I_3

To achieve this, the design of combinational circuit will be explained below. In the given circuit diagram, output of gate 1, 2, 3 and 4 will be given as,

Output of gate 1 = $I_0 \cdot \bar{S}_0 \cdot \bar{S}_1$, gate 2 = $I_1 \cdot \bar{S}_1 \cdot S_0$

gate 3 = $I_2 \cdot S_1 \cdot \bar{S}_0$, gate 4 = $I_3 \cdot S_1 \cdot S_0$

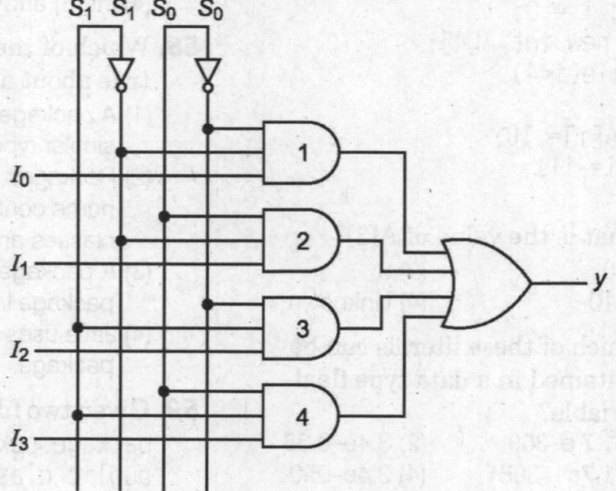

When, $S_1 = 0$ and $S_0 = 0$ output of gate 2, 3 and 4 will be 0. And the output of gate 1 will depend of I_0. (because $\bar{S}_0 = 1$ and $\bar{S}_1 = 1$ thus output of gate 1 = $I_0 \cdot 1 \cdot 1 = I_0$). In this case, we can write y as,

$$y = I_0 + 0 + 0$$
$$\Rightarrow \quad y = I_0$$

Thus, input I_0 will be propogate at output y.

Similarly, when $S_0 = 1$ and $S_1 = 0$, this time output of gate $1(\bar{S}_0 = 0)$, gate $3(\bar{S}_0 = 0)$ and output of gate $4(S_1 = 0)$ will be 0.

And output of gate 2 will be $I_1(S_0 = 1$ and $\bar{S}_1 = 1$. Thus, output of gate 2 is $I_1 \cdot S_0 \cdot \bar{S}_1 = I_1 \cdot 1 \cdot 1 = I_1$) and y will be given as

$$y = I_1 + 0 + 0 \Rightarrow y = I_1$$

We can see that for $S_1 = 1$ and $S_0 = 0$, output y will be I_2 and for $S_1 = 1$ and $S_0 = 1$, y will be I_3. Thus, by manipulating the value of S_1 and so, we can propagate any of the input to the output line.

3.12.7 Demultiplexer

A demultiplexer is a circuit that receives information on a single line and transmit that information on one of 2^n possible output lines. The output line to which input will be transmitted is selected by the selection line.

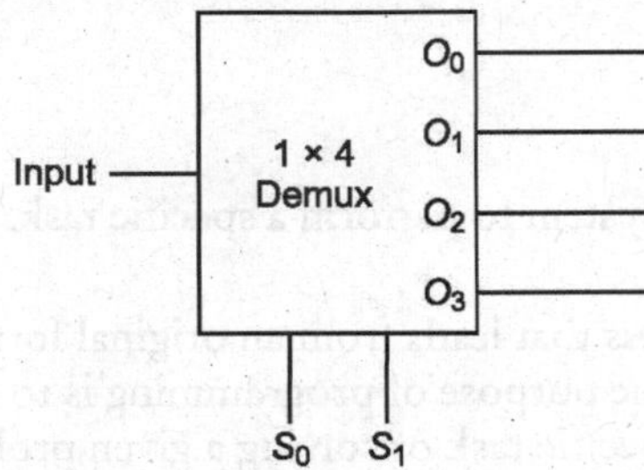

When $S_0 = S_1 = 0$, input will be transmitted to the output line O_0. Similarly, when $S_1 = 0$ and $S_0 = 1$, input will be available on output line O_1. For $S_1 = 1$ and $S_0 = 0$, output line O_2 will be selected and for $S_0 = S_1 = 1$, output line O_3 will be selected.

This is achieved from the following logic diagram:

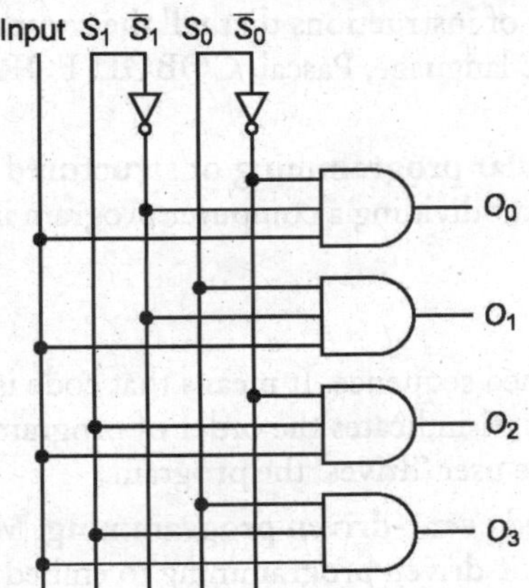

3.12.8 Multiplier

A binary multiplier is an electronic circuit used in digital electronics, such as a computer, to multiply two binary numbers.

Similar to the multiplication of decimal numbers, binary multiplication follows the same process, for producing a product of the two binary numbers. The binary multiplication is much easier as it contains only 0's and 1's.

The four fundamental rules for binary multiplication are as follow

$$0 \times 0 = 0; \quad 0 \times 1 = 0$$
$$1 \times 0 = 0; \quad 1 \times 1 = 1$$

Consider a two 4 bit binary numbers as 1010 and 1011 and its multiplication of these two is given as

```
    1010 → Multiplicand
   ×1011 → Multiplier
    1010 → Partial Product 1
   1010  → Partial Product 2
  0000   → Partial Product 3
 1010    → Partial Product 4
 1101110
```

From the above multiplication, partial products are generated for each digit in the multiplier. Then, all these partial products are added to produce the final product value. In the partial product multiplication, when the multiplier bit zero, the partial product is zero and when the multiplier bit is 1, the resulted partial product is the multiplicand.

As similar to decimal numbers, each successive partial product is shifted one position left relative to the preceding partial product before summing all partial products.

3.12.9 Parity Generator

A parity generator is a combinational logic circuit that generates the parity bits.

A parity bit is an extra bit, which is added in binary message such that the total number of 1's in the message can be either even or odd according to the parity used. There are two types of parity generators as follows:

(i) **Even Parity Generator** An even parity generator is a combinational circuit that generates a word, which always even number of 1's.

(ii) **Odd Parity Generator** Odd parity generator is a combinational circuit that generates a word which always contain odd number of 1's.

3.12.10 Parity Checker

A circuit that checks the parity in the receiver is called parity checker. Parity checker circuit checks for possible errors in the transmission. Since, the information transmitted with even parity, the receiver must have an even number of 1's.

If it has odd number of 1's, it indicates that there is a error occurred during transmission. The output of parity checker is denoted by PEC (Parity Error Checker). If there is error, that is, if it has odd number of 1's, it will indicate 1. If no then PEC will indicate 0.

Programming Tool Visual Basic

A program is a set of instructions provided to a computer system to perform a specific task. Without programs, a computer becomes useless.

Computer programming or simply programming is a process that leads from an original formulation of a computing problem to executable computer programs. The purpose of programming is to find a sequence of instructions that will automate performing a specific task or solving a given problem.

5.1 Various Programming Techniques

Every programmer follows a different programming techniques. Everyone chooses a technique according to his comfort level. Subsequently, there are various different programming techniques:

1. Procedure-Oriented Programming (POP)

Procedure-oriented programming language contains lists of instructions that tell the computer to do something such as reading, writing and calculating. e.g. C language, Pascal, COBOL, FORTRAN are the procedure-oriented programming.

Procedure-oriented programming is also known as **modular programming** or **structured programming.** Modular programming is the process of subdividing a computer program into separate sub programs.

2. Event-Driven Programming

In procedural programming, events happen in a pre-defined sequence. It means that code is executed in sequential order. But in event-driven programming, the user indicates the order of program execution, not the programmer. Instead of the program 'driving', the user 'drives' the program.

Programming, the code that responds to the event is called **event-driven programming.** Most high level GUI APIs (OWL, MFC, Turbo vision etc.) use event-driven programming to embed basic features into every program.

3. Object Based Programming

Object based programming is the style of programming that primarily supports encapsulation and object identity. That programming is a subset of object oriented programming paradigm. Major features that are required for object based programming are as follows:

(i) Data hiding and access mechanism
(ii) Data encapsulation
(iii) Automatic initialisation of objects
(iv) Operator overloading

Language that supports programming with objects are said to be object based programming languages. They do not support inheritance and dynamic binding. Ada, JavaScript, Visual Basic (VB) are typical object based programming.

4. Object Oriented Programming (OOP)

Object oriented programming approach binds the date and the functions (that operate on that data) into a single entity, such an entity is called an **object**. Functions of an object can only access its data. Thus, object oriented programming language model around objects and data rather than actions and logic. C++, Java etc., are the examples of OOP.

5.2 Introduction to Visual Basic

Visual Basic (also termed as Visual Basic.NET or VB) is a third generation event driven programming language and Integrated Development Environment (IDE) developed by Microsoft.

It was derived from BASIC (Beginner's All purpose Symbolic Instruction Code), a user-friendly programming language designed for beginners and it enables the Rapid Application Development (RAD) of Graphical User Interface (GUI) applications, access to database using Data Access Objects, Remote Data Objects or ActiveX Data Objects and creation of ActiveX controls and objects.

Visual Basic provides a GUI that allows the developer to drag and drop objects into the program as well as manually write program code. The latest version of VB is Visual Basic 10.

5.2.1 Rapid Application Development (RAD) using Visual Basic

RAD refers to a development life cycle designed to give much faster development and higher quality results than those achieved with the traditional life cycle. In general, RAD systems provide a number of tools to build graphical user interfaces that would normally take a large development effort. Two most popular RAD systems for Windows are Visual Basic and Delphi.

5.2.2 Concept of Project in Visual Basic

Every Visual Basic application is defined and saved as a project. Each project consists of a collection of files. These files can include modules, insertable objects and a single resource file. Projects themselves are tracked by a project file, which has a .VBP extension.

Four commands on the File menu allow you to create, open and save projects.

Menu Command	Description
New Project	Closes the current project, prompting you to save any files that have changed. You can select a type of project from the New Project dialog. Visual Basic then creates a new project with a single new files.
Open Project	Closes the current project, prompting you to save any changes. Visual Basic then opens an existing project, including the forms, modules and ActiveX controls listed in its project.(.vbp) file.
Save Project	Updates the project file of the current project and all of its form, standard and class modules.
Save Project As	Updates the project files of the current project, saving the project file under a File name that you specify. Visual Basic also prompts you to save any forms or modules that have changed.

It is also possible to share files between projects. A single file, such as a form, can be part of more than one project.

5.2.3 VB Project Options

As you click at New in the Visual Basic, you get a dialog box. This dialog box allows you to select the type of project you want to create. The dialog box has the following options:

1. **Standard EXE** A Standard EXE application is one that creates a standard executable file using Standard EXE project. It is the most widely used project type using VB6. Standalone programs have an .EXE file extension.
2. **ActiveX EXE** An ActiveX EXE application is one that creates an ActiveX executable file using ActiveX EXE project. ActiveX EXE are widely used in conjunction with standard EXE applications.
3. **ActiveX DLL** These files are not meant to be used by themselves. Instead, these types of files contain subprograms designed to function as building blocks when creating a standalone program. It has a .DLL file extension.
4. **ActiveX Control** Unlike an ActiveX DLL or ActiveX EXE file, an ActiveX Control file usually provides both subprograms and a user interface that you can reuse in other programs. It has an .OCX file extension.
5. **ActiveX Document EXE** An ActiveX document project is made up of a document that contains the data and a server, or application, which provides the functionality. After compilation, the document is contained in a Visual Basic Document (.VBD) file and the server is contained in either an .EXE or .DLL file.

2. Synchronous Sequential Circuits

Synchronous sequential circuit have a clock signal as one of their inputs to force the change in output only at discrete instance of time. At state transition in such circuits occurs only when the clock value is either 0 or 1 or happen at rising or falling edge of the clock.

The memory elements used in clocked sequential circuits (synchronous sequential circuit) is called **flip-flops.** These circuits are binary cells capable of storing one bit of information.

3.14 Flip-Flop

A flip-flop circuit can maintain a binary state indefinitely (as long as power is delivered to circuit) until directed by an input signal to switch states. A flip-flop circuit has two outputs, one for the normal value and one for the complement value of the bit stored in it.

3.14.1 A Basic Flip-Flop Circuit

A flip-flop circuit can be constructed from two NAND gates or two NOR gates. This is illustrated in following logical diagram:

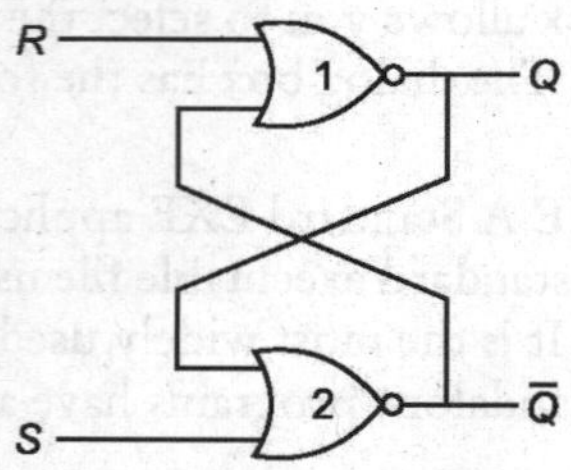

The output of NOR gate is 0, if any input is 1. At starting point, suppose R is set to 1 and S is set to 0. Since, gate 2 has an input of 1 its output $\overline{Q}$ must be 0. As the input of gate 1, R is already set to 1 the value $\overline{Q}=1$ sets the output Q to 0. Thus, for $R=1$ and $S=0$ the value of $Q=0$ and $\overline{Q}=1$.

Input		Output	
S	R	Q	$\overline{Q}$
0	0	unchanged	unchanged
0	1	0	1
1	0	1	0
1	1	undefined	undefined

Similarly, following diagram illustrates a basic flip-flop circuit using NAND gate:

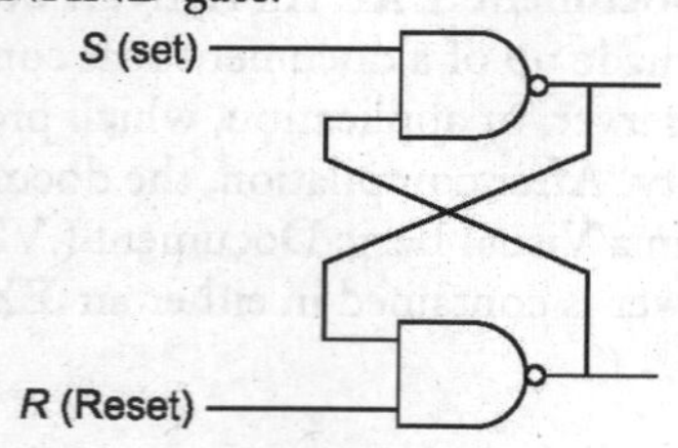

The NAND basic flip-flop circuit of previous figure operates with input normally at 1 unless the state of flip-flop has to be changed. The change in S to 0 causes output Q to set on 1 and $\overline{Q}$ to be set on 0. Similarly, when $R=0$ and $S=1$ output of gate 2 becomes 1 that is $\overline{Q}$ is set to 1 and Q set to 0. Truth table of NAND basic flip-flop is illustrated below:

Input		Output	
S	R	Q	$\overline{Q}$
0	0	×	×
0	1	1	0
1	0	0	1
1	1	no change	no change

3.14.2 Some Flip-Flop Circuits

1. RS Flip-Flop

The basic flip-flop, explained in previous section is an asynchronous sequential circuit. A circuit diagram of clocked RS flip-flop is illustrated below:

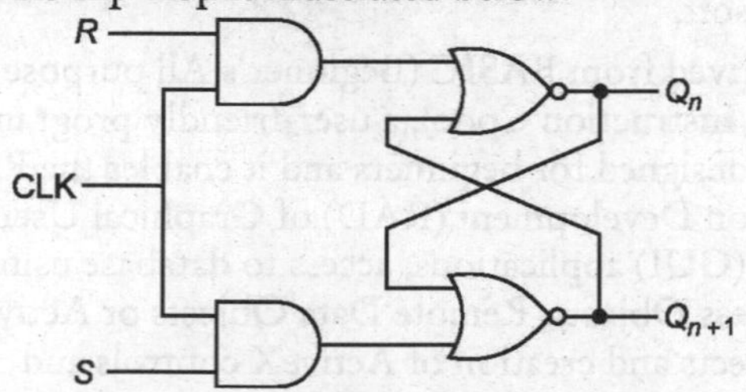

Here, in the given circuit inputs R and S will propagate to gate 1 and gate 2, respectively only when CLK input is high. Once CLK becomes high, the circuit will be equivalent to the same circuit, we have described in previous section in figure. Thus, the output of circuit diagrams shown in figure is illustrated as follows:

CLK	Q_n	S	R	Q_{n+1}
0	×	×	×	Q_n (no change)
1	0	0	0	illegal stage
1	0	0	1	0
1	0	1	0	1
1	0	1	1	0 (no change)
1	1	0	0	illegal stage
1	1	0	1	0
1	1	1	0	1
1	1	1	1	1 (no change)

2. D Flip-Flop

In case of SR flip-flop, when S and R is set to 1 the outputs (Q and $\overline{Q}$) becomes 0 that violets the rule which outputs Q and $\overline{Q}$ are the complements.

To avoid this condition, D flip-flop is introduced in which only one input (i.e. either S or R) could be high at a time and the other will be zero.

Following figure illustrates that how it is achieved:

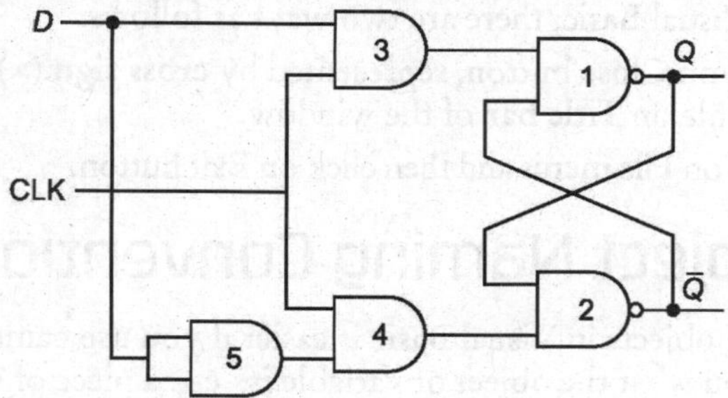

The truth table of D flip-flop will be given as follows:

CLK	D	Q_n	Q_{n+1}
0	×	×	no change
1	1	0	1
1	1	1	1
1	0	0	0
1	0	1	0

3. JK Flip-Flop

The JK flip-flop is refinement of RS flip-flop in which the condition $R = 1$ and $S = 1$ is designed in such a way that it switches the output to its complement state, that is if $Q = 1$, it switches to $Q = 0$ and *vice-versa*.

Logic diagram of JK flip-flop is illustrated as below:

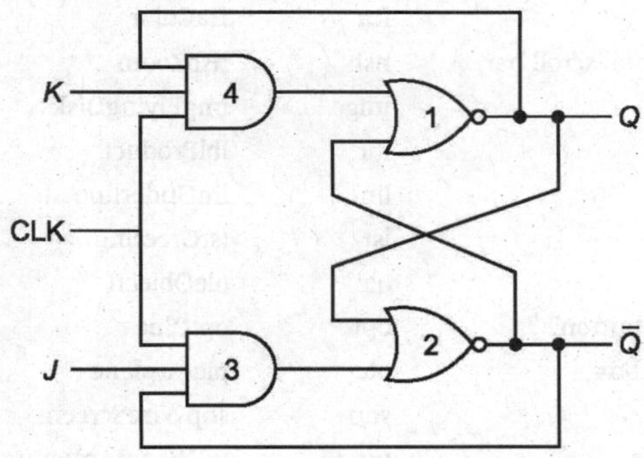

Here, J is equivalent to input S in SR flip-flop and K is equivalent to input R in SR flip-flop.

So, when J is high and K is low, i.e. $J = 1$ and $K = 0$.

In this case, if $\overline{Q} = 1$ the output of gate 3 will become high and will cause the output of gate 2 to be 0 (as one input of gate 2 become 1).

As both input of gate 1 is set to 0, the output Q will set to one. In the same case, when $J = 1$ and $Q = 0$, if $\overline{Q}$ is low in that case Q will be high, will casuse the output of gate 2 to be low (as one input of gate 2 is high) thus, again Q is set to 1.

The truth table of JK flip-flop is given below:

CLK	J	K	Q_n	Q_{n+1}
0	×	×	×	Q_n
1	1	0	×	1
1	0	1	×	0
1	0	0	×	Q_n
1	1	1	×	$\overline{Q}_n$

4. T Flip-Flop

The T flip-flop is a single input version of the JK flip-flop. As shown in figure, T flip-flop is obtained from a JK flip-flop if both inputs are tied together.

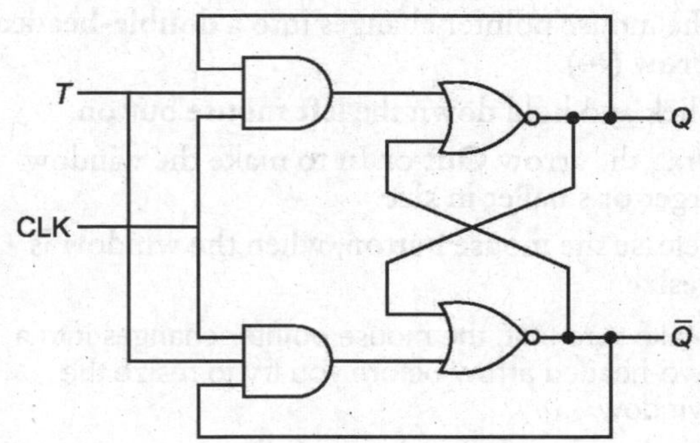

Truth table of T flip-flop is given as follows:

CLK	T	Q_{n+1}
0	×	Q_n
1	0	Q_n
1	1	$\overline{Q}_n$

5. Clocked SR Flip-Flop

The basic flip-flop as it stands is an asynchronous sequential circuit. By adding gates to the inputs of the basic circuits, the flip-flop can be made to respond to input levels during occurrence of a clock pulse.

Logic diagram of clocked SR flip-flop is illustrated as below:

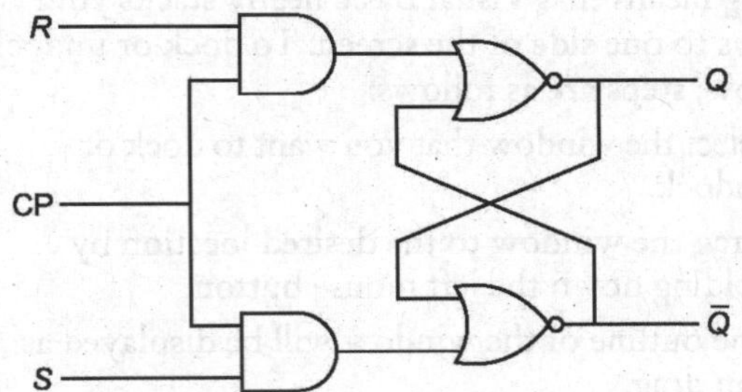

Visual Basic in Windows. You are then ready to open or start Visual Basic window.

To start Visual Basic window, steps are as follows:

(i) Click **Start** button on the Task bar.
(ii) Select **All Programs → Visual Studio → Microsoft Visual Basic.**
(iii) Double-click the **Visual Basic** icon.

You can also create a shortcut to Visual Basic on desktop and double-click the shortcut.

Resizing and Moving Window

Steps to resize the window, are as follows:

(i) Place the mouse pointer over any **corner of the window.** (You can also place the pointer over the border of the window).
(ii) The mouse pointer changes into a **double-headed arrow** (↔).
(iii) Click and hold down the **left mouse** button.
(iv) Drag the arrow **Out** or **In** to make the window larger or smaller in size.
(v) Release the mouse button, when the window is resize.

⚠ Make sure that, the mouse pointer changes into a two-headed arrow before you try to resize the window.

Steps to move the window, are as follows:

(i) Place the mouse pointer over the **title bar** (at the top of the window).
(ii) Click and hold down the **left mouse** button. (You cannot move a window that has been minimized other than to use the Minimize button).
(iii) Drag the window to the place where you want to place it and release the mouse button.

Docking Windows

Many of the windows in the IDE can be docked or connected to each other or to the edge of the screen. These include the Toolbox, Form Layout window, Project Explorer, Properties window, Color Palette and Immediate, Locals and Watch windows.

Docking means that Visual Basic neatly stacks your windows to one side of the screen. To dock or undock a window, steps are as follows:

(i) Select the window that you want to dock or undock.
(ii) Drag the window to the desired location by holding down the left mouse button.
(iii) The outline of the window will be displayed as you drag.
(iv) Release the mouse button.

Quitting Visual Basic

To quit a Visual Basic, there are two ways as follows:

(i) Click on **Close** button, represented by **cross sign** (×), available on **Title bar** of the window.
(ii) Click on **File menu** and then click on Exit button.

5.4 Object Naming Conventions

Identifying objects in Visual Basic is easier if you use name that reminds you what the object or variable is. e.g. a piece of code likes

```
x.height =y.height + z.text
```

It does not even give a hint as to whether it is changing the height of a text box, label, form, image and so on. It helps to know what the object is.

It is become a convention for Visual Basic programmers to use a three letter lower-case prefix to identify these objects. Some of the more common name prefixes are as follows:

Object	Prefix	Example
Combo box	cbo	cboCost
Check box	chk	chkAddresses
Command button	cmd	cmdRevert
Data	dat	datName
Directory list box	dir	dirSource
Drive list box	drv	drvTarget
File list box	fil	filSource
Frame	fra	fraColor
Horizontal scroll bar	hsb	hsbZoom
Image	img	imgFlyingDisk
Label	lbl	lblProduct
Line	lin	linUnderline
List box	lst	lstGreeting
OLE	ole	oleObjectl
Option button	opt	optBlue
Picture box	pic	picAirplane
Shape	shp	shpWireScreen
Text box	txt	txtWagerAmounts
Timer	tmr	tmrStopInput
Vertical scroll bar	vsb	vsbContrast

5.5 Event Procedure

Different types of controls respond in the same situation, then we write Event Procedures to handle the events generated by those controls. Event can be user or system action, whose work can be done in the form of reaction.

Visual Basic programming is predominantly based on the concept that "what action should be reacted in response to what control". Like if Command Button is click, Event Generate on cmdOK control, then the work that needs to be done should be named cmdOK_Click ( ) code is taken in the procedure. This procedure is called **Event Handler** or **Event Procedure,** which automatically gets execute in that condition when we click on the mouse on the button named cmdOK.

To create a Header of any Event Procedure, we have to double click on the control in Design Time, for which we want to create Event Handler. When we do this, then automatically becomes an Event Procedure Header with that control and its Default Event. Click Event for the Command button, the Change Event for TextBox control and the Click Event are the Default Events for the Label control. If we want to use any other event in place of the Default Event, you can create Associated New Event Handler Header with the desired control by selecting required Event from ComboBox of Events that appear in Code window.

A event procedure is a procedure block that contains the control's actual name, an underscore(_), and the event name. The following syntax represents the event procedure for a Form_Load event.

```
Private Sub Form_Load()
... Statement block..
End Sub
```

5.6 Data Types

A data type of a programming element refers to what kind of data it can hold and how it stores that data. Data types apply to all values that can be stored in computer memory or participate in the evaluation of an expression. Every variable, literal, constants, enumeration, property, procedure parameter, procedure argument and procedure return value has a data type.

The following table shows all available data types:

Type	Storage	Range
Byte	1 byte	0 to 255
Integer	2 bytes	–32,786 to 32,767
Long	4 bytes	–2,147,483,648 to 2,147,483,647
Single	4 bytes	–3.402823E+38 to –1.401298E-45 for negative values; 1.401298E –45 to 3.4028235E+38 for positive values
Double	8 bytes	–1.79769313486232E+308 to –4.94065645841247E–324 for negative values; 4.94065645841247E–324 to 1.79769313486232E+308 for positive values
Currency	8 bytes	–922,337,203,685,477.5808 to 922,337,203,685,477.5807 (the extra precision ensures that monetary calculations are kept accurate to two decimal places)
String (fixed length)	Length of string	1 to 65,400 characters
String (variable)	Length + 10 bytes	0 to 2 billion characters
Date	8 bytes	January 1, 0001 to December 31, 9999
Boolean	2 bytes	True or False
Object	4 bytes	Any embedded object
Variant (numeric)	16 bytes	Any value as large as Double
Variant (text)	Length + 22 bytes	Same as variable-length String

5.7 Variables

A variable is nothing but a name given to a storage area that our programs can manipulate. Each variable has a specific type, which determines the size and layout of the variable's memory; the range of values that can be stored within that memory and the set of operations that can be applied to the variable.

Naming a Variable

While naming a variable (or a symbolic constant), choose a meaningful name that reflects the type of data to be stored. e.g. `AnlSales, EmpName, StudMarks, Dat_of_birth.` This improves the readability of the program and makes changes to the program easier.

While declaring a variable in VB maintain the following rules:

(i) Each variable must have a unique name.
(ii) Variable must be limited to 255 characters.
(iii) Variable names must begin with an alphabets characters.
(iv) Variable names should not contain an embedded period (.).
(v) Variable cannot contain some special characters like + - */! @ # $ % ^ & ( ) = | [] {} and spaces.

Declaring Variables Explicitly

In Visual Basic, it is a good practice to declare the variables before using them by assigning names and data types. They are normally declared in the general section of the codes'. windows using the **Dim** statement.

Syntax

```
Dim VariableName As DataType
```

If you want to declare more variables, you can declare them in separate lines or you may also combine more in one line, separating each variable with a comma, as follows:

```
Dim VariableName1 As DataType1, VariableName2
As DataType2, VariableName3 As DataType3
```

e.g.

```
Dim yourName As String
Dim total As Integer
Dim password  As String, yourName As String,
firstnum As Integer
```

CHAPTER PRACTICE

1. Which system is used to refer amount of things?
(1) Number system (2) Number words
(3) Number symbols (4) All of these

2. Number system defined a set of values that is used to represent
(1) quality (2) quantity
(3) value (4) All of these

3. Bit at position zero is usually referred to as
(1) Local Bit
(2) Least Significant Bit (LSB)
(3) Most significant Bit (MSB)
(4) Least Significant Byte

4. In which system, each digit has a weight corresponding to its position.
(1) Binary number system
(2) Decimal number system
(3) Octal number system
(4) All of the above

5. If we replace each 'ON' switch with 1 and each 'OFF' switch with 0, then we get a number system, called
(1) binary number system
(2) decimal number system
(3) hexadecimal number system
(4) octal number system

6. The 2's complement representation of $(-539)_{10}$ in hexadecimal is
(1) ABE (2) DE5
(3) DBC (4) 1E5

7. When an odd number is converted into binary number the LSB is
(1) 0 (2) 1
(3) 0 or 1 (4) None of these

8. What is the octal equivalent of the hexadecimal number of 132A?
(1) 46252 (2) 11430
(3) 11452 (4) 46250

9. Binary equivalent of $(CA5)_{16}$ is
(1) 110010100101 (2) 100010010011
(3) 111001101100 (4) 101101101001

10. How many gate(s) would be required to implement the following boolean expression after simplification?

Expression : $XZ + YZ$
(1) 4 (2) 1
(3) 2 (4) 3

11. Which boolean law is represented below?

$$A + A = A$$

(1) Associative law
(2) Commutative law
(3) Idempotent law
(4) Dominant law

12. In which of the following computer code, characters are represented by eight bits?
(1) EBCDIC
(2) ASCII
(3) BCD
(4) None of the above

13. A toggle operation cannot be performed using a single
(1) NOR gate (2) AND gate
(3) NAND gate (4) XOR gate

14. Which of the following gates is called coincidence detector?
(1) XNOR gate (2) OR gate
(3) NOT gate (4) XOR gate

15. In which of the following gates, the output is 1 if and only if atleast one input is 1?
(1) NOT (2) AND
(3) OR (4) NAND

16. In which logic gate, the output is complement of the input?
(1) NOT (2) AND
(3) OR (4) XOR

17. Which method of representation has two representations for '0'?
(1) Sign-magnitude (2) 1's complement
(3) 2's complement (4) All of these

18. The arithmetic operations, addition, subtraction, multiplication and division, performed on the binary number is called
(1) binary system (2) binary arithmetic
(3) binary calculation (4) binary method

19. Which of the following is not a combinational circuit?
(1) Adder (2) Subtractor
(3) Multiplexer (4) Counter

20. The boolean expression for the sum of two variables x and y resulted by a half adder is
(1) $x \cdot y$ (2) xy
(3) $x \oplus y$ (4) $x + y$

21. All digital circuits can be realised using only
(1) XOR gate (2) multiplexer
(3) half adder (4) OR gate

22. The multiplexer with 4-bit data input is a
(1) 4:1 multiplexer (2) 2:1 multiplexer
(3) 16:1 multiplexer (4) 8:1 multiplexer

23. Decimal digits can be converted to binary format using
(1) Decoder (2) Encoder
(3) MUX (4) DE MUX

24. Carry of a full-adder is a .... function.
(1) symmetric
(2) non-symmetric
(3) cannot say
(4) None of the above

25. DEMUX can be used to realise
(1) counter
(2) shift register
(3) combinational circuit
(4) display system

26. The m-bit adder contains .... full adder.
(1) m (2) $m+1$
(3) $m/2$ (4) $m-1$

27. A demultiplexer is used to
(1) route the data from single input to one of many output.
(2) select data from several input and route to single output
(3) perform serial to parallel conversion
(4) All of the above

28. The 7-bit Hamming code is used to transmit
(1) 3 data bits (2) 7 data bits
(3) 4 data bits (4) no data bits

29. Which of the following codes is known as the 8421 code?
(1) Gray code (2) ASCII code
(3) XS-3 code (4) BCD code

30. The clock signals are used in sequential logic circuits
(1) to tell the time of the day
(2) to tell how much time has elapsed, since the system was turned on
(3) to carry serial data signals
(4) to synchronise events in various parts of a system

31. **How many full adders are required to construct an m-bit parallel adder?**
(1) $m/2$ (2) m (3) $m-1$ (4) $m+1$

32. **The dynamic race hazard problem occurs in**
(1) combination circuits only
(2) both combinational and sequential circuits
(3) sequential circuits only
(4) None of the above

33. **A shift register can be used for**
(1) serial to parallel conversion
(2) parallel to serial conversion
(3) digital delay line
(4) All of the above

34. **A full adder logic circuit will have**
(1) two inputs and one output
(2) three inputs and three outputs
(3) two inputs and two outputs
(4) three inputs and two outputs

35. **Which of the following is a sequential logic circuit?**
(1) Adder (2) Counter
(3) Multiplexer (4) Encoder

36. **Flip-flop outputs are always**
(1) complementary to each other
(2) independent to each other
(3) same
(4) same as inputs

37. **A master slave flip-flop has the characteristic that**
(1) change in the input immediately reflected in output
(2) change in the output occurs when the state of the slave is affected
(3) change in the output occurs when the state of master is affected
(4) both the master and the slaves states are affected at same time

38. **An RS latch is**
(1) combinational circuit
(2) synchronous sequential circuit
(3) one bit memory elememt
(4) one clock delay element

39. **In a positive edge triggered JK flip-flop, a low J and a low K produces:**
(1) no change (2) low state
(3) high state (4) toggle state

40. **Data can be changed from special code to temporal code by using**
(1) shift registers
(2) counters
(3) combinational circuits
(4) A/D converters

41. **Which of the following flip-flop is free from race around problem?**
(1) D flip-flop
(2) T flip-flop
(3) SR flip-flop
(4) Master-slave JK flip-flop

42. **The outputs of a sequential circuit depends on**
(1) present input only
(2) past input only
(3) both present and past inputs
(4) present output only

43. **If the radix point (binary point) is fixed and assumed to be to on the right of the right most digit, the representation of such number is called**
(1) fixed point (2) radix point
(3) floating point (4) None of these

44. **How many lines the truth table for a four-input NOR gate would contain to cover all possible input combinations?**
(1) 4 (2) 12 (3) 8 (4) 16

45. **A combinational logic circuit which is used to send data coming from a single source to two or more separate destinations is called as**
(1) decoder (2) multiplexer
(3) encoder (4) demultiplexer

46. **An odd-parity generator produces an odd-parity bit to go along with the data. The parity of the transmitted data is .... An XOR gate can test each received word for parity rejecting words with .... parity.**
(1) odd, even (2) low, high
(3) high, low (4) even, odd

47. **Identify the logic function performed by the circuit shown in the given figure**

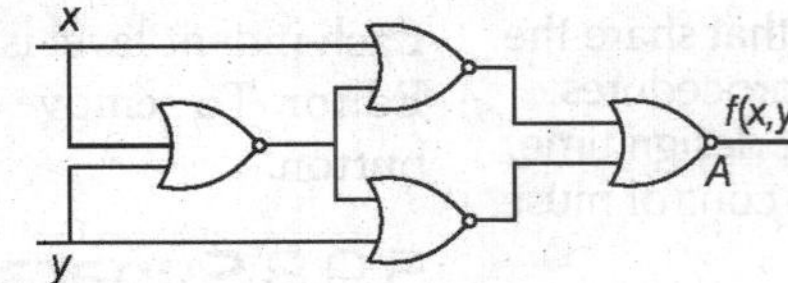

(1) Exclusive OR (2) NAND
(3) Exclusive NOR (4) NOR

48. **A .... refers to digital integrated circuit devices which are constructed with a combination of electronic circuits.**
(1) logic family (2) boolean family
(3) logic boolean (4) All of these

49. **In .... to encode a negative number, first the binary representation of its magnitude is taken, complement each bit and then add 1.**
(1) signed integer representation
(2) 1's complement representation
(3) 2's complement representation
(4) radix complement representation

50. **What does the leftmost bit represents according to IEEE standards?**
(1) Sign of the number
(2) Position of the number
(3) Weight of the number
(4) All of the above

51. **When only magnitude of numbers is considered and sign is discarded the numbers are called as**
(1) signed numbers
(2) unsigned numbers
(3) positive numbers
(4) binary numbers

52. **When the numbers are represented as positive or negative, they are called**
(1) unsigned number
(2) complement
(3) signed number
(4) binary number

53. **The sign information has to be encoded alongwith .... to represent the integer completely.**
(1) number of bits (2) position
(3) magnitude (4) weight

54. **Which method of representation of numbers occupies large amount of memory than other?**
(1) Sign-magnitude (2) 1's complement
(3) 2's complement (4) Both (1) and (2)

55. **A .... is simply an electronic circuit, which operates on one or more signals to produce an output signal.**
(1) encoder (2) adder
(3) truth table (4) logic gate

56. **Which of the following system(s) or arithmetic is/are often used in digital system?**
(1) Binary digit
(2) Decimal digit
(3) Hexadecimal digit
(4) All of the above

57. **Determine the values of the binary numbers in 2's complement number is 10101010**
(1) −86 (2) +86 (3) −98 (4) +98

5.9.4 Setting the Name Property

When assigning name for menu items, you should follow below guidelines:

(i) It should be unique within a menu.

(ii) Item names may be single, compound or multiple words.

(iii) Each item name should have a unique mnemonic access character for users who choose commands with keyboards. The access character should be the first letter of the menu title, unless another letter offers a stronger mnemonic link; no two menu titles should use the same access character.

(iv) An ellipsis(...) should follow names of commands that require more information before they can be completed, such as commands that display a dialog (Save As ....., Preferences ....).

(v) Keep the item names short.

5.9.5 Menu Naming Conventions

To make your code more readable and easier to maintain, it's a good idea to follow established naming conventions when setting the Name property in the Menu Editor. Most naming convention guidelines suggest a prefix to identify the object followed by the name of the top-level menu (e.g. File). For submenus, this would be followed by the caption of the submenu (e.g. mnuFileOpen).

5.9.6 Creating a Menu Control Array

A menu control array is a set of menu items on the same menu that share the same name and event procedures. Use a menu control array to:

(i) Create a new menu item at run time when it must be a member of a control array.

(ii) Simplify code, because common blocks of code can be used for all menu items.

⚠ A control array is a group of controls that share the same name type and the same event procedures. A control array can be created only at design time, and at the very minimum at least one control must belong to it.

Each menu control array element is identified by a unique index value, indicated in the Index property box on the Menu Editor.

To create a menu control array in the Menu Editor, steps are as follows:

(i) Select the form.

(ii) From the **Tools** menu, choose **Menu Editor.**

(iii) In the **Caption** text box, type the text for the first menu. The menu title text is displayed in the menu control list box.

(iv) In the **Name** text box, type the name for the menu control in code. Leave the **Index** box empty.

(v) At the next indentation level, create the menu item that will become the first element in the array by setting its **Caption** and **Name.**

(vi) Set the **Index** for the first element in the array to 0.

(vii) Create a second menu item at the same level of indentation as the first.

(viii) Set the **Name** of the second element to the same as the first element and set its **Index** to 1.

(ix) Repeat steps (v)-(viii) for subsequent elements of the array.

5.9.7 Creating Submenus

Each menu you create can include upto five levels of submenus. A submenu branches off another menu to display its own menu items.

You may want to use a submenu when:

(i) the menu bar is full.

(ii) a particular menu control is seldom used.

(iii) you want to emphasize one menu control's relationship to another.

In the Menu Editor, any menu control indented below a menu control that is not a menu title is a submenu control. In general, submenu controls can include submenu items, separator bars and submenu titles.

To create submenu, follows the giving steps below:

(i) Create the menu item that you want to be the submenu title.

(ii) Create the items that will appear on the new submenu and indent them by clicking the right arrow button.

Each indent level is preceded by four dots (....) in the Menu Editor. To remove one level of indentation, click the left arrow button.

5.9.8 Separating Menu Items

A separator bar displayed as a horizontal line between items on a menu. On a menu with many items, you can use a separator bar to divide items into logical groups.

e.g. the File menu in Visual Basic used separator bars to divide its menu items into three groups, as shown in figure:

To create a separator bar in the Menu Editor, steps are as follows:

(i) If you are adding a separator bar to an existing menu, choose **Insert** to insert a menu control between the menu items that you want to separate.

(ii) If necessary, click the right arrow button to indent the new menu item to the same level as the menu items it will separate.

(iii) Type a hyphen (-) in the **Caption** text box.

(iv) Set the **Name** property.

(v) Choose **OK** to close the Menu Editor.

5.9.9 Assigning Access Keys and Shortcut Keys

You can improve keyboard access to menu commands by defining access keys and shortcut keys.

1. Access Keys

You can assign an access key to your menus and menu commands.

Access keys allow the user to open a menu by pressing the **Alt key** and typing a designated letter. Once a menu is open, the user can choose a control by pressing the letter (the access key) assigned to it.

To assign an access key to a menu control in the Menu Editor, steps are as follows:

(i) Select the menu item to which you want to assign an access key.

(ii) In the **Caption** box, type an ampersand (&) immediately in front of the letter you want to be the access key.

2. Shortcut Keys

Shortcut keys run a menu item immediately when pressed. Shortcut key assignments include function key and control key combinations, such as Ctrl + F1 or Ctrl + A. They appear on the menu to the right of the corresponding menu item.

To assign a shortcut key to a menu item, steps are as follows:

(i) Open the **Menu Editor** and then select the menu item.

(ii) Select a function key or key combination in the **Shortcut** combo box.

To remove a shortcut key assignment, choose "(none)" from the top of the list.

5.9.10 Controlling Menus at Run Time

The menus you create at design time can also respond dynamically to run time conditions.

e.g. if a menu item action becomes inappropriate at some point, you can prevent users from selecting that menu item by disabling it.

Enabling and Disabling Menu Commands

All menu controls have an Enabled property and when this property is set to False, the menu is disabled and does not respond to user actions. Shortcut key access is also disabled when Enabled is set to False.

A disabled menu control appears dimmed, like the Paste menu item in below figure:

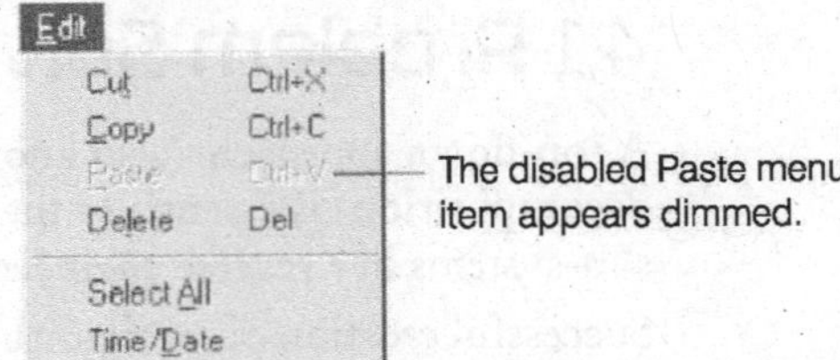

e.g. this statement disables the Paste menu item on the Edit menu of the MDI Notepad application:

```
mnuEditPaste.Enabled = False
```

Disabling a menu title in effect disables the entire menu, because the user cannot access any menu item without first clicking the menu title. e.g. the following code would disable the Edit menu of the MDI Notepad application:

```
mnuEdit.Enabled = False
```

Displaying a Check Mark on a Menu Control

Using the Checked property, you can place a check mark on a menu to:

(i) Tell the user the status of an ON/OFF condition. Choosing the menu command alternately adds and removes the check mark.

(ii) Indicate which of several modes is in effect. The Options menu of the MDI Notepad application uses a check mark to indicate the state of the toolbar.

You create check marks in Visual Basic with the Checked property. Set the initial value of the Checked property in

CHAPTER

04

Programming Fundamentals With Java

A computer program, stored in any medium, can be interpreted and executed by a computer to perform a task. A programmer writes a computer program in programming languages such as C, C++, Java etc., this form of the program is called the **source program or source code**.

For the execution of computer program, it is needed to translate it into machine language (i.e. 0 or 1), the language that the computer understands, by using the system softwares i.e. compiler and assembler.

4.1 Problem Solving Using Top-Down Design

A top-down approach (also known as **stepwise design** and in some cases used as a synonym of **decomposition**) is essentially the breaking down of a system to gain insight into its compositional sub-systems in a reverse engineering fashion.

Successful creation of an algorithm relies on solving a problem by dividing the large problem into smaller problems. Initially the high level details are solved then each of the lower level problems (modules) can be solved individually. The sum of the smaller solutions will solve the overall problem. This divide and conquer approach is called **top-down design.**

Top-down design has several main advantages as follows:

(i) Each module can be solved individually, thus reducing complexity.

(ii) The algorithm is initially functional (though limited in scope) and as more modules are added, the overall solutions becomes more and more functional.

(iii) Different modules can be written by different people, thus saving time.

(iv) Each module can be tested separately, making testing easier.

4.2 Algorithm

Algorithm is a step-by-step process of solving a well defined computational problem. It is an effective method expressed as a finite list of well defined instructions for calculating a function, starting from an initial state and initial input. It is a stepwise solution which is written in simple English language to fulfill a task. An algorithm is a set of instructions, sometimes called a **procedure** or a **function** that is used to perform a certain task.

e.g. if r is the radius of circle, then its circumference (P) is $2\pi r$ and area (A) is πr^2, where value of π is 3.1416. For this, algorithm written as

1. Read r
2. P = 2* 3.1416 * r
3. A = 3.1416 * r * r
4. Print P, A
5. Stop

Stepwise Methodology of Developing an Algorithm

The development of an algorithm (a plan) is a key step in solving a problem. Once we have an algorithm, we can translate it into a computer program in any programming language.

Algorithm development process consists of five major steps as follows:

1. Step 1 : Obtain a Description of the Problem

This step is much more difficult that it appears. In a discussion, the word client refers to someone who wants to find a solution to a problem and the word developer refers to someone who finds a way to solve the problem. The developer must create an algorithm that will solve the client's problem.

2. Step 2 : Analyse the Problem

The purpose of this step is to determine both the starting and ending points for solving the problem. This process is analogous to a mathematician determining what is given and what must be proven. A good problem description makes it easier to perform this step.

When determining the starting point, we should start by seeking answers to the following questions:

(i) What data are available?
(ii) Where is that data?
(iii) What formulas pertain to the problem?
(iv) What rules exist for working with the data?

Asking the following questions often helps to determine the ending point.

(i) What new facts will we have?
(ii) What items will have changed?
(iii) What changes will have been made to those items?
(iv) What things will no longer exist?

3. Step 3 : Develop a High Level Algorithm

An algorithm is a plan for solving a problem, but plans come in several levels of detail. It is usually better to start with a high-level algorithm that includes the major part of a solution, but leaves the details until later.

4. Step 4 : Refine the Algorithm by Adding More Details

A high level algorithm shows the major steps that need to be followed to solve a problem. Now, we need to add details to these steps, but how much detail should we add? Unfortunately, the answer to this question depends on the situation. We have to consider who (or what) is going to implement the algorithm and how much that person (or thing) already knows how to do.

When our goal is to develop algorithms that will lead to computer programs, we need to consider the capabilities of the computer and provide enough detail so that someone else could use our algorithm to write a computer program that follows the steps in our algorithm.

5. Step 5 : Review the Algorithm

The final step is to review the algorithm. What are we looking for? First, we need to work through the algorithm step by step to determine whether or not, it will solve the original problem. Once we are satisfied that the algorithm does provide a solution to the problem, we start to look for other things.

4.2.1 Analysis of Algorithm

Analysis of algorithm is common to estimate complexity of algorithm in the asymptotic sense, i.e. to estimate the complexity function for arbitrarily large input. Analysis of algorithm can known by time and space complexities of that algorithm.

1. Time Complexity

Time complexity of an algorithm signifies the total time required by the program to run to completion. The time complexity of algorithms is most commonly expressed using the big O notation.

2. Space Complexity

Space complexity of an algorithm is a function describing the amount of memory (space) an algorithm takes in terms of the amount of input to the algorithm. Space complexity includes both auxiliary space and space used by input. Auxiliary space is the extra space or temporary space used by an algorithm.

4.2.2 Asymptotic Notations

The goal of computational complexity is to classify algorithms according to their performance. We will represent the time function $T(n)$ using the 'big-O' notation to express an algorithm run time complexity.

	Worst Case Complexity	Best Case	Average Case
Linear Search	$O(n)$	$O(1)$	$O(n)$
Binary Search	$O(\log n)$	$O(1)$	$O(\log n)$
Bubble Sort	$O(n^2)$	$O(n)$	$O(n^2)$
Insertion Sort	$O(n^2)$	$O(n)$	$O(n^2)$
Merge Sort	$O(n \log n)$	$O(n \log n)$	$O(n \log n)$
Selection Sort	$O(n^2)$	$O(n^2)$	$O(n^2)$
Quick Sort	$O(n^2)$	$O(n \log n)$	$O(n \log n)$

7. Add ToolTip text that you want.
8. Click Apply.
9. Click Insert Picture and repeat the process for the second button.
10. Repeat the process for each of the buttons that will be in the toolbar.

4. To Add code for the Toolbar Buttons

Double click your first toolbar Button (like ToolStripButton1) to bring up the coding window. It should look this

```
Private Sub ToolStripButton1_Click_sender As
Object, e As EventArgs) Handles
ToolStripButton_Click
End Sub
```

You can place any code you like, here. Try a message box, as in the image below.

```
Private Sub ToolStripButton1_Click (sender As
Object, e As EventArgs)_Handles
ToolStripButton.Click
MsgBox.Show ''Save button clicked''
End Sub
```

Run your program and click your ToolStrip button. You should see the message box display.

Similarly, you can also add coding for other toolbar buttons.

5.13 Adding Status Bar

The **StatusBar** control is a ActiveX control. With the help of StatusBar, you can easily display information about the date, time and other details about the application and the environment to the user. A StatusBar control is a frame that can consist of several panels, which informs the user of the status of an application. It is made up of Panel objects, each of which displays different types of information.

(i) Click on **Start**. Then select **All Programs, Microsoft Visual Studio 6.0** and **Microsoft Visual Basic 6.0.**

(ii) Select **Standard EXE** from the list in the New Project dialog box and click on **Open**. Click on **Project** on the menu bar, then select **"Components"** from the drop down menu.

(iii) Scroll down the list in the box until **Microsoft Windows Common Controls 6.0 (SP4)** is visible. Click on the checkbox to select the component and then click on **OK**. All components show in the Toolbox.

(iv) Choose the **StatusBar** control from the list of controls in the toolbox. Place the control on the form in Visual Basic.

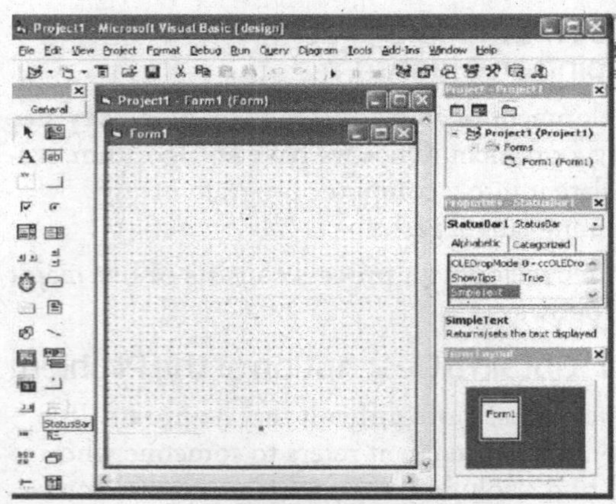

(v) By default, one panel is show on the StatusBar. Double click on StatusBar and write the following code:

```
Private Sub Form_Activate ( )
   Dim a As Panel
   StatusBar1.Panels(1).Text="Start"
   Set a=StatusBar1.Panels.Add (,,,,sbrDate)
   Set a=StatusBar1.Panels.Add (,,,,sbrTime)
End Sub
Private Sub StatusBar1_PanelClick (ByVal
                  Panel As MSComctlLib. Panel)
     MsgBox " Your page is loaded"
End Sub
```

(vi) To run the program press <F5 >. When you click on StatusBar panel then a msgbox is shown as below:

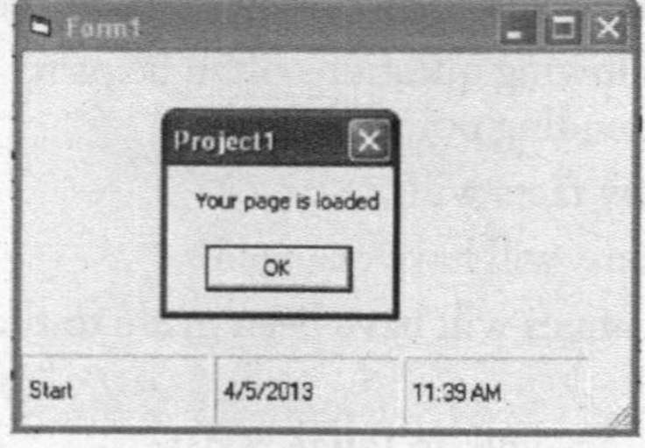

5.13.1 Adding Panels a Status Bar

To add panels to a status bar at design time:

(i) Add a **StatusBar** control to the form. For details, see Adding Controls to Windows Forms.

(ii) In the Properties window, click the **Panels** property to select it. Then, click the **Ellipsis** button to open the StatusBarPanel collection Editor.

(iii) Use the **Add** and **Remove** buttons to add and remove panels from the StatusBar control. Configure the properties of the individual panels in the Properties window that appears in the pane on the right side.

(iv) Click **OK** to close the dialog box and create the panels you specified.

(v) In the Properties window, set the **ShowPanels** property to true.

5.13.2 Adding Time and Date on the Panels

(i) Click at the Insert Panel button to add another panel.

(ii) Click the arrow button to the right of the Index box to move to the fourth panel.

(iii) Change the fourth panel's style property to 5-sbrTime.

(iv) Set the panel Alignment property to 2-sbrRight. This aligns the time in the right of the panel.

(v) Add ToolTip text for the panel.

(vi) Click Apply.

5.14 Dialog Box

A dialog box is a form defined with particular properties. It is referred to as a **container.** It is mostly used to host child controls, insuring the role of dialog between the user and the machine.

A dialog box has the following characteristics:

(i) Only system button where it is equipped with close ☒. As the only system button, this button allows the user to dismiss the dialog and ignore whatever the user would have done on the dialog box.

(ii) It cannot be minimized, maximized or restored.

(iii) It is usually modal, in which case the user is not allowed to continue any other operation on the same application until the dialog box is dismissed.

5.14.1 Predefined Dialog Box

The easiest way to add a dialog box to your application is to use a predefined dialog, because you don't have to worry about designing, loading or showing the dialog box.

However, your control over its appearance is limited. Predefined dialog boxes are always modal.

The following functions you can use to add predefined dialog box to your Visual Basic application:

Prompting for Input with InputBox

Use the InputBox function to solicit data from the user. This function displays a modal dialog box that asks the user to enter some data. The text input box shown in below figure that prompts the user for the name of the file to open.

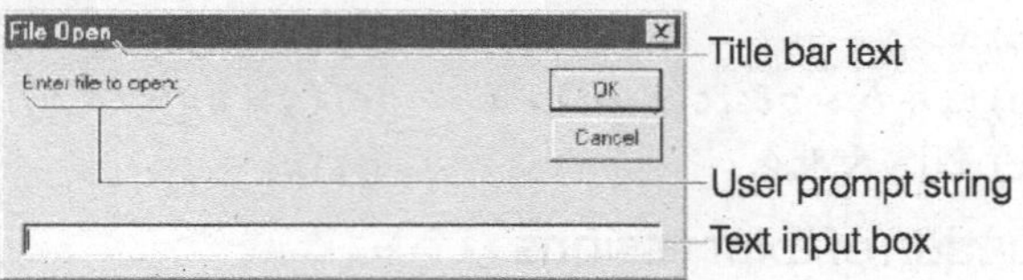

The following code displays the input box:

```
FileName = InputBox ("Enter file to open:",
                                  "File Open")
```

Displaying Information with MsgBox

Use the MsgBox function to get yes or no responses from users and to display brief messages, such as errors, warnings or alerts in a dialog box. After reading the message, the user chooses a button to close the dialog box. An application named Text Editor might display the message dialog box shown in below figure if a file cannot be opened.

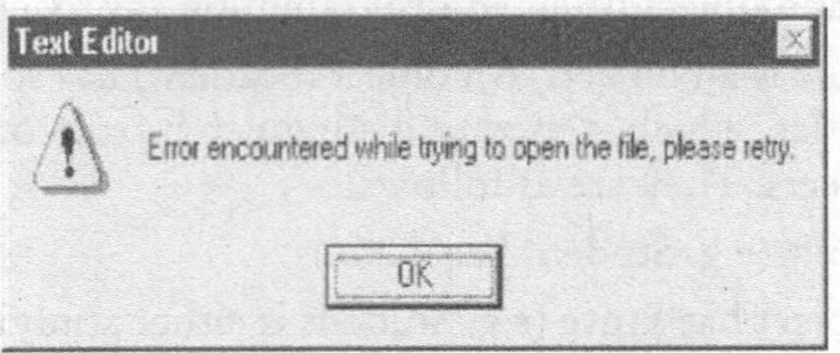

The following code displays the message box:

```
MsgBox "Error encountered while  trying to open file,
please retry.", vbExclamation, "Text Editor"
```

5.14.2 Custom Dialog Boxes

A custom dialog box is a form you create containing controls including command buttons, option buttons and text boxes that lets the user supply information to the application. You customize the appearance of the form by setting property values. You also write code to display the dialog box at run time.

To create a custom dialog box, you can start with a new form. Over time, you can build up a collection of dialog boxes that can be used in many applications.

To create a new dialog box, the steps are as follows:

(i) From the **Project** menu, choose **Add Form.** Or click the **Form** button on the toolbar to create a new form.

(ii) Customize the appearance of the form as needed.

(iii) Customize event procedures in the Code window.

You have considerable freedom to define the appearance of a custom dialog box. It can be fixed or movable, modal or modeless. It can contain different types of controls; however, dialog boxes do not usually include menu bar, window scroll bars, minimize and maximize buttons, status bars or sizable borders.

following are examples of some valid boolean expression:

(a) $x > y$ (d) $(y+z) >= (x/z)$

(b) $(a+b) > c \&\& (c+d) > a$ (e) $(y > x) || (z < y)$

(c) $x || y \&\& z$ (f) (x)

Evaluation of Expressions

Expressions are evaluated using an assignment statement of the form.

```
Variable = expression;
```

All variables used in the expression must be assigned values before evaluation is attempted.

e.g. $x = a * b - c$;

4.4.7 Objects

An object is an identifiable entity with some characteristics (attributes) and behaviour (methods). Objects are the key to understand object oriented programming approach.

e.g. **Student** is an object. An object (Student) has some characteristics, which is used to distinguish it from other similar objects. They are as follows:

(i) **Identity** (e.g. Student has name)

(ii) An object has **State** (e.g. Student is either studying or playing)

(iii) An object has **Behaviour** (e.g. Student studies, speaking etc.)

(iv) An object has **Attributes** (e.g. age, name etc.)

4.4.8 Class

A class is a group of objects that share common properties and relationships. It represents a group of similar objects. In other words, "An object is a runtime instance of a class". A class is a way to bind the data and its associated functions together.

1. Declaration and Initialisation of a Class

In general, class declarations can include following components in order:

(i) Modifiers such as public, private etc., shows the accessibility of a class.

(ii) The class name with the initial letter capitalised by convention.

(iii) The name of the class's parent (super class), if any, preceded by the keyword extends.

(iv) The class body surrounded by braces {}.

e.g.

```
class MyFirstClass
{
    public int gear;                //field
    public int speed;
    public MyFirstClass(int speedup, int
    startgear)  //Constructor
    {
        gear = startgear;
        speed = speedup;
    }
    public void setGear(int newValue)
                                    //method
    {
        gear = newValue;
    }
}
```

Class initialisation is the explicit initialisation of the class fields to values. Each class field explicitly initialises to a value *via* a class field initialiser.

e.g.
```
class Once
{
    static boolean b;
    public static void main(String[] args)
    {
        System.out.println("b="+b);
    }
}
```

Output b = false

2. Class as Composite Types

Composite types are reference type, which hold the reference id of a memory location. A class is a composite data type because it requires a reference to use its attributes. The class binds various primitive types together for using them as a unit. These primitive types can be member variables (primitive type variables) or member methods (primitive type methods). e.g. A class ABC have two values x and y and the value of these variable cannot be assigned directly. They can be assigned with the help of reference.

```
ABC  obj1;          //creating an object of ABC class
obj1.x = 5;     //referencing the variable
obj1.y  = 10;
```

3. Object as Instance of a Class

An object is an instance of a class or a class type variable that holds individual copy of data. An object can access all fields and methods of a class. The data type of an object is the class itself.

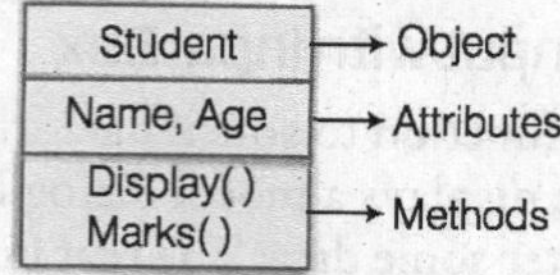

4. Creating Objects

In Java, you can create an object by creating an instance of a class in other words, instantiating a class. Objects in Java are created using the **new** keyword. The **new** keyword creates an object of the specified class and returns a reference of that object.

e.g.
```
Rectangle rect1;            //declare the object
  rect1 = new Rectangle();  //instantiate the object
```

4.4.9 The First Java Program

The first Java program may be as follows:

```
/*
comments
*/
import packagename;
class classname
{
    public static void main(String args[])
    {
        //statement block
    }
}
```

Section 1 /*comments */

It is called a comment and is important for readability of the program from programmer's point.

Section 2 `import packagename;`

In this statement, import is a keyword, which is used for reusability purpose. Package is a collection of predefined classes and interfaces. So, you can mention the name of package from which you want to reuse a class in your program.

Section 3

```
class classname
{
}
```

In this section, use the keyword class to define a new class, which is a collection of data members and methods.

Section 4

```
public static void main(String args[])
{
    //statement block
}
```

main( ) method is the entry point of control for any Java program, i.e. execution of Java program starts from main function. Hence, every Java program must contain exactly one main( ) method. Inside main( ), you can write functionality of your program as statement block.

4.4.10 Statement and Control Structure

A Java program is a set of statements, which are normally executed sequentially in order in which they appear. A statement is a single command that is executed by the Java interpreter.

Java statements can be broadly define into three categories as follows:

Single Statement

When one statement forms a complete unit of execution then it is called single statement. The following types can be made statements by terminating expression with semicolon (;).

1. Assignment expressions
2. Any use of ++ or −− operators
3. Method invocations
4. Object creating expressions
5. Control flow statement
6. Null statement

Compound Statement

It is also known as **block of statement**. Packaging several statements into a single statement between two balanced braces { }, is called a compound statement.

e.g.
```
{
   x = 1;
   y = 0;
}
```

Control Statements

Control statements are used in programming languages to cause the flow of execution in advance. These are the branch based statements where branches are depend on the state of a program.

In Java, control statements can be divided under the following three categories:

1. Selection Statements

Selection statements are used in a program to choose different paths of execution based upon the outcome of an expression or the state of a variable.

if Statement

The if statement is a powerful decision making statement and is used to control the flow of execution of statement.

Syntax
```
if(condition)
{
    statement;
}
```

Here,

- condition is a boolean expression.
- if condition is true, then the statement will execute.
- if condition is false, then the statement will be by passed.

if-else Statement

The if-else statement can be used to route program execution through two different paths.

53. ...... property is used to return or sets a value that determines whether the control can respond to user-generated events.
(1) Autosize
(2) Enable
(3) Visible
(4) Value

54. ...... allows you to position the forms in your application using a small graphical representation of the screen.
(1) Debugging window
(2) Form designer window
(3) Property window
(4) Form Layout window

55. If variables are not implicitly or explicitly type, they are assigned the type by default ....
(1) Character
(2) Integer
(3) Variant
(4) None of the above

56. All the following statements are true about variable names except
(1) the first character must be a letter
(2) they may include letters, numbers and underscore (_)
(3) can be any length
(4) you cannot use a reserved word

57. Which is true about the name and text property of a control?
(1) They are the same when the control is first created.
(2) The text property changes to match any changes in the Name property.
(3) The Name property changes to match any changes in the text property.
(4) They are never the same unless the programmer makes it that way.

58. ...... automates much of work involved in creating and deploying the files needed for our program to run on another computer.
(1) Package and deployment wizard
(2) File systems
(3) DLL
(4) None of the above

59. Which function should be used to validate that input is not a string before performing arithmetic operations?
(1) IsArithmetic
(2) IsNotString
(3) IsNumeric
(4) IsString

60. In the statement,

```
Dim Days(7) As String
```

what part of the array does the number 7 refer to?
(1) Array name (2) Datatype
(3) Lowerbound (4) Upperbound

61. Which menu object property places a check mark in the display of the menu text?
(1) Check (2) Checked
(3) CheckMark (4) CheckOn

62. Using a .... variable does not enable us to create read-only properties that are often required by a class.
(1) Public (2) Private
(3) Protected (4) Friend

63. Which of the following is the correct way of assigning value "centerscreen" for form's startposition property?
(1) StartPosition.Form1 = FormStartPosition.CenterScreen
(2) Form1.StartPosition = CenterScreen.FormStartPosition
(3) Form1.StartPosition = FormStartPosition.CenterScreen
(4) Form1.StartPosition = FormStartPosition . Location.CenterScreen

64. ...... class is built into the VB framework to display messages and accept input from the user.
(1) MsgBox
(2) MessageBox
(3) InputBox
(4) DisplayBox

65. Which of the following is/are the possible values of MsgBoxResult returned from MsgBox function?
(i) Ok (ii) Cancel
(iii) Abort (iv) Retry
(v) Ignore
(1) i, ii, iii and v only
(2) i, ii, iii and iv only
(3) ii, iii, iv and v only
(4) All i, ii, iii, iv and v

66. ...... is one of the MessageBoxDefault Button enumeration values that specifies which is the default button for the message box.
(1) DefaultButton
(2) MessageButton
(3) MessageBox
(4) DefaultMessage

67. Which of the following is/are the MessageBoxIcon enumeration values?
(i) Astrisk (ii) Error
(iii) Hand (iv) OK
(1) i, ii and iii only (2) ii, iii and iv only
(3) i, ii and iv only (4) All i, ii, iii and iv

68. ...... property of windows form sets the padding used between docked controls and the form's edge.
(1) DockPadding (2) DialogResult
(3) DialogPadding (4) DockResult

69. When you plan a Visual Basic program, you follow a three-step process that should end with....... .
(1) setting the properties
(2) writing the basic code
(3) coding all of the remark statements
(4) defining the user interface

70. Which of the following shows the correct order for creating a Visual Basic program?
(1) Set the properties, create the interface, write the code
(2) Create the interface, set the properties, write the code
(3) Create the interface, write the code, set the properties
(4) Write the code, set the properties, create the interface

71. The Visual Studio environment contains many different windows. Which window will be the user interface when the project is running?
(1) The Toolbox
(2) The Solution window
(3) The Properties window
(4) The Form Designer window

72. Which window do you open if you want to see all of the objects that you can add to a form?
(1) The Toolbox
(2) The Solution Window
(3) The Properties window
(4) The Form Designer

73. Which is true about the name and text property of a control?
(1) They are the same when the control is first created.
(2) The text property changes to match any changes in the name property.
(3) The name property changes to match any changes in the text property.
(4) They are never the same unless the programmer makes it that way.

74. Which are the standard prefixes for the text box and label controls respectively?
(1) tex and lbl
(2) tex and lab
(3) txb and lbl
(4) txb and lab

75. Which is not true about forms and controls in Visual Basic?
(1) They are pre-built.
(2) They are graphical objects.
(3) New versions of the classes must be created with each project.
(4) Buttons can be created with the drag and drop method

76. A click event procedure stud for the label control can be created by
(1) selecting the object and event from the Code Editor window's drop down boxes.
(2) typing the code in the Code Editor window.
(3) by double clicking the control.
(4) All of the above

77. Which statement will send the value generated by a function procedure, called CalculateTax, back to the calling code?
(1) Return Sales*0.08
(2) CalculateTax = Sales*0.08
(3) Return CalculateTax (Sales*0.08)
(4) Both (1) and (2)

78. Why should a variable not be declared as a module variable?
(1) It prevents a procedure from being self contained
(2) It makes it easier to document the code.
(3) Local variable names can be reused in other procedures.
(4) All of the above

79. Which Windows Media Player control property will hide the player from user's view?
(1) Anchor
(2) FileName
(3) ShowControl
(4) Visible

80. What property of controls tells the order they receive the focus when the tab key is pressed during run time?
(1) Focus order
(2) Focus number
(3) Tab index
(4) Control order

81. Sizing Handles make it very easy to resize virtually any control when developing applications with Visual Basic. When working in the Form Designer, how are these sizing handles displayed?
(1) A rectangle with 4 arrows, one in each corner, around your control.
(2) A 3-D outline around your control.
(3) A rectangle with small squares around your control.
(4) None of the above

82. The Properties window plays an important role in the development of VB applications. It is mainly used
(1) to change how objects look and feel.
(2) when opening programs stored on a hard drive
(3) to allow the developers to graphically design program components.
(4) to set program related option like Program Name, Program Location etc.

83. When creating a new application in VB, you are asked to supply a name for the program. If you do not specify a name, a default name is used. What is this default name?
(1) Wapplication followed by a number
(2) Application followed by a number
(3) Windows Application
(4) WindowsApplication followed by a number

84. What is the correct statement when declaring and assigning the value of 100 to an integer variable called numPeople?
(1) Dim numPeople =
(2) Dim numPeople = Int (100)
(3) numPeople = 100
(4) Dim numPeople As Integer = 100

85. Suppose a variable is passed by value to a parameter of a sub procedure, and the parameter has its value changed, inside the sub procedure. What will the value of the variable be after the sub procedure has executed?
(1) It will have a newly modified value from inside the sub procedure.
(2) Its value cannot be determine without more information.
(3) It will retain the value it has before the call to the sub procedure.
(4) None of the above

86. What will be the output of the following program when the button is clicked?
```
Private Sub btnDisplay_Click(...) Handles
btnDisplay.Click
Dim number As Double = 3
DoubleAndSquare(number)
txtBox.Text = CStr(number)
End Sub
Sub DoubleAndSquare(ByRef myVar As
Double)
myVar = myVar + myVar
myVar = myvar *myVar
```
(1) 3
(2) 36
(3) 6
(4) 0

87. Suppose the variable myName is declared in a Dim statement in two different Sub procedures. Which statement is true?
(1) The program will malfunction when it is executed.
(2) When the value of myName is changed in one sub procedure, it will also be changed in the other sub procedure.
(3) Visual Basic's smart editor will alert you that this is an error before the program is executed.
(4) The two variables will be local to their respective Sub procedures.

88. The arguments appearing in a Call statement must match the parameters in the appropriate Sub or Function header in all but one of the following ways. Which one?
(1) Number of arguments
(2) Names of arguments
(3) Data type of arguments
(4) Order of arguments

89. What will be the output of the following program when the button is clicked?
```
Private Sub btnDisplay_Click(...)
        Handles btnDisplays.Click
Dim word, result As String
word = "Benjamin"
result = Rotate (word)
result = Rotate (result & word)
result = Rotate (result)
textBox. Text = result
End Sub
Function Rotate (ByVal var As String) As
String
Dim varlength As Integer
varlength = var.Length
```

instead it skips the remaining part of the loop and controls go back to check the condition again.

Continue statement performs below mentioned actions:

- In while and do-while loops, a continue statement causes control to be transferred directly to the conditional expression that controls the loop.
- With the break statement, continue may specify a label to describe which enclosing loop to continue.
- It is a jumping statement and is used as keyword.
- It skips the loop and re-executes loop with new condition.
- In for loop, continue statement takes control to increment/decrement step, i.e. after continue i++/i-- will be get executed.

Return Statement

It is used to explicitly return the expression from a method. It causes program control to transfer back to the caller of the method. The return statement immediately terminate the method in which it is executed.

Syntax

```
return(expression);
```

4.4.11 Array

An array is a data structure that stores a fixed-size sequential collection of elements of the same type. It is used to store a collection of data. It is a group of contiguous or related data items that share a common name. In other words, an array is a collection of variables of the same type all of which are referred by a common name. The specific element of an array is accessed by an index.

The array can be classified into two types as follows:

One-Dimensional Array

In one-dimensional array, a single subscript or index is used, where each index value refers to an individual array element. The index of an array starts from 0 and goes upto $n-1$, i.e. the first value of the array will have an index of 0, here n is the number of elements in the array. Figure shows the Marks array with data elements.

60	58	50	78	89
Marks [0]	Marks [1]	Marks [2]	Marks [3]	Marks [4]

1. Declaring an Array

An array declaration is very similar to a variable declaration. The syntax of declaring an array is:

```
data_type Array_name[];
or data_type [] Array_name;
or data_type []Array_name;
```

e.g.
```
int marks[];
or  int[] marks;
or int []marks;
```

2. Memory Allocation in Array

Amount of memory utilised by array is estimated by specifying its size. Java allows us to create arrays using **new** operator only, as shown below:

```
Array_name = new type[size];
```

e.g.
```
number = new int[5];
average = new float[5];
```

Here, the variable number refers to an array of 5 integers and average refers to an array of 5 floating point values.

3. Initialising /Assigning an Array

Initialising an array, can be done as follows:

```
Array_name[index] = value;
```

e.g.
```
class Array
{
public static void main(String[] args)
{
int[] marks = new int[5];
//declaration of an array dynamically
marks[0] = 60;
marks[1] = 58;
marks[2] = 50;
marks[3] = 78;
marks[4] = 89;
}
}
```

Arrays can be assigned or initialised values in the same way as the variables, i.e. at the time of declaration itself. The syntax for the same can be as follows:

```
datatype ArrayName[] = {value1, value2, ....,
                                   valuen};
```

e.g.
```
int marks[] = {60, 58, 50, 78, 89};
```

Two-Dimensional Array

A two-dimensional array can be thought of as a table containing rows and columns. It contains the other properties of an array with respect to the indices, capacity and data types. Let us consider the following data table, which shows the value of sales of items by four Salesgirls:

	Item 1	Item 2	Item 3
Salesgirl #1	310	275	365
Salesgirl #2	210	190	325
Salesgirl #3	405	235	240
Salesgirl #4	260	300	380

In mathematics, we represent a particular value in a matrix by using two subscripts such as v_{ij}. Here, v denotes the entire matrix and v_{ij} refers to the value in the ith row and jth column.

The above table can be represented as

```
v[4][3];          {where, row = 4 and column = 3}
```

Syntax for Two-Dimensional Array

```
datatype[][] array_reference_name =
        new datatype[row_length][column_length];
                        (mandatory)   (optional)
```

e.g. `int[ ] array = new int [3] [4];`

We may create a two-dimensional array like this:

```
int array[][];
array = new int[3][4];
```

e.g.
```
public class LinearSearch
{
    public static void main(String[] args)
    {
        System.out.println("Linear Search
                                      List");
        int[] arr={2879, 15, 29, 78,
                   26, 24, 44,167, 12, 24, 47};
        int i;
        int num = 44;
        boolean flag = false;
        for(i=0; i<arr.length; i++)
        {
            if(arr[i] == num)
            {
                flag = true;
            }   break;
        }
        if(flag == true)
        {
            System.out.println(num+" index
                                 position" +i);
        }
        else
        {
            System.out.println(num+"
                              number not found");
        }
    }
}
```

Output

Linear Search List

44 index position 6

4.4.12 String

String represents a sequence of characters. The easiest way to represent string in Java is by using a character array.

e.g.
```
char charArray[] = new char[4];
charArray[0] = 'J';
charArray[1] = 'a';
charArray[2] = 'v';
charArray[3] = 'a';
```

Strings are class objects and implemented by using two classes, that is **String** and **StringBuffer**. A Java string is an instantiated object of the String class. It is not a character array and not NULL terminated. Strings may be declared and created as follows:

```
String stringName;
stringName = new String("string");
```

Java offers three classes to work with character data:

1. **Character class** can hold single character data.
2. **String class** can hold unchanging string, i.e. once initialised, its contents cannot be modified.
3. **StringBuffer class** can hold mutable strings, i.e. can be changed or modified.

Declaring and Allocating Strings

To create a String through assignment, we does not require the use of new operator. The most direct way to create a string is to write

```
String greeting = "Hello world!";
```

To create a String initialised by an array of characters, use following syntax :

```
String(char chars[])
```

e.g.
```
char Chars[] = {'a', 'b', 'c'};
String s = new String(Chars);
```

Here, this statements initialises s with the string "abc".

e.g.
```
public class Test
{
    public static void main(String args[])
    {
        String Str1 = new String("Welcome to
                                      string");
        String Str2 = new String("class");
        System.out.print("First String
                                    Length:");
        System.out.println(Str1.length());
        System.out.print("Second String
                                    Length:");
        System.out.println(Str2.length());
    }
}
```

Output

First String Length : 17

Second String Length : 5

4.4.13 Input-Output Interface

The java. io. Interfaces provides for system input and output through data streams, serialization and the file system.

Interface	Description
Closeable	This is a source or destination of data that can be closed.
DataInput	This provides for reading bytes from a binary stream and reconstructing from them data in any of the Java primitive types.

Modularity

The modularity is the process of partitioning program into its individual components. Some modules may be defined by standard procedures which are used and reused in different programs or parts of the same programs. A module is small enough to be understandable as a unit of code. Modules can be tested independently.

6.2 Programming with Data Structures

Programming can be done with various data structures. Some data structures are as follows:

6.2.1 Array

An array is a collection of elements of the same type of variables that are referred by a common name. Therefore, an integer array holds integers, a character array holds characters and so on. All arrays consist of contiguous memory location. The lowest address corresponds to the first element and the highest address to the last element.

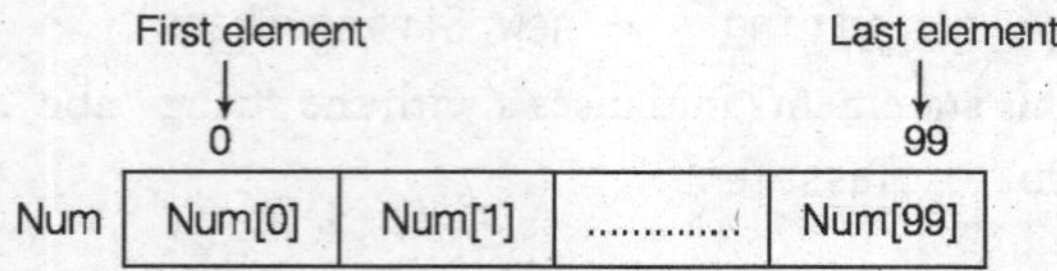

6.2.2 Stack

A stack is **Last In First Out** (LIFO) abstract data type and linear data structure. It can be implemented by both array and linked list. A stack can have any abstract data type as an element, but is characterised by only three fundamental operations : push, pop and stack top.

A stack is an ordered collection of items into which new items may be inserted and from which items may be deleted at one end, called the top of the stack.

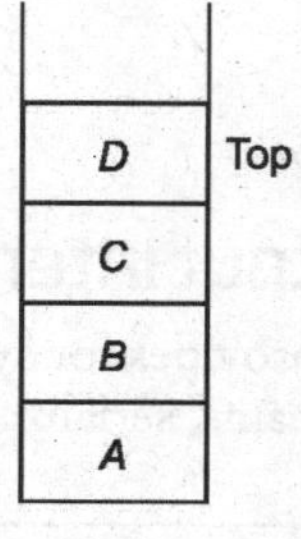

Stack

Application of Stacks

An algebraic expression can be represented using three different notations.

(i) **Infix** In this notation, operator is used in between operands. This way of writing the expressions is called **infix notation.**
e.g. x + y, 6 * 3 etc.

(ii) **Prefix** In this notation, as the name only suggests operator comes before the operands. This notation is also known as **polish notation.** e.g. +xy, * +xyz etc.

(iii) **Postfix** In this notation, the operator comes after the operands. This notation is also known as **reverse polish notation.** e.g. xy+, xyz+* etc.

Converting expressions from infix to postfix notation

In normal algebra, we use the infix notation like a + b * c. The corresponding postfix notation is abc*+. To convert an expression from infix to postfix, we are going to use a stack.

Steps of Algorithm

Step 1 Read all the symbols one by one from left to right in the given infix expression.

Step 2 If it is an operand, output it.

Step 3 If it is opening parentheses, push it on stack.

Step 4 If it is an operator, then
- if stack is empty, push operator on stack.
- if the top of the stack is opening parentheses, push operator on stack.
- if it has higher priority than the top of stack, push operator on stack.
- else pop the operator from the stack and output it, repeat step (4).

Step 5 If it is a closing parentheses, pop operators from the stack and output them until an opening parentheses is encountered. Pop and discard the opening parentheses.

Step 6 If there is more input go to step 1.

Step 7 If there is no more input, unstack the remaining operators to output.

6.2.3 Queue

A queue is an ordered collection of items from which items may be deleted at one end (called the **front** of the queue) and into which items may be inserted at the other end (called the **rear** of the queue). Sometimes, queue is also known as **FIFO** (First In First Out)

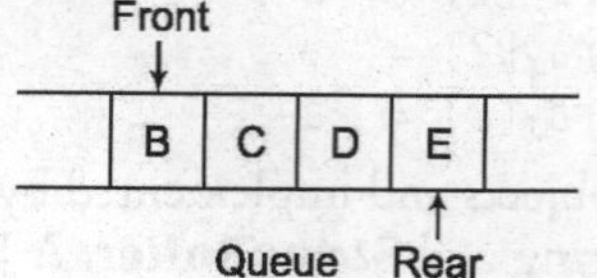

6.2.4 Linked List

A linked list is a data structure consisting of group of nodes which together represent a sequence. It is a list in which address/location of next element is embedded in the current element. They can be used to implement several other common abstract data structures including stack, queue etc.

Under the simplest form, each node is composed of a data and a reference (in other words, a link) to the next node in the sequence, more complex variants add additional links. This structure allows efficient insertion or removal of elements from any position in the sequence.

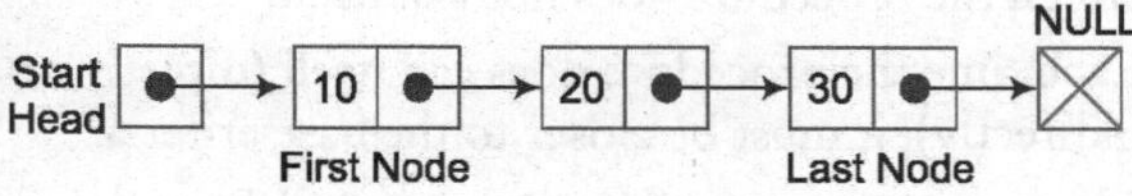

A linked list whose nodes contain two fields

(i) An integer value.
(ii) A link to the next node (link or address field).

The last node is linked to a terminator used to signify the end of the list.

6.2.5 Tree

Tree is a non-linear data structure that is used to represent data containing a hierarchical relationship between elements. e.g. records, family trees and table contents.

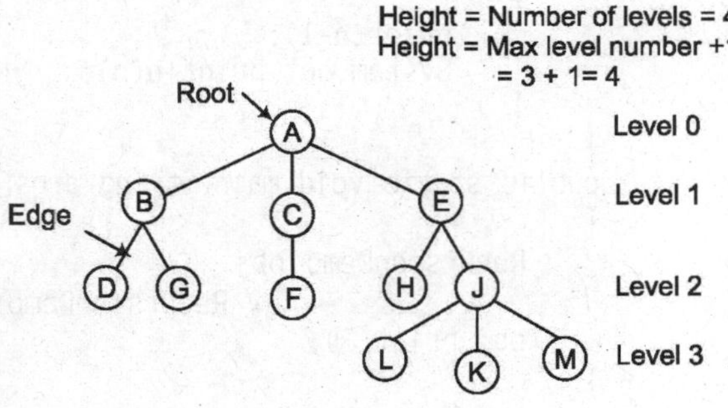

A tree diagram

For above tree, Number of level = 4

Max level number = 3

6.2.6 Binary Tree

In this kind of tree, the maximum degree of any node is at most 2. A binary tree T is defined as a finite set of elements such that:

- T is empty (called NULL tree or empty tree).

T contains a distinguished node R called the **root of** T and the remaining nodes of T form an ordered pair of disjoint binary trees T_1 and T_2.

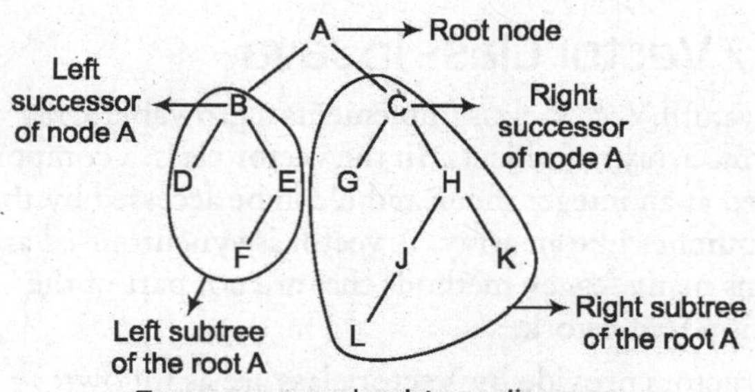

Successor and subtree diagram

Any node N in a binary tree T has either 0, 1 or 2 successors. Level r of a binary tree T can have at most 2^r nodes.

6.2.7 Balanced Binary Tree

A balanced binary tree has the minimum possible maximum height for the leaf nodes, because for any given number of leaf nodes, the leaf nodes are placed at the greatest height possible.

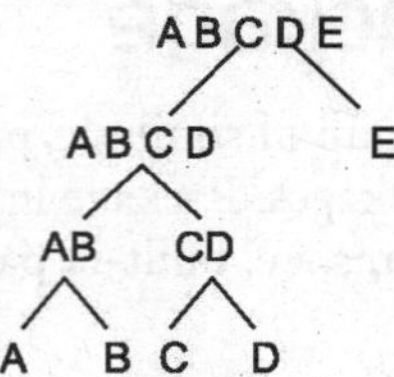

Balanced tree

One common balanced tree structure is a binary tree structure in which the left and right subtrees of every node differ in height by no more than 1. One may also consider binary trees where no leaf is much farther away from the root than any other leaf.

6.3 Exception

An exception is an event, which occurs during the execution of a program, such as invalid input or a loss of connectivity. In a program, two main types of exception such as IOException and Runtime exception.

Exception Handling

It is a construct designed to handle the occurrence of exceptions, that is special conditions that change the normal flow of program execution.

To produce high-quality programs, developers are expected to handle these exception conditions and take necessary recovery or resources-releasing actions.

C++ consists of 3 keywords for handling the exception. They are as follows:

(i) **try** try block consists of the code that may generate exception. Exception are thrown from inside the try block.

4.4.17 Vector Class in Java

The java.util.Vector class implements a growable array (dynamic array) of objects. In the vector class, a component is stored at an integer index and it can be accessed by this index number like an array. A vector is synchronised and it contains many legacy methods that are not part of the collection framework.

Constructors provide by Vector class are as follows:

Constructor	Description
Vector()	Creates a default vector, which has an initial size of 10.
Vector(int size)	Accepts an argument that equals to the required size
Vector(int size, int incr)	Creates a vector whose initial capacity is specified by size and whose increment is specified by incr.
Vector(collection C)	Creates a vector that contains the elements of collection C.

4.5 Java Package

A Java package is a group of similar types of classes, interfaces and sub-packages. Package in Java can be categorised in two forms, i.e. built-in package and user defined package.

There are many built-in packages such as, lang, awt, javax, swing, net, io, util, sql etc.

Advantages of Java Package

(i) Java package is used to categorise the classes and interfaces so that they can be easily maintained.
(ii) Java package provides access protection.
(iii) Java package removes naming collision.

e.g. The package keyword is used to create a package in Java.

```
package mypack;
public class Sample
{
    public static void main(String args[])
    {
        System.out.println("Welcome to package");
    }
}
```

How to Run Java Package Program

You need to usefully qualified name. e.g. mypack. Sample etc., to run the class.

Output

Welcome to package

4.5.1 Recursion

The idea of calling one function from another immediately suggests the possibility of a function calling itself. The function call mechanism in Java supports this possibility, which is known as recursion. A recursive method is a method that calls itself.

A recursive procedure must have the following two properties:

(i) There must be certain criteria, called **base criteria**, for which the procedure does not call itself.
(ii) Each time the procedure does call itself (directly or indirectly), it must be closer to the base criteria.

There are two types of recursion as follows:

(a) **Finite** Recursive procedure contains a valid test case.
(b) **Infinite** Recursive procedure does not contain any valid test case.

e.g.

```
public class RecursionDemo
{
    public void print(int n)
    {
        if(n<0)
            return;
        else
        {
            print(n-1);
            System.out.println(n);
        }
    }
    public static void main(String args[])
    {
        RecursionDemo obj
                = new RecursionDemo();
        obj.print(3);
    }
}
```

4.5.2 Garbage Collection

Garbage collection is done automatically by a garbage collector, which scans the references of all resident objects and removed those objects that have become orphaned. Garbage collection in the context of Java is when all references to an object are gone, the memory used by the object is automatically reclaimed.

CHAPTER PRACTICE

1. A top-down approach is also known as
(1) stepwise design
(2) top-up
(3) top-to-top design
(4) down-top design

2. In top-down approach, each module can be solved individually, thus
(1) reducing timing
(2) reducing complexity
(3) reducing memory
(4) None of the above

3. Different modules can be written by different people, thus
(1) saving memory (2) saving money
(3) saving effort (4) saving time

4. The sum of the smaller solutions will solve the overall problem. This divide and conquer approach is called
(1) top-down design
(2) bottom up design
(3) top-to-top design
(4) None of the above

5. The development of a/an .... is a key step in solving a problem.
(1) program (2) structure
(3) algorithm (4) None of these

6. Which step of an algorithm, determine both the starting and ending points for solving the problem?
(1) Analyse the problem
(2) Obtain a description of the problem
(3) Develop a high level algorithm
(4) Review the algorithm

7. What is the final step of an algorithm?
(1) Obtain a description of the problem
(2) Analyse the problem
(3) Develop a high level algorithm
(4) Review the algorithm

8. The developer must create an algorithm that will solve the ....
(1) client's questions
(2) client's confusion
(3) client's complexity
(4) client's problem

9. A .... method is a method that calls itself.
(1) calling (2) recursive
(3) structure (4) static

10. Finite recursive procedure contains a
(1) valid test case
(2) invalid test case
(3) sometime valid and sometime invalid
(4) None of the above

11. Which of the following is not a primitive data types?
(1) Byte (2) String
(3) Integer (4) Float

12. What is the range of the char type?
(1) 0 to 216 (2) 0 to 215
(3) 0 to 32767 (4) 0 to 65535

13. .... can appear anywhere in the body of a Java method.
(1) Definition (2) Declaration
(3) Determine (4) Package

14. .... must be the first non comment statement in the file.
(1) Package (2) Class
(3) Object (4) Declaration

15. .... is passed to a method by use of call by reference.
(1) Variables (2) Objects
(3) Methods (4) Operators

16. Every method of a .... is implicitly final.
(1) static class (2) dynamic class
(3) final class (4) abstract class

17. A .... object cannot be modified after it is created.
(1) double (2) int
(3) string (4) main

18. What, if anything, is wrong with following code?

```
void test(int x)
{
   switch(x)
   {
      case 1:
      case 2:
      case 0:
      default:
      case 4:
   }
}
```

(1) The variable x does not have the right type for a switch expression
(2) The case label 0 must precede case label 1
(3) Each case section must end with a break statement
(4) There is nothing wrong with the code

19. What is byte code in the context of Java?
(1) The type of code generated by a Java compiler.
(2) The type of code generated by a Java Virtual Machine.
(3) It is another name for a Java source file.
(4) It is the code written within the instance methods of a class.

20. A package is a collection of
(1) classes
(2) interfaces
(3) editing tools
(4) classes and interfaces

21. Which of these can be used to fully abstract a class from its implementation?
(1) Objects (2) Packages
(3) Interfaces (4) None of these

22. Which of these class is used to read characters in a file?
(1) FileReader
(2) FileWriter
(3) FileInputStream
(4) InputStreamReader

23. An expression involving byte, int and literal numbers is promoted to which of these?
(1) int (2) long (3) byte (4) float

24. Which of these is necessary to specify at time of array initialisation?
(1) Row
(2) Column
(3) Both row and column
(4) None of the above

25. Which data type value is returned by all transcendental math functions?
(1) int (2) float
(3) double (4) long

26. Which is a valid declaration within an interface?
(1) public static short stop= 23;
(2) protected short stop= 23;
(3) transient short stop= 23;
(4) final void start (short stop);

```
{
    clrscr();
    int a, b, sum;
    cout<<"Enter the value of a and b";
    cin>>a>>b;
    sum = a + b;
    cout<<"Sum of two numbers = "<<sum;
    getch();
}
```

Description of above program is given below:

#include<iostream.h>, #include<conio.h>

Here, '#' symbol is called *preprocessor directive*. It indicates which specified header files are included in the program.

Header files are special pre-defined files in C++ for some specified purpose. It contains the definitions of functions as well as object that is used in a program. In the given program, **<iostream.h>** is used for input/output statements such as cin and cout respectively. **<conio.h>** header file contains the definitions of clrscr( ) and getch( ) functions.

void main( )

C++ program consists of many functions, but main( ) is the most important function in C++, because it is the first execution part of a program. This function is also used to call other functions for execution. 'void' means that function will not return any value. By default, every function returns int value. Function will return one and only one value to other function. The return value can be further manipulated in other functions.

User can also define the return type such as float, char or int.

clrscr( );

This is a library function to clear the output screen.

int a, b, sum;

This line represents the declaration of three variables named 'a', 'b' and 'sum' of integer type. C++ permits declaration of variables anywhere in a program but, it should be declared before using it.

cout<<" Enter the value of a and b";

It is used to display the message on the output screen.

e.g. Enter the value of a and b

Would be displayed on the screen after the execution of the given program.

cin>>a>> b;

It extracts the input provided by user, using standard input device. Here, as soon as the user will input first integer from keyboard that will be assigned to variable 'a' and second integer will be assigned to variable 'b'.

sum = a+b;

The value of variable 'a' and variable 'b' is added and is assigned to variable 'sum'.

cout<<"Sum of two numbers =" <<sum;

This would display the message as

Sum of two numbers = include the value of sum variable, which comes out by adding the value of 'a' and 'b'.

getch( );

This is a library function used to prevent the output screen from closing until the user presses a key from keyboard.

6.7.2 C++ Basics

1. **Character Set** It is a set of valid characters that a language can recognise. A character set represents following characters:
   (i) Alphabet→ A to Z, a to z
   (ii) Digit→ 0 to 9
   (iii) Punctuators or special characters →
   + - */^\()[ ] { }@$ ' " ; : etc.
   (iv) Formatting characters → backspace, horizontal tab, vertical tab, form feed and carriage return (↵).
   (v) Other characters like 256 ASCII characters as data or literals.
2. **Tokens** It is the smallest element of a C++ program that is meaningful to the compiler. The programmer can write a program by using tokens. C++ compiler recognises these kinds of tokens as follows:
   (i) **Identifiers** An identifier is a sequence of letters and digits. The term identifiers are used to describe the name of constants, variables, functions etc. The first character must be a letter including the underscore (_). Upper and lower case letters are different. No special symbols other than underscore (_) can be used in an identifier.
   (ii) **Keywords** Keywords (also known as **reserved** or **predefined** words) have special meaning to the compiler and are always written or typed in lower case. These are reserved by the language for special purposes and cannot be redefined to use as identifiers. e.g. auto, break, if etc.
   (iii) **Literals** Literals or constants are those tokens whose value do not change during the program execution. The various literals are integer constants, character constants, floating constants and string constants.

6.7.3 C++ Operators

Operator is the term (symbol) used to describe the action to be taken between one or more data expressions. An identifier or a constant used with an operator is called an *operand.*

Some operators operate on a single operand are called *unary operators*. Some operators are indicated before operands are called *prefix operators*. The other operators indicated after operands are called *postfix operators*. Most operators are embedded between two operands are called *binary operators*. The operators that takes three operands are called *ternary operators.*

The various operators in C++ are as follows:

<table>
<tr><th>Operator's Name</th><th>Symbol</th></tr>
<tr><td>Arithmetic operators</td><td>+, –, *, /, %</td></tr>
<tr><td>Assignment operators</td><td>=, +=, –=, *=, /=, %=</td></tr>
<tr><td>Increment/Decrement operators</td><td>++, – –</td></tr>
<tr><td>Relational operators</td><td><, <=, >, >=, ==, !=</td></tr>
<tr><td>Logical operators</td><td>& &, | |, !</td></tr>
<tr><td>Conditional operators</td><td>Exp1 ? Exp2 : Exp 3</td></tr>
<tr><td>Special operators</td><td>sizeof, (,) , >>, <<</td></tr>
</table>

Precedence and Associativity

All C++ operators have two attributes. These two attributes are known as precedence and associativity. Precedence refers to the rank or urgency of an operator.

e.g. the equation a = 6 + 4 / 2 would simplify to a = 8, because the division operation has precedence over the addition and equality operations. Associativity refers to the order (direction) in which operators possessing the same precedence are to be executed.

<table>
<tr><th>Level</th><th>Operators</th><th>Kind</th><th>Associativity</th></tr>
<tr><td>Highest</td><td>: :</td><td>Unary</td><td>Both</td></tr>
<tr><td></td><td>() [] → .</td><td>Binary</td><td>Left to Right</td></tr>
<tr><td></td><td>+ ++ ! new sizeof – – –
~& delete</td><td>Unary</td><td>Right to Left</td></tr>
<tr><td></td><td>→ *, .*</td><td>Binary</td><td>Left to Right</td></tr>
<tr><td></td><td>* / %</td><td>Binary</td><td>Left to Right</td></tr>
<tr><td></td><td>+ –</td><td>Binary</td><td>Left to Right</td></tr>
<tr><td></td><td><<>></td><td>Binary</td><td>Left to Right</td></tr>
<tr><td></td><td>< <= > >=</td><td>Binary</td><td>Left to Right</td></tr>
<tr><td></td><td>== !=</td><td>Binary</td><td>Left to Right</td></tr>
<tr><td></td><td>&</td><td>Binary</td><td>Left to Right</td></tr>
<tr><td></td><td>^</td><td>Binary</td><td>Left to Right</td></tr>
<tr><td></td><td>|</td><td>Binary</td><td>Left to Right</td></tr>
<tr><td></td><td>&&</td><td>Binary</td><td>Left to Right</td></tr>
<tr><td></td><td>||</td><td>Binary</td><td>Left to Right</td></tr>
<tr><td></td><td>? :</td><td>Ternary</td><td>Left to Right</td></tr>
<tr><td></td><td>= += *= ^= &= <<=
–= /= %= != >>=</td><td>Binary</td><td>Right to Left</td></tr>
<tr><td>Lowest</td><td>,</td><td>Binary</td><td>Left to Right</td></tr>
</table>

6.7.4 Expressions

An expression may consist of one or more operands and zero or more operators to produce a value. Expressions are of six types as follows:

1. **Constant Expression** It consists of only constant values.

   e.g. `22, 275, 46/36`

2. **Integral Expression** Those expressions which produce integer results after implementing all automatic and explicit type conversions.

   e.g. `X*Y-11, (X + Y) - Z, 45 + X + int (2.5)`

3. **Float Expression** Those expressions which produce floating point results after all conversions.

   e.g. `(X+Y)/37, 37+float (16)/11`

4. **Pointer Expression** It produces a memory address values.

   e.g. `&X`

5. **Boolean Expression** These are constructed with the help of logical and relational operators.

   e.g. `a <= b , x >= y etc.`

6. **Compound Expression** These are made up of two or more expressions with the help of operators.

   e.g. `(a + b)||(c + d)`

6.7.5 C++ Comments

A comment is a text that the compiler ignores, but that is useful for programmers. Comments are normally used to annotate code for future reference. The compiler treats them as white space.

A C++ comment is written in one of the following ways:

(i) The /* (slash, asterisk) characters, followed by any sequence of characters (including new lines), followed by the */ (asterisk, slash) characters is called **multi line comment.**

(ii) The // (two slashes) characters, followed by any sequence of characters is called a **single line comment.** A new line not immediately preceded by a backslash terminates this form of comment.

6.7.6 Data Types in C++

Data types refer to the type of data used in the program. C++ supports a variety of data types and programmer can select the appropriate data type as per the need of the application.

63. In Java, elements of an array are automatically initialised to some default value. What is the default value for the elements of an array of integers?

(1) 0 (2) " 0 "
(3) null (4) 1

64. You want to initialise all of the elements of a double array a to the same value equal to 1.5. What could you write? Assume that the array has been correctly initialised.

(1) for(int i=1; i<a.length; i++)
a [i] = 1.5;
(2) for(int i=0; i<=a.length; i++)
a [i] = 1.5;
(3) for(int i=0; i<a.length; i++)
a [i] = 1.5;
(4) for(int i=0; i<a.length+1; i++)
a[i] = 1.5;

65. Consider the code

```
int[] x = {5,6,7,8,9};
int[] y=x;
y[2]= 10;
```

What is the value of x[2]?

(1) 6 (2) 7
(3) 10 (4) 8

66. Consider the following piece of code:

```
int i;
for(i=0; i<10; i++)
{
  /* some code that doesn't
  modify i */
}
System.out.println("i="+i);
/* line A */
```

What is printed by the statement on line A?

(1) i=0 (2) i=9
(3) i=10 (4) i=11

67. Which of the following while statements is equivalent to

```
do
{
  y=x+7;
  x++;
}while(x<9);
```

(1)
```
y=x+7;
x++;
while (x < 9)
{
    y = x + 7;
    x++;
}
```

(2)
```
while(x<9)
{
  y=x+7;
  x++;
}
y =x+7;
x++;
```

(3)
```
while (x<=9)
{
  y=x+7;
  x++;
}
```

(4) Both 1 and 2

68. What is printed by the following code fragment?

```
int []a= {0,1,2,3,4,5,6};
System.out.println(a.length);
```

(1) 5 (2) 6
(3) 7 (4) 8

69. How would you declare and initialise an array, palette of Color objects of size 6?

(1) Color palette = new color [5];
(2) Color palette [6];
(3) Color[5] palette;
(4) Color[ ] palette = new Color [6];

70. The documentation of a class lists a method castToIntArray that has a double array as a formal parameter and returns an array of integers. What is the signature of the method?

(1) public void castToIntArray (double [ ]a)
(2) public [ ] castToIntArray (double a)
(3) public int castToIntArray (double a)
(4) public int[ ] castToIntArray (double [ ]a)

71. From the following Java code determine the attributes of the class student:

```
class student
{
        string name;
        int marks;
}
public static void main()
{
    student S1=new student();
    student S2= new student();
}
```

(1) Only name
(2) Both name and marks
(3) Only S1
(4) Both S1 and S2

72. You read the following statement in a Java program that compiles and executes.

```
submarine.dive(depth);
```

What can you say for sure?

(1) depth must be an int
(2) dive must be a method
(3) dive must be the name of an instance field.
(4) submarine must be the name of a class

73. Analyse the following code:

```
public class Test
{
  public static void main
            (String []args)
  {
     int[] x = new int[5];
     int i;
     for(i=0 ; i<x.length; i++)
        x[i] = i;
     System.out.println(x[i]);
  }
}
```

(1) The program displays 0 1 2 3 4
(2) The program displays 4
(3) The program has a runtime error because the last statement in the main method causes ArrayIndexOutOfBounds Exception
(4) The program has syntax error because i is not defined in the last statement in the main method

74. What will be the output of the program?

```
class A
{
 int x=10;
 public void assign(int x)
 {
   x=x;
   System.out.println(this.x);
 }
 public static void main(String [] args)
 {
   new A()
 }
}
```

(1) 10
(2) No output
(3) 0
(4) Compile time error

75. Which statement does not create an object of class Student {}?

(1) new Student ();

(2) Student s1= new Student ();
s2= new Student ();

(3) Student s1;

(4) Student ss = new Student ();

76. What is the output of this program?

```
class bitwise_operator
{
  public static void main
                (String args[])
  {
    int var1 = 42;
    int var2 = ~var1;
    System.out.print(var1 +
                " "+ var2);
  }
}
```

(1) 42 43 (2)42-43

(3) 42 42 (4) 42-42

77. Which of these combinations of switch expression types and case label value types are legal within a switch statement?

(1) switch expression of type int and case label value of type int

(2) switch expression of type float and case label value of type int

(3) switch expression of type byte and case label value of type float

(4) switch expression of type char and case label value of type long

78. What will be printed as the output of the following program?

```
public class testincr
{
  public static void main
                (String args[])
  {
    int i = 0;
    i = i ++ + i;
    System.out.println("I="+i);
  }
}
```

(1) I=0 (2) I=1

(3) I=2 (4) I=3

79. Given the following code, which statement is true?

```
class MyClass
{
  public static void
  main(String[] args)
  {
    int k=0;
    int l=0;
    for(int i=0;i<=3;i++)
    {
      k++;
      if(i==2)
      break;
      l++;
    }
    System.out.println(k+","+l);
  }
}
```

(1) The program will fail to compile

(2) The program will print 3, 3 when run

(3) The program will print 4, 3 when run if break is replaced by continue

(4) The program will fail to compile if break is replaced by return

80. Consider

```
public class MyClass
{
  public MyClass (){/*code*/}
  // more code ...
}
```

To instantiate MyClass, you would write?

(1) MyClass mc = new MyClass();

(2) MyClass mc = MyClass();

(3) MyClass mc = MyClass;

(4) MyClass mc = new Myclass;

ANSWER KEY

1	(1)	2	(2)	3	(4)	4	(1)	5	(3)	6	(1)	7	(4)	8	(4)	9	(2)	10	(1)
11	(2)	12	(4)	13	(2)	14	(1)	15	(2)	16	(3)	17	(3)	18	(4)	19	(1)	20	(4)
21	(3)	22	(1)	23	(1)	24	(1)	25	(3)	26	(1)	27	(3)	28	(3)	29	(1)	30	(3)
31	(2)	32	(4)	33	(4)	34	(2)	35	(2)	36	(1)	37	(3)	38	(1)	39	(3)	40	(2)
41	(3)	42	(1)	43	(1)	44	(2)	45	(3)	46	(4)	47	(1)	48	(3)	49	(2)	50	(3)
51	(2)	52	(3)	53	(4)	54	(2)	55	(4)	56	(1)	57	(2)	58	(3)	59	(3)	60	(2)
61	(2)	62	(2)	63	(1)	64	(3)	65	(3)	66	(3)	67	(1)	68	(3)	69	(4)	70	(4)
71	(2)	72	(2)	73	(3)	74	(1)	75	(3)	76	(2)	77	(1)	78	(2)	79	(3)	80	(1)

The switch statement uses one or more case labels, each specifying a different constant to be compared to the expression. If no matches found, the default block will be executed. Each label ends with a colon (:). The expression is typically a variable name but it could be a function.

⚠ **break statement** is used to terminate execution of the loop or switch block and it will transfer the control to very next statement after the loop body or switch body.

3. Looping or Iteration Statements

Sometimes, there is a need to repeat a group of statements a number of times. Iteration statements allow a set of instructions to be performed repeatedly until a certain condition is fulfilled. Iteration continues till the loop's test condition becomes false.

C++ provides four types of iteration or loop statements as follows:

(i) **for Loop** This loop is used when we have prior knowledge of how many times the particular group of statements is to be executed. It causes statement block to be executed for fixed number of times. This loop is called an **entry control loop** because condition is checked before entering into the scope of the loop.

Syntax

```
for(expression1; expression2; expression3)
{
    statement block;
}
```

- expression1, is the initialisation part.
- expression2, is the test expression or condition.
- expression3, is update or increment/decrement expression.

(ii) **while Loop** In this loop, when a statement to be repeated till a particular condition turns false.

Syntax

```
while(condition)
{
    statement;
}
```

The condition must evaluate to a true or false. While the condition is true, the program repeatedly executes statement. Sooner or later condition must become false, so the loop ends.

(iii) **do-while Loop** This loop allows its body of instructions to be executed one or more times. A do-while loop always executes atleast once. The body of the do statement continues to execute as long as the result of the condition in the while statement remains true. This loop is often called as **exit control loop.** The do-while loop is the flip side of a while loop.

Syntax

```
do
{
    statement;
}   while(condition);
```

The only difference between while and do-while is that do-while statement executes the statement first and then evaluates condition.

Nested Loops

Any loop statement can be nested with in any other loop statement. We can say that a loop may contain another loop in its body. This form of a loop is called nested loop. In nested loop, two loops, i.e. inner loop and outer loop are executed. But the inner loop must terminate before the outer loop.

4. Jump Statements

The jump statements unconditionally transfer program control within a function. The various jump statements are as follows:

(i) **goto Statement** This statement is used to alter the program execution sequence by transferring the control to some other part of the program.

Syntax

```
goto label;
```

Here, the label is a C++ identifier used to label the destination, where the control is to be transferred the target statement will appear as

```
{
   label:statement;
}
```

(ii) **continue Statement** This statement jumps over all the rest of statements in the loop's block and goes to the next statement after the loop. The continue statement does the same thing except that, instead of terminating the loop, it goes back to the beginning of the loop's block to continue the iteration and ignores the rest of loop.

Syntax

```
continue;
```

Subtyping

Subtyping is a method for substitution and code reuse used in object oriented programming languages to prevent unnecessary copying of largely similar code and promote code readability and prevent bugs. A subtype is basically a substitute for a supertype that can fulfill all of the latter's specifications and then some.

A type B is a subtype of A, if every function that can be invoked on an object of type A can also be invoked on an object of type B.

6.7.11 Functions

A function is a self-contained block of statements, which are kept together to perform a specific task in related manner. A function has a name and it has a property, i.e. reusable. It can be executed from as many different points in a C ++ program as required. In C++, the main( ) itself is a function that means the main function is invoking the other functions to perform various tasks.

There are two types of functions in C++ are as follows:

Library Functions

Library functions are the predefined functions in programming system. These are also known as **in-built functions** Some of the library or in-built functions according to their header files are described below:

Header File	Functions
stdio.h (Standard input and output)	char gets(char str[ ]) int puts(char str[ ]) int getc(char str[ ]) int get( ) char getchar( )
ctype.h (Character tests)	int isalnum(int i) int isalpha(int i) int isdigit(int i) int islower(int i) int isupper(int i) int tolower(int i) int toupper(int i)
string.h (String operations)	char strcpy(char str1[ ], char str2[ ]) char strcat(char str1[ ], str2[ ]) int strlen(char str[ ]) int strcmp(char str1[ ], str2[ ]) int strcmpi(char str1[ ], char str2[ ]) char strrev(char str[ ]) char strupr(char str[ ]) char strlwr(char str[ ])
math.h (Mathematical functions)	double fabs(double x) double pow(double x, double y) double sqrt(double x) double sin(double x) double cos(double x) int abs(int x) double log(double or float x) double frexp(double x, int y) double exp(double x)
stdlib.h (Standard library functions)	int random(int num) randomize( )

User Defined Functions

C++ provides facility for programmers to define their own functions according to their requirements. The functions defined by programmers are known as user defined functions.

To add a user defined function in the program, there are three necessary components as given here:

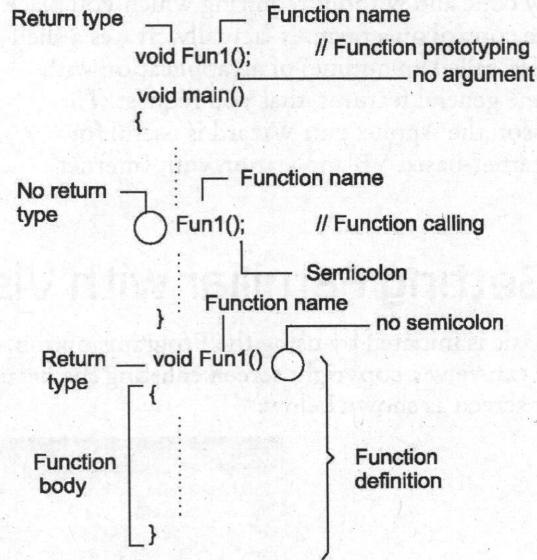

(i) Function Prototyping

It describes the function interface to the compiler by giving details such as the name of function, number and type of arguments and the type of return values.

Basically, each user defined function needs to be declared before its usage in the program. This declaration is called as **function prototype** or **function declaration**. The function prototype can be given anywhere in the program, i.e. inside or outside of any function of the program.

Function prototype is a declaration statement in the program and is of the following form:

```
return_type function_name(datatype arg1. datatype
                arg2, .... datatype argN);
```

Here,

- The return_type refers to type of value,
- The function_name can be any name,
- arg1, arg2, ..., argN are called **formal arguments** or **formal parameters** as they simply represent the name of the data items that are transferred to the function from the calling function.

6. **Addin** These are tools that you create programmatically using objects and collections in the extensibility model to customize and extend the Visual Basic environment. In a sense, add-ins "snap on" to the Visual Basic Integrated Development Environment (IDE).
7. **VB Application Wizard** It helps you to build applications without requiring that you write any code and without requiring which you place one control on a form. It actually creates a shell (also called an outline) of an application with some general features that you request. The reason the Application Wizard is useful for Internet-based VB application with Internet access that you then can complete with your own specifics to behave exactly the way you need.
8. **IIS Application** An IIS (Internet Information Sever) application is a VB application that lives on a web server and responds to requests from the browser. An IIS application uses HTML to present its user interface and uses compiled Visual Basic code to process requests and respond to events in the browser.
9. **DHTML Application** This application is a group of HTML pages that work together to perform a business process. You write Visual Basic code to handle events that occur when these pages are viewed in the browser. You can respond to events that occur on any element on the page-from clicking a button to loading an image to passing the mouse over a certain part of the page.

5.3 Getting Familiar with Visual Basic User Interface

Visual Basic is initiated by using the Programs option → Microsoft Visual Basic → Visual Basic. Clicking the Visual Basic icon, we can view a copyright screen enlisting the details of the license holder of the copy of Visual Basic. Then, it opens in to a new screen as shown below:

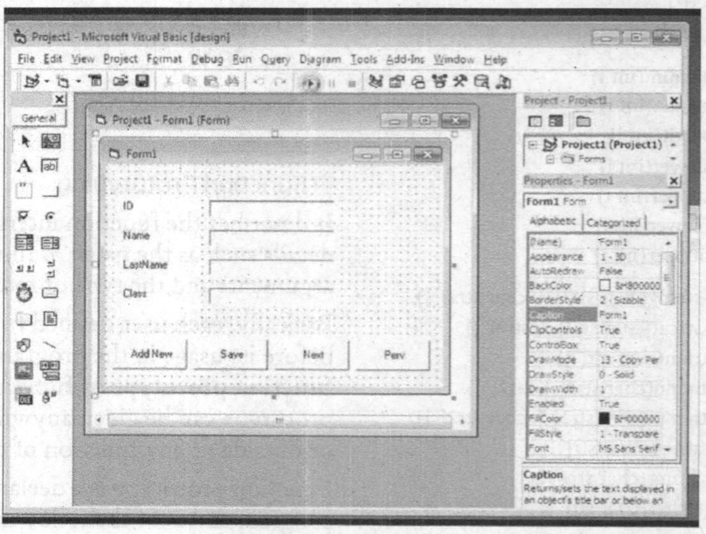

Menu Bar

The menu bar or pull down menus is dynamic, which means items are added or removed depending on what you are trying to do. It displays the commands that are required to build an application. The main menu item have sub menu items that can be chosen when needed.

Menu bar contains various tabs, some of them are as follows:

1. **File** It has become the standard where you should find, if nothing else, a way to exit the application. In this bar, you can also find ways of opening and closing single files and whole projects.
2. **Edit** This menu provides access to the common items you would expect: Undo, Redo, Cut, Copy, Paste and Delete.
3. **View** This menu provides quick access to the windows that exist in the IDE, such as the Solution Explorer, Properties window, Output window, Toolbox and so on.
4. **Project** This menu enables you to add various files to your application, such as forms and classes.
5. **Debug** This menu enables you to start and stop running your application within the Visual Basic IDE.

6. **Tools** This menu has commands to configure the Visual Studio IDE, as well as links to other external tools that may have been installed.
7. **Window** This menu has become standard for any application that allows more than one window to be open at a time. The commands on this menu enable you to switch between the windows in the IDE.
8. **Help** This menu provides access to the Visual Studio documentation. There are many different ways to access this information (e.g. through the Help contents, an index or a search).

Toolbars

Many toolbars are available within the IDE, including Formatting, Image Editor and Text Editor, which you can add to and remove from the IDE through the View → Toolbars menu option. Each one provides quick access to frequently used commands, preventing you from having to navigate through a series of menu options.

Toolbox

The toolbox is accessed through the View → Toolbox menu option, by clicking the Toolbox icon on the Standard menu bar or by pressing Ctrl+Alt+X. Alternatively, the toolbox tab is displayed on the left of the IDE; brings your mouse over this tab will cause the Toolbox window to fly out, partially covering your form.

Tools in the Visual Basic Toolbox

Icon	Tool Name	What This Tools Does
	Pointer	Selects objects
	PictureBox	Draws a box to display graphics
A	Label	Draws a box to display text
abl	TextBox	Draws a box that can display text and let the user type in text
	Frame	Groups two or more objects together
	CommandButton	Draws a command button
	CheckBox	Draws a check box
	OptionButton (or Radio Button)	Draws a radio button
	ComboBox	Draws a combo box
	ListBox	Draws a list box
	HScrollBar	Draws a horizontal scroll bar
	VScrollBar	Draws a vertical scroll bar
	Timer	Places a timer on a form
	DriveListBox	Draws a drive list box that displays all the disk drives available
	DirListBox	Draws a directory list box that displays a directory on a particular disk drive
	FileListBox	Draws a file list box that displays files in a specific directory
	Shape	Draws a geometric shape such as a circle or a square
	Line	Draws a straight line
	Image	Draws a box to display graphics but less capability than the PictureBox
	Data	Draws a control to link a program to a database file
OLE	OLE	Draws a box to insert an OLE object

Project Explorer

It is a list of the forms and modules for the current projects. It is a hierarchical tree-branch structure, where the project at top of tree and other parts like forms, modules descend from this tree.

Properties Window

It is a list of properties settings for a selected form or a control. These properties are characteristics (such as size, visible or color) of the selected object. It provides an easy way to set properties.

Form Layout Window

The Form Layout Window is a small screen, which is used to reposition the form of the application so that it appears in proper place when project is run.

Form

The form is the most important visible object, without it no control can be displayed. It is a window that can be designed and modified to fit user applications.

Immediate Window

It is used to debug and evaluate expressions, execute statements, print variable values and so forth. It allows you to enter expressions to be evaluated or executed by the development language during debugging.

Code Editor Window

It is used to write a VB code for an application. For each form, there is a separate code editor window. It is displayed when user clicks on form or object in form.

Opening the Visual Basic IDE Window

When you run the Visual Basic set-up program, it allows you to place the program items in an existing program group or create a new program group and new program items for

26. Which of the following term is related to the stack?
(1) TOP (2) PUSH
(3) POP (4) All of these

27. Stack is also called ....
(1) First In First Out (FIFO)
(2) Last In First Out (LIFO)
(3) First In Last Out (FILO)
(4) First Come First Served (FCFS)

28. Stack is useful for implementing
(1) recursion
(2) breadth first search
(3) depth first search
(4) Both (1) and (3)

29. Which of the following name does not related to stacks?
(1) FIFO lists (2) LIFO lists
(3) Piles (4) Push down lists

30. Queue serves a major role in
(1) simulation of recursion
(2) simulation of arbitrary linked list
(3) simulation of limited resource allocation
(4) expression evaluation

31. In queue, an element can be inserted and deleted by using
(1) rear and front
(2) front and rear
(3) top
(4) None of the above

32. Queue can be used to implement
(1) radix sort
(2) quick sort
(3) recursion
(4) depth first search

33. Insert operation on queue has to be done after testing
(1) overflow
(2) memory space
(3) underflow
(4) no need to test anything

34. Which of the following is appropriate to represent a queue?
(1) a circular linked list
(2) doubly linked list
(3) linear link list
(4) None of the above

35. In a linked list
(i) **each link contains a pointer to the next link**
(ii) **an array of pointers point to the links**
(iii) **each link containing data or pointer to data**
(iv) **the links are stored in an array**

Which of the following is correct?
(1) (i) and (iii) (2) Only (i)
(3) Only (iii) (4) (ii) and (iv)

36. Which is true about linked list?
(1) A list is a dynamic structure
(2) A list is a static structure having variable storage
(3) A stack cannot be implemented by linear linked list
(4) Both (1) and (2)

37. Linked list uses null pointer to signal
(1) end of the list
(2) beginning of the list
(3) Middle of the list
(4) Neither (1) nor (2)

38. A list with no nodes is called
(1) error list (2) empty list
(3) unique lis (4) None of these

39. In a linked list, an element can be inserted to or deleted from
(1) front of the list only
(2) end of the list only
(3) middle of the list only
(4) All of the above

40. Linked list can be used to implement
(1) stack
(2) queue
(3) Both (1) and (2)
(4) Neither (1) nor (2)

41. Which one is true about binary search tree?
(1) Key of every node of right sub-tree of tree is greater than the root
(2) Key of every node in the left sub-tree of tree is less than the key at the root
(3) Both of them are true
(4) None of the above

42. The address field of linked list
(1) contains address of the next node
(2) contains address of next pointer
(3) may contain NULL character
(4) Both (1) and (3)

43. Through linked list one can implement
(1) stack (2) graph
(3) queue (4) All of these

44. Linked lists are best suited
(1) for relatively permanent collections of data
(2) for the size of the structure and the data in the structure are constantly changing
(3) Both (1) and (2)
(4) None of the above

45. A binary tree with 20 nodes has ...... branch.
(1) 21 (2) 17 (3) 19 (4) 10

46. Which of the following sorting algorithms uses recursion?
(1) Insertion sort
(2) Heap sort
(3) Merge sort
(4) Bubble sort

47. Recursive procedures is implement using
(1) string
(2) queue
(3) stack
(4) linked list

48. The postfix expression for the infix expression ((A + B) * (C + D)) / (F + D * E) is
(1) (AB + CD + * F) / D + E*
(2) (AB CD * + F) / (+DE * +)
(3) (A * B + CD) / F * DE + +
(4) None of the above

49. Binary search algorithm cannot be applied to
(1) sorted linked list
(2) sorted binary trees
(3) sorted linear array
(4) pointer array

50. The infix notation for the postfix notation ABC + * D/ is
(1) A * (B + C) / D
(2) / * A + B C D
(3) A * B C + / D
(4) A * / B C + D

51. Finding the location of the element with a given value is
(1) traversal
(2) search
(3) sort
(4) None of the above

52. Which of the following sorting algorithm is of divide and conquer type?
(1) Bubble sort
(2) Insertion sort
(3) Quick sort
(4) All of the above

53. Which of the following structure is FIFO (First In First Out)?
(1) Stack (2) Array
(3) Queue (4) Graph

54. The postfix equivalent of the prefix * + ab − cd is
(1) ab + cd − * (2) abcd + − *
(3) ab + cd * − (4) a b + − cd *

55. The postfix form of A$B * C − D / E / F (G + H) is
(1) AB $C * D − EF / GH+ / +
(2) AB $ * C − D + EF / GH / +
(3) AB$ * C + D − EF / GH / * +
(4) AB$C − D * EF / GH / + +

56. The memory address of the first element of an array is called
(1) floor address
(2) foundation address
(3) first address
(4) base address

57. Which of the following is not a limitation of binary search algorithm?
(1) must use a sorted array
(2) requirement of sorted array is expensive when a lot of insertion and deletions are needed
(3) there must be a mechanism to access middle element directly
(4) binary search algorithm is not efficient when the data elements are more than 1000.

58. Each data item in a record may be a group item composed of sub-items; those items which are indecomposable are called
(1) elementary items
(2) atoms
(3) scalars
(4) All of the above

59. The difference between linear array and a record is
(1) An array is suitable for homogeneous data but the data items in a record may have different data type
(2) In a record, there may not be a natural ordering in opposed to linear array.
(3) A record form a hierarchical structure but a linear array does not
(4) All of the above

60. Type of search in which record is checked and read for desired items in file is classified as
(1) search
(2) linear research
(3) linear search
(4) quadratic search

61. Arrangement of data into a specific order is classified as
(1) sorting (2) ordering
(3) learning (4) enquiring

62. Pick the odd one out
(1) array type
(2) character type
(3) boolean type
(4) integer type

63. The value 132.54 can represented using which data type?
(1) double
(2) void
(3) int
(4) bool

64. What are the parts of the literal constants?
(1) Integer numerals
(2) Floating-point numerals
(3) Strings and boolean values
(4) All of the mentioned

65. Which operator is having right to left associativity in the following?
(1) Array subscripting
(2) Function call
(3) Addition and subtraction
(4) Type cast

66. The if..else statement can be replaced by which operator?
(1) Bitwise operator
(2) Conditional operator
(3) Multiplicative operator
(4) None of the mentioned

67. The destination statement for the goto label is identified by what label?
(1) $ (2) @
(3) * (4) :

68. What is a comment in C++?
(1) Comments are parts of the source code disregarded by the compiler
(2) Comments are executed by compiler to find the meaning of the comment
(3) Comments are executable
(4) None of the mentioned

69. Which looping process is best used when the number of iterations is known?
(1) for
(2) while
(3) do-while
(4) all looping processes require that the iterations be known

70. Where does the execution of the program starts?
(1) User-defined function
(2) main function
(3) void function
(4) None of the mentioned

71. What are mandatory parts in function declaration?
(1) Return type, function name
(2) Return type, function name, parameters
(3) Parameters
(4) Function name

72. How many minimum numbers of functions are need to be presented in C++?
(1) 0 (2) 1
(3) 2 (4) 3

73. Consider the situation in which assignment operation is very costly. Which of the following sorting algorithm should be performed so that the number of assignment operations is minimized in general?
(1) Insertion sort
(2) Selection sort
(3) Heap sort
(4) None of the above

74. Assume that the operators +, −, *, are left associative and ^ is right associative. The order of precedence is ^, *, +, −. The postfix expression corresponding to the infix expression a + b* c − d ^ e ^ f is
(1) abc * + def ^ ^ −
(2) abc * + de ^f^
(3) ab + c * d − e ^ f ^
(4) abc * + de ^ f ^

75. Which of the following is true about the characteristics of abstract data types?
(i) It exports a type
(ii) It exports a set of operations
(1) True, False (2) False, True
(3) True, True (4) False, False

76. Which of the following keyword is used to declare the header file?
(1) include (2) exclude
(3) string (4) namespace

77. Which of the following header files is required for creating and reading data files?
(1) ofstream.h (2) fstream.h
(3) ifstream.h (4) console.h

78. The best data structure, to check whether an arithmetic expression has balanced parentheses or not, is a
(1) queue (2) stack
(3) tree (4) list

You can also combine variables of the same data type on one line

e.g. Dim total, firstnum As Integer.

Unlike other programming languages, Visual Basic actually doesn't require you to specifically declare a variable before it's used. If a variable is not declared, VB will automatically declare the variable as a Variant. A variant is data type that can hold any type of data.

Scope of Variables

Other than using the Dim keyword to declare the data, you can also use other keywords to declare the data. Three other keywords are private, static and public. The forms are as shown below:

```
Private VariableName As Datatype
Static VariableName As Datatype
Public VariableName As Datatype
```

The above keywords indicate the scope of declaration. **Private** declares a local variable or a variable that is local to a procedure or module. However, Private is rarely used, we normally use Dim to declare a local variable. The **Static** keyword declares a variable that is being used multiple times, even after a procedure has been terminated. Most variables created inside a procedure are discarded by Visual Basic when the procedure is finished, Static keyword preserves the value of a variable even after the procedure is terminated. **Public** is the keyword that declares a global variable, which means it can be used by all the procedures and modules of the whole program.

Assigning Values to Variables

After declaring various variables using the Dim statements, we can assign values to those variables.

Syntax

```
Variable=Expression
```

The variable can be declared variable or a control property value. The expression could be a mathematical expression, a number, a string, a boolean value (True or False) and more.

e.g.
```
firstNumber=100
secondNumber = firstNumber-99
```

5.8 Concept of Menus

You must have seen the various menus Visual Basic has. Some menus items perform an action directly; e.g. the Exit menu item on the File menu closes the application. Other menu items display a dialog box-a window that requires the user to supply information needed by the application to perform the action. These menu items should be followed by an ellipsis (.....). e.g. when you choose Save As.... from the File menu, the Save File As dialog box appears.

Pop-up Menus

Pop-up menus are sometimes referred to as **speed menus, right-click menus** or **context menus.** A pop-up menu is a floating menu that is displayed over a form, independent of the menu bar. The items displayed on the pop-up menu depend on where the pointer was located when the right mouse button was pressed.

Shortcut Menus

It appears when the user right-clicks a selection, toolbar, or taskbar button. The shortcut menu lists commands pertaining to that screen region or selection only.

5.9 Menu Editor

Menu Editor utility of VB can be accessed from Tools menu in the forms design screen. This utility is used for creating menus. It allows you to create custom menus for your application and to define their properties. Menus contain a list of related commands when you click a menu title in a Windows-based program, a list of menu commands should always appear in a well organised list.

5.9.1 Creating Menu Editor

To start the Menu Editor,

Click on **Tools → Menu Editor**

or

Click the Menu Editor button on the toolbar.

The Menu Editor appears, as shown in fig:

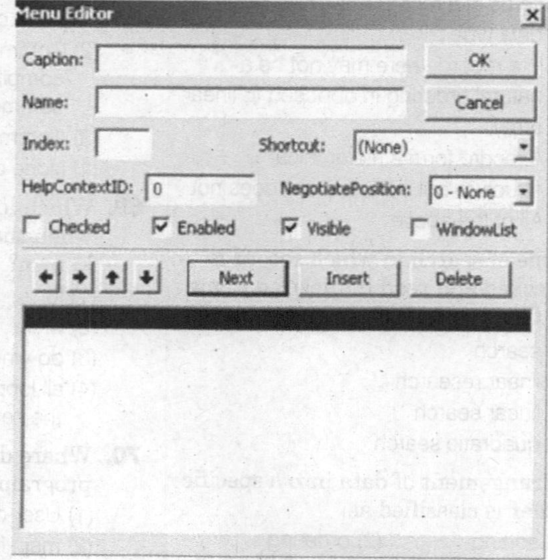

5.9.2 Menu Editor Dialog Box Options

1. **Caption** Allows you to enter the menu or command name that you want to appear on your menu bar or in a menu. If you want to create a separator bar in your menu, you can type a single hyphen(-) in the Caption box.
2. **Name** Allows you to enter a control name for the menu item. A control name is an identifier used only to access the menu item in code, it dose not appear in a menu.
3. **Index** Allows you to assign a numeric value that determines the control's position within a control array. This position is not related to the screen position.
4. **Shortcut** Allows you to select a shortcut key for each command.
5. **HelpContextID** Allows you to assign a unique numeric value for the context ID. This value is used to find the appropriate Help topic in the help file identified by the HelpFile property.
6. **NegotiatePosition** Allows you to select the menu's NegotiatePosition property. This property determines whether and how the menu appears in a container form.
7. **Checked** Allows you to have a check mark appear initially at the left of a menu item. It is generally used to indicate whether a toggle option is turned ON or OFF.
8. **Enabled** Allows you to select whether you want the menu item to respond to events or clear if you want the item to be unavailable and appear dimmed.
9. **Visible** Allows you to have the menu item appear on the menu.
10. **WindowsList** Determines if the menu control contains a list of open MDI child forms in an MDI application.
11. **Right Arrow** Moves the selected menu down one level each time you click it. You can create up to four levels of submenus.
12. **Left Arrow** Moves the selected menu up one level each time you click it. You can create up to four levels of submenus.
13. **Up Arrow** Moves the selected menu item up one position within the same menu level each time you click it.
14. **Down Arrow** Moves the selected menu item down one position within the same menu level each time you click it.
15. **Menu List** A list box that displays a hierarchical list of menu items. Submenu items are indented to indicate their hierarchical position of level.
16. **Next** Move selection to the next line.
17. **Insert** Inserts a line in the list box above the currently selected line.
18. **Delete** Deletes the currently selected line.
19. **OK** Closes the Menu Editor and applies all changes to the last form you selected. The menu is available at design time, but selecting a menu at design time opens the Code windows for that menu's Click event rather than executing any event code.
20. **Cancel** Closes the Menu Editor and cancels all changes.

5.9.3 To Create Menu Controls in the Menu Editor

(i) Select the form.

(ii) From the **Tools** menu, choose **Menu Editor.**

(iii) In the **Caption** text box, type the text for the first menu title. Also, place an ampersand (&) before the letter you want to be the access key for that menu item. This letter will automatically be underlined in the menu.
The menu title text is displayed in the menu control list box.

(iv) In the **Name** text box, type the name for menu control in code.

(v) Click the left arrow or right arrow button to change the indentation level of the control.

(vi) Set other properties for the control, if you choose. You can do this in the Menu Editor or later, in the **Properties** window.

(vii) Choose **Next** to create another menu control.

or

Click **Insert** to add a menu control between existing controls.

You can also click the up arrow and down arrow buttons to move the control among the existing menu controls.

(viii) When you have created all the menu controls for that form, choose **OK** to close the Menu Editor.
The menu titles you create are displayed on the form. At design time, click a menu title to drop down its corresponding menu items.

```
int a = 10;
if(a < 10)
{       for(i = 0; i
                < 10; i++)
        cout<<i;
}
else
{
        cout<<i;
}
}
```

(1) 0123456789 (2) 123456789
(3) 0 (4) error

110. **What is the output of the following C++ program?**

```
#include<iostream.h>
void main()
{
    int a;
    a = 5 + 3 * 5;
    cout<<a;
}
```

(1) 35 (2) 20
(3) 25 (4) 30

111. **What is the output of this program?**

```
#include<iostream.h>
int max(int a, int b)
{
        return( a > b ? a : b );
}
void main()
{
        int i = 5;
        int j = 7;
        cout<< max(i, j );
}
```

(1) 5
(2) 7
(3) Either (1) or (2)
(4) 12

ANSWER KEY

1	(4)	2	(4)	3	(4)	4	(3)	5	(3)	6	(4)	7	(1)	8	(3)	9	(4)	10	(1)
11	(2)	12	(1)	13	(3)	14	(3)	15	(4)	16	(1)	17	(3)	18	(1)	19	(2)	20	(3)
21	(2)	22	(4)	23	(4)	24	(4)	25	(3)	26	(4)	27	(2)	28	(4)	29	(1)	30	(3)
31	(1)	32	(1)	33	(1)	34	(1)	35	(1)	36	(2)	37	(1)	38	(2)	39	(4)	40	(3)
41	(3)	42	(2)	43	(4)	44	(2)	45	(1)	46	(2)	47	(3)	48	(4)	49	(1)	50	(1)
51	(2)	52	(3)	53	(3)	54	(1)	55	(1)	56	(4)	57	(4)	58	(4)	59	(4)	60	(3)
61	(1)	62	(1)	63	(1)	64	(4)	65	(4)	66	(2)	67	(4)	68	(1)	69	(1)	70	(2)
71	(1)	72	(2)	73	(2)	74	(1)	75	(3)	76	(1)	77	(2)	78	(2)	79	(1)	80	(1)
81	(2)	82	(2)	83	(2)	84	(2)	85	(1)	86	(2)	87	(2)	88	(2)	89	(2)	90	(2)
91	(3)	92	(1)	93	(1)	94	(3)	95	(2)	96	(3)	97	(3)	98	(1)	99	(1)	100	(2)
101	(3)	102	(1)	103	(3)	104	(2)	105	(2)	106	(1)	107	(1)	108	(1)	109	(4)	110	(2)
111	(2)																		

CHAPTER

07

OOP With C++

C++ is the superset of the C programming language that supports both procedural and object oriented programming. The object oriented programming approach has attempted to handle the large complexities in programs giving more reliable, clear and easily maintainable products. C++ is today's dominant Object Oriented Programming (OOP) language due to its striking features like data abstraction, encapsulation, polymorphism, inheritance etc.

OOP approach binds the data and the functions (that operate on that data) into a single entity, such an entity is called object. Functions of an object can only access its data. Thus, object oriented programming language model around 'objects' rather than 'actions' and 'data' rather than 'logic'.

7.1 Concepts of Object Oriented Programming

Different people interpret the concept of object oriented programming differently. The care of the pure object oriented programming is to create an object that has certain properties and methods. There are a few principle concepts that form the foundation of OOP.

1. Objects

In object oriented programming, a program is divided into objects. In our daily life, we come across a number of objects. Some examples are TV, telephone, car, computer, table, chair etc.

Each object has the following two characteristics:

(i) **State or Attribute** The state or attribute refers to the built-in characteristics of an object. e.g. a colour TV has the following attributes:
(a) Volume control (b) Picture control (c) 75 channels (d) Remote control unit

(ii) **Behaviour or Operation** The operation of an object refers to its action. e.g. a TV can have following operations:
(a) Switched ON (b) Switched OFF (c) Display pictures

⚠ Object is also an entity or instance which have some characteristics and behaviour of a class.

2. Classes

A class is a group of objects that share common properties and behaviours. Classes are user defined data types and behave like the built-in types of a programming language. Objects are variables of the type class. e.g. a class Fruit has mango, apple and banana as objects. Classes are the basic building blocks of object oriented programming.

3. Data Abstraction

Abstraction refers to the act of representing essential features of real world concept without including the background details. e.g. a TV user can switch ON the TV set and enjoy the various TV programs or they can switch from one channel to another for selecting the desired TV program without knowing its complete technical details.

the Menu Editor by selecting the check box labeled Checked. To add or remove a check mark from a menu control at run time, set its Checked property from code.

e.g.

```
Private Sub mnuOptions_Clicks( )
  'Set the state of the check mark based on
  'the Visible  property.
  mnuOptionsToolbar.Checked=picToolbar.Visible
 End Sub
```

Making Menu Controls Invisible

In the Menu Editor, you can set the initial value of the Visible property for a menu control by selecting the check box labeled Visible. To make a menu control visible or invisible at run time, set its Visible property from code.

```
e.g. mnuFileArray(0).Visible=True 'Make the
                            control 'visible.
  mnuFileArray(0).Visible=False 'Make the control
                                  'invisible.
```

When a menu control is invisible, the rest of the controls in the menu move up to fill the empty space. If the control is on the menu bar, the rest of the controls on the menu bar move left to fill the space.

Adding Menu Controls at Run Time

A menu can grow at run time, In following figure, as files are opened in the SDI Notepad application, menu items are dynamically created to display the path names of the most recently opened files.

Menu control array elements created and displayed at run time.

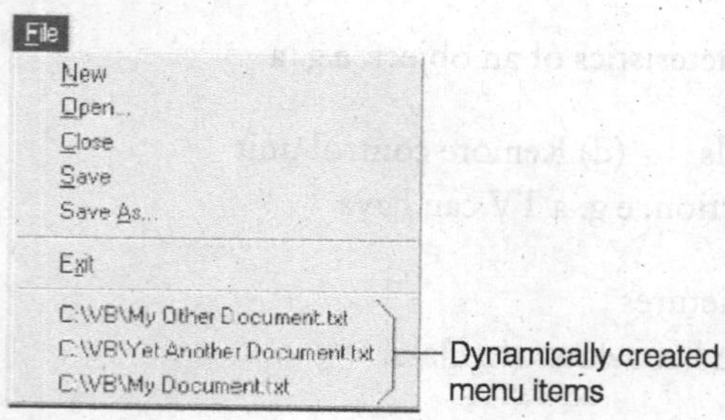

You must use a control array to create a control at run time. Because the mnuRecentFile menu control is assigned a value for the Index property at design time, it automatically becomes an element of a control array – even though no other element have yet been created.

When you create mnuRecentFile(0), you actually create a separator bar that is invisible at run time. The first time a user saves a file at run time, the separator bar becomes visible and the first file name is added to the menu. Each time you save a file at run time, additional menu controls are loaded into the array, making the menu grow.

Controls created at run time can be hidden by using the Hide method or by setting the control's Visible property to False. If you want to remove a control in a control array from memory, use the Unload statement .

5.9.11 Displaying Pop-up menus

Any menu that has at least one menu item can be displayed at run time as a pop-up menu. To display a pop-up menu, use the PopupMenu method. This method uses the following syntax:

```
[object.] PopupMenu menuname [.flags[.x[.y[.bold
command]]]]
```

e.g. the following code displays a menu named mnuFile when the user clicks a form with the right mouse button. You can use the MouseUp or MouseDown event to detect when the user clicks the right mouse button, although the standard is to use the MouseUp event:

```
Private Sub Form_MouseUp (Button As Integer, Shift
                As_ Integer, X As Single, Y As Single)
If Button = 2 Then ' Check if right mouse button
                                    was clicked.
PopupMenu mnuFile ' Display the file menu as a
                                      pop-up menu.
End If
End Sub
```

Any code following a call to the PopupMenu method is not run until the user selects an item in the menu or cancels the menu. Often you want a pop-up menu to access options that are not usually available on the menu bar.To create a menu that will not display on the Menu bar, make the top-level menu item invisible at design time. When VB displays a pop-up menu, the Visible property of the specified top-level menu is ignored.

5.10 String Functions

Visual Basic has numerous built-in string functions for processing strings. Most VB string-handling functions return a string, although some return a number. The functions that return strings can be coded with or without the dollar sign($) at the end.

Some important string functions are as follows:

1. **Mid** Returns a substring containing a specified number of characters from a string.
2. **Left** Returns a substring containing a specified number of characters from the beginning (left side) of a string.
3. **Instr** Returns a long specifying the position of one string within another. The search starts either at the first character position or at the position specified by the start

argument and proceeds forward toward the end of the string.

4. **Replace** Returns a string in which a specified substring has been replaced with another substring a specified number of times.

5.11 General Controls (Advance) in Visual Basic

Some common general controls (advance) in VB are as follows:

1. ImageList

An ImageList control contains a collection of images that can be used by other windows Common Controls.

e.g. the ImageList control can store all the images that appear on a Toolbar control's buttons.

2. CommonDialog Box

It provides a standard set of dialog boxes for operations such as opening and saving files, setting print options and selecting colors and fonts. The control also has the ability to display help by running the windows Help engine.

The Common Dialog control provides an interface between Visual Basic and the routines in the Microsoft Windows dynamic link library commdlgdll.

3. ADO DC

The ADO DC (ActiveX Data Object Data Control) is the primary interface between a Visual Basic application and a database. It can be used without writing any code at all or it can be a central part of a complex DBMS.

4. DBCombo

This control is a data bound combo box with a drop down list box which is automatically populated from a field in an attached Data control and optionally updates a field in a related table of another Data control. The text box portion of DBCombo can be used to edit the selected field.

5. Media Player Control

It is a command line audio and video player. It can play audio or video file using several different output drivers.

6. DB Grid

It is a spreadsheet like bound control that displays a series of rows and columns representing records and field from a Recordset object. This control is included with VB in the Tools directory.

5.12 Adding a Toolbar

The toolbar (also called a **ribbon** or **control bar**) has become a standard feature in many Windows-based applications. A toolbar provides quick access to the most frequently used menu commands in an application. Creating a toolbar is easy and convenient using the toolbar control, which is available with the Professional and Enterprise editions of Visual Basic.

To build or add the Toolbar to the form, the steps are as follows:

1. To add the toolbar to the form, firstly you must make sure that the form is open.
2. Double click the Toolbar control in Toolbar.
3. You can name it according to your liking in the Properties window.
4. Now, when you run the project, you will see the toolbar aligned at the top of the form.

1. Adding an ImageList

To add an ImageList steps are as follows:

1. Double click the ImageList control in the Toolbox.
2. An image list is added to the form.

2. Adding an ImageList with Images

To add an ImagList with images, steps are as follows:

1. Use the Properties window to change the name of the ImageList to imgDemo.
2. Open the Property pages for the ImageList.
3. Click at the General tab.
4. Click the Images tab.
5. Click Insert Picture.
6. The Select Picture dialog box opens.
7. Select the picture.
8. Click open to use the picture.
9. A small icon of the picture will be seen in the Image tab
10. If you have to add more pictures repeat the process.
11. Click when you have all the pictures required.

3. Adding Images to the ToolBar Buttons

1. With the Property pages for the toolbar open, select the Buttons tab. Notice that the Index field is grayed.
2. Click Insert Picture. The Index field is now active.
3. In the Image field, put the number of the picture in the ImageList.
4. Tab away from the field. A button with the first ImageList picture appears in the toolbar.
5. Add a caption if you want text to appear on the button.
6. Add a name to the Key field that will be used to reference the button in code.

Members of a Class

Two types of members are supported by a class as follows:

(i) **Data Members** The variables declared inside the class definition are called as data members or member variables of the class. And, variables are said to have class scope, i.e. they will exist in the memory as long as the object of class exist. As soon as the object of class goes out of scope, these will be destroyed.

(ii) **Member Functions** A member function or method of a class is a function that has its definition or its prototype within the class definition like any other variable.

e.g.

```
class Box
{
     public:
          double length;       } Data
          double breadth;      } members
          double height;
          double getVolume (void); } Member
          void setValues(void);    } functions
};
```

Visibility Modes or Access Specifiers

C++ offers the flexibility to decide which data members or class methods should be accessible outside the class or which should not. Class members fall under one of three different access permission categories:

(i) **Public members** are accessible by all class members.

(ii) **Private members** are only accessible by the class members within the class.

(iii) **Protected members** are only accessible by the class members and the members of a derived class.

The data type defined by a class is used in exactly the same way as a built-in data type.

The format of the class declaration is given below:

```
class <class_name>
{            //opening of class
  private:   //cannot be accessed from outside
             //the class
     variable declaration;
     function declaration;
  public:    //can be accessed from outside the
             //class
     variable declaration;
     function declaration;
  protected: //accessible by the class members
          //and the members of a derived class only
     variable declaration;
     function declaration;
};           //closing of class with semicolon
```

Where, class is a keyword and <class_name> is the user defined name of the class. The body of the class is enclosed within curly braces { } and terminated by semicolon(;) The term private, public and protected are access specifiers.

Access specifier is a way to specify the scope and accessibility of members of a class. The private brings out the data hiding feature of object oriented programming. By default, the members of the class are private. Therefore, it is not necessary to write the keyword private.

Member Function Definition

The member functions may be defined in two places as follows:

(i) **Inside the Class Definition** In this method, the function is defined in the class itself as the place of declaration. This function is treated as an **inline function**. The coding of normal functions and inline functions is similar except that inline functions definitions start with the keyword inline.

e.g. function definition inside the class to find the value of a Box.

```
class Box
{
   public:
      double length, breadth, height;
      double getVolume()
      {
           return length*breadth*height;
      }
};
```

(ii) **Outside the Class Definition** When the member functions are to be defined outside the class definition, the following declaration is to be made:

(a) Declare the prototype of the member functions inside the class definition.

(b) Bind the member function definition for a class to whom it belongs. This is done using the scope resolution operator (::).

e.g.

```
class Sample
{
  int a, b;
  public:
  int s;
  void add();
};
void Sample::add(int a, int b)
       //function definition outside the class
{
  cout<<"Addition="<<(a+b);
}
```

⚠ The symbol :: tells the compiler that the function add ( ) belongs to class Sample.

7.4.2 Objects

Objects are the variables of a user defined data type called class. In other words, the class acts as a data type and the object acts as its variable. When we define a class, it does not define or create objects of that class, rather it only specifies what type of information the objects of this class type will be contained. Once a class has been defined, its object can be defined like any other variable.

The syntax for creating objects is:

```
classname objectname(s);
```

For the above declared class Sample, an object x can be created like

```
Sample x;
```

Objects can also be created when a class is defined by placing their name immediately after closing the brackets. Consider this

```
class Student
{
  private:
     int roll;
     int age;
     void pri();
  public:
     void getdata(void);
     void display(void);
} x,y;    // x,y are the objects of class student
```

Accessing Class Members from Object

The class members that are declared to be public can be accessed from outside the class. We can access them using the following syntax:

```
Objectname.functionname (actual arguments);
                  //accessing member function
Objectname.datamember = Some value;
                       //accessing data member
```

Dot operator(.) is used to access members of class either data members or member functions.

e.g.

```
Student x;
x.getdata();
x.age = 25; or cin>>x.age;
```

Arrays of Objects

We know that an array can be of any data type. Similarly, we can also have arrays of variables that are of the type class. Such variables are called arrays of objects.

Consider the following class definition:

```
class Employee
{
  char name[30];
  float age;
  public:
     void getdata(void);
     void putdata(void);
};
```

The identifier employee is a user defined data type and can be used to create objects that relate to different categories of the employees.

e.g.

```
Employee manager[3];          //array of manager
Employee foreman[15];         //array of foreman
Employee worker[75];          //array of worker
```

We can use the usual array accessing methods to access individual elements and then the dot operator to access the member functions.

e.g. `manager[i].putdata();`

will display the data of the ith element of the array manager, i.e. this statement requests the object manager [i] to invoke the member function putdata( ).

Objects as Function Arguments

An object can be used as a function argument. It can be done in the following ways:

Pass by Value

A copy of the object is passed to the function and any change made is not reflected back. An object may be passed by value to the member function and friend functions are permitted to access the private and protected members of the passed object. The non-member functions can only access the public members of the passed object.

e.g. To show the data members are passed by value.

```
#include<iostream.h>
#include<conio.h>
class time
{
  public:
     int hours,minutes.seconds;
     void enter();
     void addtime(time, time);
};
void time::enter()
{
  cout<<"Enter the time";
  cout<<"HOURS";
  cin>>hours;
  cout<<"MINUTES";
  cin>>minutes";
  cout<<"SECONDS";
  cin>>seconds;
}
void time :: addtime(time t1,time t2)
{
  int hr,min,sec;
```

CHAPTER PRACTICE

1. **...... is a set of instructions provided to a computer system to perform a specific task.**
(1) Algorithm
(2) Steps
(3) Program
(4) Pseudocode

2. **The process of subdividing a computer program into separate sub programs is known as**
(1) modular programming
(2) event-driven programming
(3) object-based programming
(4) object-oriented programming

3. **Most high level GUI APIs (OWL, MFC, Turbo vision etc.) use ...... programming to embed basic features into every program.**
(1) modular
(2) object-based
(3) object-oriented
(4) event-driven

4. **Which of the following programming technique do not support inheritance and dynamic binding?**
(1) object-oriented
(2) object-based
(3) event-driven
(4) procedure-oriented

5. **Object oriented programming language model around ...... and data rather than actions and logic.**
(1) objects
(2) classes
(3) procedures
(4) keywords

6. **Visual basic and Delphi are the two most popular ...... systems for Windows.**
(1) CAD
(2) POP
(3) RAD
(4) OOP

7. **...... files are not meant to be used by themselves.**
(1) Standard EXE
(2) ActiveX EXE
(3) Addin
(4) ActiveX DLL

8. **It has an .OCX file extension.**
(1) ActiveX Control
(2) ActiveX Document EXE
(3) IIS Application
(4) ActiveX DLL

9. **Visual Basic is a tool that allows you to develop application in ....**
(1) Real time
(2) Graphical User Interface
(3) Character User Interface
(4) None of the above

10. **In Visual Basic, ... is the extension to represent project file.**
(1) .frm (2) .vbp
(3) .cls (4) .vb

11. **...... is used for finding out about objects, properties and methods.**
(1) Form Layout window
(2) Code Editor window
(3) Object browser
(4) None of the above

12. **In Visual Basic, a variable name cannot be more than ...... characters.**
(1) 255 (2) 300
(3) 355 (4) 400

13. **The variable that does not change the value during execution of program is ....**
(1) numeric
(2) string
(3) constant
(4) None of the above

14. **The function procedures are ...... by default.**
(1) public
(2) private
(3) protected
(4) None of the above

15. **...... is a data type that can be used to declare a text of maximum 10 million characters.**
(1) Date (2) Ulong
(3) Numeric (4) String

16. **In ......, we can write code.**
(1) Immediate window
(2) Locals window
(3) Code Editor window
(4) None of the above

17. **Mouse down event takes place when you**
(1) click the left mouse button
(2) press the mouse button
(3) mouse is moved over the control
(4) All of the above

18. **In ...... , there is no need to declare a variable before using it.**
(1) Implicit declaration
(2) Explicit declaration
(3) Option explicit
(4) General declarations

19. **In ...... scope, variables are available only to the module in which they are declared.**
(1) Private (2) Public
(3) Module (4) Static

20. **...... control provides all standard dialog boxes into VB form.**
(1) Common dialog
(2) Rich text box
(3) Input box
(4) All of the above

21. **In event-driven programming, an event is generated by**
(1) the system
(2) user's action
(3) the program itself
(4) All of the above

22. **The scope of a variable refers to**
(1) the length of the variable.
(2) the name of the variable.
(3) the accessibility of the variable.
(4) the datatype of the variable.

23. **Which symbol creates an access key in the text of a menu item?**
(1) @ (2) &
(3) $ (4) %

24. **...... is a string expression displayed as the message in the dialog box.**
(1) Prompt
(2) Message
(3) Expression
(4) Dialog

25. **Which of the following is not the MessageBoxButtons enumeration value?**
(1) Ok (2) OkCancel
(3) None (4) YesNo

26. **...... property returns a value of the enumeration when the dialog box is closed.**
(1) DockPadding (2) DialogResult
(3) DialogPadding (4) DockResult

27. **In Visual Basic, the declaration of variables is done by ...... keyword.**
(1) Int (2) Dim
(3) Static (4) Declare

28. **Which is not a main component of the Visual Studio IDE?**
(1) Tool Box
(2) Start Menu
(3) Designer Window
(4) Properties Window

29. **Which are the standard prefixes for the Button and Combo box controls respectively?**
(1) btn and chb
(2) btn and cbo
(3) bto and chb
(4) cmd and cbo

30. **The Date data type does not hold which type of information.**
(1) Seconds (2) Hours
(3) Months (4) Quarters

31. **The Boolean data type:**
(1) is unsigned
(2) has two states.
(3) is displayed by the program as yes or no.
(4) Both (1) and (2)

32. **Which is a valid statement for declaring a variable?**
(1) Const Form As Integer
(2) Const myForm As Integer
(3) Dim Form As Integer
(4) Dim myForm As Integer

33. **Which is true about the prompt argument?**
(1) It can be made of multiple values concatenated into one string.
(2) It can include the vbCrLf constant.
(3) It can include the ampersand symbol to concatenate strings.
(4) All of the above

34. **Which is a valid way to write a sub procedure declaration?**
(1) Use the Class and Method combo boxes in the Code Editor window.
(2) Double click on the object in the Form Designer window.
(3) Type the procedure declaration in the Code Editor window.
(4) Both (1) and (2)

35. **How are dialog boxes implemented in a program?**
(1) A dialog box is generated programmatically.
(2) A dialog control is placed in the component tray.
(3) A dialog control is placed on the form.
(4) Both (1) and (2)

36. **Which type of file can be played with the Windows Media Player control?**
(1) MPEG (2) AVI
(3) WAV (4) All of these

37. **The Windows Media Player control**
(1) is located in the toolbox by default.
(2) is located in the toolbar.
(3) can be added to the toolbar.
(4) All of the above

38. **What is the syntax for creating and using an application variable?**
(1) Application. VariableName = Value
(2) Application(VariableName) = Value
(3) Application (VariableName) = (Value)
(4) Application("VariableName") = Value

39. **To run an application in Visual Basic**
(1) click on the Start button (blue arrow)
(2) use the File Menu
(3) use the Project Menu to select Run
(4) None of the above

40. **To exit Visual Basic**
(1) Click Alt-E
(2) Use the File Menu to select Exit
(3) Use the Window Menu to select Exit
(4) Click on the diskette icon

41. **Each individual variable in the list student (0), student (1) student (2) is known as *a (n)***
(1) subscript
(2) dimension
(3) element
(4) type

42. **Which of the following is true?**
(1) "Cat" = "cat"
(2) "Cat" < "cat"
(3) "Cat" > " cat"
(4) Relational operators are only valid for numeric values.

43. **Which of the following is a valid Visual Basic conditional statement?**
(1) 2<n<5
(2) 2 < n or < 5
(3) 2 < n or 5
(4) (2 < n) or (n < 5)

44. **Asc("A") is 65. What is displayed by txtBox.Text = Chr(65) & "BC"?**
(1) ABC (2) A BC (3) 656667
(4) Not enough information is available.

45. **What is the proper syntax when using a message dialog box?**
(1) MsgBox.Show("Hi there", "Hi")
(2) MsgBox.Show(Hi there, Hi)
(3) MsgBox.Show "Hi There", "Hi"
(4) MsgBox.Show Hi There, Hi

46. **Which of the following converts the expression to Byte data type?**
(1) CBool(expression)
(2) CByte(expression)
(3) CChar(expression)
(4) CDate(expression)

47. **Which of the following statement declares and defines one or more constants?**
(1) Dim (2) Const
(3) Enum (4) Class

48. **Variables are named storage locations in memory, the value of which does not change during program ....**
(1) debug (2) design
(3) execution (4) All of these

49. **Which window displays a list of all forms and modules making up your application?**
(1) Project window
(2) Properties window
(3) Form Layout window
(4) All of the above

50. **Which of the following windows is the central to the development of Visual Basic applications?**
(1) Project window
(2) Form window
(3) Properties window
(4) All of the above

51. **Which of the following provides quick access to commonly used commands in the programming environment?**
(1) Toolbox (2) Object browser
(3) Toolbar (4) None of these

52. **What is the output of the following code?**

```
MyString = "Hello World"
LeftString = left
(MyString,3)
```

(1) Hel (2) Hello World
(3) World (4) Wor

```
INTEREST:: INTEREST(int p , int t, int r)
{
   principal = p;
   year=t;
   rate = r;
}
```

(iv) **Overloaded Constructor** A class can have any number of constructors. All the constructors in the class have the same data members as that of the class but with different parameters, which is known as constructor overloading. That is, when more than one constructor function is defined in a class with different arguments, we can say that constructor is overloaded.

```
class Circle
{
   float radius;
   public:
       Circle()      //Default constructor
       {
           radius = 0;
       }
       Circle(int r)
                    //Parameterized constructor
       {
           radius = r;
       }
};
```

(v) **Copy Constructor** The initialisation of an object when done by another object is called copy constructor. In simple words, we can say that if we have an object (obj1) and we want to create a new object (obj2) with the same values that obj1 has, then the copy constructor should be used.

The copy constructor is defined in the class as a parameterized constructor receiving an object as argument passed-by-reference.

Syntax

```
Classname obj1;
Classname obj2(obj1);
```

or

```
Classname obj2 = obj1;
```

e.g.

```
class Sample
{
   int i, j;
   public:
       Sample(int a, int b)   //parameterized
                              //constructor
       {
           i = a;
           j=b;
       }
};
void main()
{
       Sample S1(4, 6);   //S1 initialise first
                          //constructor used
       Sample S2(S1);     //S1 copied to S2. Copy
                          //constructor called.
       Sample S3=S1;      //S1 copied to S3. Copy
                          //constructor called again
}
```

7.5.2 Destructor

A destructor is a member function that is used to destroy the object that has been created by a constructor. Destructor will have exactly same name as the class and tilde sign (~) precede their name.

Special Characteristics of a Destructor

(i) A destructor has the same name as that of the class prefixed by a tilde character (~).
(ii) No arguments can be provided to a destructor.
(iii) It has no return type, not even void type.
(iv) Destructors cannot be inherited.
(v) Destructors cannot be overloaded.
(vi) Destructor functions are invoked automatically, when the object goes out of scope.
(vii) If there is no destructor in a class, a default destructor is generated by the compiler automatically.

Declaration and Definition

A destructor can be defined like any other member function. However, it does not take any argument and does not return any value. A general syntax to declare a destructor is ~classname ( );

Like a constructor, destructor can also be define inside the class or outside the class (using scope resolution operator (::)).

e.g.

```
class Sale
{
   int a, b;
   public:
       Sale(int i,int j);
       ~Sale();          //Destructor declaration
};
Sale :: Sale(int i,int j)
{
   a = i;
   b = j;
}
Sale :: ~Sale()               //Destructor definition
{
   cout<<"\nDestructor Called";
}
```

7.6 Inheritance (Extending Classes)

Inheritance is one of the most important concepts of object oriented programming. It allows us to define a class to acquire properties and characteristics from another class. It means that when creating a new class, instead of writing all members, the programmer can designate that the new class should inherit the all members of an existing class.

Inheritance also provides an opportunity to reuse the code functionality (i.e. when we inherit an existing class, all its members become available in the new class) and fast implementation time.

7.6.1 Base and Derived Classes

The class whose properties are inherited by other class is called the Parent or Base or Super class. And, the class which inherits properties of other class is called Child or Derived or Sub class. A class can be derived from more than one class, which means it can inherit data and functions from multiple base classes.

Whenever a derived class is defined, we have to specify its relationship with the base class. The general form of specifying a base and derived class is:

```
class base_classname
{
   ..........
   ..........         //Members of base class
   ..........
};
class derived_classname: visibility_mode
                                  base_classname
{
      ..........
      ..........      //Members of derived class
      ..........
};
```

Where, colon (:) symbol shows the relationship of a derived class to its base class and visibility mode may be private, public or protected. The default mode is private.

e.g.

```
class b
{
      ..........      //Members of base class
};
class a:public b
{
      ..........      //Members of derived class
};
```

7.6.2 Access Control in Inheritance

Access restrictions can be imposed not only within a class but also imposed when deriving the class. The access specifier or visibility mode can be public, protected or private.

Access Specifier	Base Class Member		Derived Class Member
public	public	⟶	public
	protected	⟶	protected
	private	⟶	Not accessible
protected	public	⟶	protected
	protected	⟶	protected
	private	⟶	Not accessible
private	public	⟶	private
	protected	⟶	private
	private	⟶	Not accessible

To illustrate the access control, declarations of a DERIVED class from a BASE class are shown below. In each of the three cases, the access specifier is different.

Access Specifiers in Inheritance

Case 1	Case 2	Case 3
`class BASE { private: int a,b; protected: int c,d; public: int e; int Fn(); }; class DERIVED : public BASE { private: int p,q; protected: int r,s; public: int t; int D(); };`	`class BASE { private: int a,b; protected: int c,d; public: int e; int Fn(); }; class DERIVED :protected BASE { private: int p,q; protected: int r,s; public: int t; int D(); };`	`class BASE { private: int a,b; protected: int c,d; public: int e; int Fn(); }; class DERIVED :private BASE { private: int p,q; protected: int r,s; public: int t; int D(); };`

The visual representation of the members of the DERIVED class is shown below:

p, q	Private members	p, q	Private members	c, d, p, q, e, Fn()
c, d, r, s	Protected members	c, d, e, r, s, Fn()	Protected members	r, s,
e, Fn(), t, D()	Public members	t, D()	Public members	t, D()

Return var.Substring (1) &
var.Substring(0, 1)
End Function

(1) jaminBBenjaminen
(2) BenjaminBenjamin
(3) njaminBe
(4) None of the above

90. In the context of Visual Basic, multiple controls of the same type can be grouped into an array, in the same manner as a collection of data items, such a grouping is known as

(1) control array
(2) primary array
(3) secondary array
(4) an integer array

91. Which of the following Visual Basic statement will assign the value "QUICK" from the variable *y* to the string variable *x*?

y= "The QUICK RED FOX JUMPED OVER THE DOG"

(1) x= Middle (y,5,5)
(2) x= left (y,5)
(3) x= Mid (y,5,5)
(4) x= Instr (5,y,"QUICK")

92. Which of the following statements is guaranteed to pass the variable number by value to the sub procedure Tally?

(1) Tally(numVar)
(2) Tally(ByVal numVar)
(3) Tally(numVar)
(4) Tally(ByVal numVar As Double

93. What happens to a variable declared locally inside a Sub procedure after the procedure terminates?

(1) It maintains its value even after the End Sub statement executes.
(2) It ceases to exist after the End Sub statement executes.
(3) It loses its value temporarily after the End Sub statement executes, but regains that value upon re-entry to the Sub procedure.
(4) It is reset to its default value.

94. Suppose a variable is passed by reference to a parameter of a Sub procedure and the parameter has its value changed inside the Sub procedure. What will the value of the variable be after the Sub procedure has executed?

(1) It will have the newly modified value from inside the Sub procedure.
(2) Its value can't be determined without more information.
(3) It will retain the value it had before the call to the Sub procedure.
(4) None of the above

95. Which of the following expressions has as its value the words "Hello World" surrounded by quotation marks?

(1) "Hello World"
(2) Chr(34) & "Hello World"
(3) Chr(34) & "Hello World & Chr(34)
(4) Chr(34) & "Hello World" & Chr(34)

96. Which of the following statement declares the name, parameters and code that define a function procedure?

(1) Structure (2) Module
(3) Interface (4) Function

97. Which of the following statement declares the name, parameters and code that define a Sub procedure?

(1) Sub (2) Declare
(3) Operator (4) Property

ANSWER KEY

1	(3)	2	(1)	3	(4)	4	(2)	5	(1)	6	(3)	7	(4)	8	(1)	9	(2)	10	(2)
11	(3)	12	(1)	13	(3)	14	(1)	15	(4)	16	(3)	17	(2)	18	(1)	19	(4)	20	(1)
21	(4)	22	(3)	23	(2)	24	(1)	25	(3)	26	(2)	27	(2)	28	(2)	29	(2)	30	(4)
31	(4)	32	(4)	33	(4)	34	(3)	35	(4)	36	(4)	37	(3)	38	(4)	39	(1)	40	(2)
41	(3)	42	(2)	43	(4)	44	(1)	45	(1)	46	(2)	47	(2)	48	(3)	49	(1)	50	(2)
51	(3)	52	(1)	53	(2)	54	(4)	55	(3)	56	(3)	57	(1)	58	(1)	59	(3)	60	(4)
61	(2)	62	(1)	63	(3)	64	(2)	65	(4)	66	(1)	67	(1)	68	(1)	69	(2)	70	(2)
71	(4)	72	(1)	73	(1)	74	(3)	75	(3)	76	(4)	77	(4)	78	(4)	79	(4)	80	(3)
81	(3)	82	(1)	83	(4)	84	(4)	85	(3)	86	(2)	87	(4)	88	(2)	89	(1)	90	(1)
91	(3)	92	(4)	93	(2)	94	(1)	95	(1)	96	(4)	97	(1)						

CHAPTER

06

Data Structure and Introduction To C++

6.1 Data Structure

A data structure is a group of similar or different types of data elements that can be processed as a single unit. It is a specialised format for organising and storing data in memory. General data structure types include array, file, record, table, tree, graph and so on. A data structure can be viewed as consisting of a set of algorithms for performing operations on the data it stores.

Data structures are classified into following two types:

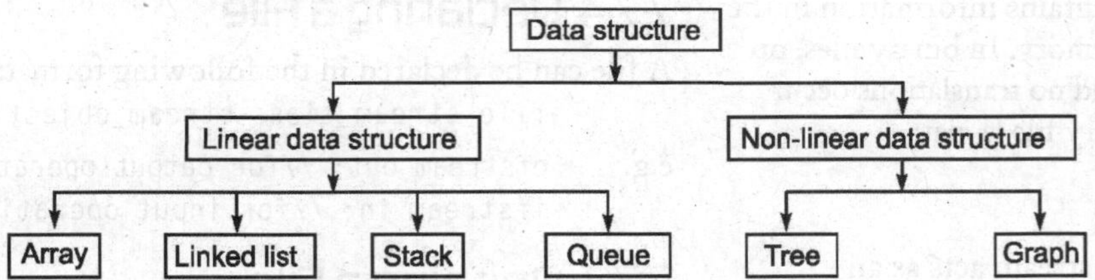

1. Linear Data Structure

A linear data structure is single level data structure and it traverses the data elements sequentially in which only one data element can directly be reached. e.g. arrays, linked list, stack and queue.

2. Non-Linear Data Structure

These are multilevel data structures and every data item is attached to several other data items in a way that is specific for reflecting relationships. The data items are not arranged in a sequential structure. e.g. tree and graph.

6.1.1 Record

A record is a special type of data structure that, unlike arrays, collects different data types that define a particular structure such as book, product, person and many others. Each record consists of several fields, including the information fields that contain the actual data. Other fields of a record may contain links, which hold addresses of other records.

6.1.2 Abstract Data Type

An abstract data type or ADT is a mathematical model of a data structure. It is a logical description of how we view the data and the operations that are allowed without regard to how they will be implemented. This means that we are concerned only with what the data is representing and not with how it will eventually be constructed.

7.7.1 Data File

A data file is a bunch or stream of bytes stored on some secondary storage devices. These files store data concerning to a specific application for later use.

The following are the most important needs of a data file:

(i) It is a convenient way to deal with large quantities of data.

(ii) To store data permanently (until file is deleted). File save over data for future use, as RAM is not able to hold our data permanently.

(iii) To avoid input of data multiple times during program execution.

(iv) To share data between various programs.

Types of Data Files

The C++ language supports two types of data files as follows:

(i) **Text File** It is a file that stores information in ASCII characters. In text files, each line of text is terminated with a special character known as **EOL** (End of Line) **character** or **delimiter character.** When this EOL character is read or written, certain internal translations take place. The file extension of text file is .txt.

(ii) **Binary File** It is a file that contains information in the same format, as it is held in memory. In binary files, no delimiters are used for a line and no translations occur here. The file extension of binary file is .dat.

7.7.2 File Stream

A stream is a sequence of bytes. A stream acts as an interface between program and the input/output devices.

The input/output system of C++ handles file operations, which are very similar to control input/output operation.

It uses file stream that supplies data to program is known as **input stream** and the stream that receives the data from the program is known as **output stream.**

The file input operation involves the creation of an input stream and linking it with the program and the input file. Similarly, the file output operation involves establishing an output stream with necessary links with the program and the output file.

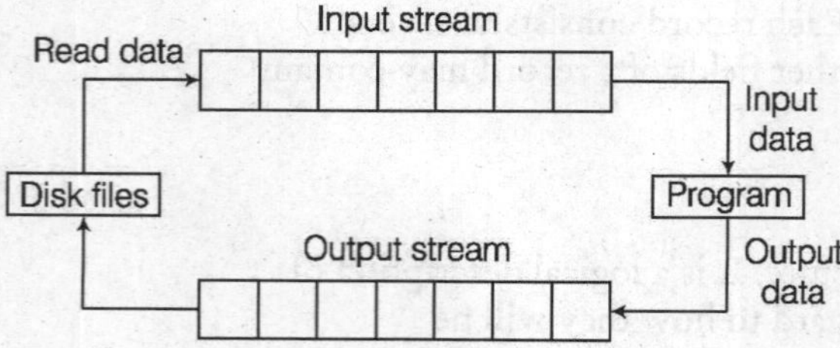

File input and output streams

7.7.3 Classes for File Stream Operations

The I/O system of C++ contains a set of classes that define the file handling methods. These include ifstream, ofstream and fstream. These classes are designed to manage the disk files, are declared in fstream.h header file and therefore, we must include this file in program that uses file.

Details of File Stream Classes

Classes	Contents
ifstream	This class is used to provide input operations from a files, i.e. to read data from files. It contains open() with default input mode. It inherits the functions get(), getline(), read(), seekg() and tellg() from istream class.
ofstream	This class is used to provide output operations to a file, i.e. to write data to a file. It contains open() function with default output mode. It also inherits put(), seekp(), tellp() and write() functions from ostream class.
fstream	It provides function for simultaneous input and output operations into a file. It inherits all the functions from istream and ostream classes through iostream class.

⚠ The fstream also includes the iostream.h header file, so if you are using fstream.h, there is no need to include iostream.h header file in a program.

7.7.4 Declaring a File

A file can be declared in the following format:

```
file_stream_class stream_object;
```

e.g.

```
ofstream out; //for output operation
ifstream in; //for input operation
```

7.7.5 Opening a File

Before a file is used, it must be opened. No I/O functions on a stream can be performed, unless it is opened.

There are two methods of opening a file as follows:

1. Opening Files using Constructor Function

A constructor is a function which automatically creates and initialises an object at the time of creation. To open a file using constructor, the syntax is

```
file_stream_class stream_object
("filename.extension");
```

e.g.

```
ifstream fin("abc");
```

This statement opens a file named "abc" for input (reading) with the help of stream object fin.

Similarly,

```
ofstream fout( "xyz");
```

This statement opens a file named 'xyz" for output (writing) with the help of stream object fout.

This method is useful when we use only one file with the one stream at a time.

⚠ When a file is opened for output only, a new file is created if there is no file of that name. If a file by that name exists already, then the contents are deleted and the file is represented as a new one.

2. Opening a File using open( ) Function

This method is useful when we want to manage multiple files using one stream.

To open a file with a stream object, we use its member function open( ).

Syntax

```
file_stream object;
object.open(filename, mode);
```

Where, filename is a null-terminated character sequence representing the name of the file to be opened and the mode describes how a file is to be used, i.e. to read from it, to write it, append it and so on.

e.g.

```
ofstream myfile;
myfile.open("abc", ios::out);
```

Mode is an optional parameter with a combination of the following flags:

Mode	Description
ios::in	Open for input operations.
ios::out	Open for output operations.
ios::binary	Open in binary mode.
ios::app	All output operations are performed at the end of the file, appending the content to the current content of the file. This flag can only be used in these streams that are open for output only operations.

All these flags can be combined using the bitwise operator OR (|).

e.g.

```
ofstream myfile;
myfile.open("abc",ios::out|ios::app|ios::binary);
```

Each one of the open( ) member functions of the classes ofstream, ifstream and fstream has a default mode that is used, if the file is opened without a second argument.

Classes	Default Mode Parameter	Means
ofstream	ios::out	Memory to file
ifstream	ios::in	File to memory
fstream	ios::in | ios::out	File to memory/Memory to file

We can also combine object construction and stream opening in a single statement as below. Both forms to open a file are valid and equivalent.

```
ofstream myfile("abc", ios::out
                      |ios::app|ios::binary);
```

To check, if a file stream was successful created while opening a file, you can do it by calling member function is_open( ) with no arguments. This member function returns a boolean value of True, in the case that indeed the stream object is associated with an open file or False otherwise.

```
if(myfile.is_open())
{
    /* ok,proceed with output */
}
```

Checking for Successful File Opening

It is important to check that the file has open or not. e.g. the open fails, if the file does not exist or if it cannot be read because another program is writing in it. A failure can be detected with the help of the code given below, using the ! (logical NOT) operator.

e.g.

```
ofstream out("abc");
if(!out)  //code to check about opening of file
{
    cout<<"cannot open the file";
    exit(1);      //call system to stop
}
```

If the file out is not opened, then the compiler assigns a value 0 (null). Therefore, the condition (!out) becomes True. Next statement displays the message and terminate the program.

7.7.6 Detecting End of File

Detection of the end of file condition is necessary for preventing any further attempt to read data from the file. There are two methods for it:

(i) **Without using eof( ) Function** We can simply detect end of file by placing the object of file in the while loop.

Syntax

```
while(stream_name/stream_object)
```

The while loop is executed until end of file is not encountered.

e.g. `while(fin)`

(ii) **Using eof( ) Function** An eof ( ) function is used to check the end of file condition. eof ( ) function returns a non-zero value, if the end of file condition is encountered, otherwise return zero.

Syntax

```
while(!stream_name.eof())
```

e.g. `while(!fin.eof())`

7.7.7 Closing a File

When we are finished with our input and output operations on a file, we shall close it, so that its resources become available again. In order to do that, we have to call the

(ii) **throw** throw keyword is used to throw an exception encountered inside try block. After the exception is thrown, the control is transferred to catch block.

(iii) **catch** catch block catches the exception thrown by throw statement from try block. Then, exception are handled inside catch block.

Syntax

```
try
{
    statements;
    ..........
    throw exception;
}
catch(type argument)
{
    statements;
    ..........
}
```

6.4 Sparse Array

A sparse array is simply an array most of whose entries are zero (or null, or some other default value).

e.g. Suppose 2-dimensional array of course grades, whose rows are Penn students and whose columns are Courses.

(i) There are about 22,000 students.

(ii) There are about 5000 courses.

(iii) This array would have about 110,000,000 entries.

(iv) Since, most students take fewer than 5000 courses, there will be a lot of empty spaces in this array.

Sparse array as linked list

We will start with sparse one-dimensional arrays, which are simpler.

Here is an example of a sparse one dimensional array.

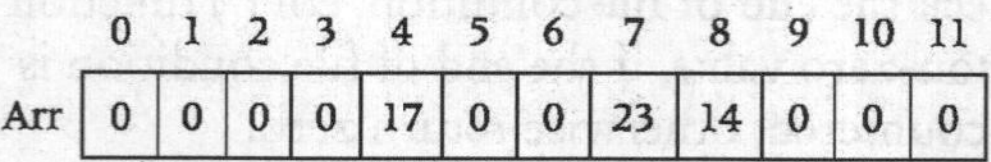

	0	1	2	3	4	5	6	7	8	9	10	11
Arr	0	0	0	0	17	0	0	23	14	0	0	0

Here is how it could be represented as a linked list.

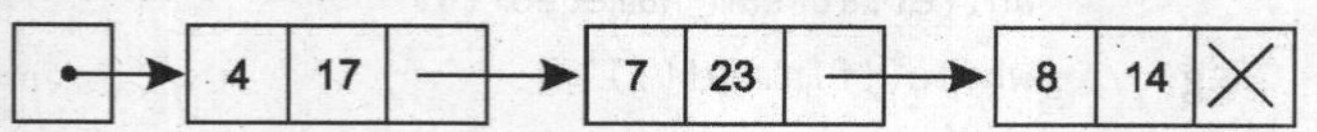

Sparse array can be represented as

Sparse_Array [{pos 1 → val 1, pos 2 → val 2,...}] or

Sparse_Array [{pos 1 , pos 2, ...} → {val 1, val 2......}]

6.5 Searching

Searching is the process of finding the position of a particular element in an array.

We can do searching in two ways as follows:

6.5.1. Linear Search

In linear search, each element of array is compared with the item to be searched for, one by one. This method which traverses the array sequentially to locate the given item, is called *linear search* or *sequential search*.

In this algorithm, several steps are to be performed as follows:

Step 1 Read the search element from the user.

Step 2 Compare the search element with the first element in the list.

Step 3 If both are equal, then display "Given element found!" and terminate the loop.

Step 4 If both are not equal, then compare search element with the next element in the list.

Step 5 Repeat steps 3 and 4 until the search element is compared with the last element in the list.

Step 6 If the last element in the list is also not match, then display "Element not found!!" and terminate the loop.

6.5.2 Binary Search

Binary search or half-interval search or logarithmic search is an alogorithm used to search for an element (item) in a sorted array in any order (ascending or descending).

In this algorithm, several steps are to be performed as follows:

Step 1 Firstly the middle element of array is found and compared with the given item which user wanted to search in an array.

Step 2 If they are same then it will return the location of the required value.

Step 3 If they are not equal then it will break the array in half.

Step 4 If the middle element of array is smaller than the given item then it will search the first half of an array.

Step 5 If the middle element of array is greater than the given item then it will search the second half of an array.

This process will continue until the given item is found or until the loop terminates.

6.6 Sorting

Sorting is defined as arranging data in a specific order (either ascending or descending order). It is a very common activity in data processing. The following methods can be used for sorting:

6.6.1 Selection Sort

Selection sort is probably the easiest sort to understand. The basic idea of a selection sort is to repeatedly select the smallest key in the remaining unsorted array.

Selection sort performs the following steps:

***Step* 1** Starting at index 0, search the entire array to find the smallest value.

***Step* 2** Swap the smallest value found with the value at index 0.

***Step* 3** Repeat steps (1) and (2) starting from the next index.

6.6.2 Bubble Sort

The basic idea of bubble sort is to compare two adjoining values and exchange them, if they are not in proper order.

Bubble sort performs following steps:

***Step* 1** Compare adjacents elements. If the first is greater than the second, swap them.

***Step* 2** Do, this for each pair of adjacent elements, starting with the first two and ending with the last two. At this point, the last element should be the greatest.

***Step* 3** Repeat the steps for all elements except the last one.

***Step* 4** Continue for one less element each time, until there are no more pairs to compare.

6.6.3 Insertion Sort

This sorting is generally used for small set of data. In this sorting, initially the first element is picked up in the unsorted part and is then appropriately inserted in the sorted part, this process will repeat till the final list in ordered accordingly.

This is not a popular method of sorting with compare to selection sort and bubble sort.

In this algorithm, several steps are to be performed as follows:

***Step* 1** Pick the element if it is the first element, it is already sorted return 1.

***Step* 2** Pick next element.

***Step* 3** Compare with all elements in the sorted sub-list.

***Step* 4** Shift all the elements in the sorted sub-list that is greater than the value to be sorted.

***Step* 5** Insert the value.

***Step* 6** Repeat until list is sorted.

6.6.4 Merge Sort

Merge sort keeps on dividing the list into equal halves until it can no more be divided. By definition, if it is only one element in the list, it is sorted. Then, merge sort combines the smaller sorted lists keeping the new list sorted too.

In this algorithm, several steps are to be performed as follows:

***Step* 1** If it is only one element in the list it is already sorted, return.

***Step* 2** Divide the list recursively into two halves until it can no more be divided.

***Step* 3** Merge the smaller lists into new list in sorted order.

6.6.5 Quick Sort

Quick sort sorts by employing a divide and conquer strategy to divide a list into sublists.

The steps are as follows:

***Step* 1** Pick an element, called a pivot from the list.

***Step* 2** Reorder the list so that all the elements which are less than the pivot come before the pivot and so that all elements greater than the pivot come after it. After this partitioning, the pivot is in its final position.

***Step* 3** Recursively sort the sublist of lesser elements and the sublist of greater elements.

⚠ **Heap sort** is a comparison based sorting technique based on binary heap data structure. It is similar to selection sort where we first find the maximum element and place the maximum element at the end.

6.7 Introduction to C++

C++ was developed by **Bjarne Stroustrup** at AT&T Bell laboratories in the early 1980s. He combined the features of C and SIMULA 67 to form a more powerful language that could support the concepts of object oriented programming. C++ is an object oriented programming language that allows programmers to build large and complex applications in a useful and efficient way.

6.7.1 Structure of C++ Program

A C++ program is a collection of functions. The program also contains the list of library files included for adding the contents to the program.

Sample program in C++:

```
#include<iostream.h>
#include<conio.h>
void main()
```

```
        student:";
        gets(name);
    }
    void showdata()
    {
        cout<<"\nAdmission no:"<<admno;
        cout<<"\nStudent name:";
        puts(name);
    }
    int retadmno()
    {
        return admno;
    }
};
```

1. Creating/Writing in a Binary File

For creating/writing data into binary file, we have to perform the following operations:

(i) First, we have to create an object of ofstream class.
(ii) Open the binary file by specifying "filename.dat" in open( ) function and specify its mode ios::out | ios:: binary mode. If binary file does not exist, it will create a blank binary file. Otherwise, it will take the given binary file as blank file.
(iii) Write the data into binary file by using write( ) function.

write_data() function to create/write a binary file:

```
void write_data()
{
    Student obj;
    ofstream fp2;
    fp2.open( "Student.dat", ios::binary|
                                  ios::out);
    obj.getdata();
    fp2.write((char*)&obj,sizeof(obj));
    fp2.close();
}
```

2. Appending Data to a Binary File

Appending data means adding the data into existing binary file, the previous information is retained and new data gets appended to the binary file.

append_data( ) function to add the data into existing binary file:

```
void append_data()
{
  Student obj;
  ofstream fp2;
  fp2.open("Student.dat", ios::binary|ios::app);
  obj.getdata( );
  fp2.write((char*)&obj,sizeof(obj));
  fp2.close();
}
```

3. Reading Data from Binary File

For reading data from binary file, we have to declare an object of ifstream class, after then, binary file is opened in binary mode. The data of binary file is read by using read( ) function. The data is read until the end of file is not occurred.

read_data( ) function to read the data from binary file:

```
void read_data()
{
  Student obj;
  ifstream fp1;
  fp1.open("Student.dat", ios::binary);
  while(fp1.read((char*)&obj,sizeof(obj)))
  {
      obj.showdata();
  }
  fp1.close();
}
```

4. Insertion of Data in Sorted Binary File

The insertion of data in sorted binary file requires another binary file. First of all open the given data file, which is already sorted in reading mode (input mode) and open a temporary file in writing mode (output mode).

As the data in the temporary file must be kept in sorted order, the data from the already existing binary file, which come earlier to the data to be inserted are copied to the temporary file. Now, copy the given data in it and after that the remaining data from existing files are copied to the temporary file. Close the both files. Now, rename this temporary file as master file (a file which is relatively permanent to an organisation or person), if needed.

insert_data( ) function to insert the data in a sorted binary file:

```
void insert_data()
{
  Student obj;
  Student ob;
  char ch='n';
  ifstream fp1("Student.dat",ios::in|ios::binary);
  ofstream fp2("new.dat",ios::out|ios
                          ::binary |ios::app);

  ob.getdata();
  fp1.read((char*)&obj,sizeof(obj));
  while(!fp1.eof() && ch== 'n')
  {
      if(ob.retadmno()<=obj.retadmno())
      {
          fp2.write((char*)&ob,sizeof(ob));
          ch='y';
          break;
      }
      else
```

```
        {
            fp2.write((char*)&obj,sizeof(obj));
        }
        fp1.read((char*)&obj,sizeof(obj));
    }
    if(ch = ='y')
        while(!fp1.eof())
        {
            fp2.write((char*)&obj,sizeof(obj));
            fp1.read((char*)&obj,sizeof(obj));
        }
    else
        fp2.write((char*)&ob,sizeof(ob));
    fp1.close();
    fp2.close();
    remove("Student.dat");
    rename("new.dat","Student.dat");
}
```

5. Searching for Required Data from Binary File

In searching, the first data will be read and it will be checked whether, it satisfies the given condition or not. If not, the successive data will be retrieved till the condition is satisfied. If the desired data is not found in the binary file, an error message will be displayed.

search_data( ) function to search the required data from binary file:

```
void search_data(int n)
{
        Student obj;
        ifstream fp1;
        fp1.open("Student.dat",ios::binary);
        while(fp1.read((char*)&obj,sizeof(obj)))
        {
            if(obj.retadmno() == n)
                obj.showdata();
        }
        fp1.close();
}
```

6. Deletion of Data from Binary File

For a data to be deleted, following steps are to be performed:

***Step* I** Determine the position of the data to be deleted by searching.

***Step* II** Keep copying the data other than the data to be deleted in a temporary file say Temp.dat.

***Step* III** Delete original file say student.dat as
`remove("Student.dat");`

***Step* IV** Rename Temp.dat as Student.dat as:
`rename("Temp.dat", "Student.dat");`

delete_data( ) function to delete the data from binary file:

```
void delete_data(int n)
{
    Student obj;
    ifstream fp1;
    fp1.open("Student.dat",ios::binary);
    ofstream fp2;
    fp2.open("Temp.dat",ios::out|ios::binary);
    while(fp1.read((char*)&obj,sizeof(obj)))
    {
        if(obj.retadmno()!= n)
            fp2.write((char*)&obj,sizeof(obj));
    }
    fp1.close();
    fp2.close();
    remove("Student.dat");
    rename("Temp.dat","Student.dat");
}
```

7. Modification of Data in a Binary File

The modification of data in a binary file can be done sequentially or randomly. The sequential modification requires open the file for input/output, retrieval of data, modify it as desired and then it is written back in the same location from which it was read. The modified data must be of the same length as the data retrieved. In a random way, we directly reach the desired data and then make the specified modifications. The modified data is rewritten to the file in the same location.

modify_data ( ) function to modify the data in a binary file:

```
void modify_data(int n)
{
    Student obj;
    ifstream fp1;
    fp1.open("student. dat ",ios ::binary);
    ofstream fp2;
    fp2.open("Temp.dat",ios::out|ios::
                                binary|ios::app);
    while(fp1.read((char*)&obj,sizeof(obj)))
    {
        if(obj.retadmno() == n)
        {
            fp2.seekp(-1*sizeof(obj),ios::cur);
            obj.getdata( );
        }
        fp2.write((char*)&obj,sizeof(obj));
    }
    fp1.close();
    fp2.close();
    remove("Student.dat");
    rename("Temp.dat","Student.dat");
}
```

C++ supports following data types:

1. **Built in Data Types** These data types are known as **basic** or **fundamental** data types. These are the data types that are not composed of any other data type. These are already defined in compiler program.

   e.g. char, int, float, double, void etc.
2. **Derived Data Types** These are the data types that are composed of fundamental data types. e.g. array, function, pointer, reference etc.
3. **User Defined Data Types** These are the data types that enable a programmer to invent his/her own data types and define, what value it can take? e.g. class, structure, union etc.

6.7.7 Variables

Variables are identifiers, which can hold value. And the value of variable can be manipulated during program execution, i.e in a program, we need to use values, which must be stored in memory cell. In order to refer to that value in our program, we give a name to memory cell. So, in order to use a variable in our program, first we need to declare a variable which means assigning a name to a memory location (or) reserve it. Secondary, we need to initialise it, i.e. we need to store some value in it.

Syntax

```
data-type variable-name;
                              //variable declaration
variable-name= value;   //initialisation
```

e.g.

```
int num;
num = 2;
```

Variable may be declared as globally or locally.

6.7.8 Type Conversion

In certain situation, some variables are declared as integers but sometimes it may be required to get the result as floating point numbers. The type conversion is the process to convert the set of declared data type to another required data type. It is easy to convert a value from one type to another type in a C++ program.

Type conversions are in two forms as follows:

1. **Implicit Type Conversion** It is performed automatically by the compiler without programmer's intervention.

   e.g.
   ```
   int x = 10;
   int y = 2.5*x; //implicit conversion
   ```
   here, y = 25
2. **Explicit Type Conversion** C++ allows the programmer to create a variable and to change its type by using the type cast operator and this process is called **type casting.**

   e.g.
   ```
   float x = 3.5;
   int y = int (x);
   //explicit conversion
   ```
   here, y = 3

⚠ **endl** is used to insert a line feed into the stream. It has the same effects as using the new line character '\n'.

e.g. `cout<<"a =" <<a<<endl;`

6.7.9 Errors

Errors may be made during program creation even by the programmers. Such types of errors are detected by the compiler. The errors are of following types:

1. **Syntax Error** This means that the compiler could not compile a line of code. Such as identifier not declare, statement not terminated by semicolon etc.
2. **Runtime Error** These errors may be detected at runtime due to division by zero, stack overflow etc.
3. **Logical Error** This error would not be displayed on the screen. However, it will lead to display wrong results. e.g. infinite loop.
4. **Linking Error** These errors are occur during the linking process.

6.7.10 Control Flow

A computer program is a set of instructions known as **statements.** These statements are executed sequentially one after the other as they appear in a program and each statement is terminated with a semicolon(;). Not many programs execute all their statements in a sequential order from beginning to end. The flow of control jumps from one part of the program to another, depending on calculations performed in the program. Program statements that cause such jumps are called **control statements.** C++ identifies a compound statement by enclosing its sequence of statements in curlybraces { }.

e.g.

```
{
    int temp = X;
    X = Y;
    Y = temp;
}
```

The braces that enclose these statements form a block. Statements are classified into four types

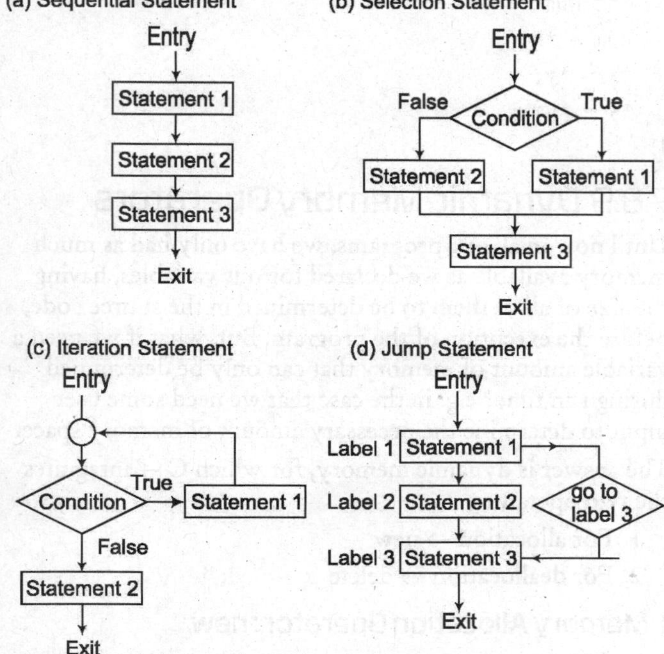

1. Sequence Statements

Sequence statements are being executed sequentially. Sequence structure is also known as **straight line path.**

2. Selection or Branching Statements

When programmers are required to execute a particular set of statements depending upon a particular test condition, a branching statement is required.

Following are the branching statements supported by C++:

(i) **if Statement** The if statement is the most extensively used conditional statement.

Syntax
```
if(condition)
    statement;
```

A statement or set of statements are executed when the condition is true, otherwise these are skipped.

(ii) **if-else Statement** This statement executes one of two alternative statements, according to the specified condition.

Syntax
```
if(condition)
    statement1;
else
    statement2;
```

When the if expression evaluates as true, statement1 is executed and else is ignored. When the if expression evaluates as false, statement1 is ignored and statement2 is executed.

(iii) **if-else-if Statement** This statement executes more than two alternative conditional statements according to the specified conditions.

Syntax
```
if(condition1)
        statement1;
else if(condition2)
        statement2;
else if(condition3)
        statement3;
:
:
:
else
        statmentn;
```

In the given syntax, if the condition1 is true then statement1 will be executed else, if condition2 is true then statement2 will be executed and so on. If none of the given conditions are true then statement under else part, i.e. statement*n* will be executed.

(iv) **Nested if Statement** if statement can be used within another if or else statement. This is called nested if statement.

Syntax
```
if(condition1)
{
    statement1;
    if(condition2)
        statement2;
}
else
if(condition3)
    statement3;
```

In the given syntax, the condition1 is checked first. If it is true, then the program control flow goes inside the braces and again checks the next condition. If it is true, then it executes the block of statements associated with it, otherwise execute else part.

(v) **switch Statement** This statement provides an alternative to if-else-if construct. It is a multiway branching statement. This statement causes a particular group of statements to be chosen from several available groups.

Syntax
```
switch(expression)
{
    case val_1:
        statement block_1;
        break;
    case val_2:
        statement block_2;
        break;
    ........
    ........
    case val_n:
        statement block_n;
        break;
    default:
    statement block_default;
}
```

7.8.7 Function Returning a Pointer

A function can also return pointer. The method is same as used for returning other data types such as int, char, float etc.

Syntax

```
type *name_of_function(parameterlist);
```

Here, type specifies the pointer type to be returned by the function.

e.g.

```
#include<iostream.h>
#include<iomanip.h>
int *getdata(): //function prototype
void main()
{
   int *p:
   p=getdata():
                    //invoke function to get int value
   cout<<"The value returned by the function is
                                               "<<*p;
}
int *getdata()   //function definition
{
   int num;
   int *ptr:
   cout<<"Enter a number: ";
   cin>>num;
   ptr=&num;
   return (ptr); //return pointer
}
```

7.8.8 Function Call by Reference using Pointer

In the call by reference method, instead of passing values to the function being called, references/pointers to the original variables are passed. When parameters are passed to the functions by reference, then the formal parameters become references to the actual parameters in the calling function. Which means the called function does not creates its duplicate copy of original values, rather, it refers to the original values by different names. If any changes made to reference variable, it will also reflect to original argument.

e.g.

```
#include<iostream.h>
void main()
{
   void swap(int *, int *);
   int a=8,b=2;
   cout<<"Original values are\n";
   cout<<"a = "<<a<<"b = "<<b<<"\n";
   swap(&a,&b);
   cout<<"Swapped values are\n";
   cout<<"a  = ''<<a<<"b = "<<b<<"\n";
}
void swap(int *x, int *y)
{
   int num;
   num = *x;
   *x = *y;
   *y = num;
}
```

7.8.9 Dynamic Memory Operators

Until now in all our programs, we have only had as much memory available as we declared for our variables, having the size of all of them to be determined in the source code, before the execution of the program. But, what if we need a variable amount of memory that can only be determined during run time? e.g. in the case that we need some user input to determine the necessary amount of memory space.

The answer is dynamic memory, for which C++ integrates the two operators:

1. For allocation → new
2. For deallocation → delete

1. Memory Allocation Operator : new

In order to request dynamic memory, we use the 'new' operator which is followed by a data type specifier and if a sequence of more than one element is required, the number of elements is typed in brackets [ ]. It returns a pointer to the beginning of the new block of memory allocated. Its forms are

```
pointer = new type;
pointer = new type[number_of_elements];
```

Where, new is a reserved word and type is a dynamic variable.

The first expression is used to allocate memory to contain one single element of data type. The second one is used to assign a block (an array) of elements of datatype, where number_of_elements is an integer value representing the amount of these.

e.g.

```
int *bobby;
bobby= new int[5];
```

2. Memory Deallocation Operator : delete

The necessity of dynamic memory is usually limited to specific moments within a program, once it is no longer needed it should be freed, so that the memory becomes available again for other requests of dynamic memory. This is the purpose of the operator delete.

Syntax

```
delete ptr;
```

Where, delete is a reserved word and ptr is the pointer to dynamic variable.

Every variable created through the new operator must be destroyed through the delete operator otherwise a large amount of memory will continue to be allocated by the new operator resulting in a possible non-availability of memory, crash of system, assigning a pointer variable already allocated to an object.

7.8.10 Pointers to Structures ('->' Arrow Operator)

It is possible to create a pointer to almost any type in C++, including user-defined types. Pointer to structure is a very common in C++. For this, a special operator is used for accessing struct elements *via* pointers. The pointer to a struct member operator (- >) is used to access a member of a struct using a pointer variable.

e.g.

```
#include<iostream.h>
#include<string.h>
struct Student
{
    char name[35];
    int no;
    float marks;
};
void main()
{
    Student r,*p;
    p=&r;
    strcpy(p->name, "anumita");
    p->no=31;
    p->marks=89.5;
    cout<<p->name<<" "<<p->no<<" "<<p->marks;
}
```

Output

anumita 31 89.5

⚠ Arrow operator (->) is used to refer to the public member of the class or structure with a pointer to an object.

7.8.11 Self-Referential Structures

The self-referential structures are structures that include a member which is a pointer to the another structure of the same type.

Syntax

```
struct name
{
    datatype member1;
    datatype member2;
    :
    :
    name *ptr;
};
```

Where, ptr refers to the name of a pointer variable. Thus, the structure of type name will contain a member that points to another structure of type name.

e.g.

```
struct list
{
    char info[35];
    list *p;
};
```

This is a structure of type list.

(ii) **Defining a Function**

A function definition has a name, a parentheses pair containing zero or more parameters and a body. For each parameter, there should be a corresponding declaration that occurs before the body.

The general format of function definition is as follows:

```
    return_type function_name(datatype arg 1,
                              datatype arg2, ....)
{
           // body of function
           ..........
           ..........
           return(expression);
}
```

e.g.

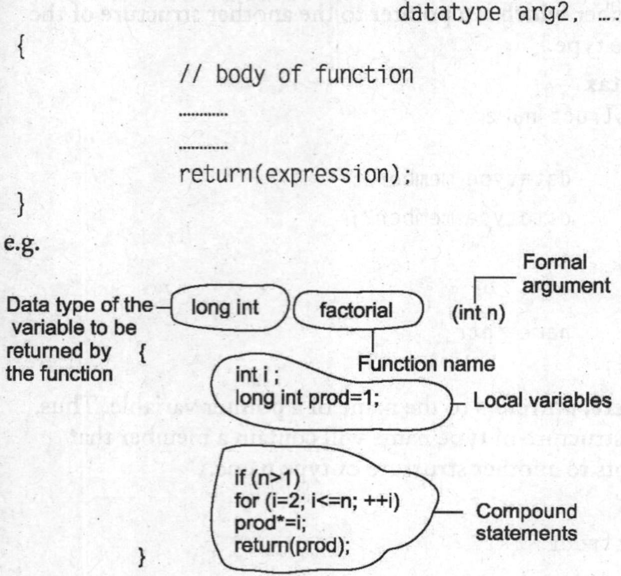

(iii) **Calling a Function**

A function can be called by specifying its name followed by list of arguments separated by commas, enclosed in parentheses. If no arguments are required, then these must be empty pair of parentheses. The function, which calls any other function is known as **caller function** and this function is known as **called function**.

e.g. `factorial (5);`

6.7.12 Function Templates

Function template defines a general set of operations that will be applied to various types of data. The type of data that the function will operate upon is passed to it as a parameter.

Depending on the program, the compiler creates different versions of function template associated with different data types. Generic function is created using the keyword **template**. It is used to create a template that describes what a function will do.

The format for declaring function templates with type parameters is:

```
template <class identifier> function_declaration;
template < typename identifier > function_declaration;
```

The only difference between both prototypes is the use of either the keyword class or the keyword typename.

Command Line Argument in C++

If any input value is passed through command prompt at the time of running of program is known as command line argument. In C++, it is possible to accept command line arguments. These arguments are given after the name of a program in command line operating systems like DOS or Linux. To use command line arguments in your program, you must first understand the full declaration of the main function, which previously has accepted no arguments.

The full declaration of main:

```
int main (int argc, char *argv[ ])
```

Here, the integer argc is the argument count. It is the number of arguments passed into the program from the command line, including the name of the program. The array of character pointers is the listing of all the arguments argv[0] is the name of the program, or an empty string if the name is not available. After that, every element number less than argc is a command line argument.

Separate Compilation

The process of dividing a large program into many smaller source files is called **separate compilation.** Separate compilation of program units is a practical necessity. Its basic goals are to permit the separation of large programs into simpler, more manageable parts and to create libraries of program units. Separate compilation helps to reduce compilation costs and to simplify the development and management of program corrections and modifications.

For large projects involving several programmers, separate compilation permits program texts to be separated physically in a way that reflects the division of work and responsibilities. Once the common interface between two parts has been agreed upon and recorded, the two parts can be developed and compiled separately.

CHAPTER PRACTICE

1. Among the following which is not primitive data structure.
(1) Array (2) Stack
(3) Queue (4) Tree

2. Data structure mainly specifies which of the following?
(1) Organisation of data
(2) Accessing methods
(3) Degree of associativity
(4) All of the above

3. Which of the following operations can be performed on data structures?
(1) Data organisation
(2) Accessing technique
(3) Manipulating selections for information
(4) All of the above

4. Data structure which is capable of expressing more complex relationship than that of physical adjacency is called ....
(1) linear data structure
(2) linked list
(3) non-linear data structure
(4) data structure

5. Which of the following data structure is linear data structure?
(1) Tree
(2) Graph
(3) Array
(4) None of the above

6. Which of the following data structure is not a linear data structure?
(1) Array (2) Linked list
(3) Queue (4) None of these

7. Arrays are best data structures
(1) for relatively permanent collections of data
(2) for the size of the structure and the data in the structure are constantly changing
(3) for both the above situation
(4) for none of above situation

8. Which of the following is/are the levels of implementation of data structure?
(1) Abstract level
(2) Application level
(3) Implementation level
(4) All of the above

9. ...... is not the component of data structure.
(1) Operations
(2) Storage structure
(3) Algorithms
(4) None of the above

10. Which of the following data structure can't store the non-homogeneous data elements?
(1) Arrays (2) Records
(3) Pointers (4) Stacks

11. Which data structure is used in breadth first search of a graph to hold nodes?
(1) Stack (2) Queue
(3) Tree (4) Array

12. Term data structure refers to ...... and interrelationship between them.
(1) organisation of data element
(2) coding standards
(3) programming language statement
(4) Both (1) and (2)

13. Abstract Data Type (ADT) specifies
(1) the components, their structuring relationship
(2) the list of operations that are allowed to be performed
(3) Both (1) and (2)
(4) None of the above

14. ADT contains
(1) a value definition
(2) an operator definition
(3) Both (1) and (2)
(4) None of the above

15. eof( ) is the function used for
(1) asserting no errors in a file
(2) appending data to a file
(3) counting the amount of data in a file
(4) checking for end of file

16. What is meant by template parameter?
(1) It can be used to pass a type as argument
(2) It can be used to evaluate a type
(3) It can no return type
(4) None of the above

17. Which keyword can be used in template?
(1) class
(2) typename
(3) Both (1) and (2)
(4) function

18. What is a function template?
(1) Creating a function without having to specify the exact type.
(2) Creating a function with having a exact type.
(3) Both (1) and (2)
(4) None of the above

19. In the template' <class T> declaration, T stands for
(1) an integer data type
(2) a generic data type
(3) a class defined earlier
(4) None of the above

20. Stack can be represented by
(1) array
(2) linked list
(3) Both (1) and (2)
(4) Neither (1) nor (2)

21. In a stack, the data item placed on the stack first is
(1) the first data item to be removed
(2) the last data item to be removed
(3) given an index zero
(4) not given as index number

22. Stack cannot be used to
(1) evaluate an arithmetic expression in postfix form
(2) implement recursion
(3) convert a given arithmetic expression in infix form to its equivalent postfix form
(4) allocate resource (like CPU) by the operating system

23. Stack is not used in
(1) compilers
(2) system programming
(3) operating system
(4) process scheduling

24. Which of the following applications may use a stack?
(1) A parentheses balancing program
(2) Keeping track of local variables at run time
(3) Syntax analyser for a compiler
(4) All of the above

25. Stacks are used in
(1) compilers in parsing an expression by recursion
(2) memory management in operating system
(3) Both (1) and (2)
(4) None of the above

51. **The operator used for dereferencing or indirection is ..... .**
(1) * (2) &
(3) -> (4) ->>

52. **Choose the right option**
`string* x, y;`
(1) x is a pointer to a string, y is a string
(2) y is a pointer to a string, x is a string
(3) Both x and y are pointer to string types
(4) None of the mentioned

53. **Which one of the following is not a possible state for a pointer?**
(1) Hold the address of the specific object
(2) Point one past the end of an object
(3) Zero
(4) Point to a type

54. **Which of the following is illegal?**
(1) int *ip;
(2) string s, *sp;
(3) int i; double* dp = &i;
(4) int* pi = 0;

55. **Only functions of the class can access the data of the class and they (functions) provide the interface between data, objects and the program. This kind of isolation of the data from direct access by the program is called ... .**
(1) data abstraction
(2) data hiding
(3) data binding
(4) data encapsulation

56. **...... is the OOP feature and mechanism that binds together code and the data it manipulates, and keep both safe from outside world.**
(1) Data binding
(2) Data encapsulation
(3) Data storing
(4) data abstraction

57. **The feature in object oriented programming that allows the same operation to be carried out differently, depending on the object, is ....**
(1) inheritance
(2) polymorphism
(3) over functioning
(4) overriding

58. **Consider an operation of addition. For two numbers the operation will generate a sum. If the operands are strings, and the same operation would produce a third string by concatenation. This feature is called**
(1) inheritance (2) encapsulation
(3) polymorphism (4) binding

59. **A C++ program contains a function with the header `int function (double d, char c)`. Which of the following function headers could be used within the same program?**
(1) char function (double d, char c)
(2) int function (int d, char c)
(3) Both (1) and (2)
(4) float function (double d, char c)

60. **In C++, we can use the same function name to create functions that perform a variety of different tasks. This is known as**
(1) global function
(2) function overloading
(3) inheritance
(4) All of the above

61. **The feature that allows you to use the same function name for separate functions that have different argument lists is called ....**
(1) overriding (2) overloading
(3) constructing (4) destructing

62. **What is the term used to describe the situation when a derived class provides a function already provided in the base class?**
(1) Overloading
(2) Overriding
(3) Polymorphism
(4) Encapsulation

63. **The dot operator connects the following two entities (reading from left to right)**
(1) a class member and a class object
(2) a class object and a class
(3) a class and a member of that class
(4) a class object and a member of that class

64. **...... is a blueprint or prototype that defines the variables and the methods common to all objects of a certain kind.**
(1) Class (2) Inheritance
(3) Object (4) Polymorphism

65. **Which of these following members are not accessed by using direct member access operator?**
(1) public
(2) protected
(3) private
(4) Both (2) and (3)

66. **Which of the following remarks about the differences between constructors and destructors are correct?**
(1) Constructors can take arguments but destructors cannot
(2) Constructors can be overloaded but destructors cannot be overloaded.
(3) Destructors can take arguments but constructors cannot
(4) Both (1) and (2)

67. **If default constructor is not defined, then how the objects of the class will be created?**
(1) The compiler will generate error
(2) Error will occur at run time
(3) Compiler automatically provides its default constructor to build the object
(4) None of the above

68. **Assume a class TEST. Which of the following statements is/are responsible to invoke copy constructor?**
(1) TEST T2 (T1) (2) TEST T4 = T1
(3) T2 = T1 (4) Both (1) and (2)

69. **When the compiler cannot differentiate between two overloaded constructors, they are called**
(1) overloaded
(2) destructed
(3) ambiguous
(4) dubious

70. **If you omit any constructor argument when you instantiate an object, you must use default values**
(1) for all parameters to the constructor
(2) for all parameters to the right of the argument
(3) for all parameters to the left of the argument
(4) for no other parameters

71. **Assume that we have constructor functions for both base class and derived class. Now consider the declaration in main( ).**
`Base * P = New Derived;`
In what sequence will the constructor be called?
(1) Derived class constructor followed by base class constructor
(2) Base class constructor followed by derived class constructor
(3) Base class constructor will not be called
(4) Base class constructor will not be called

72. Which of the following is the valid class declaration header for the derived class d with base classes b1 and b2?
(1) class d : public b1, public b2
(2) class d : class b1, class b2
(3) class d : public b1, b2
(4) class d : b1, b2

73. Let class APE be a friend of class SAPIEN. Let class HUMAN be a child class of SAPIEN and let MONKEY be a child class of APE. Then
(1) SAPIEN is not a friend of APE
(2) APE is not a friend of HUMAN
(3) MONKEY is not a friend of SAPIEN
(4) All of the above

74. When a child class inherits traits from more than one parent class, this type of inheritance is called ...... inheritance.
(1) hierarchical (2) hybrid
(3) multilevel (4) multiple

75. During a class inheritance in C++, if the visibility mode or mode of derivation is not provided, then by default visibility mode is ....
(1) public (2) protected
(3) private (4) friend

76. What is difference between protected and private access specifier in inheritance?
(1) private member is not inheritable but accessible in derived class
(2) protected member is inheritable and also accessible in derived class
(3) Both are inheritable but private is accessible in the derived class
(4) Both are inheritable but protected is not accessible in the derived class

77. In case of inheritance where both base and derived classes are having constructors, when an object of derived class is created then ....
(1) constructor of derived class will be invoked first
(2) constructor of base class will not be invoked
(3) constructor of derived class will be executed first followed by base class
(4) constructor of base class will be executed first followed by derived class

78. If base class has constructor with arguments, then it is ...... for the derived class to have constructor and pass the arguments to base class constructor.
(1) optical
(2) mandatory
(3) compiler dependent
(4) error

79. When a child class function is called, the compiler looks first for matching function name in the ....
(1) class of the object using the function name
(2) immediate ancestor class
(3) base class
(4) descendant class

80. Assume the C++ definition:
`class circle : public point`
which of the following is false?
(1) 'point' is the base class and circle is the derived class.
(2) The colon (:) in the header of class definition indicates inheritance.
(3) The keyword 'public' indicates type of inheritance
(4) All the public and protected members of class 'circle' are inherited as public and protected members respectively, into class 'point'.

81. Which one of the following accurately describes "multiple inheritance"?
(1) When a child class has both an " is a" and a "has a" relationship with its parent class.
(2) When two classes inherit from each other
(3) When a base class has two or more derived classes
(4) When a child class has two or more parent classes.

82. Streams that will be performing both input and output operations must be declared as class ....
(1) iostream (2) fstream
(3) stdstream (4) stdiostream

83. If we have object from ofstream class, then default mode of opening the file is
(1) ios::in
(2) ios::out
(3) ios::in |ios :: trun
(4) ios::out |ios::trunc

84. If we have object from fstream class, then default mode of opening the file is ....
(1) ios::in|ios::out
(2) ios::in|ios::out|ios::trunc
(3) ios::in|ios::trunc
(4) Default mode depends on compiler

85. Which of the following is correct syntax with respect to data file handling?
(1) myfile:open ("example.bin", ios:: out);
(2) myfile.open ("example.bin", ios:: out);
(3) myfile::open ("example.bin", ios::out);
(4) mylife.open ("example.bin", ios:in);

86. What does the following segment of code do?
`fprintf(fp, "Copying");`
(1) It writes "Copying!" into the file pointed by fp
(2) It reads "Copying!" from the file and prints on display
(3) It writes as well as reads "Copying!" to and from and file and prints it
(4) None of the mentioned

87. Which is among following is used to open a file for output and move the read/write control to the end of the file?
(1) ios::ate (2) ios::at
(3) ios::ann (4) ios::end

88. What will happen in this code?
```
int a =100, b = 200;
int* p = &a, *q = &b;
p = q;
```
(1) b is assigned to a
(2) p now points to b
(3) a is assigned to b
(4) q now points to a

89. The correct statement for a function that takes pointer to a float, a pointer to a pointer to a char and returns a pointer to a pointer to a integer is
(1) int** fun(float**, char**)
(2) int** fun(float*, char*)
(3) int*** fun(float*, char**)
(4) int***fun(*float, **char)

90. In C++, which of the following statements correctly returns the memory from the dynamic array pointer pp to the free store?
(1) delete pp; (2) delete pp [ ];
(3) delete [ ] pp; (4) delete *pp;

91. Object based language differ from object oriented language as it does not support features
(i) encapsulation
(ii) inheritance
(iii) abstraction
(iv) polymorphism
(1) (iii), (iv) (2) (i), (iii), (iv)
(3) (ii), (iii) (4) (ii), (iv)

79. **From the given syntax, the corresponding expression is**

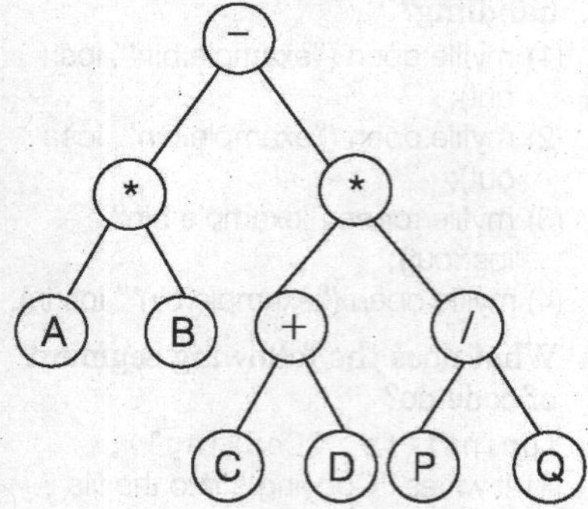

(1) A * B – (C + D)* (P/Q)
(2) – ** AB + /CDPQ
(3) (C + D)* (P/Q) – (A * B)
(4) (C + D)* A* B/P* Q

80. **What data structure would you mostly likely see in a non-recursive implementation of a recursive algorithm?**

(1) Stack (2) Linked list
(3) Queue (4) Tree

81. **Which of the following data structures is most efficient in terms of both space and time to reverse a string of characters?**

(1) Linked list (2) Stack
(3) Array (4) Tree

82. **Which of the following data structure is most suitable for evaluating positive expression?**

(1) Tree (2) Stack
(3) Linked list (4) Queue

83. **When new data are to be inserted into a data structure, but there is no available space, this situation is called**

(1) underflow (2) overflow
(3) housefull (4) saturated

84. **...... is a pile in which items are added at one end and removed from the other.**

(1) Stack
(2) Queue
(3) List
(4) None of the above

85. **...... is very useful in situation when data have to stored and then retrieved in reverse order.**

(1) Stack
(2) Queue
(3) List
(4) Link list

86. **Which data structure allows deleting data elements from the inserting at rear?**

(1) Stacks
(2) Queues
(3) Dequeues
(4) Binary search tree

87. **If we delete 50 from the given binary search tree the root of the new binary tree will be**

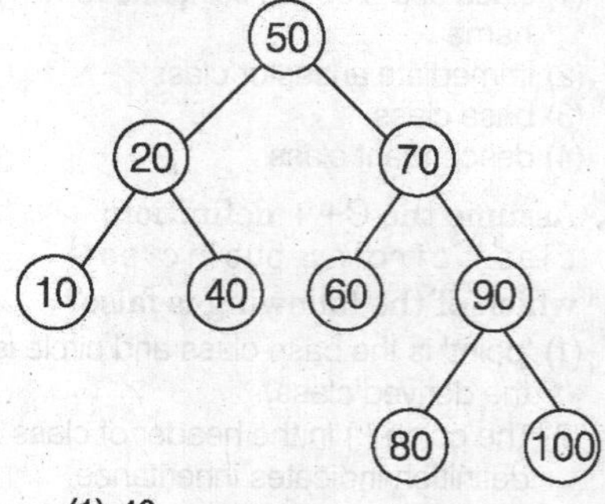

(1) 40
(2) 60
(3) Both (1) and (2) is possible
(4) Neither (1) nor (2) is possible

88. **A linear list in which elements can be added or removed at either end but not in the middle is known as**

(1) queue (2) deque
(3) stack (4) tree

89. **After deletion of a node from a linked list, it is compulsory to do**

(1) getnode operation
(2) freenode operation
(3) freelist operation
(4) getlist operation

90. **Match List I with List II and select the correct answer using the codes given below the lists.**

	List I		List II
P.	Base address of an array	1.	Stack
Q.	The term push and pop is related to	2.	refers combining two or more than two data structure into a one structure in sorted order
R.	Merging	3.	is a data structure consisting of a group of nodes which together represent a sequence
S.	A linked list	4.	address of the first element of an array

Codes

	P	Q	R	S		P	Q	R	S
(1)	2	4	3	1	(2)	4	1	2	3
(3)	2	1	3	4	(4)	3	4	2	1

91. **Match List I with List II and select the correct answer using the codes given below the lists.**

	List I		List II
P.	Stack	1.	First In First Out
Q.	Queue	2.	Last In First Out
R.	An array	3.	Has no children
S.	A leaf node in a tree	4.	Stores several elements of same data type

Codes

	P	Q	R	S		P	Q	R	S
(1)	2	4	3	1	(2)	2	1	3	4
(3)	2	1	4	3	(4)	3	4	2	1

92. **A linear list of elements in which deletion can be done from one end and insertion can take place only at other end, is known as**

(1) queue
(2) stack
(3) tree
(4) branch

93. **The given tree is**

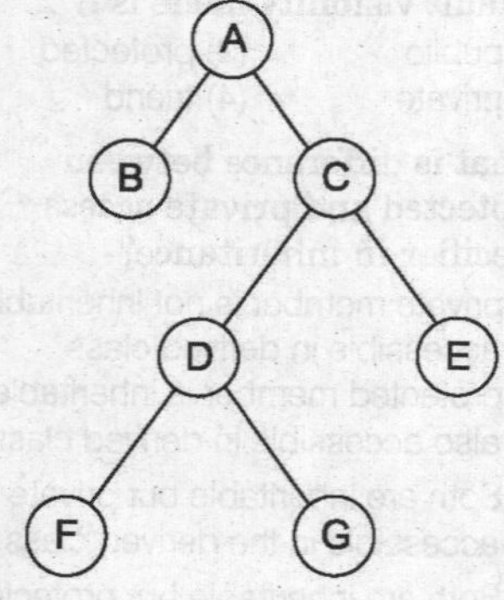

(1) strictly binary tree
(2) complete binary tree
(3) Both (1) and (2)
(4) None of the above

94. **Out of the following which cannot be used as an identifier in C++?**

(1) Name7
(2) _Average
(3) if
(4) Switch

95. **In tree construction, which one will be suitable and efficient data structure?**

(1) Array
(2) Linked list
(3) Stack
(4) Queue

96. **In the given binary search tree, if we want to insert 18. What will be the correct position?**

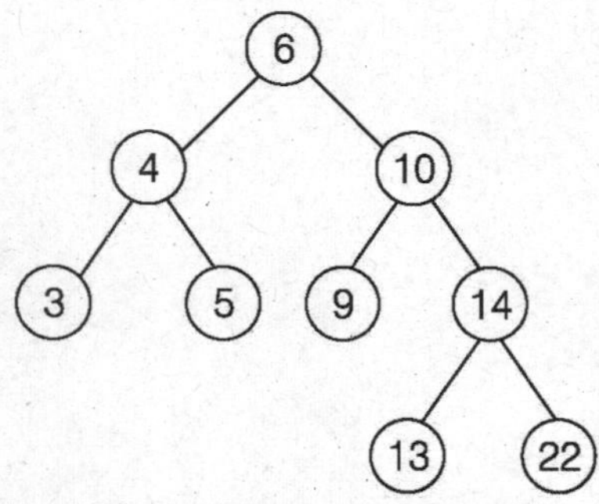

(1) Left child of node labelled 9
(2) Left child of node labelled 13
(3) Left child of node labelled 22
(4) Cannot be inserted

97. **A binary tree whose every node has either zero or two children is called**
(1) complete binary tree
(2) binary search tree
(3) extended binary tree
(4) None of the above

98. **Which of the following is represent correct expression for given syntax tree?**

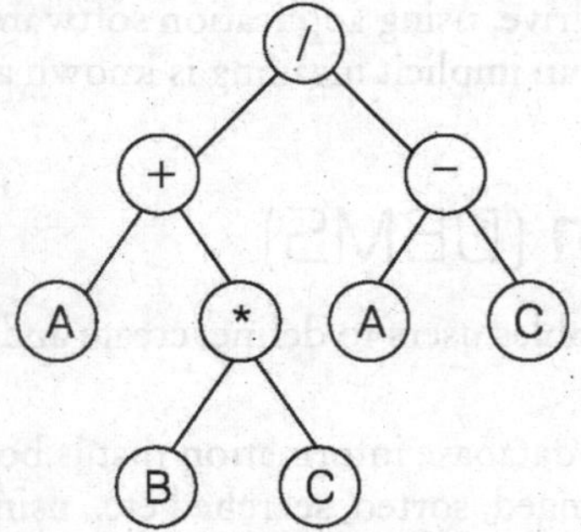

(1) (A + B * C) / (A – C)
(2) (A + B)* /A – C
(3) A + (B * C) / (A / C)
(4) None of the above

99. **Suppose we are sorting an array of eight integers using quick sort, and we have just finished the first partitioning with the array looking like this**
2, 3, 1, 7, 9, 12, 11, 10
Which statement is correct?
(1) The pivot could be either the 7 or the 9.
(2) The pivot could be the 7, but it is not the 9.
(3) The pivot is not the 7, but it is could be the 9.
(4) Neither the 7 nor the 9 is the pivot

100. **Merge sort makes two recursive calls. Which statement is true after, these recursive calls finish, but before the merge step?**
(1) The array element form a heap
(2) Elements in each half of the array are sorted amongst themselves
(3) Elements in the first half of the array are less than or equal to elements in the second half of the array
(4) None of the above

101. **When is insertion sort a good choice for sorting an array?**
(1) Each component of the array requires a large amount of memory
(2) Each component of the array requires a small amount of memory
(3) The array has only a few items out of place.
(4) The processor speed is fast

102. **Consider the following statements:**
(i) **First-in-first out types of computations is efficiently supported by stacks**
(ii) **Implementing lists on linked lists is more efficient than implementing lists on an array for almost all the basic list operations**
(iii) **Implementing queues on a circular array is more efficient than implementing queues on a linear array with two indices**
(iv) **Last-in-first out type of computations is efficiently supported by queues**

From the above, which statement (s) is (are) incorrect?
(1) (i) and (iv)
(2) (i) and (ii)
(3) (iii) and (iv)
(4) (ii) and (iv)

103. **Which of the following is not required condition for binary search algorithm?**
(1) The list must be sorted
(2) There should be the direct access to the middle element in any subject
(3) There must be mechanism to delete and/or insert element in list
(4) None of the above

104. **In a selection sort of n elements, how many times is the swap function called in the complete execution of the algorithm?**
(1) 1 (2) $n-1$
(3) $n \log n$ (4) n^2

105.

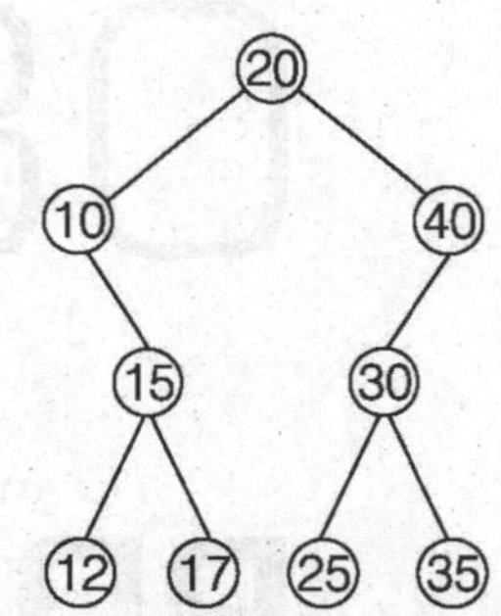

In the above binary search tree, if we delete 20 then the root will be
(1) 17
(2) 25
(3) 40
(4) 10

106. **[(A $ B) * C – D] + [(E / F) / (G + H)]**
Convert the above infix operation into postfix form.
(1) AB $C * D – EF / GH + / +
(2) AB $CD * – EF / GH + / +
(3) AB $C * D – E / FG + / + / +
(4) AB $C * D – / EF + G H / +

107. **A condition that is caused by run time error in a computer program is known as**
(1) exception
(2) syntax error
(3) semantic
(4) fault

108. **What is the output of the following program?**

```
#include<iostream.h>
void addprint()
{
    static int s = 1;
    s++;
    cout<<s;
}
void main()
{
    addprint();
    addprint();
    addprint();
}
```

(1) 234 (2) 111
(3) 123 (4) 235

109. **What is the output of the following program?**

```
#include<iostream.h>
void main()
{
```

CHAPTER

08

RDBMS

8.1 Database

A database can be defined as a collection of organised information in such a way that user can retrieve data quickly. The main purpose of a database is that the same collection of data should serve as many applications as possible.

A database has the following properties:

(i) It is a collection of related data elements representing real-world information.

(ii) It is logical, coherent and internally consistent.

e.g. consider the names, telephone numbers and addresses of the relatives. You may have recorded this data in an indexed address book or you may have stored it on a hard drive, using application software such as MS-Access, MS-Excel etc. This collection of related data with an implicit meaning is known as a **database**.

8.2 Database Management System (DBMS)

A Database Management System (DBMS) is a set of programs that enables users to define, create and maintain the database and provides controlled access to this database.

The primary goal of a DBMS is to provide a way to store and retrieve database information that is both convenient and efficient. Data in a database can be added, deleted, changed, sorted, searched etc., using a DBMS. e.g. MySQL, Ingres, MS-Access, Oracle etc., are the most popular DBMS softwares.

View of Data (Data Abstraction)

A major purpose of a database system is to provide users with an abstract view of data. That is, the system hides certain details about how the data is stored and maintained.

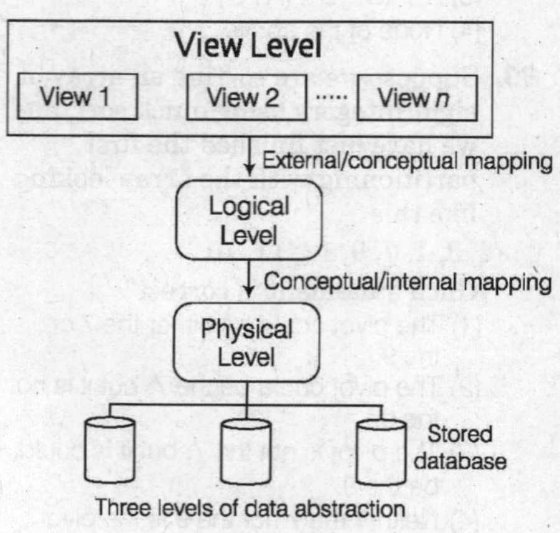

Three levels of data abstraction

View is a virtual table that does not really exist in its own right but is instead derived from one or more base table(s). Each view is defined according to an outline or a plan called **schema**. The description of a database is called the **database schema**, which is specified during database design and is not expected to change frequently.

Many database system users are not computer trained, so developers hide the complexity from users through several levels of abstraction, to simplify user's interactions with the system. This concept is known as **data abstraction**.

Several levels of abstraction are described below:

1. Internal Level

It is the lowest level of abstraction that describes how the data is physically stored and organised on storage medium. It describes complex low-level data structures and access method to be used by the database. It is defined by the internal schema. It is also known as **physical level** or **physical view.**

2. Conceptual Level

The conceptual level presents a logical view of the entire database and thus, it is also known as **logical level** or **global view**. It describes what data is stored in the database, the relationships among the data and complete view of user's requirements without any concern for physical implementation.

Conceptual schema hides the complexity of physical storage structures. Database administrator, who must decide what information to keep in the database, uses the this level of abstraction.

3. External Level

It is the highest level of database abstraction and also known as **view level or user view.** The external level describes a part of database for a particular group of users. In general, most of the users need to access only a part of the database.

The view level of abstraction exists to simplify their interaction with the system. An external schema is used to define each external view, which contains definition of logical records and relationships. It permits users to access data in a way that is customised to their needs, so that the same data can be seen by different users in different ways, at the same time.

8.3 Relational DataBase Management System (RDBMS)

A Relational Database Management System (RDBMS) is a database management system. It is developed by Dr. E.F. Codd of IBM's SAN Jose Research Laboratory.

RDBMS stores data in the form of related tables. RDBMS are powerful because they require few assumptions about how data is related or how it will be extracted from the database.

An important feature of relational system is that a single database can be spread across several tables. Today, popular RDBMS include Oracle, SQL Server, MySQL, PostgreSQL etc.

Various terms related to relational database are as follows:

1. Relation

A relation is a table with columns and rows, which represent the data items and relationships among them. Relations have three important properties as a name, a cardinality and a degree. These properties help us to further define and describe relations. These properties are as follows:

(i) **Name** The first property of a relation is its name, which is represented by the title or the entity identifier.

(ii) **Cardinality** The second property of a relation is its cardinality, which refers to the number of tuples (rows) in a relation.

(iii) **Degree** The third property of a relation is its degree, which refers to the number of attributes (columns) in each tuple.

2. Domain

A domain is a collection of all possible values from which the values for a given column or an attribute is drawn. A domain is said to be atomic if elements are considered to be indivisible units. e.g. in below table, the domain of attribute Book_id contains following values 100, 101, 102.

3. Attributes

The heading columns of a table relation are known as attributes. Each attribute of a table has a distinct name. Attributes are also called **fields.**

4. Tuples

The rows in a relation are also known as tuple. Each row or tuple has a set of permitted values for each attribute.

Attributes

Book_id	Author_id	Emp_Salary	Years
100	Jim	20000	2
101	James	21000	1
102	Anne	21001	3

Tuples

8.3.1 Data

It is an important component of database. Most of the organisations generate, store and process large amount of data. The data act as a bridge between the hardware, software and the users.

A database contains various types of data as follows:

(i) **User Data** It contains a table of data in the form of rows (records) and columns (fields).

(ii) **Meta Data** Simply it defines as data about data. In other words, the data that describes the properties or keeps the information of the other data.

4. Data Encapsulation

The wrapping up of data (member variables) and functions into a single unit is known as data encapsulation. It is the most fundamental concept of OOPs. The data is not accessible to the outside world and only those functions which are wrapped in that class can access it. These functions are referred to as member functions and also provide the interface between the object's data and the program.

5. Data Hiding

When member data and member function are binded into a single unit then the data is not accessible to the outside world and only those functions, which are wrapped in that class can access it. These functions are referred to as member functions and also provide the interface between the object's data and the program. This insulation of data from direct access by the program is called data hiding or information hiding. In other words, we can say that encapsulation is implemented through data hiding.

⚠ Encapsulation is implemented in C++ with the help of classes. Data hiding is implemented in C++ with the help of private and protected keywords.

6. Inheritance

Inheritance is the process by which objects of one class acquire the properties of objects of another class. It supports the concept of hierarchical classification. The principle behind inheritance is that each derived class shares common characteristics with the class from which it is derived. e.g. the class Scooter has inherited the properties of class Two wheelers, which is a member of Automobile class.

7. Abstract Class

Abstract class is a class that defines an interface, but does not necessarily provide implementation for all its member functions. No object of an abstract class exists, i.e. it cannot be instantiated.

8. Concrete Class

A concrete class is a derived class of an abstract class that implements all the missing functionality. This class can be instantiated, i.e. its object can be created.

9. Polymorphism

Polymorphism means processing of data or messages in more than one form. It is the phenomenon, where different objects take different set of actions for the same message. It is implemented using function overloading and operator overloading.

⚠ The process of making an operator to exhibit different behaviour in different instances is called operator overloading.

Overloading refers to the use of the same things for different purposes. Overloading can make programs easier to write and understand. Overloading is a kind of polymorphism.

Types of Polymorphism

There are two types of polymorphism as follows:

(i) **Compile Time Polymorphism** Binding the code associated with the function call at compile time is known as compile time polymorphism. Function overloading implements compile time polymorphism.

(ii) **Run Time Polymorphism** Binding the code associated with a function at run time is called run time polymorphism. Virtual function implements the run time polymorphism.

7.2 Function Overloading

Function overloading refers to the use of one function name to perform different tasks. C++ allows you to use the same name for different functions, as long as they have different parameter type lists, the compiler will regard them as different functions. e.g. a single function named, area ( ) can be used to find the area of Circle, Rectangle or Triangle depending upon the number of arguments.

To correctly implement function overloading, the parameter lists must contain either a different number of parameters or there must be atleast one position in their parameter lists, where the types are different. The correct function to be invoked is determined by checking the number and type of the arguments.

1. Different Number of Arguments

e.g.
```
int area(int a);                  //P1
int area(int a, int b);           //P2
int area(int a, int b, int c);    //P3
cout<<area(10, 20);               //call P2
```

2. Different Type of Arguments

e.g.
```
float add(float a, float b);      //P4
float add(float a, int b);        //P5
cout<<add(0.75, 6);               //call P5
```

e.g. To illustrate the working of function overloading.

```
#include<iostream.h>
#include<conio.h>
int area(int side)
{
    return(side*side);
}
int area(int length, int breadth)
{
    return(length*breadth);
}
```

```
float area(float radius)
{
    return(3.14*radius*radius);
}
float area(int base, float height)
{
    return(base*height/2);
}
float area(float base, int height)
{
    return(base*height/2);
}
void main()
{
    cout<<"For computing the area of a(an)";
    cout<<"Square(side=5)";
    cout<<area(5)<<endl;
    cout<<"Rectangle(length=5, breadth=10)";
    cout<<area(5, 10)<<endl;
    cout<<"Circle(radius=5.5)";
    cout<<area(5. 5f)<<endl;
    cout<<"Triangle(base=3, height=5.4)";
    cout<<area(3, 5.4f)<<endl;
    cout<<"Triangle(base= 4.5, height=6)";
    cout<<area(4.5f, 6)<<endl;
    getch();
}
```

7.3 Advantages of Object Oriented Programming over Earlier Programming Methodologies

Advantages of object oriented programming over earlier programming methodologies are as follows:

Difference between Object Oriented Programming and Procedure-Oriented Programming

Difference between object oriented programming and procedure oriented programming are as follows:

Parameters	Object Oriented Programming (OOP)	Procedure-Oriented Programming (POP)
Divide into	In the OOP, program is divided into parts called objects.	In POP, program is divided into small parts called functions.
Data Moving	In OOP, objects can move and communicate with each other through member functions.	In POP, data can move freely from function to function in the system.
Expansion	OOP provides an easy way to add new data and function.	To add new data and function in POP is not so easy.
Importance	In OOP, importance is given to data rather than procedure or function because it works as a real world/entity.	In POP, importance is not given to data but the function as well as sequence of action to be done on data.
Approach	OOP follows bottom up approach.	POP follows top down approach.
Access Specifier	OOP has access specifier public, private and protected.	POP does not have any access specifier.
Data Hiding	OOP provides data hiding that provides more security.	POP does not have any proper way for data hiding so it is less secure.
Data Access	In OOP, data cannot move easily from function to function. It can be kept public or private so we can control the access of data.	In POP, most function uses the global data for sharing that can be accessed freely from function to function in the system.
Overloading	In OOP, overloading is possible in the form of function overloading and operator overloading.	In POP, overloading is not possible.
Example	C++, Java, VB.NET, C#, .NET etc.	C, FORTRAN, Pascal etc.

Difference between Object Oriented Programming and Object Based Programming

Difference between object oriented programming and object based programming are as follows:

Object Oriented Programming	Object Based Programming
It supports all features of OOPs, i.e. encapsulation, inheritance, polymorphism etc.	It doesn't support OOPs concept except polymorphism and inheritance.
No built-in type of objects are available.	Built-in type objects are available.
It is object oriented, where one can acquire or hide property of objects.	It is also called prototype based programming.
e.g. Eiffel, Python, Ruby, Java, C# etc.	e.g. Ada, JavaScript, Visual Basic (VB) etc.

7.4 Implementation of OOPs Concept in C++

The most important feature of C++ is the 'class'. A class is an extension of the idea of structure used in C. It is a new way of creating and implementing a user defined data type.

7.4.1 Classes

A class is user defined data type which holds binds the both the data and its associated functions together.

A class definition consists of two parts: header and body. The class header specifies the class name. The class body defines the class members.

8.4.4 Login Screen

Capture Login
User Name:
Password:
OK Cancel Help

Use this screen to log in the Oracle.

1. **User Name** Enter the user name assigned to you by a database administrator. User names are case insensitive.
2. **Password** Enter the password assigned to you by a database administrator. Passwords are also case sensitive.

8.5 SQL (Structured Query Language)

SQL is a non-procedural computer language, aimed to store, manipulate and query data stored in a relational database and also used to create interface between user and database. SQL provides variety of tasks such as follows:

(i) Querying data.
(ii) Creating, replacing, altering and dropping tables.
(iii) Inserting, updating and deleting rows/columns in a table.
(iv) Controlling access to the database.
(v) Guaranteeing database consistency and integrity.

8.5.1 Data Types

A data type is a data storage format that can contain a specific type or range of values. The fields within a database often require a specific type of data to be input.

e.g. a school's record for a table Student may use a character data type for the students firstname and last name. The student's date of admission and date of birth would be stored in a date format, while his or her marks in each subject may be stored as a numeric.

Some mainly used data types in DBMS are as follows:

1. Numeric Data Types

It allows the database server to store numbers such as integers and real numbers in a column. Various numeric data types are as follows :

Types	Length in Bytes	Minimum Value (Signed)	Maximum Value (Signed)	Minimum Value (Unsigned)	Maximum Value (Unsigned)
TINYINT	1	-128	127	0	255
SMALLINT	2	-32768	32767	0	65535
MEDIUMINT	3	-8388608	8388607	0	16777215
INT	4	-2147483648	2147483647	0	4294967295
BIGINT	8	-9223372036854775808	9223372036854775807	0	18446744073709551615

(i) **FLOAT** (N, D) A small number with floating decimal point. It cannot be unsigned. It's size is 4 bytes. Here, N represents the total number of digits (including decimals) and D represents the number of decimals.

(ii) **DOUBLE** (N, D) A large number with floating decimal point. It cannot be unsigned. It's size is 8 bytes.

(iii) **DECIMAL** (N, D) It cannot be unsigned. The maximum number of digits may be specified in the N parameter. The maximum number of digits to the right of the decimal point is specified in the D parameter.

2. String/Text Data Types

It allows the database server to store string values. Various string/text data types are as follows:

Types	Description	Display Format	Range in Characters
CHAR	Contains non-binary strings. Length is fixed as you declare while creating a table. When stored, they are right-padded with spaces to the specified length.	Trailing spaces are removed	The length can be any value from 0 to 255.
VARCHAR	Contains non-binary strings. Columns are variable length strings.	As stored	A value from 0 to 255 before MySQL 5.0.3.
BLOB or TEXT	BLOB are "Binary Large Objects" and are used to store large amount of binary data.	As stored	0 to 65535 characters.

3. Date and Time Data Types

It allows the database server to store a date using the fields YEAR, MONTH and DAY in the format YYYY-MM-DD. Various date and time data types are as follows:

Types	Description	Display Format	Range
DATETIME	Use when you need values containing both date and time information.	YYYY-MM-DD HH:MM:SS	'1000-01-01 00:00:00' to '9999-12-31 23:59:59'
DATE	Use when you need only date information.	YYYY-MM-DD	'1000-01-01' to '9999-12-31'.
TIMESTAMP	Values are converted from the current time zone to UTC (Co-ordinated Universal Time) while storing and converted back from UTC to the current time zone when retrieved.	YYYY-MM-DD HH:MM:SS	'1970-01-01 00:00:01' UTC to '2038-01-19 03:14:07' UTC

8.5.2 SQL Statements

SQL command or statement is a special kind of sentence that contains clauses and all end with a semicolon (;) just as a sentence ends with a period. There are four types of SQL statements as follows:

1. DDL (Data Definition Language)

It provides statements for creation and deletion of the database tables, views etc. The DDL provides a set of definitions to specify the storage structure in a database system. Create, Alter, Drop, Rename, Truncate are the DDL statements.

2. DML (Data Manipulation Language)

It provides statements for manipulating the database objects. It is used to query the databases for information retrieval. Select, Insert, Update, Delete are the DML statements.

3. DCL (Data Control Language)

It is used to assign security levels in a database, which involves multiple user setups. They are used to grant defined role and access privileges to the users. Grant and Revoke are the DCL statements.

4. TCL (Transaction Control Language)

It is used for controlling the transactions in a database system. These are also used to manage the changes made by DML. Commit, Savepoint, Rollback and Set Transaction are the TCL statements.

NULLs or Null Values

If a column in a table row has no value, then the column is said to be a null. NULL values are treated differently from other values.

NULLs can appear in columns of any data type provided they are not restricted by NOT NULL or PRIMARY KEY integrity constraints. It is used as a placeholder for unknown or inapplicable values, but NULL and 0 are not equivalent.

Comments

It is the text that is not executed and is used only for documentation purpose. Comments within SQL statement do not affect the statement execution. Comments can be written in SQL in following three ways:

(a) Double hyphen "--" precedes a comment within a single line.

(b) Comment beginning with a # symbol. This is a single line comment.

(c) Comment enclosed in /*......*/. This is multiline comment.

```
    sec = t1.seconds + t2.seconds;
    min = t1.minutes + t2.minutes + sec/60;
    sec %= 60;
    hr = t1.hours + t2.hours+min/60;
    min %= 60;
    cout<<"Resultant time"\n;
    cout<<"HOURS";
    cout<<hr;
    cout<<"\nMINUTES";
    cout<<min;
    cout<<"\nSECONDS";
    cout<<sec;
}
void main()
{
    time ob1,ob2,ob3;
    clrscr();
    ob1.enter();
    ob2.enter();
    ob3.addtime(ob1, ob2);
    getch();
}
```

Output

Enter the time
HOURS 10
MINUTES 50
SECONDS 30
Enter the time
HOURS 12
MINUTES 15
SECONDS 40
Resultant time
HOURS 23
MINUTES 6
SECONDS 10

Pass by Reference

The memory address of the object is passed to the function and the called function operates on the original object being passed. No separate memory is allocated for the data members of the passed object, i.e. any change made to object inside the function will reflect in the actual argument.

e.g. To show the use of call by reference.

```
#include<iostream.h>
#include<conio.h>
class Number
{
    int num;
    public:
        void modify(Number &N)
        {
            N.num++;
        }
        void get()
        {
            num = 10;
        }
        void put()
        {
            cout<<num<<endl;
        }
};
void main()
{
    Number obj1,obj2;
    obj2.get();
    obj2.put();
    obj1.modify(obj2);
    obj2.put();
    getch();
```

Output

10
11

7.5 Constructor and Destructor

The objects of a class type have to be created and initialised separately in broader sense, is a region of memory storage. There are two special kinds of member functions that you should create for every object, they are called constructors and destructors. Constructors are called every time you create an object and destructors are called every time you destroy an object.

7.5.1 Constructor

A constructor is a special member function of a class that is automatically executed or called whenever an object of that class is created. It will have exact same name as the class and it does not have any return type at all, not even void. The primary job of a constructor is to set initial values for certain member variables.

Special Characteristics of a Constructor

(i) A constructor name must be the same as that of its class name.

(ii) It is declared with no return type (not even void).

(iii) It is declared in the public section of the class.
(iv) It is automatically invoked when an object is created.
(v) It can have default arguments.
(vi) It cannot refer to its own address.

Declaration and Definition

A constructor can be defined like any other member function of a class, i.e. either inside the class or outside the class (using scope resolution (::) operator). But, it must have same name as that of class and must not have any return type.

Following example illustrates the declaration and definition of a constructor within a class:

```
class Sample
{
  public:
      int a;
      Sample()      //Default constructor defined
      {
            a = 10;
      }
};
```

However, we can also create a constructor outside the class as an outline function, as illustrated below:

```
class Sample
{
  public:
      int a;
      Sample();
};
Sample:: Sample()
{
  a = 10;
}
```

Generally, constructors are public, but they can be defined as private or protected as well. In that case, object of the class cannot be created outside the class and cannot be accessed outside the class definition directly.

Types of Constructor

There are five types of constructor as given below:

(i) **Default Constructor** A constructor having no arguments is called a default constructor. The previous example is an example of a default constructor.

⚠ No object of a class is created without a constructor. If the programmer does not include any constructor at the time of coding, then this job is done by the compiler. The compiler automatically provides a default constructor for creating the objects with some dummy values.

(ii) **Parameterized Constructor** The constructor with arguments is known as parameterized constructor. Parameterized constructors are very helpful in a situation, where the programmer wants to initialise various data elements of different objects with different values when they are created.

There are two ways of passing initial values to the parameterized constructor as follows:

(a) **Explicit Call to Constructor** It means that the name of constructor is explicitly provided to invoke it, so that the object can be initialised. Where, the initial value of the private data member can retrieve the constructor explicitly.

Syntax

```
Classname objectname =
Constructor_name(arguments);
```

(b) **Implicit Call to Constructor** It means that the constructor is called even when its name has not been mentioned in the statement.

Syntax

```
Classname objectname(arguments);
```

This method is sometimes called the **shorthand method** and it is used very often as it is shorter, looks better and easy to implement.

e.g.

```
class Student
{
     public:
     int Marks;
     Student(int y)      //Parameterized
                         //constructor
     {
          Marks=y;
     }
};
 void main()
{
     Student S1=Student(86); //Explicit call
     Student S2(76);          //Implicit call
     cout<<S1.Marks<< "\n";
     cout<<S2.Marks;
}
```

(iii) **Constructor with Default Arguments** We can define a constructor with default arguments.

e.g.

```
class INTEREST
{
   long principal,rate,year;
   float interest;
   public:
      INTEREST(int p, int t , int r=10);
                                 //Default argument
};
```

Syntax

```
SELECT <Expression1> <arithmetic
                    operator> <Expression2>
FROM <table_name>
WHERE <condition>;
```

Null Values in Arithmetic Expression

Columns with NULL value can be selected in a SELECT query and can be the part of an arithmetic expression.

Any arithmetic expression using NULL values results into NULL.

e.g. `SELECT 7 + NULL;`
Result is NULL.

(b) Comparison Operators

These operators are used to test or compare the value of two operands, i.e. between two variables or between a variable and a constant.

If the condition is false, then the result is zero (0) and if the condition is true, then the result is non-zero. These operators are also called **relational operators.**

Some of the comparison/relational operators are as follows:

Operators	Description
=	Equals to
>	Greater than
<	Less than
>=	Greater than or equal to
<=	Less than or equal to
<> or !=	Not equal to (not ISO standard)
!<	Not less than (not ISO standard)
!>	Not greater than (not ISO standard)

Syntax

```
SELECT <column_name>|*|expression
FROM <table_name>
WHERE <expression>
<comparison operator> <expression>;
```

(c) Logical Operators

The logical operators compare two conditions at a time to determine whether a row can be selected for the output or not. Logical operators are also called **boolean operators** because these operators return a boolean data type value as TRUE or FALSE.

Some of the boolean/logical operators are as follows:

Operators	Description
AND	Logical AND compares two expressions and return TRUE, when both expressions are TRUE otherwise FALSE.
OR	Logical OR compares two expressions and return TRUE, when atleast one of the expressions is TRUE otherwise FALSE.
NOT	NOT takes a single expression as an argument and changes its value from FALSE to TRUE or from TRUE to FALSE. You can use an exclamation point (!) in place of NOT operator.

Syntax

```
SELECT <column_name>|*|<expression>
FROM <table_name>
WHERE <expression> <boolean operator>
<expression>;
```

(d) BETWEEN Operator

The BETWEEN operator is used in a WHERE clause to check that, the field values are within a specified inclusive range. The values can be numbers, text or dates. The range consists of a beginning expression, followed by an AND keyword and an end expression.

The operator returns 1 if the search value is present within the range otherwise returns 0. BETWEEN clause is sensitive in order and the first value in the clause must be first in alphabetic or numeric order.

Syntax

```
SELECT <column_name>|*| <expression>
FROM <table_name>
WHERE <column_name> BETWEEN <value1> AND <value2>;
```

(e) IN Operator

This operator checks a value within a set of values separated by commas and retrieve the rows from the table, which are matching. The IN operator returns 1 when the search value is present within the set, otherwise returns 0. The IN operator allows you to specify multiple values in a WHERE clause.

Syntax

```
SELECT <column_name>|*|<expression>
FROM <table_name>
WHERE <column_name> IN <(value1, value2,...
                                      valuen)>;
```

(f) LIKE Operator

This operator is used to search a specified pattern in a column. It is useful when you want to search rows to match a specific pattern, or when you do not know the entire value. The SQL LIKE clause is used to compare a value to similar values using wildcard operators.

We describe patterns by using two special wildcard operators, given below :

- **The Percent Sign** (%) It is used to match any substring.
- **The Underscore** (_) It is used to match any character.

These symbols can also be used in combinations.

Syntax

```
SELECT <column_name> |*| <expression> <column_name>
FROM <table_name>
WHERE <column_name> LIKE <pattern>;
```

(g) IS NULL Operator

A null in a table column has a special meaning the value of the column is not currently known (missing), however its value may be known at a later time. Since, two null columns may eventually be assigned different values, one null cannot be compared to another in the conventional way. The following syntax is illegal in SQL.

```
WHERE qty = NULL
```

A special comparison operation IS NULL, tests a column for null.

(h) Concatenation Operator

This operator can be used to join two string values or expressions in a SELECT query. The double vertical bar (II) symbol is used as string concatenation operator. It is applicable only for character and string column values resulting into a new character expression.

Syntax

```
SELECT "String1" || "String2"
FROM table_name;
```

This syntax shows concatenation of two character literals values.

Operator Precedence

Precedence is the order in which SQL database evaluates different operators in the same expression. When evaluating an expression containing multiple operators, SQL evaluates operator with higher precedence before evaluating those with lower precedence. SQL evaluates operators with equal precedence from left to right within an expression.

Operator Precedence Table

Operator	Operation
+, ~	identity, negation
*, /	multiplication, division
+, −, ||	addition, subtraction, concatenation
=, !=, <, >, <=, >=, IS NULL, LIKE, BETWEEN, IN	comparision
NOT	logical
AND	logical AND
OR	logical OR

Data Type Conversion Functions

There are two data type conversion as follows:

(a) Implicit Data Type Conversion

This conversion can have a negative impact on performance, especially if the datatype of a column value is converted to that of a constant rather than the other way round. Implicit conversion depends on the context in which it occurs and may not work the same way in every case.

e.g. The text literal 10 has datatype CHAR. SQL implicitly converts it to the number datatype if it appears in a numeric expression as in the following statement:

```
SELECT salary + '10'
FROM employees;
```

(b) Explicit Data Type Conversion

SQL conversion functions are single row functions which are capable of typecasting column value, literal or an expression. TO_CHAR, TO_NUMBER and TO_DATE are the three functions which perform cross modification of data types.

To_CHAR () Function This function is used to type cast a numeric or data input to character type with a format model.

Syntax

```
TO_CHAR (number1, [format], [nls_parameter])
```

TO_NUMBER () Function This function converts a character value to a numeric datatype. If the string being converted contains non-numeric characters, the function returns an error.

Syntax

```
TO_NUMBER (string1, [format], [nls_parameter])
```

TO_DATE Function This function allows users to enter a date in any format and then it converts the entry into the default format used by SQL.

Syntax

```
TO_DATE (string1, [format_mask], [nls_language])
```

- **General Functions** These functions are used to handle NULL values in database.

  NVL Function The NVL function substitutes an alternate value for a NULL value.

  Syntax

  ```
  NVL(Arg1, replace_with)
  ```

- **Conditional Functions** SQL provides conditional functions DECODE to impose conditions even in SQL statements.

  DECODE Function This function is the SQL equivalence of IF...THEN...ELSE conditional procedural statement. DECODE works with values/columns/expressions of all data types.

  Syntax

  ```
  DECODE(expression,search,result[,search,result]…[,default])
  ```

(iii) UPDATE Statement

The UPDATE statement is used to update existing records in a table.

Syntax

```
UPDATE table_name
SET column1=value1, column2=value2,...
WHERE condition;
```

⚠ The WHERE clause specifies, which record or records that should be updated. If you omit the WHERE clause, all records will be updated.

Members of the DERIVED class in case 1-public access specifier	Members of the DERIVED class in case 2-protected access specifier	Members of the DERIVED class in case 3-private access specifier

In the code shown previously, e is a public data member of the BASE class. As you can see from the visual representation of members, the data member e has public access in the DERIVED class, if BASE class inherits publicly. It has a protected access in the DERIVED class, if BASE class inherits protectedly. It has a private access in the DERIVED class, if BASE class inherits privately.

⚠ Only public members of a class are accessible by the object of that class. Private and protected members are not accessible.

7.6.3 Types of Inheritance

Inheritance may take place in many forms, which are being discussed below:

1. Single Inheritance

When a derived class inherits only from one base class, it is known as single inheritance. It is also known as **single level inheritance.** Figure illustrates single inheritance. Here, class B inherits the properties and behaviour of class A.

A Base class
B Derived class

e.g. C++ program to illustrate the use of single inheritance in which derived class (Number2) inherits the base class (Number) in public mode.

```
class Number          //Base class
{
  protected:
    int n1;
  public:
    void Get_n1()
    {
        cout<<"Enter the value of n1:";
        cin>>n1;
    }
};
class Number2 : public Number        //Derived class
{
  private:
    int n2;
  public:
    void Get_n2()
    {
        cout<<"Enter the value of n2 :";
    }
    void Display()
    {
        cout<<"Value of n1 :"<<n1<<endl
                                  <<"Value of n2:"<<n2;
    }
};
```

2. Multiple Inheritance

When a derived class inherits from multiple base classes, it is known as multiple inheritance. Figure illustrates multiple inheritance.

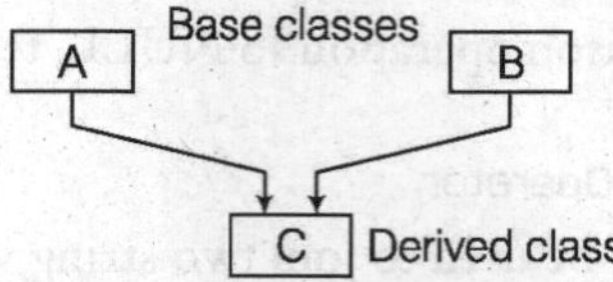

Here, class C inherits the properties and behaviours of both classes A and B.

e.g. A program illustrating how all the three classes are implemented in multiple inheritance.

```
class M                    //Base class
{
  protected:
     int m;
  public:
     void get_M(int x)
     {
          m = x;
     }
};
class N                    //Base class
{
  protected:
     int n;
  public:
     void get_N(int y)
     {
          n = y;
     }
};
class B : public M, public N //Derived class
{
  public:
     void display()
     {
        cout<<"m = "<<m<<endl<<"n = "
                            <<n<<"\n m + n = "<<m+n;
     }
};
```

3. Multilevel Inheritance

In multilevel inheritance, a derived class can be used as a base class for another derived class, creating a multilevel class hierarchy. In this case, the original base class is said to be **an indirect base class of the second derived class.** Figure illustrates multilevel inheritance.

A Base class of B and indirect base class of C
B Derived class of A and base class of C
C Derived class of B

Here, class C inherits the properties of class B and class B inherits the properties of class A. So, indirectly class C inherits the properties of class A.

The transitive nature of inheritance is reflected by this type of inheritance.

e.g. C+ + program to illustrate the use of multilevel inheritance.

```
class A                    //Base class
{
   public:
      int a;
      void get_a()
      {
         cout<<"Enter value of a:";
         cin>>a;
      }
};
class B : public A         //class A is publicly
                           //derived by class B
{
   protected:
      int b;
   public:
      void get_b()
      {
         cout<<"Enter the value of b :";
         cin>>b;
      }
};
class C : public B         //class B is publicly
                           //derived by class C
{
   public:
      void output()
      {
         cout<<"The value of :\n";
         cout<<"a = "<<a<<endl<<"b = "<<b;
      }
};
```

4. Hierarchical Inheritance

When many derived classes inherited from a single base class, it is known as hierarchical inheritance. This type of inheritance is helpful in class hierarchies. In this inheritance, the base class will include the features that are common to all the sub classes.

Figure illustrates hierarchical inheritance

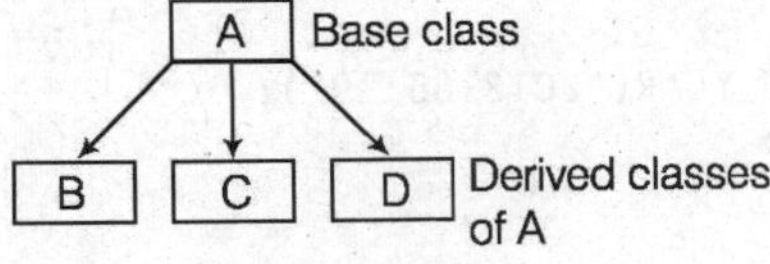

Here, class B, C and D inherits the properties and behaviours of class A.

e.g. C++ program to illustrate the use of hierarchical inheritance.

```
class A                          //Base class
{
   protected:
      int x, y:
   public:
      void get()
      {
         cout<<"\nEnter two values\n";
         cin>>x>>y;
      }
};
class B: public A                //Derived class
{
   private:
      int m;
   public:
      void add()
      {
         m=x+y;
         cout<<"The Sum is "<<m;
      }
};
class C : public A               //Derived class
{
   private:
      int n;
   public:
      void mul()
      {
         n=x*y;
         cout<<"The Product is "<<n;
      }
};
class D : public A               //Derived class
{
   private:
      float l;
   public:
      void division()
      {
         l=x/y;
         cout<<"The Quotient is "<<l;
      }
};
```

7.7 Data File Handling

Many applications require large amounts of data. In such situation, we need to use some devices such as hard disk or floppy disk to store the data. Therefore, programs need to read and write data from and to disk files. In C++, file handling provides a mechanism to store output of a program in file and read from a file on the disk.

Functions	Description	Example
LPAD()	This function pad the given string upto a specific length with a given character. **Syntax** `LPAD(string1, padded_length[, pad_string])`	`SELECT LPAD('tech', 8, '0');` **Output** '0000tech'

2. Mathematical Functions

SQL provides a number of functions used for performing mathematical calculations on database data. These mathematical or number functions accept numeric values and after performing the required operation, return numeric values.

Some mathematical functions are explained with examples are as follows:

Functions	Description	Example
MOD( )	It returns the remainder of one expression by dividing by another expression. **Syntax** `MOD(Dividend, Divisor)`	`SELECT MOD(11, 4);` **Output** 3
ROUND( )	This function rounds up the number to the upwards or downwards to the nearest whole number. **Syntax** `ROUND(number, decimal place)`	`SELECT ROUND(4.65,1);` **Output** 4.7
TRUNCATE( )	This function returns a number as an argument truncated upto a specified number of decimal places. **Syntax** `TRUNCATE(number, decimal)`	`SELECT TRUNCATE(1.999, 1);` **Output** 1.9

3. Date / Time Functions

SQL stores date in date/time format, representing the century, month, year, day and hours. The date and time functions are used to perform operations on the date/time data stored in the database. The default date format is YYYY-MM-DD in SQL.

Some basic functions for date and time are as follows:

Functions	Description	Example

CURDATE( ) /CURRENT_DATE( )	This function returns the current date in 'YYYY-MM-DD' or YYYYMMDD format, depending on whether the function is used in a string or numeric context.
	Syntax
	`CURDATE()`
	or
	`CURRENT_DATE`
		`SELECT CURRENT_DATE;`
		Output
		Let the today is 10-June-2015. It displays current date as, 2015-06-10.

DATE( )	This function returns only DATE part from the given date/time argument. **Syntax** `DATE(date time)`	`SELECT DATE("2013-12-31 01:02:03");` **Output** 2013-12-31
MONTH( )	This function returns the MONTH part from the date argument within a range of 1 to 12 (January to December) and it returns 0 if MONTH part of the date contains null. **Syntax** `MONTH(date/column_name)`	`SELECT MONTH("2009-06-18");` **Output** 06
YEAR( )	This function returns the YEAR part from the given date argument. The return value is in the range of 1000 to 9999 or 0 for null date. **Syntax** `YEAR(date/column_name)`	`SELECT YEAR("2012-05-19");` **Output** 2012

Functions	Description	Example
DAYNAME( )	It returns the name of the week day from a date specified as an argument. **Syntax** `DAYNAME(date/column_name)`	`SELECT DAYNAME("2013-02-18");` **Output** Monday
DAYOFMONTH( )	This function returns the day of the month for a given date argument. The day returned will be within the range of 1 to 31. **Syntax** `DAYOFMONTH(date/column_name)`	`SELECT DAYOFMONTH("2009-05-15");` **Output** 15
DAYOFWEEK( )	This function returns the week day number (1 for Sunday, 2 for Monday and so on) for a date specified as an argument. **Syntax** `DAYOFWEEK(date/column_name)`	`SELECT DAYOFWEEK("2008-05-15");` **Output** 5
DAYOFYEAR( )	It returns day of the year for a given date in numeric format. The return value is within the range of 1 to 366. **Syntax** `DAYOFYEAR(date/column_name)`	`SELECT DAYOFYEAR("2007-07-09");` **Output** 190
NOW( )	This function returns the current date and time in the format 'YYYY-MM-DD HH:MM:SS' or YYYYMMDD HHMMSS format. **Syntax** `NOW()`	`SELECT NOW( );` **Output** Let today date is 10-June-2015 and time is 01:15:20. Now it displays the output as: 2015-06-10 01:15:20
SYSDATE( )	This function returns the current date and time at which the function executes as a value in 'YYYY-MM-DD HH:MM:SS' or YYYYMMDD HHMMSS format. **Syntax** `SYSDATE()`	`SELECT SYSDATE( );` **Output** Let currently function execute on 10-June-2015 and time is 01:18:30. Now, it displays the output as: 2015-06-10 01:18:30.

Some Important SQL Oracle Functions

ADD_MONTHS	This function adds the specified number of months to a datetime value. **Syntax** `ADD_MONTHS(date1, number_months)`	`SELECT ADD_MONTHS('01-Aug-03',3);` **Output** '01-Nov-03'
MONTHS_BETWEEN	This function calculates the number of months between two dates. **Syntax** `MONTHS_BETWEEN(date1, date2)`	`SELECT MONTHS_BETWEEN('06-Jul-05','17-Jul-03');` **Output** 23.65
NEXT_DAY	The NEXT_DAY function returns the date of the first instance of a particular day of the week that follows the specified date. **Syntax** `NEXT_DAY(date, weekday)`	`SELECT NEXT_DAY('01-Aug-03','Tuesday');` **Output** '05-Aug-03'
INITCAP	This function returns capitalise string/char (capitalise first letter of each word). **Syntax** `INITCAP(string)`	`SELECT INITCAP('computer science');` **Output** Computer Science
LAST_DAY	This function returns the date of the last day of the month that contains date. **Syntax** `LAST_DAY (date);`	`Last_DAY (2017-05-18)` **Output** 2017-05-31

stream's member function close( ). This member function takes no parameters and what it does to flush the associated buffers and close the file.

```
out.close();
```

Once this member function is called, the stream object can be used to open another file and the file is available again to be opened by other processes. In that case, an object is destructed while still associated with an open file, the destructor automatically calls the member function close( ).

7.7.8 Basic Operations on Text File

1. Writing to a File

When you want to write in a text file, you have to first declare the ofstream class, then open the text file name and then check whether, it is opened or not. If opened successfully, then write in it and then close it.

e.g.

```
//writing to a text file
#include<fstream.h>
void main()
{
   ofstream myfile("example.txt");
          //opening file using constructor method
   if(myfile)
        //checks whether the file is opened or not
   {
      myfile<<"This is a line.\n"        ]
      myfile<<"This is another           } writing in
      line.\n";                          } the file
      myfile.close();                    ]
   }
   else
      cout<<"Unable to open file";
}
```

Now, you will see the contents of file you've created just now through your program, i.e. you will see these two lines in the text file "example.txt".

This is a line.

This is another line.

• **put( )** This function is a member of ofstream class. It writes single character at a time.

e.g.

```
//writing on a text file using put() function
#include<fstream.h>
#include<string.h>
void main()
{
   ofstream myfile;
   myfile.open("abc.txt",ios::out);
          //using open() and file mode out
   char str[80] = "we are writing in file";
   if(myfile)
      //checks whether the file is opened or not
   {
      int len = strlen(str);
      for(int i=0;i<len;i++)
         myfile.put(str[i]);
      myfile.close();          //close the file
   }
   else
      cout<<"Unable to open the file";
}
```

2. Reading from a File

For reading from a file, we need ifstream class. There are two functions defined in ifstream class that are used for reading purpose.

(i) **get( )** This function is used for reading one character at a time.

e.g.

```
//reading from text file abc.txt using get()
                                      //function
#include<fstream.h>
#include<string.h>
void main()
{
   char c;
   ifstream infile;
   infile.open ("abc.txt",ios::in);
        //using open() and filemode in
   while(infile)
   {
      infile.get(c);
      cout<<c;
   }
   infile.close();
}
```

(ii) **getline ( )** This function is used with input stream and read characters into buffer until either
- num-characters have been read
- a new line is encountered
- or, optionally, until the character delim is read. The delim character is not put into the buffer.

Syntax

```
obj.getline(charline, size, 'terminating-char');
```

where, obj is an object of ifstream class and terminating char is an optional parameter. This function reads character, input into the variable named charline and this reading is terminated as so on as either the newline character '\n' is encountered or given character's size is read (which ever occurs first).

3. Using Cascading Operators (>>,<<) for Reading and Writing Text File

Generally, when using text files, we shall use the same << and >> operators that we used in communication with the console (cin and cout). e.g. In the following program segment, we use the overloaded insertion operator << and extraction operator >>.

e.g. To read and write the text file using cascading operator (> >,< <)

```
#include<fstream.h>
void main()
{
   int rollNo, marks;
   char name[20];
   ofstream fout("ITEM.txt");
   cout<<"\nEnter RollNo, Name and Marks of
                                        Student";
   cin>>rollNo>>name>>marks;
   cout<<"RollNo="<<rollNo<<"\nName="<<name
   <<"\nMarks="<<marks;
         //cascading of << operator to write the
         //content in a text file
   fout.close();
   ifstream fin("ITEM.txt"),arr1[50],
                              arr2[50], arr3[50];
   while(!fin.eof())
   {
      fin>>arr1>>arr2>>arr3;
      //cascading of >> operator to read the
                              content of text file
      cout<<"\n"<<arr1<<"\n"<<arr2<<"\n"
                                   <<arr3<<endl;
   }
   fin.close();
}
```

Output

Enter RollNo, Name and Marks of Student
1001
Amar
345
RollNo = 1001
Name = Amar
Marks = 345

4. Accessing File Sequentially

e.g. To count the number of characters in a file.

```
#include<fstream.h>
void main()
{
   ifstream fin;
   fin.open("out.txt");
   char ch;
   int count = 0;
   while(!fin.eof())
   {
      fin.get(ch);
      count++;
   }
   cout<<"Number of characters in file is";
   cout<<count;
   fin.close();
}
```

e.g. To count the number of words in a file.

```
#include<fstream.h>
void main()
{
   ifstream fin;
   fin.open("out.txt");
   char word[30];
   int count = 0;
   while(!fin.eof())
   {
      fin>>word;
      count++;
   }
   cout<<"Number of words in file is";
   cout<<count;
   fin.close();
}
```

e.g. To count the number of lines in a file.

```
#include<fstream.h>
void main()
{
   ifstream fin;
   fin.open("out.txt");
   char str[80];
   int count = 0;
   while(!fin.eof()
   {
      fin.getline(str,80);
      count++;
   }
   cout<<"Number of lines in file is";
   cout<<count;
   fin.close();
}
```

7.7.9 Basic Operations on Binary File

Consider the following student class to perform basic operations on binary file:

```
class Student
{
   int admno;
   char name[20];
   public:
      void getdata()
      {
         cout<<"\nEnter the admission no:";
         cin>>admno;
         cout<<"\nEnter the name of the
```

(ii) Outer Join

The outer join includes rows in a joined result even when they have no match in the joined table. An outer join returns all rows that satisfy the join condition and also returns those rows from one table for which no rows from the other satisfy the join condition.

(a) Left Outer Join

The left outer join returns all the rows from the left table, even if there are no matches in the right table.

Syntax

```
SELECT col1, col2
FROM table1 LEFT JOIN table2
ON table1.col_name = table2.col_name;
```

(b) Right Outer Join

The right outer join returns all the rows from the right table, even if there are no matches in the left table.

Syntax

```
SELECT column1, column2
FROM table1 RIGHT JOIN table2
ON table1.column_name=table2.column_name;
```

2. Self Join

A self join is a join, where we join a particular table to itself. Here in this case, it is necessary to ensure that the join statement defines an ALIAS name for both the copies of the tables to avoid column ambiguity.

Syntax

```
SELECT Alias_Name1.col1, Alias_Name2.col2
FROM table1<Alias_Name1>,
table2<Alias_Name2>
WHERE Alias_Name1.col_name = Alias_Name2.col_name;
```

3. Non-Equi Join

Non-equi join is used to return the result from two or more tables, where exact join is not possible. The SQL non-equi join uses comparison operators instead of the equal sign like >, <, >=, <= alongwith conditions.

Syntax

```
SELECT * FROM table1, table2
WHERE table1.column > table2.column;
```

4. Natural Join

The natural join is a type of equi join and is structured in such a way that, columns with same name of associate tables will appear once only.

Syntax

```
SELECT * FROM table1 NATURAL JOIN table2;
```

8.10 Cartesian Product

The cartesian product is also referred as cross-join. The cartesian product is a binary operation and is denoted by (×). The degree of new relation is the sum of the degrees of two relations on which cartesian product is operated. The number of tuples, of the new relation is equal to the product of the number of tuples, of the two relations on which cartesian product is performed.

Syntax

```
SELECT * FROM table1 CROSS JOIN table2;
```

Some facts about cartesian product are as follows:

(i) A cartesian product is formed, when join conditions are omitted and invalid.
(ii) All rows in the first table are joined to all rows in the second table.
(iii) If you want to avoid cartesian product, then you should use a join condition in a WHERE clause.
(iv) Using cartesian product, it gives us a large number of rows and is rarely useful.

Consider the following tables GAMESCORES and DEPARTMENTS

TABLE: GAMESCORES

PlayerName	DeptID	Scores
Jason	1	3000
Irene	1	1500
Jane	2	1000

TABLE: DEPARTMENTS

DeptID	DeptName
1	IT
2	Marketing

e.g. To perform the Cross Join on two tables GAMESCORES and DEPARTMENTS.

```
SELECT * FROM GAMESCORES CROSS JOIN DEPARTMENTS;
```

Output

PlayerName	DeptID	Scores	DeptID	DeptName
Jason	1	3000	1	IT
Jason	1	3000	2	Marketing
Irene	1	1500	1	IT
Irene	1	1500	2	Marketing
Jane	2	1000	1	IT
Jane	2	1000	2	Marketing

8.11 Constraints

Constraints are rules enforced on data column that the table must satisfy. These are used to limit the type of data that can go into table. This ensures the accuracy and reliability of the data in the database.

These can be specified at the time of creating table or can also be added to table by using ALTER table statement. Constraints prevent the table from deletion, if there is any dependency.

Constraints can be defined at two level as follows:

(i) **Column level** At Column level, the constraints are referred for a single column and is defined within a specification.

(ii) **Table level** When constraints are defined at table level, then it can be referred to one or more columns and it can also be defined separately from the definitions of the columns in the table.

The basic syntax to apply constraints on columns are as follows:

```
CREATE TABLE table_name
(column1 datatype column1_constraint,
column2 datatype column2_constraint,
column3 datatype);
```

8.11.1 Types of Constraints

There are six types of constraints as follows:

(i) NOT NULL Constraint

NOT NULL constraint is used when we do not want null values to be allowed. It also ensures that null values are not permitted in the column.

The columns without the NOT NULL constraint can have null values. By default, a column can contain NULL values. If you do not want to allow null values in a column, you would have to use NOT NULL constraint to a specific column.

(ii) UNIQUE Constraint

The UNIQUE constraint is used to uniquely identify each record in a database. It requires that, each value in a column should be unique, i.e. no two rows of same column should have duplicate values.

It provides you the guarantee for uniqueness in a column or set of columns and allows us to input the NULL values, unless there is not defined NOT NULL constraint for the same column. It can be defined at table level or at column level.

(iii) PRIMARY KEY Constraint

A PRIMARY KEY constraint is a field in a table which uniquely identifies each rows/records in a database table.

- PRIMARY KEY constraint must contain unique values.
- PRIMARY KEY constraint column cannot have NULL values.

A table can have only one primary key. If multiple fields are used as a primary key, then they are called as composite key. When a table has been assigned a PRIMARY KEY constraint on any field, then you cannot insert two same values in that field.

(iv) FOREIGN KEY Constraint

A foreign key is a field, which points to the primary key of another table. Means that, the same value in one table must also appear in another table. The reference table, means the table, which contains primary key is called the **parent table** and the table with the foreign key is called the **child table**.

A foreign key field cannot contain values, which are not present in the parent table. Primary key field cannot contain null values but foreign key field can contain null values. A FOREIGN KEY constraint can refer to the columns of tables in the same database or within the same table.

Syntax

```
CREATE TABLE table_name
(column1 datatype NULL/NOT NULL,
column2 datatype NULL/NOT NULL, ...
CONSTRAINT fk_column
FOREIGN KEY(column1, column2,..., columnn)
REFERENCES parent_table(column1,
                        column2, ..., column_n));
```

(v) CHECK Constraint

The CHECK constraint is used to check the value, which is entered into a record. It is used to define condition, which each row must satisfy.

If the condition value evaluates to false, then the record violates the constraint and you cannot enter into the table.

⚠ We cannot define CHECK constraint on SQL VIEW.

The CHECK constraint can be applied to one column in a table. It cannot refer to columns in other tables. The sub query also cannot use the CHECK constraint.

The CHECK constraint can be defined by CREATE TABLE statement or ALTER TABLE statement.

A single column can contain *n* number of CHECK constraints. It can be defined at the table level or column level.

Syntax

```
CREATE TABLE table_name
(column1 data type,
column2 data type,
.....
CONSTRAINT constraint_name CHECK
                        (column_name_condition));
```

(vi) DEFAULT Constraint

This constraint is used to provide a default value for a column. The default value will be added to all new records IF no other value is specified.

Syntax

```
CREATE TABLE table_name
(column1 datatype,
column2 datatype,
.....
columnN datatype DEFAULT <value>,
...);
```

7.7.10 Functions for Manipulation of File Pointers

We can move the file pointer to any desired position inside the file. This makes random access possible in file.

This is possible by using the following functions of file stream classes:

Function	Purpose
tellg( )	Returns the current position of the get pointer.
seekg( )	Moves the get pointer (input) to the specified location.
tellp( )	Returns the current position of the put pointer.
seekp( )	Moves the put pointer (output) to the specified location.

e.g. `int pos = fin.tellg();`

This statement returns the current position of get pointer in terms of number of bytes and store it into the variable pos. Similarly, the statement

```
fout.seekp(20);
```

moves the put pointer of file to the byte number 20.

Specifying the Offset

We moved the file pointer using seekg( ) and seekp( ) functions. These functions can also be used with two arguments as given below:

```
seekg(offset,position);
seekp(offset,position);
```

The offset is the number of characters by which the pointers should move. Position denotes the initial position of the file pointer.

The position takes one of the following three constants defined in ios class:

ios::beg	Offset counted from the beginning of the stream.
ios::cur	Offset counted from the current position of the stream pointer.
ios::end	Offset counted from the end of the stream.

e.g. The statement

```
fin.seekg(20,ios::beg);
```

will move the get pointer by 20 bytes from the beginning of the file.

7.8 Pointers

A pointer is a variable, which holds a memory address. This address is the location of another object (typically another variable) in memory. e.g. if one variable contains the address of another variable, the first variable is said to be a pointer to the second variable.

Memory Address	Variable in Memory
2000	2003
2001	
2002	
2003	

Here, the address 2003 is assumed once, it may be some other address also. There are three useful reasons for proper utilisation of pointers as follows:

(i) The memory location can be directly accessed and manipulated.

(ii) Dynamic memory allocation is possible.

(iii) Efficiency of some particular routines can be improved.

7.8.1 The 'Address of' and the 'Indirection' Operators

There are mainly two operators when we deal with pointers. They are as follows:

(i) **Address of (&) or Reference Operator** It gives the address occupied by a variable.

(ii) **Indirection or Value at Address (*) or Dereference Operator** It gives the value stored at a particular address.

e.g. To illustrate the use of address of (&) and dereference (*) operators.

```
#include<iostream.h>
void main()
{
  int alpha=1;
  cout<<"\nThe value "<<alpha<<" is stored at
                                address "<<&alpha;
  cout<<"\nThe value  "<<*(&alpha)<< " is stored
  at address "<<&alpha;
}
```

Output

The value 1 is stored at address 0x8f97fff4

The value 1 is stored at address 0x8f97fff4

Here, &alpha gives the address associated with the variable alpha and *(&alpha) gives the value stored at alpha's address.

7.8.2 Declaration and Initialisation of a Pointer Variable

We can declare a pointer variable similar to other variables in C++. The declaration is based on the data type of the variable that is going to point.

Syntax

```
date_type *pointer_variable;
```

Here, pointer_variable is the name of the pointer and the data_type refers to one of the valid C++ data types, such as int, char, float etc. The data type is followed by an asterisk (*) symbol, which distinguishes a pointer variable from other variables to the compiler. Dereference operator (*) is applied for dereferencing pointer when the pointer can access the value of pointer that points to.

e.g. `int *iptr;`

iptr can hold the address of an integer variable. We can initialise a pointer variables as follows:

```
int num = 25;
int *iptr; //declaration
iptr = &num; //initialisation
```

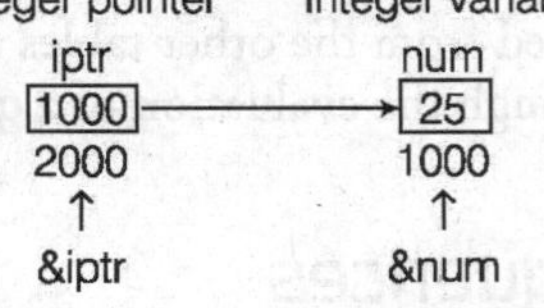

The pointer variable iptr contains the address of an integer variable num. The third statement assigns the address of the variable num to the pointer iptr.

To print num using iptr and indirection operator (*)

```
cout<<iptr; //prints 1000 (address of num)
cout<<*iptr; //prints 25 (dereferencing of iptr)
```

Similarly, the following declaration shows.

```
char *cptr;
float *fptr;
```

cptr is a pointer to character and fptr is a pointer to float value.

7.8.3 Pointer Arithmetic

Following arithmetic operators can be used with pointers:

(i) Increment (++) and decrement (– –) operators.

(ii) Integers can be added to, or subtracted from pointers using the operators +, –, + = and – =.

When a pointer is incremented, it points to the memory location of the next element of its base type and when it is decremented, it points to the memory location of the previous element of the same base type. If 'p' is a character pointer then 'p++' will increment 'p' by 1 byte. If 'p' is an integer pointer, then 'p++' will incremented by 2 bytes.

⚠ No addition, multiplication and division can be performed on two pointers variables.

7.8.4 Reference Variables and Use of Alias

C+ + supports a new type of variable known as the reference variable. A reference provides an alias, i.e. a different name for the variable which means the same variable's value can be used by two different names, the original name and the alias name.

Syntax

```
type &reference_name=variable_name;
```

e.g.

```
float total;
float &sum=total;
```

Here, sum is another name (alias) for total and can be used interchangeably.

7.8.5 Pointers and Arrays

Pointers and arrays are very closely linked to each other. An array name is a pointer to the first element in that array. Therefore, if x is a one-dimensional array, then the address of the first array element can be expressed as either x[0] or simply x. Moreover, the address of the second array element can be written as either x[1] or (x+1) and so on. Since, &x[i] and (x+i) both represent the address of the ith element of x, it would seem reasonable that x[i] and *(x+i) both represent the contents of that address, i.e. the value of the ith element of x.

We know that array elements are always stored in contiguous memory locations. A pointer when incremented always points to an immediately next location of its type.

1. Pointers to an Array (One-Dimensional Array)

Pointers can also be used to point to arrays. If we declared p as an integer pointer, then we can make the pointer p to point to the array a by the following assignment:

```
p=a;
```

This is equivalent to

```
p=&a[0];
```

2. Array of Pointers

Like any other array, we can also have an array of pointers. Each element of such array can point to a data item such as variable, array etc. An array of pointers will contain list of addresses. e.g. consider the following declaration

```
float *name[20];
```

In this declaration, name is an array of 20 elements and each element is a pointer to a variable of type float.

7.8.6 Pointer to a Function

Using pointers, you can access a function. Every function has an address location in the memory and if you know the address of the function, you can access the function through its address directly. A pointer to a function is declared as follows:

```
return_type (*ptr)(formal arguments);
```

This statement tells the compiler that ptr is a pointer to a function, which returns value of the given return_type. The parentheses around *ptr are necessary for precedence reasons.

The function will be accessed as

```
*ptr(actual arguments);
```

Before using this function, it is assumed that the address of the function is assigned to a variable ptr.

Dropping a View

You can delete a view with the DROP view command.

Syntax

```
DROP VIEW view_name;
```

8.13.2 Synonyms

A synonym is an alias for a database object (table, view, sequence etc). Synonyms may be used to reference the original object in SQL as well as PL/SQL. They can be used to hide ownership and location of the database objects they refer to and minimize the impact of moving or renaming the database objects.

With the help of synonym, you can reduce the effort of referencing the object.

There are two categories of synonyms : public and private. A public synonym can be used to allow easy access to an object for all system users. Private synonym, on the other hand, belong to the system user that creates them and reside in that user's schema.

To creat a synonyms, syntax is :

```
CREATE [PUBLIC|PRIVATE] SYNONYM [synonym_name]
FOR object;
```

To remove a synonym from the database or to change the definition of a synonym by dropping and re-creating it, use the DROP SYNONYM statement :

```
DROP [PUBLIC|PRIVATE] SYNONYM [Synonym_name];
```

8.13.3 Table

A table comprises of a number of column object and contains rows of data. A row is a non-empty sequence of values that correspond to the column object in the table.

Every row of the same table has the same number of columns and contains a value for every column of that table.

The following are two types of tables used in the RDBMS:

Base Table

A table whose data is actually stored in the database.

Derived Table

A table obtained from the other tables directly or indirectly through the evaluation of a query expression.

8.13.4 Sequences

Oracle provides the capability to generate sequence of unique numbers. Generally, sequences are used to generate unique, sequential integer values that are used as primary key values is database tables. A sequence of number can be generated in either ascending or descending order. A number once generated by sequence cannot be rolled back.

8.13.5 Index

Indexes are used to retrieves data from the database very fast. These are special lookup tables that the database search engine can use to speed up data retrieval. An index in a database is very similar to an index in the back of book.

To create an index on a table, duplicate values are allowed:

```
CREATE INDEX index_name
ON table_name (column1, column2,…);
```

CHAPTER PRACTICE

1. Which of the following is not an advantage of the database approach?
(1) Increased security
(2) Elimination data redundancy
(3) Ability to associate related data
(4) None of the above

2. Rows of a relation are called
(1) relation (2) tuples
(3) data structure (4) an entity

3. In a relational database, this is a data structure that organises the information about a single topic into rows and columns.
(1) Blocks (2) Record
(3) Tuple (4) Table

4. A database management system
(1) allows simultaneous access to multiple files.
(1) can do more than a record management system.
(3) is a collection of programs for managing data in a single file.
(4) Both (1) and (2)

5. The property/properties of a database is/are
(1) an integrated collection of logically related records.
(2) consolidate separate files into a common pool of data records.
(3) data stored in a database is independent of the application programs using it.
(4) All of the above

6. The primary goal(s) of a DBMS is/are to
(1) provide an environment that is congenial to user
(1) store the information
(3) retrieve information
(4) All of the above

7. A good candidate for a primary key in a database would be a(n)
(1) last name
(1) birth date
(3) employee position tittle
(4) student id number

8. The .... database is the most widely used database structure.
(1) hierarchical
(2) general
(3) standard
(4) relational

9. Course (course_id, sec_id, semester)
Here, the course_id, sec_id and semester are .... and Course is a ....
(1) relations, attribute
(2) attributes, relation
(3) tuple, relation
(4) tuple, attributes

10. In relational database model, after conceptually designing your database, the information contained in a single class would be stored in a
(1) database (2) field
(3) property (4) table

11. In the relational models, a cardinality is termed as
(1) number of tuples
(2) number of attributes
(3) number of tables
(4) number of constraints

12. A .... in a table represents a relationship among a set of values.
(1) column (2) key
(3) row (4) entry

13. 1NF was defined to disallow
(1) multi valued attributes
(2) composite attribute
(3) Both (1) and (2)
(4) None of the above

14. Which normal form is considered adequate for relational database design?
(1) 2NF (2) 3NF (3) 4NF (4) BCNF

15. A primary key if combined with a foreign key creates
(1) parent-child relationship between the tables that connect them.
(2) many-to-many relationship between the tables that connect them.
(3) network model between the tables that connect them.
(4) All of the above

16. An attribute of a relation that references the primary key of another relation is known as the ....
(1) foreign key
(2) unique key
(3) parent key
(4) child key

17. An attribute of one table matching the primary key of another table, is called as
(1) foreign key (2) secondary key
(3) candidate key (4) composite key

18. A group of related fields in a relational database is called a(n)
(1) record (2) object
(3) memo (4) table

19. A primary key that consists of more than one field is called a
(1) composite key
(2) secondary key
(3) group key
(4) All of the above

20. In a relational model, relations are termed as
(1) tuples (2) attributes
(3) tables (4) rows

21. If a relation is in 2NF and 3NF forms, then
(1) no non-prime attribute is functionally dependent on other non-prime attributes.
(2) no non-prime attribute is functionally dependent on prime attributes.
(3) all attributes are functionally independent.
(4) prime attribute is functionally independent of all non-prime attributes.

22. The end of an SQL command is denoted by
(1) an end of line character
(2) an enter-key marker
(3) entering F4 key
(4) a semicolon (;)

23. In a database table, the category of information is called
(1) tuple
(2) field
(3) record
(4) All of the above

24. Which of the following statements is true?
(1) Foreign key fields do not allow duplicate values
(2) In primary key field, you can enter duplicate value
(3) In an indexed field, you may or may not enter duplicate value depending upon setting
(4) All of the above

CHAPTER PRACTICE

1. The basic unit of object-oriented programming is a
(1) method (2) class
(3) overloading (4) object

2. Classes in C++ are …… .
(1) derived data types
(2) user defined data types
(3) built-in data types
(4) All of the above

3. Reusability of the code can be achieved in C++ through
(1) polymorphism
(2) encapsulation
(3) inheritance
(4) Both (1) and (3)

4. The entire set of data and code of an object can be made a user defined data type with the help of …… .
(1) object (2) class
(3) binding (4) abstraction

5. Paying attention to the important properties while ignoring inessential details is known as
(1) selectiveness (2) polymorphism
(3) abstraction (4) summarising

6. …… refers to the act of representing only essential features without including the background details.
(1) Data hiding
(2) Data encapsulation
(3) Data abstraction
(4) All of the above

7. The classes which are intended for the creation of objects or instances, are called …… .
(1) abstract class
(2) concrete class
(3) binding
(4) polymorphism

8. In object oriented programming, by wrapping up characteristics and behaviour into one unit, we achieve
(1) data abstraction
(2) data encapsulation
(3) data hiding
(4) All of the above

9. The major goal of object oriented programming is
(1) top-down program development
(2) speed
(3) user interface
(4) reuse

10. The mechanism by which the data and functions are bound together with an object definition.
(1) Inheritance
(2) Encapsulation
(3) Abstraction
(4) Polymorphism

11. Which of the following operators can be overloaded in C++?
(1) Scope resolution operator
(2) sizeof operator
(3) Conditional operator
(4) Arithmetic operator

12. Overloading involves writing two or more functions with …… .
(1) different names and different argument lists
(2) different names and the same argument list
(3) the same name and different argument lists
(4) the same name and the same argument list

13. In C++, overloaded functions
(1) are the group of functions with the same name
(2) all have the same name and type of arguments
(3) may fall unexpectedly due to stress
(4) All of the above

14. By default, members of the class are …… in nature.
(1) protected (2) private
(3) public (4) static

15. Which operator is used to define the member of class externally?
(1) : (2) ::
(3) # (4) None

16. Which of the following is a valid class declaration?
(1) class A {int x;};
(2) class B {}
(3) public class A {}
(4) object A {int x;};.

17. Pick out the other definition of objects.
(1) Member of the class
(2) Associate of the class
(3) Attribute of the class
(4) Instance of the class

18. How many objects can present in a single class?
(1) 1
(2) 2
(3) 3
(4) as many as possible

19. Private data can be accessed by
(1) class member functions
(2) functions in derived classes
(3) Both (1) and (2)
(4) public classes

20. Objects of a class can directly use any member function declared in the
(1) private and protected sections only
(2) public and protected section only
(3) public section only
(4) public, protected and private section

21. The scope resolution operator usually
(1) specifies a particular class
(2) one base class and more than one derived class
(3) resolve ambiguities
(4) All of the above

22. Constructors are used to
(1) initialise the object
(2) Both (1) and (2)
(3) construct the data members
(4) None of the above

23. How to access the object in the class?
(1) Scope resolution operator
(2) Direct member access operator
(3) Ternary operator
(4) None of the above

24. In which case is it mandatory to provide a destructor in a class?
(1) Almost in every class
(2) Class for which two or more than two objects will be created
(3) Class for which copy constructor is defined
(4) Class whose object will be created dynamically.

25. A constructor that does not have any parameter is called ...... constructor.
(1) custom (2) static
(3) dynamic (4) default

26. A class named Student must have a constructor whose name is
(1) Student
(2) ~Student
(3) student
(4) any legal C++ name

27. A function that is called automatically each time an object is created, is a
(1) constructor (2) destructor
(3) destroyer (4) terminator

28. The return type you code for all constructors is ....
(1) void
(2) the class type
(3) the same type as the first data member defined in the class
(4) no type

29. A function that is called automatically each time an object is destroyed is a
(1) constructor (2) destructor
(3) destroyer (4) terminator

30. class X, class Y and class Z are derived from class BASE. This ...... inheritance.
(1) multiple (2) multilevel
(3) hierarchical (4) single

31. The derivation of Child class from Base class is indicated by ...... symbol.
(1) :: (2) :
(3) ; (4) |

32. When a base class is privately inherited by the derived class, then ....
(1) protected members of the base class become private members of derived class
(2) public members of the base class become private members of derived class
(3) Both (1) and (2)
(4) Only 2

33. Inheritance is the principle that
(1) classes with the same name must be derived from each another
(2) knowledge of a general category can be applied to more specific objects
(3) C++ functions may be used only if they have logical predecessors
(4) one function name may invoke different methods

34. Which of the following is true?
(1) A derived class may have more than one base class
(2) A base class may have more than one derived class
(3) Both (1) and (2)
(4) A base class is not a super class

35. When a class serves as a base class to others, ...
(1) all of its members are inherited
(2) all of its members are inherited, except for any private members
(3) all of its members are inherited, except for any protected members
(4) None of its members is inherited unless specifically listed

36. If we create a file by 'ifstream', then the default mode of the file is ....
(1) ios :: out (2) ios :: in
(3) ios :: app (4) ios :: binary

37. To perform file I/O operations, we must use ...... header file.
(1) <ifstream> (2) <ofstream>
(3) <fstream> (4) Any of these

38. To create an output stream, we must declare the stream to be of class ....
(1) ofstream (2) ifstream
(3) iostream (4) None of these

39. Which of the following is not a file opening mode?
(1) ios::out (2) ios::in
(3) ios::app (4) ios::truncate

40. ...... is return type of is_open () function.
(1) int (2) bool
(3) float (4) char*

41. Which of the following is not used to seek a file pointer?
(1) ios::cur (2) c:ios::end
(3) ios::set (4) ios:beg

42. Which among following is correct syntax of closing a file in C++?
(1) myfile$close( ); (2) myfile@close( );
(3) myfile:close( ); (4) myfile.close( );

43. What is the use of eof( )?
(1) Returns true if a file open for reading has reached the next character.
(2) Returns true if a file open for reading has reached the next word.
(3) Returns true if a file open for reading has reached the end.
(4) Returns true if a file open for reading has reached the middle.

44. Which functions allow to change the location of the get and put positions?
(1) sg( ) and sp( )
(2) sekg( ) and sekp( )
(3) gog( ) and gop( )
(4) seekg ( ) and seekp( )

45. Which is correct syntax for position n bytes back from end of fileObject?
(1) fileObject.seekg(ios::end,n);
(2) fileObject.seekg(n, ios:end);
(3) fileObject.seekg(n, ios::end);
(4) fielObject.seekg(ios:end, n);

46. The first and second arguments of fopen are
(1) a character string containing the name of the file and the second argument is the mode.
(2) a character string containing the name of the user and the second argument is the mode.
(3) a character string containing file pointer and the second argument is the mode.
(4) None of the above

47. How to get position n bytes forward in fileObject?
(1) fileObject.seekg (ios::cur, n);
(2) fileObject.seekg(n, ios::cur);
(3) fileObject.seekg(n, ios::cur);
(4) fileObject.seekg(ios:cur, n);

48. How to get position to the nth byte of fileObject?
(1) fileObject.seekg ('filename', n);
(2) fileObject.seekg (n, 'filename');
(3) fileObject.seekg (n);
(4) fileObject.seekg (n, ios::app);

49. Which of the following fopen statements are illegal?
(1) fp = fopen("abc.txt", "r");
(2) fp = fopen("/home/user1/abc.txt", "w");
(3) fp = fopen("abc", "w");
(4) None of the mentioned

50. What does the following statement mean?
`int(*fp)(char*)`
(1) pointer to a pointer
(2) pointer to an array of chars
(3) pointer to function taking a char* argument and returns an int
(4) function taking a char* argument and returning a pointer to int

77. Which of the following is false?
(1) Normal forms when considered in isolation from other factors do not guarantee a good database design.
(2) The lossless join property guarantees that spuriors tuple generations problem does not occur with respect to relation schemas created after decomposition.
(3) The dependency preservation property ensures that each functional dependency is represented in some individual relations resulting after decomposition.
(4) All of the above

78. The database design that consists of multiple tables that are linked together through matching data stored in each table is called a
(1) hierarchical database
(2) network database
(3) object oriented database
(4) relational database

79. A Relational Database Management System (RDBMS) package manages data in more than one file at once. How does it organise these files?
(1) Tables (2) Relations
(3) Tuple (4) Both (1) and (2)

80. In a table, there can be more than one field that can uniquely identify each tuple of relation known as
(1) candidate key (2) foreign key
(3) primary key (4) super key

81. Which one of the following statements about normal forms is false?
(1) BCNF is stricter than 3NF
(2) Loss-less, dependency preserving decomposition into 3NF is always possible
(3) Loss-less, dependency preserving decomposition into BCNF is always possible
(4) Any relation with two attributes is BCNF

82. Consider two database relation R and S having 3 tuples in R and 2 tuples in S. What is the maximum number of tuples that could appear in the natural join of R and S?
(1) 6 (2) 2 (3) 3 (4) 5

83. Which of the following SQL commands can be used to modify existing data in a database table?
(1) MODIFY (2) UPDATE
(3) CHANGE (4) NEW

84. Which of the following is not included in DML (Data Manipulation Language)?
(1) INSERT
(2) UPDATE
(3) DELETE
(4) CREATE

85. The relational model includes two general integrity rules. Integrity rule 1 is concerned with .... and integrity rule 2 is concerned with ....
(1) primary key, foreign key
(2) primary key, composite key
(3) unique key, foreign key
(4) composite key, foreign key

86. The language used in application programs to request data from the DBMS is referred to as the
(1) QUERY language
(2) DDL
(3) DML
(4) None of the above

87. Which is the correct order, if all the six clauses given below appears in a query?
(1) SELECT, FROM, WHERE, GROUP BY, HAVING, ORDER BY
(2) SELECT, FROM, WHERE, ORDER BY, HAVING, GROUP BY
(3) SELECT, FROM, WHERE, HAVING, ORDER BY, GROUP BY
(4) SELECT, FROM, WHERE, HAVING, GROUP BY, ORDER BY

88. The .... operator is used to compare a value to a list of literals values that have been specified.
(1) BETWEEN (2) ANY
(3) IN (4) ALL

89. What is the language used by most of the DBMS for helping their users to access data?
(1) High level language
(2) Query language
(3) SQL
(4) UGL

90. With SQL, how can you return the number of records in the "Persons" table?
(1) SELECT COUNT (*) FROM Persons
(2) SELECT COUNT ( ) FROM Persons
(3) SELECT COLUMN ( ) FROM Persons
(4) SELECT COLUMN (*) FROM Persons

91. To remove duplicate rows from the result of an SQL SELECT statement, the ...... qualifier specified must be included.
(1) ONLY (2) UNIQUE
(3) DISTINCT (4) SINGLE

92. When three or more AND and OR conditions are combined, it is easier to use the SQL keyword(s)
(1) LIKE only
(2) IN only
(3) NOT IN only
(4) Both IN and NOT IN

93. Which character function can be used to return a specified portion of a character string?
(1) INSTR (2) SUBSTRING
(3) SUBSTR (4) POS

94. Which of the following is an exception to the return values of a DATE type single row function?
(1) TO_DATE
(2) SYSDATE
(3) MONTHS_BETWEEN
(4) TO_NUMBER

95. What result set is returned from the following SQL query?
```
SELECT customer_name, telephone
FROM customers
WHERE city IN ('Jaipur', 'Delhi', 'Agra');
```
(1) The customer_name of all customer who are not living in Jaipur, Delhi or Agra
(2) The customer_name and telephone of all customers
(3) The customer_name and telephone of all customer
(4) The customer_name and telephone of all customers living in either Jaipur, Delhi or Agra

96. Find the SQL statement below that is equal to the following:
```
SELECT NAME FROM CUSTOMER
WHERE STATE = 'VA';
```
(1) SELECT NAME IS CUSTOMER WHERE STATE IN ('V A');
(2) SELECT NAME IN CUSTOMER WHERE STATE = 'V, A';
(3) SELECT NAME IN CUSTOMER WHERE STATE = 'V';
(4) SELECT NAME FROM CUSTOMER WHERE STATE IN ('VA');

97. The SQL statement
SELECT SUBSTR ('123456789',
```
INSTR ('abcabcabc', 'b'), 4)
FROM EMP;
```
prints
(1) 6789 (2) 2345
(3) 123 (4) 456789

98. What will be the output of the following query?
```
SELECT ROUND(144.23, -1)
FROM dual;
```
(1) 140 (2) 144 (3) 150 (4) 100

99. What will be the output of the following query?
```
SELECT LOWER ('HI WORLD
!!!') FROM dual;
```
(1) Hi World (2) Hi World
(3) hi world !!! (4) HI WORLD !!!

100. What will be the output of the following query?
```
SELECT LENGTH ('hi') FROM
dual;
```
(1) 2 (2) 3 (3) 1 (4) hi

101. What will the following query show as a result?
```
SELECT LENGTH ('It is a
lovely day today!') FROM
dual;
```
(1) 25 (2) 19 (3) 20 (4) 0

102. What will be returned as a result of the following query?
```
SELECT INSTR ('James', 'x')
FROM dual;
```
(1) 1 (2) 2 (3) 0 (4) 3

103. Assuming the SYSDATE is 13-JUN-13, what will be the outcome of the following query?
```
SELECT SUBSTR (SYSDATE, 10,
7) FROM dual;
```
(1) 3 (2) N-13 (3) 0 (4) Null

104. What will be the outcome of the following query?
```
SELECT ROUND (148.50) FROM
dual;
```
(1) 148.50 (2) 140
(3) 150 (4) 149

105. Assuming the sysdate is 10-JUN-13, What will be the outcome of the following query?
```
SELECT(SYSDATE, 'mon') FROM
dual;
```
(1) 10-JUN-13
(2) 1-JUN-13
(3) Error as the TRUNC function can't have an input parameter when used with dates
(4) 31-JUN-13

106. What will be the outcome of the following query?
```
SELECT MONTHS_BETWEEN
('21_JUN-13', '19-JUN-13')
FROM dual;
```
(1) Error
(2) A positive number
(3) A negative number
(4) 0

107. Match the List I with List II and find the correct answer using the codes given below the lists.

	List I	List II
P.	3 NF	1. Functional dependencies
Q.	BCNF	2. Multi valued dependencies
R.	4 NF	3. Join dependencies
S.	5 NF	

Codes

	P	Q	R	S
(1)	1	1	3	2
(2)	1	2	3	3
(3)	1	1	2	3
(4)	1	2	2	3

108. Indicate which of the following statements are true :
A relation database which is in 3NF may still have undesirable data redundancy because there may exist
(1) transitive functional dependencies
(2) non-trivial functional dependencies involving prime attributes on the right side
(3) non-trivial functional dependencies involving prime attributed only on the left side
(4) non-trivial functional dependencies involving only prime attributes

109. An entity has
(i) a set of properties
(ii) a set of properties and values for all the properties
(iii) a set of properties and the values for some set of properties may non-uniquely identify an entity
(iv) a set of properties and the values of some set of properties may uniquely identify an entity
Which of the above are valid?
(1) Only (i) (2) Only (ii)
(3) Only (iii) (4) Only (iv)

110. 3 NF is preferred than BCNF because
(i) we normally choose to retain dependency preservation.
(ii) a high penalty in system performance is to be paid or risk the integrity of the data in our database.
(iii) there is not any problem of repetition of information.
(iv) Given statement is wrong.
(1) Only (iv) is true
(2) (ii) and (iii) are true
(3) (i) and (ii) are true
(4) Only (iii) is true

111. Which of the following statements best describes the main reasons for normalising relations database?
(i) To achieve physical data independence
(ii) To remove data anomalies (insertion, updation, deletion anomalies)
(iii) To save space on disk
(1) (i), (ii) and (iii) (2) (i) and (ii)
(3) (i) and (iii) (4) (ii) and (iii)

112. Null values in SQL indicate
(i) Zero value
(ii) Value is unknown
(iii) Value does not exist
(1) Only (iii) (2) (ii) and (iii)
(3) (i) and (ii) (4) All of these

113. Would the user use the DML or the DDL to do each task?
(i) Define a new table for keeping soil and light needs.
(ii) Add a flower to the inventory.
(iii) Add a new zone to the zone table.
(1) DDL, DML, DML
(2) DML, DDL, DDL
(3) DML, DML, DDL
(4) DDL, DDL, DML

114. Consider the query:
```
SELECT student_name
FROM Student
WHERE class_name = (SELECT
class_name FROM Student WHERE
math_marks = 100);
```
What will be the output?
(1) The list of names of students with 100 marks in mathematics
(2) The names of all students of all classes in which atleast one student has 100 marks in mathematics
(3) The names of all students in all classes having 100 marks in mathematics
(4) The names and class of all students whose marks in mathematics are 100

92. Match the following with their description.

List I	List II
a Encapsulation	i The capability to write on function or method that works in variety of different ways.
b Aggregation	ii The capability of a class or relay upon another class.
c Inheritance	iii The capability to store one object inside of another object
d Polymorphism	iv The capability to store related information

(1) a-iv, b-iii, c-ii, d-i
(2) a-iii, b-i, c-ii, d-iv
(3) a-iii, b-iv, c-i, d-ii
(4) a-i, b-iii, c-iv, d-ii

93. Consider the following statements:

```
char *ptr;
ptr = "Hello";
cout<<*ptr;
```

What will be printed?
(1) first letter
(2) entire string
(3) it is a syntax error
(4) last letter

94. Which of the followings are true about constructors?
(i) A class can have more than one constructor
(ii) They can be inherited
(iii) Their address can be referred
(iv) Constructors cannot be declared in protected section of the class
(v) Constructors cannot return values
(1) (i), (ii), (iv)
(2) (i), (ii), (v)
(3) (i), (iii), (v)
(4) (i), (iv), (v)

95. Which of the following statements are not true about destructor?
(i) It is invoked when object goes out of the scope
(ii) Like constructor, it can also have parameters
(iii) It can be virtual
(iv) It can be declared in private section
(v) It bears same name as that of the class and precedes Lambda singh
(1) (ii), (iii), (v)
(2) (ii), (iii), (iv)
(3) (ii), (iv), (v)
(4) (iii), (iv), (v)

96. Match the following.

Table: Execution of base class constructors

Method of Inheritance	Order of Execution
P class B : public A	I B (); C (); A ();
Q class A : public B, public C	II A (); B (); A ();
R class A : public B, virtual public C	III A (); B ();
	IV C (); B (); A ();
	V B (); A ();

(1) P-III, Q-II, R-I (2) P-V, Q-I, R-IV
(3) P-III, Q-I, R-IV (4) P-V, Q-II, R-I

97. Which constructor will be called by the following lines of code?
(i) `Student s1;`
(ii) `Student s2 = s1;`
(1) First copy constructor, then default constructor
(2) First default constructor, then copy constructor
(3) Default constructors for both lines of code
(4) Copy constructor for both lines of code.

98. Which of the statements are true?
(i) Function overloading is done at compile time.
(ii) Protected members are accessible to the member of derived class.
(iii) A derived class inherits constructors and destructors.
(iv) A friend function can be called like a normal function
(v) Nested class is a derived class.
(1) (i), (ii), (iii) (2) (iii), (iv), (v)
(3) (ii), (iii), (v) (4) (i), (ii), (iv)

99. When base class is derived in protected mode, then ....
(i) public members of base class become private members of derived class
(ii) public members of base class become protected members of derived class
(iii) public members of base class become public members of derived class
(iv) protected members of base class become protected members of derived class
(v) protected members of base class become private members of derived class
(vi) protected member of base class become public members of derived class
(1) (i), (v) (2) (i), (vi)
(3) (ii), (vi) (4) (ii), (iv)

100. In case of inheritance, where both base and derived classes are having constructor and destructor, then which if the following are true?
(i) Constructor are executed in their order of derivation
(ii) Constructors are executed in reverse order of derivation
(iii) Destructors are executed in their order of derivation
(iv) Destructors are executed in reverse order of derivation
(1) (ii), (iv) (2) (i), (iii)
(3) (i), (iv) (4) (ii), (iii)

101. Which of the following are member dereferencing operators in CPP?
(i) . * (ii) ::
(iii) – >* (iv) :*
(1) (i) and (iii)
(2) (i) and (v)
(3) (iii) and (iv)
(4) (iii), (iv), (v)

102. The return value of the following code is

```
class1 & test (class1 obj)
{
  class1 *ptr = new
                    class1();
  .......
  return ptr;
}
```

(1) object of class1
(2) reference to ptr
(3) reference of class1
(4) object pointed by ptr

103. If an integer occupies 4 bytes and a character occupies 1 byte of memory, each element of the following class would occupy how many bytes?

```
class Name
{
  int age;
  char name[20];
}
```

(1) 5 (2) 24
(3) 21 (4) 22

104. Consider the following class definitions:

```
class A
{
};
```

```
class B : protected A
{
};
```

What happens when we try to compile this class?

(1) will not compile because class body of A is not defined

(2) will not compile because class body of B is not defined

(3) will not compile because class A is not public inherited

(4) will compile successfully

105. **What is the output of this program?**

```
class rect
{
    int x, y;
    public:
      void val(int, int);
      int area( )
        {
            return(x*y);
        }
};
void rect :: val(int a,int b)
{
    x = a;
    y = b;
}
void main( )
{
    rect r;
    r.val(3, 4);
    cout<<"react area:"
                <<r.area(
);
}
```

(1) rect area:3 (2) rect area:12

(3) rect area:24 (4) None of these

106. **What is the output of the following program?**

```
class Box
{
    public:
    double length,breadth;
    double height;
};
void main( )
{
    Box Box1;
    double volume;
    Box1.height = 5;
    Box1.length = 6;
    Box1.breadth = 7.1;
    volume = Box1.height*
    Box1.length*
    Box1.breadth;
    cout<<volume;
```

(1) 210 (2) 213 (3) 215 (4) 217

107. **What is the output of this program?**

```
class sample
{
    private:
      int var;
    public:
    void input()
    {
      cout<<var;
    }
    void output()
    {
      cout<<"Variable
                entered is";
      cout<<var<<"\n";
    }
};
void main()
{
    sample object;
    object.input();
    object.output();
    object.var();
}
```

(1) Enter an integer 5
Variable entered is 5

(2) runtime error

(3) error

(4) None of the mentioned

108. **What is the output of this program?**

```
void main( )
{
    int a = 5, b = 10, c = 15;
    int *arr[]= {&a,&b,&c};
    cout<<arr[1];
}
```

(1) 5

(2) 10

(3) 15

(4) it will return some random number

109. **What is the output of this program?**

```
void main( )
{
    char arr[20];
    int i;
    for(i = 0;i < 10; i++)
        *(arr + i) = 65 + i;
    (arr + i) = '\0';
    cout<<arr;
}
```

(1) ABCDEFGHIJ

(2) AAAAAAAAAA

(3) JJJJJJ

(4) None of the mentioned

110. **What is the output of this program?**

```
void main( )
{
    char *ptr;
    char Str[ ] = "abcdefg";
    ptr = Str;
    ptr += 5;
    cout<<ptr;
}
```

(1) fg (2) cdef

(3) defg (4) abcd

ANSWER KEY

1	(4)	2	(2)	3	(3)	4	(2)	5	(3)	6	(3)	7	(2)	8	(2)	9	(4)	10	(2)
11	(4)	12	(3)	13	(1)	14	(2)	15	(2)	16	(1)	17	(4)	18	(4)	19	(1)	20	(3)
21	(1)	22	(1)	23	(2)	24	(4)	25	(4)	26	(1)	27	(1)	28	(4)	29	(2)	30	(3)
31	(2)	32	(3)	33	(2)	34	(3)	35	(2)	36	(2)	37	(3)	38	(1)	39	(4)	40	(2)
41	(3)	42	(4)	43	(3)	44	(4)	45	(3)	46	(1)	47	(3)	48	(3)	49	(4)	50	(3)
51	(1)	52	(1)	53	(4)	54	(4)	55	(2)	56	(2)	57	(2)	58	(3)	59	(2)	60	(2)
61	(2)	62	(2)	63	(4)	64	(1)	65	(4)	66	(4)	67	(3)	68	(4)	69	(3)	70	(2)
71	(2)	72	(1)	73	(4)	74	(4)	75	(3)	76	(2)	77	(4)	78	(2)	79	(1)	80	(4)
81	(4)	82	(2)	83	(4)	84	(4)	85	(2)	86	(1)	87	(1)	88	(2)	89	(3)	90	(1)
91	(4)	92	(1)	93	(1)	94	(4)	95	(3)	96	(3)	97	(2)	98	(4)	99	(4)	100	(3)
101	(1)	102	(2)	103	(2)	104	(4)	105	(2)	106	(2)	107	(3)	108	(4)	109	(1)	110	(1)

9.1.3 Examples of Front-End Software

Some of the common examples of front-end software are as follows :

1. Oracle SQL Developer

It is the Oracle Database IDE. A free graphical user interface, Oracle SQL developer allows database users and administrators to do their database tasks in fewer clicks and keystrokes.

A productivity tool, SQL developer's main objective is to help the end user as save time and maximise the return on investment in the Oracle database technology stack.

2. Visual Basic

Visual Basic (VB) is a programming software from Microsoft in which a programmer uses a Graphical User Interface (GUI) to choose and modify pre-selected sections of code written in the Basic programming language.

3. Visual C++

Microsoft Visual C++ is an Integrated Development Environment (IDE) product from Microsoft for the C, C++ and C++/CLI programming languages. It features tools for developing and debugging C++ code, especially code written for Windows API, DirectX and .NET framework.

Many applications require redistributable visual C++ packages to functions correctly. These packages are often installed independently of applications, allowing multiple applications to make use of the package while only having to install it once.

4. PowerBuilder

It is a popular Rapid Application Development (RAD) tool for building object oriented programming client/server applications, the part of which can be distributed within a network. A major feature of PowerBuilder is the ability to create databases using an object oriented interface.

Applications created with PowerBuilder can access other popular types of databases on other major platforms using Open Database Connectivity (ODC).

5. Delphi

It is a Rapid Application Development (RAD) tool for Windows, Delphi, part of RAD studio, includes a code editor with Code Insight (code completion), Error Insight (real time error-checking) and other features; refactoring; a visual forms designer for both VCL (native windows) and FMX (cross-platform, partially native per platform); an integrated debugger for all platforms including mobile; source control and support for third party plugins. It has strong database support.

9.2 Back-End Database

A back-end database is a database that is accessed by users indirectly through an external application rather than by an application programming stored within the database itself or by low level manipulation of the data. A back-end database stores data, but does not include end user application elements such as stored queries, forms, macros or reports.

9.2.1 Small Database Systems

The term back-end database is most widely used among developers using small database programming systems, which can contain the end user application programming within the database as a single item.

The developer must decide whether to include the application programming with the data in a single database or whether to separate them into two database files, according to the client/server model.

For simple database applications, it is common for all programs to be stored with the data. This results in a single file and is easier to develop at the expense of scalability and concurrency.

9.2.2 Examples of Common Database Management Systems (Back-End)

There are several database management systems used to manage the data in an effective way.

Some of the common examples of DBMS are given below:

1. MySQL

It is the most popular open source SQL or relational database management system developed, distributed and supported by Oracle corporation. It runs as a server, providing multi-user access of data to a number of databases. It uses SQL (Structured Query Language) for data manipulation and retrieval.

2. Oracle

Oracle is a fourth generation relational database management system, developed, distributed and supported by Oracle corporation. It is one of the most widely used and trusted relational database engine. This system is built upon a relational database frameworks in which data objects may be accessed by users through SQL.

3. Ingres

Ingres stands for Interactive Graphics Retrieval System. It is a commerically supported, open source SQL relational database management system. It is fully open with a growing global community of contributors. Ingres has created a number of commercial database applications like action.

4. DB2

It is a Relational Database Management System (RDBMS), initially designed to work exclusively on IBM mainframe platforms but later ported to other widely used operating systems like Unix, Windows and presently in Linux. DB2 is an integral part of IBM's information management portfolio.

It is a fully-featured, high-performance database engine capable of handling large quantities of data and concurrently serving many users.

5. MS SQL

MS SQL or Microsoft SQL server is a client/server RDBMS, developed, distributed and supported by Microsoft corporation.

It is a fully-featured database primarily designed to compete against competitors like Oracle database and MySQL. It supports the standard SQL language known as **ANSI SQL**. This MS SQL database splits the database processing between two systems, the client PC and the remote database server.

6. Sybase

Sybase database also known as **Sybase SQL server** or **Sybase ASE** (Adaptive Server Enterprise), developed and marketed by a computer software company named as 'Sybase Solutions Corporation'.

9.3 System Development Life Cycle

System Development Life Cycle (SDLC) is a series of six main phases to create a hardware system only, a software system only or a combination of both to meet or exceed customer's expectations.

"A **system** is a set of interacting or interdependent components forming an integrated whole" it's a term that can be used in different industries, therefore **Software Development Life Cycle** is a limited term that explains the phases of creating a software component that integrates with other software components to create the whole system.

System development life cycle phases are as follows:

1. System Planning

The planning phase is the most crucial step in creating a successful system, during this phase you decide exactly what you want to do and the problems you're trying to solve, by:

- Defining the problems, the objectives and the resources such as personnel and costs.
- Studying the ability of proposing alternative solutions after meeting with clients, suppliers, consultants and employees.
- Studying how to make your product better than your competitors'.

After analysing this data, you will have three choices:

(i) develop a new system
(ii) improve the current system
(iii) leave the system as it is.

2. System Analysis

The end-user's requirements should be determined and documented, what their expectations are for the system, and how it will perform. A feasibility study will be made for the project as well, involving determining whether it's organisationally, economically, socially, technologically feasible. It's very important to maintain strong communication level with the clients to make sure you have a clear vision of the finished product and its function.

3. System Design

The design phase comes after a good understanding of customer's requirements, this phase defines the elements of a system, the components, the security level, modules, architecture and the different interfaces and type of data that goes through the system.

A general system design can be done with a pen and a piece of paper to determine how the system will look like and how it will function, and then a detailed and expanded system design is produced, and it will meet all functional and technical requirements, logically and physically.

4. Implementation and Deployment

This phase comes after a complete understanding of system requirements and specifications, it's the actual construction process after having a complete and illustrated design for the requested system.

In the Software Development Life Cycle, the actual code is written here, and if the system contains hardware, then the implementation phase will contain configuration and fine-tuning for the hardware to meet certain requirements and functions.

In this phase, the system is ready to be deployed and installed in customer's premises, ready to become running, live and productive, training may be required for end users to make sure they know how to use the system and to get familiar with it, the implementation phase may take a long time and that depends on the complexity of the system and the solution it presents.

5. System Testing and Integration

Bringing different components and subsystems together to create the whole integrated system and then

(iii) **Application Data** It contains the structure and format of queries, reports and other application components.

8.3.2 Keys

The key is defined as the column or attribute or a combination of attributes that is used to identify records of the database table. Sometimes, we might have to retrieve data from more than one table, in those cases we require to join tables with the help of keys.

It also controls and maintains the integrity of information stored in the database.

Candidate Keys | Alternate Key | Relationship (Foreign Key) | Primary Key

studentId	firstname	lastname	courseId
L0002345	Jim	Black	C002
L0001254	James	Harradine	A004
L0002349	Amanda	Holland	C002
L0001198	Simon	McCloud	S042
L0023487	Peter	Murray	P301
L0018453	Anne	Norris	S042

Primary Key

Student table

courseId	courseName
A004	Accounts
C002	Computing
P301	History
S042	Short Course

Course table

There are various types of keys, which are as follows:

1. Primary Key

The primary key of a relational table uniquely identifies each record in the table. In some tables, combination of more than one attribute can be declared as primary key. In that case, primary key is known as **composite key**. The value of primary key should be unique and not null. Every relation does have a primary key.

e.g. in the given student table studentId works as a primary key because it contains Id's, which are unique for each student.

2. Candidate Key

The set of all attributes, which can uniquely identify each tuple of a relation are known as candidate keys. Each table may have one or more candidate keys and one of them will become the primary key. e.g. columns studentId and the combination of firstname and lastname work as the candidate keys for the given Student table.

3. Alternate Key

A candidate key that is not the primary key is known as alternate key. These keys are also unique but they allow nulls. e.g. from the candidate keys (studentId, firstname and lastname), studentId chosen as a primary key then the firstname and lastname columns work as a alternate key.

4. Foreign Key

A foreign key is a non-key attribute, whose value is derived from the primary key of another table. The relationship between two tables is established with the help of foreign key.

8.3.3 Normalisation

The normalisation is the process of transformation of the relationship among data elements in a record. Normalisation replaces a collection of data in a record structure by another record design which is simpler, more predictable and therefore more manageable.

Some important form of normalisation are as follows:

1. First Normal Form (1NF)

Any table is in 1NF if the values in the domain of each attribute of the relation are "atomic". We can say, only one value is associated with each attribute and the value is not a set of values or a list of values. It does not have any repeating groups. It does not allow multi-valued attributes, composite attributes and their combinations.

2. Second Normal Form (2NF)

To be in 2NF, a table must be in 1NF and no attributes of the table should be functionally dependent on only one part of a concatenated primary key. Thus, 2NF can be violated only when a key is a composite key, or in other words, one that consists of more than one attributes.

3. Third Normal Form (3NF)

A table is said to be in the 3NF, if all the non-key fields of the table are independent of all other non-key fields of the table.

Functional Dependency

It is a relationship that exists between any two attributes or fields.

In a relation R, attribute B of R is functionally dependent on attribute A of R, if and only if each value of A uniquely determine the values of B.

The notation form of functional dependency is $A \rightarrow B$.

4. Boyce-Codd Normal Form (BCNF)

A relation R is in BCNF if every determinant is a candidate key. Let $X \rightarrow A$ is a functional dependency, in relation schema R is in 3NF, if X is a super key of R.

This is more restrictive than 3NF. While decomposing relation to make them in BCNF we may loose some dependencies. 3NF is better than BCNF.

8.4 Oracle

Oracle Database (commonly referred to as Oracle RDBMS or simply as Oracle) is an object relational database management system. Users of Oracle database refer to the server side memory structure. The Oracle DBMS can store and execute stored procedure and functions within itself. The Oracle RDBMS stores data logically in the form of tablespaces and physically in the form of data files.

Table describes various Oracle versions

Oracle Versions	PL/SQL Version	Characteristics
Oracle6	1.0	Initial version of PL/SQL used primarily as a scripting language in SQL*Plus and also as a programming language in SQL*Forms 3.
Oracle7	2.0	Major upgrade to version 1. Adds support for stored procedures, functions packages, programmer-defined records, PL/SQL tables, and many package extensions.
Oracle7.1	2.1	Supports programmer-defined subtypes, enables the use of stored functions inside SQL statements, and offers dynamic SQL with the DBMS_SQL package. With version 2.1, you can now execute SQL DDL statements from within PL/SQL programs.
Oracle7.3	2.3	Enhances functionality of PL/SQL tables, offers improved remote dependency management, adds file I/O capabilities to PL/SQL.
Oracle8	8.0	The new version number reflects Oracle's effort to synchronize version number across related products. PL/SQL8 that supports the many enhancements of Oracle8, including, object-oriented design and development.
Oracle8*i*	8.1	The First or Oracle's *i* series (the "Internet database"), the corresponding release of PL/SQL offers a truly impressive set of added functionality, including a new version of dynamic SQL (native dynamic SQL), support for Java in the database.
Oracle9*i* Release1	9.0	Oracle9*i* came fairly quickly on the heels of Oracle8*i* . The first release of this version show cases the following features for PL/SQL developers; support for inheritance in object types, table functions and cursor expression.
Oracle9*i* Release2	9.2	The most recent version of the Oracle product set, Oracle Release2 puts a major emphasis on XML (eXtensible Markup Language), but also has some treats for PL/SQL developers, including associative arrays (index-by tables that can be indexed by VARCHAR 2 strings in addition to integers), record-based DML.

8.4.1 Two-Tier Architecture

The two-tier is based on client-server architecture. This model consists of a client tier and a database server tier. Processing tasks and application logic are shared between the database server and the client.

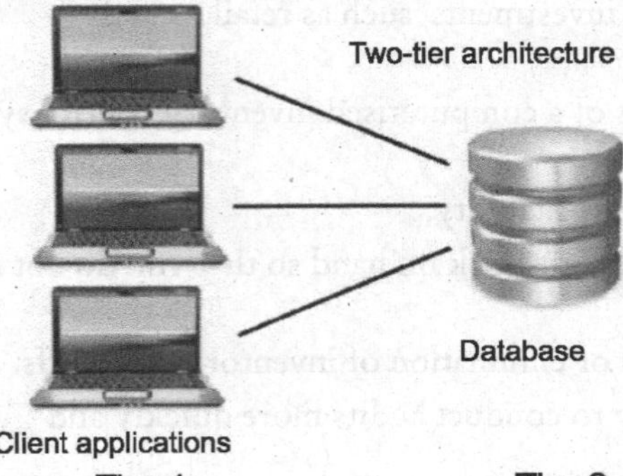

•The above figure shows the architecture of two-tier. Two layers of two-tier architecture are Database (Data tier) and Client applications (Client tier).

8.4.2 Three-Tier Architecture

This model evolved to address the problems of the two-tier model. Three-tier architecture having three layers. They are as follows:

1. **Client Layer** This layer is used for the design purpose where data is presented to the user or input is taken from the user.
2. **Business Layer** It is the intermediate layer which has the functions for client layer and it is used to make communication faster between client and data layer. It provides the business processes logic and the data access.
3. **Data Layer** In this layer, actual database is comes.

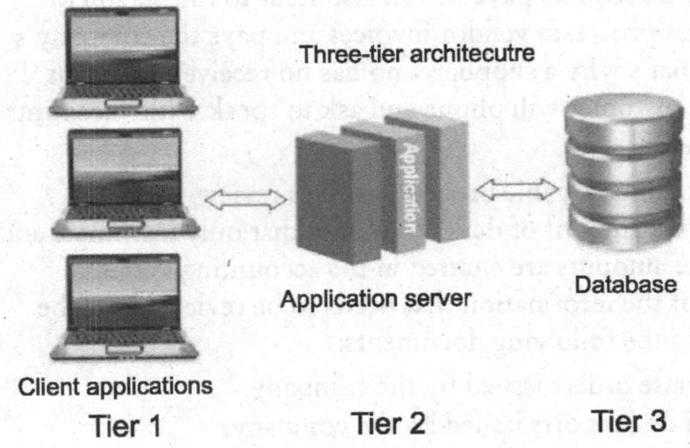

8.4.3 Oracle Call Interface (OCI)

The Oracle Call Interface (OCI) is an Application Programming Interface (API) that allows applications written in C to interact with one or more Oracle server. OCI gives the capability to your programs to perform the full range of database operations that are possible with Oracle9i database including SQL statement processing and object manipulation.

OCI is highly reliable. OCI libraries are included by default in Oracle database.

Given the impact on customers and profits, inventory control is one of the chief concerns of businesses that have large inventory investments, such as retailers and distributors.

Typical benefits of a computerised inventory control system include:

(i) Increased profitability.
(ii) Having enough stock on hand so that you do not run out.
(iii) Reduction or elimination of inventory write-offs.
(iv) The ability to conduct audits more quickly and efficiently.

2. Financial Accounting

It is a specialised branch of accounting that deals with evaluating and preparing companies financial information and records. Financial accounting is used to prepare financial document for people outside the organisation or not involved in the day-to-day running of the company such as creditors, investors, banks and government agencies. It is the process of recording, summarising and reporting the transactions resulting from business operations over a period of time. These transactions are summarised in the preparation of financial statements, including the balance sheet, income statement and cash flow statement, that encapsulates the company's operating performance over a specific period.

3. Accounts Payable

The term accounts payable can also refer to the person or staff that processes vendor invoices and pays the company's bills. That's why a supplier who has no received payment from a customer will phone and ask to speak with "accounts payable".

The accounts payable process involves reviewing an enormous amount of detail to ensure that only legitimate and accurate amounts are entered in the accounting system. Much of the information that needs to be reviewed will be found in the following documents:

- Purchase orders issued by the company.
- Receiving reports issued by the company.
- Invoices from the company's vendors.
- Contracts and other agreements.

4. Invoice Management System

It is an internal business function responsible for managing documents from vendors or suppliers. Invoices represent a source document in accounting. Companies use invoice management processes to ensure vendors and suppliers receive payment in a timely manner.

A common invoice management process is the three way match system found in accounts payable functions. Purchase orders represent the company's internal information that provides individuals specific authorisation to purchase items from vendors or suppliers. Two copies of purchase orders usually exist in a business. One is sent to the vendor or supplier and one is retained in the company's accounting department. This document comes into play later on during the invoice management process.

5. Personal Information Management System

It is a system that manages all the information of a person. It refers to both the practice and the study of the activities a person performs in order to acquire or create, store, organise, maintain, retrieve, use and distribute the information needed to meet life's many goals and to fulfill life's many roles and responsibilities. It places special emphasis on the organisation and maintenance of personal information collections in which information items such as paper documents, electronic documents, E-mail messages, web references, handwritten notes etc., are stored for later use and repeated reuse.

6. Fees Management System

It is the most important module that helps an institution to maintain a financial record of an institution. It takes care of the amount of fees paid by students for the respective course opted by them. Fees management system is a kind of module specially designed to give a precise idea to parents regarding the fee structure of the institution.

It becomes easy for them to analyse the exact amount that parents are investing for a particular course.

7. Result Analysis System

Student result analysis system is a software which helpful for students as well as college authorities. In the current system, all activities are done manually. It is very time consuming and costly. Our student result analysis system deals with the various activities related to the students. During analysis, data collected on the various files, decision points and transactions handled by the present system. The commonly used tools in the system are data flow diagram, interviews, etc. The success of the system depends on how clearly the problem is defined thoroughly investigated and properly carried out through the choice of solution.

8. Admission Management System

It allows you to manage the admission of all the students easily alongwith student's basic details family information, previous school details, transfer and birth certificate and report card with passport sized photo.

This system provides online registration system where parents can register their child for the upcoming academic session. Proposed system is an online registration system which is accessed by parents, account executive and interview committee.

The data is maintained in the DBMS. Parents should be able to take appointment for the required slot with their own time preferences. Account executive can update the student payment details in case not paid online. He can provide day/slot/class wise payment details for the interview committee. Required reports will be produced.

9. Income Tax Management System

It is a process which is related to proper management and synchronised way for collecting tax by filling up return form and getting Tax Identification Number (TIN). Our government can get the thorough information of income and expenditure for any single people who pay taxes.

9.7 Terms Related to Data

Some common terms related to data are as follows :

1. Data Dictionary

The data dictionary, also called a **system catalog** is an important part of the DBMS. It contains metadata, that means, it contains the database descriptions used by the DBMS. In most DBMS, the data dictionary is active and integrated.

It holds the following information about each data element in the database and normally includes :

(i) Names (ii) Data type
(iii) Range of values (iv) Source
(v) Access authorisation
(vi) Indicates which application programs use which data.

Data dictionary may be either **active** or **passive**. An active **data dictionary** (also called **integrated data dictionary**) is managed automatically by the database management software. The **passive data dictionary** (also called **non-integrated data dictionary**) is the one used only for documentation purposes. It is managed by the users of the system and is modified whenever the structure of the database is changed.

2. Data Warehouse

The term **"Data Warehouse"** was first coined by Bill Inmon in 1990. According to Inmon, a data warehouse is a subject oriented, integrated, time-variant and non-volatile collection of data. This data helps analysts to take informed decisions in an organisation.

A data warehouses provide us generalised and consolidated data in multidimensional view. Alongwith generalised and consolidated view of data, a data warehouses also provides us Online Analytical Processing (OLAP) tools. These tools help us in interactive and effective analysis of data in a multidimensional space. This analysis results in data generalisation and data mining.

3. Data Mining

Data mining is defined as extracting the information from the huge set of data. In other words, data mining is mining the knowledge from data.

Data mining is a powerful new technology with great potential to help companies focus on the most important information in the data they have collected about the behaviour of their customers and potential customers. It discovers information within the data that queries and reports can't effectively reveal.

4. Meta Data

Meta Data means 'Data about Data'. This is the documentation stored in the database repository, and which holds information about your database objects.

e.g. in Oracle, the table USER_TABLES holds vital information about your tables.

9.8 Object Modeling

It is the process of designing the objects or classes through which an object oriented application examines and manipulates some service.

Introduction to Object Oriented Modeling using Unified Modeling Language

Object oriented modeling is an approach to modeling an application that is used at the beginning of the software life cycle when using an object oriented approach to software development.

Object oriented modeling is typically done *via* use cases and abstract definitions of the most important objects. The most common language used to do object oriented modeling is the Object Management Group's Unified Modeling Language (UML).

The UML is inherently object oriented modeling language and was designed for use in object oriented software applications. The application could be based on the object oriented technologies recommended by the Object Management Group (OMG), which owns the UML.

8.6 SQL Queries

SQL queries using various commands are as follows:

8.6.1. Using DDL Commands

Some queries using DDL commands are as follows:

(i) CREATE Statement

The CREATE statement is used to create a table in a database. In this command, we need to give information about table like number of columns, rows and its types etc.

Syntax

```
CREATE TABLE <table_name>
(
    <column_name1><data_type>[(<size>)]   [constraints],
    <column_name2><data_type>[(<size>)]   [constraints],
    <column_name3><data_type>[(<size>)]   [constraints],
    ....
 );
```

The data type specifies what type of data, the column can hold and the size is optional.

(ii) DROP Statement

The SQL DROP command is used to remove the table definition and all data, constraints and permission specified, etc. for that table. You have to be careful while using the DROP command because once the table is deleted, then all the information available in the table would be lost forever. But there is a condition for dropping a table; it must be empty. A table with rows in it cannot be dropped.

Syntax

```
DROP TABLE table_name;
```

(iii) ALTER Statement

The SQL ALTER TABLE command is used to add, delete or modify columns and constraints in the existing table.

To ADD a Column

```
ALTER TABLE table_name ADD column_name data_type;
```

To DROP Column

```
ALTER TABLE table_name DROP COLUMN column_name;
```

To MODIFY Column Data Type

```
ALTER TABLE table_name MODIFY column_name
                                    data_type;
```

To DELETE a Constraint

```
ALTER TABLE table_name DROP Constraint_Name;
```

(iv) RENAME Statement

The SQL RENAME statement is used to rename a table.

Syntax

```
RENAME old_table_name TO new_table_name;
```

(v) Truncate Statement

The SQL TRUNCATE TABLE command is used to delete complete data from an existing table. You can also use DROP TABLE command to delete complete table but it would remove complete table structure from the database and you would need to re-create this table once again if you wish to store some data.

Syntax

```
TRUNCATE TABLE table_name;
```

8.6.2 Using DML Commands

Some queries using DML commands are as follows:

(i) INSERT Statement

The INSERT statement is used to insert a new row/data in a table.

Syntax

```
INSERT INTO table_name VALUES
(value1, value2, value3,...);
                    or
INSERT INTO table_name(column1, column2,
         column3,...) VALUES (value1, value2,
                                    value3,...);
```

The SQL INSERT statement can also be used to insert NULL value for a column.

```
INSERT INTO table_name (column1,column2,
         column3,)VALUES (value1, NULL, value3);
```

INSERT INTO SELECT Statement

This statement copies data from on table and inserts it into another table. This statement requires that data types in source and target tables match. The existing records in the target table are unaffected.

To copy all columns/row from one table to another table:

```
INSERT INTO table_name2
SELECT*FROM table_name1
WHERE condition;
```

To copy only some specific columns from one table to another table:

```
INSERT INTO table_name2 (column1, column2, ......)
SELECT column1, column2, ......
FROM table_name1
WHERE condition;
```

(ii) SELECT Statement

The SELECT statement is used to select data from a database or view table information. The result is stored in a result table, called the **result set**.

Syntax

To select some specify columns

```
SELECT column_name(s) FROM table_name;
```

To select all columns

```
SELECT * FROM table_name;
```

The asterisk (*) is a quick way of selecting all columns. SQL is not case sensitive. SELECT is the same as select.

DISTINCT Keyword

In a table, some of the columns may contain duplicate values. This is not a problem, however sometimes you may want to list only the different (distinct) values in a table.

The DISTINCT keyword can be used to return only distinct (different) values in a particular column or a whole table.

Syntax

```
SELECT DISTINCT column_name(s) FROM table_name;
```

Column Alias

Column alias is used to temporarily rename a table's column for the purpose of a particular query. This renaming is a temporary change and the actual column name does not change in the database.

Syntax

```
SELECT column_name1 AS Alias_name
FROM table_name;
```

WHERE Clause

The WHERE clause is used to extract only those records that fulfill a specified criteria.

Syntax

```
SELECT column_name
FROM table_name WHERE condition;
```

ORDER BY Clause

The ORDER BY keyword is used to sort the result set along a specified column. The ORDER BY keyword sorts the records in ascending order by default. If you want to sort the records in a descending order, you can use the DESC keyword.

Syntax

```
SELECT column_name(s)
FROM table_name
ORDER BY column_name(s) ASC/DESC;
```

(a) Sorting in Ascending Order

Table: COMPANY

Emp_Code	Emp_Name	Emp_Salary	Emp_Dep	Joining_Date
101	Ravi	28000	D02	2010-10-10
102	Neeru	70000	D03	2013-06-04
103	Swarg	60000	D05	2011-03-02
104	Puneet	15000	D07	2009-05-01
105	Sneha	12000	D08	2008-04-03

To display employee's records in ascending order of name. The SQL query is :

```
SELECT * FROM COMPANY ORDER BY Emp_Name;
```

By default, the sort order is ASC or Ascending.

or

```
SELECT * FROM COMPANY ORDER BY Emp_Name ASC;
```

Emp_Code	Emp_Name	Emp_Salary	Emp_Dep	Joining_Date
102	Neeru	70000	D03	2013-06-04
104	Puneet	15000	D07	2009-05-01
101	Ravi	28000	D02	2010-10-10
105	Sneha	12000	D08	2008-04-03
103	Swarg	60000	D05	2011-03-02

(b) Sorting in Descending Order

To display employee's records in descending order of name. The SQL query is :

```
SELECT * FROM COMPANY ORDER BY Emp_Name DESC;
```

Output

Emp_Code	Emp_Name	Emp_Salary	Emp_Dep	Joining_Date
103	Swarg	60000	D05	2011-03-02
105	Sneha	12000	D08	2008-04-03
101	Ravi	28000	D02	2010-10-10
104	Puneet	15000	D07	2009-05-01
102	Neeru	70000	D03	2013-06-04

(c) Sorting by Column Alias

If a column alias declared anywhere in the statement then it can also be used even for the sorting records.

e.g. To display the Emp_Code, Emp_Name and Joining_Date as Date_of_Joining (change the name of the column by column alias) in ascending order of Date_of_Joining. The SQL query is :

```
SELECT Emp_Code, Emp_Name,
Joining_Date AS Date_of_Joining
FROM COMPANY ORDER BY Date_of_Joining;
```

Output

Emp_Code	Emp_Name	Joining_Date
105	Sneha	2008-04-03
104	Puneet	2009-05-01
101	Ravi	2010-10-10
103	Swarg	2011-03-02
102	Neeru	2013-06-04

Operators used in SELECT and WHERE Statement

SQL supports different types of operators. Some of them are described below:

(a) Arithmetic Operators

They can be used in SELECT statement to retrieve information from table. The arithmetic operators used in SQL are as follows:

Operators	Description
+	Addition
–	Subtraction
*	Multiplication
/	Division

45. ...... **can also refer to the person or staff that processes vendor invoices and pays the company's bills.**
(1) Income tax
(2) Financial account
(3) Account payable
(4) Invoice management

46. ...... **are responsible for running queries and reports against data warehouse tables.**
(1) Hardwares (2) Softwares
(3) End users (4) Middlewares

47. ...... **is an essential process where intelligent methods are applied to extract data patterns.**
(1) Data warehousing
(2) Data mining
(3) Text mining
(4) Data selection

48. The easiest way to gain access to the data and facilitate effective decision making is to set-up a ....
(1) database (2) datamart
(3) data warehouse (4) operational

49. This phase of SDLC comes after a complete understanding of system requirements and specifications.
(1) System maintenance
(2) Implementation and deployment
(3) System testing and integration
(4) System analysis

50. Which of the following is a specialised branch of accounting that deals with evaluating and preparing companies financial information and record?
(1) Financial accounting
(2) Accounts payable
(3) Invoice management system
(4) Financial management

51. Which of the following refers to something that can be identified in the users', work environment, something that the users want to track?
(1) Entity (2) Attribute
(3) Identifier (4) Relationship

52. When a user accesses any website (like, www. google.com) on their web browser (which acts as a user interface) is called ....
(1) user's response
(2) user's acknowledge
(3) user's request
(4) None of the above

53. A back-end database is a database that is accessed by users indirectly through an external application. Which of the following is not back-end?
(1) MySQL (2) Ingres
(3) Sybase (4) Delphi

54. .... **process involves reviewing an enormous amount of detail to ensure that only legitimate and accurate amounts are entered in the accounting system.**
(1) Accounting system
(2) Account management
(3) Accounts payable
(4) Invoice management

55. Which of the following system is a kind of module specially designed to give a precise idea to parents regarding the fee structure of the institution?
(1) Result analysis system
(2) Fees management system
(3) Structure management system
(4) Fees structure

56. ...... **is the process of designing the objects or classes through which an object oriented application examines and manipulates some service.**
(1) Data mining (2) Data warehouse
(3) Data dictionary (4) Object modeling

57. ...... **refers to computing technologies in which the hardware and software components are distributed across a network.**
(1) Client and server
(2) User and system
(3) User and file server
(4) User and database server

58. In two -tier client/server architecture, running of application programs and user interface programs is in control of
(1) modulation side
(2) client side
(3) server side
(4) host side

59. Consider a directed line(→) from the relationship set advisor to both entity sets instructor and student. This indicates ...... **cardinality**
(1) One-to-many (2) One-to-one
(3) Many-to-many (4) Many-to-one

60. If you were collecting and storing information about your music collection, an album would be considered a(n) ....
(1) relation (2) entity
(3) instance (4) attribute

61. What term is used to refer to a specific record in your music database; for instance; information stored about a specific album?
(1) Relation (2) Instance
(3) Table (4) Column

62. In a relation between the entities, the type and condition of the relation should be specified. That is called as ...... **attribute.**
(1) descriptive (2) derived
(3) recursive (4) relative

63. The attribute name could be structured as a attribute consisting of first name, middle initial and last name. This type of attribute is called
(1) simple attribute
(2) composite attribute
(3) multi-valued attribute
(4) derived attribute

ANSWER KEY

1	(2)	**2**	(1)	**3**	(1)	**4**	(3)	**5**	(4)	**6**	(3)	**7**	(4)	**8**	(1)	**9**	(2)	**10**	(3)
11	(2)	**12**	(1)	**13**	(4)	**14**	(1)	**15**	(3)	**16**	(3)	**17**	(4)	**18**	(4)	**19**	(1)	**20**	(4)
21	(1)	**22**	(4)	**23**	(4)	**24**	(4)	**25**	(3)	**26**	(3)	**27**	(4)	**28**	(3)	**29**	(1)	**30**	(3)
31	(2)	**32**	(1)	**33**	(4)	**34**	(3)	**35**	(1)	**36**	(4)	**37**	(1)	**38**	(1)	**39**	(3)	**40**	(4)
41	(4)	**42**	(1)	**43**	(3)	**44**	(3)	**45**	(3)	**46**	(3)	**47**	(2)	**48**	(3)	**49**	(2)	**50**	(1)
51	(1)	**52**	(3)	**53**	(4)	**54**	(3)	**55**	(2)	**56**	(4)	**57**	(1)	**58**	(2)	**59**	(2)	**60**	(2)
61	(2)	**62**	(1)	**63**	(2)														

CHAPTER 10

HTML and CSS

HTML (HyperText Markup Language) and CSS (Cascading Style Sheet) are two of the core technologies for building web pages. HTML provides the structure of the page, CSS the layout, for a variety of devices. Along with graphics and scripting, HTML and CSS are the basis of building web pages and web applications.

10.1 HTML

HTML is a markup language, which is used to define the layout and attributes of a World Wide Web (WWW) document as well as to create links between web pages. It is the underlying foundation of website design. HTML is a subset of SGML (Standard Generalised Markup Language), which is a high-level markup language. HTML is used to inform browsers, how to display web pages.

HTML stands for **HyperText Markup Language.** Where, **HyperText** is simply a piece of text that has some extra features like formatting, images, multimedia and links to another document. **Markup Language** is a way of writing layout information within documents. HTML is a document layout and hyperlink specification language. It allows images and other objects to be embedded and can be used to create interactive forms. HTML documents are described through HTML tags or elements and their attributes. The extension of HTML language is .htm or .html.

10.1.1 History of HTML

It was originally developed by **Tim Berners Lee** at CERN in 1990 and popularised by the Mosaic browser developed at NCSA. During the course of the 1990s, it has blossomed with the explosive growth of the web. During this time, HTML has been extended in a number of ways. The web depends on web page authors and vendors sharing the same conventions for HTML. This has motivated joint work on specifications for HTML. HTML is a product of SGML which is a complex, technical specification describing markup languages, especially those used in electronic document exchange, document management and document publishing.

10.1.2 Standard Generalised Markup Language (SGML)

SGML is a standard for how to specify a document markup language or tag set. Such a specification is itself a **Document Type Definition** (DTD). SGML is not in itself a document language, but a description of how to specify one. It is a metadata. SGML is based on the idea that documents have structural and other semantic elements that can be described without reference to how such elements should be displayed.

The syntax for the UPDATE statement when updating one table with data from another table:

```
UPDATE table_name1
SET column1 = (SELECT expression1 FROM
              table_Name2. WHERE conditions)
                        [WHERE conditions];
```

or

```
UPDATE table_name1
SET table_name1.column = table_name2.
                             expression1
FROM table_name1 INNER JOIN table_name2
ON (table_name1. column1 = table_name2. column1)
(WHERE conditions);
```

(iv) DELETE Statement

The DELETE statement is used to delete rows in a table.

Syntax

```
DELETE FROM table_name
WHERE condition;
```

Delete All Rows

It is possible to delete all rows in a table without deleting the table. This means that the table structure, attributes and indexes will be intact.

Syntax

```
DELETE FROM table_name;
```

Using EXISTS with the DELETE Statement

If you may wish to delete records in one table based on values in another table, then you can use the EXISTS clause.

Syntax

```
DELETE FROM table_name1
WHERE EXISTS
(SELECT * From table_name2
WHERE Conditions);
```

8.6.3 Using DCL Commands

Some queries using DCL commands are as follows:

(i) GRANT

This command is used to give user's access privileges to database.

Syntax

```
GRANT privilege_name ON object_name TO
  {user_name |PUBLIC| role_name} [with GRANT option]
```

(ii) REVOKE

This command is used to withdraw access privileges given with the GRANT command.

Syntax

```
REVORE privilege_name ON object_name
FROM {user_name |PUBLIC| role_name}
```

8.6.4 Using TCL Commands

Some transaction control queries using TCL commands are as follows:

(i) COMMIT

It is used to save the work done.

Syntax `COMMIT;`

(ii) SAVEPOINT

It is used to identify a point in a transaction to which you can later rollback.

Syntax

```
SAVEPOINT savepoint_name;
```

(iii) ROLLBACK

It is used to restore database to original since the last COMMIT.

Syntax `ROLLBACK;`

8.7. SQL Functions

A SQL function performs a pre-defined task and returns some type of result, such as a numerical, string or date/time value.

While using a function, arguments or parameters are often supplied that provides function with the information it needs to perform the task. These arguments are usually in the form of column names, literal values or other expressions.

SQL supports number of built-in functions that are already implemented in SQL. These functions allow to perform different types of operations on the data such as find the ASCII value of the string stored in column or convert all characters of a string to uppercase and so on.

To use any function, you need to specify the column to which the function should be applied.

Syntax

```
SELECT function (column_name)FROM table_name;
```

On a broader category, there are two types of function as follows :

(i) **Single Row Function** These functions are the one who work on single row and return one output per row. e.g. length and case conversion functions are single row functions.

(ii) **Multiple Row Function** These functions work upon group of rows and return one result for the complete set of rows. They are also known as **group functions.**

The SQL functions have been categorised into various categories such as follows:

1. String Functions

The string or character functions of SQL are used to extract, change, format or alter character strings. It accepts a character string as an input and provides character string or numeric values as an output.

String functions are broadly divided into two parts as follows:

(i) Case-Manipulation Functions

These functions are convert case for character strings:

Functions	Description	Example

LCASE( ) or LOWER( )	This function converts the characters of an argument string to the lowercase characters. The return value has the same data type as the argument.
	Syntax
	`LCASE(str/column_name)`
	or
	`LOWER(str/column_name)`
		`SELECT LCASE("INFORMATION PRACTICES");`
		Output
		information practices

UPPER( ) or UCASE( )	This function converts the characters of an argument string to the uppercase characters.
	Syntax
	`UCASE(str/column_name)`
	or
	`UPPER(str/column_name)`
		`SELECT UPPER("Price");`
		Output
		PRICE

(ii) Character-Manipulation Functions

These functions manipulate character strings:

Functions	Description	Example
CONCAT( )	This function can have one or more arguments and it returns a string that is the result of concatenating the arguments. **Syntax** `CONCAT(string1/column_name1, string2/column_name2, string3/column_name3...)`	`SELECT CONCAT("India","is","best");` **Output** Indiaisbest
SUBSTR( )	This function returns the specified number of characters from a particular position of a given string. **Syntax** `SUBSTR(str/column_name, pos, len)`	`SELECT SUBSTR("EASYCALCULATION", 5,11);` **Output** CALCULATION
INSTR( )	This function takes a string and a substring of it as arguments and returns an integer which indicates the position of the first occurrence of the substring within the string. **Syntax** `INSTR(ori_str/column_name, sub_str)`	`SELECT INSTR("Footbar", "bar");` **Output** 5
LENGTH( )	This function returns the length of the string in bytes. The length of the string also includes all the blanks. **Syntax** `LENGTH(string/column_name)`	`SELECT LENGTH("environment");` **Output** 11

TRIM( )	This function is used to return a string after removing all prefix or suffix spaces from the given string.
	Syntax
	`TRIM([{BOTH | LEADING | TRAILING} [remstr] FROM] str/column_name)`
		`SELECT TRIM(" India ");`
		Output
		India
		`SELECT TRIM(LEADING "!" FROM "!!!!India!!!!");`
		Output
		India!!!!

This tag is generally used for changing the appearance of a short segment of text. Font tags can be set for a character, sentence or entire document. This tag starts with <font> tag and ends with </font> tag. <font> tag contains, various attributes, some are given below:

Attribute	Use	Syntax
size	This attribute specifies the size of the text inside a <font> tag. The range of accepted values goes from 1 (the smallest) to 7 (the largest). We can also set the relative size to the current size using (+)ve or (–)ve sign. e.g. size = +2	`<font size= "number">`
face	This attribute specifies the font name or type face of the text inside a <font> tag.	`<font face = "font_family">`
color	This attribute specifies the color of the text inside a <font> tag.	`<font color= "color_name|hex_number|rgb_number">`

6. <basefont> Tag

This tag specifies a default font color, font size or font face for all the text in a document that follows it. This tag is only supported by Internet Explorer web browser. Ending tag </basefont> of basefont is optional.

The < basefont > can also have face, size and color attributes, which can be used exactly in the same way as face, size and color attributes of < font > tag. The < basefont > tag contains various attributes, some are given below:

Attribute	Use	Syntax
color	It specifies the default color for a text.	`<basefont color= "color_name|hex_number|rgb_number">`
face	It specifies the default font for text in document.	`<basefont face= "font_family">`
size	It specifies the default size of text in a document.	`<basefont size= "number">`

Colors and their hexadecimal & RGB values

Color Name	Hexadecimal Value	RGB Value
Aqua	#00FFFF	rgb (0,255,255)
Black	#000000	rgb (0,0,0)
Blue	#0000FF	rgb (0,0,255)
Fuchsia	#FF00FF	rgb (255,0,255)
Gold	#FFD700	rgb (255, 215, 0)
Gray	#808080	rgb (128, 128, 128)
Green	#008000	rgb (0, 128, 0)
Khaki	#F0E68C	rgb (240, 230, 140)
Lime	#00FF00	rgb (0, 255, 0)

Color Name	Hexadecimal Value	RGB Value
Maroon	#800000	rgb (128, 0, 0)
Navy	#000080	rgb (0, 0, 128)
Olive	#808000	rgb (128, 128, 0)
Orange	#FFA500	rgb (255, 165, 0)
Pink	#FFC0CB	rgb (255, 192, 203)
Purple	#800080	rgb (128, 0, 128)
Red	#FF0000	rgb (255, 0, 0)
Silver	#C0C0C0	rgb (192, 192, 192)
Skyblue	#87CEEB	rgb (135, 206, 235)
Teal	#008080	rgb (0, 128, 128)
White	#FFFFFF	rgb (255, 255, 255)
Yellow	#FFFF00	rgb (255, 255, 0)

7. <center> Tag

This tag is used to centralise a segment of text to be displayed on browser's window. With the <center> tag, closing tag </center> is always used. Anything between these two tags will be centered including text, images and tables.

Syntax

```
<center>...</center>
```

8. Comment <!--...--> Tag

The comment tag is used to insert comments in the source code of the web pages.

Comments are not displayed in the browser's window. All the text inserted inside this tag (<!– – ...– – >) will be ignored by the browser and made invisible for the user. You can use comments to explain your code, it can help you, when you edit the source code at a later date. This is especially useful, when you have a lot of codes.

Syntax

```
<! -- ... -->
```

9. Heading Tags

In HTML, heading tags are used to display the text as some heading. Heading element can be used to give section headings.

There are six levels of headings, ranging from <h1>...</h1> to <h6>...</h6>. <h1> defines the most important largest heading level and <h6> defines the smallest heading level.

Syntax

```
<hn>
:
</hn>
```

Where, *n* may be any number from 1 to 6. Attribute of heading tag is as follows:

Attribute	Value	Syntax
align	left, right, center, justify	`<hn align= "value">`

10. Paragraph <p> Tag

To separate our text by paragraphs, we use the <p> tag. It is an empty tag. Normally, all text in a HTML document is treated like one long paragraph.

Indented or blank lines, which normally indicates start of paragraphs in text are ignored.

The <p> tag is used to separate paragraphs of text within a HTML document. The <p> tag forces end to the line and a blank line before the next paragraph.

Syntax

```
<p>
 :
</p>
```

Attribute of paragraph tag is as follows:

Attribute	Value	Syntax
align	left, right, center, justify	`<p align="value">`

11. Line Break
 Tag

A <br> tag will insert a line break, which means the text/image following this tag will be moved to the next line when displayed in the browser.

To add a single line of space, you use break tag, i.e.
. This is an empty element, i.e. no need of closing tag. You can use the <br> tag to insert one or more blank lines.

12. Horizontal Rule <hr> Tag

A<hr> tag is also known as **section separator** as it separates the field into two sections by forming a rule or line.

Section separator is formed by using <hr> tag and the size of different sections can be fixed.

Attributes of horizontal rule tag are as follows:

Attribute	Use	Syntax
align	This attribute specifies the alignment of a horizontal line. The value of align may be left, right, center.	`<hr align="value">`
size	This attribute specifies the height of the rule in pixels. Its default value depends directly on the browser. The default size of a rule is 3 pixels.	`<hr size="pixels">`
noshade	When this boolean attribute is present, the rule is drawn with a solid black line as 2D effect instead of the default 3D effect, i.e. without shading.	`<hr noshade>`
width	This attribute specifies the width of a horizontal line, in pixels or per cent. Its default value is 100%.	`<hr width="pixels or%">`
color	This attribute specifies the color of the horizontal line.	`<hr color="color_name|hex_number|rgb_number">`

e.g. To display text using heading, horizontal rule, line break and paragraph tags.

```
<html>
<head><title>Home Page</title></head>
<body>
<h1 align="center">WELCOME PAGE</h1>
<hr align="center" size="3" color="blue">
<h2 align="left">ARIHANT PRAKASHAN</h2>
<h3 align="left">ARIHANT PUBLICATIONS (INDIA)
LIMITED<br>which was incorporated as a public
limited company in the year 2011</h3>
<h4 align="justify">ARIHANT MEDIA
PROMOTERS</h4>
<h5 align="left">Arihant Samsamayiki
Mahasagar </h5>
<p>ARIHANT EDU WEB(P)LTD<br>ARIHANT PRINT
SOLUTION</p>
<hr noshade width="50%" align="right">
<h6 align="right">THANKS!!!</h6>
</body></html>
```

13. <bgsound> Tag

This tag is used to play a soundtrack in the background. This tag is for Internet Explorer only.

Syntax

```
<bgsound src = "soundURL" loop = "value">
```

The HTML < bgsound> tag also supports following attributes:

Attribute	Value	Description
loop	number	Lets you replay a background soundtrack a certain number of times.
src	URL	Specifies the path of the sound file

14. <embed> Tag

In HTML, this tag is a block element used to designate an area for interactive content (plug in) or an external application. It is useful when you want to add content that might not be natively supported by an Internet browser.

e.g. `<embed src =" ../m/example.mp3"></embed>`

8.8 SQL Aggregate Functions

SQL aggregate or group functions return a single value, which is calculated from values in a column. These functions are called aggregate functions because they operate on aggregates of tuples. These functions are also known as group functions.

Some useful aggregate functions are as follows:

1. AVG( ) Function

This function returns the average value of a specified column.

Syntax

```
SELECT AVG(column_name)
FROM table_name;
```

Consider the following table PAYMENTS:

Empid	Emp_Name	Salary	Department
1	Ridhi	20000	D1
2	Rohit	25000	D2
3	Rakesh	20000	D2
4	Roshan	44000	D1
5	Rohini	15000	D3
6	Radha	14000	D1

e.g. To display the average of employees salary from PAYMENTS table.

```
SELECT AVG(Salary) FROM PAYMENTS;
```

Output

AVG(Salary)
23000

2. COUNT( ) Function

This function returns the total number of values in the specified field. COUNT returns the total number of rows in a query. COUNT (*) is a special function, as it returns the count of all rows in a specified table. It includes all the null and duplicate values.

Syntax

```
SELECT COUNT(*) FROM table_name;
```

e.g. To count the total number of employees from PAYMENTS table.

```
SELECT COUNT(*) "Employees" FROM PAYMENTS;
```

Output

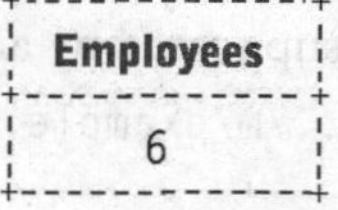

Employees
6

DISTINCT Clause with COUNT( ) Function

The DISTINCT keyword helps us in removing the duplicates from our result. When it is used with aggregate function COUNT, it returns the number of distinct rows in a specified table.

Syntax

```
SELECT COUNT(DISTINCT column_name)
FROM table_name;
```

e.g. To count distinct values of column Department from PAYMENTS table.

```
SELECT COUNT(DISTINCT Department) "Deptid"
FROM PAYMENTS;
```

Output

Deptid
3

3. MAX( ) Function

This function returns the largest value from the selected column.

Syntax

```
SELECT MAX(column_name)
FROM table_name;
```

e.g. To find the maximum salary of employee from PAYMENTS table.

```
SELECT MAX(Salary) "Maximum"
FROM PAYMENTS;
```

Output

Maximum
44000

4. MIN( ) Function

This function returns the smallest value from the selected column.

Syntax

```
SELECT MIN(column_name)
FROM table_name;
```

e.g. To display the minimum salary of employee from PAYMENTS table.

```
SELECT MIN(Salary) "Minimum"
FROM PAYMENTS;
```

Output

Minimum
14000

5. SUM( ) Function

This function returns the sum of values in the specified column.

The sum works on numeric fields only. Null values are excluded from the result returned.

Syntax
```
SELECT SUM(column_name)
FROM table_name;
```

e.g. To display sum of employee's salary from PAYMENTS table.
```
SELECT SUM(Salary) "Salary"
FROM PAYMENTS;
```

Output

Salary
138000

8.8.1 GROUP BY Statement

The GROUP BY statement is used with the aggregate functions to group the result set by one or more columns.

Syntax
```
SELECT column_name, aggregate_function (column_name)
FROM table_name
WHERE condition GROUP BY column_name;
```

Nested Group Functions

Group functions may only be nested two levels deep. A GROUP BY clause is mandatory since the G2 value of the group_item per group is calculated before being aggregated by the G1 function.

Syntax
```
SELECT G1/G2(Column_name1)
FROM table_name
GROUP BY Column_name2;
```

Where, G1 → first group function
G2 → second group function

8.8.2 HAVING Clause

The HAVING clause is used with GROUP BY clause to place condition because the WHERE keyword could not be used with aggregate functions.

Syntax
```
SELECT column_name,aggregate_function(column_name)
FROM table_name
WHERE condition GROUP BY column_name
HAVING aggregate_function(column_name) <condition>;
```

8.8.3 Illegal Queries Using Group/Aggregate Functions

- Any column or expression in the SELECT statement that is not an aggregate function must be in the GROUP BY clause.

  e.g.
  ```
  SELECT deptno, COUNT(ename)
  FROM emp;
  ```
  ERROR Column "comp.deptno" must appear in the GROUP BY clause.

- You cannot use the WHERE clause to restrict groups whereas you can use the HAVING clause to restrict groups. It means you cannot use group functions in the WHERE clause.

  e.g.
  ```
  SELECT deptno, AVG(sal)
  FROM emp
  WHERE Avg(sal) > 8000
  GROUP BY deptno;
  ```
  ERROR Aggregate functions are not allowed in WHERE clause.

8.8.4 Nulls and Aggregate Functions

All aggregate functions except COUNT (*) and GROUPING ignore nulls. You can use the NVL function in the argument to an aggregate function to substitute a value for a null. COUNT () function never returns null but returns either a number or zero. For all the remaining aggregate functions, if the data set contains no rows or contains only rows with nulls as arguments to the aggregate function, then the function returns NULL.

8.9 Join

A join is a query that combines rows from two or more tables. In a join query, more than one tables are listed in FROM clause. The function of combining data from multiple tables is called **joining**. SQL can obtain data from several related tables by performing either a physical or virtual join on the tables.

The SQL join condition is always used in the WHERE clause of SELECT, UPDATE and DELETE statements.

There are different kind of SQL joins as follows:

1. Equi Join

Equi join is a simple SQL join condition that uses equal sign as a comparison operator. It combines rows that have equivalent values for the specified columns.

Syntax
```
SELECT col1, col2, col3
FROM table1, table2
WHERE table1.col1 = table2.col1;
```

SQL equi joins are further classified into two categories as follows:

(i) Inner Join

The inner join using either of the equivalent queries give the intersection of two tables, i.e. it returns us the rows, which are common in both the tables.

Syntax
```
SELECT col1, col2
FROM table1 INNER JOIN table2
ON table1.column_name=table2.column_name;
```

<img> tag have various attributes, some are given below:

Attribute	Use	Syntax
src	The source (src) attribute is used to display an image. It takes URL of an image file as value which points to the directory location of an image file.	`<img src = "path/file name">`
alt	The alternate (alt) attribute is used to provide alternate text when an image on a web page cannot be displayed.	`<img alt="text">`
align	It is used to set the position of an image according to the user's requirement.	`<img align = "left/right/ middle/top/bottom">`
height	It is used to set the height of an image.	`<img height = "pixels">`
width	It is used to set the width of an image.	`<img width = "pixels">`

e.g.
```
<img src="f:\Wallpapers\rigid.jpg" align
 = "left"  width="145" height="126" alt="rigid">
```

10.1.11 Hyperlinks

A key feature of the HTML is its ability to link text and/or image to each other. If you are on a web page and see the colored and/or underlined text, that is a hyperlink. It is also known as **hypertext link** or just **link**.

In HTML, links can be created by using <a> anchor tag. <a> tag is a container tag that means it requires a starting as well as ending tag.

Syntax

```
<a href ="URL">....</a>
```

Attributes of <a> tag are as follows:

Attribute	Use	Syntax
href	The href attribute is used to specify the URL of the target document and destination of web page which is linked.	`<a href ="URL"> Some Text </a>`
title	The title attribute is used to specify the title of the document to which we are linking.	`<a href ="URL" title ="text"> Some Text</a>`
name	The name attribute specify the name of an anchor. This attribute is used to create a bookmark inside a document.	`< a name="name"> Some Text</a>`

e.g.

```
<a href = "http://www.google.com" name=
    "Google" title =  "It is a hyperlink">Click
                                     Here </a>
```

- To create a link to a named anchor in HTML, # symbol is to be specified.

  e.g.

  ```
  <a href = "# aa" > Click Here </a> Google"
  ```

  where, "aa" is the name of fragment/segment you want to refers (like top, bottom etc).

- Inserting the sound file in an <a href> tag allows the browser to open and play the audio file if the viewer of your web page has properly configured their Internet browser.

  e.g.

  ```
  <a href ="../jargon/m/example. mp3"> Play
  sound file </a>
  ```

10.1.12 Images as Links

Images can also be used as hyperlinks. To create image as a link, following is syntax:

```
<a href = "URL"> <img src = "image1.jpg"> </a>
```

10.1.13 HTML List

Sometimes, we are in a hurry and do not like to read a lot of text. So, putting important information in the form of a list seems to be helpful. HTML supports several elements for making lists. They can be divided into two types-glossary lists and regular lists.

Glossary lists are denoted by the element <dl>, while **Regular lists** are denoted by the elements <ul>, <ol>, <menu> and <dir>. Lists can be nested, i.e. you can have a list within a regular list, a regular list within a glossary list and so on.

If you want to make a list of items in the form of terms and their description, you should create a definition list. Apart from this, you can also create nested lists. These list tags are responsible for affecting the spacing and layout of text, not the emphasis, so they are applied to groups of text and allow individual formatting tags within them.

There are actually three different types of HTML lists:

1. Unordered List <ul>

An unordered list is also known as **unnumbered list** or **bulleted list**. It is an indented list with a bullet symbol infront of each list item.

An unordered list starts with the <ul> tag. Each list item starts with the <li> tag. The list items are marked with bullets (typically small black circles).

The unordered list tag is a container tag. The default bullet type for most web browsers is a full disc (black circle), but this can be adjusted using HTML attribute called **type**.

Syntax

```
<ul type = "Value">
    <li> First item of list
    <li> Second item of list
    ⋮
</ul>
```

Where, <li> element is used to indicate a list item as contained in an unordered or ordered list. The closing tag of the <li> tag (</li>) is optional.

Attribute of unordered list is as follows:

Attribute	Use	Syntax
type	This attribute is used to change the bulleted symbol in a list. The attribute may have a value of circle (○), disc (•) or square (■).	`<ul type = "value">`

2. Ordered List <ol>

An ordered list is also known as **numbered list**. An ordered list starts with the <ol> tag. Each list item starts with the <li> tag. The list items are marked with numbers. The ordered list tag is a container tag and is used for numbered lists.

By default, the numbering will be 1, 2, 3.... You can also adjust the numbering using **type** attribute.

Syntax

```
<ol>
<li> First item of list
<li> Second item of list
⋮
</ol>
```

Attributes of ordered list are as follows:

Attribute	Use	Syntax
type	The numbering of an HTML list can be changed to letters or roman numerals by the type attribute.	`<ol type ="value">` where, value = 1, I, i, A or a.
start	The start attribute is used to change the beginning value of an ordered list. Normally, the ordered list begins with 1. It lets you further customise an HTML ordered list by setting a new starting digit for the ordered list element.	`<ol start="value">`

3. Definition List

A definition list is a list of items, with a description of each item. HTML definition lists (<dl>) are list elements that have a unique array of tags and elements; the resulting lists are similar to those you would see in a dictionary. Tags used in definition lists are as follows:

```
<dl> Opening tag that defines the start of the list.
<dt> List item that defines the definition term.
<dd> Definition of the list item.
</dl> Closing tag that defines the end of the list.
```

Syntax

```
<dl>
<dt>Term 1</dt>
<dd>Definition of Term 1
<dt>Term 2</dt>
<dd>Definition of Term 2
</dl>
```

4. Nested List

List can be nested, that means one list can be placed inside another. In the nested list, one or more items can contain sub-items.

```
<ul>
    <li>Fruits
    <ol type ="i">
        <li>Mango
        <li>Apple
    </ol>
    <li>Vegetables
    <ol type="i">
        <li>Onion
        <li>Tomato
    </ol>
</ul>
```

10.1.14 HTML Table

Table allows you to arrange the data in the form of rows and columns.

The data could be in any form whether it may be text, tables, images etc., and you can use tables to arrange data, either horizontally or vertically.

Tables may have an associated caption with it.

A table is divided into rows with <tr> tag, tr stands for table row and each row is divided into data cells with the <td> tag, td stands for table data and it can contain text, links, images, lists, forms, other tables etc, i.e. content of a data cell.

To specify the header of each column, <th> tag is used, th stands for table header.

Tags used in HTML tables are as follows:

(i) Table tag <table>...</table>
(ii) Row tag <tr>...</tr>
(iii) Table heading <th>...</th>
(iv) Cell tag <td>...</td>
(v) Caption tag <caption>...</caption>

Data Integrity It means that you can correctly and consistently navigate and manipulate the tables in the database. There are two basic rules to ensure data integrity: entity integrity and referential integrity.

(i) **Entity Integrity** The entity integrity rule states that the value of the primary key can never be a null value.

(ii) **Referential Integrity** It states that if a relational table has a foreign key, then every value of the foreign key must either be null or match the value in the relational table in which that foreign key is primary key.

8.11.2 Altering Table with Constraints

The SQL ALTER command is used to add, delete or modify columns and constraints in the existing table. The ALTER command is used to perform following functions:

(i) Add and Drop Constraints

Syntax

To ADD PRIMARY KEY or UNIQUE KEY constraint

```
ALTER TABLE table_name
ADD CONSTRAINT constraint_name
PRIMARY KEY/UNIQUE KEY column_name;
```

To ADD FOREIGN KEY constraint

```
ALTER TABLE table_name
ADD CONSTRAINT constraint_name
FOREIGN KEY(col1, col2,...., coln)
REFERENCES parent_table(col1, col2,...,coln);
```

To ADD CHECK constraint

```
ALTER TABLE table_name
ADD CONSTRAINT constraint_name CHECK
(column_name condition);
```

To DROP constraint

```
ALTER TABLE table_name
DROP CONSTRAINT constraint_name;
```

(ii) Disable and Enable Constraints

Syntax

To DISABLE constraints

```
ALTER TABLE table_name
DISABLE CONSTRAINT constraint_name;
```

To ENABLE constraints

```
ALTER TABLE table_name
ENABLE CONSTRAINT constraint_name;
```

8.11.3 Viewing Constraints and their Columns

In SQL, to view all the constraints and columns on your table query, you can use SHOW CREATE TABLE command and DESC command.

SHOW CREATE TABLE Command

If the table has already been created, you can confirm the existence by making use of the following statement:

```
SHOW CREATE TABLE table_name;
```

DESC Command

The DESC, DESCRIBE and EXPLAIN statements are synonyms. This provides information about the columns and constraints in a table.

Syntax

```
DESC table_name;
```

8.12 Sub Queries

A subquery is a query that is nested inside a SELECT, INSERT, UPDATE or DELETE statement, or inside another subquery. A subquery can be used anywhere an expression is allowed.

A subquery is also called an **inner query or inner select.** While the statement containing a subquery is also called an **outer query or outer select.**

The inner query executes first before its parent query so that the results of an inner query can be passed to the outer query.

8.12.1 Guidelines for using Sub Queries

There are some guidelines to consider when using subqueries as follows:

(i) A subquery must be enclosed in parentheses.

(ii) A subquery must be placed on the right side of comparison operator.

(iii) Subqueries cannot manipulate their results internally, therefore ORDER BY clause cannot be added into a subquery. You can use an ORDER BY clause in the main SELECT statement (outer query) which will be the last clause.

(iv) Use single row operators with single row subqueries.

(v) If a subquery (inner query) returns a null value to the outer query, the outer query will not return any rows when using certain comparison operators in a WHERE clause.

8.12.2 Types of Subquery

There are various types of subquery as follows:

(i) Single Row Subquery

A single row subquery is used when the outer query's results are based on a single, unknown value. Although this query type is formally called single row, the name implies that the query returns multiple columns, but only one row of results. However, a single row subquery can return only one row of results consisting of only one column to the outer query.

(ii) Multiple Row Subquery

Multiple row subqueries are nested queries that can return more than one row of results to the parent query.

(iii) Multiple Column Subquery

A multiple column subquery returns more than one column to the outer query and can be listed in the outer's query FROM, WHERE or HAVING clause.

8.12.3 Creating a Table using a Subquery

A table can be created using a combination of the CREATE TABLE statement and the SELECT statement. The new table has the same column definitions. All columns or specific columns can be selected. When you create a new table using existing table, new table would be populated using existing values in the old table.

Syntax

```
CREATE TABLE NEW_TABLE_NAME AS
SELECT [column1, column2…columnN]
FROM EXISTING_TABLE_NAME
[WHERE];
```

Here, column1, column2 … are the fields of existing table and same would be used to create fields of new table.

8.13 Database Object

A database object in a relational database is a data structural used to either store or reference data. The most common object that people interact with is the table. Other objects are indexes, stored procedures, sequences, views and many more.

When a database object is created, a new object type cannot be created because all the various object types created are restricted by the nature, or source code, of the relational database model being used, such as Oracle, SQL server or Access.

8.13.1 View

Views are virtual tables that are compiled at run time. The data associated with views are not physically stored in the view, but it is stored in the base tables of the view. A view can be made over one or more database tables. Once you have created the view, you can view the query like as table. In SQL, a view is a virtual table based on the result set of an SQL statement. A view contains rows and columns, just like a real table. The fields in a view are fields from one or more real tables in the database.

Types of View

There are two types of view as follows:

(i) Simple View

Simple views are created from tables and are used for creating secure manipulation over the tables or structures of the database. Views make the manipulations easier to perform on the database. Simple view does not contain functions and groups of data.

(ii) Complex View

Complex views are by definition views of type which may comprise of many of elements, such as tables, view sequences and other similar objects of the database. When talking about the views, we can have views of one table, and one view, views of multiple tables, views of multiple views and so on. Complex view created from one or more table. Complex view contains functions and groups of data.

SQL Create View Statement

The view is created in SQL as follows:

```
CREATE VIEW view_name AS
SELECT Column1, Column2,...
FROM table_name
WHERE condition;
```

Retrieving Data from a View

After creating the view, you can retrieving data from a view using following query:

```
SELECT Column_Name FROM View_Name;
```

Updating a View

A view can be updated under certain conditions:

(i) The SELECT clause may not contain the keyword DISTINCT.
(ii) The SELECT clause may not contain summary functions.
(iii) The SELECT clause may not contain set functions.
(iv) The SELECT clause may not contain set operators.
(v) The SELECT clause may not contain an ORDER BY clause.
(vi) The FROM clause may not contain multiple tables.
(vii) The WHERE clause may not contain subqueries.
(viii) The query may not contain GROUP BY or HAVING.
(ix) Calculated columns may not be updated.
(x) All NOT NULL columns from the base table must be included in the view in order for the INSERT query to function.

Syntax

```
UPDATE View_name
SET Column_Name = Value
WHERE [Condition];
```

Attribute	Use	Syntax
size	It is used to resize the field such as set the length of text box.	`<input size = "value">`
height and width	This attribute is used to set the height and width of any field.	`<input height ="pixels" width ="pixels">`
maxlength	It allows to specify the maximum number of characters a user can enter into the text box.	`<input maxlength ="value">`
align	It defines the alignment of content.	`<input align = "left|right|top|middle|bottom">`

Different field types (values of type attribute) or controls supported by HTML

Field Type	Use	Additional Attribute
Text	It provides a single line text input field where the user can enter the text.	**size="n"** Sets the visible size of the text field to n characters. **maxlength="n"** Sets the maximum number of character that can be input in the text field to n.
Password	It provides a single line text input field where the user can enter password. A password field shows one dot for each character input by the user. This is to prevent other from seeing the password.	Same as those for text field.
Radio	It provides a radio button on the form. Only one radio button of a group can be selected at one time. When a form is submitted, selected radio button's value (specified by the value attribute) is submitted to the destination.	**Checked** Indicates that the radio button is selected, which can be deselected when another choice is made. This attribute is optional.
Checkbox	It provides a check box on the form. With checkboxes, we can give the users a list of items to choose from. The user can choose more than one items from the list. When a form is submitted, selected checkboxes' values (specified by the VALUE attribute) are submitted to the destination.	Checked – Indicates that the checkbox is to be displayed with a tick mark to show selection. This attribute is optional.
Submit	This provides a button on the form. When this button is clicked, the form is submitted to the destination.	—
Reset	This provides a button on the form. When this button is clicked, the input fields on the form are reset to their default state.	—
Hidden	This controls are used to hide data inside the page which later on can be pushed to the server.	—
Image	This control defines an image as the submit button	**src = " URL"** defines the URL of the image to display.

2. <select> Tag

Use the <select> container tag to create drop-down menus and scrolled lists.

Attributes of <select> tag are as follows:

Attribute	Use	Syntax
name	It shows the name of drop-down.	`<select name ="name">`
size	It displays height of the list. If it is 1 (or omitted), the list is a drop-down menu, otherwise it is a scrolled list.	`<select size ="value">`
disabled	It specifies that a drop-down list should be disabled.	`<select disabled>`

3. <option> Tag

This tag occurs only within the select element or tag and is used to represent each choice of the select.

An <option> tag can have a value attribute, which is what sent to the CGI script, if that item is selected. If there is no value attribute, the value sent is the text following the <option> tag. To make an item selected by default, use the selected attribute in the <option> tag. An example of a <select> drop-down list is:

Syntax

```
<select name ="name">
<option value ="value 1">text</option>
<option value ="value 2">text</option>
:
:
more options
</select>
```

Attributes of <option> tag are as follows:

Attribute	Use	Syntax
label	It specifies a shorter label for an option.	<option label ="text">
selected	It defines the default option to be selected when page is loaded.	<option selected>
value	It specifies the value to be sent to the server when form is submitted.	<option value ="value">

4. <textarea> Tag

Use the <textarea> container tag to create multiline, scrollable, text entry boxes. Whatever is between the <textarea> and </textarea> tags will be the initial contents of the entry box, so put them right next to each other, if you do not want initial contents. The <textarea> tag has a name attribute like every input field.

Use the rows and cols (columns) attributes to set the displayed height and width of the text area.

Note textarea scrolls as much as needed, so you are only setting the display size, not the data size.

Syntax

```
<textarea name="name" rows="number"
cols="number">Text</textarea>
```

Attributes of <textarea> tag are as follows:

Attribute	Use	Syntax
name	It is used to identify the input field.	<textarea name ="text">
rows and cols	This attribute is used to arrange the height and width of a row and column.	<textarea rows ="number" cols ="number">

e.g. To display the form using form's attributes.

```
<html>
<head><title>FORM</title></head>
<body>
<h1>FORM</h1>
<form action="submission.html" method="GET">
User Name
<input type="text" name="Name" value="Enter your
Name" size="30" height="15" width="80"><br>
Password
<input type="password" name="Password"
value="Pass" size="30" height="15"
width="80"><br>
Address
<textarea rows="2" cols="30" name="Address">
Enter your Address</textarea><br>
Country
<select name="s1" size="1">
<option label="America">America</option>
<option value="US">US</option>
<option value="India"
selected>India</option>
<option value="Japan">Japan</option>
</select><br>
Gender
<input type="radio" name="Radio
Button">Male
<input type="radio" name="Radio
                    Button">Female<br>
Hobbies
<input type="checkbox" name="Check
Box">Drawing
<input type="checkbox" name="Check
Box">Story
                           Writing<br>
<input type="submit" value="Submit">
<input type="reset" value="Reset">
<input type="button" value="Cancel">
</form>
</body>
</html>
```

Output

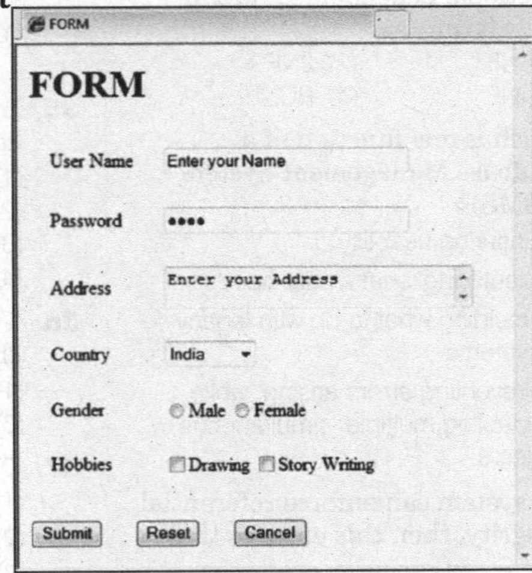

10.1.16 Frames

Frames allow you to divide a browser window into several independent parts. It is a way of displaying two or more pages at once. The window is divided into frames in a similar way the tables are organised into rows and columns.

Following tags are used to create frames in HTML:

1. <frameset> Tag

To use frames on a page, we use <frameset> tag instead of < body> tag. This tag is a frame container for dividing a window into rectangular subspaces called frames.

Attributes of <frameset> tag are as follows:

25. An advantage of the database management approach is
(1) data is dependent on programs
(2) data redundancy increases
(3) data is integrated and can be accessed by multiple programs
(4) None of the above

26. A DBMS query language is designed to
(1) support end users who use English-like commands
(2) support in the development of complex applications software
(3) specify the structure of a database
(4) All of the above

27. If a relation is in 2NF, then
(1) every candidate key is a primary key.
(2) every non-prime attribute is fully functionally dependent on each relation key.
(3) every attribute is functionally independent.
(4) every relational key is a primary key.

28. A function that has no partial functional dependencies are in .... form.
(1) 3NF (2) 2NF
(3) 4NF (4) BCNF

29. Which is one function of a Database Management System (DBMS)?
(1) Ensuring usability
(2) Identifying what a user needs
(3) Deciding what to do with legacy systems
(4) Preventing errors arising, while enabling multiple, simultaneous users

30. If a system can enforce referential integrity, then this ensures that
(1) a record can never contain a null value for a foreign key attribute
(2) a non-null foreign key attribute always refers to another record
(3) a foreign key attribute in a record always refers to another record which contains nulls
(4) a foreign key attribute in a record always refers to another record which does not contain nulls

31. The database environment has all of the following components except
(1) users
(2) separate files
(3) database
(4) database administration

32. In a large DBMS
(1) each sub schema contains every field in the logical schema
(2) each user can access every subschema
(3) each user can see only a small part of the entire database
(4) All of the above

33. When using a database management sysem, the first thing that we must do is to
(1) load the software into our micro-computer
(2) activate file editor
(3) create a database file
(4) keep a floppy disk in readiness

34. Which of the following statements is false with respect to relational DBMS?
(1) A disadvantage of highly normalised tables is that queries may require to many time consuming joins
(2) Foreign key constraints are referential integrity constraints
(3) A primary key uniquely identifies a row in a table
(4) Nulls reduce space requirement in tables

35. In a relational database model, cardinality of a relation means
(1) the number of constraints
(2) the number of tuples
(3) the number of attributes
(4) the number of tables

36. To discard all pending data changes
(1) COMMIT (2) ROLLBACK
(3) SAVEPOINT (4) LOCK

37. TRUNCATE statement in SQL is a
(1) DML statement
(2) DDL statement
(3) DCL statement
(4) DSL statement

38. In SQL, CREATE TABLE is used
(1) to create a table, defining its columns, integrity constraint and storage allocation
(2) to add a column/integrity constraint to a table
(3) to redefine a column
(4) to change a table's storage characteristics

39. In SQL, which of the following is a data manipulation language command?
(1) RENAME (2) REVOKE
(3) GRANT (4) UPDATE

40. In SQL, which command is used to changes data in a data table?
(1) UPDATE (2) INSERT
(3) BROWSE (4) APPEND

41. Which command(s) is (are) used to redefine a column of the table in SQL?
(1) ALTER TABLE
(2) DEFINE TABLE
(3) MODIFY TABLE
(4) All of the above

42. Which of the following is not a type of SQL statement?
(1) Data Manipulation Language (DML)
(2) Data Definition Language (DDL)
(3) Data Control Language (DCL)
(4) Data Communication Language (DCL)

43. The Data Control Language (DCL)
(1) is used to manage user access to databases
(2) is used to manipulate the contents of a database in some form
(3) Both (1) and (2)
(4) Used for inserting, deleting and updating data in a database
(5) None of the above

44. To modify existing rows of the table .... statement is used.
(1) ALTER (2) MODIFY
(3) UPDATE (4) COMMIT

45. In a relational schema, each tuple is divided into fields called
(1) relations (2) domains
(3) queries (4) All of these

46. The language used in application programs to request data from the DBMS is referred as the
(1) DML (2) DDL
(3) Query language (4) DCL

47. To delete a particular column in a relation, the command used is
(1) DELETE (2) UPDATE
(3) DROP (4) ALTER

48. Which of the following is used to add new attribute (column) in the existing relation schema?
(1) DROP (2) CREATE
(3) INSERT (4) ADD

49. In SQL, which command is used to add a column line integrity constraint to a table?
(1) ALTER TABLE
(2) MODIFY TABLE
(3) INSERT COLUMN
(4) ADD COLUMN

50. In SQL, which command is used to change a table's storage characteristics?
(1) CHANGE TABLE
(2) MODIFY TABLE
(3) ALTER TABLE
(4) None of the above

51. In SQL, GRANT command is used to
(1) choose auditing for specific SQL commands
(2) grant system privileges, roles and object privileges to uses and roles
(3) allow user to create databases
(4) allow user to access databases

52. In SQL, which command is used to remove rows from a table?
(1) TRUNCATE
(2) DELETE
(3) REMOVE
(4) Both (1) and (2)

53. For comparing multiple value, we used .... operator.
(1) LIKE (2) IN
(3) SELECT (4) Both (1) and (3)

54. Indexes are used to arrange the database constraints such as
(1) unique key (2) foreign key
(3) primary key (4) All of these

55. The five aggregation operators in SQL are
(1) SUM, AVG, IN, DISTINCT, COUNT
(2) SUM, AVG, MIN, MAX, COUNT
(3) SUM, AVG, MIN, MAX, DISTINCT
(4) SUM, AVG, IN, ALL, ANY

56. Cartesian product in relational algebra is
(1) a unary operator
(2) a binary operator
(3) a ternary operator
(4) not defined

57. .... produces the relation that has attributes of R_1 and R_2.
(1) Cartesian product
(2) Difference
(3) Intersection
(4) Product

58. Which type of join returns all rows that satisfy the join condition?
(1) Inner join (2) Outer join
(3) Semi join (4) Anti join

59. Which of the following is not a transaction management SQL command?
(1) Rollback (2) Commit
(3) Select (4) Savepoint

60. In relational databases, the natural join of two tables is
(1) cartesian product always
(2) combination of union and filtered cartesian product
(3) combination of selection and filtered cartesian product
(4) combination of projection and filtered cartesian product.

61. The SQL WHERE clause
(1) limits the column data that are returned
(2) limits the row data are returned
(3) Both (1) and (2) are correct
(4) Neither (1) nor (2) are correct

62. A subquery in an SQL SELECT statement is enclosed in
(1) braces…{…}
(2) CAPITAL LETTERS
(3) parentheses…(…)
(4) brackets…[…]

63. The result of a SQL SELECT statement is a(n)… .
(1) report (2) form
(3) file (4) table

64. The HAVING clause does which of the following?
(1) Acts like a WHERE clause but is used for groups rather than rows
(2) Acts like a WHERE clause but is used for rows rather than columns.
(3) Acts like a WHERE clause but is used for columns rather than groups.
(4) Acts EXACTLY like a WHERE clause.

65. Which of the following do you need to consider when you make a table in SQL?
(1) Data types (2) Primary keys
(3) Default values (4) All of these

66. The SQL keyword BETWEEN is used
(1) for ranges
(2) to limit the columns displayed
(3) as a wildcard
(4) None of the above

67. A subquery in a SQL SELECT statement:
(1) can only be used with two tables
(2) can always be duplicated by a join
(3) has a distinct form that cannot be duplicated by a join
(4) cannot have its results sorted using ORDER BY

68. Which operator performs pattern matching?
(1) BETWEEN operator
(2) LIKE operator
(3) EXISTS operator
(4) None of the above

69. What is the most appropriate about multiple ROW functions?
(1) They return multiple values per each row.
(2) They return one result per group of rows and can manipulate group of rows.
(3) They return one result per row and can manipulate groups of rows.
(4) They return multiple values per a group of row.

70. Which of the following are also called group functions?
(1) Single row functions
(2) Multi group functions
(3) Multiple row functions
(4) Single group functions

71. What is true regarding the TRIM function?
(1) It is similar to SUBSTR function
(2) It removes spaces from the beginning or ending of string literals, columns or expression
(3) TRIM function cannot be applied on expression and NUMBERS
(4) TRIM function can remove character only from both sides of a string

72. What is the syntax of the MOD function in SQL DB?
(1) MOD (divisor, dividend)
(2) MOD (divisor, 1)
(3) MOD (dividend, divisor)
(4) None of the above

73. How many parameters does the SYSDATE function take?
(1) 1 (2) 2
(3) 4 (4) 0

74. Which of the following is illegal?
(1) SELECT SYSDATE - SYSDATE FROM DUAL;
(2) SELECT SYSDATE - (SYSDATE-2) FROM DUAL;
(3) SELECT SYSDATE - (SYSDATE+2) FROM DUAL;
(4) None of the above

75. Which of the following join is also called as an 'inner-join'?
(1) Non-equi join
(2) Self-join
(3) Equi join
(4) None of the above

76. Which of the following is not a type of SQL constraint?
(1) PRIMARY KEY
(2) ALTERNATE KEY
(3) FOREIGN KEY
(4) UNIQUE

Syntax

A CSS rule-set consists of a selector and a declaration block:

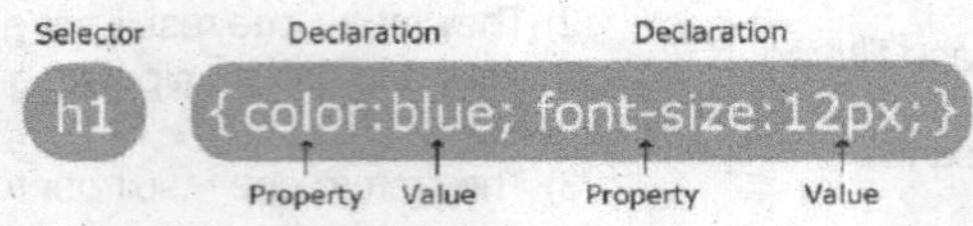

The selector points to the HTML element that you want to style. The declaration block contains one or more declarations separated by semicolons. Each declaration includes a CSS property name and a value that separated by a colon.

A CSS declaration always ends with a semicolon and declaration blocks are surrounded by curlybraces.

e.g.

```
p
{
   color: red;
   text-align: center;
}
```

Declaration of CSS in HTML is as follows:

```
p
{
  color:red;
  text-align:center;
}
body
{
  background-color:yellow;
}
h1
{
  font-size:36pt;
}
h2
{
  color:blue;
}
p
{
  margin-left:50px;
}
```

Above code is Style-01.css file. CSS file declares as follows in which HTML document save as CSS-Example-01.html.

```
<html>
<head>
<link rel="stylesheet" type="text/css"
                    href="Style-01.css"/>
</head>
<body>
<h1>This header is 36 pt</h1>
<h2>This header is blue</h2>
<p>This paragraph has a left margin of
                              50 pixels</p>
</body>
</html>
```

Output

This header is 36 pt

This header is blue

This paragraph has a left margin of 50 pixels

10.3.1 Inserting CSS

In HTML, CSS can be inserted in various ways which are as follows:

1. External Style Sheet

With an external style sheet, you can change the look of the entire website by changing just one file.

Each page must include a reference to the external style sheet file inside the <link> element. The <link> element goes inside the <head> section.

e.g.

```
<head>
   <link rel="stylesheet" type="text/css"
                         href="mystyle.css">
</head>
```

An external style sheet can be written in any text editor. The file should not contain any html tags. The style sheet file must be saved with a .css extension.

```
hr
{ color:white; }
h1
{ font-size=40 }
p
{ margin-left:20px; }
body { background-image:url("E:\Projects
\PGT\Web Design Concepts\colorful.jpg");}
```

Above code is a file as Style-02.css.

e.g.

In HTML code, which is save as CSS-Example-04.html.

```
<html>
<head>
<link rel="stylesheet"
 type="text/css"href="Style-02.css"/>
<title>Arihant BOOKS</title>
</head>
<body>
<h1>Arihant Books</h1>
<p>A wide range of books for school
   curricula, polytechnic, competitive and
   recruitment examinations are published by
   <b>Arihant Publications India Ltd.</b></p>
```

```
<hr>
For any query e-mail at info@arihantbooks.com
and crm@arihantbooks.com or dial+91-11-40546380
</body>
</html>
```

Output

2. Internal Style Sheet

An internal style sheet may be used if one single page has a unique style. Internal styles are defined within the <style> element, inside the <head> section of an HTML page. This style sheet is also known as embedded style sheet.

e.g.

HTML code saves as CSS-Example-05.html.

```
<html>
<head>
<style type="text/css">
hr
{color:white;}
h1
{font-size=40;
p
{margin-left:20px;}
body
{background-image:url("E:\Projects\copa\PGTW
eb Design Concepts\colorful.jpg");}
</style>
<title>Arihant BOOKS</title>
</head>
<body>
<h1>Arihant Books</h1>
<p>A wide range of books for school curricula,
polytechnic, competitive and recruitment
examinations are published by <b>Arihant
Publications India Ltd.</b></p>
<hr>
For any query e-mail at info@arihantbooks.com
and crm@arihantbooks.com or dial
+91-11-40546380
</body>
</html>
```

Output

3. Inline Style Sheet

An inline style may be used to apply a unique style for a single element. To use inline styles, add the style attribute to the relevant element. The style attribute can contain any CSS property.

e.g. HTML code saves as CSS-Example-06.html.

```
<html>
<head>
<style type="text/css">
hr{color:white;}
h1 {font-size=40 }
p{margin-left:20px; }
body
{background-image:url("E:\Projects\PGT\Web
Design Concepts\colorful.jpg"); }
</style>
<title>Arihant BOOKS</title>
</head>
<body>
<h1>Arihant Books</h1>
<p>A wide range of books for school curricula,
polytechnic, competitive and recruitment
examinations are published by <B>Arihant
Publications India Ltd.</b></p>
<hr style="color:black">
For any query e-mail at info@arihantbooks.com
and crm@arihantbooks.com or dial
                                  +91-11-40546380
</body>
</html>
```

Output

4. Multiple Style Sheet

If some properties have been defined for the same selector (element) in different style sheets, the value from the last read style sheet will be used. e.g. h3 selector for properties value of external style sheet in HTML document are as follows:

```
h3
{
   color : red;
   text-align : left;
   font-size : 8pt;
}
```

115. **Consider the query:**

```
SELECT student_name
FROM student_data
WHERE roll_no=(SELECT
roll_no FROM student_marks
WHERE Sem1_mark =
Sem2_mark);
```

Which of the following is true?

(1) It gives the name of the student whose marks in semester 1 and semester 2 are same
(2) It gives all the names and roll numbers of those students whose marks in semester 1 and semester 2 are same
(3) It gives the name of all students whose marks in semester 1 and semester 2 are same
(4) It gives the roll no of all students whose marks in semester 1 and semester 2 are same

116. **Which of the following queries will give the same result as given in the query given below?**

```
SELECT CONCAT(first_name,
last_name) FROM employees;
```

(1) SELECT first_name || last_name FROM employees;
(2) SELECT first_name ||''|| first_name FROM employees;
(3) SELECT last_name ||','|| first_name FROM employees;
(4) SELECT first_name ||','|| last_name FROM employees;

117. **Consider the database table "Persons" having Person_ID as the primary key:**

Person_ID	Name	Age
1000	Rajan	40
----	Jatin	45
1001	Rajesh	35

What are the constraints violated by the above table?

(1) Relationship integrity
(2) Referential integrity only
(3) Entity and domain integrities
(4) Referential and domain integrities

Directions (Q. Nos. 118-120)

Table :

MNO	Name	Fee	Type	Joining
1101	Shreya	10000	Life	28-Jan-2017
1105	Rahul	5000	Annual	17-Feb-2017
1005	Muskan	800	Monthly	25-Dec-2016
1111	Aryan	12000	Life	16-Sep-2016
1009	Prerna	1000	Guest	01-Mar-2008
1012	Asad	6000	Annual	05-Apr-2010
1019	Swati	700	Monthly	30-Jun-2009

In the above table MEMBER, Type column has Type of membership and Fee contains membership fee as per the type of membership. Life members have paid one time fee, whereas Annual members pay fee every year one the day and month of their joining, Monthly members pay fee every month on day of their Joining, Guest members pay fee daily from the day they have joined.

118. **Based on table MEMBER, which of the following SQL query will display earliest and latest joining under each type?**

(1) SELECT MIN(Joining), MAX (Joining) FROM MEMBER;
(2) SELECT MIN(Joining), MAX(Joining) FROM MEMBER GROUP BY Type;
(3) SELECT MIN(Joining), MAX(Joining), Type FROM MEMBER GROUP BY Type;
(4) SELECT MIN(Joining), MAX (Joining), Type GROUP BY Type FROM MEMBER;

119. **Based on table MEMBER, find out the most appropriate SQL statememt from the following to display the total amount of fee collected from monthly members till date:**

(1) SELECT SUM (MONTHS_BETWEEN (SYSDATE, Joing)*Fee) FROM MEMBER WHERE Type="Monthly";
(2) SELECT SUM (MONTH_BETWEEN (Joining, SYSDATE)*Fee) FROM MEMBER WHERE Type = "Monthly";
(3) SELECT SUM (MONTH_BETWEEN (Joining, SYSDATE)* Fee) FROM MEMBER WHERE Type = "Monthly";
(4) SELECT MONTHS_BETWEEN (SYSDATE, Joining)* Fee FROM MEMBER WHERE Type = "Monthly";

120. **Based on table MEMBER, which of the following SQL statement will delete the information of those members who are either Annual members or those who are having joining on or after "01-Jan-2010".**

(1) DELETE FROM MEMBER WHERE Type = "Annual" AND Joining >= "01-Jan-10";
(2) DELETE FROM MEMBER WHERE Type = "Annual" OR Joining > "01-Jan-10";
(3) DELETE * FROM MEMBER WHERE Type = "Annual" OR Joining > "01-Jan-10";
(4) DELETE FROM MEMBER WHERE Type = "Annual" OR Joining >= "01-Jan-10";

ANSWER KEY

1	(4)	2	(2)	3	(4)	4	(4)	5	(4)	6	(4)	7	(4)	8	(4)	9	(2)	10	(4)
11	(1)	12	(2)	13	(3)	14	(2)	15	(1)	16	(1)	17	(1)	18	(1)	19	(1)	20	(3)
21	(4)	22	(4)	23	(2)	24	(3)	25	(3)	26	(4)	27	(2)	28	(2)	29	(4)	30	(4)
31	(2)	32	(4)	33	(3)	34	(4)	35	(2)	36	(2)	37	(2)	38	(1)	39	(4)	40	(1)
41	(1)	42	(4)	43	(1)	44	(3)	45	(2)	46	(1)	47	(4)	48	(4)	49	(4)	50	(3)
51	(2)	52	(4)	53	(2)	54	(4)	55	(2)	56	(2)	57	(1)	58	(2)	59	(3)	60	(4)
61	(2)	62	(3)	63	(4)	64	(1)	65	(4)	66	(1)	67	(3)	68	(2)	69	(2)	70	(3)
71	(2)	72	(3)	73	(4)	74	(4)	75	(3)	76	(2)	77	(4)	78	(4)	79	(4)	80	(1)
81	(3)	82	(1)	83	(2)	84	(4)	85	(1)	86	(1)	87	(1)	88	(1)	89	(2)	90	(1)
91	(3)	92	(4)	93	(3)	94	(3)	95	(4)	96	(4)	97	(2)	98	(1)	99	(3)	100	(1)
101	(1)	102	(3)	103	(4)	104	(4)	105	(2)	106	(1)	107	(3)	108	(1)	109	(4)	110	(3)
111	(4)	112	(2)	113	(1)	114	(3)	115	(3)	116	(1)	117	(3)	118	(2)	119	(1)	120	(3)

Business Computing

Business computing system is any application that directly or indirectly deals or supports financial, administrative, or other information that is an integral part of running the business. Business computing is any digitised process that facilitate the operations of any enterprise. It is a computer based system used to achieve business objectives.

9.1 Front-End Interface

It is a user interface that the user sees and it receives input from user in the form of query, request etc., and passes them to the back-end. When a user accesses any website (like, www.google.com) on their web browser (which acts as a user interface) is called **user's request** and the response is also displayed on the same web browser.

In client/server application, the client side program is called **front-end** and server side program is called **back-end**.

The goal of user interface is to make the user interaction simple and efficient.

Front-end interface is mainly divided into two parts as follows :

9.1.1 Command Line Interface (CLI)

It is a type of human computer interface (i.e. a way for human to interact with computers) that relies only on textual input and output. That is the entire display screen on the current active portion of it, shows only characters (and no images) and input is usually performed entirely with a keyboard.

The CLI gets its name from the fact that it is an interface, which contains command lines. A command line is a space on the display screen in which commands (i.e. instructions telling a computer to do something) are typed by the user.

e.g. The most familiar example of a CLI used by many people is MS-DOS.

9.1.2 Graphical User Interface (GUI)

It is a type of front-end user interface in which user interacts with computer using windows, icons, menus and other graphical components, which can be manipulated by a mouse or any other device and a limited use of keyboard.

A window is a (usually) rectangular portion of the monitor screen that can display its contents (e.g. a program, icons, a text file or an image) seemingly independently of the rest of the display screen. A major feature of GUI is the ability for multiple windows to be opened simultaneously. Each window can display different application or file (e.g. text, image or spreadsheet files) that have been opened/created with a single application.

1. **Padding-bottom** specifies the bottom padding of an element.
2. **Padding-top** specifies the top padding of an element.
3. **Padding-left** specifies the left padding of an element.
4. **Padding-right** specifies the right padding of an element.
5. **Padding** serves as shorthand for the preceding properties.
6. **Vertical-align** This property vertical align an image.
   e.g.
   ```
   <img style = " vertical-align:text-top;
                                ">......</img>
   ```
7. **Direction** This property sets the text direction to "right-to-left".
   e.g.
   ```
   <div style = "direction:rtl;">......</div>
   ```

10.3.9 CSS Layers

CSS gives you opportunity to create layers of various divisions. The CSS layers refer to applying the z-index property to elements that overlap with each other.

The z-index property is used along with the position property is used along with position to create an effect of layers. You can specify which element should come on top and which element should come at bottom.

<layer> tag can be explicitly positioned by setting the LEFT and TOP attributes.

<ilayer> tag appears whenever they naturally fall in the flow of the documents.

10.4 Additional Features

Some additional features of CSS are as follows:

10.4.1 Grouping Style Sheets or CSS Combinations

A combinator is something that explains the relationship between the selectors. A CSS selector can contain more than one simple selector. Between the simple selectors, we can include a combinator.

There are various different combinators in CSS:

1. Descendant Selectors (space)

This selector matches all elements that are descendants of a specified element.

e.g
```
div p
{
   background-color : yellow;
}
```

2. Child Selector (>)

This selector selects all elements that are the immediate children of a specified element.

e.g.
```
div>p
{
  background-color:yellow;
}
```

3. Adjacent Sibling Selector (+)

This selector selects all elements that are the adjacent siblings of a specified element.

e.g.
```
div + p
{
   background-color:yellow;
}
```

4. General Sibling Selector (~)

This selector selects all elements that are siblings of a specified element.

e.g.
```
div ~ p
{
   background-color:yellow;
}
```

10.4.2 CSS. class Selector

This selector selects elements with a specific class attribute. To select elements with a specific class, write a period (·) character, followed by the name of the class.

Syntax
```
.class
{
   CSS declarations;
}
```

You can also specify that only specific HTML elements should be affected by a class. To do this, start with the element name, then write the period (·) character, followed by the name of the class.

e.g

1. ```
   p.hometown
   {
      background-color:yellow;
   }
   ```
   In above example, style all <p> elements with class = "hometown".
2. <p class = " center bold"> This paragraph refers to two classes. </p>
   In above example, this <p> element will be styled according to class = "center" AND to class = " bold".
   ```

CHAPTER PRACTICE

1. **To create HTML page, you need**
(1) text editor
(2) web browser
(3) Both (1) and (2)
(4) None of the above

2. **Markup tags tell the web browser**
(1) how to organise the page
(2) how to display the page
(3) how to display message box on page
(4) None of the above

3. **The web standard allows programmers on many different computer platforms to dispersed format and display the information server. These programs are called**
(1) web browsers
(2) HTML
(3) Internet Explorer
(4) None of the above

4. **Which of the following is the appropriate format for graphics that can be embedded within an Internet document?**
(1) HTML (2) BMP
(3) TIFF (4) GIF

5. **Which of the following tag identifies the document as an HTML document?**
(1) <html> (2) <head>
(3) <body> (4) <p>

6. **Tags and text that do not display directly on the page are placed in**
(1) body (2) tables
(3) head (4) title

7. **Which of the following is not the appropriate format for graphics that can be embedded withing a Internet document?**
(1) XBM (2) JPG
(3) GIF (4) TIFF

8. **Which section is used for text and tags that are shown directly on your web pages?**
(1) Meta (2) Head
(3) Body (4) Table

9. **Choose the correct HTML tag for the largest heading.**
(1) <h2> (2) <h4>
(3) <h6> (4) <h1>

10. **To create a square bulleted list, use**
(1) <ul type = "circle">
(2) <ol type = "square">
(3) <ul type = "square">
(4) <ul start ="square">

11. **To start a numbered list with regular numerals, use**
(1) <ol type = "a">
(2) <ol type = "1">
(3) <ol type = "I">
(4) <ol type = "u">

12. **The ...... attribute is used to specify the location of the image file.**
(1) alt (2) src (3) align (4) name

13. **The tag used in HTML to link a web page with other web page is**
(1) <a> (2) <h>
(3) <u> (4) <l>

14. **From which tag the descriptive list starts?**
(1) <ll> (2) <dd>
(3) <dl> (4) <ds>

15. **The common element which describes the web page, is**
(1) heading (2) paragraph
(3) list (4) All of these

16. **Symbol used at the beginning of HREF text is**
(1) # (2) $ (3) & (4) ^

17. **The tag used to create a new list item and also includes a hyperlink is**
(1) <li> (2) <dl>
(3) <dd> (4) <ul>

18. **The text inside the <textarea> tag works like**
(1) <p> formatted text
(2) <t> formatted text
(3) <pre> formatted text
(4) None of the above

19. **......... is the default color of a hyperlink.**
(1) Red (2) Blue
(3) Green (4) Black

20. **A much better approach to establish the base URL is to use**
(1) base elements
(2) head elements
(3) Both (1) and (2)
(4) None of the above

21. **Which of the following tags that are all in sequence in TABLE ?**
(1) <thread>,<body>,<tr>
(2) <table>,<head>,<tfoot>
(3) <table>,<tr>,<td>
(4) <table>,<tr>,<tt>

22. **border, frame, cellspacing, cellpadding, align are the attributes of**
(1) <body> (2) <img>
(3) <table> (4) <head>

23. **Which attribute tells, how many rows a cell should span?**
(1) colspan = n
(2) rowspan = n
(3) Both (1) and (2)
(4) None of the above

24. **Which of the following is an attribute of <table> tag?**
(1) src (2) cellpadding
(3) link (4) bold

25. **The GET and POST methods are specified in**
(1) a CGI program (2) a Java program
(3) an HTML form (4) a URL string

26. **The attribute is used to set the border color of a table is**
(1) border (2) bordercolor
(3) color (4) border color

27. **The attribute is used to specify the background color of a table is**
(1) color (2) bgtable
(3) backcolor (4) bgcolor

28. **The .... attribute helps to align data vertically in a single cell.**
(1) align (2) valign
(3) halign (4) Both (2) and (3)

29. **Which of the following tags gives a caption to the table?**
(1) <caption> (2) <summary>
(3) <frame> (4) <cap>

30. **The attribute of <form> tag is**
(1) method
(2) action
(3) Both (1) and (2)
(4) None of the above

31. **Which of the following is a container?**
(1) <select> (2) <value>
(3) <input> (4)

introducing the system to different inputs to obtain and analyse its outputs and behaviour and the way it functions. Testing is becoming more and more important to ensure customer's satisfaction, and it requires no knowledge in coding, hardware configuration or design.

Testing can be performed by real users, or by a team of specialised personnel, it can also be systematic and automated to ensure that the actual outcomes are compared and equal to the predicted and desired outcomes.

6. System Maintenance

In this phase, periodic maintenance for the system will be carried out to make sure that the system won't become obsolete, this will include replacing the old hardware and continuously evaluating system's performance, it also includes providing latest updates for certain components to make sure it meets the right standards and the latest technologies to face current security threats.

These are the main six phases of the System Development Life Cycle, and it's an iterative process for each project. It's important to mention that excellent communication level should be maintained with the customer, and prototypes are very important and helpful when it comes to meeting the requirements. By building the system in short iterations; we can guarantee meeting the customer's requirements before we build the whole system.

9.4 Entity Relationship Model

The Entity Relationship (ER) data model is based on a perception of a real world, which consists a set of basic objects called **entities** and **relationships** among these objects. The ER model was introduced by Peter Chen. but he also introduced a corresponding diagramming technique.

In software engineering, an Entity Relationship model (ER model in short) is an abstract way to describe a database. It usually starts with a relational database, which stores data in tables. Some of the data in these tables point to data in other tables.

Some terminology related to ER model are as follows:

1. Entity

An 'Entity' is an object that exists and is distinguishable from other objects. An entity is any object, place, person, concept or activity about which an enterprise records data. While diagramming, entities are named and represented by a rectangle as shown in figure:

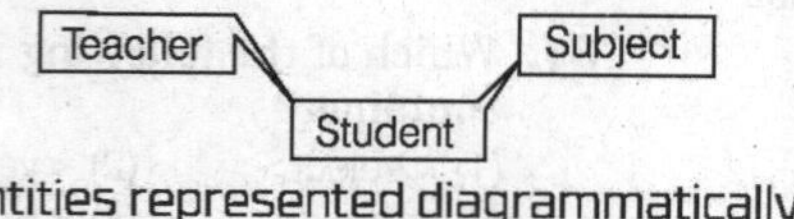

Entities represented diagrammatically

(i) **Entity Type** An entity type (also called entity set) is a set of entities of same type, i.e. which share common properties. e.g. the set of all persons having an account at a bank, can be defined as the entity type CUSTOMER. Similarly, TEACHER, SUBJECT and STUDENT are also entity types or entity sets.

(ii) **Entity Instance** An entity instance is an instance of entity type, i.e. an entity instance is a specific individual, thing or object, e.g. 'Shyam' is an instance of entity type STUDENT; 'Computer' is an instance of entity type SUBJECT and so on.

2. Relationship

A relationship is defined as an association among several entities. It connects two or more entities into a relationship. It represented by a diamond ◇. e.g. there is a relationship between artist and song.

This relationship represents the fact that an artist performs several songs and a song is performed by many artists. You may name this relationship as PERFORMS.

A relationship type defines the association of entity types (e.g. artist-song relationship) and a relationship instance is an association of entity instances (e.g. shyam - tumbin relationship).

A relationship between ARTIST and SONG entities

An entity can associate with itself also. e.g. in an organisation, one employee may marry another employee. Such a relationship can be represented diagrammatically as shown in figure.

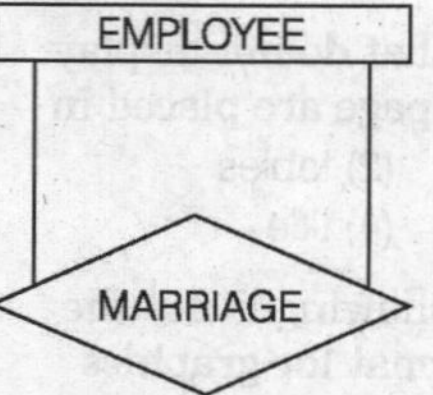

An entity associated with result

There can be following types of relationship:

(i) **One-to-One Relationship** When one entity is related with another entity through a common attribute. Then such relation is known as one-to-one relationship.

(ii) **One-to-Many Relationship** When one entity is related with more than one entities through a common attribute or one attribute of an entity is related with more than one attributes of another table. Then such relation is known as one-to-many relationship.

(iii) **Many-to-Many Relationship** When more than one attributes of one entity is related with more than one attributes of another table. Then such relation is known as many-to-many relationship.

3. Attributes

An entity is represented by a set of attributes. An attribute is a property of a given entity. An attribute instance is a particular property of an individual entity instance. An attribute type is a property of an entity type.

Attributes are represented through ellipses, labelled with the name of the property. The 'key attributes' are underlined.

Figure shows an entity alongwith its attributes.

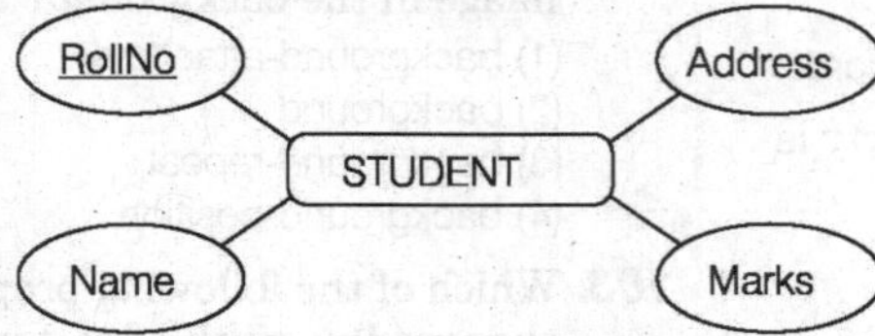

An entity alongwith its attributes

In figure, RollNo is underlined because it is the key attribute. It has unique value for each student.

There are two types of attributes as follows:

(i) **Composite Attribute** If an attribute is a group of properties, it is called composite attribute. e.g. address is a composite attribute as it is a group of sub-properties such as house no., area, city, state etc.

(ii) **Single-Valued and Multi-Valued Attribute** Attributes can either be single-valued if they are capable of storing single value or be multi-valued if they are capable of storing multiple values. e.g. if an entity STUDENT has following attributes:

RollNo, Name, Class, Subject.

Then, the attributes RollNo, Name and Class can hold one value whereas, attribute Subject can hold multiple values as the student can study multiple subjects.

Thus, the attributes RollNo, Name and Class are single valued attributes but the attribute Subject is a multi-valued attribute.

9.5 Front-End and Back-End Connectivity

The front-end and back-end interact with one another through database connectivity. Database connectivity refers to a programming interface that lets a front-end access a database on a back-end, *via* some means. When database connectivity is implemented in a Java application, then it is known as Java Database Connectivity, i.e. JDBC.

JDBC was based largely on Microsoft's ODBC (Open Database Connectivity) but has largely surpassed it. Compared to ODBC, JDBC has more flexible APIs which programmers can use in their applications. JDBC has all the advantages that ODBC has and caters to the need of programmers under a variety of platforms.

JDBC provides Java developers with an industry standard API (An API or Application Programming Interface is a set of classes, methods and resources that programmers can use to do their work.) for database independent connectivity between Java Applications (Applets, Servlets, JSPs, EJBs etc.) and a wide range of RDBMS such as Oracle, Informix, Microsoft SQL Server and Sybase. JDBC accomplishes most of what it does through a native API, that translates Java methods to native calls.

In its simplest form, JDBC makes it possible to do the following:

(i) Connect to a database.

(ii) Execute SQL statements to query your database.

(iii) Generate query results.

(iv) Perform updates, inserts and deletions.

(v) Execute stored procedures.

The only requirement to create a JDBC application is that the driver for JDBC connectivity should be available and installed.

Benefits of Database Connectivity

Some common benefits of databases connectivity are as follows :

(i) Any database can be accessed from within the application code if its connectivity driver is available.

(ii) Distribution of application logic in terms of front-end and back-end leads to better performance.

(iii) Since, database handling is entirely with back-end. The data is safely and securely processed. In other words, enhanced database security.

(iv) Some connectivity drivers lead to better performance, portability, optimised performance of the application.

9.6 More Application Areas of Database

There are various application areas of database as follows:

1. Inventory Control

Inventory control, also known as **stock control,** involves regulating and maximising your company's inventory. The goal of inventory control is to maximise profits with minimum inventory investment, without impacting customer satisfaction levels.

84. **Which of the following symbol is used to create a link to a named anchor in HTML?**
(1) & (2) @
(3) # (4) $

85. **The attribute, which defines the relationship between current document and href URL is**
(1) rel (2) url
(3) rev (4) All of these

86. **Which of the following property specifies the top margin of an element?**
(1) margin
(2) margin-bottom
(3) margin-top
(4) margin-left

87. **Which of the following property is used to set the background color of an element?**
(1) background-color
(2) background-image
(3) background-repeat
(4) background-position

88. **Which of the following is a way to associate styles with your HTML document?**
(1) External CSS - The Element
(2) Important CSS - @import Rule
(3) Both (1) and (2)
(4) None of the above

89. **Which of the following property is used to increase or decrease how bold or light a font appears?**
(1) font-family
(2) font-style
(3) font-variant
(4) font-weight

90. **Which of the following property is used to make a font italic or oblique?**
(1) font-family
(2) font-style
(3) font-variant
(4) font-weight

91. **Which of the following property is used to underlined, overline and strikethrough text?**
(1) text-indent
(2) text-align
(3) text-decoration
(4) text-transform

92. **Which of the following property specifies the left padding of an element?**
(1) padding-bottom
(2) padding-top
(3) padding-left (4) padding-right

93. **Which of the following property specifies the left margin of an element?**
(1) margin (2) margin-bottom
(3) margin-top (4) margin-left

94. **The ...... property allows to specify how much space appear between the content of an element and it's border.**
(1) spacing (2) marking
(3) padding (4) content-border

95. **Which of the following property is used to align the text of a document?**
(1) text-indent
(2) text-align
(3) text-decoration
(4) text-transform

96. **Which of the following property specifies whether a border should be solid, dashed line, double line or one of the other possible values?**
(1) border-color
(2) border-style
(3) border-width
(4) border-bottom-color

97. **Which of the following property is used to capitalise text or convert text to uppercase or lowercase letters?**
(1) text-indent
(2) text-align
(3) text-decoration
(4) text-transform

98. **Which of the following property specifies the top padding of an element?**
(1) padding-bottom
(2) padding-top
(3) padding-left
(4) padding-right

99. **Where in an HTML document is the correct place to refer to an external style sheet?**
(1) At the end of the document
(2) In the <head> section
(3) At the top of the document
(4) In the <body> section

100. **Which of the following property is used to control the repetition of an image in the background?**
(1) background-color
(2) background-image
(3) background-repeat
(4) background-position

101. **Which of the following property of a anchor element signifies an element on which the user is currently clicking?**
(1) link (2) visited
(3) hover (4) active

102. **Which of the following property is used to control the scrolling of an image in the background?**
(1) background-attachment
(2) background
(3) background-repeat
(4) background-position

103. **Which of the following property changes the width of bottom border?**
(1) border-bottom-width
(2) border-top-width
(3) border-left-width
(4) border-right-width

104. **Which of the following is a valid value of the frameborder attribute of the <frameset> tag?**
(1) yes
(2) no
(3) Either yes or no
(4) None of the above

105. **The tags used for specifying style in HTML are**
I. <b> II. <i>
III. <u> IV. <I>
Choose the correct one
(1) I and II (2) I and III
(3) II and IV (4) I, II and III

106. **Observe the HTML code given below and identify the line that will be ignored and not displayed by the browser:**

```
<html>
<head><title> Web Page
</title></head>
<body> Welcome to Page
<! -- check-- >
</body>
</html>
```

(1) <title> Web Page </title>
(2) <body> Welcome to Page
(3) <! -- check -->
(4) None of the abvoe

107. **Given below are several usages of the anchor tag in HTML.**

(i) **<a href="http://www.gate.ac.in /HTML/BASIC/testpage.html"> Test Me</a>**

(ii) **<a href="/BASIC/testpage.html ">Test Me</a>**

(iii) **<a href="testpage. html">Test Me</a>**

(iv) **<a href="testpage.html# test">Test Me</a>**

Which of the above are valid?

(1) (i) and (ii) (2) (i) and (iii)
(3) (i), (ii) and (iii) (4) All of these

108. **How do you display a border like this:**
The top border = 10 pixels
The bottom border = 5 pixels
The left border = 20 pixels
The right border = 1 pixels?

(1) border-width : 10px 20px 5px 1px
(2) border-width : 10px 1px 5px 20px
(3) border-width : 5px 20px 10px 1px
(4) border-width : 10px 5px 20px 1px

ANSWER KEY

1	(3)	**2**	(2)	**3**	(1)	**4**	(4)	**5**	(1)	**6**	(3)	**7**	(4)	**8**	(3)	**9**	(4)	**10**	(3)
11	(2)	**12**	(2)	**13**	(1)	**14**	(3)	**15**	(4)	**16**	(1)	**17**	(1)	**18**	(3)	**19**	(2)	**20**	(1)
21	(3)	**22**	(3)	**23**	(2)	**24**	(2)	**25**	(3)	**26**	(2)	**27**	(4)	**28**	(2)	**29**	(1)	**30**	(3)
31	(1)	**32**	(4)	**33**	(1)	**34**	(1)	**35**	(4)	**36**	(1)	**37**	(3)	**38**	(1)	**39**	(3)	**40**	(2)
41	(1)	**42**	(2)	**43**	(4)	**44**	(4)	**45**	(1)	**46**	(3)	**47**	(3)	**48**	(1)	**49**	(3)	**50**	(3)
51	(3)	**52**	(2)	**53**	(2)	**54**	(3)	**55**	(3)	**56**	(1)	**57**	(3)	**58**	(4)	**59**	(3)	**60**	(2)
61	(4)	**62**	(1)	**63**	(2)	**64**	(4)	**65**	(2)	**66**	(3)	**67**	(2)	**68**	(1)	**69**	(2)	**70**	(2)
71	(3)	**72**	(2)	**73**	(3)	**74**	(2)	**75**	(1)	**76**	(3)	**77**	(2)	**78**	(2)	**79**	(3)	**80**	(4)
81	(2)	**82**	(1)	**83**	(2)	**84**	(3)	**85**	(3)	**86**	(3)	**87**	(1)	**88**	(3)	**89**	(4)	**90**	(2)
91	(3)	**92**	(3)	**93**	(4)	**94**	(3)	**95**	(2)	**96**	(2)	**97**	(4)	**98**	(2)	**99**	(2)	**100**	(3)
101	(4)	**102**	(1)	**103**	(1)	**104**	(3)	**105**	(4)	**106**	(3)	**107**	(4)	**108**	(2)				

9.9 Client/Server Computing

Client/Server computing is a computing model in which client and server computers communicate with each other over a network. In client/server computing, a server takes requests from client computers and shares its resources, applications and/or data with one or more client computers on the network, and a client is a computing device that initiates contact with a server in order to make use of shareable resource.

Client server computing is dividing into three components, a client process requesting service and a server process providing the requested service, with a middleware in between them for their interaction.

(i) A client server process usually manages the user interface portion of the applications, validate data entered by the user, dispatch requests to server programs. It is the front-end of the application that the user sees and interacts with.

(ii) The server process fulfills the client requests by performing the service requested. After the server receives requests from clients, it executes database retrieval, updates and manages data integrity and dispatches responses to client requests.

(iii) Middleware allows applications to transparently communicate with other programs or processes regardless of location.

CHAPTER PRACTICE

1. **In client server application, the client side program is called**
(1) back-end (2) front-end
(3) database (4) program

2. **In client server application, the server side program is called**
(1) back-end (2) front-end
(3) metadata (4) program

3. **Which of the following is not an inventory?**
(1) Machines
(2) Raw materials
(3) Finished products
(4) Consumable tools

4. **The cost of insurance and taxes are included in**
(1) cost of ordering
(2) set-up cost
(3) inventory carrying cost
(4) cost of shortages

5. **Which of the following is true for inventory control?**
(1) Economic order quantity has minimum total cost per order.
(2) Inventory carrying costs increases with quantity per order
(3) Ordering cost decreases with low size
(4) All of the above

6. **An example of purchasing costs include**
(1) incoming freight (2) storage costs
(3) insurance (4) spoillage

7. **Costs of not carrying enough inventory include**
(1) lost sales
(2) customer disappointment
(3) possible worker layoffs
(4) All of the above

8. **Cost of capital is helpful in corporative analysis of various**
(1) source of finance
(2) source of services
(3) source of material
(4) product

9. **Which of the following has the highest cost of capital?**
(1) Loans
(2) Equity shares
(3) Bonds
(4) Preference shares

10. **Which one is not an element of internal environment?**
(1) Marketing capabilities
(2) Operational capabilities
(3) Money and capital market
(4) Personal capabilities

11. **An RPC (Remote Procedure Call) is initiated by the**
(1) server (2) client
(3) Both (1) and (2) (4) None of these

12. **A server cannot serve on which of the following levels?**
(1) Client layer (2) Business layer
(3) Database layer (4) All of these

13. **The entity relationship set is represented in E-R diagram as**
(1) double diamonds
(2) undivided rectangles
(3) dashed lines
(4) diamond

14. **The rectangles divided into two parts represents …… .**
(1) entity set
(2) relationship set
(3) attributes of a relationship set
(4) primary key

15. **Weak entity set is represented as**
(1) underline
(2) double line
(3) double diamond
(4) double rectangle

16. **A data dictionary is created when a …… created.**
(1) instance (2) segment
(3) database (4) dictionary

17. **The statement that is true about data mining is …… .**
(1) data mining is not a single technique
(2) it finds the hidden patterns from data set
(3) it is a real discovery process
(4) all forms of pollutions are found during the data mining state itself

18. **The following classes of costs are usually involved in inventory decisions except**
(1) cost of ordering
(2) carrying cost
(3) cost of shortages
(4) machining cost

19. The time period between placing an order its receipt in stock is known as
(1) lead time (2) carrying time
(3) shortage time (4) over time

20. Which of the following relationships hold true for safety stock?
(1) The greater the risk of running out of stock, the smaller the safety of stock
(2) The larger the opportunity cost of the funds invested in inventory, the larger the safety stock
(3) The greater the uncertainty associated with fore costed demand, the smaller the safety stock
(4) The higher the profit margin per unit, the higher the safety stock necessary

21. Indian business encounter the following problem in the globalisation.
(1) Infrastructural Bottleneck
(2) Lack of interest shown by MNC's
(3) Both (1) and (2)
(4) None of the above

22. Which of the following items are not necessary for client/server?
(1) Assure that tools will connect with middleware
(2) Understand the requirements
(3) Determine network bandwidth capabilities
(4) Include the use of a file server

23. Client/server security includes which of the following?
(1) Physical security
(2) Change control security
(3) Measures taken to secure all systems
(4) All of the above

24. One of the most common technique used for conceptual design is …… .
(1) logical design (2) database design
(3) physical design (4) E-R model

25. Cost of product failure, error prevention and appraisals are classified as
(1) stocking costs (2) stock-out costs
(3) costs of quality (4) shrinkage costs

26. Activities related to coordinating, controlling and planning activities of flow of inventory are classified as
(1) decisional management
(2) throughput management
(3) inventory management
(4) manufacturing management

27. Purchase order lead time is multiplied to number of units is sold per unit of time to calculate
(1) carrying costs
(2) relevant total cost
(3) economic order quantity
(4) reorder point

28. The process of providing financial information to external decision makers is referred to as
(1) public accounting
(2) government accounting
(3) financial accounting
(4) business accounting

29. The role of financial management does not usually include responsibility for
(1) compliance with accounting standards
(2) treasury management
(3) corporate finance
(4) risk management

30. Use the new system as the same time as the old system to compare the results. This is known as
(1) procedure writing
(2) simultaneous processing
(3) parallel operation
(4) file conversion

31. Which of the following is not a likely configuration of a client–server system?
(1) Single client - single server
(2) Single client - multiple server system
(3) Multiple clients - multiple servers system
(4) None of the above

32. Which of the following gives a logical structure of the database graphically?
(1) Entity-relationship diagram
(2) Entity diagram
(3) Database diagram
(4) Architectural representation

33. We indicate roles in E-R diagrams by labeling the lines that connect …… to …….. .
(1) diamond, diamond
(2) rectangle, diamond
(3) rectangle, rectangle
(4) diamond, rectangle

34. An entity set that does not have sufficient attributes to form a primary key is termed a …… .
(1) strong entity set (2) variant set
(3) weak entity set (4) variable set

35. For a weak entity set to be meaningful, it must be associated with another entity set, called the
(1) identifying set
(2) owner set
(3) neighbour set
(4) strong entity set

36. The attribute AGE is calculated from DATE_OF_BIRTH. The attribute AGE is
(1) single-valued (2) multi-valued
(3) composite (4) derived

37. An …… is a set of entities of the same type that share the same properties, or attributes.
(1) entity set (2) attribute set
(3) relation set (4) entity model

38. In one-to-many relationship, the entity that is on the one side of the relationship is called a(n) … entity.
(1) parent (2) child
(3) instance (4) subtype

39. An Oracle …… is a set of tables and views that are used as a read-only reference about the database.
(1) database dictionary
(2) dictionary table
(3) data dictionary
(4) dictionary

40. Relational schemas and other metadata about relations are stored in a structure called the
(1) metadata (2) catalog
(3) log (4) data dictionary

41. The important aspect of the data warehouse environment is that data found within the data warehouse is,
(1) subject-oriented (2) time-variant
(3) integrated (4) All of these

42. …… maps the core warehouse metadata to business concepts, familiar and useful to end users.
(1) Application level metadata
(2) User level metadata
(3) End user level metadata
(4) Core level metadata

43. Data warehouse contains …… data that is never found in the operational environment.
(1) normalised (2) informational
(3) summary (4) denormalised

44. A directory to help the DSS analyst locate the content of the data warehouse is seen in …… .
(1) current detail data
(2) lightly summarised data
(3) metadata
(4) older details data

11.3 Structure of XML Document System

When it is felt that the need to process an XML document on web in the desired format, a complete XML document system is required.

XML defines certain rules for syntax that specify how to structure an XML document. The syntax used to create an XML document is called **markup syntax.**

The XML document system is a combination of the following types of documents:

1. **Semantic of data** (XML file or document) It contains the actual data.
2. **DTD** It refers to Document Type Definition. It defines the structure and grammar rules for an XML document. DTD provides a framework to validate XML documents. Also, it defines the structure of an XML document with a list of legal elements.
3. **StyleSheet** It refers to document that defines the style or appearance for the XML document. It will define the styles of the elements, i.e. their color, font, alignment etc.

There are two types of stylesheets used in XML as follows:

(i) XSL (eXtensible StyleSheet Language)

(ii) CSS (Cascading StyleSheet)

11.4 Structure of XML-File/Document

Every XML document includes both physical and logical structures as follows :

11.4.1 Physical Structure

It contains the actual data used in a document. The basic storage unit called **entity,** each of which may refer to other entities. An entity has a name and content. It contains references to other entities. There is a special entity called **document entity** or **root** that serves as a main storage unit. XML processor always start document processing from that unit. We have three classifications of entities, these are as follows:

i. Internal and External Entities

For internal entity, there is no separate physical storage object and the content of the entity is given in the declaration. It contained inside the document. If the entity is not internal, then it is an external entity.

ii. General and Parameter Entities

General entities are entities which are used within the document content. In this specification, general entities are sometimes referred to with the unqualified entity, when this leads to no ambiguity. Generally, entities are declared and used differently. Parameter entities are parsed and used only in the DTD part of the XML document.

iii. Parsed and Unparsed Entities

Parsed entities contain text that is referred as replacement text intended to be processed by the XML software such as XML parser and is considered as an integral part of the document. Unparsed entities are resources that can be of any type including text objects. This type of entity is never process by XML parser.

11.4.2 Logical Structure

It is a template that enables the elements to be included in a document and in the order in which they have to be included. The logical structure includes the basic components of the XML document. It indicates how a document is built, irrespective of what a document contains. The first structural element is prolog which is the base for the logical structure.

The structure of the document of example code:

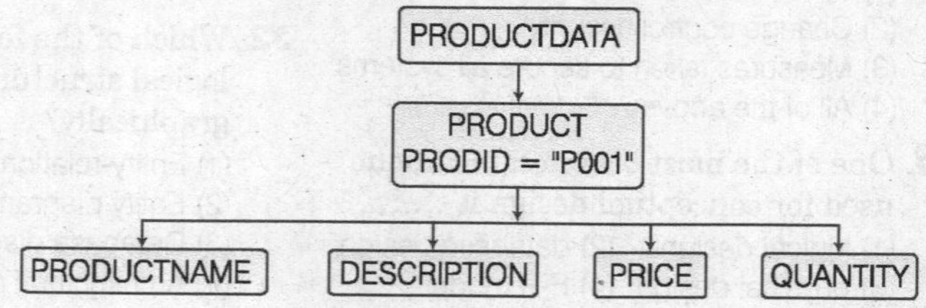

11.5 Components of XML Document

An XML document is composed of many things like declarations, list of instructions to be processed, elements and comments. An XML document contains the following two components:

11.5.1 Prolog

The prolog is an introduction to the XML document. It outlines the order and content of initial prolog in an XML document. It should be the first logical component. But, the XML prolog is an optional piece of information.

The prolog contains the following components, all of these are optional, either we can use it in syntax or not.

i. XML Declaration

XML declaration refers to a statement, which is used to indicate the specified XML document. It is the first line in the document and defines the XML version and character encoding used in the document.

The following code shows the XML declaration statement:

```
<?xml version = "1.0" encoding = "UTF-8"
standalone = "no"?>
```

The following are the attributes of declaration:

(a) **version** It identifies the version of XML which is using pseudo-attribute (value) must be provided in the declaration, i.e. document belongs to XML recommendation version 1.0.

(b) **encoding** It specifies the character set which is optional. By default, the character set is UTF-8.

(c) **standalone** It specifies whether document needs external entities or not. The 'yes' value specifies that the XML document has a DTD and the 'no' value specifies that the XML document is linked to an external entity. By default, value is yes.

An XML declaration is made up of as many as three name/value pairs, syntactically identical to attributes. The three attributes are a mandatory version attribute and optional encoding and standalone attributes.

ii. Processing Instructions (PI)

Processing instructions can be used to pass information to applications in such a way that escapes most XML rules. Its main use is of linking to an XML stylesheet in the prolog of an XML document. Processing instructions do not have to follow much internal syntax, it can include markup characters without escaping them and can appear anywhere in the document.

The following is the processing instruction syntax:

```
<?xml-stylesheet type="type" href="uri"?>
```

Name of the PI | Specify the type of stylesheet | Specify the name of stylesheet

e.g.

```
<?xml-stylesheet type = "text/xsl"
href = "show_book.xsl"?>
```

or

```
<?xml-stylesheet type="text/css"
href="example.css"?>
```

The following are the attributes of PI as follows:

(a) href refers to the name of stylesheet.

(b) type refers to the type of stylesheet.

iii. Document Type (DOCTYPE) Declaration

The document type declarations (DTD) are used in XML to specify information about a document, including the document's root element and Data Type Definitions.

The DTD consists of an internal or references an external Document Type Declaration. It can also have a combination of both internal and external DTD.

DOCTYPE declaration can contain:

(a) The name of the document or root element.

(b) Define elements, attributes, entities, notations and comments to the document (internal) DTD.

(c) Identifies an external DTD for the document.

The document type declaration begins with the <!DOCTYPE> declaration.

Syntax

```
<!DOCTYPE dtd_name SYSTEM="dtd_file_name.dtd">
```

e.g.

```
3<!DOCTYPE PRODUCT SYSTEM="pro.dtd">
```

The simplest DOCTYPE declaration identifies only the root element of the document.

```
<!DOCTYPE rootelement>
```

DOCTYPE declarations can also include declarations directly, in which it is referred to as an internal subset. If a DOCTYPE declaration includes the entire DTD directly, about reference to external files or external subset, it uses following syntax:

```
<!DOCTYPE rootelement SYSTEM
                    ="URIreference" [declarations]>
```

iv. Comments

It explains how comments can be made in XML markup as a means of annotating in a XML document.

It is used to leave a note or to temporarily edit out a portion of XML code that appears in the code of an XML document to understand the code better. XML comments have the exact same syntax as HTML comments have.

Syntax

```
<!--This is a comment-->
```

e.g.

```
<!--Students grades are updated bi-monthly-->
```

Make sure that two "hyphens" do not appear in a comment except in the beginning (<! – –) or the end (– –>).

v. White Space and New Line

It refers to the blank or empty spaces in the XML document. White spaces include spaces, tabs, CR-Carriage Returns, blank lines and LF-Line Feed. XML stores a new lines as LF. You can add white spaces by spacebar, TAB or

10.1.3 Main Features of HTML

Main features of HTML are as follows:

1. **Linking** Data can be linked in HTML, this allows user to move from one page to another page, from top of the page to bottom of the page by a mouse click and *vice-versa.*
2. **Portability** HTML can be opened across networks as it uses ASCII format, i.e. HTML is a platform independent.
3. **Simplicity** HTML is simple, easy to use and understand.

10.1.4 HTML Elements or Tags

HTML is written in the form of tags. A tag refers to a string enclosed within angular brackets (< and >). HTML elements represent semantics or meaning.

(i) HTML tags are predefined and are not case-sensitive.

(ii) All the HTML tags are typed inside the angular brackets (< and >) and the text between these brackets are called **elements.**

(iii) The opening tags are written within the less than (<) and greater than (>) signs. e.g. `<html>`

(iv) The closing tags are written within the < and > signs with a forward slash (/) appended before the name of the tag. e.g. `</html>`

(v) The attributes are always specified in the opening tag, which provide additional information about that tag.

There are two kinds of elements as follows:

1. Container Elements

These type of HTML elements always wrap around text or graphics and come in a set with opening as well as closing tag.

e.g.
```
<html>...</html>
<head>...</head>
```

2. Empty Elements

These type of HTML elements are standalone tags, i.e. empty tags do not have to be wrapped around text or graphics and not require a closing tag.

e.g.
```
<hr> inserts a horizontal line
<br> adds a line break
```

10.1.5 HTML Tag Structure

Consider the following syntax to understand the HTML tag structure:

```
<Tag_Name Attribute_Name
    ="Attribute_Value">Content</Tag_Name>
```

HTML tag consists of the following elements:

Tag_Name This is the name of the opening HTML tag. In case of container elements, the tag structure should also contain a similar ending tag with forward slash.

Attribute_Name It contains either a single or list of attributes. If more than one attributes are listed, then these attributes should be separated by a comma or space.

Attribute_Value In case an attribute of a tag has a value, it is specified after the attribute name along with the equal (=) sign and quotes (optional).

e.g. `<font size ="5">`

Some examples of tags with their attributes:

(i) `<body bgcolor="red">` (ii) `<ul type = "circle">`
(iii) `<font face ="Arial">` (iv) `<hr width=20%>`

The most basic structure, need for creation of any web page is shown below:

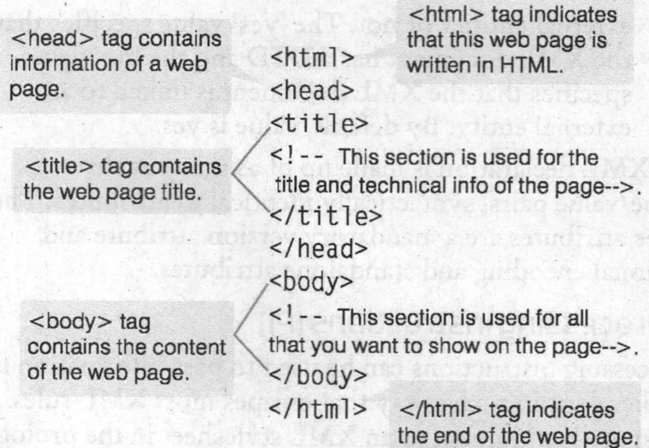

10.1.6 Basic HTML Tags

1. <html> Tag

The <html> tag represents the root of an HTML document, so it acts as the container for all other HTML elements. <html> tag informs the web browser that the document is a web page and is created by using HTML coding.

It is very important to place both of these tags (open and close html tags) in your documents as they tell the browser, where your page begins and ends. The entire coding is done between the <html> and </html> tags.

Syntax

```
<html>
  :
</html>
```

<html> tag contains many attributes. Some important attributes are as follows:

Attribute	Use	Syntax
dir	This attribute of HTML tag specifies the type of text to be presented by the browser. The attribute can have values either ltr(left to right) or rtl (right to left). By default, the value of attribute is ltr. The rtl is used for language like Chinese or Hebrew.	`<html dir= "ltr">` or `<html dir= "rtl">`
lang	This attribute specifies the language of the text. As we know, these days web pages are designed in many languages. e.g. English, Hindi, French, Italian, German etc.	`<html lang ="en">`

2. <head> Tag

This element is a container for all the header elements. The <head> tag must include a title for the document and can include scripts, styles, meta information and more. The second line of your HTML document should be <head>.

The text contained in the head section of your document provides information to browsers and search engines but it is not displayed to the person viewing the web page.

This tag is written inside the <html> and </html> tags.

Syntax

```
<head>......</head>
```

3. <title> Tag

This tag defines the title of the document. Title must be a simple text and not needed to be same as the file name. This tag is placed between <head> and </head> tags.

The text between the <title> and </title> tags will appear in the title bar of the browser's window.

Syntax

```
<title>
   Name of the title of a web page
</title>
```

4. <body> Tag

This tag defines the document's body. It is used to set basic page characteristics. It contains all the necessary contents of an HTML document, such as text, hyperlinks, images, tables, lists etc. The content of your web page is placed in between the <body> and </body> tags.

The <body> tag is opened just after the head section is closed. The <body> tag is closed just before closing the <html> tag.

Syntax

```
<body> The content of the body. </body>
```

<body> tag contains many attributes. Some important attributes are as follows:

Attribute	Use	Syntax
background	This attribute specifies a background image for a document. HTML supports various graphics format such as .gif, .jpg etc.	`<body background ="URL of the image">`
text	This attribute specifies the foreground color of the text in a document. By default, the text color is black.	`<body text="color_name|hex_number|rgb_number">`
bgcolor	This attribute specifies the background color of a document.	`<body bgcolor ="color_name |hex_number|rgb_number">`
link	This attribute specifies the color of unvisited links in a document. The default color of link attribute is blue (#0000FF).	`<body link ="color_name |hex_number |rgb_number">`
alink	This attribute specifies the color of an active link in a document (a link get activated when it is clicked). The default color of alink attribute is red (#FF0000).	`<body alink ="color_ name |hex_number| rgb_number">`
vlink	This attribute specifies the color of visited links in a document. The default color of vlink attribute is purple (#800080).	`<body vlink ="color_name |hex_number |rgb_number">`
topmargin	Sets a top margin (distance between the top of the document and top of the browser window) of your body element.	`<body topmargin= "value">`
leftmargin	Sets a left hand margin (distance between the left side of the document and the left edge of the browser window) of your body element.	`<body leftmargin = "value">`

e.g.

```
<body background="flowers.jpg" bgcolor="pink"
leftmargin="50" topmargin="100" text = "blue">
   This is my first page
</body>
```

5. <font> Tag

This tag specifies the font style, font size and font color of the text. The <font> tag provides no real functionality by itself but with the help of a few attributes, this tag is used to change style, size and color of HTML text.

(v) **XML elements must be properly nested** The parent element has to be opened before the child element and closed after the child element.

e.g.

```
<College>
<Student>
<RollNo> 10 </RollNo>
<Name> Aoin </Name>
<Class> X </Class>
</Student>
</College>
```

Well-formed

```
<College>
<Student>
<RollNo> 10 </RollNo>
<Name> Aoin </Name>
<Class> X </Class>
</College>
</Student>
```

Not well-formed

This code is not well-formed because the root element (College) is closed before the parent element (Student).

(vi) **XML tags are case sensitive** XML tags are case sensitive means the opening and ending tags must be in the same case.

e.g.

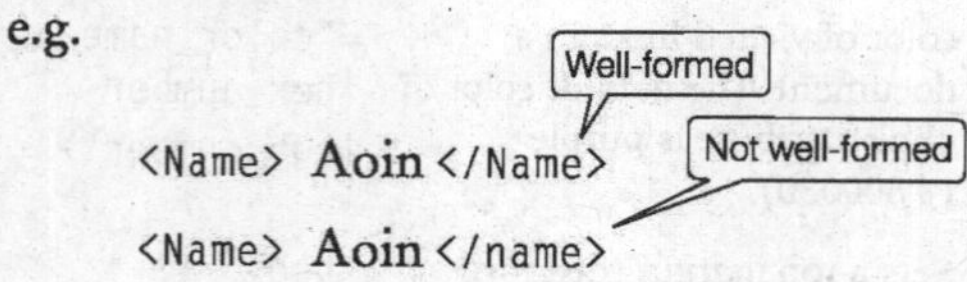

(vii) **XML attribute values should be in double quotation marks** The attribute value in an XML document should be enclosed in proper quotes.

e.g.

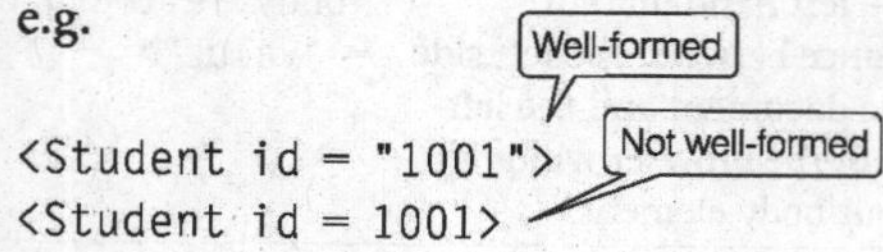

11.6.2 Valid XML Document

A valid XML document is not only a well-formed document but as well as they also checked error against a DTD (Document Type Definition) or schema.

DTD is a set of rules that defines what tags appear, what value those tags may contain and how the tags are related to each other in an XML document.

Validation can be done only if the XML document has valid DTD. When an XML document is checked or parsed according to a particular structure or guidelines, the process is known as **validation of the document.**

11.7 Software that Validate XML Documents

There are two types of software, which enable DTD to run XML document in proper manner, when it gets executed.

11.7.1 XML Validator

XML validators are the software packages that validate your XML document according to the DTD specification and give information about the document, i.e. program will stop processing an XML document if it finds an error because XML software is small, fast and compatible.

Some common XML validators on web are as follows:

Validator	Source
W3C Validation Service	http://validator.w3.org/
Brown University's	http://www.stg.brown.edu/service/xml-valid/
RUWF? XML.com's	http://www.xml.com/pub/a/tools/ruwf/check.html
Tidy	http://www.w3.org/People/Raggett/tidy/

11.7.2 PCDATA

PCDATA (Parsed Character Data) : XML parsers are used to parse all the text in an XML document.

PCDATA is the text that will be parsed by a parser. Tags inside the PCDATA will be treated as markup and entities will be expanded.

The role of an XML parser is to cut a part of a valid XML document to obtain actual data from the XML document.

If the parser reads the file against the DTD description, it is known as a **validating parser.** An XML parser converts an XML document into an XML DOM (Document Object Model) object which can be manipulated with JavaScript.

Some XML parsers are as follows:

XML Parser	Source
LT-XML	http://www.ltg.ed.ac.uk/software/xml/
SAX (Simple API for XML)	http://www.saxproject.org/
expat	http://expat.sourceforge.net/
TclXML	http://tclxml.sourceforge.net/
XML4J(XML for Java)	http://alphaworks.ibm.com/tech/xml4j
Xerces	http://xerces.apache.org/

11.8 Validation Process

XML validation is the process of validating an XML document.

11.8 Validation Process

XML validation is the process of validating an XML document.

e.g.

DTD start from here

```
<?xml version = "1.0"?>
<!DOCTYPE e-mail[
<!ELEMENT e-mail (to, from, heading, body)>
<!ELEMENT to (#PCDATA)>
<!ELEMENT from (#PCDATA)>
<!ELEMENT heading (#PCDATA)>
<!ELEMENT body (#PCDATA)>
]>
<e-mail>
<to>abc@kogentindia.com</to>
<from>xyz@kogentindia.com</from>
<heading>Welcome</heading>
<body>This is an example of DTD</body>
</e-mail>
```

All the elements are defined

#PCDATA means all the contents help by these elements will be validated by the XML parser

DTD end here

Above example means an e-mail can contain the fields, as to, from, heading and body. To define the structure of this document, a DTD can be created which can be a part of the XML document itself. Order of the tags is maintained.

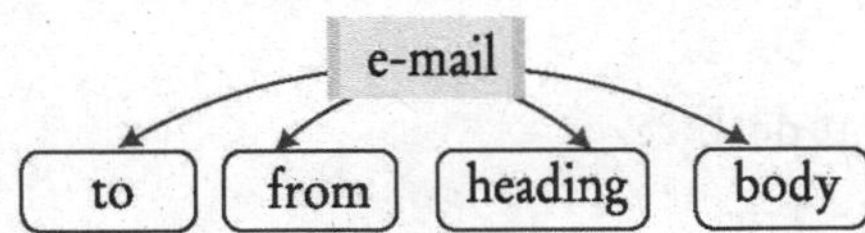

11.9 Using CSS with an XML Document

To link an XML document with a stylesheet, perform the following steps :

(i) Create a stylesheet and save it as a file with the .css extension.

(ii) Create an XML document and save it as a file with the .xml extension.

(iii) Link both the files in the XML document by using the PI.

```
<?xml-stylesheet href = "test.css"
type = "text/css"?>
```

e.g. The following is the **CSS document:**

```
People
{
    background-color : green;
    display : block;
    padding : 5px;
    font-family : arial;
}
Person
{
    background-color : pink;
    border : 2px solid black;
    display : block;
    margin-bottom : 5px;
}
Name
{
    font-family : bold;
    display : block;
}
Birthdate
{
    display : block;
}
Eyes
{
    display : block;
}
```

Now, save it as test.css

The following is the **XML document:**

```
<?xml version="1.0" encoding="UTF-8"?>
<?xml-stylesheet type = "text/css"
href= "test.css"?>
<People>
<Person><Name>A</Name>
<Birthdate>Jan 24, 1987</Birthdate>
<Eyes>Blue</Eyes></Person>
<Person><Name>B</Name>
<Birthdate>Dec 15, 2009</Birthdate>
<Eyes>Brown</Eyes></Person>
</People>
```

Now, save it as test1.xml

11.10 Viewing the XML Document in the Browser

To see the XML document in the browser, you have to take the same steps as you do in HTML.

Once the CSS and XML documents are created in the same folder, double-click the XML document and see the document browsing on the web browser as per stylesheet or CSS file.

e.g. double click on the file test1.xml to open it in the browser. It will look as follows:

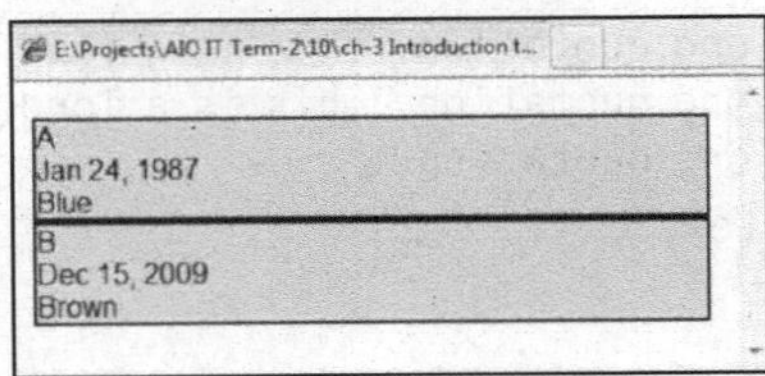

10.1.7 Text Formatting Tags

1. <q> Tag

<q> tag defines the short quotation tag.

e.g. `Here comes a short quotation: <q> This is a short quotation </q>`

Output

Here comes a short quotation : "This is a short quotation"

2. <span> Tag

<span> tag is used to add styles to the content or manipulate the content with for example, JavaScript.

3. <strong> Tag

This tag is also used to display the text in bold format.

e.g. `Hello <strong>how r u </strong>`

Output

Hello **how r u**

4. <sub> Tag

This tag defines subscript text. Subscript text appears half a character below the baseline. Subscript text can be used for chemical formulas, like H_2O.

e.g.

```
H<sub>2</sub>O
```

Output

H_2O

5. <sup> Tag

This tag defines superscript text. Superscript text appears half a character above the baseline. Superscript text can be used for footnotes.

e.g.

```
This is 4<sup>th</sup>edition.
```

Output

This is 4th edition.

6. <blockquote> Tag

This tag defines a long quotation. A browser inserts white space before and after a blockquote element. It also insert margins for the blockquote element.

e.g.

```
Here comes a long quotation
<blockquote>
This is a long quotation. This is a long quotation.
This is a long quotation. This is a long quotation.
This is a long quotation.
</blockquote>
```

Output

Here comes a long quotation

This is a long quotation. This is a long quotation. This is a long quotation. This is a long quotation. This is long quotation.

7. <del> Tag

This tag is used to define the text that has been deleted from a document.

e.g.

```
The leader of this class is <del>Rahul</del>Neha
```

Output

The leader of this class is ~~Rahul~~ Neha

8. <strike> Tag

Anything that appears with <strike>...</strike> elements is displayed with strikethrough.

e.g.

```
Arihant Publications <strike> Company</strike>
```

Output

Arihant Publications ~~Company~~.

9. <big> Tag

This tag is displayed one font size larger than the rest of the text surrounding it.

e.g.

```
This is <big> Great </big> deal.
```

Output

This is Great deal.

10. <small> Tag

This tag is displayed one font size smaller than the rest of the text surrounding it.

e.g.

```
This is <small> Great </small> deal.
```

Output

This is Great deal.

11. <pre > Tag

This tag is used for indicating preformatted text. The code tag surrounds the code being marked up. Browsers normally render pre text in a fixed pitched font, with whitespace in tact and without word wrap.

e.g.

```
<pre>
    This text is
in a fixed-pitch
    font, and it preserves
both speces and line breaks
</pre>
```

Output

```
        This text is
    in a fixed-pitch
        font, and it preserves
    both spaces and line breaks
```

12. <address>Tag

This tag is used for indicating an address. The address usually renders in italic.

e.g.

```
<address>
    600 Wisdom Apartments <br>
    filmcity, kondiura <br>
    New Delhi-50027
</address>
```

Output

600 Wisdom Apartments
filmcity, kondiura
New Delhi-50027

10.1.8 Applying Styles to Individual Words or Sentences

The text which is entered in HTML format on Notepad displays in its default format on the web browser. To give an attractive look, you have to apply formatting or style on text.

There are two types of styles as follows:

1. Logical Text Styles

This style tag gives a different look to the text when it is displayed by browsers. These tags are preferred because they let the browser, handle the look and feel of the logical tag. It is also known as **idiomatic style tag.**

Some logical text styles are as follows:

Tag Name	Tag	Use
Citation	<cite>	It is used to display the title of book and name of character.
Code	<code>	It is used to indicate the code of text.
Emphasis	<em>	It is used for emphasising phrases.
Keyboard	<kbd>	It defines text that should be entered by user.
Sample	<samp>	It indicates a sequence of literal character.
Variable	<var>	This style is used for variables.

2. Physical Text Styles

We can apply physical text styles like bold, italic etc., to change physical appearance of the text in your web page.

Some physical text styles are as follows:

Tag Name	Use	Syntax
Bold	The <b> tag is used to make the text in bold form. It is a container element.	<b>....</b>
Italic	The <i> tag is used to make the text in italic form. It is also a container element.	<i>....</i>
Underline	The <u> tag underlines the specified text. It is also a container element.	<u>....</u>
Teletype	The<tt> tag creates teletype or monospaced font of the enclosed text.	<tt>....</tt>

10.1.9 Universal Resource Identifier (URI)

URI is a string of characters used to identify names or resources on the Internet. The URI describes the mechanism used to access resources, the computer on which resources are housed and the names of the resources on each computer.

1. Fragment identifiers

Some URI's refer to a location within a resource. The kind of URI ends with "#" followed by an anchor identifier (called the fragment identifier).

e.g. here is a URI pointing to an anchor named section:
http://somesite.com/html/top.html# section

2. Relative URI

A relative URI does not contain any naming scheme information. Its path generally refers to a resource on the same machine as the current document. Relative URIs may contain relative path components and may contain fragment identifiers. Relative URIs are resolved to full URIs using a base URI.

10.1.10 Inserting an Image in a Web Page

The <img> tag is used to insert an image in a web page. It is very important to know that images are not technically part of the web page file, they are separate files which are inserted into the web page when it is viewed by a browser. So, a simple web page with one image is actually two files.

When an HTML file is displayed in a browser, it requests the image file and places it on the page where the tag appears an image is by default placed **inline with text.** <img> tag is an empty element.

Images displayed by web browser are in GIF (Graphics Interchange format), XBM (X Bitmap), JPEG (or JPG) (Joint Photographic Experts Group) and PNG (Portable Network Graphics) formats.

24. **DTD's**
(1) don't follow inheritance principle
(2) follow the inheritance principle
(3) are recommendation only
(4) None of the above

25. **Document type declaration and document type are**
(1) different terms (2) same
(3) uncertain (4) can't say

26. **Which of the following is a valid name?**
(1) <person> (2) <123 person>
(3) Both (1) and (2) (4) None of these

27. **Can the element <First> be replace with <first>**
(1) no, they represent different elements altogether
(2) both are same
(3) <First> is correct
(4) <first> is correct

28. **Valid XML document means**
(1) the document has one root element
(2) the document contains one or more root element
(3) the document has a DTD and compiles to it
(4) each element must be in capital letters

29. **To link an XML document with a stylesheet, you need to**
(1) use the PI component in the XML document
(2) use the document declaration component in the XML document
(3) add the <link> tag in the XML document
(4) None of the above

30. **Which of the following is a prolog component?**
(1) Element
(2) Tab
(3) White space
(4) All of the above

31. **Comments in XML are**
(1) having the same syntax as that of comments in HTML
(2) used to add additional notes
(3) not displayed on the final web pages
(4) All of the above

32. **An XML parser is used to**
(1) extract data from the XML file and build tree like structure
(2) check whether or not an XML document is well-formed
(3) Both (1) and (2)
(4) None of the above

33. **An XML document that follows the XML syntax is called a**
(1) valid XML document
(2) well-formed XML document
(3) correct XML document
(4) All of the above

34. **Which of the following XML fragments are well-formed?**
(1) <element attribute = value>
(2) <element attribute = "value">
(3) <element attribute = !value>
(4) <element attribute = 'value'>

35. **DTD definition is used along with XML to specify**
(1) the presentation of XML document
(2) the links with other documents
(3) the structure of XML document
(4) None of the above

36. **How is an empty element defined in XML?**
(1) <name> </name>
(2) <name/>
(3) name/
(4) All of the above

37. **Well-formed XML document means**
(1) it contains a root element
(2) it contains an elements
(3) it contains one or more elements
(4) must contain one or more elements, and root element must contain all other elements

38. **To declare the version of XML, the correct syntax is**
(1) <?xml version = "1.0?">
(2) <?xml version = "1.0">
(3) </xml version = "1.0">
(4) <? xml version = "1.0">

39. **The comment in XML document is given by**
(1) </... ...> (2) <?... ...>
(3) <!— — —> (4) <... ...!>

40. **The function of the XML parser is to**
(1) convert XML content into HTML content
(2) convert XML content into DHTML content
(3) convert XML content into XML DOM content
(4) convert XML content into binary code

41. **PI is a component of**
(1) prolog
(2) data instance
(3) element
(4) root element

42. **Which of the following is not an online XML validator?**
(1) W3C validation service
(2) Tidy
(3) XML.com's
(4) Expat

43. **Attribute standalone = "no" should be included XML declaration if a document**
(1) is linked to an external XSL stylesheet
(2) has external general references
(3) has processing instructions
(4) has an external DTD

44. **In XML,**
(1) the internal DTD subset is read before the external DTD
(2) the external DTD subset is read before the internal DTD
(3) there is no external type of DTD
(4) there is no internal type of DTD

45. **The syntax for parameter entity is**
(1) <!ENTITY % NAME DEFINITION>
(2) <ENTITY % NAME DEFINITION>
(3) <!ENTITY $ NAME DEFINITION>
(4) None of the above

46. **The use of a DTD in XML development is**
(1) required when validating XML documents.
(2) no longer necessary after the XML editor has been customised.
(3) used to direct conversion using an XSLT processor.
(4) a good guide to populating a templates to be filled in when generating an XML document automatically

47. **In order to interpret XML documents, one should**
(1) use standardised tags
(2) have a document type definition which defines the tags
(3) define the tags separately
(4) specify tag filename

48. **Which of the following XML fragments are well formed?**
(1) <myElement myAttribute>= "someValue"/>
(2) <myElement myAttribute = some Value/>
(3) <myElement myAttribute ='some Value'>
(4) <myElement myAttribute = "some Value">

49. When processing an output XML, "new line" symbols are
(1) copied into output "as is" i.e. "CR + LF" for Windows, CR for Macintosh, LF for Unix
(2) converted to single LF symbol
(3) converted to single CR symbol
(4) discarded

50. Which of the following strings is a correct XML name?
(1) _myElement
(2) my Element
(3) #myElement
(4) None of the above

51. Which of the following strings can be included as correct name in XML?
(1) xmlExtension
(2) xslNewElement
(3) XMLElement#123
(4) All of the above

52. Which of the following XML fragments are well formed?
(1) <?xml?>
(2) <?xml version = "1.0"?>
(3) <?xml version = "JIS"?>
(4) <?xml encoding = "JIS" version = "1.0"?>

53. What are predefined attributes
(1) xml:lang
(2) xml:space
(3) Both (1) and (2)
(4) None of the above

54. The most popular way to materalize XML document is to use
(1) DTD
(2) XSLT
(3) HTML
(4) SOAP

55. With XML
(1) views are not limited to one multi-valued path only
(2) documents can automatically be generated from database data only
(3) database data can automatically be extracted from XML documents only
(4) All of the above

56. Valid XML document means (most appropriate)
(1) the document has root element
(2) the document contains atleast one or more root element
(3) the XML document has DTD associated with it and it complies with that DTD
(4) Each element must nest inside any enclosing element property

57. What is the correct way of describing XML data?
(1) XML uses a DTD to describe data
(2) XML uses a description node to describe data
(3) XML uses XSL to describe the data
(4) XML uses a validator to describe the data

58. XML validated against a .... is considered as valid XML.
(1) JQuery (2) Parser
(3) CFG (4) DTD

59. Which of the following statement is not true about XML schemas?
(1) They are used to define the content and structure of data
(2) They define a set of symbols and the relationship of those symbols
(3) They are themselves XML documents
(4) They have their own syntax

60. DTD includes the specifications about the markup that can be used within the document, the specifications consist of all except
(1) the browser name
(2) the size of element name
(3) entity declarations
(4) element declarations

61. The words document node, nodelist, element node, named node map etc are
(1) interfaces (2) objects
(3) attributes (4) elements

62. Which of the following XPath expression selects all student elements that are children of class?
(1) ./class/student
(2) ../class/student
(3) @ class/student
(4) class/student

63. If an XML document uses internal as well as external DTD sub sets and both sub sets have declaration for the same element type or entity, which sub set will have the precedence?
(1) External
(2) Internal
(3) Can't be determined
(4) None of the above

64. What is the full form of DTD that is used to describe content in an XHTML document?
(1) Document To Definition
(2) Document Type Definition
(3) Document Towards Definition
(4) Document Text Definition

65. To add the attribute named Type to the <customer> tag, the syntax will be
(1) <customer attribute Type = "exelent">
(2) <customer Type attribute = "exelent">
(3) <customer Type attribute _ type = "exelent">
(4) <customer Type = "exelent">

66. The XSLT processor copies the elements of the stylesheet unit it finds a command in the format
(1) SELECT...FROM...WHERE
(2) {item, action}
(3) {for-each select}
(4) <HTML>...</HTML>

67. DTD includes the specifications about the markup that can be used within the document, the specification consists of all except
(1) the browsers name
(2) the size of element name
(3) entity declarations
(4) element declarations

68. Observe the given DTD

```
<? XML version = "1.0"?>
<! DOCTYPE SITES[
<! ELEMENT SITES (SITES *)>
<! ELEMENT SITE (ADDRESS,
                  QUALITY)>
<! ELEMENT ADDRESS
                 (# PCDATA)>
<! ELEMENT QUALITY
                 (# PCDATA)>
]>
```

Choose the statement that is true about the above DTD
(1) The SITE element is optional
(2) Elements ADDRESS and QUALITY both are to be present in specified order
(3) Root element is SITE which in turn contains two sub elements.
(4) ADDRESS and QUALITY elements are empty elements.

69. Choose the attribute of the XML declaration statement from the following attributes that specifies whether document needs external entities or not.
(1) version
(2) encoding
(3) standalone
(4) doctype

Attributes of <table> tag are as follows:

Attribute	Use	Syntax
border	This attribute is used to display border around the cells. If we do not specify a border attribute, the table will display without border.	<table border ="value">
bordercolor	This attribute defines the color of the table's border. We can use any of the standard colors provided.	<table bordercolor= "color_name|hex_number| rgb_number">
frame	This attribute allows us to state, which portion of the border should be displayed and which portion should not be displayed.	<table frame="value"> where, value = void, above, below, hside, vside, box, border etc.
cellspacing	It controls or sets the amount of space between table cells.	<table cellspacing ="pixels">
cellpadding	It controls or sets the amount of space between the contents of the cell and the cell wall. By default, cellpadding is 1.	<table cellpadding="pixels">
align	This attribute is used to align the table completely.	<table align= "left/ right/center">
bgcolor	This attribute is used to specify any desired background color to the table.	<table bgcolor="color_name| hex_number|rgb_number">
height and width	By using height and width attributes, we are able to specify the height and width of the table according to our wish. For this, we have to specify the height and width in terms of pixels or percentage of browser window.	<table height="pixels or %" width="pixels or%">

1. The <tr> Tag

The <tr> tag denotes table row. This tag is used to create a new row of data in a table. <tr> tag contains the following attributes:

Attribute	Use	Syntax
align	It is used to align the content in a table row.	<tr align ="left|right|center| justify">
bgcolor	It is used to specify a background color for a table row.	<tr bgcolor="color_name| hex_number| rgb_number">
valign	It specifies the vertical alignment of the content in a table row.	<tr valign ="top|middle|bottom| baseline">

2. The <th> Tag

The <th> tag denotes table header. This tag is used for specifying a table's header. It displays the content of a table in heading style and this content appears in bold.

Apart from this difference, both the <th> tag and <td> tag are similar in function.

<th> tag contains the following attributes:

Attribute	Use	Syntax
align	It is used to align the content in a header cell.	<th align ="left | right |center|justify">
bgcolor	It specifies the background color of a header cell.	<th bgcolor="color_name |hex_number|rgb_number">
colspan	It specifies the number of columns, a header cell should span.	<th colspan="number">
rowspan	It defines the number of rows, a header cell should span.	<th rowspan ="number">
height and width	It specifies the height and width of a header cell.	<th height ="pixels or %" width= "pixels or %">

3. The <td> Tag

The <td> tag denotes table data. The <td> tag is used with specifying a cell or table data within a table. It is a container tag that is why it must contain matching closing </td> tag.

Some attributes used with <td> tag are given below:

Attribute	Use	Syntax
align	The table data can be aligned using align attribute. By default, the content of a cell are left aligned.	<td align ="left |right|center| justify">
height and width	It sets the height and width of a cell.	<td heigth= "pixels or %" width= "pixels or %">
colspan	It allows the user to strech a cell to span multiple columns.	<td colspan= "number">
rowspan	It is used to span multiple rows.	<td rowspan= "number">
valign	It determines the placement of content in a cell.	<td valign="top| middle|bottom">

4. The <caption> Tag

The <caption> tag is used to define a table caption. Its attribute is align, which is used to set the position of caption.

Syntax

```
<caption align="left|right|top|bottom|center">
```

e.g. To create a table in HTML:

```
<table align="center" border="4"
  bordercolor="blue" cellspacing="5"
  cellpadding="4" height=20% width=20%
                           bgcolor="pink">
  <tr align="right" bgcolor="skyblue"
                        valign="middle">
  <th align="center" colspan=2
          bgcolor="white">Production</th>
  <th rowspan=8>Welcome</th>
  </tr> <tr>
  <td>Rahul Choudhary</td>
  <td>1493</td>
  </tr> <tr>
  <td>Shalu Bhusan</td>
  <td>3829</td>
  </tr> <tr>
  <th colspan=2 bgcolor="white">Sales</th>
  </tr> <tr>
  <td>Neha Jain</td>
  <td>4827</td>
  </tr> <tr>
  <td>Shubhi Nigam</td>
  <td>7246</td>
  </tr>
  <caption align="center">Production and
                      Sale Table</caption>
  </table>
```

10.1.15 HTML Form

HTML forms are very effective because they can easily collect data from the Internet and utilise that information in other web page. Form starts with the <form> tag and ends with the </form> tag.

The information collected from a form can be as follows:

(i) written to a file
(ii) Submitted to a database such as Informix, MS-Access or Oracle
(iii) E-mailed to someone in particular.

Forms involve two-way Communication

The input-catching programs on our server reply on an interface between web browsers and servers called the **Common Gateway Interface** (CGI). This interface codifies how browsers can send information back to servers. It sets up the formatting for the user supplied input information, so that forms handling programs know what to expect and how to deal with what they receive.

It contains various attributes, some are as follows:

1. **Name** It specifies the name of the form. The name attribute is optional if there is only one form on the web page.
2. **Action** It provides the URL of the program (in the server) that receives the information from the form and processes it.
3. **Method** A method attribute, which is the HTTP method used to submit the form data. The method attribute of <form> tag can take one of the following three values:
   (a) **GET** method send the information to the server.
   (b) **POST** method send the form information in the HTTP environment.
   (c) **Form** method opens a new form as per the URL specified in the action attribute.

So, a typical <form> tag is,

```
<form name="form_name"
          action="URL" method="method">
```

In the form, you can still put any HTML codes as you want. We can also use following tags in the <form> tags.

1. <input> Tag

It defines text entry fields, check boxes, radio buttons or push buttons. It is an empty element specified by <input> tag. The <input> tag defines an object on the form which can receive user input.

Syntax

```
<input type ="fieldtype" name = "fieldname"
                     value = "fieldtext">
```

Attributes of <input> tag are as follows:

Attribute	Use	Syntax
type	It specifies the type of <input> element to display fieldtype can be one of the following: Text, Password, Radio, Checkbox, Submit, Reset Button, Image, hidden.	`<input type = "fieldtype">`
name	It specifies the fieldname of <input> tag. It is required for the identification of form.	`<input name ="field name">`
value	It specifies the value of an <input> tag. It is used to represent the default value of any type field.	`<input value = "fieldtext">`

The process of serving an HTML page can be broken into the following steps:

1. A user enters the Internet address of an HTML file into the address bar of a web browser and presses Enter to request a web page (e.g. http:// www.aspsite.com/hello.htm).
2. The browser sends a request for the web page to a web server such as IIS.
3. The web server receives the request and recognises that request is for an HTML file because the requested file has the extension .htm or .html.
4. The web server retrieves the proper HTML file from disk or memory and sends the file back to the browser.
5. The HTML file is interpreted by the user's web browser and the result are displayed in the browser window.

This process is often more complicated but in broad strokes, these steps outline the moment-to-moment activity of a typical web server. A server receives requests for particular files and responds by sending the correct file, retrieving it from the hard drive or memory.

Although IIS can be used to server static HTML pages. ASPs enable IIS to serve dynamic content as well. Using ASP, you can create pages with new content in response to user requests. The web server itself becomes active in the process of creating the web page.

It's important to understand how this process of serving an ASP contrasts with the normal process of serving an HTML page, so we'll break it into steps:

1. A user enters the Internet address of an ASP file into the address bar of a web browser and presses Enter to request an ASP (e.g. http://www.aspsite.com/hello.asp).
2. The browser sends a request for the ASP to IIS.
3. The web server receives the request and recognises that the request is for an ASP file because the requested file has the extension .asp.
4. The web server retrieves the proper ASP file from disk or memory.
5. The web server sends the file to a special program named ASP.dll.
6. The ASP file is processed from top to bottom and any commands it encounters are executed. The result of this process is a standard HTML file.
7. The HTML file is sent back to the browser.
8. The HTML file is interpreted by the user's web browser and the results are displayed in the browser window.

From the perspective of the web server, an ASP is very different from a normal HTML page. A normal HTML file is sent without processing to the browser. All the commands in an ASP, on the other hand, must first be executed to create an HTML page. This allows an ASP to contain dynamic content.

From the perspective of the browser, on the other hand, an ASP is almost exactly the same as a normal HTML page. The only difference is that an ASP typically must end with the extension .asp rather than .htm or .html. When a request is made for an ASP, the browser receives a normal HTML page. This enables an ASP to be compatible with all browsers.

12.3 Other Equivalent Tools

1. **JSP** (Java Server Pages) It is a server side programming technology that enables the creation of dynamic, platform independent method for building web based application. It has access to the entire family of Java APIs, including the JDBC API to access enterprise databases.
2. **PHP** (PHP : Hypertext Preprocessor) It is a widely used, open source scripting language that allows web developers to create dynamic content that interacts with database. It is basically used for developing web based software applications.

12.4 Data Types

Data type refers to an extensive system used for declaring variables or functions of different types. The type of a variable determines how much space it occupies in storage and how the bit pattern stored is interpreted.

Following table shows all the data types available:

Type	Storage	Range
Byte	1 byte	0 to 225
Integer	2 bytes	−32,768 to 32,767
Long	4 bytes	−2,147,483,648 to 2,147,483,647
Single	4 bytes	−3.402823E + 38 to −1.401298E −45 for negative values; 1.401298E-45 to 3.402823E+38 for positive values
Double	8 bytes	−1.79769313486232E+308 to − 4.94065645841247E-324 for negative values 4.94065645841247E-324 to 1.79769313486232E+308 for positive values
Currency	8 bytes	−922,337,203,685,477.5808 to 922,337,203,685,477.5807 (the extra precision ensures that monetary calculations are kept accurate to two decimal places)

Type	Storage	Range
String (fixed length)	Length of string	1 to 65,400 characters
String (variable)	Length +10 bytes	0 to 2 billion characters
Date	8 bytes	January 1,100 to December 31,9999
Boolean	2 bytes	True or False
Object	4 bytes	Any embedded object
Variant (numeric)	16 bytes	Any value as large as Double
Variant (text)	Length +22 bytes	Same as variable - length String

12.5 Variables

A variable is nothing but a name given to a storage area that our programs can manipulate. Each variable has a specific type, which determines the size and layout of the variable's memory: the range of values that can be stored within that memory and the set of operations that can be applied to the variable.

1. Rules for Declaring Variables

Some rules for declaring variables are as follows:

(i) Variable names must begin with an alphabet.
(ii) Variable names cannot exceed 255 characters.
(iii) Variable names should not contain a period(·).
(iv) Variable names should be unique in the declared context.

2. Declaring Variables

In ASP, a variable is declared with the Dim keyword. This is the same methodology as with VBScript.

Syntax `Dim variableName`

e.g. `<% Dim title%>`

You can declare variable separately or all at once.

Declaring variables separately

```
<% Dim title Dim numPages Dim author Dim genre %>
```

Declaring variables all at once

```
<% Dim title, numPages, author, genre %>
```

3. Assigning Values to Variables

You can assign values to variables using the "=" sign.

e.g. `<% Dim title = "A book to read", numPages = 84 %>`

4. Variable Declaration Implicit vs Explicit

We have to change the data that we are using. Sometimes this change may change the value of the data or sometimes it just changes the memory space allocated by the data. This change is called **data type conversion**. Data type is converted in two ways.

They are as follows:

(i) **Implicit Conversion** It converts data automatically without losing any data. Normally, data types can implicitly converted into the data types those contains more memory space.

(ii) **Explicit Conversion** It converts data that are automatically can't be converted. It may convert data from bigger size to smaller size or convert data from one type into totally different type.

e.g.
```
short firstNumber = 65
long secondNumber = firstNumber
                    //implicit conversion
short thirdNumber
= (short) secondNumber
   //Explicit conversion: outputs 65
char a = (char) firstNumber
  // Explicit conversion: outputs A
```

12.6 Constants

Constants just as variables are used to store information. The main difference between constants and variables is that constant value cannot be changed in the process of running program. If we attempt to re-assign the value of the constant we will get a run time error. To declare a constant in ASP, we use the Const keyword.

e.g. (i) `Const myConst = "myText"`

(ii) `Const PI = 3.14, Wg = 2.78`

12.7 ASP Comments

ASP uses VBScript as its default programming language. This means VBScript comments are ASP comments. To create a comment in ASP, you simply place an apostrophe in front of what you want commented out.

e.g.
```
<%
 'Hello I am a comment
  Dim newVar1, newVar2
 'Dim oldVar1, oldVar2
%>
```

In the above example, we had two comments. The first comment was note style comment. Programmers often use these kinds of comments to leave information to people who are going to read their code or to themselves.

The second comment we created commented out "Dim oldVar1, oldVar2" preventing the ASP interpreter from reading this line of code. This kind of comment is a block-out comment that is often used to temporarily remove code from a file that may be causing errors of is just unnecessary at the time.

Attribute	Description

cols	Specifies how many columns are contained in the frameset and the size of each column. You can specify the width of each column in one of four ways.
	(i) Absolute values in pixels:
	`<frameset cols ="100,70">`
	(ii) A percentage of the browser
	`<frameset cols="50%,70%">`
	(iii) Using a wildcard symbol
	`<frameset cols ="70%,*">`
	In this case, wildcard (*) takes remainder of the window.
	(iv) As relative widths of the browser window
	`<frameset ="3*,2*,1*">`

rows	This attribute works just like the cols attribute and takes the same values, but it is used to specify the rows in the frameset.
border	This attribute specifies the width of the border of each frame in pixels. e.g. `<frameset border= "5">` A value of zero means no border.
frame border	This attribute specifies whether a three dimensional border should be displayed between frames. This takes value either 1(yes) or 0(no). e.g.`<frameset frameborder = "0">`
framespacing	Specifies the amount of space between frames in the frameset. This can take any integer value. e.g. `<frameset framespacing ="8">`

2. <frame> Tag

Each frame is indicated by <frame> tag and it defines which HTML document shall open into the frame.

Attribute of <frame> tag are as follows:

Attribute	Description
src	This attribute is used to give the filename that should be added in the frames. Its value can be any URL.
name	This attribute allows you to give a name to a frame.
marginwidth	This attribute allows you to specify the width of the space between the left and right of the frame's borders and the frame's content. This value is given in pixels.
marginheight	This attribute allows you to specify the height of the space between the top and bottom of the frame's borders and its contents. This value is given in pixels.
noresize	This attribute prevents a user from being able to resize the frame.
scrolling	This attribute controls the appearance of the scrollbars that appear on the frame. This takes values either yes, no or auto.

3. <noframes> Tag

If a user is using any browser which does not support frames then <noframes> element should be displayed alternate text message to the user.

You can put some nice message for your user having old browsers.

e.g.

```
<html>
<head>
<title>HTML FRAME</title>
</head>
<frameset rows = "50%, 50%">
<frameset cols = "50%, 50%">
<frame src ="A.html" name ="First Frame">
<frame src ="B.html" name =" Second Frame">
</frameset>
<frameset cols ="50%, 50%">
<frame src ="C.html" name ="Third Frame">
<frame src = "D.html" name ="Forth Frame">
</frameset>
<noframes>
<body>
Sorry, your browser does not support frame.
</body>
</noframes>
</frameset>
</html>
```

10.2 Document Object Model (DOM)

It is a programming API for HTML and XML documents. It defines the logical structure of documents and the way a document is accessed and manipulated. In the DOM specification, the term "document" is used in the broad sense-increasingly, XML is being used as a way of representing many different kinds of information that may be stored in diverse systems and much of this would traditionally be seen as data rather than as documents. Nevertheless, XML presents this data as documents and the DOM may be used to manage this data.

With the document object model, programmers can create and build documents, navigate their structure and add, modify, or delete elements and content. Anything found in an HTML or XML document can be accessed, changed, deleted, or added using the DOM, with a few exceptions in particular, the DOM interfaces for the internal subset and external subset, have not yet been specified.

e.g.

```
<html>
<head>
<title> Sample page </title>
</head>
< body>
<p> Hello World ! </p>
</body>
</html>
```

When this HTML code is loaded into memory of web browser, then different HTML elements are shown in hierarchy level, which is as follows:

```
<html>
    <head><title> Sample page </title> </head>
    <body>
        <p> Hello World ! </p>
    </body>
</html>
```

In the document object model, documents have a logical structure which is very much like a tree; to be more precise, it is like a "forest " or "grove" which can contain more than one tree. However, the document object model does not specify that documents be implemented as a tree or a grove, nor does it specify how the relationships among objects be implemented in any way. In other words, the object model specifies the logical model for the programming interface and this logical model may be implemented in any way that a particular implementation finds convenient.

In this specification, we use the term structure model to describe the tree-like representation of a document; we specifically avoid terms like "tree" or "grove" in order to avoid implying a particular implementation.

One important property of DOM structure models is structural isomorphism: if any two document object model implementations are used to create a representation of the same document, they will create the same structure model, with precisely the same objects and relationships.

The name "Document Object Model" was chosen because it is an "object model" is used in the traditional object oriented design sense: documents are modeled using objects and the model encompasses not only the structure of a document, but also the behaviour of a document and the object of which it is composed.

As an object model, the document object model identifies:

1. The interfaces and objects used to represent and manipulate a document.
2. The semantics of these interfaces and objects-including both behaviour and attributes.
3. The relationships and collaboration among these interfaces and objects.

Dynamic HTML and DOM

The term Dynamic HTML often abbreviated as DHTML, refers to the techniques of making web pages dynamic by client-side scripting to manipulate the document content and presentation.

In the past , DHTML relies on browser/vendor specific feature to work. Making such pages work for all browsers require much effort, testing and unnecessarily long programs.

Standardisation efforts at W3C and elsewhere are making it possible to write standard-based DHTML that work for all compliant browsers. Standard-based involves three aspects:

1. **JavaScript** for cross-browser scripting.
2. **Cascading Style Sheets** (CSS) for style and presentation control.
3. **Document Object Model** (DOM) for a uniform programming interface to access and manipulate the web page as a document.

When these three aspects are combined, you get the ability to program changes in web pages in reaction to user or browser generated events and therefore to make HTML pages more dynamic.

Popular with web developer, supported by all major browsers, and standardised, JavaScript provides the ability to program browser actions in response to events. To have true cross platform DHTML, we still need a uniform way for JavaScript to access and manipulate web documents. This bring us to the DOM.

10.3 Cascading Style Sheet (CSS)

It is a style sheet language used for describing the presentation of a document written in a markup language. CSS is designed primarily to enable the separation of document content from document presentation, including aspects such as the layout, colors and fonts. This separation can improve content accessibility, provide more flexibility and control in the specification of presentation characteristics, enable multiple HTML pages to share formatting by specifying the relevant CSS in a separate .css file and reduce complexity and repetition in the structural content, such as semantically insignificance tables that were widely used to format pages before consistent CSS rendering was available in all major browsers.

CSS makes it possible to separate presentation instructions from the HTML content in a separate file or style section of the HTML file. For each matching HTML element, it provides a list of formatting instructions.

2. If ...... Then ...... Else Statement

It selects one of two sets of lines to execute. If you want to execute a statement when a condition is true and execute another statement when the condition is not true, you must add the "Else" keyword.

e.g.
```
i= hour(time)
    If  i < 10 Then
        response.write("Good morning!")
    Else
        response.write("Have a nice day!")
    End If
```

In this example, the first block of code will be executed if the condition is true, otherwise the other block will be executed (if i is greater than or equal to 10).

3. If...Then...ElseIf Statement

You can use the If…Then…ElseIf statement if you want to select one of many blocks of code or set of lines to execute.

e.g.
```
i = hour(time)
    If i = 10 Then
        response.write("Just started.!")
    ElseIf i = 11 Then
        response.write("Hungry !")
    ElseIf i = 12 Then
        response.write("Ah,lunch-time!")
    ElseIf i = 16 Then
        response.write("Time to go home!")
    Else
        response.write("Unknown")
    End If
```

4. Select Case Statement

You can also use the "Select Case" statement if you want to select one of many blocks of code or sets of lines to execute.

e.g.
```
d= weekday(date)
    Select Case d
      Case 1
         response.write("Sunday")
      Case 2
         response.write("Monday")
      Case 3
         response.write("Tuesday")
      Case 4
         response.write("Wednesday")
      Case 5
         response.write("Thursday")
      Case 6
         response.write("Friday")
      Case else
         response.write("Saturday")
    End Select
```

In this statement, first we have a single expression (most often a variable), that is evaluated once. The value of the expression is then compared with the values for each Case in the structure. If there is a match, the block of code associated with that Case is executed otherwise case else is executed.

12.12 Looping Statements

Looping statements are used to run the same block a specified number of times. In ASP, we have following looping statements:

1. For...Next Statement

Use the For…Next statement to run a block of code a specified number of times. The For statement specifies the counter variable (i) and its start and end values. The Next statement increases the counter variable (i) by one.

e.g.
```
For i = 0 To 5
    response.write ("The number is" & i &" <br/>")
Next
```

2. For Each...Next Statement

A For Each…Next loop repeats a block of code for each item in a collection or for each element of an array.

e.g.
```
Dim cars(2)
cars(0) = "Volvo"
cars(1) = "Saab"
cars(2) = "BMW"
For Each x In cars
    response.write (x & "<br/>")
Next
```

3. Do...Loop Statement

The Do…Loop statement repeats a block of code while a condition is true or until a condition becomes true.

1. **Repeat Code While a Condition is True** You use the While keyword to check a condition in a Do…Loop statement.

```
Do While i>10
    'some code
Loop
```

If i equals to 9, the code inside the above loop will never be executed.

```
Do
    'some code
Loop While i>10
```

The code inside the loop will be executed at least one time, even if i is less than 10.

2. **Repeat Code Until a Condition Becomes True** You use the Until keyword to check a condition in a Do…Loop statement.

```
Do Until i = 10
    'some code
Loop
```

If i equals to 10, the code inside the loop will never be executed.

```
Do
    'some code
Loop Until i = 10
```

The code inside the loop will be executed at least one time, even if i is equal to 10.

12.13 Procedures and Functions

Procedures and functions provide a way to create re-usable modules of programming code and avoid rewriting the same block of code every time you do the particular task.

ASP procedures and functions are executed only when they are called, not inline with the rest of the code. A function or sub procedure can be reused as many times as required, thus saving your time and making for as less clustered looking page. You can write functions in ASP similar to the way you write them in VB.

To declare a subroutine (a function that does not return a value, starts with the Sub keyword and ends with End Sub), you simply use the following syntax:

```
Sub subroutineName(parameter_1,…,
parameter_n)
        statement_1
        statement_2
        :
        statement_n
End Sub
```

A function differs from a subroutine in the fact that it returns data, starts with Function keyword and end with End Function. These are especially good for doing calculations and returning a value.

To declare a function, the syntax is:

```
Function functionName(parameter_1, …,parameter_n)
        statement_1
        statement_2
        statement_3
        :
        statement_n
End Function
```

e.g. The code for a procedure that is used to print the information on the page:

```
Sub GetInfo(name, phone, fee)
    response.write("Name:" & name & "<br>")
    response.write("Telephone:"& phone & "<br>")
    response.write("Fee:" & fee & "<br>")
End Sub
```

There are two ways to call the Sub:

First Method `Call GetInfo("Mr. Donnel", " 555-5555", 20)`

Second Method `GetInfo "Mr. Donnel", "555-5555", 20`

In each calling method, the actual argument is passed into the sub procedure in the corresponding position.

Note If you use the call statement, the arguments must be enclosed in parentheses otherwise parentheses are not used.

e.g. The code for a function that takes an integer value and returns the square of that value. Also included code to call the function.

```
Function Square(num)
    Square = num * num
End Function
response.write(Square(5))
If 40<Square(7) Then
    response.write("40 is less than 8^2")
Else
    response.write("8^2 is less than 40")
End If
```

To return a value from a function, you need to name the output value the same as your function.

12.14 ASP Object Model

The interaction between web clients and servers is complex, with many messages passed between the two. However, most of the time, we only need to work with one part of this complex interaction, e.g. a cookie sent by a user's browser to our web server.

One of the goals of ASP is to hide unneeded complexity from the developer. The designers of ASP have built a model of this complex interaction in the ASP object model. ASP server component contains built-in objects that are readily available to users when an ASP application is created.

h3 selector for internal style sheet are as follows:

```
h3
{
    text-align : right ;
    font - size : 20 pt;
}
```

If the internal style is defined after the link to the external style sheet, the h3 elements will be

color : red ; text - align : right ; font - size : 20 pt;

<div> tag

This tag defines a division or a section in an HTML document. This tag is used to group block-elements to format them with CSS.

e.g.
```
<div style = "color:#0000FF">
    <h3> This is a heading</h3>
    <p> This is a paragraph.</p>
</div>
```

From above coding, display a section in a document in blue color.

10.3.2 CSS Color

CSS uses color values to specify a color. Typically, these are used to set a color either for the foreground of an element or else for the background of the element.

Some common color properties are as follows:

1. color

This property sets the text-color for different elements.

e.g.
```
<p style = "color:red;">......</p>
```

2. opacity

This property sets the opacity level for a <div> element.

```
<div style = "opacity:0.5;">.......</div>
```

Lists all the Possibles Formats

Format	Syntax	Example
Hexcode	#RRGGBB	p{color : #FF0000;}
Short Hexcode	#RGB	p{color : # 6A7;}
RGB%	rgb(rrr%, ggg%, bbb%)	p{color : rgb (50%, 50%, 50%);}
RGB Absolute	rgb (rrr, ggg, bbb)	p{color : rgb (0, 0, 255);}
Keyword	aqua, back etc.	p{color: teal;}

10.3.3 CSS Background

The CSS background properties are used to define the background effects for elements. Some properties are as follows:

1. background-color

This property is used to set the background color of an element.

e.g.
```
<body>
<p style = "background-color:yellow;">
This is Arihant </p>
</body>
```

2. background-image

This property is used to set the background image of an element.

e.g.
```
body
{
    background-image:url;
}
```

3. background-repeat

By default, the background-image property repeats an image both horizontal and vertically. This property is used to control the repetition of an image in the background.

This property has following possible values:

- **repeat** causes the background image to be repeated along both the horizontal and vertical axes.
- **repeat-x** causes the background image to be repeated along the x-axis.
- **repeat-y** causes the background image to be repeated along the y-axis.
- **no-repeat** prevents the background image from being repeated at all.

4. background-attachment

This property sets whether a background image is fixed or scrolls with the rest of the page.

e.g
```
body
{
    background-attachment : fixed;
}
```

10.3.4 CSS Fonts

The CSS font properties define the font family boldness, size and the style of a text. Some properties are as follows:

1. font-family

This property is used to change the face of a font.

e.g.
```
<body>
    <p style = "font-family : georgia,
                              serif;">…</p> </body>
```

2. font-style

This property is used to make a font italic or oblique.

e.g.
```
<body>
    <p style = "font-style : italic;">…</p>
    </body>
```

3. font-size

This property is used to increase or decrease the size of a font.

e.g.
```
<p style = "font-size : 10px/small;">…</p>
```

4. font-variant

This property is used to create a small caps effect.

e.g.
```
<p style = "font-variant : small - caps;" >…</p>.
```

5. font-weight

This property is used to increase or decrease how bold or light a font appears.

e.g.
```
<p style ="font-weight : 500;">…</p>
```

10.3.5 CSS Text

This text is styled with some of the text formatting properties. Some common text properties are as follows:

1. word-spacing

This property is used to add or subtract space between the words of a sentence.

e.g.
```
<p style = "word-spacing:5px;">……</p>
```

2. letter-spacing

This property is used to add or subtract space between the letters that make up a word.

e.g.
```
<p style = "letter-spacing:6px;" >……</p>
```

3. text-decoration

This property is used to underline, overline and strikethrough text.

e.g.
```
<p style = "text-decoration:overline;">……</p>
```

4. text-transform

This property is used to capitalise text or convert text to uppercase or lowercase letters.

e.g.
```
<p style = "text-transform:uppercase;">……</p>
```

5. text-align

This property is used to align the text of a document.

e.g.
```
<p style = "text-align:center ;">……</p>
```

6. text-indent

This property is used to indent the text of a paragraph.

e.g.
```
<p style = "text-indent:2cm;">……</p>
```

7. line-height

This property is used to specify the space between lines.

e.g.
```
<p style = "line-height:1.8;">.......</p>
```

10.3.6 CSS Border

The border properties allow you to specify how the border of the box representing an element should look. There are three properties of a border you can change:

1. **Border-color** specifies the color of a border.
2. **Border-style** specifies whether a border should be solid, dashed line, double line or one of the other possible values.
3. **Border-width** specifies the width of a border.

10.3.7 CSS Margins

The margin property defines the space around an HTML element. It is possible to use negative values to overlap content. The following properties to set an element margin:

1. **Margin** specifies a shorthand property for setting the margin properties in one declaration.
2. **Margin-bottom** specifies the bottom margin of an element.
3. **Margin-top** specifies the top margin of an element.
4. **Margin-left** specifies the left margin of an element.
5. **Margin-right** specifies the right margin of an element.

10.3.8 CSS Paddings

The padding property allows you to specify how much space should appear between the content of an element and its border. You can also set different values for the padding on each side of the box using the following properties:

Methods	Description
WriteLine	Writes a specified text and new-line character to a TextStream file.
WriteBlankLine	Writes a specified number of new-line character to a TextStream file.

12.17 ActiveX Data Objects (ADO)

ADO is a Microsoft technology that can be used to access databases from your web pages. It is automatically installed with Microsoft IIS. ADO is specifically used as means to communicate and manipulate a database. The types of databases ADO will allow your ASP program to interact with MS-Access, MySQL, Oracle etc.

12.17.1 Accessing a Database from an ASP Page

The common steps to access a databases from inside an ASP page are as follows:

(i) Create an ADO connection to a database.
(ii) Open the database connection.
(iii) Create an ADO recordset.
(iv) Open the recordset.
(v) Extract the data you need from the recordset.
(vi) Close the recordset.
(vii) Close the connection.

12.17.2 Creation of DSN

To create a system Data Source Name (DSN) for an Access database on your local machine, follow these steps:

(i) Open the 'ODBC Data Source Administrator' (Start-> Control Panel -> Administrative Tools -> Data Sources).
(ii) Choose the System DSN tab.
(iii) Click on Add in the System DSN tab.
(iv) In the box that will appear, you should select the Microsoft Access driver and click Finish.
(v) Type in a name that is easily remembered and relevant to your database in the 'Data Source Name' textbox.
(vi) Click Select and browse to your local database file.
(vii) Click OK all the way out.
(viii) You have now created a DSN which will come in handy when you try to connect and retrieve information from your database.

12.17.3 Create a Database Connection from an ASP Page in IIS

Before a database can be accessed from a web page, a database connection has to be established. The following are the requirements for connecting to a database:

(i) Active Server Pages (ASP) enabled Internet Information Service (IIS) version 5.0 web server with Microsoft Data Access Components (MDAC) version 2.5 or 2.6 (with a Jet database engine).
(ii) Connectivity to a local or remote database.
(iii) ASP enabled Microsoft Internet Explorer version 5.0 or later.

12.17.4 Sample Database Connection Strings

These examples are for demonstration purposes only. You must paste this code in your ASP code to make a connection to the specified database. Note that you must change elements such as database name, server name, database location, Data Source Name (DSN) and so on.

12.17.5 Microsoft Access

1. OLE DB

```
<%
    Set Cnn = Server.CreateObject
                                  ("ADODB.Connection")
    Cnn.open "PROVIDER = MICROSOFT.JET.OLEDB .4.0;
DATA SOURCE = c:\mydatabase.mdb"
%>
```

2. With DSN and no User ID/Password

```
<%
    Set Conn = Server.CreateObject
                                  ("ADODB.Connection")
    Conn.open" DSNname"
%>
```

3. With DSN and User ID/Password

```
<%
    Set Conn = Server.CreateObject
                                  ("ADODB.Connection")
    Conn.open "DSNname", "username," "password"
%>
```

12.17.6 Microsoft SQL Server

1. OLE DB

```
<%
    Set cnn = Server.CreateObject
                                  ("ADODB.Connection")
    cnn.open "PROVIDER = SQLOLEDB;
    DATA SOURCE = sqlservername; UID = username;
    PWD = password; DATABASE = mydatabase"
%>
```

2. With DSN

```
<%
    Set Conn = Server.CreateObject
                        ("ADODB.Connection")
    Conn.open "DSN = MyDSN;UID = user;
         PWD = Password; DATABASE = mydatabase"
%>
```

12.17.7 ADO Recordset

To be able to read database data, the data must first be loaded into a recordset.

1. Create an ADO Table Recordset

After an ADO Database Connection has been created, it is possible to create an ADO recordset.

e.g. Suppose we have a database named "wind", we can get the access to the "Students" table inside the database with the following lines:

```
<%
    Set Conn = Server.CreateObject
                        ("ADODB.Connection")
    Conn.Provider = "Microsoft.Jet.OLEDB.4.0"
    Conn.Open "C:/webdata/wind.mdb"
    set rs = Server.CreateObject
                        ("ADODB.recordset")
    rs.Open "Students",Conn
%>
```

We can also get access to the data in the Students table using SQL:

```
<%
    Set Conn = Server.CreateObject
                        ("ADODB.Connection")
    Conn.Provider = "Microsoft.Jet.OLEDB.4.0"
    Conn.Open "C:/webdata/wind.mdb"
    set rs = Server.CreateObject
                        ("ADODB.recordset")
    rs.Open "Select * From Students", Conn
%>
```

2. Extract Data from the Recordset

After a recordset is opened, we can extract data from recordset.

e.g.

```
<%
    Set Conn = Server.CreateObject
                        ("ADODB.Connection")
    Conn.Provider = "Microsoft.Jet.OLEDB.4.0"
    Conn.open "C:/webdata/wind.mdb"
    set rs = Server.CreateObject
                        ("ADODB.recordset")
    rs.Open "Select * From Students", Conn
    For Each x in rs.fields
        response.write(x.name)
        response.write(" = ")
        response.write(x.value)
    Next
%>
```

3. Insert a Record to a Table in a Database

We may use the SQL INSERT INTO command to insert a record to a table in a database. We want to insert a new record to the Students table in the wind database. We first create a form that contains the fields we want to collect data from:

```
<html>
  <body>
    <form method = "post" action
                        = "demo_add.asp">
      Student RollNo: <input name = "stroll">
      Student Name: <input name = "schname">
      Student Name: <input name = "stname">
                        <br> <br>
      <input type = "submit" value = "Add New">
      <input type = "reset" value = "Cancel">
    </form>
  </body>
</html>
```

When the user presses the Submit button, the form is sent to a file called "demo_add.asp". The "demo_add.asp" file contains the code that will add a new record to the Students table:

```
<html>
  <body>
    <%
set conn = Server.CreateObject
                        ("ADODB.Connection")
conn.Provider
                = "Microsoft.Jet.OLEDB.4.0"
conn.Open "C:/webdata/wind.mbd"
sql= "INSERT INTO Students
            (StudentRollNo, SchoolName,"
sql = sql & "StudentName)"
sql = sql & "VALUES"
sql = sql & "('" & Request.Form
                        ("stroll")& "',"
sql = sql & "'" & Request.Form
                        ("schname") & "',"
sql = sql  & "'," & Request.Form
                        ("stname") & "')"
on error resume next
conn.Execute sql, recaffected
```

32. **Which of the following creates push button?**
(1) Check box (2) Radio
(3) Reset (4) Input

33. **DOM is a**
(1) parser (2) specification
(3) coding style (4) None of these

34. **Which 'HTML' tag is used to define an internal style sheet?**
(1) <style> (2) <css>
(3) <script> (4) <font>

35. **Which HTML attribute is used to define inline styles?**
(1) font (2) class
(3) styles (4) style

36. **Which is the correct CSS syntax?**
(1) body {color : black}
(2) {body; color : black}
(3) {body; color : black (body)}
(4) body : color = black

37. **How do you change the text color of an element?**
(1) text-color= (2) fgcolor:
(3) color: (4) text-color:

38. **Which CSS property controls the text size?**
(1) font-size (2) font-style
(3) text-style (4) text-size

39. **How do you display hyperlinks without an underline?**
(1) a {text-decoration : no underline}
(2) a {decoration : no underline}
(3) a {text-decoration : none}
(4) a {underline : none}

40. **Which of the following property is used to set the text direction?**
(1) color
(2) direction
(3) letter-spacing
(4) word-spacing

41. **How do you change the font of an element?**
(1) font-family: (2) font=
(3) f: (4) font = family

42. **How do you make the text bold?**
(1) font:b
(2) font-weight:bold
(3) style:bold
(4) font-style = Bold

43. **Which of the following is a component of CSS style rule?**
(1) Selector
(2) Property
(3) Value
(4) All of the above

44. **What is the correct syntax in HTML for creating a link on a web page?**
(1) <link src = "ghumti.html">
(2) <body link = "ghumti.html">
(3) <a src = "ghumti.html">
(4) <a href = "ghumti.html">

45. **Which of the following creates a text field in an HTML form?**
(1) <input type = "text" name = "mi" size = "5">
(2) <input type = "radio" name = "gender" value = "M" checked>
(3) Major <select name = "major" size = "5" ><option value = "CS"> Computer Science <option value = "Math">Mathematics <option>English <option>chinese </select>
(4) <input type = "checkbox" name = "tennis">tennis

46. **Which of the following tag is used to add sound file in your web page?**
(1) <add> (2) <img>
(3) <embed> (4) <bold>

47. **To display $(X+Y)^2$, the correct HTML code is**
(1) _{(X +Y)2}
(2) X+Y<sup>2</sub>
(3) (X+Y)²
(4) _{(X +Y)2}

48. **Which option do you have while making bulleted lists?**
(1) Disc, circle, square
(2) Square, polygon
(3) Disc, circle, rectangle
(4) Disc, oval, polygon

49. **In HTML, external linking implies linking two different.**
(1) Sections
(2) Documents
(3) Both (1) and (2)
(4) None of the above

50. **Which of the following tag is used to mark a being of a paragraph?**
(1) <td> (2)
(3) <p> (4) <tr>

51. **What is correct HTML for making a hyperlink?**
(1) < a url = "http://www.company .com">company.com</a>
(2) <a>http://www.company.com</a>
(3) <a href = "http:// www.company. com"> company</a>
(4) < a name="http://www.company. com">company.com<(1)w>

52. **...... attribute is used to set the color of a link while it is active.**
(1) vlink
(2) alink
(3) Both (1) and (2)
(4) link

53. **Which is not a valid value in the align attribute of <img>?**
(1) top (2) center
(3) bottom (4) right

54. **The elements <div> and <span> have the following characteristics**
(1) element <div> inherits properties defined for <span> in a stylesheet
(2) <div> and <span> have no real meanings as html tags unless stylesheet is applied
(3) elements <span> and <div> define content to be inline or block-level
(4) <div> and <span> are used as alternatives for the element <p>

55. **The correct HTML code for inserting an image is**
(1) <img href="image.gif">
(2) <img> image.gif</gif>
(3) <img src = "image.gif">
(4) <image src = "image.gif">

56. **Which of the following tag of CSS can be explicitly positioned by setting the left and top attributes?**
(1) <layer> (2) <ilayer>
(3) <style> (4) <body>

57. **What is the correct HTML add for adding a background color?**
(1) <background>yellow <background>
(2) <body color = "yellow">
(3) <body bgcolor = "yellow">
(4) <body bg = "yellow">

58. **Which of the following statements are true?**
(1) When issuing a request from an HTML form, either a GET method or a POST method can be used. The form explicitly specifies which of the two is used
(2) If the GET method is used, the data in the form are appended to the request string as if they were submitted using a URL
(3) If the POST method is used, the data in the form are packaged as part of the request file. The server program obtains the data by reading the file
(4) All of the above

59. Internal linking with respect to HTML means
(1) linking one part of the document on one computer, to another part of the document on some other computer with the same file name
(2) linking one part of the document on one computer, to another part of the document on some other computer in the same LAN
(3) linking one part of the document to another part of the same document
(4) linking one part of the document to another document on the same computer

60. What is the correct HTML code to left align the content inside a table cell?
(1) <td valign = "left">
(2) <td align = "left">
(3) <td left align>
(4) <td left>

61. Which of the following is correct about CSS?
(1) Style sheets allow content to be optimised for more than one type of device
(2) CSS can store web applications locally with the help of an offline cache
(3) Using CCS, we can view offline websites. The cache also ensures faster loading and better overall performance of the website
(4) All of the above

62. Which of the following property changes the style of bottom border?
(1) border-bottom-style
(2) border-top-style
(3) border-left-style
(4) border-right-style

63. Which of the following property is used to set the height of an image?
(1) border (2) height
(3) width (4) moz-opacity

64. Which of the following property changes the color of bottom border?
(1) border-color
(2) border-style
(3) border-width
(4) border-bottom-color

65 Which of the following property changes the style of top border?
(1) border-bottom-style
(2) border-top-style
(3) border-left-style
(4) border-right-style

66. Which of the following property changes the width of left border?
(1) border-bottom-width
(2) border-top-width
(3) border-left-width
(4) border-right-width

67. What is the correct CSS syntax for making all the <p> element bold?
(1) <p style = "text-size : bold">
(2) p {font-weight : bold}
(3) p {text size : bold}
(4) < p style = "font-size : bold">

68. How do you make each word in a text starts with a capital letter?
(1) text-transform : capitalise
(2) You cannot do that with CSS
(3) text-transform : uppercase
(4) text-transform

69. To bind the HTML element <input> type in text with the datasource "dsoCustomer" we use
(1) <input type = "text" datafield = "#dsoCustomer">
(2) <input type = "text" datasrc = "dsoCustomer">
(3) <input type = "text" datasrc = "#dsocustomer">
(4) <input type = "text" datafld = "#dsoCustomer">

70. Which of the following tag is displayed one font size larger than the rest of the text surrounding it?
(1)<small> (2) <big>
(3) <large> (4) <span>

71. Which of the following HTML container tags do you apply to text for formatting the text as a paragraph?
(1) <paragraph>...</paragraph>
(2) <para> .... </para>
(3) <p> .... </p>
(4) None of the above

72. The style element holds the document for setting
(1) font, color and alignment
(2) font, color, alignment and border
(3) color, alignment and border
(4) None of the above

73. Which of the following tag is used to make a list that lists the items with numbers?
(1) <dl>
(2) <ul>
(3) <ol>
(4) None of the above

74. ...... attribute of the <a> tag is used to name the section in a web page to create an internal link.
(1) href (2) name
(3) align (4) link

75. Which of the following attribute of <img> tag is used to provide alternate text when an image on a web page cannot be displayed?
(1) alt (2) src
(3) align (4) usemap

76. Method used to send the data is stored in an environment variable on the web server is
(1) content-length (2) get
(3) request (4) post

77. <dt> tag is designed to fit a single line of our web page but <dd> tag will accept a
(1) line of text (2) full paragraph
(3) word (4) request

78. When creating a web document, which unit is used to express an image's height and width?
(1) Centimetres (2) Pixels
(3) Dots per inch (4) Inches

79. For internal linking, the section names are provided by .... attribute of <a> tag.
(1) title (2) href
(3) name (4) None of these

80. If a user is not able to see the image on the web page, the text is displayed in place of the image, is specified, by which of the following attributes in HTML?
(1) Alternate (2) All_Text
(3) Alt_link (4) Alt

81. Which of the following is used to specify the beginning of a table's row?
(1) <table> (2) <tr>
(3) <row> (4) <begin>

82. If your request is not time sensitive, such as finding the address of a student in the database, use the .... method to speed up the performance.
(1) GET (2) POST
(3) DELETE (4) UPDATE

83. Which attribute of the <table> tag is used to set an image in the background of a table?
(1) bgcolor (2) background
(3) frame (4) rules

CHAPTER PRACTICE

1. ASP code is .... .
(1) a client-side executable code
(2) a server-side executable code
(3) a world-wide-web executable code
(4) All of the above

2. ASP pages can contain embedded ...... code.
(1) HTML (2) DOM
(3) XML (4) CSS

3. Which of the following is the default scripting language in Active Server Pages (ASP)?
(1) JavaScript
(2) PHP
(3) HTML
(4) VBScript

4. If the default pages in HTML are index.htm, default.html etc., what are the default pages in ASP?
(1) index. asp
(2) default.asp
(3) home.asp
(4) Both (1) and (2)

5. How ASP.Net different from classic ASP?
(1) Scripting is separated from the HTML, Code is interpreted separately
(2) Scripting is separated from the HTML, Code is compiled as a DLL, the DLLs can be executed on server
(3) Code is separated from the HTML and interpreted Code is interpreted separately
(4) All of the above

6. When an .aspx page is requested from the web server, the output will be rendered to browser in following format.
(1) HTML
(2) XML
(3) WML
(4) JSP

7. When an ASP. NET file is placed on an IIS server and viewed through a browser, the resulting HTML page contains?
(1) a mix of ASP. NET and HTML code
(2) All ASP. NET code
(3) all HTML code
(4) as much ASP. NET code as is in the ASP. NET file

8. In OLEDB, a service provider
(1) does not own data only
(2) transforms data through OLE DB interface only
(3) is both a consumer and a provider of data only
(4) All of the above are true of an OLE DB service provider.

9. The name of a constant
(1) must both begin with a letter and be all uppercase.
(2) does not have to begin with a letter but must be all uppercase.
(3) does not have to begin with a letter and be either upper or lowercase.
(4) None of the above

10. The End If statement is required
(1) in all If ... Then statements.
(2) in all multi-line statements with Else.
(3) in single line statements.
(4) Both (1) and (2)

11. The For ... Next Loop is used when
(1) a choice is made based on a boolean condition.
(2) a block of statements is executed an unknown number of times.
(3) a block of statements is executed a known number of times.
(4) Both (1) and (2)

12. Which of the following object is not an ASP component?
(1) LinkCounter
(2) Counter
(3) AdRotator
(4) Permission Checker

13. Difference between response.write ( ) and response.output.write( ).
(1) response.output.write( ) allows you to buffer output
(2) response.output.write( ) allows you to write formatted output
(3) response.output.write( ) allows you to flush output
(4) response.output.write( ) allows you to stream output

14. Which object can help you maintain data across users?
(1) Application object
(2) Session object
(3) Response object
(4) Server object

15. Which of the following ASP object encapsulates the state of the client?
(1) Session object
(2) Application object
(3) Response object
(4) Server object

16. Which of the following can done using ASP scripts?
(1) Edit, change or add content to a web page on the fly
(2) Respond to user queries or data submitted through HTML forms
(3) Access any data or database and return results to the browser
(4) All of the above

17. Which of the following is not the way to maintain state?
(1) View state
(2) Cookies
(3) Hidden fields
(4) Request object

18. In ASP, a request object retrieves information from a user by ....
(1) a collection of values sent as cookies in a HTTP header
(2) a collection of data sent with a submitted form
(3) from client variables described from within an object
(4) Both (1) and (2)

19. Which of the following are ASP standard objects?
(1) Server (2) Response
(3) Session (4) All of these

20. How do you comment a line in ASP using VBScript?
(1) (< Comment a line in ASP >)
(2) < Comment a line in ASP>
(3) 'Comment a line in ASP
(4) <% Comment a line in ASP %>

21. The Application object is similar to the Session object except that
(1) it stores public data whereas a session object stores private data
(2) it stores global information whereas a session object stores information about an individual user
(3) there may exist many instances of an application object, whereas there can be only one instance of a session object for each user
(4) None of the above

22. Which of these is OKAY to use for a variable name?
(1) employee salary
(2) 2nd_employee
(3) employee_hire_date
(4) date-of-birth

23. What happens when a user types in a URL that requests an ASP page?
(1) Browser requests ASP code, server returns code, browser executes code into HTML form.
(2) Browser requests ASP code, server executes ASP code and returns HTML document to browser.
(3) Browser requests code, server returns code, Windows executes code, since ASP is Microsoft code.
(4) All of the above

24. When writing ASP code, what are the correct delimiters to use?
(1) % code % (2) < code>
(3) <% code> (4) <% code %>

25. Which of the following is the root of the .NET type hierarchy?
(1) System.Object (2) System.Type
(3) System. Base (4) System.Pare

26. Which of the following is not a valid data type in ASP?
(1) Byte (2) Date
(3) Currency (4) Data

27. This operator's syntax consists of an expression + expression:
(1) Addition (2) Sum
(3) Expression (4) Result

28. Use this function to return a data with a time interval:
(1) DateAdd (2) Return
(3) Date (4) Time

29. In ASP, the session variables can be used to
(1) store data and information for a particular page.
(2) store data and information for a particular user and for a particular page.
(3) store information about a single user and these are also available to all pages in an application
(4) All of the above

30. ODBC minimum SQL grammar contains which of the following?
(1) INSERT, UPDATE, DELETE only
(2) Stored Procedures only
(3) Literals for date, time and timestamp only
(4) CREATE VIEW, DROP VIEW only

31. Which of the following are goals of OLE DB?
(1) Create object interfaces for DBMS functionality pieces only.
(2) Increase flexibility only.
(3) Object interface over any type of data only.
(4) All of the above as goals of OLE DB.

32. Syntax for closing and opening the connection in ADO is:
(1) sqlConn.Open( ) and sqlConn.close( )
(2) sqlConn.open( ) and sqlConn.Close( )
(3) sqlConn.Open( ) and sqlConn.Close( )
(4) None of the mentioned

33. With A = False and B = True, which statement evaluates as True?
(1) A AND A
(2) A AND B
(3) B AND B
(4) None are true

34. With A = False and B = True, which statement evaluates as False?
(1) A OR A
(2) A OR B
(3) B OR A
(4) B OR B

35. The left side of an assignment statement will hold
(1) a variable.
(2) an object property.
(3) an expression.
(4) Both (1) and (2)

36. When a condition in an If ...Then statement tests true then
(1) the next Else statement is activated.
(2) the next If statement is activated.
(3) the next Then statement is activated.
(4) the End If statement is activated

37. Which statements are optional in an If ... Then statement?
(1) If
(2) Then
(3) Else
(4) Both (1) and (2)

38. Do...Loop is an iterative statement because it
(1) selects a block of statements to run.
(2) runs the same block of statements repeatedly.
(3) selects a block of statements and runs it repeatedly.
(4) selects a block of statements and runs it a specified number of times.

39. The advantage of For ... Next loops over Do...Loop is that they are
(1) easier to read and maintain.
(2) less prone to being infinite loops.
(3) good for working with arrays.
(4) All of the above

40. Which of the following is true to declare variable for ASP?
(1) Var (2) Dim
(3) $ (4) Set

41. Which of the following denote ways to manage state in an ASP application?
(1) Session objects
(2) Application objects
(3) ViewState
(4) All of the above

42. Which is better in managing your code when writing with ASP or any other scripting code?
(1) Break it up into smaller easier-to-manage files that can serve as subroutines and function calls.
(2) Keep it nice and simple in one file and use subroutines and function calls.
(3) Both (1) and (2)
(4) None of the above

43. You want to add ASP capability to your company's website. What is the first thing you would check?
(1) That all pages are saved in .asp extensions.
(2) Check that the web server has Microsoft FrontPage extensions installed.
(3) Make sure the web server is capable of hosting ASP pages.
(4) Check the coding and be sure the ASP code is surrounded with <% and %>

44. It is imperative when writing ASP code is to begin every file with which statement?
(1) <% Language=VBScript %>
(2) <% ASPLanguage = VBScript %>
(3) <%@ Language=VBScript %>
(4) <% @ ASPLanguage = VBScript %>

45. Which web server control is used to display advertisements in ASP web page?
(1) Image
(2) Imagemap
(3) Panel
(4) AdRotator

CHAPTER

11

eXtensible Markup Language

XML stands for eXtensible Markup Language. It is a software and hardware independent tool for carrying information. It is a way to apply structure to a Web page. It provides a standard open format and mechanisms for structuring a document, so that it can be exchanged and manipulated. In recent years, XML has evolved as the efficient standard for document markup because, it provides customised tags to format and display textual information.

XML will not change the way of your web pages look, but it will change the way, the documents are read and the way documents are filled and stored. The XML format can be used by any individual or group of individuals or companies that want to share information in a consistent way. XML is actually easier-to-use and simpler subset of the Standard Generalised Markup Language (SGML), which is the standard to create a document structure.

History of XML

XML history begins with the development of Standard Generalised Markup Language (SGML) by Charles F.GoldFarb, alongwith Ed Mosher and Ray Lorie in the 1970's while working at IBM. The first markup language, introduced in 1969, was Generalised Markup Language (GML).

The main disadvantage of GML is a different file created by using GML required different parsers. This led to the development of Standard Generalised Markup Language (SGML) in 1986. It allowed the user to define and create platform-independent files. Since, the software used to create SGML files was complex and expensive, this led to the development of HTML by Tim Berners Lee in the late 1980's.

Since, HTML (Subset of SGML) has somewhat become a victim of it's own popularity, as it was rapidly adopted and extended in many ways beyond it's original vision. But HTML is only intended for displaying files in a browser. This led to the development of XML. Since, XML is originated from SGML, which is a system for defining new markup languages. A system that allows defining new markup language is known as **meta language** and hence SGML and XML are both the meta languages.

Features of XML

The most common features of XML are as follows:

(i) **XML simplifies data description** The focus of XML is on the description of data, not its presentation.

(ii) **XML is a structured format** We can define exactly how the data is to be arranged, organised and expressed within the file. When we are given a file, we can validate that it confirms to a specific structure, prior to importing the data. XML is a user defined language, implying that it allows you to create your own tags.

(iii) **XML can easily describe hierarchical data and the relationships between data** It provides the relationship between root element and its child element. The hierarchical structure is suitable for most types of documents.

(iv) **XML is platform independent** XML can run on all platforms. It enables you to execute XML-based applications on any operating system such as Windows, Macintosh and UNIX etc.

(v) **XML has user defined and extensible tags** XML tags are not predefined. It means it supports user-defined tags which user can define as per the requirement.

(vi) **XML is a global format** There is only one way to express a number in an XML file and only one way to express a date.

(vii) **XML is a meta language** It can be used to create new languages. There are several languages derived from XML such as MathML, which is a markup language used for the representation of mathematical formulae and scientific data. Similarly, Wireless Markup Language (WML), which is used for web applications that can be accused by using a cellular phone is also derived from XML.

Some other languages are:

(a) Ink Markup Language (InkML)
(b) Business Narrative Markup Language (BNML)
(c) Financial Product Markup Language (FPML)
(d) Virtual Human Markup Language (VHML)
(e) Architecture Description Markup Language (ADML)
(f) Artificial Intelligence Markup Language (AIML)
(g) Chess Markup Language (ChessML), etc.

(viii) **XML is a W3C recommendation** It is descriptively identified in the XML 1.0 W3C recommendation. XML was initially developed by a W3C Generic SGML editorial Review Board formed under the conservancy of the W3.

11.1 Comparing XML and Other Technologies

XML is a markup language, but there are various other markup languages, such as HTML and SGML which are also available.

1. Comparing XML and SGML

XML	SGML
XML is a markup language.	SGML is a meta language used to define and describe generic markup language.
It does not include complex and optional features of SGML.	It was complex and requires overheads to use it.
It allows creation of new tags to describe and present your data.	It is an ISO standard for specifying a set of tags.
It allows data validation.	It does not allow data validation.
It describes the data and transfer data between applications.	It allowed you to define and create platform-independent files.

2. Comparing HTML and XML

HTML	XML
HTML tags are predefined.	XML tags are not predefined.
HTML is case insensitive.	XML is case sensitive.
HTML is markup language that creates the form and appearance of the web page.	XML is neither a programming nor a presentation language.
HTML documents are viewable in a browser.	XML documents can be viewed only if proper stylesheet file is also available alongwith XML file.
HTML tags may not have closing tags.	XML tags must have a closing tags.

11.2 Working with XML

Before you create an XML document, you need to understand how data is stored in an XML document and the various components of an XML document.

XML provides a way to store structured data that is capable of being recognised by different kinds of **devices**.

e.g. the code of XML document is following:

XML declaration

```
<?xml version="1.0" encoding="UTF-8"?>
<!--PRODUCTDATA is the root element-->
<PRODUCTDATA>
<!--PRODUCT is the element-->
<PRODUCT PRODID="P001">
<PRODUCTNAME> Barbie Doll </PRODUCTNAME>
<DESCRIPTION> This is a toy for children
in the age group of 5-10 years </DESCRIPTION>
<PRICE> $20.00 </PRICE>
<QUANTITY>12 </QUANTITY>
</PRODUCT>
</PRODUCTDATA>
```

Child elements

End of document

XML declaration line specifies the version and encoding format of the XML document.

CHAPTER

13

Web Scripting

A script language (or web scripting) is a programming language that supports scripts, programs written for a special run time environment that automate the execution of tasks that could be executed one by one. Scripting languages can be embedded within HTML are commonly used to add functionality to a web page, such as different menu styles, graphic displays or to serve dynamic advertisements. Perl, Hypertalk, Lingo, AppleScript, JavaScript, VBScript etc, are the examples of scripting languages.

13.1 VBScript

VBScript stands for Visual Basic Scripting that forms a subset of Visual Basic for Applications (VBA). It is a general-purpose, light-weight and active scripting language developed by Microsoft that is modelled on Visual Basic.

It allows Microsoft Windows administrators to generate powerful tools for managing computers with error handling, subroutines and other programming constructs. It can give the user complete control over many aspects of their computing environment.

Features of VBScript

(i) It is a light-weight scripting language, which has a lighting fast interpreter.
(ii) It is a case insensitive language. It has a very simple syntax, easy to learn and implement.
(iii) Unlike or Java, it is an object-based scripting language and not an object oriented programming language.

13.1.1 Adding VBScript Code to HTML Page

VBScript code can be included in HTML file anywhere but we include VBScript ideally only in following four positions:

(i) Inside <head> ...... </head> section.
(ii) Inside <body>...... </body> section.
(iii) Inside <body> ...... </body> and <head> ...... </head> sections .
(iv) Inside external file.

To insert a VBScript into an HTML page, we use the <script> tag. Inside the <script> tag, we use the type or language attribute to define the scripting language.

So, the <script type = "text/vbscript"> and </script> tell where the starts and ends:

e.g.

```
<html>
     <body>
          <script type = "text/vbscript">
               document.write("Hello World")
          </script>
     </body>
</html>
```

Here, document.write command is a standard VBScript command for writing output to a page. By entering the document.write command between the <script> and </script> tags, the browser will recognise it as a VBScript command and execute the code line. In the above example, the browser will write Hello World to the page.

13.1.2 VBScript Data Type

VBScript has only one datatype called a Variant. It is a special kind of data type that can contain different kinds of information, depending on how it is used.

A Variant can contain either numeric or string information. It behaves as a number when you use it in a numeric context and as a string when you use it in a string context.

Variant Subtype

Beyond the simple numeric or string classifications, a Variant can make further categorisation about the specific nature of numeric information. These different categories of information in a Variant are called subtypes.

The following table shows the subtypes of data that a Variant can contain:

Subtype	Description
Empty	Variant is uninitialised. Value is 0 for numeric variables or a zero-length string (" ") for string variables.
Null	Variant intentionally contains no valid data.
Boolean	Contains either True or False.
Byte	Contains integer in the range 0 to 255.
Integer	Contains integer in the range -32,768 to 32,767.
Currency	-922,337,203, 685,477.5808 to 922, 337,203, 685, 477.5807.
Long	Contains integer in the range -2,147, 483,648 to 2,147,483,647.
Single	Contains a single-precision, floating point number in the range -3.402823E38 to -1.401298E-45 for negative values; 1.401298E-45 to 3.402823E38 for positive values.
Double	Contains a double-precision, floating point number in the range -1.79769313486232E308 to –4.94065645841247E-324 for negative values; 4.94065645841247E-324 to 1.79769313486232E308 for positive values.
Date (Time)	Contains a number that represents a data between January 1,100 to December 31,9999.
String	Contains a variable-length string that can be upto approximately 2 billion characters in length.
Object	Contains an object.
Error	Contains an error number.

13.1.3 VBScript Variables

Variable is a named memory location used to hold a value that can be changed during the script execution. It can store the information required to use in our programming. When we are working with data, we deal with different types of data, so we need different types of variables to store the data.

Naming Restrictions

Variable names follow the standard rules for naming anything in VBScript. A variable name:

(i) must begin with an alphabetic character.

(ii) cannot contain an embedded period.

(iii) must not exceed 255 characters.

(iv) must be unique in the scope in which it is declared.

Declaring Variables

You can declare variables explicitly in your script using the Dim, Public or Private statement. Generally, we use Dim statement for declaring variables.

e.g. `Dim a`

You can declare multiple variables by separating each variable name with a comma.

e.g. `Dim a, b, c`

Assigning Values to the Variables

Values are assigned similar to an algebraic expression. The variable name on the left hand side followed by an equal to (=) symbol and then its values on the right hand side.

Rules

(i) Numeric value should be declared without double quotes.

(ii) String value should be enclosed within a double quotes (" ").

(iii) Date and time value should be enclosed within hash symbol (#).

e.g.

(i) `Num = 25`

(ii) `StrValue = "VBScript"`

(iii) `Date1 = #01/01/2020#`

(iv) `Time1 = #12:30:44 PM#`

Scalar Variables and Arrays Variables

Most of the time, you just want to assign a single value to a single variable. A variable containing a single value is known as **scalar variable.** Other times, you want to assign more than one related values to a single variable. A variable containing a series of values is known as **array variable.**

ENTER key. White space is generally provided to enhance the reliability of the document.

XML parser ignores these white spaces. You must notice in HTML, the multiple spaces between the words are reduced to a single space, when HTML code is navigated in the web browser.

e.g. **when white space in HTML**

HTML It is my HTML code.

Output It is my HTML code.

e.g. **when white space in XML**

XML It is my XML code.

Output It is my XML code.

11.5.2 Data Instance

Sometimes, data instance is also referred to as **body of the XML document**. It follows the prolog and consists of one or more elements, which contains the actual data. The basic building blocks of data instance are elements, which contain the data items present in the XML document and begins with a start tag and ends with an end tag. Data instance contains the following components as follows:

i. Root/Document Element

Each XML document has exactly one single root element. This element is known as the **document or root element.** It encloses all the other elements and therefore atleast one element will be their that will be sole parent to all the other elements. Root elements are also called **parent element.** Root or document elements are not any keywords.

Syntax

```
<Root>
<Child>
<Subchild> ...... </Subchild>
</Child>
</Root>
```

e.g.

```
<School>
<Student>
<Roll_No> 12 </Roll_No>
</Student>
</School>
```

In the above example, <School> is a root element.

ii. Elements

Elements are the basic units used to identify and store data and are represented by using tags. Also, an element can contain another element text.

Elements are divided into two basic categories empty and nested (child):

(a) **Empty Elements** If an element does not have any content, it is called an empty element. It can have attributes that help to identify an entity. An empty element can be written without the end tag.

e.g.

```
<Product>
<Item item_id="24"/>   } Empty element
</Product>
```

(b) **Child Elements** A child element is a nested element, i.e. element inside another element. An element that contains child element is known as the **parent element.**

e.g. (Parent element)

```
<book>
<title> Harry Potter </title>        } Child
<author> J.K. Rowling </author>      } elements
</book>
```

Rules for Defining Elements

- Element names must start either with a letter or underscore (_) character.
- After the first character, you can use numbers, letters, underscore characters, the dot (.) or a hyphen (-) in the element name.
- Spaces are not allowed in element names.
- Element names cannot have a blank space after the opening character but there can be space before the closing character.
- By convention, XML elements are written in lowercase.
- XML is case sensitive.
- Element names cannot start with the word "xml" or "Xml" or "XML". It is reserved for the XML specification.

iii. Tags

Tags are used to identify elements in an XML document. XML tags consist of opening and closing angular brackets (<>). You can use tags to mark the start and end of elements, which are the logical units of information in an XML document. An element consists of a start tag, possibly followed by content and other complete elements, followed by an end tag.

e.g.

Start tag: <P>   Content: Tony Blair   End tag: </P>

Three types of tags are as follows:

(a) **Start Tag** It is a tag name, which is placed inside angle brackets (<>). It starts the definition of an element.

e.g. <tag>

(b) **End Tag** It is a tag name, which has same name as that of its start tag but alongwith a slash before the name.
e.g. </tag>

(c) **Empty Tag** It is a tag without end tag. It is a tag name following slash.
e.g. <tag/>

iv. Attributes

In addition to marking the beginning of an element, XML will start with tags to provide a place to specify attributes. An attribute specifies a single property of an element, using a **name-value pair**. Every attribute assignment consists of two parts as the attribute name and the attribute value.

e.g.

Attribute value

```
<PRODUCT PRODUCTID ="P001" CATEGORY
= "Books">
```

Attribute name

All attributes value must be enclosed in single or double quotation marks.

v. Content

The content of an XML document is contained in the elements used in the document.

e.g.

```
<PRODUCTNAME> Books </PRODUCTNAME>
```

Content of <PRODUCTNAME> element

vi. Special Characters

Special characters are also known as **predefined entities.** It is a short name given to a set of information. When a special character is used in an XML document, it expands its full definition. It is a shortcut for the associated block of data. Special characters are also called **references.**

Some special characters are as follows:

Character	Predefined Entity
&	&
<	< ;
>	> ;
"	"
'	'

e.g.

```
<NAME> HTML &apos; XML </NAME>
```

Output HTML' XML

11.6 Types of XML Documents

There are two types of XML documents as follows:

11.6.1 Well-Formed XML Documents

A "Well-Formed" XML document means that the document has the correct XML syntax.

The XML document that follows XML grammar rules is called **well-formed document.** A document that includes sequence of markup characters that cannot be parsed or are invalid cannot be well-formed.

The following points are to be kept in mind for a valid XML document:

(i) **The document must contain atleast one element**

e.g.

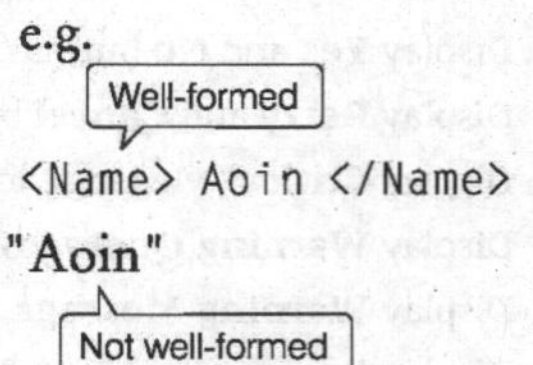

Above syntax is not well-formed because it is not marked up as an element.

(ii) **The document must have a root element** A root element is a unique element in the XML document, which contains the complete document.

e.g.

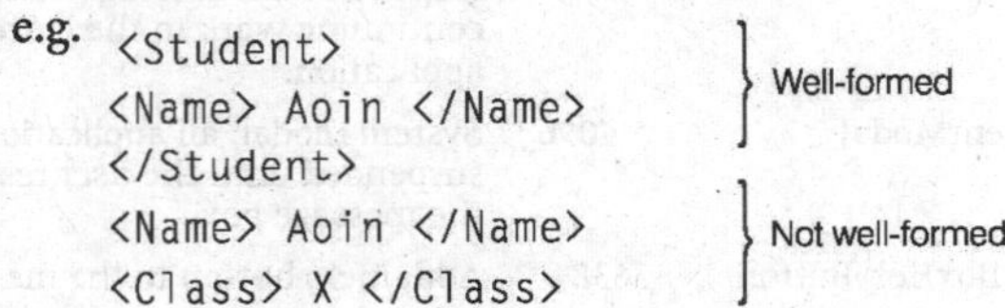

(iii) **The element must have the opening and closing tags** To close a tag, you need to prefix the forward slash with the normal tag.

e.g.

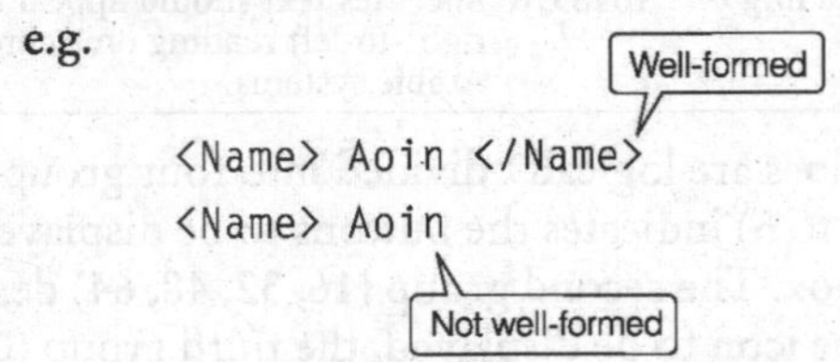

(iv) **XML tags must be closed properly** There must be a proper closing tag. In XML, empty tags must end with a following slash.

e.g.

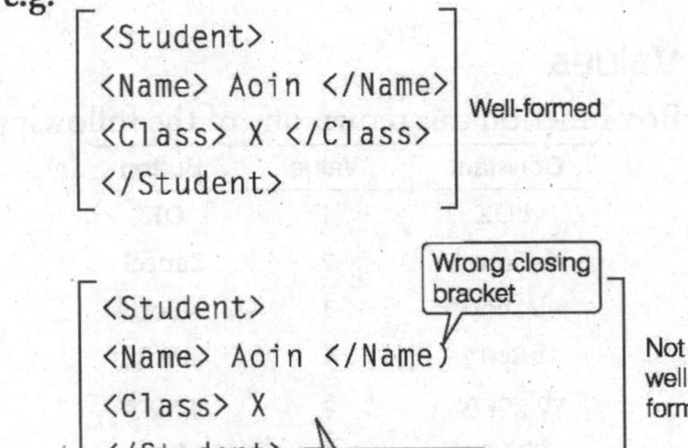

Button Argument Setting

The **Buttons** parameter can take any of the following values:

Constant	Value	Description
vbOKOnly	0	Display **OK** button only.
vbOKCancel	1	Display **OK** and **Cancel** buttons.
vbAbortRetryIgnore	2	Display **Abort, Retry** and **Ignore** buttons.
vbYesNoCancel	3	Display **Yes, No** and **Cancel** buttons.
vbYesNo	4	Display **Yes** and **No** buttons.
vbRetryCancel	5	Display **Retry** and **Cancel** buttons.
vbCritical	16	Display **Critical Message** icon.
vbQuestion	32	Display **Warning Query** icon.
vbExclamation	48	Display **Warning Message** icon.
vbInformation	64	Display Information Message icon.
vbDefaultButton1	0	First button is default.
vbDefaultButton2	256	Second button is default.
vbDefaultButton3	512	Third button is default.
vbDefaultButton4	768	Fourth button is default.
vbApplicationModal	0	Application modal; the user must respond to the message box before continuing work in the current application.
vbSystemModal	4096	System modal; all applications are suspended until the user responds to the message box.
vbMsgBoxHelpButton	16384	Adds Help button to the message box.
vbMsgBoxSetForeground	65536	Specifies the message box window as the foreground window.
vbMsgBoxRight	524288	Text is right aligned.
vbMsgBoxRtlReading	1048576	Specifies text should appear as right-to-left reading on Hebrew and Arabic systems.

The above values are logically divided into four groups: The first group (0 to 5) indicates the buttons to be displayed in the message box. The second group (16, 32, 48, 64) describes the style of the icon to be displayed, the third group (0, 256, 512, 768) indicates which button must be the default and the fourth group (0, 4096) determines the modality of the message box. When adding numbers to create a final value for the buttons argument, use only one number from each group.

Return Values

The MsgBox function can return one of the following values:

Constant	Value	Button
vbOK	1	OK
vbCancel	2	Cancel
vbAbort	3	Abort
vbRetry	4	Retry
vbIgnore	5	Ignore
vbYes	6	Yes
vbNo	7	No

e.g.

```
<html>
    <body>
        <script language ="vbscript" type
        ="text/vbscript">
            MsgBox("Welcome")
            a = MsgBox("Do you like blue color?",3,
            "Choose options")
            document.write("The Value of a is" & a)
        </script>
    </body>
</html>
```

When the above script is executed, the message box is displayed and if user click on No button, then the output is:

The Value of a is 7

13.1.8 Conditional Statements

These statements allow programmers to control the execution flow of a script or one of its sections. The execution is governed by one or more conditional statements. The following conditional statements are available in VBScript:

(i) If … Then … Else statement
(ii) Select Case statement

Making Decisions Using If ...Then...Else

The If …Then…Else statement is used to evaluate whether a condition is True or False and depending on the result, to specify one or more statements to run. Usually, the condition is an expression that uses a comparison operator to compare one value or variable with another.

Running Statements if a Condition is True

To run only one statement when a condition is True, use the single line syntax for the If …Then statement. or, To run more than one line of code, you must use the multiline (or block) syntax. This syntax includes the End If statement.

e.g.

```
Dim a, b
a=20
b=10
If a > b Then
    document.write "a is greater than b"
End If
```

Running Certain Statements if a Condition is True and Running Others if a Condition is False

You can use an If…Then…Else statement to define two blocks of executable statements: one block to run if the condition is True, the other block to run if the condition is False.

e.g.

```
Dim a, b
a = 20
b = 10
If a > b Then
   document.write "a is greater than b"
Else
   document.write "b is greater than a"
End If
```

Deciding between Several Alternatives

A variation on the If… Then…Else statement allows you to choose from several alternatives. Adding ElseIf clauses expands the functionality of the If…Then…Else statement so you can control program flow based on different possibilities.

e.g.

```
Dim a
a = -5
If a > 0 Then
   document.write "a is positive"
ElseIf a < 0 Then
   document.write "a is negative"
Else
   document.write "a is zero"
End If
```

You can add as many ElseIf clauses as you need to provide alternative choices. A better way to choose between several alternatives is the Select Case statement.

Making Decisions with Select Case

When a user wants to execute a group of statements depending upon a value of an expression, then Select Case is used. Each value is called a case and the variable being switched ON based on each case. Case Else statement is executed if test expression does not match any of the case specified by the user. Case Else is an optional statement within Select Case, however it is good programming practice to always have a Case Else statement.

e.g.

```
Dim MyVar
MyVar = 1
Select Case MyVar
  Case 1
        document.write "The Number is the Least
                                  Composite Number"
  Case 2
        document.write "The Number is the only Even
                                      Prime Number"
  Case 3
        document.write "The Number is the Least Odd
                                      Prime Number"
  Case Else
        document.write "Unknown Number"
End Select
```

13.1.9 Loops

There may be a situation when you need to execute a block of code several number of times. In general, statements are executed sequentially. The first statement in a function is executed first, followed by the second and so on. Programming language provides various control structures that allow for more complicated execution paths. A loop statement allows us to execute a statement or group of statements multiple times.

The following looping statements are available in VBScript:

Do Loops

You can use Do … Loop statements to run a block of statements an indefinite number of times. The statements are repeated either while a condition is True or until a condition becomes True.

(i) Do ... While Loop

A Do ... While loop is used when we wan to repeat a set of statements as long as the condition is True. The condition may be checked at the beginning of the loop or at the end of the loop.

e.g.

```
(i) Dim i
  i = 0
  Do While i <5
      i=i+1
      document.write"The value of i is:" & i
  Loop
(ii) Dim i
  i = 10
  Do
      i=i+1
      document.write "The value of i is:" & i
  Loop While i<3
```

(ii) Do...Until Loop

A Do...Until loop is used when we want to repeat a set of statements as long as the condition is False. The condition may be checked at the beginning of the loop or at the end of loop.

e.g.

```
(i) Dim i
  i=10
  Do Until i > 15
      document.write "The value of i is :" & i
      i = i + 1
  Loop
(ii) Dim i
  i = 1
  Do
     document.write "The value of i is" & i
  i = i + 1
  Loop Until i=10
```

11.11 Choice Element

The choice element provides an XML representation for describing a selection from a set of element types. An XML instance contains elements that corresponds to a selection from the set of element types defined by the choice element in an XML schema document. The minOccurs and maxOccurs attributes may permit the XML instance to select several occurrence of element types from the set.

Attributes of Choice element

id

The ID of this element. The id value must be of type ID and be unique within the document containing this element.

maxOccurs

The maximum number of times the choice can occur. The value can be an integer greater than or equal to zero. To set no limit on the maximum number, use the string "unbounded". Default value is 1.

minOccurs

The minimum number of times of choice can occur. The value can be an integer greater than or equal to zero. To specify that, this choice group is optional, set this attribute to zero. Default value is 1.

11.12 Element Occurrence Indicators

The plus (+), star (*) and question mark (?) characters in the element content are occurrence indicators. They indicate whether and how element in the child list can repeat.

(i) An element followed by no occurrence indicator must appear once and only once in the element being defined.

(ii) An element followed by a "+" character must appear one or several times in the element being defined. The element can repeat.

(iii) An element followed by a "*" character can appear zero or more times in the element being defined. The element is optional but, if it is included, it can repeat indefinitely.

(iv) An element followed by a "?" character can appear once or not at all in the element being defined. It indicates the element is optional and if included, cannot repeat.

11.13 XML with Data Source Object

XML Data Source Object (XML-DSO) is a Microsoft ActiveX Object built into the web browser so we can use ActiveX control to extract data from the XML code embedded directly in the HTML file and the external XML file using data binding into HTML web pages.

You can either use the <OBJECT> element to refer to the XML data source object, or you can use data islands and the <XML> element.

The CLASSID for the XML-DSO is:

```
CLSID : 550dda30 - 0541 - 11d2 - 9Ca9 -
                                0060boec3d39
```

The above ID uniquely identifies the XML-DSO, and we initialise this control in a web page as follows:

```
<OBJECT ID = "SomeID" CLASSID.= "CLSID :
550dda30-0541 - 11d2 - 9Ca9 - 0060b0ec3d39">
</OBJECT>
```

Most OBJECTs have a number of parameters associated with them, but the XML-DSO does not require any such parameters.

Now, we can either extract the data from one external XML file or we can use XML Data Islands, where we embed XML code in the HTML page itself.

11.14 XSL (eXtensible Style Sheet Language)

XSL is a language for expressing style sheets. An XSL style is, like with CSS, a file that describes how to display an XML document of a given type. XSL shares the functionality and is compatible with CSS2 (although it uses a different syntax).

e.g. in an XML page, that describes the characteristics of one or more automobiles. Using XSL, you could tell the web browser that the auto manufacturer name should be displayed, where to display it on a page and that it should be displayed in a bold font.

Think of an XML page as similar to an HTML page, but containing data in identified fields rather than text and graphics. XSL gives a developer the tools to describes exactly which data fields in an XML file to display and exactly where and how to display them. Like any style sheet language, XSL can be used to create a style definition for one XML document or reused for many other XML documents.

CHAPTER PRACTICE

1. XML allows you to

(1) create new tags
(2) arrange your tags in any order
(3) closing tags are not required
(4) All of the above

2. What makes XML more powerful than HTML?

(1) The fact that it's supported by all of the major software vendors
(2) Not as much coding is needed
(3) Its ability to adopt to new uses
(4) None of the above

3. The way of describing XML data is

(1) XML uses XSL to describes data
(2) XML uses a descritption node to describe data
(3) XML uses a DTD to describe the data
(4) None of the above

4. The XML document is like a

(1) tree structure
(2) inverted tree structure
(3) flat structure
(4) None of the above

5. There is a way of describing XML data, how?

(1) XML uses a DTD to describe the data
(2) XML uses XSL to describe the data
(3) XML uses a description node to describe the data
(4) Both (1) and (3)

6. Which of the following programs supports XML or XML applications?

(1) Internet Explorer 5.5
(2) Netscape 4.7
(3) Real player
(4) Both (1) and (2)

7. Which of the following statement is true?

(1) All XML elements must have a closing tag
(2) All XML elements must be lower case
(3) All XML documents must have a DTD
(4) All the statements are true

8. What is the full form of SGML from which XML is originated, is the standard to create a document structure?

(1) Standard Generalised Markup Language
(2) Standard Generalised Meta Language
(3) Standard Genuine Markup Language
(4) None of the above

9. Output of XML document can be viewed in a

(1) Word processor
(2) Web browser
(3) Notepad
(4) None of the above

10. Which of the following statement is true?

(1) An XML document can have one root element
(2) An XML document can have one child element
(3) XML elements have to be in lower case
(4) All of the above

11. White space in XML includes

(1) thing like space character, new lines and tabs
(2) only spaces
(3) space between double quotes
(4) None of the above

12. How can we make attributes have multiple values?

(1) <myElement myAttribute = "value1 value 2"/>
(2) <myElement myAttribute = "value1" myAttribute = "value2"/>
(3) <myElement myAttribute = "value1, value2"/>
(4) Attribute cannot have multiple values

13. XSL is

(1) an XML based language to create style sheets
(2) a language which is not used in XML
(3) eXtensible solution language
(4) eXtensible stylesheet language

14. To create a choice in XML schemas, we use the

(1) <xsd : select> element
(2) <xsd : multi> element
(3) <xsd : choice> element
(4) <xsd : single> element

15. Node in XML is

(1) any part of the document whether it is element attribute or otherwise
(2) referred only to attributes
(3) referred to the top elements in the documents
(4) None of the above

16. A root element is

(1) a bridge between HTML and XML
(2) the parent of all other element
(3) child element of the parent
(4) None of the above

17. Which of them is the correct statement?

(1) An XML element must have a closing tag
(2) An XML element must be lowercase
(3) An XML documents must have a DTD
(4) All of the above

18. Which is not a correct name for an XML element?

(1) <xmldocument>
(2) <7eleven>
(3) <phone_number>
(4) <root>

19. Is this, a "well-formed" XML document?

```
<?xml version = "1.0"?>
<note>
<to age = "29"> Tove </to>
<from> Jani </from>
```

(1) Yes
(2) No
(3) Cannot be determined without the DTD
(4) None of the above

20. Name space

(1) distinguishes one XML vocabulary from another
(2) provides the spaces in the names
(3) is a querying language
(4) None of the above

21. DTD that used to describe content in an XHTML document is

(1) way to create templates
(2) document type declaration in XML
(3) part of name spaces
(4) None of the above

22. Schema is

(1) template written in XML and can be modified at runtime
(2) read only for all practical purpose
(3) a global name space
(4) None of the above

23. A document have how many DTD's?

(1) Two
(2) None
(3) Three
(4) All of the above

```
        CheckFileExists
                    = objFso.FileExists(StrFilePath)
    End Function
```

3. **Write data to file**

```
    Function WriteToFile(byref FileRef, str)
        FileRef.WriteLine(str)
    End Function
```

4. **Read line from file**

```
    Function ReadLineFromFile(byref FileRef)
        ReadLineFromFile = FileRef.ReadLine
    End Function
```

5. **Read entire text file test**

```
    Function ReadTextFileTest(StrFilePath)
        Const ForReading = 1, ForWriting = 2,
                                ForAppending = 8
        Dim fso, f, Msg
        Set fso
        = CreateObject("Scripting.FileSystemObject")
        Set f = fso.OpenTextFile(StrFilePath,
                                    ForReading)
        ReadTextFileTest = f.Readall()
    End Function
```

6. **Closes an open file**

```
    Function CloseFile(byref FileRef)
        FileRef.close
    End Function
```

7. **Delete a file**

```
    Sub FileDelete(StrFilePath)
        objFso.DeleteFile(StrFilePath)
    End Function
```

13.1.13 String Functions

There are predefined VBScript String functions, which help the developers to work with the strings very effectively. Below are String methods that are supported in VBScript:

Function	Description
InStr	Returns the first occurrence of the specified substring. Search happens from left to right.
InstrRev	Returns the first occurrence of the specified substring. Search happens from right to left.
Lcase	Returns the lower case of the specified string.
Ucase	Returns the upper case of the specified string.
Left	Returns a specific number of characters from the left side of the string.
Right	Returns a specific number of characters from the right side of the string.
Mid	Returns a specific number of characters from a string based on the specified parameters.
Ltrim	Returns a string after removing the spaces on the left side of the specified string.
Rtrim	Returns a string after removing the spaces on the right side of the specified string.
Trim	Returns a string value after removing both leading and trailing blank spaces.
Len	Returns the length of the given string.
Replace	Returns a string after replacing a string with another string.
Space	Fills a string with the specified number of spaces.
StrComp	Returns an integer value after comparing the two specified strings.
String	Returns a string with a specified character the specified number of times.
StrReverse	Returns a string after reversing the sequence of the characters of the given string.

13.1.14 Date and Time Functions

VBScript Date and Time Functions help the developers to convert date and time from one format to another or to express the date or time value in the format that suits a specific condition.

Date Functions

Function	Description
Date	A function, which returns the current system date.
CDate	A function, which converts a given input to date.
DateAdd	A function, which returns a date to which a specified time interval has been added.
DateDiff	A function, which returns the difference between two time period.
DatePart	A function, which returns a specified part of the given input date value.
DateSerial	A function, which returns a valid date for the given year, month and date.
FormatDateTime	A function, which formats the date based on the supplied parameters.
IsDate	A function, which returns a Boolean value whether or not the supplied parameter is a date.
Day	A function, which returns an integer between 1 and 31 that represents the day of the specified date.
Month	A function, which returns an integer between 1 and 12 that represents the month of the specified date.
Year	A function, which returns an integer that represents the year of the specified date.
MonthName	A function, which returns name of the particular month for the specified date.
WeekDay	A function, which returns an integer(1 to 7) that represents the day of the week for the specified day.
WeekDayName	A function, which returns the weekday name for the specified day.

Time Functions

Function	Description
Now	A function, which returns the current system date and time.
Hour	A function, which returns an integer between 0 and 23 that represents the Hour part of the given time.
Minute	A function, which returns an integer between 0 and 59 that represents the Minutes part of the given time.
Second	A function, which returns an integer between 0 and 59 that represents the Seconds part of the given time.
Time	A function, which returns the current system time.
Timer	A function, which returns the number of seconds and milliseconds since 12:00 AM.
TimeSerial	A function, which returns the time for the specific input of hour,minute and second.
TimeValue	A function, which converts the input string to a time format.

13.2 JavaScript

JavaScript is a dynamic computer programming language. It is lightweight and most commonly used as a part of web pages, whose implementations allow client-side script to interact with the user and make dynamic pages. It is an interpreted programming language with object-oriented capabilities. JavaScript is complimentary to and integrated with Java.

JavaScript was first known as **LiveScript,** but Netscape changed its name to **JavaScript,** possibly because of the excitement being generated by Java. It made its first appearance in Netscape 2.0 in 1995 with the name LiveScript.

13.2.1 Adding JavaScript in an HTML Page

In HTML, JavaScript code must be inserted between <script> and </script> tags. Inside <script> tag, we use various attributes to define the scripting language. Some are as follows:

Attribute	Value	Description
type/language	text/javascript application/ javascript text	Specifies the scripting language as a content-type.
src	URL	Specifies a URI/URL of an external script.

There is a flexibility given to include JavaScript code anywhere in an HTML document. However, the most preferred ways to include JavaScript in an HTML file are as follows:

1. **JavaScript in <head>...</head> section**

   If you want to have a script run on some event, such as when a user clicks somewhere, then you will place that script in the head as follows:

```
<html>
    <head>
        <script type="text/javascript">
        <!–
        function sayHello()
                            { alert("Hello World") }
        //–>
        </script>
    </head>
    <body>
        <input type="button"
                            onclick="sayHello()"
                              value="Say Hello"/>
    </body>
</html>
```

   Output

   Click here for the result

   Say Hello

2. **JavaScript in <body>...</body> section**

   If you need a script to run as the page loads so that the script generates content in the page, then the script goes in the <body> portion of the document. In this case, you would not have any function defined using JavaScript. Take a look at the following code:

```
<html>
    <body>
        <script type="text/javascript">
        <!– document.write("Hello World") //–>
        </script>
        <p>This is web page body </p>
    </body>
</html>
```

   Output

   Hello World

   This is web page body

3. **JavaScript in <body> and <head> sections**

   You can put your JavaScript code in <head> and <body> section altogether as follows:

```
<html>
    <head>
        <script type="text/javascript">
        <!–
        function sayHello()
                            { alert("Hello World") }
        //–>
        </script>
    </head>
    <body>
```

70. **Disadvantages of DTD are**

(i) DTDs are not extensible
(ii) DTDs are not into support for name spaces
(iii) there is no provision for inheritance from one DTD to another

(1) (i) is correct
(2) (i), (ii) are correct
(3) (ii), (iii) are correct
(4) (i), (ii), (iii) are correct

71. **The advantage of XML over HTML is**

(i) it allows processing of data stored in web pages
(ii) it uses meaningful tags which aid in understanding the nature of a document
(iii) is simpler than HTML
(iv) it separates presentation and structure of a document

(1) (i), (ii) and (iii)
(2) (i), (ii) and (iv)
(3) (ii), (iii) and (iv)
(4) (i), (iii) and (iv)

72. **Name the root element in the following XML document:**

```
<father> <child1>
<name> Megha </name>
<age> 12 </age>
</child1>
<child2> <name> Mana </name>
<age> 15 </age> </child
2></father>
```

(1) child1 (2) child2
(3) father (4) name

73. **To use the external DTD, we have the syntax**

(1) <?xml version = "1.0" standalone = "no"?>
<!DOCTYPE DOCUMENT SYSTEM = "order.dtd"?>

(2) <?xml version = "1.0" standalone = "yes"?>
<!DOCTYPE DOCUMENT SYSTEM = "ordere.dtd"?>

(3) <?xml version = "1.0" standalone = "no"?>
<!DOCTYPE DOCUMENT "order.dtd"?>

(4) <?xml version = "1.0" standalone = "yes"?>
<!DOCTYPE DOCUMENT SYSTEM = "order.dtd"?>

74. **Which of the following XML documents as well formed?**

(1) <firstElement> some text goes here <secondElement> another text goes here </secondElement> </firstElement>

(2) <firstElement> some text goes here </first Element><secondElement> another text goes here </secondElement>

(3) <firstElement> some text goes here <second Element> another text goes here</firstElement> </second Element>

(4) </firstElement> some text goes here </secondElement> another text goes here <secondelement>> <firstElement> </secondelement>>

ANSWER KEY

1	(2)	2	(3)	3	(3)	4	(1)	5	(4)	6	(4)	7	(1)	8	(1)	9	(2)	10	(1)
11	(1)	12	(4)	13	(4)	14	(2)	15	(1)	16	(2)	17	(1)	18	(2)	19	(2)	20	(1)
21	(2)	22	(4)	23	(4)	24	(3)	25	(2)	26	(1)	27	(1)	28	(3)	29	(1)	30	(1)
31	(4)	32	(2)	33	(2)	34	(2)	35	(3)	36	(2)	37	(4)	38	(1)	39	(3)	40	(3)
41	(1)	42	(4)	43	(4)	44	(1)	45	(1)	46	(1)	47	(2)	48	(1)	49	(2)	50	(1)
51	(2)	52	(2)	53	(3)	54	(2)	55	(4)	56	(3)	57	(3)	58	(4)	59	(4)	60	(1)
61	(2)	62	(4)	63	(2)	64	(2)	65	(4)	66	(2)	67	(1)	68	(2)	69	(3)	70	(2)
71	(2)	72	(3)	73	(1)	74	(1)												

CHAPTER 12

Active Server Pages

Microsoft introduced Active Server Pages or ASP in December 1996, beginning with version 3.0. Microsoft officially defined ASP as:

"ASP is an open, compile-free application environment in which you can combine HTML, scripts and reusable ActiveX server components to create dynamic and powerful web based business solutions. It enables server-side scripting for IIS (Internet Information Services) with native support for both VBScript and JavaScript".

The default scripting language in ASP is VBScript. A scripting language is a light weight programming language. ASP documents have a file extension is .asp.

12.1 Features of ASP

The features of ASP are as follows:

1. **Dynamic Web Page** ASP supports scripting languages, which run on the web server, your web page can be dynamically created. e.g. you can create your web page so as to greeting each user when they log into your page differently.
2. **Browser Independent** ASP is browser independent because all the scripting code runs on the server. The browser only gets the results from the server in a standard HTML page.
3. **Database Access** One of the greatest assets of ASP is database connectivity. ASP enables you to easily build rich database functionality into your website, such as form processing.
4. **Read and Write Cookies** A cookie is a small text file stored by a website on a user's hard drive. With ASP, you can create cookies to store on a user's hard drive and later read them.
5. **Implement Sessions** A session is a way to store information about what happens during a user's visit to a website. Through this mechanism, you can store information about the user such as at what time they visited a page.

12.2 Concept of ASP

ASP program contains two parts : Programming code and Embedded HTML. The programming code can be written in number of scripting languages. A scripting language is used to execute commands on a computer. Server side scripts are processed completely on the web server. The client does not receive any code from server side scripts rather the client receives the output of server side script.

Client side and server side scripts cannot interact with each other because client side scripts are executed on the client after the server side scripts have finished processing completely. These features define an ASP. An ASP is a standard HTML page that has been extended with server side scripts, objects and components. By using ASP, you can create websites with dynamic content.

(ii) **Postfix Notation** In this notation, operator uses after operand. e.g. (i++)

Following unary operators are available in JavaScript:

Operator	Uses
–	Negation
~	One's complement
++	Increment
– –	Decrement
!	Logical NOT

2. Binary Operator

This operator has need two operands. Following binary operators are available in JavaScript:

(i) **Assignment Operators** These operators which assign a value to a variable. The assignment operation returns the assigned values. Chaining the assignment operator is possible in order to assign a single value to the multiple variables.

Assignment operators in JavaScript are as follows:

Operator	Description
=	Assignment
+=	Addition and assignment
–=	Subtraction and assignment
*=	Multiply and assignment
/=	Division and assignment
%=	Modules and assignment
&=	Binary AND and assignment
|=	Binary OR and assignment
^=	Binary exclusive OR and assignment
<<=	Bitwise left side shift and assignment
>>=	Bitwise right side shift and assignment

(ii) **Comparison Operators** These operators are used in logical statements to determine equality or difference between variables or values. Comparison operators in JavaScript are as follows:

Operator	Description
==	Equality
!=	Inequality
===	Identity
!==	Non - identity
<	Less than
>	Greater than
<=	Less than or equals to
>=	Greater than or equals to

(iii) **Arithmetic Operators** These operators take numerical values (either literals or variables) as their operands and return a single numerical value. Arithmetic operators in JavaScript are as follows:

Operator	Description
+	Addition
–	Subtraction
*	Multiply
/	Division
%	Remainder

(iv) **Bitwise Operators** These operators treat their operands as a sequence of 32 bits (zeros and ones) rather than as decimal, hexadecimal, or octal numbers.

Bitwise operators in JavaScript are as follows:

Operator	Description
&	Binary AND
|	Binary OR
^	Binary Exclusive OR
~	Bitwise NOT (one's complement)
<<	Bitwise left shift
>>	Bitwise right shift
>>>	Bitwise right shift and zero fill

(v) **Logical Operators** These operators are typically used with boolean (logical) values. When they are used in conditional expression, they return a boolean value. However, the && and || operators actually return the value of one of the specified operands, so if these operators are used with non-boolean values, they may return a non-boolean value. Logical operators in JavaScript are as follows:

Operator	Description
!	Logical NOT
&&	Logical AND
||	Logical OR

(vi) **Special Operators** Some special operators are available in JavaScript, which are as follows:

(a) **String Operator** When working with JavaScript, strings sometimes you need to join two or more strings together into a single string. Joining multiple strings together is known as concatenation.

Syntax

```
string3 = string1 + string2
```

(b) **Conditional** (Ternary) **Operator** It is the only JavaScript operator that takes three operands. This operator is frequently used as a shortcut for the if statement.

Syntax

```
condition ? exp1 : exp2
```

13.2.7 Operator Precedence

This describes the order in which operations are performed when an expression is evaluated. Operations with a higher precedence are performed before those with a lower precedence. e.g. multiplication is performed before addition. Following table is showing the precedence from highest to lowest. Which operators have same precedence, these will be evaluated from left to right.

Operator	Description
++ --- !	Increment, decrement, negation, logical NOT
* / %	Multiply, division, remainder
+ - +	Addition, subtraction, concatenation operator
<< >> >>>	Bit shifting
< <= > >=	Less than, less than or equals to, greater than, greater than or equals to
== !=, === !==	Equality, inequality, identity, non - identity
&	Binary AND
^	Binary Exclusive OR
|	Binary OR
&&	Logical AND
||	Logical OR
? :	Conditional operator
= OP =	Assignment, operation with assignment (such as, += ,& =)

13.2.8 Branching and Looping Statements

Branching and looping statements are required to control the flow of program. Branching statements are also known as **control structure.**

Branching Statements

It is very essential to execute program with respect to certain condition. Here, we will see how to use some keyword to implement program flow. Some control structures which are used in JavaScript are as follows:

(i) if Statement

The simplest and most common selection structure is the if statement. The if statement allows branching depending upon the value or state of variables. If the condition evaluates True, an action is followed otherwise, the action is ignored.

Syntax

```
if(condition)
{
    statements;
}
```

(ii) if else Statement

This statement also tests a conditional expression. If the condition is True, the entire block of statements following the if will be executed. Otherwise the entire block of statements following the else will be executed.

Syntax

```
if(condition)
{
    statements;
}
else
{
    statements;
}
```

Conditional (Ternary) operator can use in place of if...else statement. if ...else if ...else statement can use to testing the more than two situations.

```
if(condition1)
{
    statements;
}
else if(condition2)
{
    statements;
}
else
{
    statements;
}
```

(iii) switch Statement

The selection statement is provided when you have multiple branching and all decisions depend upon the value of the same variable. Multiple branch selection statements are known as **switch**. It is a replacement of a long series of if-else-if statement.

A switch statement allows a variable to be tested for equality against a list of values. Each value is called a case and the variable being switched is checked for each case value until a match is found.

Syntax

```
switch(expression)
{
    case constant1:
    statement-block1;
    break;
    case constant2:
    statement-block2;
    break;
    :
    :
    default:
    statement-block;
}
```

If none of the case expressions match with the switch expression, the **default** case block will be executed. The

12.8 ASP Operators

Operators have many purposes such as adding values, joining text strings, setting decisions on what code should be executed and more.

1. Arithmetic Operators

These operators are used to perform mathematical calculations.

Operator	Function	Example	Result
+	Addition	Num = 3+ 4	Num =7
–	Subtraction	Num = 4–1	Num =3
*	Multiplication	Num = 3*2	Num =6
/	Division	Num = 9/3	Num =3
^	Exponential	Num 2^4	Num =16
Mod	Modulus	Num = 23 Mod 10	Num =3
-	Negation	Num =-10	Num =-10
\	Integer division	Num = 9/3	Num 3

2. Comparison Operators

These operators are used to compare two values and make a decision. Comparison operator return a value either true or false.

Operator	Function	Example	Result
=	Equal to	4=3	False
<	Less than	4<3	False
>	Greater than	4>3	True
<=	Less than or equal to	4<=3	False
>=	Greater than or equal to	4>=3	True
<>	Not equal to	4<>3	True

3. Logical Operators

These operators take the result produced by comparison operators and compares them to create new true or false value.

Operator	Function	Example	Result
AND	Both must be True	True AND False	False
OR	One must be True	True OR False	True
NOT	Flips Truth value	NOT True	False
XOR	Number of TRUE inputs is odd	True XOR False	True
EQV	Both must be SAME	True EQV True	True
IMP	Return FALSE if only first operand is TRUE	True IMP False	False

4. String Operators

There is only one string operator and that is the concatenation operator "&". This operator is used to combine text strings.

Operator	English	Example	Result
&	String concatenation	string4 = "Bob" & "runs"	string4 = "Bobruns"

12.9 Function

There are various functions used in ASP are as follows:

12.9.1 Conversion Functions

These functions are used to convert to a specific format.

Function	Description
Asc	Converts the first letter in a string to ANSI code
CBool	Converts an expression to a variant of subtype Boolean
CByte	Converts an expression to a variant of subtype Byte
CDate	Converts a valid date and time expression to the variant of subtype Date
CInt	Converts an expression to a variant of subtype Integer
CIng	Converts an expression to a variant of subtype Long
CSng	Converts an expression to a variant of subtype Single
CStr	Converts an expression to a variant of subtype String

e.g.
```
If isNumeric(request.form("age")) Then
    X = CInt(request.form("age"))
End If
```

12.9.2 String Manipulation Functions

There are predefined ASP String functions, which help the developers to work with the strings very effectively. Below are String methods that are supported in ASP:

Function	Description
InStr	Returns the positions of the first occurrence of one string within another. The search begins at the first character of the string.
LCase	Converts a specified string to lowercase.
Left	Returns a specified number of characters from the left side of a string.
Len	Returns the number of characters in a string.
LTrim	Removes spaces on the left side of a string.
RTrim	Removes spaces on the right side of a string.
Trim	Removes spaces on both the left and the right side of a string.
Mid	Returns a specified number of characters from a string.
Right	Returns a specified number of characters from the right side of a string.
UCase	Converts a specified string to uppercase.

e.g.
```
If len(x)=0 Then
    response.write("It was empty!")
End If
```

12.9.3 Date/Time Functions

These functions help the developers to convert date and time from one format to another or to express the date or time value in the format that suits a specific condition.

Function	Description
Date	Returns the current system date.
Day	Returns a number that represents the day of the month (between 1 and 31, inclusive).
Hour	Returns a number that represents the hour of the day (between 0 and 23, inclusive).
Minute	Returns a number that represents the minute of the hour (between 0 and 59, inclusive).
Month	Returns a number that represents the month of the year (between 1 and 12, inclusive).
MonthName	Returns the name of specified month.
Now	Returns the current system date and time.
Second	Returns a number that represents the second of the minute (between 0 to 59, inclusive).
Time	Returns the current system time.
Year	Returns a number that represents the year.

e.g.

```
x=date()
    response.write(year(x))
```

12.10 Array

An array is a contiguous space of memory allocated for storing some data. Each memory allocation in the array is referred to as a **cell** or **index**. It is used to store multiple values in a single variable.

Types of Array

There are two types of array as follows:

1. **One Dimensional Array** The one or single dimensional array is the simplest type of array that contains only one row for storing data. It is declared with the keyword Dim.

   Syntax `Dim ArrayName(ArraySize)`

   In the above statement, ArrayName is the name of the array and ArraySize is the size of the array.

   e.g. `Dim Names(2)`

   In this example, number shows in the parentheses is 2. We start at zero so this array contains 3 elements. It is a fixed-size array. You can assign data to each of the elements of the array:

   ```
   Names(0) = "Tove"
   Names(1) = "John"
   Names(2) = "Stale"
   ```

   Similarly, the data can be retrieved from any element using the index of the particular array element you want:

   ```
   mother=Names(0)
   ```

2. **Two Dimensional Array** 2D arrays are generally known as **matrix.** Like a 1D array, 2D array is a collection of data cells, all of the same type, which can be given a single name.

   However, a 2D array is organised with a number of rows and columns.

   Syntax `Dim ArrayName (No_of_rows, No_of_columns)`

   e.g. `Dim Names(2,2)`

   Here, a 2D array Names consisting of 3 rows and 3 columns.

Assign data to 2 D array

```
Names(0, 0) = "Volvo"
Names(0, 1) = "BMW"
Names(0, 2) = "Ford"
Names(1, 0) = "Apple"
Names(1, 1) = "Orange"
Names(1, 2) = "Banana"
Names(2, 0) = "Coke"
Names(2, 1) = "Pepsi"
Names(2, 2) = "Frooti"
```

12.11 Conditional Statements

Conditional statements are used to perform different actions for different decisions. In ASP, we have four conditional statements:

1. If Statement

It executes a set of code when a condition is true. If you want to execute only one statement when a condition is true, you can write the code on one line.

e.g.

```
If i = 10 Then
    response.write("Hello")
```

In this example, you just tell the code to perform one action if a condition is true.

If you want to execute more than one statement when a condition is true, you must put each statement on separate lines and end the statement with the keyword "End If":

e.g.

```
If i = 10 Then
    response. write("Hello")
    i = i + 1
End If
```

In this example, you just tell the code to perform multiple actions if the condition is true.

(a) **new Array ()** By this, we can create an array without declare its size.

Syntax

```
var array_name = new Array[];
```

(b) **new Array** (size) By this, we can create an array with declare its size.

Syntax

```
var array_name = new Array[array_size];
```

(c) **new Array** (element1, element2, ... elementN) By this, we can create array as well as declare its different elements. This array is also known as dense array. In this, element1, element2,... elementN are saved elements in array.

Syntax

```
var array_name = new Array[value1, .... value N];
```

(ii) **Two Dimensional Array** JavaScript does not support multidimensional array but you can use two dimensional array to making array of arrays.

Syntax

```
var array_name = new Array [row_size]
                                    [column_size];
```

or

```
var array_name = new Array [row_size, column_size];
```

13.2.10 JavaScript Strings

A JavaScript string stores a series of characters like "John Doe". A string can be any text inside double or single quotes.

e.g.

```
var carname = "Volvo XC60";
var carname = 'Volvo XC60';
```

String indexes are zero-based: The first character is in position 0, the second in 1 and so on.

13.2.11 JavaScript Objects, Methods and Properties

JavaScript is used to manipulate or get information about objects in the HTML DOM. Objects in an HTML page have methods (actions, such as opening a new window or submitting a form) and properties (attributes or qualities, such as color and size).

e.g.

```
<html>
    <head>
        <title>JavaScript Page</title>
        <link href="style.css" rel="stylesheet"
                                    type="text/css">
        <script type="text/javascript">
            //Pop up an alert
            window.alert("The page is loading");
        </script>
    </head>
    <body>
        <p>
            <span onclick="document.bgColor
                        = 'red';"> Red</span>
            <span onclick="document.bgColor
                        = 'white';"> White</span>
            <span onclick="document.bgColor
                        = 'green';"> Green</span>
            <span onclick="document.bgColor
                        = 'blue';"> Blue</span>
        </p>
        <script type="text/javascript"
                        src="script-2.js"></script>
    </body>
</html>
```

Methods

Methods are the verbs of JavaScript. They cause things to happen.

(i) **window.alert()** HTML pages are read and processed from top to bottom. Above JavaScript calls the alert() method of the window object. When the browser reads that line of code, it will pop up an alert box and will not continue processing the page until the user presses the OK button. Once the user presses the OK button, the alert box will disappear and the rest of the page loads.

(ii) **document.write()** The write() method of the document object is used to write out code to the page as it loads. It is more often used to write out dynamic data, such as the date and time on the user's machine.

Arguments

Methods can take zero or more arguments separated by commas.

Syntax

```
object.method(argument1, argument2);
```

The alert() and write() methods shown in the above example, each take only one argument: the message to show or the HTML to write out to the browser.

Properties

Properties are the adjectives of JavaScript. They describe qualities of objects and in some cases are writable (can be changed dynamically).

(i) **document.bgColor** The bgColor property of the document object is read-write. In above example, the four span elements use the onclick event handler to catch click events. When the user clicks on a span, JavaScript is used to change the value of the bgColor property to a new color.

The bgColor property of document is deprecated, meaning it should not be used anymore. Instead, document.body.style.backgroundColor should be used to change the background color of the page. However, we do not get to the style property in this course, so we use bgColor for learning purposes. In practice, you can substitute document.body.style.backgroundColor for document.bgColor.

(ii) **The Implicit Window Object** The window object is always the implicit top-level object and therefore does not have to be included in references to objects. e.g. window.document.write() can be shortened to document.write(). Likewise, window.alert() can be shortened to just alert().

13.2.12 Event Handling

JavaScript's interaction with HTML is handled through events that occur when the user or the browser manipulates a page. When the page loads, it is called an **event**. When the user clicks a button, that click too is an event. Other examples include events like pressing any key, closing a window, resizing a window etc.

Some common event handler with their description are as follows:

Event Handler	Description
onclick	a pointer button was clicked
ondblclick	a pointer button was double clicked
onkeypress	a key was pressed and released
onmousedown	a pointer button was pressed down
onmousemove	a pointer was moved within
onmouseout	a pointer was moved away
onmouseover	a pointer was moved onto
onmouseup	a pointer button was released
onreset	the form was reset
onselect	some text was selected
onsubmit	the form was submitted

e.g.

```
<html>
    <head>
        <script type="text/javascript">
        <!--
            function sayHello()
            {
                alert("Hello World")
            }
            //-->
        </script>
        </head>
    <body>
        <p>Click the following button and see
                                            result</p>
        <form>
            <input type="button"
                                        onclick="sayHello()"
                                        value="Say Hello" />
        </form>
    </body>
</html>
```

13.2.13 The Window Object

The window object represents a window in browser. An object of window is created automatically by the browser. Window is the object of browser, it is not the object of JavaScript. The JavaScript objects are string, array, date etc.

Methods

Methods	Description
alert()	Displays the alert box containing message with OK button.
confirm()	Displays the confirm dialog box containing message with OK and Cancel button.
prompt()	Displays a dialog box to get input from the user.
open()	Opens the new window.
close()	Closes the current window.
setTimeout()	Performs action after specified time like calling function, evaluating expressions etc.

13.2.14 Document Object Model

The document object, represents the whole HTML document. When HTML document is loaded in the browser, it becomes a document object. It is the root element that represents the HTML document. It has properties and methods. By the help of document object, we can add dynamic content to our web page.

Properties

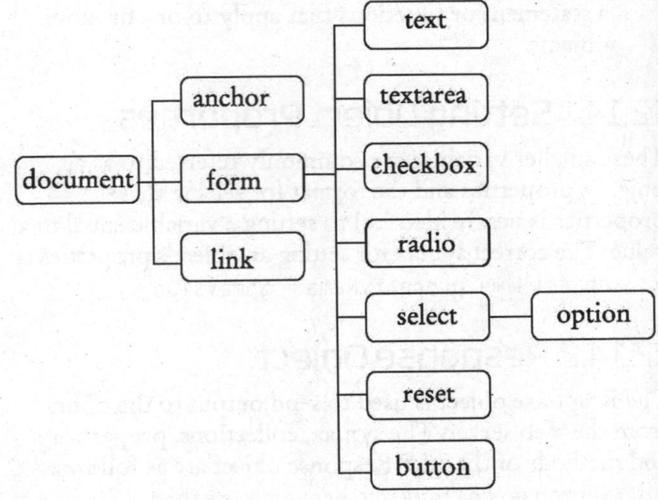

There are six main objects in ASP object model:

1. **Response Object** This object is used to send responses to the request made by the user's browser.
2. **Request Object** This object handles all the requests from the user, including data from cookies, forms and security certifications.
3. **Application Object** This object can be used to share some information among several clients who are visiting same group of pages.
4. **Session Object** This object holds the information that is unique to specific user's current session on the web server and hence different instances are created for different sessions.
5. **Server Object** This object provides an access to the server itself, i.e. to incorporate some of server's own functionality into the ASPs.
6. **ASP Error Object** This object can be used to receive error information about an error that is present in the scripts.

These objects are known as the **Intrinsic ASP Object**. They are built-in and do not require additional files. Each of the objects can contain properties, collection, events and methods:

1. **Properties Store an Object-Specific Value** A property is an attribute of an object to which a value can be assigned. The properties of this object would be Min, Max and Current.
2. **Collections are Containers that hold Objects** A collection is an object that contains the other object, i.e. object in the collection will have some relation to each other that contains.
3. **Events let Objects Respond to Specific Action** An event results in an action.
4. **Methods are Executable Functions** A method is like a statement or functions that apply to one or more objects.

12.14.1 Setting Object Properties

These smaller variables are commonly referred to as an object's properties and the format for setting these properties is nearly identical to setting a variable equal to a value. The correct syntax for setting an object's properties is

```
objectName.propertyName = SomeValue
```

12.14.2 Response Object

The Response object is used to send output to the client from the web server. The syntax, collections, properties and methods of the ASP Response object are as follows:

```
Response.collection|property|method
```

1. Collection

Collection	Description
Cookies	Sets a cookie value. If the cookie does not exist, it will be created and take the value that is specified.

2. Properties

Properties	Description
Buffer	Specifies whether to buffer the page output or not.
Charset	Appends the name of a character-set to the content type header in the Response object.
ContentType	Sets the HTTP content type for the Response object.
Status	Specifies the value of the status line returned by the server.

3. Methods

Methods	Description
AddHeader	Adds a new HTTP header and a value to the HTTP response.
AppendToLog	Adds a string to the end of the server log entry.
BinaryWrite	Writes data directly to the output without any character conversion.
Clear	Clears any buffered HTML output.
End	Stops processing a script and returns the current result.
Flush	Sends buffered HTML output immediately.
Write	Writes a specified string to the output.

12.14.3 Request Object

The Request object retrieves the values that the client browser passed to the server during an HTTP request. It is used to get information from the user. The syntax, collections, properties and methods of the ASP Request object are as follows:

```
Request[.collection|property|method]
                                  (variable)
```

1. Collections

Collections	Description
ClientCertificate	Contains all the field values stored in the client certificate.
Cookies	Contains all the cookie values sent in a HTTP request.
Form	Contains all the form (input) values from a form that uses the post method.
QueryString	Contains all the variable values in a HTTP query string.
ServerVariables	Contains all the server variable values.

2. Property

Property	Description
TotalBytes	Returns the total number of bytes the client sent in the body of the request.

3. Method

Method	Description
BinaryRead	Retrieves the data sent to the server from the client as part of a post request and stores it in a safe array.

12.14.4 Application Object

An ASP application is actually collection of ASP files in a virtual directory and associated sub-directories. The Application object is used to control and manage all items that are available to all users of an Active Server application.

The Application object is initialised by IIS when the first .asp page from within the given virtual directory is requested. It remains in the server's memory until either the web service is stopped or the application is explicitly unloaded from the web server (using the Microsoft Management Console). The syntax, collections, methods and events of the ASP Application object are as follows:

```
Application.method
```

1. Collection

Collection	Description
Contents	Contain all the items appended to the application through a script command.

2. Methods

Methods	Description
Contents.Remove	Deletes an item from the Contents collection.
Contents.RemoveAll()	Deletes all items from the Contents collection.
Lock	Prevents other users from modifying the variables in the Application object.
Unlock	Enables other users to modify the variables in the Application object (after it has been locked using the Lock method).

3. Events

Events	Description
Application_OnEnd	Occurs when all user sessions are over and the application ends.
Application_OnStart	Occurs before the first new session is created (when the Application object is first referenced).

12.15 ASP Components

Like the built-in objects, ASP components can be used to extend the power of your scripts. Components differ from the built-in objects because they are typically used for more specialised tasks.

Some of the components bundled with ASP are as follows:

1. **AD Rotator** It is used to display banner advertisements on the web pages of a website. You can use this to specify how frequently different banner advertisements should be displayed.
2. **Content Rotator** It enables you to rotate through HTML content on a page. e.g. you can use the component to randomly display different announcements on the home page of your website.
3. **Counters** It can be used to keep track of the number of visitors to your website. You can use this components to add a hit counter to a web page.
4. **Page Counter** It is exactly like the counter, in that it can be used to track the number of visitors and to add a hit counter to particular web page.
5. **Permission Checker** It can be used to display links to web pages only to those users who have permission to see them. You can use this component to create web pages that can be viewed only by the administrators of a website.

12.16 TextStream Object

The TextStream object provides sequential access to the contents of text files. This allows you to read, write or append characters or lines to a text file.

The properties and methods of TextStream object are as follows:

1. Properties

Properties	Description
AtEndOfLine	Returns true if the file pointer is positioned immediately before the end-of-line marker in a TextStream file and false if not.
AtEndOfStream	Returns true if the file pointer is at the end of a TextStream file and false if not.
Column	Returns the column number of the current character position in an input stream.
Line	Returns the current line number in a TextStream file.

2. Methods

Methods	Description
Close	Closes an open TextStream file.
Read	Reads a specified number of characters from a TextStream file and returns the result.
ReadAll	Reads an entire TextStream file and returns the result.
ReadLine	Reads one line from a TextStream file and returns the results.
Write	Writes a specified text to a TextStream file.

13.2.23 Password Object

The password field (<input type="password">) within your form can be accessed and manipulated using JavaScript *via* the corresponding Password object.

Properties

Properties	Description
disabled	Boolean value that sets/ returns whether the field is disabled.
form	References the form that contains the password field.
name	Reflects the name of the password field (the name attribute).
type	A property available on all form elements, "type" returns the type of the calling form element, in this case, "password".
value	A read/write string that specifies the value of the password field. Note that due to security reasons, some browsers may not return the actual value of the password when this property is invoked.

Methods

Methods	Description
blur()	Removes focus away from the password field.
focus()	Sets focus on the password field.
select()	Selects the input area of the password field.

13.2.24 Text Object

Text fields (<input type="text">) within your form can be accessed and manipulated using JavaScript, *via* the corresponding Text object.

Properties

Properties	Description
accessKey	String value that sets/ returns the accessKey for the field.
disabled	Boolean value that sets/ returns whether the field is disabled.
form	References the form that contains the text field.
name	Reflects the name of the text field (the name attribute).
type	A property available on all form elements, "type" returns the type of the calling form element, in this case, "text".
value	Read/write string that specifies the value of the text field.

Methods

Methods	Description
blur()	Removes focus away from the text field.
focus()	Sets focus on the text field.
select()	Highlights the content of the text field.

13.2.25 TextArea Object

Textareas (<textarea> </textarea>) within your form can be accessed, validated and manipulated using JavaScript, *via* the corresponding Textarea object.

Properties

Properties	Description
accessKey	String value that sets/ returns the accessKey for the field.
disabled	Boolean value that sets/ returns whether the field is disabled.
form	References the form that contains the textarea.
name	Reflects the name of the textarea (the name attribute).
type	A property available on all form elements, "type" returns the type of the calling form element, in this case, "Textarea".
value	Read/write string that specifies the value of the textarea.

Methods

Methods	Description
blur()	Removes focus away from the textarea.
focus()	Sets focus on the textarea.
select()	Highlights the content of the textarea.

13.2.26 Date Object

The Date object is used to work with dates and times. Date objects are created with new Date().

Property

Property	Description
prototype	Use this property to attach additional properties and/or methods that get reflected in all instances of the Date object.

Methods

Methods	Description
getFullYear()	Returns year in full 4 digit format (i.e. 2004).
getYear()	Returns the year, in 4 digit format or otherwise depending on browser. Deprecated in favor of getFullYear().
getMonth()	Returns the month. (Range is 0-11)
getDate()	Returns the day of the month (Range is 1-31)
getDay()	Returns the day of the week (Range is 0-6). 0=Sunday, 1=Monday etc.
getHours()	Returns the hour (Range is 0-23).
getMinutes()	Returns the minutes. (Range is 0-59).
getSeconds()	Returns the seconds. (Range is 0-59).
getMilliseconds()	Returns the milliseconds. (Range is 0-999).
getTime()	Returns the millisecond representation of the current Date object. In the words, the number of milliseconds between 1/1/1970 (GMT) and the current Date object.

CHAPTER PRACTICE

1. Why is a scripting language called a scripting language?

(1) Scripting languages, like JavaScript and VBScript are designed as an extension to XML.
(2) Scripting languages, like JavaScript and VBScript are designed as an extension to XHTML.
(3) Scripting languages, like JavaScript and VBScript are designed as an extension to HTML.
(4) Scripting languages, like JavaScript and VBScript are designed as an extension to DHTML.

2. Which of the following is true about VBScript?

(1) VBScript is an object-based scripting language and NOT an object-oriented programming language.
(2) VBScript uses Component Object Model (COM) in order to access the elements of the environment in which it is executing.
(3) VBScript is a case-insensitive language.
(4) All of the above

3. What is the output of A + B in VBScript if A = 5 and B = 10?

(1) 15 (2) 510
(3) 5 (4) 2

4. Which of the following is true about time value assignment in VBScript?

(1) The time values should be assigned without double quotes.
(2) The time values should be enclosed within double quotes (" ").
(3) The time values should be enclosed within hash symbol (#).
(4) The time values should be assigned within single quotes.

5. Which of the following is true about VBScript?

(1) Microsoft VBScript (Visual Basic Script) is a general-purpose, lightweight and active scripting language developed by Microsoft that is modeled on Visual Basic.
(2) VBScript is the primary scripting language for Quick Test Professional (QTP), which is a test automaton tool.
(3) VBScript, for the most part, is case insensitive. It has a very simple syntax, easy to learn and to implement.
(4) All of the above

6. What is the scope of a constant declared using Public in VBScript?

(1) The Public constants are available for all the scripts and procedures.
(2) The Public constants are available within the procedure or class.
(3) The Public constants are available within the procedure only.
(4) None of the above

7. What is the output of A & B in VBScript if A = "VB" and B = "Script"?

(1) VBScript (2) Error
(3) VB (4) Script

8. Which of the following is a valid scope in VBScript?

(1) Dim (2) Public
(3) Private (4) All of these

9. Which of the following is a correct way to declare array in VBScript?

(1) Dim arr1()
(2) Dim arr2(5)
(3) Dim arr3 = Array ("apple", "Orange", "Grapes")
(4) All of the above

10. Which of the following is correct about subprocedures in VBScript?

(1) Sub procedures do not return a value while functions may or may not return a value.
(2) Sub procedures can be called without call keyword.
(3) Sub procedures are always enclosed within Sub and End Sub statements.
(4) All of the above

11. Which of the following is true about numeric value assignment in VBScript?

(1) The numeric values should be assigned without double quotes.
(2) The numeric values should be enclosed within double quotes (" ").
(3) The numeric values should be enclosed within hash symbol (#).
(4) None of the above

12. What is the scope of a constant declared using Private in VBScript?

(1) The Private constants are available for all the scripts and procedures.
(2) The Private constants are available within the procedure or class.
(3) The Private constants are available only for one scripts.
(4) All of the above

13. Which of the following is true about string value assignment in VBScript?

(1) The string values should be assigned without double quotes.
(2) The string values should be enclosed within double quotes (" ").
(3) The string values should be enclosed within hash symbol (#).
(4) The string values should be enclosed within single quotes.

14. Which of the following operator can be used to do an XOR operation in VBScript?

(1) ~ (2) ^ (3) XOR (4) &

15. Which of the following keyword is used to declare a variable in VBScript?

(1) variant (2) var
(3) Dim (4) public

16. Which of the following operator can be used to get the exponent of two numbers in VBScript?

(1) EXP (2) ^
(3) EXPONENT (4) ~

17. Which statement is true for VBScript names, e.g. variable names or procedure names?

(1) They are case sensitive.
(2) They are case insensitive.
(3) They are case insensitive but should be written consistently for readability.
(4) Only variable names are case insensitive.

18. What is the datatype of a variable in VBScript?

(1) String
(2) Variant
(3) It is the datatype specified when that variable is declared.
(4) Integer

```
If err <> 0 Then
    response.write
              ("No update permissions!")
Else
    response.write ("<h3>" &
    recaffacted &" record added </h3>")
End If
conn.close
%>
</body>
</html>
```

4. Update /Modify a Record in a Table

We may use the SQL UPDATE command to update a record in a table in a database. We want to update a record in the Students table in the wind database. We first create a table that lists all records in the Students table:

```
<html>
  <body>
  <%
    set conn=Server.CreateObject
                    ("ADODB.Connection")
    conn.Provider="Microsoft.Jet.OLEDB.4.0"
    conn.Open "C:/webdata/wind.mdb"
    set rs = Server.CreateObject
                    ("ADODB.Recordset")
    rs.open "SELECT * FROM Students", conn
  %>
  <h2>List Database</h2>
  <table border="1" width="100%">
    <tr>
    <%
    For Each x in rs.Fields
        response.write("<th>" &
                 ucase(x.name) &"</th>")
    Next
    %>
    </tr>
    <% Do Until rs.EOF %>
    <tr>
    <form method = "post"
           action="demo_update.asp">
    <%
    For Each x in rs.Fields
      If lcase(x.name)=
                "studentrollno" Then%>
        <td>
          <input type="submit" name
                    ="StudentRollNo"
          value ="<%=x.value%>">
        </td>
    <%Else%>
        <td><%response.write(x.value)%></td>
    <%End If
    Next
    %>
    </form>
    <%rs.MoveNext%>
    </tr>
    <%
      Loop
      conn.close
    %>
  </table>
  </body>
</html>
```

If the user clicks on the button in the "StudentRollNo" column he or she will be taken to a new file called "demo_update.asp". The "demo_update.asp" file contains the source code on how to create input fields based on the fields from one record in the database table. It also contains a "Update record" button that will save your changes:

```
<html>
  <body>
  <h2>Update Record</h2>
  <%
    set conn=Server.CreateObject
                    ("ADODB.Connection")
    conn.Provider
          ="Microsoft.Jet.OLEDB.4.0"
    conn.Open "C:/webdata/wind.mdb"
    cid=Request.Form("StudentRollNo")
    If Request.form("schoolname")="" Then
    set rs=Server.CreateObject
                    ("ADODB.Recordset")
    rs.open "SELECT * FROM customers
  WHERE StudentRollNo=" & cid & "'",conn
  %>
  <form method="post" action
              ="demo_update.asp">
  <table>
    <%For Each x in rs.Fields%>
      <tr>
        <td><%=x.name%></td>
        <td><input name
              ="<%=x.name%>" value
              ="<%=x.value%>"></td>
    <%Next%>
    </tr>
  </table>
  <br><br>
  <input type="submit"
              value="Update record">
  </form>
  <%
```

```
        Else
            sql="UPDATE Students SET "
            sql=sql & "schoolname='" &
                    Request.Form("schoolname") & "',"
            sql=sql & "studentname='" &
                  Request.Form("studentname") & "',"
            sql=sql & " WHERE StudentRollNo ='" &
                                          cid & "'"
            on error resume next
            conn.Execute sql
            If err<>0 Then
                response.write
                        ("No update permissions!")
            Else
                response.write("Record " & cid & "
                                       was updated!")
            End If
        End If
        conn.close
        %>
        </body>
    </html>
```

12.18 ASP ServerVariables

The ServerVariables collection is used to retrieve the server variable values.

Syntax

```
Request.ServerVariables(server environment variable)
```

Parameter

Server environment variable It specifies the name of the server environment variable to retrieve. It can be one of the following values:

Variable	Description
HTTP_USER_AGENT	Returns a string describing the browser that sent the request.
REMOTE_ADDR	Returns the IP address of the remote host making the request.
REMOTE_HOST	Returns the name of the host making the request.
SERVER_NAME	Returns the server's host name, DNS alias or IP address as it would appear in self-referencing URLs.

Examples

The following examples uses the Request object to display several server variables:

You are browsing this site with:

```
<%= Request.ServerVariables("HTTP_USER_AGENT")%>
```

Your IP address is:

```
<%= Request.ServerVariables("remote_addr")%>
```

The DNS lookup of the IP address is:

```
<%= Request.ServerVariables("remote_host")%>
```

The server's domain name:

```
<%= Request.ServerVariables("server_name")%>
```

60. **What should appear at the very end of your JavaScript?**
The <script language ="JavaScript" > tag
(1) The </script>
(2) The <script>
(3) The END statement
(4) None of the above

61. (i) `var arr = "Quality Point";`
(ii) `var arr1 = new String ("Quality Point");`

In JavaScript, which of the above Statement can used for string declaration?
(1) Either (i) or (ii)
(2) Only (i)
(3) Neither (i) nor (ii)
(4) Only (ii)

62. **Which of the following is not a valid JavaScript variable name?**
(1) 2names
(2) _first_and_last_names
(3) FirstAndLast
(4) Name5

63. **......... tag is an extension to HTML that can enclose any number of JavaScript statements.**
(1) <script> (2) <body>
(3) <head> (4) <title>

64. **Which of the following attribute can hold the JavaScript version?**
(1) language (2) script
(3) version (4) ver

65. **What is the correct JavaScript syntax to write "Hello World"?**
(1) System.out.println("Hello World")
(2) println(" Hello World")
(3) document.write("Hello World")
(4) response.write("Hello World")

66. **Which of the following way can be used to indicate the language attribute?**
(1) <language = "javascriptversion " >
(2) <script language = "javascript Version">
(3) <script language = "javascript Version"> JavaScript statements ... </script>
(4) <script language = "javascript Version" > JavaScript statements...... < / script >

67. (i) //, /* .... **/
(ii) /, /** .... /, /*
(iii) /* .... */, //
(iv) * .... *\, //

In JavaScript, which of the above comments lines are used?
(1) Only (iv)
(2) Only (iii)
(3) Either (iii) or (iv)
(4) Only (ii)

68. **Which is the correct way to write a JavaScript array?**
(1) var txt = new Array(1:"tim", 2:"kim", 3:"jim")
(2) var txt = new Array:1=("tim") 2=("kim") 3=("jim")
(3) var txt = new Array("tim","kim","jim")
(4) var txt = new Array="tim","kim","jim"

69. **Which of the following is not considered a JavaScript operator?**
(1) new (2) this
(3) delete (4) typeof

70. **Which of the following event fires when the form element loses the focus: <button>, <input>, <label>, <select>, <textarea>?**
(1) onfocus (2) onblur
(3) onclick (4) ondblclick

71. **Using ...... statement is how you test for a specific condition.**
(1) Select (2) If
(3) Switch (4) For

72. **Which of the following is the structure of an if statement?**
(1) if (conditional expression is true) then execute this code end if
(2) if (conditional expression is true)execute this code end if
(3) if (conditional expression is true) {then execute this code>->}
(4) if (conditional expression is true) then {execute this code}

73. **If x = 103 and y = 9, then x%= y, what is the value of x after executing x%= y?**
(1) 4 (2) 3
(3) 2 (4) 5

74. **The syntax of a blur method in a button object is ....**
(1) blur () (2) blur(contrast)
(3) blur(value) (4) blur(depth)

75. **Which of the followng is true?**
(1) If onkeyDown returns false, the key press event is cancelled.
(2) If onKeyPress returns false, the key down event is cancelled.
(3) If onKeyDown returns false, the key-up event is cancelled.
(4) If onKeyPress returns false, the key-up event is cancelled.

76.
```
<script type="text/javascript">
  x=4+"4";
  document.write(x);
</script>
```
Output------ ?
(1) 44 (2) 8
(3) 4 (4) Error output

77.
```
<script language="javascript">
function x()
{document.write(2+5+"8");
</script>}
```
Output ....?
(1) 258 (2) Error
(3) 7 (4) 78

78. **Which of the following is true about typeof operator in JavaScript?**
(1) The typeof is a unary operator that is placed before its single operand, which can be of any type.
(2) Its value is a string indicating the data type of the operand.
(3) Both of the above
(4) None of the above

79. **Which built-in method calls a function for each element in the array?**
(1) while( )
(2) loop( )
(3) For Each( )
(4) None of the above

80. **Study the code given below:**
```
<html>
  <head>
    <script language
            = "JavaScript">
      function Test()
      {
          alert("checked")
      }
    </script></head>
    <body onLoad = "Test()">
    <H2>Guess the condition
    </H2>
  </body>
</html>
```
How many times will the function Test() be called?
(1) Once every time the system starts
(2) Once every time the web page is refreshed
(3) Only once when the window is opened
(4) will not be called as the event handler is wrong.

81. Which of the following methods in JavaScript will display a window having a dialog box with a specified message alongwith an OK and a CANCEL button as options?

(1) prompt( )
(2) alert( )
(3) confirm( )
(4) request( )

82. Consider the following statements will respect to JavaScript:

(i) A variable is created using the var keyword
(ii) JavaScript is untyped language

Which of the above are true?

(1) Neither (i) nor (ii)
(2) Only (i)
(3) Only (ii)
(4) Both (i) and (ii)

83.
```
<script type =
"text/javascript" language
            = "JavaScript">
var arr = new Array();
arr[0] = "webDevelopment";
arr[1] = "HTML";
arr[2] = "Testing";
arr[3] = "Technology";
document.write(arr[0,1,2,3])
</script>
```
What is the output of the above code snippet?

(1) Error
(2) Technology
(3) WebDevelopment
(4) WebDevelopment, HTML, Testing, Technology

84.
```
<script type =
"text/javascript" language =
" javascript">
arr = ((45%2)==0)?"Hello" :
"Bye"
document.write (arr);
</script>
```
What is the output of the above code snippet?

(1) Hello
(2) Bye
(3) error in string handing
(4) None of the above

85. The statement (a == b) refers to

(1) Both a and b are equal in value
(2) Both a and b are equal in value and type
(3) Both a and b are equal in value, type and reference address.
(4) None of the above

86. Which of the following is a JavaScript data type?

(1) Null (2) Undefined
(3) Object (4) All of these

87. Which of the following is not a JavaScript data type?

(1) Boolean (2) String
(3) Number (4) Function

88. What is the output? X = 1001/"Mango";

(1) null (2) NaN
(3) undefined (4) infinity

89. Which is the correct order of precedence of arithmetic operators?

(1) + / * – b * / + –
(3) + – * / (4) + * – /

90. Identify the statement that is equivalent to the given statement: `document.write("Hello")`

(1) window.document.write ("Hello")
(2) body.document.write ("Hello")
(3) location.document.write ("Hello")
(4) document.writeln ("Hello")

91. Among the following, which one is a ternary operator?

(1) + (2) :
(3) – (4) ?:

92. A statement block is a

(1) conditional block
(2) block that contains a single statement.
(3) Both (1) and (2)
(4) block that combines multiple statements into a single compound statement.

93. The "var" and "function" are

(1) keywords
(2) declaration statements
(3) data types
(4) prototypes

94. JavaScript entities start with …… and end with …… .

(1) semicolon, colon
(2) semicolon, ampersand
(3) ampersand, colon
(4) ampersand, semicolon

95. A function definition expression can be called

(1) function prototype
(2) function literal
(3) function definition
(4) function declaration

ANSWER KEY

1	(3)	2	(4)	3	(1)	4	(3)	5	(4)	6	(1)	7	(1)	8	(4)	9	(4)	10	(4)
11	(1)	12	(2)	13	(2)	14	(3)	15	(3)	16	(2)	17	(3)	18	(2)	19	(3)	20	(1)
21	(4)	22	(2)	23	(3)	24	(1)	25	(3)	26	(1)	27	(2)	28	(4)	29	(4)	30	(1)
31	(1)	32	(3)	33	(2)	34	(4)	35	(3)	36	(4)	37	(1)	38	(3)	39	(4)	40	(3)
41	(1)	42	(2)	43	(2)	44	(4)	45	(1)	46	(1)	47	(2)	48	(3)	49	(1)	50	(3)
51	(2)	52	(2)	53	(1)	54	(4)	55	(1)	56	(2)	57	(3)	58	(1)	59	(1)	60	(1)
61	(4)	62	(1)	63	(1)	64	(1)	65	(3)	66	(3)	67	(2)	68	(3)	69	(2)	70	(2)
71	(2)	72	(3)	73	(1)	74	(1)	75	(1)	76	(1)	77	(4)	78	(3)	79	(3)	80	(3)
81	(1)	82	(4)	83	(2)	84	(2)	85	(2)	86	(4)	87	(4)	88	(2)	89	(2)	90	(4)
91	(4)	92	(4)	93	(2)	94	(4)	95.	(4)										

46. To add two strings, you can use which of the following operator in ASP?
(1) Add (2) Two
(3) Concatenation (4)Joint

47. Use this function to return a value using a currency symbol as up on your system.
(1) Currency
(2) FormatCurrency
(3) Symbol
(4) Format

48. ....is considered to be one of the foundations of data access in the Microsoft world.
(1) ODBC
(2) OLE DB
(3) JPCD
(4) ADO

49. In OLEDB, which of the following represents characteristics of the recordset abstraction?
(1) Properties
(2) Collections
(3) Methods
(4) Abstractions

50. Using ...... as the data provider, you can obtain from source such as Access, Orcale, Sybase or DB2.
(1) OLEDB
(2) SQLClient for SQLServer
(3) ODBC
(4) Oracle

51. Which selection process is an example of multiple branches from a single expression?
(1) If…Then
(2) Select Case
(3) Do… Loop
(4) For… Next

52. How many times is the test expression of a Select Case evaluated?
(1) 0
(2) 1
(3) Once for each Case.
(4) It depends on the value of the test expression.

53. What happens in a Select Case construct when a test value matches the test expression?
(1) The corresponding block of statements is run.
(2) The next Case test value is checked.
(3) The Case Else statement is run.
(4) The Select Case construct is exited.

54. My ASP page won't work is a common complaint for those new to ASP. Which of these can be the cause?
(1) Syntax error such as missing parentheses, comma or quotation mark.
(2) Comments in your code are not tagged properly as comments.
(3) Make sure function names have both opening and closing parentheses.
(4) All of the above

55. You need to store state data that is accessible to any user who connects to your web application. Which object should you use?
(1) Session
(2) Application
(3) Response.ViewState
(4) Response.Cookies

56. You have determined that your company's website is housed on a web server that cannot handle ASP. What would you do?
(1) Contact the ISP and have them switch the website to have ASP capability.
(2) Have your ISP install the Microsoft FrontPage extensions
(3) Develop a transition plan first that includes a step-by-step plan on every detail prior to contacting the ISP.
(4) All of the above

57. Variable are used to hold both numerical and text values. Which of the following is not a valid variable name?
(1) X
(2) X1
(3) 1X
(4) x1X

58. ....is a simple object model that is easier to understand and use than OLEDB and is frequently used for database applications.
(1) ASP
(2) XML
(3) ODBC
(4) ADO

59. A doctor's office uses a database to store information about each of the patients. All of the information about a patient is stored in a ....
(1) file in the database
(2) record in the database table
(3) field in the database table
(4) key field

60. Which Do...Loop statement should be used to process test scores where a test score over 100 is a signal to stop the processing?
(1) Do While Score > 100
(2) Do Until Score > 100
(3) Loop While Score > 100
(4) Loop Until Score > 100

61. If one has two different web form controls in a application and if one wanted to know whether the values in the above two different web form control match what control must be used?
(1) DataList
(2) GridView
(3) CompareValidator
(4) Listview

62. Suppose one wants to modify a SOAP message in a SOAP extension then how this can be achieved. Choose the correct option from below:
(1) One must override the method ReceiveMessage
(2) One must override the method InitializeMethod
(3) Both (1) and (2)
(4) One must override the method ProcessMessage

63. If I'm developing an application that must accommodate multiple security levels though secure login and my ASP.NET web application is spanned across three web-servers (using round-robin load balancing) what would be the best approach to maintain login-in state for the users?
(1) Maintain the login state security through a database.
(2) Maintain the login state security through a Session.
(3) Maintain the login state security through a View State.
(4) All of the above

64. Some say that JavaScript is easier to use than ASP and will run regardless of whatever operating system the web server is using Unix, Linux, Windows 2000 etc. Then others say that ASP has advantages over JavaScript such as what?
(1) ASP does not depend upon which browser the viewer is using.

(2) ASP code does not show up in the source code; thus, the code is protected.
(3) ASP can easily interact with a database.
(4) All of the above

65. You have a long piece of code tracking employee salaries. In your opinion, which of these variables is the best (shortest yet most descriptive) to use throughout the code to track the salaries of the managers? Keep in mind that you may try to analyse your

(1) manager_salaries
(2) SalariesOfManagers
(3) Salaries_Of_Managers
(4) mgmtSalary

66. Which of the following is the common property of web server controls that assigns a small piece of text when a mouse pointer is held over the control for a short period of time?

(1) Accesskey
(2) ToolTip
(3) skinID
(4) TabIndex

67. You are creating a project which stores small amount of frequently changing information about a page on the client. Which is the best method to use?

(1) Cookie
(2) Query String
(3) Hidden Form Field
(4) None of the above

68. An organisation has developed a web service in which the values of the forms are validated using ASP application. Suppose this web service is got and used by a customer then in such a scenario which of the following is TRUE?

(1) Such a situation cannot happen at all
(2) The customer must be having technology that run ASP.
(3) The customer can run on any platform.
(4) None of the above

ANSWER KEY

1	(2)	**2**	(1)	**3**	(4)	**4**	(4)	**5**	(2)	**6**	(1)	**7**	(3)	**8**	(2)	**9**	(4)	**10**	(2)
11	(3)	**12**	(1)	**13**	(2)	**14**	(1)	**15**	(1)	**16**	(4)	**17**	(4)	**18**	(4)	**19**	(4)	**20**	(3)
21	(2)	**22**	(3)	**23**	(2)	**24**	(4)	**25**	(1)	**26**	(4)	**27**	(1)	**28**	(1)	**29**	(3)	**30**	(1)
31	(4)	**32**	(3)	**33**	(3)	**34**	(1)	**35**	(4)	**36**	(3)	**37**	(3)	**38**	(2)	**39**	(4)	**40**	(2)
41	(4)	**42**	(1)	**43**	(3)	**44**	(3)	**45**	(4)	**46**	(3)	**47**	(2)	**48**	(2)	**49**	(1)	**50**	(1)
51	(2)	**52**	(2)	**53**	(1)	**54**	(4)	**55**	(2)	**56**	(3)	**57**	(3)	**58**	(4)	**59**	(2)	**60**	(2)
61	(3)	**62**	(1)	**63**	(1)	**64**	(4)	**65**	(4)	**66**	(2)	**67**	(1)	**68**	(3)				

items on the artwork are very important both from the outlook of the design and its appeal.

9. Color Harmony

Which color goes with which color, it is very important to know. The combination of colors should be such that the whole product does not hide below the color.

10. Unity

Whichever way user choose to have the text and graphics placed on the artwork, they should compliment each other in such a way that the artwork should look like one piece not standing alone, they should have unity among them.

11. Balance

The items on the artwork should balance themselves. They should compliment each other and not reject or over shadow each other.

12. Proportion

User cannot have the graphic holding only 20% of the artwork and the text holding rest of 80%. There should be some proportion of each other. Neither should be very big nor very small.

13. Rhythm

This means that both the text and graphics should be in rhythm, complimenting each other.

14. Repetition

One must make sure that on the artwork nothing is repeated. However, if the space permits, you can highlight the main points again but do not repeat.

15. Variety

One must make sure that even if the ad is copied, it should have variety of its own so that it does not look like the original.

16. Economy

Everybody is concerned about the money. So, the ad should be such that it takes less space and has maximum impact.

17. Still life

It is very important to know the life span of the ad. You must withdraw it before it gets overexposed.

18. Light and Shade

Using in the print media, the lights and shades do not matter much. They are of more significance in the multimedia environment.

19. Poster Design

This is used to support the artwork. You have to be careful to know the impact it is going to have in the form of a poster.

14.2.1 Applications of Print Media

The above mentioned all points have their own significance when applied to the various applications in general. So far we have learned what these items mean. Now, we understand how they are created:

1. Colored Layout

First of all, a layout of the job is created. Similarly, for the books, magazines etc., a layout is first made. For the color based jobs, it is very important since the various combination of color are used.

2. Poster Design

A poster can be designed using any of the graphics programs like CorelDRAW or Adobe Photoshop.

3. Designing of Books

Most of books are designed on the computer. But, I have seen some people who making a rough work on paper and then transcribing it on the computer. The other best way, user can have the idea in their mind before to start the working on computer. If users are working with both graphics and text, then CorelDRAW is the best option.

4. Magazines Brochures

To promote a magazine a brochure is must. The brochure for these is no doubt very colorful and appealing so that you are tempted to subscribe the magazine. Since here the major part of the brochure is in color, you have to use a good color and text mixing software such as CorelDRAW or Adobe Photoshop.

5. Children's Literature

To attract children to books, you need to have catchy literature. Your literature should be such that it forces children to leave the TV sets and go to books for reading.

6. Narrative Text Handling

It is possible to record now the spoken words too in the form of text in computer. For this you have software, which converts the spoken words into files and then records them in computer.

7. Scripts in Indian Languages

In India, people using the languages like Tamil, Telgu run into crores. The software developers look into this aspect because they consider them as their prospective buyers.

8. Picture Books

It combines visual and verbal narratives in a book format, most often aimed at young children. The images in picture books use a range of media such as oil paints, acrylics, watercolor and pencil, among others.

9. Comics

A comic refers to a magazine or book of narrative artwork and virtually always, dialogue and descriptive prose. Despite the term, the subject matter in comic is not necessarily humorous; in fact, it is often serious and action oriented.

14.2.2 Illustrations with Photographs

An illustration is a visualisation such as a drawing, painting, photograph or other work of art that stresses subject more than form. Illustrations add excitement and character to your book.

1. Scientific Illustration

It reflects the findings of science and technology. Scientific illustration takes the viewer to the often unobservable from molecules and viruses to the universe from depiction of the internal anatomy of arthropods and plants.

2. Conceptual Illustration

It is gaining popularity today. This type of illustration is used in almost all the fields today that includes areas such as digital art, illustrations, painting, sculpture, video art etc.

14.2.3 Handling of Assignment for the Market

Good marketing makes the company look smart, Great marketing makes the customer feel smart, so handling of assignment for the market is very important in artwork.

14.3 Image Scanning with the Help of Scanner

An image scanner is a digital device used to scan images, pictures, printed text and object and then convert them to digital images. The most widely used type of scanner in offices or homes is a flatbed scanner, also known as a **Xerox machine.**

Follow the steps for performing the scan:

(i) Double click on the Scanning Wizard icon on the desktop.

(ii) When the new scan window appears, place the original on the scanner glass; face down in the upper right hand corner.

(iii) From the Profile drop down list select Photo or Document.

(iv) From the Color Format drop down list, select Color, Greyscale or Black and White. Change the Resolution (dpi) if required and ensure you select the correct file type such as JPEG, TIFF, PNG, BMP etc.

(v) Click on Preview. The four square handles and dotted line surrounding the preview image indicates what will be scanned. Use the handles to select a section of the image if appropriate.

(vi) Click on Scan. The Picture Name and Destination window will be displayed.

1. Setting up Resolution

While scans can be created with up to a 4800 dpi, this uses a lot of memory and creates very large files, which take longer to print. In most cases, scanning at a lower resolution will give acceptable results. The following settings are recommended:

(i) Photographs to be displayed on a monitor, e.g. web pages-75 dpi;

(ii) Scans to be printed (Information Services printers print at 600 dpi), 100 dpi (for 300 dpi printers), 150 dpi (for 600 dpi printers), 300 dpi (for 1200 dpi printers).

(iii) Drawings (black and white and color) - 600 dpi (irrespective of printer).

(iv) Text-300 dpi.

2. Size

Most of the scanner would allow you to use the document in the shape of visiting card to A4 size paper. If you have to use a bigger paper, then you will have to use the drum scanner.

3. Image Preview

Before scanning user can see the scanned picture on the screen. Scanners allow user to select a portion from the preview. Then you have the option to see the preview again or just go ahead with the actual scanning.

4. Grey Scale and Color Options

Scanners allow user to scan color images and the resultant color images are stored in their hard disk as per their requirements. It is upto them to choose which color option they want to have.

14.4 Significance of PDF

PDF (Portable Document Format) is a file format that has captured all the elements of a printed document as an electronic image that you can view, navigate, print or forward to someone else. PDF files are created using Adobe Acrobat, Acrobat capture or similar products.

1. Creating PDF documents

Creating PDF documents is usually a very straight forward process, depending on the software package that you are using.

Both variables are declared in the same way, except that the declaration of an array variable uses parentheses () following the **variable name.**

e.g.

```
Dim A(10)
```

In this example, single-dimension array contains 11 elements. You assign data to each of the elements of the array using an index into the array. Beginning at zero and ending at 10 as follows:

```
A(0) = 56
A(1) = 24
 :
A(10) = 50
```

Similarly, the data can be retrieved from any element using an index into the particular array element you want.

Arrays are not just limited to a single dimension and can have a maximum of 60 dimensions. Multiple dimensions are declared by separating an array's size numbers in the parentheses with commas.

e.g.

```
Dim A (5,10)
```

Number of rows ← → Number of columns

You can also declare an array whose size changes during the time your script is running. This is called **dynamic array**. The array is initially declared within a procedure using Dim or ReDim statement. However, for a dynamic array, no size or number of dimensions is placed inside the parentheses.

e.g.

```
Dim A()
ReDim B()
```

To use dynamic array, you must subsequently use ReDim to determine the number of dimensions and the size of each dimension. In the following example, ReDim sets the initial size of the dynamic array to 25. A subsequent ReDim statement resizes the array to 30, but uses the Preserve keyword to preserve the contents of the array as the resizing takes place.

```
ReDim A(25)
 :
ReDim Preserve A(30)
```

There is no limit to the number of times you can resize a dynamic array, but you should know that if you make an array smaller than it was you lose the data in the eliminated elements.

13.1.4 VBScript Constants

Constant is a named memory location used to hold a value that cannot be changed during the script execution. If a user tries to change a constant value, the script execution ends up with an error. Constants are declared the same way the variables are declared. Constants are also define as variables.

You can create user-defined constants in VBScript using the Const statement.

Syntax

```
[Public|Private] const constant_name = Value
```

The constant can be of type Public or Private. The use of Public or Private is optional. The Public constants are available for all the scripts and procedures while the Private constants are available within the procedure or class. One can assign any value such as number, String or date to the declared constant.

e.g.

```
Const MyStr = "This is a VBScript"
Const a=50
```

13.1.5 VBScript Operators

An operator is an object is capable of manipulating a value or operator. e.g. in "1+2", the "1" and "2", are the operands and the plus symbol is the operator.

VBScript supports different types of operators, which are as follows:

Arithmetic Operators

There are following arithmetic operators supported by VBScript language: Assume variable A holds 5 and variable B holds 10, then:

Operator	Description	Example
+	Adds two operands	A+B will give 15
–	Subtracts second operand from the first	A – B will give – 5
*	Multiply both operands	A * B will give 50
/	Divide numerator by denominator	B/A will give 2
%	Modulus operator and remainder of after an integer division	B MOD A will give 0
^	Exponentiation operator	B ^ A will give 100000

Comparison Operators

There are following comparison operators supported by VBScript language: Assume variable A holds 10 and variable B holds 20, then:

Operator	Description	Example
==	Checks if the value of two operands are equal or not, if yes then condition becomes true.	(A==B) is False
<>	Checks if the value of two operands are equal or not, if values are not equal then condition becomes true.	(A<>B) is True
>	Checks if the value of left operand is greater than the value of right operand, if yes then condition becomes true.	(A>B) is False

Operator	Description	Example
<	Check if the value of left operand is less than the value of right operand, if yes then condition becomes true.	(A < B) is True
>=	Check if the value of left operand is greater than or equal to the value of right operand, if yes then condition becomes true.	(A >=B) is False
<=	Checks if the value of left operand is less than or equal to the value of right operand, if yes then condition becomes true.	(A<=B) is True.

Logical Operators

There are following logical operators supported by VBScript language:

Assume variable A holds 10 and variable B holds 0, then:

Operator	Description	Example
AND	Called logical AND operator. If both the conditions are True then expression becomes true.	a<>0 AND b<>0 is False.
OR	Called logical OR operator. If any of the two conditions are True then condition becomes true.	a<>0 OR b<>0 is True.
NOT	Called logical NOT operator. Use to reverses the logical state of its operand. If a condition is True then Logical NOT operator will make False.	NOT (a<>0 OR b<>0) is False.
XOR	Called logical exclusion. It is the combination of NOT and OR operator. If one, and only one, of the expressions evaluates to True, result is True.	(a<>0 XOR b<>0) is False.

Concatenation Operators

There are following concatenation operators supported by VBScript language:

Assume variable A holds 5 and B holds 10, then:

Operator	Description	Example
+	Adds two values as variable values are numeric	A + B will give 15
&	Concatenates two values	A & B will give 510

Assume variable A="Microsoft" and variable B= "VBScript", then:

Operator	Description	Example
+	Concatenates two values	A + B will give MicrosoftVBScript
&	Concatenates two values	A & B will give MicrosoftVBScript

13.1.6 Operator Precedence

When several operations occur in an expression, each part is evaluated and resolved in a predetermined order called operator precedence. You can use parentheses to override the order of precedence. When expressions contain operators from more than one category, arithmetic operators are evaluated first, comparison operators are evaluated next and logical operators are evaluated last. Comparison operators all have equal precedence; that is, they evaluated in the left-to-right order in which they appear.

Arithmetic and logical operators are evaluated in the following order of precedence:

Arithmetic Operator		Logical Operator	
Description	Symbol	Description	Symbol
Exponentiation	^	Logical negation	NOT
Unary negation	-	Logical conjunction	AND
Multiplication	*	Logical disjunction	OR
Division	/	Logical exclusion	XOR
Integer division	\		
Modulus arithmetic	Mod		
Addition	+		
Subtraction	-		
String concatenation	&		

13.1.7 MsgBox() Function

The MsgBox() function displays a message box and waits for the user to click a button and then an action is performed based on the button clicked by the user.

Syntax

```
MsgBox(prompt [, buttons][, title][, helpfile, context])
```

Parameters

(i) **prompt** String expression presented as the message in the window. The maximum length of prompt is 1024 characters (approx). If the message extends to more than a line, then we can separate the lines using a carriage return character or a linefeed character between each line.

(ii) **buttons** [optional] Numeric expression that is the sum of values specifying the number and type of buttons to show, the icon style to use, the identity of the default button and the modality of the message box. If omitted, the default value for buttons is vbOKOnly.

(iii) **title** [optional] String expression presented in the title bar of the window. If you omit title, the application name is placed in the title bar.

(iv) **helpfile** [optional] String expression that identifies the Help file to use to provide context-sensitive Help for the window. If helpfile is provided, context parameter must also be provided.

(v) **context** [optional] Numeric expression that identifies the Help context number assigned by the Help author to the appropriate Help topic. If context is provided, helpfile parameter must also be provided.

Creating a File in Photoshop

To follow the steps for creating new files in Photoshop:

(i) Click File and then New.

(ii) Set the height, width and resolution of the new file in the box.

(iii) Click OK button.

Opening an Existing File

To follow the steps for opening an existing file in Photoshop:

(i) Click File menu.

(ii) Now, click on Open option from dropdown list.

Once you've created or opened a file and edited it, you can save your file in a number of different formats.

Saving a File

To follow the steps for saving a file in Photoshop.

(i) Choose File> Save As.

(ii) Specify a filename and location and choose the Format as per your need from the format list.

Your image is saved as a copy in the specified directory.

(iii) Click Save.

14.8.3 Image Handling

Image handling with Photoshop can be done in various ways, are as follows:

Creating New Images

To create new images, follow these steps:

(i) Choose File → New.

(ii) Type a name for the new file.

(iii) In the New dialog box, select a preset image category from the Preset pop-up menu.

(iv) If you selected an image category from the Preset menu in step 3, select your desired preset size for that category.

(v) Or, if you choose Custom in step 4, enter the width and height of your image manually by typing the width and height of your choice in the text boxes.

(vi) Enter the resolution for the new document.

(vii) From the Color Mode drop down list, select a color mode.

(viii) Select your desired color depth for your document.

(ix) In the Background Contents drop down list, select an option for how you want the background layer to be filled.

(x) Click the Advanced button to display a couple of additional options: Color Profile and Pixel Aspect Ratio.

(xi) Click OK when you finish entering your options.

Scan an Image using TWAIN

TWAIN is a widely-used program that lets you scan an image (using a scanner) directly into the application (such as Photoshop) where you want to work with the image. TWAIN usually comes as part of the software package you get when you buy a scanner. It's also integrated into Photoshop and similar image manipulation programs. Steps to scan an image using TWAIN are as follows:

(i) Load the image on the scanner.

After loading the image, go to the front of the computer to perform TWAIN scanning.

(ii) Start Adobe Photoshop.

(iii) In the File menu, select [Import], and select your TWAIN driver.

- The TWAIN driver is displayed "KONICA MINOLTA TWAIN".

(iv) Select this sacnner in the [Select Devices] screen, then click [Connect].

- The main dialog box appears.
- If necessary, use the [Settings] tab to configure scan settings.

(v) Click [Scan].

The image is scanned, and an image appears in the application window of the computer.

Cropping an Image

Cropping is the removal of the outer parts of an image to improve framing, accentuate subject matter or change aspect ratio.

In the photo editor Adobe Photoshop, an image can be cropped with the Crop tool or the Crop command.

To crop an image with the Crop tool, follow these instructions:

(i) Choose the Crop Tool from the Tool Panel or press C.

(ii) Bring the cursor to a point on the image, where a corner of the cropped image will be and left click the mouse.

(iii) Moving the cursor diagonally, keep the left mouse button pressed.

(iv) Release the left mouse button. A box will appear over the image with marked corners, indicating the area that will be preserved. This box can be moved, resized and rotated.

Resizing an Image

If you have an image that's monstrously large, don't be afraid to resize any image in order to suit your needs. It is actually quite a simple procedure. Here's an easy way to do it using Adobe Photoshop:

(i) Open an image that you need to resize.

(ii) Produce a duplicate of the file just in case the resized image is not what you intended.

(iii) Go to Image → Image Size.

(iv) Type the new dimensions to the Width and Height box.

(v) To change the locked proportions, simply uncheck the box next to "Constrain Proportions".

(vi) If you would like to resize an image by a certain percent, click the "Percent" option beside the width and height dimensions.

(vii) Finished.

Changing the Canvas Size

The canvas in Photoshop is the term for the image area. When you increase the size of the canvas, Photoshop fills the expanded area outside the image with your chosen color.

To change the canvas size, follow these steps:

(i) Choose Image → Canvas Size.

(ii) Enter new values in the Width and Height text boxes.

(iii) Specify your desired anchor placement.

(iv) Select your canvas color from the Canvas extension color pop-up menu and click OK.

14.8.4 Layer

Layers are useful because they let you add components to an image and work on them one at a time, without permanently changing your original image. For each layer, you can adjust color and brightness, apply special effects, reposition layer content, specify opacity and blending values and so on.

Adding Layer

By default a Photoshop image has one layer, called background. If you look in the Layers palette you can add more layer using:

(i) Select Layer > New > Layer.

(ii) A window will appear. In this window, enter a descriptive name for the layer - you can usually ignore the other options.

(iii) The new layer will appear above the currently selected layer in the Layer palette.

Dragging Selection into Layers

The Move tool lets you cut and drag a pixel selection to a new location in the photo. To drag selection into layers, follow these steps:

(i) Select the Move tool.

(ii) Move the pointer inside the selection border and drag the selection to a new position. If you selected multiple areas, all move as you drag.

Pasting Selection into Layers

You can use the Paste into Selection command to paste clipboard or copied content, within a selection. To paste selection into layers, follow these steps:

(i) In the Edit workspace, use the Copy command to copy the part of the photo that you want to paste.

(ii) Make a selection in the photo into which you want to paste the copied photo.

(iii) Choose Edit> Paste Into Selection.

(iv) With your pointer within the selection border, drag the pasted image to the proper location.

(v) When you're satisfied with the results, deselect the pasted image to commit the changes.

Hiding and Viewing Layers

You can also quickly hide a layer by the following steps:

(i) Clicking the eye icon at the left side of the layer that you want to hide.

(ii) You can restore or unhide a layer at any time by clicking the empty box where the eye icon used to be.

Editing Layer

You can edit part of an image without changing the rest of it by making changes to a particular layer in Adobe Photoshop Elements. To edit a layer, steps are as follows:

(i) Open the multilayer image that you want to edit in elements.

(ii) In the Layers palette, click the layer that you want to edit.

(iii) Make the changes you want to the active layer.

(iv) Choose File → Save to save your work.

Rotating Selections

To rotating a selection use the following steps:

(i) Open your image.

(ii) Select that layer and then select the object.

(iii) Click Edit on the toolbars.

(iv) Rotate the object and press Enter.

(iii) Exiting a Do...Loop Statement

You can exit a Do...Loop by using the Exit Do statement. Because you usually want to exit only in certain situation such as to avoid an endless loop, you should use the Exit Do statement in the True statement block of an If...Then...Else statement. If the condition is False, the loop runs as usual.

e.g.

```
Dim i, counter
counter = 0
i =9
Do Until i =10
   i = i -1
   counter = counter +1
   If i < 10 Then Exit Do
Loop
```

While...Wend

In a While...Wend loop, if the condition is True, all statements are executed until Wend keyword is encountered. If the condition is False, the loop is exited and the control jumps to very next statement after Wend keyword.

e.g.

```
Dim Counter
Counter =10
While Counter <15 'Test value of Counter
   Counter = Counter + 1 'Increment Counter
   document.write "The Current Value of the
                          Counter  is :" & Counter
Wend
```

For...Next

You can use For...Next statement to run a block of statements a specific number of times. For loops, use a counter variable whose value is increased or decreased with each repetition of loop.

e.g.

```
Dim a
a =10
For i =0 To a
    document.write "The value of i is : " & i
Next
```

Using the Step keyword, you can increase or decrease the counter variable by the value you specify.

e.g.

```
Dim i, Sum
Sum = 0
For i =2 to 10 Step 2
  Sum = Sum + i
  document.write "The value of sum is" & sum
Next
```

In this example, the counter variable i is incremented by 2 each time the loop repeats.

To decrease the counter variable, you can use a negative Step value.

e.g.

```
Dim i, Sum
Sum =0
For i =20 to 2 Step -2
  Sum = Sum + i
  document.write "The value of sum is" & sum
Next
```

You can also exit any For...Next statement before the counter reaches its end value by using the Exit For statement.

For Each...Next

A For Each...Next loop is similar to For...Next loop. Instead of repeating the statements a specified number of times, a For Each...Next loop is used when we want to execute a statement or a group of statements for each element in an array or collection.

e.g.

```
fruits = Array("apple", "orange","cherries")
Dim fruitnames
For  Each item in fruits
  fruitnames = fruitnames & item & vbnewline
Next
```

13.1.10 VBScript Procedure

A procedure is a group of reusable code which can be called anywhere in your program. This eliminates the need of writing same code over and over again. This will enable programmers to divide a big program into a number of small and manageable procedures.

In VBScript, there are two kinds of procedures as follows:

1. Sub Procedures

A Sub procedure is a series of VBScript statements, enclosed by Sub and End Sub statements, that perform actions but do not return a value. It can take arguments (constants, variables or expressions that are passed by a calling procedure).

If a Sub procedure has no arguments, its Sub statement must include an empty set of parentheses ().

e.g.

```
Sub ConvertTemp()
   temp = InputBox("Please enter the temperature in
                                         degrees F.",1)
   MsgBox "The temperature is " & Celsius(temp)
                                       & "degrees C."
End Sub
```

In above example, Sub procedure ConvertTemp( ) uses two built-in VBScript functions, i.e. MsgBox and InputBox, to promt a user for some information. It then displays the results of a calculation based on that information.

2. Function Procedures

A Function procedure is a series of VBScript statements enclosed by the Function and End Function statements. A Function procedure is similar to a Sub procedure but can also return a value. A Function returns a value by assigning a value to its name in one or more statements of the procedure. The return type of a Function is always a Variant.

e.g.

```
Sub ConvertTemp()
    temp = InputBox("Please enter the temperature in
                                              degrees. F",1)
    MsgBox "The temperature is " & Celsius(temp)
                                              & "degrees C."
End Sub
Function Celsius(fDegrees)
    Celsius = (fDegrees - 32)*5/9
End Function
```

In above example, the Celsius function calculates degrees Celsius from degrees Fahrenheit. When the function is called from the ConvertTemp Sub procedure, a variable containing the argument value is passed to the function. The result of the calculation is returned to the calling procedure and displayed in a message box.

13.1.11 Using VBScript with HTML Form Controls

As the popularity of web page forms increase, so does the need to be able to validate data before the client browser submits it to the web server. As a scripting language, VBScript is well suited for this task. Once the form has been validated, the same script can be used to forward the data on to the server.

Validating Your Forms

The process of validating forms involves checking the form to see if:

(i) All of the required data is proved

(ii) The data provided is valid

Checking Form Input

This example is pretty simple. It has a single field in which the user can enter their age and a single command button that is used to submit their age to the server.

```
<html>
    <head>
        <title>Working With VBScript</title>
        <script language="vbscript">
        <!--
        Sub cmdSubmit_OnClick
          If(Len(document.frm.txt.value)= 0) Then
            MsgBox "You must enter your age
                                    before submitting."
            Exit Sub
          End If
          If(Not(IsNumeric(document.frm.txt.value
                                              ))) Then
            MsgBox "You must enter a number for
                                           your age."
            Exit Sub
          End If
          If(document.frm.txt.value<0) or
                        (document.frm.txt.value>100) Then
            MsgBox "The age you entered is invalid."
            Exit Sub
          End If
          MsgBox "Thanks for providing your age."
                                    document.frm.submit

        End Sub
        -->

        </script>
    </head>
    <body>
        <h1>A VBScript Example on Variables</h1>
        <p> This example demonstrates validation
                              techniques in VBScript.</p>

        <form NAME="frm">
          Enter your age:<INPUT TYPE="Text"
                      NAME="txt" SIZE="12"><br><br>
            <INPUT TYPE="Button" NAME="cmdSubmit"
                                      VALUE="Submit">

        </form>
    </body>
</html>
```

In above example, if the user entered anything at all into the field using VBScript's Len function. This function returns the length of a string. Then, according to condition appropriate message will be displayed.

13.1.12 Data Handling Functions

1. **Create a new txt file**

```
Function CreateFile(StrFilePath)
    Dim NewFile
    Set NewFile = objFso.CreateTextFile
                                    (StrFilePath,True)

    Set CreateFile = NewFile
End Function
```

2. **Check if a specific file exist**

```
Function CheckFileExists(StrFilePath)
```

Options Palette

Most tools have an Options palette. Depending on the tool selected, the palette's appearance and available choices change.

To display the Options palette : Do one of the following:

(i) Choose Window > Show Options.

(ii) Double-click a tool in the toolbox (except the zoom or hand tool).

(iii) Click a tool or press its keyboard shortcut and press Enter.

Setting Brush Options

Basic Settings

Along the brush's options bar are some simple yet powerful settings that determine the strength and shape of your brush. These settings have a large impact on the how the brush applies paint, so they're definitely important to understand.

(i) **Brush** The brush menu, which is accessible by clicking the drop-down menu next to the brush preview or by right-clicking within the canvas, presents three options to control the shape of your brush: "Master Diameter," "Hardness" and "Brush Shape."

(ii) **Mode** The brush's mode sets how painted pixels affect those already on the current layer. These modes work in the same way that Blend Modes work on the layer's palette, except that they're converted to absolute values when the stroke is finished.

(iii) **Opacity, Flow And Airbrush** These three settings work in unison to determine the amount of paint laid on the canvas. The opacity setting is the master control; it sets the maximum amount that can be painted with each stroke, mouse down to mouse up, regardless of any other setting. Flow, on the other hand, sets the amount of paint applied to an area every time the brush moves. Finally, the Airbrush setting allows you to build up paint based on time instead of movement; by simply holding the mouse down in one area, you can multiply the brush's effect.

Advanced Settings

Within the Brushes palette (F5) are dozens of settings that control the way the brush paints, from shape and size to flow and scatter. Understanding how to use these options is the key to creating wonderful brushes.

(i) **Brush Presets** The Brush Presets menu lists all of the currently available brushes. While some of the presets simply change the shape of the brush, others have advanced settings.

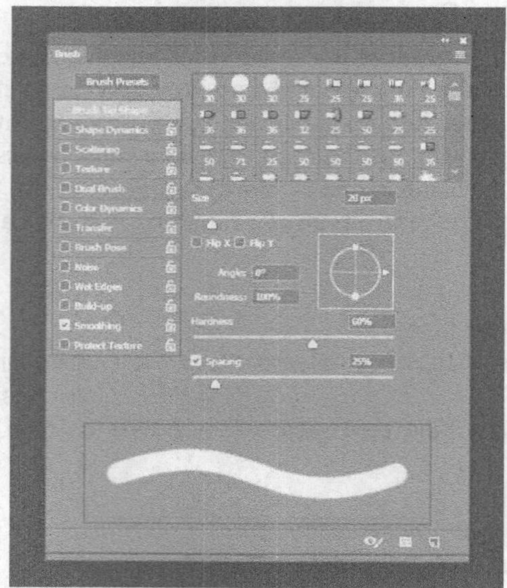

(ii) **Brush Tip Shape** This group allows you to control the primary shape of the brush. Many of the settings are also found in the Brushes toolbar, but here we also have options for flipping, rotation, roundness and spacing.

(iii) **Brush Control Methods** A number of the settings in the Brushes palette allow you to set a method for controlling values. They include "Off," "Fade," "Pen Pressure," "Pen Tilt," "Stylus Wheel," "Rotation," "Initial Direction" and "Direction."

(iv) **Shape Dynamics** Now you have a basic shape and size set, you can add some variance using Shape Dynamics. Here, three different types of jitters are available, which control the amount of variation allowed for size, angle and roundness.

(v) **Scattering** The Scattering menu allows you to vary where each sample of the brush is placed and how many samples are placed per step. Three sliders are here for you to control: "Scatter," "Count" and "Count Jitter."

(vi) **Texture** Adding a texture to your brush can give a wonderful sense of depth. Photoshop allows you to apply any of your Texture presets to your brush. You can then modify the Scale or Invert it.

(vii) **Dual Brush** As the name implies, this setting uses two different brush shapes to create the final sample. The primary brush is basically used as the mask that the dual brush is contained within. The Dual Brush menu has a few settings for the second brush, which work in the same manner as they do for the primary brush.

(viii) **Color Dynamics** The Color Dynamics menu helps you interject some color variation into your brush strokes. You can control the colors by using the Foreground/Background Jitter, or you can allow Photoshop to randomly select values using the Hue, Saturation and Brightness Jitters.

(ix) **Other Dynamics** With the Other Dynamics menu, you can jitter and set controls for varying the brush's opacity and flow. Both of these jitters depend on the brush's current settings in the Properties bar.

Other Settings

(i) **Noise** Generates random noise within the gray values of your brush shape.

(ii) **Wet Edges** Decreases the interior values of your brush, while leaving the edges at full opacity. Doing so, the brush creates an effect similar to watercolor with its "wet edges."

(iii) **Airbrush** Allows paint to build up incrementally based on the Flow setting and limited by the Opacity setting.

(iv) **Smoothing** Smoothes the curves of the stroke to prevent polygonal curvatures. Turning this off may help if your brush is rendering slowly.

(v) **Protect Texture** Ensures that the same texture is used for every brush with a texture.

Other Palette Options Link

(i) **Lock Setting** Next to each menu name in the Brushes Palette is a padlock icon. These allow you to lock a setting so that when you switch to a different brush preset, the settings from that menu carry over to the new preset. This can be very helpful when you need a similar effect but don't want to have to rebuild it with a new brush shape.

(ii) **Resetting** The Brushes Palette has two different ways to reset controls in its fly-out menu: "Clear Brush Controls" and "Reset All Locked Settings." Clear Brush Controls will turn off all controls except for Smoothing but keeps the locked settings locked. Reset All Locked Settings also turns off all controls but will also unlock everything.

Opacity, Pressure and Exposure

Another way to change the performance of paint or an edit tool is to adjust the Pressure, Opacity, or Exposure value, depending on what tool you're using. In version 6, the controls appear on the Options bar, which replaces the former Options palette. Regardless of which setting you want to change, you click the triangle to display a slider bar, drag the slider to raise or lower the value, and then press Enter. Alternatively, you can double-click the option box, type a value, and press Enter. Here's a look at how these options work:

1. **Opacity** The Opacity value determines the translucency of colors applied with the paint bucket, gradient, line, pencil, paintbrush, eraser, or rubber stamp tools. At 100 percent, the applied colors appear opaque, completely covering the image behind them. At lower settings, the applied colors mix with the existing colors in the image.
   You can change the opacity of pixels that you just altered by choosing Edit ^ Fade (Ctrl+Shift+F) and dragging the Opacity slider in the Fade dialog box.
2. **Pressure** The Pressure value affects different tools in different ways. When you use the airbrush tool, the Pressure value controls the opacity of each spot of color the tool delivers. The effect appears unique because the airbrush lays each spot of color onto the previous spot, mixing them together. This results in a progressive effect. Meanwhile, the paintbrush and pencil tools are not progressive, so their spots blend to form smooth lines.
3. **Exposure** Available when you select the dodge or burn tool, Exposure controls how much the tools lighten or darken the image, respectively. A setting of 100 percent applies the maximum amount of lightening or darkening, which is still far short of either absolute white or black.
   The factory default setting for all Exposure and Pressure values is 50 percent; the default setting for all Opacity values is 100 percent.

Paint Fade-out Rate

The rate at which the Photoshop paintbrush and airbrush tools fade out as you paint with them to simulate an actual brush stroke.

Making Selections

Making selections is one of the toughest things to master in Photoshop, mostly because there are so many tools to use and so many features to take advantage of. Using a Wacom Pen Tablet, pressure sensitivity and a few lesser known tricks can turn frustration into fun.

Selection Tools

The selection tools are used to facilitate the process of making selections of shapes, colors and objects inside of Photoshop and positioning them in the working image area. With tools like the magnetic lasso and magic wand, Photoshop packs a powerful array of selection gadgets.

In Photoshop, selections are used to work in a specified area, while not altering any of the area around it. In many regards, a selection is a lot like a stencil. Basically you are enabling yourself to only paint in one area while the rest of your canvas is left unaffected.

```
        <script type="text/javascript">
        <!- document.write("Hello World") //->
        </script>
        <input type="button"
        onclick="sayHello()" value="Say Hello"/>
    </body>
</html>
```

Output

Say Hello

4. **JavaScript in external file**

You are not restricted to be maintaining identical code in multiple HTML files. The script tag provides a mechanism to allow you to store JavaScript in an external file and then include it into your HTML files.

Here is an example to show how you can include an external JavaScript file in your HTML code using script tag and its src attribute:

```
<html>
    <head>
        <script type="text/javascript"
                    src="filename.js"></script>
    </head>
    <body>
    ........
    </body>
</html>
```

To use JavaScript from an external file source, you need to write all your JavaScript source code in a simple text file with the extension ".js" and then include that file as shown above.

e.g. you can keep the following content in filename.js file and then you can use sayHello function in your HTML file after including the filename.js file.

```
function sayHello() {alert("Hello World")}
```

13.2.2 Variables

It is the basic unit of storage in JavaScript or we can say that, variable is a container object that stores a meaningful value that can be used throughout the program.

Each variable has a specific type, which determines the size and layout of the variable's memory, the range of values that can be stored within that memory and the set of operations that can be applied to the variable.

There are two types of variables in Javascript : local variable and global variable.

In JavaScript, the rules for variables are as follows:

(i) Only alphabets, digits and underscores are permitted.
(ii) Variable name cannot start with a digit.
(iii) Reserved keywords cannot be used as variable.
(iv) Uppercase and lowercase letters are distinct because JavaScript is a case sensitive language.
(v) Special characters are not allowed.

Declaring the Variables

Before you use a variable in a JavaScript program, you must declare it. You declare variables in JavaScript with the var keyword.

e.g.
```
var money;
var name;
```

You can also declare multiple variables with the single var keyword as follows:

```
var money, name;
```

Assigning the Value to the Variables

After you declare a variable, you can assign a value to a variable. Assigning a value to a variable means storing a value to a variable. Storing a value in variable is called **variable initialisation**. You can do variable initialisation at the time of variable creation or at a later point in time when you need that variable.

e.g.
```
var name = "Ansh";
var money;
money = 2500;
```

13.2.3 Data Types

A value is a piece of information that can be a Number, String, Boolean, Null etc. JavaScript recognises the following data types of values:

1. Number Data Type

In JavaScript, there is no distinction between integer and floating point values; a JavaScript number can be either (internally, JavaScript represents all numbers as floating point values).

(i) **Integer Values** It can be positive whole numbers, negative whole numbers and 0. They can be represented in Base 10 (decimal), Base 16 (hexadecimal) and Base 8 (octal).

(ii) **Floating Point Values** It can be whole numbers with a decimal portion. They can be expressed in scientific notation. JavaScript represents numbers using the eight byte IEEE 754 floating point standard for numerical representation.

2. String Data Type

String is a series of characters enclosed in quotation marks. A string must be delimited by quotation marks of the same type, either single quotation marks (' ') or double quotation marks (" ").

3. Boolean Data Type

Whereas the string and the number data types can have a virtually unlimited number of different values, the Boolean data type can only have two. They are the literals True and False.

4. Null Data Type

A special keyword denoting a null value (i.e. empty value or nothing). Since, JavaScript is case sensitive, null is not the same as Null, NULL or any other Variant.

5. Undefined Data Type

The undefined value is returned when you use an object property that does not exist, or a variable that has been declared but has never a value assigned to it.

13.2.4 Data Type Conversion

JavaScript is a dynamically typed language. Therefore, there is no need to specify the data type of a variable at the time of declaring it. Data types are converted automatically as needed during script execution.

e.g. Study the below codes

```
var name = "Manesh";    typeof(name) //returns "string"
var age = 42;     typeof(age) //returns "number"
var bDate = new Date(1965, 7, 17);
typeof(bDate) //returns "object"
typeof(null) //returns "string"
typeof(Date) //returns "function"
typeof(unknown Var)//returns "undefined"
typeof(false) //returns "boolean"
```

JavaScript converts implicit data type according to context of Script. e.g. If context required that value should be string type, then JavaScript will change this value in string data type. Apart from this, JavaScript provides some methods and functions, by which explicit string data type can change into numeric type and objects can change into string.

Some functions and methods are as follows:

1. parseInt() Function

This function is used to convert a string value to an integer. parseInt( ) returns the first integer contained in a string or 0 if the string does not begin with an integer.

e.g.

```
var Num = parseInt("123XYZ");
```

results in the integer 123 being assigned to the variable Num.

```
var string = parseInt("XYZ");
```

results in NaN (Not a Number) being assigned to the variable string.

2. parseFloat() Function

This function returns the first floating point number contained in a string or 0 if the string does not being with a valid floating point number.

e.g.

```
var Num = parseFloat("1.32XYZ");
```

results in the float 1.32 being assigned to the variable Num.

```
var str = parseFloat("XYZ");
```

results in NaN (Not a Number) being assigned to the variable str.

13.2.5 Comments

Comments are the remark statements of a program. These remark statements are used to describe the objective of program, function or statement. Any number of comments can be used in a program.

Nested comments (i.e. comments in comment) cannot be used in the program. In actual, comments are used to improve the readability and understandability of a program.

In JavaScript, two types of comments are as follows:

1. Single Line Comment (//)

The // (double forward slashes), followed by a sequence of characters, is used to represent single line comment. Two slash signs indicate that the rest of the line is a comment inserted by a programmer which does not effect the behaviour of the program; because whatever is written after the double slash till the end of the line is ignored by the compiler. Programmers use them to include short explanations or observations concerning the code or program.

e.g.

```
// Declares two integer variables
```

2. Multiline Comment (/*)

The /* (slash, asterisk) characters, followed by any sequence of characters (including new line) followed by the */ characters, is used to represent multiline comment. That means, everything that falls between /* and */ is ignored by the compiler even though it is spread across multi lines. It is also called **block comment**.

e.g.

```
/*Declares two
 integer variables */
```

13.2.6 Operators

Operators are the symbols between values that allow different operations like addition, subtraction, multiplication and more.

Operators in JavaScript are very similar to operators that appear in other programming languages.

There are two types of operators in JavaScript as follows:

1. Unary Operator

This operator has need only one operand. Unary operator can use with following two types of notation:

(i) **Prefix Notation** In this notation, operator uses before operand. e.g. (++i)

3. Video

Digital video appears in many multimedia applications, particularly on the web. As with audio, websites can stream digital video to increase the speed and availability of playback. Common digital video formats include Flash, MPEG, AVI, WMV and Quick Time. Most digital video requires use of browser plug-in to play the video.

14.9.2 Sound

Recording Sound using Sound Recorder

Windows comes with a sound recorder program that allows you to record, edit and playback your voice or audio from a recorded device. To record sound using sound recorder, follow these steps:

(i) Tap the Sound Recorder icon from application.
(ii) Tap the Microphone icon to start recording your voice.
(iii) If you make a mistake or finished while recording, tap the Stop icon and tap Delete or Done.

Sound Capture through Sound Editing Software (Sound Forge)

Sony Sound Forge (formerly known as Sonic Foundry Sound Forge) is a digital audio editing suite by Sony Creative Software which is aimed at the professional and semi-professional markets.

Before you begin, please take a moment to locate each piece of equipment that you will be using to complete this task.

(i) Kramer VS-100 Input Selector
(ii) Multimedia rack components

Steps

1. Select your source.
2. Adjust Play Control.
3. Launch Sound Forge.
4. Record your audio.
5. Edit and save your file.

Sound Editing

Sound editing is the process by which all of the talking, music and sound effects are put together to form the final sound track. The sound editor is responsible for taking all of the sound elements and placing them in the right spots in relation to the visual elements of the film.

Noise Correction

Noise reduction is the process of removing noise from a signal. Noise reduction can reduce constant background sounds such as hum, whistle, whine, buzz and hiss, such as tape hiss, fan noise or FM/webcast carrier noise. It is not suitable for individual clicks and pops, or irregular background noise such as from traffic or an audience. To use Noise Reduction, you need a region in the waveform that contains only the noise you want to reduce.

Sound Effects

Sound effects (or audio effects) are artificially created or enhanced sounds or sound processes used to emphasize artistic or other content of films, television shows, live performance, animation, video games, music or other media.

In motion picture and television production, a sound effect is a sound recorded and presented to make a specific story telling or creative point without the use of dialogue or music. The term often refers to a process applied to a recording, without necessarily referring to the recording itself.

14.9.3 Voice Recognition Software

Voice recognition software lets you talk to your computer using a microphone normally on a headset.

This software lets you dictate letters and as you talk the words appear on the Word processor. Some voice recognition software also allows you to navigate around your computer like what you can do with your mouse. It's like magic however it isn't always easy to set-up and keep working.

Philips

Philips SpeechLive is your personal assistant in the cloud. The new dictation workflow service increases your productivity by allowing you to focus on your core business. You can now take full control of your entire dictation workflow, whether you are in the office or on the road.

Dragon

DragonDictate, Dragon Dictate or Dragon for Mac, is proprietary speech recognition software. DragonDictate for Windows was the original speech recognition application from Dragon Systems and used discrete speech where the user must pause between speaking each word. It has been replaced by Dragon Naturally Speaking, which allows continuous speech recognition and correction and training of words *via* the keyboard.

14.9.4 MIDI Player

MIDI Player is a simple, yet effective utility that helps you to play audio MIDI files while adjusting the volume, bass, balance and treble. MIDI Player enables you to edit melodies in MIDI file format. With this software, you can enhance loudness, tempo, pitch, notes and more.

14.9.5 Sound Recorder

It is a device for recording sound on disc, tape or film usually by electronic means. Sound Recorder can record audio from a microphone or headset. In addition, many modern sound cards allow their output channels to be recorded through a loopback channel, typically called **Wave-Out Mix** or **Stereo Mix.**

14.9.6 MONO & Stereo

Mono & Stereo are two classifications of reproduced sound. Mono is the term used to describe sound that is only from one channel while stereo uses 2 or more channels to provide an experience much like being in the same room where the sound was created.

Stereo is essential for broadcasting and listening to music since Mono provides inadequate sound quality. Mono is used widely in talk radio and mobile communications since stereo doesn't really provide any practical advantages in these situations.

14.9.7 Sound File Format

An audio/sound file format is a file format for storing digital audio/sound data on a computer system.

Some common sound file formats are as follows:

1. AIFF

AIFF is short for Audio Interchange File Format, which is an audio format initially created by Apple Computer for storing and transmitting high-quality sampled audio data. It supports a variety of bit resolutions, sample rates and channels of audio. This format is quite popular upon Apple platforms and is commonly adopted in professional programs that handle digital audio waveforms.

2. MIDI

MIDI (Musical Instrument Digital Interface) is a protocol designed for recording and playing back music on digital synthesizer that is supported by many makes of personal computer sound cards. Originally intended to control one keyboard from another, it was quickly adopted for the personal computer. Rather than representing musical sound directly, it transmits information about how music is produced.

3. WAV

WAV is an audio file format that was developed by Microsoft. It is so wide spread today that it is called a standard PC audio file format. A Wave file is identified by a file name extension of WAV (.wav). Used primarily in PCs, the Wave file format has been accepted as a viable interchange medium for other computer platforms, such as Macintosh.

4. MP3

MP3 (MPEG-1 Audio Layer-3) is a standard technology and format for compressing a sound sequence into a very small file (about one-twelfth the size of the original file) while preserving the original level of sound quality when it is played.

MP3 provides near CD quality audio. It is one of the most common music file types. It is not an MPEG 3 but uses the audio compression found in layer III in MPEG 1 or 2 video files, the audio stream layer.

5. ASF

ASF stands for Advanced Systems Format. It was developed by Microsoft as part of the Windows Media framework. ASF is most commonly used for streaming media purposes. The format doesn't specify the way video or audio should be encoded. ASF specifies the structure of video or audio stream. Due to this encoded with different audio or video codec the files will still have .asf extension.

Importing Audio from Audio CD

You can import audio from audio CDs into Cubase projects in 2 ways:

(i) To import the CD tracks directly into project tracks, choose the "Audio CD..." option from the Import submenu of the File menu.

The imported audio CD track(s) are inserted on the selected audio track(s) at the project cursor position.

(ii) To import the CD tracks into the Pool, select "Import Audio CD..." from the Media menu.

This might be the preferred method if you want to import several CD tracks in one go.

Saving Audio Files from Audio CD

Here's how to save the file to your computer so you can burn a CD or transfer it to your portable player.

For Windows PC or Linux, right-click on the link to the MP3 file and choose the option for Saving the link (or target).

It will say "Save Target As..." or "Save Link As..." or "Download Link ...". On most systems, double-clicking the downloaded file will open it and begin playback.

14.9.8 Sound Quality

Sound quality is typically an assessment of the accuracy, enjoyability or intelligibility of audio output from an electronic device. Quality can be measured objectively, such as when tools are used to gauge the accuracy with which the device reproduces an original sound; or it can be measured subjectively, such as when default statement is optional and if it is missing, no action will take place if all matches fail.

When a break statement is encountered in a switch statement, program execution jumps to the line of code following the switch statement, i.e. outside the body of switch statement.

Looping Statements

JavaScript performs several types of repetitive operations called **looping**. Loops are set of instructions used to repeat the same block of code till a specified condition returns false or true depending on how you need it. To control the loops you can use counter variable that increments or decrements with each repetition of the loop.

There are various types of loops as follows.

(i) for() Loop

The for statement encloses one or more statements that form the body of the loop, the statement in the loop repeat continuously a certain number of times. A for loop has three parts, i.e. the variable initialisation, loop-condition update expression and logic to continue loop. This loop is also known as **Entry Control Loop**, as condition is checked before entering into the scope of the loop.

Syntax

```
for (Initialization; Condition, Increment/Decrement)
{
    //Here goes the script lines that you want.
}
```

e.g. To make the table to comparison of Fahrenheit and Celsius using for( ) loop.

```
<html>
    <head> <title>Celsius-Fahrenheit
                                Converter</title>
    </head>
    <body>
    <table border=3>
    <tr><td>celsius</td><td>fahrenheit</td></tr>
    <script language="javascript">
    var celsius;
    for(celsius=0; celsius<=10;celsius=celsius+1)
    {
        document.write("<tr><td>"+celsius+"
                    </td><td>" +((celsius*9/5)+32)
                                +"</td></tr>");
    }
    </script>
    </table>
    </body>
</html>
```

(ii) for-in() Loop

This loop is used to loop through an object's properties. As we have not discussed objects yet, you may not feel comfortable with this loop. But once you understand how objects behave in JavaScript, you will find this loop very useful.

Syntax

```
for(variablename in object)
{
        statements;
}
```

In each iteration, one property from object is assigned to variablename and this loop continues till all the properties of the object are exhausted.

(iii) while() Loop

A while loop tests for its ending condition before executing the statements enclosed in the loop body even the first time. So, if the ending condition is met when the while loop begins, the lines of instruction it contains will never be carried out.

Syntax

```
Initialization;
while (Condition)
{
    // Here goes the script lines that you want
    Increment/Decrement;
}
```

A while continues iteration-cycle till its loop-condition is evaluated as True.

If the loop-condition is False for the first time iteration then loop will not be execute even once.

e.g. To make a table to comparison between Fahrenheit and Celsius using while() loop.

```
<html>
    <head> <title>Celsius-Fahrenheit
                                Converter</title>
    </head>
    <body>
    <table border=3>
    <tr><td>celsius</td><td>fahrenheit</td></tr>
    <script language="javascript">
    var celsius=0;
    while(celsius<=10)
    {
        document.write("<tr><td>"+celsius+"</td>
          <td>"+((celsius*9/5)+32)+"</td></tr>");
        celsius=celsius+1;
    }
    </script>
    </table>
    </body>
</html>
```

(iv) do-while() loop

A do-while loop is identical to a while loop. It guarantees the execution of the instruction inside the do-while loop body atleast once before testing for the loop condition.

The do-while loop is a post-test or bottom-test loop. That is, it executes its body atleast once without testing specified conditional expression and then makes test.

Syntax

```
Initialization;
do
{
    //Here goes the script that you want
    Increment/Decrement;
}
while(Condition);
```

In do-while loop, the looping condition is evaluated at the end of the loop's scope, i.e. after the last statement in the scope of loop. This type of checking is called **Exit Control Checking.** do-while () loop is often called as **Exit Control Loop.**

e.g. To show the table of 2 using do-while() loop.

```
<html>
    <head> <title>table of 2</title>
    </head>
    <body> <h4>table of 2</h4>
        <script language="javascript">
        var i=0;
        do
        {
            i=i+2;
            document.write("<br>"+i);
        }
        while(i != 20);
        </script>
    </body>
</html>
```

Break and Continue Statements

The **break** statement terminates the current loop, switch or label statement and transfers program control to the statement following the terminated statement.

e.g.

```
<html>
    <head><title>EXAMPLE OF BREAK
                    STATEMENT</title>
    </head>
    <body>
    <script type="text/javascript">
        var i=0;
        for(i=0; i<10; i++)
        {
            if(i == 3){ break; }
            document.write("The Number is "+ i
                                    +"<BR>");
        }
        </script>
        <p><b>Explanation:</b>
        The Loop will break when i =3.</p>
    </body>
</html>
```

The **continue** statement terminates execution of the statements in the current iteration of the current or labeled loop and continues execution of the loop with the next iteration.

e.g.

```
<html>
<head> <title>EXAMPLE OF CONTINUE
                            STATEMENT</title>
</head>
<body>
    <script type="text/javascript">
        var i=0;
        for(i=0; i<10; i++)
        {
            if(i == 3)    { continue; }
            if(i == 4)    { continue; }
            if(i == 5)    { continue; }
        document.write("The Number is "+ i
                                    +"<br>" );
        }
        </script>
        <p><b>Explanation:</b>
        The Loop will break current loop and
                continue with the next value.</p>

    </body>
</html>
```

13.2.9 Arrays in JavaScript

Arrays are fundamental part of most programming languages and scripts. Arrays are simply an ordered stack of data items. Each element of the array can store its own data, just like a variable, thus you can say arrays are collection of variables. Items can be added or removed from the array at any time, also their value can be changed easily. One other feature of the arrays, which is specific to JavaScript is that the elements in the array can be of different types.

We have to make an object of array class to creating the array in JavaScript. new operator is used to create array class, which allows us that how we want to create the array.

Types of Array

The two types of array are as follows:

(i) **One Dimensional Array** It is a type of variable. Before using it, you have to declare it. We can use it in three types, which are as follows:

(vi) Select different colors and stroke widths and then try drawing some objects to see how the changes affect your drawing.

(vii) Click frame 1 in the timeline to select it. This will change the Properties panel options so that you can add frame labels, apply a tween, add sounds, and so on,

(viii) Add a frame label and see how it appears in the timeline.

(ix) Drag the Properties panel back to the bottom of the Flash window until it docks in place below the stage. You may need to use the zoom control above the right side of the stage or the options on the View Magnification menu to once again see the entire stage.

14.10.3 Change Background and Stage Size

The Stage provides a preview of how your Flash content will appear in your published file. You'll change the size of the Stage to accommodate artwork designed for a larger Stage, and you'll change the background color of the Stage.

To change background and stage size,steps are as follows.

(i) In the Tools panel, click the Selection tool.

(ii) On the Stage, click anywhere in the gray workspace that surrounds the Stage, or on the background area of the Stage, so that no objects are selected.

The Property inspector, under the Stage, displays properties for the document when no objects are selected.

(iii) To change the Stage background color, click the Background color box and select a light shade of gray, such as gray with the hexadecimal value of #CCCCCC.

(iv) To change the Stage size, click Size in the Property inspector. In the Document Properties dialog box, enter 750 for the Stage width, and then click OK.

The Stage resizes to 750 pixels wide.

14.10.4 Concept of Scene

A Scene is only a portion of the Timeline, including everything (layers, frames ...).

Its main aim is to ORGANIZE the movie, so that the parts with no connection could be one after another (following in the Timeline). This way, if we divide the movie in 3 scenes, we will get 3 timelines, 3 groups of layers and 3 groups of frames, that we will see and edit apparently in 3 different movies.

We must not forget that in spite of being apparently 3 different movie, they have the same Timeline and after the end of the first will begin the second and so on.

The Scenes can be added, deleted, edited ...from the Menu Scene that you can access from Window → Other Panels → Scene

Add Scene

(i) Select Window> Other Panels> Scene.

(ii) Select Insert> Scene or click the Add Scene button in the Scene panel.

Duplicate Scene

(i) Select Window> Other Panels> Scene.

(ii) Click the Duplicate Scene button in the Scene panel.

Delete Scene

(i) Select Window> Other Panels> Scene.

(ii) Click the Delete Scene button in the Scene panel.

(iii) Click OK to confirm the deletion.

Navigating between Scenes

To navigate between scenes, do one of the following:

(i) From the scene list in the Scene panel, click the name of the scene that you want to navigate to.

or

(ii) From the View menu, choose Go To and then specify one of the available scenes from the list.
The timeline will automatically jump to that scene.

14.10.5 Concept of Layer

Layers help you organise the artwork in your document. You can draw and edit objects on one layer without affecting objects on another layer. In areas of the stage with nothing on a layer, you can see through it to the layers below.

To draw, paint or otherwise modify a layer or folder, select the layer in the Timeline to make it active. A pencil icon next to a layer or folder name in the Timeline indicates that the layer or folder is active. Only one layer can be active at a time.

Types of Layer

There are many types of layers, as you can see in the general properties of a layer:

1. **Normal Layers** These are the layers of Flash by default. They are used most commonly and for almost everything to place objects, sounds, actions and helps.

2. **Guide Layers** These are layers for special or specific content. They are used in the animations of objects movement and its only aim is to set the trajectory that this object must follow. Because its mission is to represent the trajectory of an animated object, its content usually is a line (straight, curve etc).

3. **Mask Layers** These layers can be seen as groups that keep the unmasked layers off (we'll see them immediately). The use of these layers is something difficult (but not too much).

Layer Properties

The Layer Properties dialog box makes it easy to changes several layer options at once. You can change a layer name, show or lock a layer, change a layer type or outline color, and modify the layer height to show more information in the Timeline.

Setting layer properties of a folder automatically sets the properties for all the layers within that folder. To change layer properties, steps are as follows:

(i) Select the layer in the Timeline.
(ii) Click the Modify menu, point to Timeline, and then click Layer Properties.
(iii) Select from the following options:
  (a) **Name** Enter a new name.
  (b) **Show** Select this check box to show the layer.
  (c) **Lock** Select this check box to lock the layer or clear it to unlock the layer.
  (d) **Type** Select a layer option: Normal, Guide, Guided, Mask, Masked, or Folder.
  (e) **Outline Color** Click the Color box, and then select a color.
  (f) **View Layer As Outlines** Select this check box to view the layer as outlines.
  (g) **Layer Height** Click the popup, and then select a percentage to display more information in the Timeline.
(iv) Click OK.

Create a Layer and Layer Name

To create a new layer, do one of the following.

(i) Insert -> Timeline-> Layer.
(ii) Click the New Layer button at the bottom of the Timeline.
(iii) Right-click a layer name in the Timeline and select insert Layer from the context menu.

As soon as you create a new layer, you should give it meaningful name. Right-click on its name (something like Layer 2), select Properties and change the name.

Show or Hide a Layer or Folder

A red X next to the name of a layer or folder in the Timeline indicates that a layer or folder is hidden. In the publish settings, you can choose whether hidden layers are included when you publish a SWF file.

(i) To hide a layer or folder, click in the Eye column to the right of the layer or folder name in the Timeline. To show the layer or folder, click it again.
(ii) To hide all the layers and folders in the Timeline, click the Eye icon. To show all layers and folders, click it again.
(iii) To show or hide multiple layers or folders, drag through the Eye column.
(iv) To hide all layers and folders other than the current layer or folder, Alt+click in the Eye column to the right of a layer or folder name. To show all layers and folders, Alt-click it again.

Lock or Unlock One or More Layers or Folders

Follow the steps to lock or unlock one or more layers or folders:

(i) To lock a layer or folder, click in the Lock column to the right of the name. To unlock the layer or folder, click in the Lock column again.
(ii) To lock all layers and folders, click the padlock icon. To unlock all layers and folders, click it again.
(iii) To lock or unlock multiple layers or folders, drag through the Lock column.
(iv) To lock all other layers or folders, Alt-click in the Lock column to the right of a layer or folder name. To unlock all layers or folders, Alt+click in the Lock column again.

Delete a Layer or Folder

To delete a layer or folder, steps are as follows:

(i) To select the layer or folder, click its name in the Timeline or any frame in the layer.
(ii) Do one of the following:
  (a) Click the Delete Layer button in the Timeline.
  (b) Drag the layer or folder to the Delete Layer button.
  (c) Right-click the layer or folder name and select Delete Layer from the context menu.

View the Contents of a Layer as Outlines

To distinguish which layer an object belongs to, display all objects on a layer as colored outlines.

(i) To display all objects on that layer as outlines, click in the Outline column to the right of the layer's name. To turn off outline display, click it again.
(ii) To display objects on all layers as outlines, click the outline icon. To turn off outline display on all layers, click it again.
(iii) To display objects on all layers other than the current layer as outlines, Alt+click in the Outline column to the right of a layer's name. To turn off the outline display for all layers, Alt-click in it again.

Methods

Methods	Description
write("string")	Writes the given string on the document.
writeln("string")	Writes the given string on the document with newline character at the end.
getElementById()	Returns the element having the given id value.
getElementsByName()	Returns all the elements having the given name value.
getElementsByTagName()	Returns all the elements having the given tag name.
getElementsByClassName()	Returns all the elements having the given class name.

13.2.15 The Location Object

A location object holds information on the current URL. It cannot be created by the user. It is a predefined object. It can be accessed by the location property of a window object.

Properties

Properties	Description
host	Specifies the host and domain name, or IP address of a network host.
hostname	Specifies the host:port portion of the URL.
href	Specifies the entire URL.
pathname	Specifies the URL-path portion of the URL.
protocol	Specifies the beginning of the URL, including the colon.

Methods

Methods	Description
reload	Forces a reload of the window's current document.
replace	Loads the specified URL over the current history entry.

13.2.16 The Form Object

The JavaScript Form Object is a property of the document object. This corresponds to an HTML input form constructed with the <form> tag. A form can be submitted by calling the JavaScript submit method or clicking the form submit button.

Properties

Properties	Description
action	Read/write string that reflects the action attribute of the form.
elements[]	An array containing all of the elements of the form. Use it to loop through form easily.
encoding	Read/write string that specifies how the form data is encoded.
length	The number of elements in the form.
method	Read/write string that specifies how the method the form is submitted.
name	The name of the form.
target	The name of the target frame or window form is to be submitted to.

Methods

Methods	Description
reset()	Resets the form
submit()	Submits a form

13.2.17 Button Object

A button object refers to a clickable button in an HTML page.

Properties

Properties	Description
accessKey	String value that sets/ returns the accessKey for the button.
disabled	Boolean value that sets/ returns whether the button is disabled.
form	References the form that contains the reset button.
name	Reflects the name of the button (the name attribute).
type	A property available on all form elements, "type" returns the type of the calling form element, in this case, "button".
value	A read only string that specifies the value of the button.

Methods

Methods	Description
blur()	Removes focus away from the button.
click()	Simulates a user clicking on the form button.
focus()	Sets focus on the button.

13.2.18 Reset Object

The reset button (<input type="reset">) within your form can be accessed and manipulated using JavaScript, *via* the corresponding Reset object.

Properties

Properties	Description
disabled	Boolean value that sets/ returns whether the reset button is disabled.
form	References the form that contains the reset button.
name	Reflects the name of the reset button (the name attribute).
type	A property available on all form elements, "type" returns the type of the calling form element, in this case, "reset".
value	A read only string that specifies the value of the reset button.

13.2.19 Submit Object

The submit button (<input type="submit">) within your form can be accessed and manipulated using JavaScript, *via* the corresponding Submit object.

Properties

Properties	Description
disabled	Boolean value that sets/ returns whether the submit button is disabled.
form	References the form that contains the submit button.
name	Reflects the name of the submit button (the name attribute).
type	A property available on all form elements, "type" returns the type of the calling form element, in this case, "submit".
value	A read only string that specifies the value of the submit button.

13.2.20 Checkbox Object

Checkboxes (<input type="checkbox">) within your form can be accessed and manipulated using JavaScript *via* the corresponding Checkbox object. There are two ways to access a checkbox, depending on whether it unique in the form (distinct name), or part of a group of checkboxes, all sharing the same name.

Properties

Properties	Description
accessKey	String value that sets/ returns the accessKey for the checkbox.
checked	Boolean property that reflects the current state of the checkbox, "True" if it's checked, and "False" if not.
defaultChecked	Boolean property that reflects the value of the CHECKED attribute.
disabled	Boolean value that sets/ returns whether the checkbox is disabled.
form	References the form that contains the checkbox.
name	Reflects the name of the checkbox (the name attribute).
type	A property available on all form elements, "type" returns the type of the calling form element, in this case, "checkbox".
value	A read/write string that specifies the value of the checkbox (the value attribute).

Methods

Methods	Description
blur()	Removes focus away from the checkbox.
click()	Simulates a user clicking on the checkbox.
focus()	Sets focus on the checkbox.

13.2.21 Radio Object

Radio buttons (<input type="radio">) within your form can be accessed and manipulated using JavaScript *via* the corresponding Radio object. There are two ways to access a radio button, depending on whether it unique in the form (distinct name), or part of a group of radio buttons, all sharing the same name.

Properties

Properties	Description
checked	Boolean property that reflects the current state of the radio button, "True" if it's checked, and "False" if not.
defaultChecked	Boolean property that reflects the value of the CHECKED attribute.
form	References the form that contains the radio button.
name	Reflects the name of the radio button (the name attribute).
type	A property available on all form elements, "type" returns the type of the calling form element, in this case, "radio".
value	A read/write string that specifies the value of the radio button (the value attribute).

Methods

Methods	Description
blur()	Removes focus away from the radio button.
click()	Simulates a user clicking on the radio button.
focus()	Sets focus on the radio button.

13.2.22 Select Objects

Form SELECT elements (<select>) within your form can be accessed and manipulated in JavaScript *via* the corresponding Select object.

Properties

Properties	Description
disabled	Boolean value that sets/ returns whether this SELECT element is disabled.
form	References the form that contains the selection list in question.
length	Returns the number of options in the SELECT element.
multiple	Boolean that indicates whether this SELECT allows more than one option to be selected simultaneously.
name	Reflects the name of the SELECT element (the name attribute).
size	An integer reflecting the number of OPTIONs being displayed at once within this SELECT element.
type	A property available on all form elements, "type" returns the type of the calling form element. For SELECT, the two possible values are "select-one" or "select-multiple", depending on the type of selection list.

Methods

Methods	Description
add(newoption, beforeoption*)	Dynamically adds a new OPTION to the SELECT element, where: • **newoption** The new option to add, created using new Option(). • **beforeoption*** This parameter differs depending on the browser used.
remove (optionindex)	Removes an existing option within SELECT at the specified position, where 0=1st option, 1=2nd option etc.
blur()	Removes focus away from the selection list.
focus()	Sets focus on the selection list.

animate the motion of an object. Instead of defining the location of the object in every frame, you can create a motion tween, which will automatically move the object from the beginning location to ending location.

2. Shape Tweening

Macromedia Flash is known as one of the greatest animation tools around. Using the Flash authoring tool you can create frame-by-frame animations, motion-tweened animations which are created by specifying the first and the last frames only and dynamic animations that are generated *via* Action Script. In addition to all these animations, Flash can create morphing animations, in which you can specify the first and the final shapes so that all the frames in between are created by the authoring tool. This is called Shape Tween.

14.10.8 Tweening Color Effects

A fade-out effect is achieved in Flash by creating a Motion Tween, and adjusting the Alpha property of a Symbol. A simple example of creating this effect is provided below. The Symbol created will fade out over the duration of ten frames. The instructions provided are written for Flash 5. However, if you are using a previous version of Flash, the basic method is the same.

This process can be applied to any Symbol, including those containing text. Make sure that the object has been converted to a Symbol before applying a Motion Tween.

A basic example: To fade a blue circle to white over ten frames, do the following:

1	Open a new document, with a white background.
2	Select the Circle Tool, using a blue color. (Or any other desired color).
3	Draw a circle on the Stage.
4	Double-click the circle to highlight both the line and fill.
5	Choose Insert > Convert to Symbol. Select "Graphic" and click OK.
6	Select frame 10 in the Timeline. Choose Insert > Keyframe.
7	Highlight the Symbol on the Stage. Select Modify > Instance.
8	Choose the Effects Panel. Note:In previous versions, this is called the "Color Effect" panel.
9	Choose "Alpha" from the pop-up menu.
10	Enter the number "0" as the percent. Hit the Enter key on your keyboard to activate the change.
11	Highlight frame 1 and choose Modify > Frame, to access the Frame panel.
12	In the Tweening dialog box, choose "Motion" from the menu. Note:In previous versions, this can be found as a Tweening tab. Hit the Enter key to activate the change.
13	Choose Control> Test Movie to see the fade effect.

14.10.9 Inserting Sound Layer

An audio gives additional effect to the flash file and often adds to the viewers interest, audio files can also be used as event sounds, button sounds etc. To insert sound layer, steps are as follows:

(i) Open Adobe Flash (or Macromedia flash) and select actionscript 2.0 or 3.0 as your version.
(ii) Create a new layer.
(iii) Then go to "file" menu on the top and select "import to library" from the dropdown ,browse to the location on to the hard disk and select the audio file.
(iv) Drag the audio file from the library on to the stage, make sure the layer currently selected is the new blank layer.
(v) Add a new keyframe to the layer after any number of frames, the audio can be clearly seen as a waveform.
(vi) Go to "control" menu from the top and select play from drop down, the play head moves forward and the sound plays.
(vii) Go to Properties panel and select sound, the option if set to stream plays the sound up to the number of frames in the layer whereas selecting event option plays the whole audio irrespective of number of frames.

14.10.10 Testing a Scene and Movie

Follow the steps for testing a scene and movie:

(i) If your movie is not already open, go ahead and open it now.
(ii) Choose Control> Test Movie.
(iii) Flash will export the movie to a SWF file and then open a Preview window. The size of the preview may be different from your original movie. To view it at actual size, choose View> 100%.
(iv) You can control playback by choosing Window> Controller. Use the Controller as you normally would to stop and start playback.

14.10.11 Macromedia Flash: Importing Objects

In Flash, you are able to import audio, video and images. All of your imported objects will be placed in the library (whether you import directly to the library or to the stage).

To import images, go to File > Import > Import to Library (If you wish to place an object directly onto the stage in the current layer and frame, choose Import to

Stage). Flash will import .AI, .BMP, .EPS, .GIF, .JPG, .PCT, .PNG, .PSD, .TIF, .WMF and other image formats.

Select the images you would like to import and click OK. You will find all of your imported images in the Library panel.

To import audio, go to File > Import > Import to Library. Flash will import .MP3, .WAV, .AIF, and .AU audio formats. To apply an audio file, select or create the keyframe where you would like the audio to start. Select the keyframe in the Timeline, and choose your desired audio clip from the Sound drop down menu in the Properties panel. In the Properties panel, you can also change the loop (repetition), fade in, fade out, or customize fading effects. To stop an audio file, select or create a keyframe where you want the audio to stop. In the Properties panel, select the audio that would be playing and choose Stop from the Sync drop down menu or choose Fade Out from the Effect drop down menu.

To import video, go to File > Import > Import Video. Flash will import .MOV, .AVI, .MPG, .MPEG, .DV, .DVI, .WMV, and .FLV video formats. If the video file is on your computer, enter the file path. If the video file is on a web server, select the "web server…" radio button and enter the full URL. Select Next. Now, we recommend you select the "Progressive download from a web server." Choose the desired video quality. Choose Next.

14.10.12 Macromedia Flash: Saving Your Flash Movie

Generally, you will want to save/export your Flash animation as a .SWF. When you preview your animation in Flash Player by hitting Ctrl+Enter (or Control >Test Movie), Flash automatically creates a .SWF in the same folder as your Flash Document (.FLA).

To export your Flash animation in an HTML web page, go to File>Publish Settings. Click the HTML tab, customize your settings and click Publish. Flash will save the .HTML file in the same folder as your Flash Document. In the Formats tab of Publish Settings (File>Publish Settings), you can also choose from .GIF, .JPG, .PNG, .EXE, .HQX, and .MOV.

To export your Flash animation in another video format, go to File>Export>Export Movie. Change "Save as type" to your desired format. Flash will export to .SWF, .AVI, .MOV and more. Depending on the video format, you may have to select video compression settings in a dialog box. Flash will save the exported video in the same folder as the Flash Document.

14.10.13 Publish a Flash Movie

After you have made the appropriate changes to the flash animated header of your web design template you should publish and update it. To Publish a Flash movie, follow these steps:

1. Click on **File** menu and select **Publish Settings.**
2. A **Publish Settings** dialog box appears. By default in this dialog box, **Formats** tab appears. In Formats tab, there are publishing options. From here you can select the types of files you want Flash to generate.

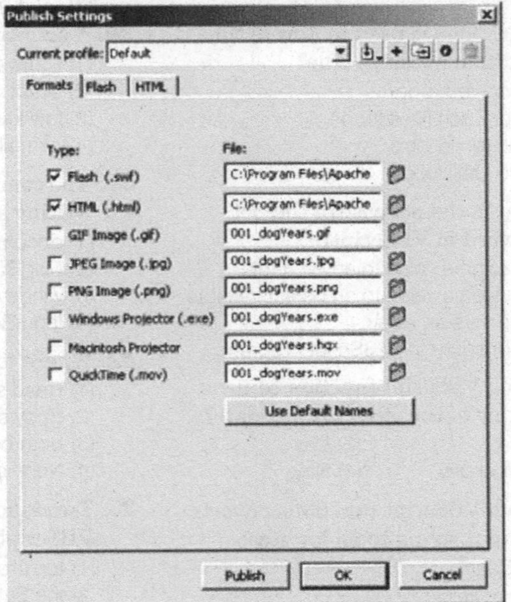

Types of files are as follows:

a. **Flash (.swf)** Web browsers must have flash player or Shockwave player installed to view any movies.

b. **HTML (.html)** This file is needed in order for the flash file to be contained somewhere. If an .swf is directly linked to in a web browser, the movie will automatically resize to the dimensions of the viewer's web browser, possibly causing some distortion or scaling in any graphics used within the movie.

c. **GIF Image (.gif)** This format saves the movie as animated or still GIF images. The tab for it offers various optimization options.

d. **JPEG Image (.jpg)** This format will publish the first frame of the movie.

e. **PNG image (.png)** This format is not supported by all browsers or computers yet, but it also contains optimization options. Will publish the first frame of the movie.

19. What is the difference between the Sub procedure and Function procedure?
(1) Only the Sub procedure can perform actions
(2) Both procedures can take arguments
(3) Only the Function procedure can return a value
(4) All of the above

20. In the Select Case statement, which case is used for unknown cases?
(1) Else (2) Default
(3) Unknown (4) Not

21. Which loop is used to iterate till a condition becomes true?
(1) For Next loop
(2) For Each Next loop
(3) Do While loop
(4) Do Until loop

22. What is the purpose of the Set keyword in VBScript?
(1) Assign a value to any variable.
(2) Assign a value to an object variable.
(3) Declare an array.
(4) Configure the VBScript program.

23. Which VBScript function returns the day of the week for any date?
(1) Date (2) Day
(3) Weekday (4) Now

24. Which VBScript function converts an input string to all lowercase?
(1) LCase
(2) LowerCase
(3) Lower
(4) There is no such function to directly convert to lowercase.

25. Which VBScript function can compare two strings?
(1) StringCompare
(2) Compare
(3) StrComp
(4) StrCompare

26. What language is VBScript based on?
(1) VBScript, Microsoft's Visual Basic Scripting Edition, is a scaled down version of Visual Basic.
(2) JScript and JavaScript.
(3) HTML
(4) XML

27. There are two methods for declaring variables in VBScript
(1) option explicit and option explicit.
(2) explicitly and implicitly.
(3) using VB and Java.
(4) using JavaScript and Perl variable.

28. What two VBScript commands can be used to make decisions?
(1) If ..Then …Else
(2) Select …Case
(3) For ...Next
(4) (1) and (2) are correct.

29. Which of these VBScript commands can be used to iterate through loops?
(1) For ...Next.
(2) While … Wend
(3) If … Then Else
(4) (1) and (2) are correct

30. A scripting language is a
(1) lightweight programming language
(2) script
(3) low level language
(4) compiled language

31. The command used in VBScript for writing some text on a page is
(1) document.write( )
(2) MsgBox
(3) window.write( )
(4) InputBox

32. Where to put the VBScript code?
(1) Head section
(2) Body section
(3) Both body and head section
(4) None of the above

33. Two kinds of procedures in VBScript
(1) top procedure and bottom procedure.
(2) the Sub procedure and the Function procedure.
(3) low procedure and high procedure
(4) None of the above

34. Which of these are string functions available in VBScript?
(1) Chr (2) InStr
(3) LCase (4) All of these

35. Which of these are Time and Date functions available in VBScript?
(1) DateSerial
(2) DateDifference
(3) (1) and (2) are correct
(4) DateValue

36. Which of the following is true about variable naming conventions in VBScript?
(1) Variable name must begin with an alphabet.
(2) Variable names cannot exceed 255 characters.
(3) Variables should not contain a period(.)
(4) All of the above

37. Which of the following operator can be used to get the modulus of two numbers in VBScript?
(1) Mod (2) %
(3) Remainder (4) Remain

38. How will you get the integer part of a number in VBScript?
(1) Using FormatNumber function
(2) Using FormatPercent function
(3) Using Int function
(4) Using Log function

39. How will you trim the spaces on the right of a string using VBScript?
(1) Using Lcase function
(2) Using Ucase function
(3) Using Ltrim function
(4) Using Rtrim function

40. Which of the following is correct about variable declared using 'Dim' in VBScript?
(1) Variables declared using 'Dim' keyword at a Procedure level are available only within the same procedure.
(2) Variables declared using 'Dim' keyword at script level are available to all the procedures within the same script.
(3) Both of the above
(4) None of the above

41. How will you increase the size of an array in VBScript?
(1) Using RiDim statement
(2) Using LBound function
(3) Using UBound function
(4) Using split function

42. Which of the following operator can be used to check if two numbers are equal or not in VBScript?
(1) != (2) <>
(3) not (4) ~

43. How to return a value from a function in VBScript?
(1) Using return keyword.
(2) Assign the value to the function name itself.
(3) Using ret keyword.
(4) Using back keyword.

44. Which of the following is correct about features of JavaScript?
(1) JavaScript is a lightweight, interpreted programming language.
(2) JavaScript is designed for creating network-centric applications.
(3) JavaScript is complementary to and integrated with Java.
(4) All of the above

45. Which of the following is the correct syntax to print a page using JavaScript?

(1) window.print( ):
(2) browser.print( );
(3) navigator.print( );
(4) document.print( );

46. Consider the following code snippet

```
function printArray (a)
{
  var len = a.length. i = 0;
  if(len == 0)
   console.log("Empty Array");
  else
  {
   do
   {
     console.log(a[i]);
   } while (++i < len);
  }
}
```

What does the above code result?

(1) Prints the numbers in the array in ascending order.
(2) Prints the numbers in the array in the reverse order.
(3) Prints 0 to the length of the array.
(4) Prints "Empty Array".

47. What are the three important manipulations done in a for loop on a loop variable?

(1) Updation, Incrementation, Initialisation.
(2) Initialisation, Testing, Updation.
(3) Testing, Updation, Testing.
(4) Initialisation,Testing,Incrementation.

48. Consider the following code snippet

```
function tail(o)
{
 for(; o.next; o = o.next);
 return 0;
}
```

Will the above code snippet work? If not, what will be the error?

(1) No, this will throw an exception as only numerics can be used in a for loop
(2) No, this will not iterate
(3) Yes, this will work
(4) No, this will result in a runtime error with the message "Cannot use Linked List"

49. Consider the following code snippet

```
for(var p in o)
   console.log(o[p]);
```

The above code is equivalent to which code?

(1) for(var i = 0;i < a.length;i++)
console.log(a[i]);
(2) for(int i = 0;i < a.length;i++)
console.log(a[i]);
(3) for(var i = 0;i <= a.length;i++)
console.log(a[i]);
(4) for(var i = 1;i < a.length;i++)
console.log(a[i]);

50. Consider the following code snippet

```
while(a != 0)
{
 if(a == 1)
  continue;
 else
  a++;
}
```

What will be the role of the continue keyword in the above code snippet?

(1) The continue keyword restarts the loop
(2) The continue keyword skips the next iteration
(3) The continue keyword skips the rest of the statements in that iteration
(4) None of the above

51. You can redirect the web page in JavaScript by using...... method.

(1) window.reload (2) window.location
(3) page.location (4) url.newlocation

52. ....are usually variables that are used internally in the objects methods, but can also be globally visible variables that are used through the page.

(1) Object properties
(2) Variable properties
(3) Method properties
(4) Internal properties

53. State whether the following statements are True or False.

(i) **JavaScript ignores spaces, tabs and newlines that appear in JavaScript program.**
(ii) **Semicolons are necessary while writing JavaScript statements.**
(iii) **JavaScript is a case-sensitive language.**

(1) i- True, ii- False, iii-True
(2) i- False, ii- True, iii-True
(3) i-True, ii-True, iii-False
(4) i- False, ii- False, iii-True

54. Which of the following is not an operator used in JavaScript?

(1) Arithmetic operator
(2) Comparison operator
(3) Conditional operator
(4) Static operator

55. JavaScript for loop contains the following important parts.

(i) **The loop initialisation to start value.**
(ii) **The test statement to test if the given condition is True or not.**
(iii) **The iteration statement to increase or decrease counter.**
(iv) **The end statement to finish the loop.**

(1) i, ii and iii
(2) i, iii and iv
(3) i, ii and iv
(4) All i, ii, iii, and iv

56. In JavaScript, a ...... is simply an identifier followed by a colon that is applied to a statement or block of code.

(1) bookmark (2) label
(3) break (4) continue

57. Match the following JavaScript function with their description.

i. onblur	a. script runs when element changes
ii. onmouseup	b. script runs when the form is reset
iii. onchange	c. script runs when the element lost focus.
iv. onreset	d. script runs when mouse button is released.

(1) i-d, ii-c, iii-a, iv-b
(2) i-b, ii-c, iii-a, iv-d
(3) i-c, ii-d, iii-a, iv-b
(4) i-a, ii-c, iii-d, iv-b

58. What are variables used for in JavaScript programs?

(1) Storing numbers, dates, or other values
(2) Varying randomly
(3) Causing high-school algebra flashbacks
(4) None of the above

59. .... JavaScript statements embedded in an HTML page can respond to user events such as mouse-clicks, form input and page navigation.

(1) Client-side (2) Server-side
(3) Local (4) Native

CHAPTER PRACTICE

1. ...... refers to any type of application or presentation that involves more than one type of media, such as text, graphics, video, animation and sound.
(1) An executable file
(2) Desktop publishing
(3) Multimedia
(4) Hypertext

2. One of the disadvantages of multimedia is
(1) cost (2) adaptability
(3) usability (4) relativity

3. The text color in a presentation should contrast with the .... color.
(1) CPU (2) frame
(3) stack (4) background

4. A smaller version of an image is called a
(1) clipart
(2) bitmap
(3) portable network graphic
(4) thumbnail

5. Images included in many software titles are called ....
(1) clipart (2) popups
(3) .jpg files (4) .tiff files

6. In the top level domains, .nom specifies
(1) commercial entities
(2) personal sites
(3) non-government organisations
(4) cooperatives

7. Space between lines
(1) leading (2) kerning
(3) extrude (4) expanded

8. Computer monitor works in which color space?
(1) RGB (2) CMYK
(3) RBG (4) None

9. There are how many types of 2D graphics?
(1) 2 (2) 3 (3) 4 (4) 5

10. Bitmap is sometimes referred as
(1) JPEG (2) GIF (3) Raster (4) None

11. The .... shows the frames in the movie .
(1) Toolbar (2) Properties pane
(3) Timeline (4) Scene

12. Hardware that creates sound from a mathematical representation.
(1) Sound Synthesizer
(2) Stampers
(3) Speaker
(4) Sons

13. The typical size for a graphic design is measured in
(1) pica (2)pixels
(3) points (4) inches

14. The tool allows you the magnify an area of the design for detail work.
(1) Zoom (2) Filters
(3) Crop (4) Eraser

15. By changing the % of, you can blend multiple layers with one another.
(1) Transparency (2) Opacity
(3) Blending options (4) Both (1) and (2)

16. Which tool allows you to reposition an object in your layer
(1) Move (2) Marquee
(3) Crop (4) Hand

17. The name of the area upon which the graphic design is completed is
(1) gradient (2) canvas
(3) smudge (4) stage

18. Computer monitor palette does not hold which color?
(1) blob of black paint
(2) blob of red paint
(3) blob of green paint
(4) blob of blue paint

19. Computer monitor primary color allows how many individual shades?
(1) 300 (2) 255 (3) 200 (4) 256

20. This is, by far, the most tedious way to create animations.
(1) Shape Tween (2) Motion Tween
(3) Mask (4) Frame by Frame

21. Which of the following best describes the process of streaming?
(1) Playing audio files.
(2) Delaying playing a multimedia element until enough data has been buffered so the element can play uninterrupted.
(3) Reducing the load time of a web page by streamlining operations.
(4) Sending packets to a web server so improve server performance.

22. Empty key frames are indicated by a .... circle on the timeline.
(1) hollow (2) black
(3) open eye (4) closed eye

23. Which one of the following audio formats was developed by Microsoft?
(1) AIFF (2) MIDI
(3) RealAudio (4) WAV

24. Which of the following statements is true?
(1) MIDI files are generally larger than WAV files.
(2) Video files are generally much larger than audio files.
(3) Audio and video are one and the same.
(4) Nearly all 5 minute movie clips are under 1M in size.

25. Which company developed the Quick Time format?
(1) Microsoft
(2) Juniper
(3) Apple
(4) Silicon graphics

26. An audio repository is which of the following?
(1) A web presentation that warehouse audio files
(2) A library cataloging all MIDI music
(3) A website that provides tutorials on sound
(4) A web server capable of playing audio files.

27. Which of the following is the best definition for Virtual Reality?
(1) Any computer game involving graphics.
(2) A 3D simulation of a real or imagined environment using computers.
(3) A simulator which requires special eye glasses.
(4) The process of coding in another dimension.

28. What is another term to describe vector animation?
(1) Animation (2) Vector
(3) Alpha (4) Path animation

29. What type of animation is best for creating a flat appearance?
(1) SWF (2) Path animation
(3) 3D animation (4) 2D animation

30. How is the movement of text or graphics classified?
(1) Animation (2) Alpha
(3) Vector (4) MOV

31. A .... displays a list of commands and usually appears in the toolbar at the top of the screen.
(1) view (2) menu
(3) kit (4) list

32. Quick access to frequently used commands can be found in the ...... toolbar.
(1) view (2) drawing
(3) kit (4) menu

33. To cut down the size of the entire graphic design, including all layers, you should select the ...... tool.
(1) marquee (2) magic wand
(3) eraser (4) crop

34. Drop shadow, inner glow and bevel are examples of ...... you need to use with text.
(1) filters
(2) blending options
(3) image adjustments
(4) layer modes

35. The tool allows you to copy one area of the layer to another area of the layer.
(1) Magic wand (2) Clone stamp
(3) Marquee (4) Gradient

36. The ...... tool allows you to select a rectangular or circular area of an layer to change or delete.
(1) marquee (2) crop
(3) hand (4) zoom

37. To delete a series of steps that have been used in a graphic design, you would need to use the ...... pallette.
(1) layer (2) action
(3) history (4) path

38. To undo the last change made to your graphic design, the keys may be used.
(1) Ctrl + D (2) Ctrl + Z
(3) Shift + D (4) Shift + Z

39. Which of these is not likely to be the responsibility of a multimedia project?
(1) Create interfaces
(2) Ensure the visual consistency of the project
(3) Structure content
(4) Create budgets and timelines for the project

40. MIDI is a protocol designed for recording and playing back music on digital synthesizer. MIDI stands for:
(1) Musical Instrument Digital Interface
(2) Musical Instrument Digital Instruction
(3) MP3 Instrument Digital Interface
(4) Musical Instrument Design Interface

41. Interleaving the audio and video segments of a video clip together in a data file is
(1) flare (2) flattening
(3) hot spot (4) helical scan

42. Pixels represent tiny ...... of color, which are typically unseen by the naked eye.
(1) circles (2) squares
(3) inches (4) swatches

43. To resize a graphic in a layer, select the ...... tool, then check mark ...... to see selection handles.
(1) marquee; resize
(2) move; show bounding box
(3) move; resize
(4) marquee; show bounding box

44. The ...... tool is best selected when you need to select an abnormally shaped image in a layer.
(1) marquee (2) lasso
(3) magic wand (4) clone stamp

45. Once you build the layers in your graphic design, you cannot rearrange them.
(1) True (2) False
(3) Both (1) and (2) (4) None

46. The tool allows you to cut text out of a scenic background for use in your design.
(1) Blending options
(2) Image adjustments
(3) Layer modes
(4) Text mask

47. If you have a solid color to select and delete, the tool is the quickest and most effective.
(1) Magic wand (2) Color picker
(3) Zoom (4) None

48. When deleting detailed areas of your image by hand, the tool is the best option.
(1) Magic wand (2) Clone stamp
(3) Gradient (4) Eraser

49. You must select which tool to give your text perspective against your background.
(1) Blending option (2) Transparency
(3) Layer effect (4) Both (1) and (3)

50. The name of the areas that include the color swatches, layers and toolbox
(1) Layer (2) Layer effect
(3) Blending option (4) Palette

51. The .... panel contains the basic tools needed to draw and modify objects.
(1) Actions (2) Properties
(3) Tools (4) Layers

52. The .... is a holding place for all symbols and imported images and sounds within a single Flash file .
(1) Library (2) Timeline
(3) Properties (4) Tools panel

53. A key frame that contains objects will be represented by a .... circle.
(1) Hollow (2) Black
(3) Blue (4) Gray

54. Which of the following tags cannot be used to include audio on a web page?
(1) BG SOUND (2) EMBED
(3) MUSIC (4) OBJECT

55. Which of the following file extensions would be used for a Quick Time movie?
(1) avi (2) mpg (3) mov (4) sgi

56. Short films that use stop motion techniques are what type of animation?
(1) Production
(2) Frame-based animation
(3) Animation
(4) HTML

57. Which type of animation uses still frames with a graphic that slightly changes position?
(1) Pre-production
(2) Animation
(3) Frame-based animation
(4) Vector animation

58. Which type of animation is best suited for creating a flipbook animation?
(1) Frames Per Second
(2) Animation
(3) SWF
(4) Frame-based animation

59. Which type of animation is best for developing characters that would showcase depth and realism?
(1) 3D animation (2) 2D animation
(3) Vector (4) Alpha

CHAPTER

14

Multimedia & Authoring Tools

Multi means many and media means different medium to communicate. Multimedia is an integration of T, G, V, I, A. Here T
stands for Text, G signifies Graphics, V stands for Video, I signifies Images and A stands for Animation. Multimedia is best used for presenting things in interactive and attractive manner so that they (concepts) are never forgotten.

Multimedia authoring tools provide the important framework you need for organising and editing the elements of multimedia like graphics, sounds, animations and video clips. Some of the examples are Macromedia Flash, Macromedia Director, Author ware and Quest.

One can also say that multimedia authoring is the creation of multimedia production, sometimes called Movies or Presentations.

14.1 Graphics Devices

Graphics devices are the computer hardware that generates computer graphics and allows them to be shown on a display, usually using a graphics card or video card in combination with a device driver to create images on the screen.

Graphic devices use an approach which assumes that every dot on the screen is separately accessible. Graphic devices are output devices, but their physical characteristics restrict them from taking data as represented in the computer's memory and displaying the data directly.

14.1.1 Graphic Accelerator Card

It is also known as a 3D accelerator. The graphics accelerator card is an internal board that generally installed into the PCI or AGP slot and reduces the time it takes to produce images on the computer screen by incorporating its own processor and memory. These days almost all graphics cards are accelerator cards.

14.1.2 Monitor Display Configuration

Using screen resolution menu:

(i) Close all open programs

(ii) Right click on blank area on your desktop and then click Screen resolution.

(iii) Click the image of the monitor that you want to configure.

(iv) To change the screen size for the selected monitor, select a resolution from the **Resolution** drop down list.

We recommend in most circumstances to use the native resolution of the monitor, which is marked as recommended.

(v) To change the orientation between landscape and portrait or to flip the orientation, select an option from the **Orientation** drop down list.

(vi) After changing the display setting, click on **Apply**.

(vii) A confirmation window opens. Click **Keep changes** to save the settings, or click **Revert** to cancel the change.

14.1.3 Digital Image

A digital image is composed of an array of picture elements or pixels. Each pixel represents a single color and value. The computer arranges the pixels to create the illusion of a continuous image, in a manner similar to that of a television screen or a Pointillist painting. Every image has an absolute width and height in pixels.

Image Formats

Image file formats are standardised means of organising and storing digital images. Image files are composed of digital data in one of these formats that can be rasterised for use on a computer display or printer. An image file format may store data in uncompressed, compressed or vector formats.

Extension	Name	Description
.TIFF,.TIF	Tagged Image File Format	TIFF images create very large file sizes. TIFF images are uncompresses and thus contain a lot of detailed image data.
.BMP	BitMap	This format handles graphic files within the Microsoft Windows OS. There is no compression or information loss with BMP files which allow images to have very high quality, but also very large file sizes.
.JPG/JPEG	Joint Photographic Experts Group	A JPEG is compressed in a way that losses some of the image detail during the compression in order to make the file small. JPEG files are usually used for photographs on the web.
.GIF	Graphics Interchange Format	This format compresses image but, as different from JPEG, the compression is lossless (no detail is lost in the compression, but the file can't be made as small as a JPEG). This format is never used for photography, because of the limited number of color. It can also be used for animations.
.PIC	Macintosh Picture	This format is a standard for encoding graphical images, both object oriented and bitmapped. It is used in Macintosh applications, but many PC applications can read format too.
.PDF	Portable Document Format	This format is used to present documents in an independent manner of application software, hardware and operating systems. To display or print a PDF file, the user should obtain the freeware Adobe Acrobat Reader.
.PSD	Photoshop Document	A PSD file stores an image with support for most imaging options available in Photoshop. These include layers with masks, transparency, text, alpha channels and spot color, clipping paths and duotone settings.

14.2 Graphic Formats

This is the kind of multimedia where print media is involved. You can create a graphic design with the help of various sort of fonts, lines, pictures etc.

Various aspect of drawing formats are as follows:

1. Theory of Design

Before proceeding on to designing the artwork, you must know what is to be there on the artwork. The complete knowledge of the subject is must. Remember, well begun is half done. So, once you are ready with all the complete details you can start the work.

2. Form

It is a platform on which the all main artwork is to be done. It can be one of the various size which are available in the market. The most popular one of size is A4 size.

3. Line

User can have the various lines which thickness ranging starts from $\frac{1}{2}$ point to 12 points. It depends on user's artwork, what type of line they want to use in their artwork.

4. Space

In artwork, white space is most important. The white space gives the energetic good look and appear of the artwork. More the white space, more the readability of the various objects on the artwork.

5. Texture

It also concerns the base of the artwork, i.e. type of base that user is going to use for the artwork. It can be paper, matte etc.

6. Color

It is most appealing part of the artwork because there are few people who have real color combination sense, both the mixing and contrasting. This has to be decided in such a way that the result is not goddy and too light that it skips the eyes.

7. Typography

There are more than 1000 fonts available. One has to be very choosy while selecting the font. Not only it should suit the product which is being advertised but it should be more readable too.

8. Layout

User can have their text on the right and graphic on the left or *vice-versa*. This emphasis on the layout of the

15.2 Networking

The term communication means sending or receiving information. A communication system can be defined as the collection of hardware and software that facilitates intersystem exchange of information between different devices.

A computer network is a collection of two or more computers, which are connected together to share information and resources. It is a combination of hardware and software that allows communication between computers over a network.

Evolution of Networking

Evolution of networking has the following networks:

1. ARPANET

The Advanced Research Projects Agency NETwork (ARPANET) was the world's first operational packet switching network, the first network to implement TCP/IP.

The U.S department of defence sponsored a project named ARPANET, whose goal was to connect computers at different universities and U.S defence.

In 1969, the University of California at Los Angeles, the University of California and the University of Utah were connected as the beginning of the ARPANET using 50 Kbits circuits.

In mid 80's, the National Science Foundation created a new network called NSFnet, which was more capable than ARPANET.

2. Internet (INTERconnection NETwork)

The Internet, in simple terms, is a network of the interlinked computer networking worldwide, which is accessible to the general public. Internet is such a huge network of several different interlinked networks relating to the business, government, academic and even smaller domestic networks.

Therefore, Internet is known as the network of all the other networks. These networks enable the Internet to be used for various important functions, which include the several means of communications like the file transfer, the online chat and even the sharing of the documents and websites on the WWW or the World Wide Web.

3. Interspace

Interspace is a client/server software program that allows multiple users to communicate online with real-time audio, video and text chat in dynamic 3D environments.

Interspace provides the most advanced form of communication available on the Internet today.

The Interspace is a vision of what the Internet will become tomorrow, when users cross-correlate information in multiple sources. It is an application environment for interconnecting spaces to manipulate information such as the Internet.

15.3 Switching Techniques

Switching techniques are used for transmitting data across networks. Different types of switching techniques are employed to provide communication between two computers. These are as follows:

15.3.1 Circuit Switching

Circuit switching is a methodology of implementing a telecommunication network in which two network nodes establish a dedicated communication channel (circuit), first through the network and then the message is transmitted through the channels.

The main advantage of circuit switching is guaranteed delivery. The circuit switching guarantees the full bandwidth of the channels and remains connected for the duration of the communication session.

15.3.2 Packet Switching

In packet based networks, the message gets broken into small data packets. These packets are sent out from the computer and they travel around the network seeking out the most efficient route to travel as circuits become available.

15.3.3 Message Switching

Message switching is a network switching technique, in which data is routed entirely from the source node to the destination node. In this technique, no physical path is established between source and destination in advance. During message routing, every intermediate switch in the network stores the whole message.

15.4 Data Communication Terminologies

The various data communication terminologies are as shown below:

15.4.1 Channel

A communication channel is a medium that is used in the transmission of a message from one point to another. In simple terms we can say that, it is a pathway over which data is transferred between remote devices. It may refer to the entire physical medium such as a telephone line, optical fibre, co-axial cable or twisted pair wire, it may refer to one of the several carrier frequencies transmitted simultaneously within the line.

Depending on their speed, there are three broad categories of communication channels – **narrow band**, which is slow and used for telegraph lines and low speed terminals; **voice band** used for ordinary telephone communication and **broadband,** which is fastest and used for transmitting large volumes of data at high speeds.

15.4.2 Baud Rate

It is a measure of the number of symbols (signals) transferred or line changes every second. It may represent more than one binary bit. Each symbol can represent or convey one (binary encoded signal) or several bits of data. For a binary signal of 20 Hz, this is equivalent to 20 baud (there are 20 changes per second).

15.4.3 Bandwidth

Bandwidth is the frequency range of a channel, measured as the difference between the highest and lowest frequencies that the channel supports. The maximum transmission speed is dependent upon the available bandwidth.

The larger the bandwidth, the higher the transmission speed. Frequency is measured in cycles per second, i.e. hertz (Hz). One Hz equals one cycle per second.

Note Frequency and period are the inverse of each other.

$$f = \frac{1}{T} \text{ and } T = \frac{1}{f}$$

Table : Units of period and frequency

Unit	Equivalent
Seconds (s)	1 s
Milliseconds (ms)	10^{-3} s
Microseconds (μs)	10^{-6} s
Nanoseconds (ns)	10^{-9} s
Picoseconds (ps)	10^{-12} s
Hertz (Hz)	1 Hz
Kilohertz (KHz)	10^{3} Hz
Megahertz (MHz)	10^{6} Hz
Gigahertz (GHz)	10^{9} Hz
Terahertz (THz)	10^{12} Hz

15.4.4 Data Transfer Rate (DTR)

A data transfer rate (or just data rate) is the amount of digital data that is moved from one place to another in a given time, usually in a second time on a network. In telecommunication, data transfer is usually measured in bits per second.

Bits Per Second (bps)

This is an expression of the number of data bits per second. Where, a binary signal is being used, this is same as the baud rate. When the signal is changed to another form, it will not be equal to the baud rate, as each line change can represent more than one bit (either two or four bits).

Measurement of Data Transfer Rate

The data rate of a computer network connection is normally measured in units of Bits Per Second (bps).

Network equipment makers typically rate their products using related, larger units of kbps, mbps, gbps and tbps.

One **Kilobit Per Second** (Kbps) equals 1000 bits per second (bps). (Kbps is sometimes also written as 'kbps' both carry the same meaning.)

One **Megabit Per Second** (Mbps) equals 1000 kbps or one million bps.

One **Gigabit Per Second** (Gbps) equals 1000 mbps or one million kbps or one billion bps.

One **Terabit Per Second** (Tbps) equals 1000 gbps or one million mbps or one trillion bps.

Data rates for non-network equipment are sometimes shown in Bytes Per Second (BPS) rather than bits per second.
In those cases:

- One KBPS equals one kilobyte per second.
- One MBPS equals one megabyte per second.
- One GBPS equals one gigabyte per second.
- One TBPS equals one terabyte per second.

Finally, one kilobyte per second equals 8 kilobits per second.

15.5 Transmission Media

Communication media of a network refer to the transmission media or the connecting media used in the network. It carries a signal from one computer to another. The communication media can also be referred as **communication channels.** Transmission media is grouped into two types as follows:

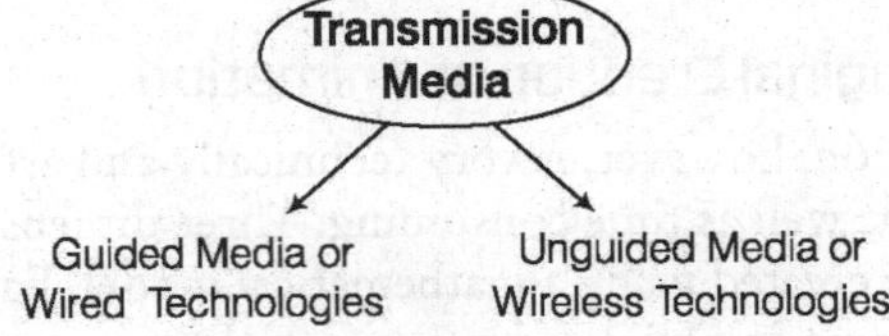

15.5.1 Guided Media or Wired Technologies

In guided media or wired technologies, the computers in a network are connected through wire or cable. The data signal physically gets transferred from the transmitting computer to the receiving computer through the wired e.g. the suite of Microsoft Office (versions 2010 and later) applications, including Microsoft Word and Excel, provides the PDF format as an option in the "Save As" dialog box. This enables you to create your documents as you normally would and then simply choose Save As → PDF, when saving. You can also add this functionality to earlier versions of Microsoft Office products by using this add on from Microsoft.

2. PDF Modification

Adobe Acrobat is the most popular PDF editor, but Microsoft Word will do it too.

PDFescape, DocHub and PDF Buddy are a few free to use online PDF editors that make it really easy to fill out forms like ones you sometimes see on a job application.

Just upload your PDF to the website to do things like insert images, text, signatures, links and more and then download it back to your computer as a PDF.

14.5 Animation

It is the process of making the illusion of motion and the illusion of change by means of the rapid display of a sequence of images that minimally differ from each other. Animation can be recorded with either analogue media, a flip book, motion picture film, video tape, digital media, including formats with animated GIF, Flash animation and digital video.

Type of Animation

There are two main types of animations which are used in multimedia applications:

1. The First Type of Animation

2D animation or linear animation is the simple movement of objects on the screen, generally through linear translation. Multimedia development environments often provide the necessary tools to perform this simple animation procedure.

2. The Original Creation of Animation

3D animation, however, is very technically and artistically involved, as well as time consuming. Three dimensional objects are created using a mathematical model. Each object may be shown in various views, giving the user a realistic sense of third dimension.

14.6 Morphing

Morphing is the process of converting of an image to another image. Morphing is a part of animation where you start with an object and end up with another object. In between the first object keeps on fading and the second one starts appearing. You must have seen the use in various TV program titles, movie titles etc.

1. Morphing Process

(i) Morphing is basically done by matching image shapes with color interpolations.

(ii) Morphing cannot be done directly one image to another image within one step. So its takes gradual steps.

(iii) There are two kinds of images in MORPHING process. They are as follows:
  (a) Source image (Very first object)
  (b) Destination Image (Very last Image)

(iv) So, morphing process goes in several steps by applying steps gradually.

(v) For the first process, the source image is gradually distorted and ultimately this source image gets vanished as we are looking for the target image (Destination Image).

(vi) If you have observed the objects from left side are similar to the left meet image. And likewise the objects from right side are similar to the rightmost image. (As distoration is taking place).

2.Morphing Applications

Some common morphing applications, are as follows:

(i) Electronic book illustrations
(ii) Education field
(iii) Computer training centers
(iv) Movies
(v) Animation industry (Mostly Used)
(vi) Medical field
(vii) Entertainment industry

14.7 Image Editing Software

It is a software program used to edit or otherwise manipulate an image, a picture or other graphic. The most popular and powerful image editing softwares are:

1. **Photoshop** It is the leading professional image editing program released by Adobe. It is useful for both creating and editing images to be used in print or online.
2. **Corel Draw** It is a vector graphics editor developed and marketed by corel corporation. It provides tools and effects that make it possible to work efficiently to produce high-quality graphics.

14.8 Photoshop

It is Adobe's photo editing, image creation and graphic design software. This software provides many image editing features for raster images as well as vector graphics. It uses a layer based editing system that enables image creation and altering with multiple overlays that supports transparency. Photoshop actions include automation features to reduce the need of repetitive tasks.

To start Adobe photoshop in windows:

Choose Start → All Programs → Adobe Photoshop CS6.

14.8.1 Menu commands of Photoshop

Various commands in the menus of photoshop are given below:

1. **File Menu** This menu is home to commands that let you open and close documents, import and export files, browse files in Adobe Bridge, print documents and so on. It includes New, Open, Browse, Save As etc.
2. **Edit Menu** This menu is where you'll find the Copy and Paste commands, Transform options and keyboard and menu shortcut settings, among other items. If you use a PC, you'll also find Photoshop's preferences here. It includes Cut, Copy, Paste, Clear etc.
3. **Image Menu** The Image menu groups together features for working with images and your canvas. You can resize documents, adjust Curves and Levels, duplicate images and rotate images from here. It includes Mode, Adjustments, Auto Tone etc.
4. **Layer Menu** This menu has controls for working with your document layers. From here you can add and delete layers, create layer masks and merge layers, among other things. It includes Duplicate Layer, Delete Layer Properties etc.
5. **Select Menu** Items in this menu let you grab layers, pick colors, use Quick Mask mode and more. It includes All, Deselect, Reselect, Inverse etc.
6. **Filter Menu** This menu is packed with all kinds of effects you can apply to your images. It groups filters by type: Artistic, Blur, Sharpen and so on. It includes Last Filter, Filter Gallery, Liquify etc.
7. **Analysis Menu** This menu appears only in Photoshop CS4 Extended. It includes tools for analysing data in scientific images, counting objects, setting data points and recording measurements. It includes Set Measurement Scale, Select Data Points, Record Measurements etc.
8. **3D Menu** This menu is another Photoshop CS4 Extended-only feature. It includes tools for working with 3D images. It includes New Layer from 3D File, New 3D Postcard From Layer etc.
9. **View Menu** This menu gives you all sorts of different ways of looking at your images, from zooming in or out to adding guides and rulers. It includes Proof Setup, Proof Colors etc.
10. **Window Menu** Use this menu to change what you see in Photoshop; it lets you arrange your open documents, view or hide panels and so on. It includes Arrange, Workspace etc.
11. **Help** Some interactive help is right at your mouse-tip on the Help menu. The menu also offers links to the Adobe website for more information and a little assistance, courtesy of the tutorials accessible from this menu.

14.8.2 Toolbox

The toolbox contains the main tools for working on images. Click any tool to select and use it.

A small arrow next to a tool in the toolbox indicates that the tool also has additional options available. In Photoshop, click and hold your mouse on a tool to see its options.

e.g. if you click and hold on the select tool, you'll see select options such as elliptical selection, single row selection etc.

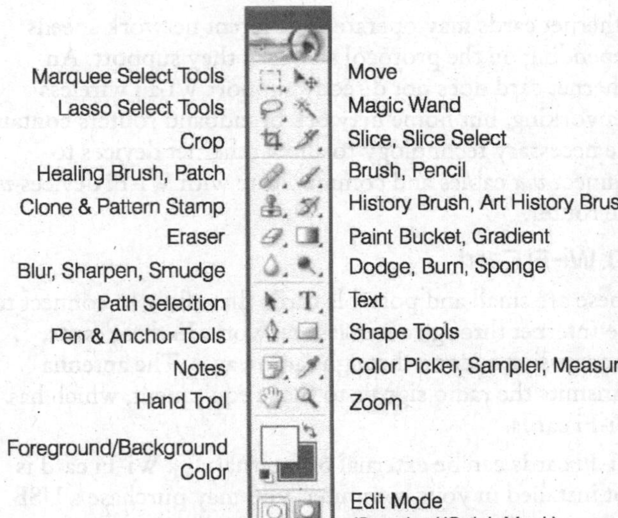

7. Modem (MOdulator DEModulator)

Modem is a device that converts digital signal to analog signal (modulator) at the sender's site and converts back analog signal to digital signal (demodulator) at the receiver's end, in order to make communication possible *via* telephone lines.

It enables a computer to transmit data over telephone or cable lines.

Modems are of two types as follows:

(i) **Internal Modem** Fixed within a computer.

(ii) **External Modem** Connected externally to a computer.

8. RJ45 Connector

RJ45 stands for Registered Jack-45. It is an eight wire connector. RJ45 connector is used to connect computers onto a Local Area Network (LAN).

It is commonly used in telephony applications and networking. It is also used for serial connections.

9. Ethernet Card

An ethernet card is a kind of network adapter. These adapters support the ethernet standard for high-speed network connections *via* cables. Ethernet cards are sometimes known as **Network Interface Cards** (NICs).

Ethernet cards are available in several different standard packages called **form factors**. Newer ethernet cards installed inside desktop computers use the PCI standard and are usually installed by the manufacturer.

Ethernet cards may operate at different network speeds depending on the protocol standard they support. An ethernet card does not directly support Wi-Fi wireless networking, but home network broadband routers contain the necessary technology to allow ethernet devices to connect *via* cables and communicate with Wi-Fi devices *via* the router.

10. Wi-Fi Card

These are small and portable cards that allow to connect to the Internet through a wireless network. In these cards, transmission is done through radiowaves. The antenna transmits the radio signals to those equipment, which has Wi-Fi cards.

Wi-Fi cards can be external or internal. If a Wi-Fi card is not installed in your computer, you may purchase a USB antenna attachment and have it externally connected to your device. Many newer computers, mobile devices etc., are equipped with wireless networking capability and do not require a Wi-Fi card.

15.7 Network Topology

Network topology is the arrangement of the various elements (links, nodes etc.) of a computer or biological network. The main network topologies are as follows:

15.7.1 Bus Topology (Linear Topology)

A bus topology is an arrangement in which the computers and the peripheral devices are connected to a common single length data line.

Bus topology

All the computers or devices are directly connected to the data line. The data is transmitted in small blocks known as **packets.** Each packet has a header containing the destination address. When data is transmitted on the cable, the destination node identifies the address on the packet and thereby processes the data.

15.7.2 Ring or Circular Topology

In this type of topology, the node is connected to two and only two neighbouring nodes. The data travels in one direction only from node to node around the ring. After passing through each node, the data returns to the sending node.

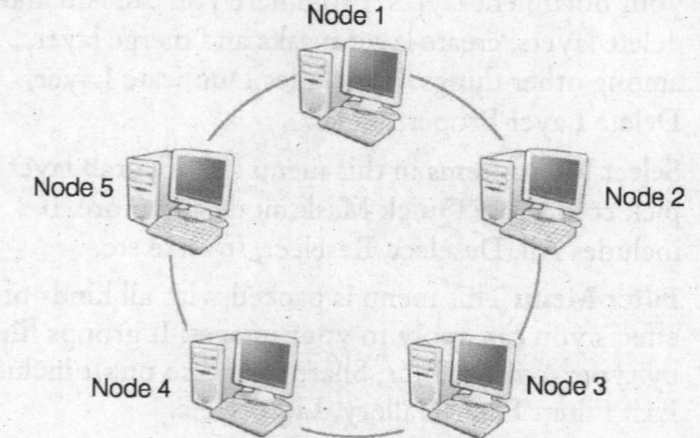

Ring or circular topology

15.7.3 Star Topology

In star topology, there persists a central node (hub), which is connected to all other nodes directly.

If one node has to take information from second node, then the data is taken from the second node to the first node through the central node or server.

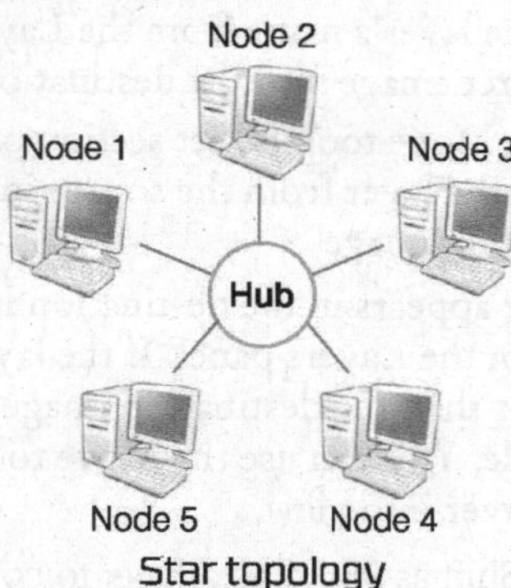

Star topology

15.7.4 Tree Topology

A tree topology is an extension and variation of bus topology. Its basic structure is like an inverted tree, where the root acts as a server. In tree topology, the nodes are interlinked in the form of tree. If one node fails, then the node following that node gets detached from the main tree topology.

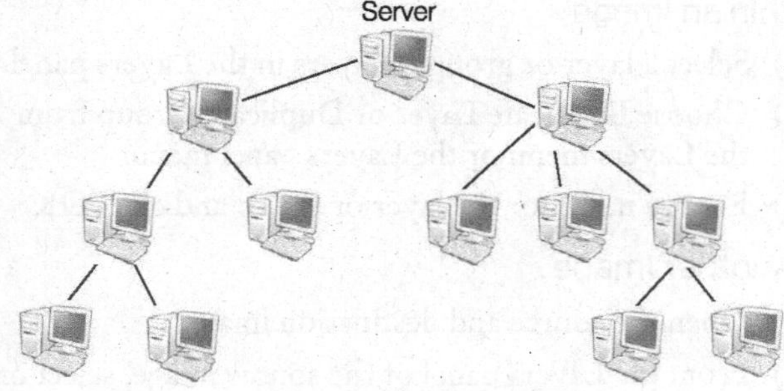

Tree topology

15.7.5 Mesh Topology

In mesh topology, each node is connected to all other nodes, so that it provides alternative route, in case, if the host is either down or busy. We can also call it as extension of Point-to-Point (P2P) network.

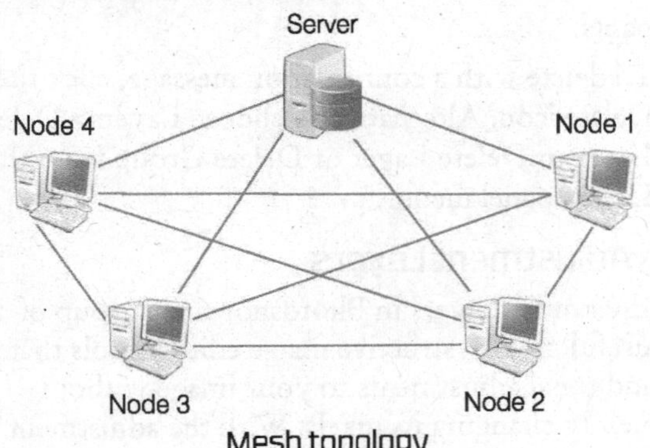

Mesh topology

15.8 Types of Network

On the basis of coverage or geographical spread, a network can be divided mainly into three types as follows:

15.8.1 Local Area Network (LAN)

In a LAN, a group of computers and its devices are connected over a relatively short distance. Generally, it is a privately owned networks within a single building or campus, upto a few kilometres in size. Users can share expensive devices, such as laser printers, as well as data on the LAN and can also use the LAN to communicate with each other, by sending mails or engaging in chat sessions.

One LAN can even be connected to other LANs over any distance *via* telephone lines and radiowaves. However, there is also a limit on the number of computers that can be attached to a single LAN.

Now-a-days, we also have WLAN(Wireless LAN) which is based on wireless network.

15.8.2 Metropolitan Area Network (MAN)

This is basically a bigger version of LAN and normally uses similar technology. It might cover few buildings in a city and might either be private or public. This is a network which spans a physical area (in the range of 5 and 50 km diameter) that is larger than a LAN but smaller than a WAN.

MANs are usually characterised by very high-speed connections using optical fibres or other digital media and provides uplink services to Wide Area Networks (WANs) and the Internet. e.g. in a city, a MAN, which can support both data and voice might even be related to local cable television network.

The MAN, its communications links and equipment are generally owned by either a consortium of users or by a single network provider who sells the service to the users.

Since, MAN adopts technologies from both LAN and WAN to serve its purpose, it is also frequently used to provide a shared connection to other networks using a link to a WAN.

15.8.3 Wide Area Network (WAN)

As the term implies, WAN spans a large geographical area, often a country or a continent and uses various commercial and private communication lines to connect computers. Typically, a WAN combines multiple LANs that are geographically separated.

This is accomplished by connecting the different LANs using services such as dedicated leased phone lines, dial-up

Scaling an Object

You can scale by dragging a handle. Hold down the Shift key as you drag a corner handle to scale proportionately. Hold down the Option (Alt) key to scale in both directions simultaneously. To scale numerically, enter a value in the Options bar.

Merging Layers

Merging layers can help to decrease your file size and make your document more manageable. To do this, steps are as follows:

(i) Position the layer or layer groups that you want to merge adjacent to each other in the Layers panel.
(ii) Select the top layer of those you want merged.
(iii) Choose Merge Down from the Layers panel menu or the Layer menu.

Move the Content of Layers

To move the content of layers, steps are as follows:

(i) From the Layers panel, select the layers containing the objects you want to move.
(ii) Select the Move tool.

You can select the layers that you want to move directly in the document window. In the Move tool's options bar, select AutoSelect, the choose Layer from the drop down menu. Shift-click to select multiple layers. Select AutoSelect, then choose Group, to select the entire group when you select one layer in the group.

(iii) Do one of the following:
 (a) In the document window, drag any object onto one of the selected layers. (All objects on the layer will move together.)
 (b) Press an arrow key on the keyboard to nudge the objects by 1 pixel.
 (c) Hold down Shift and press an arrow key on the keyboard to nudge the objects by 10 pixels.

Copy a Layer from One Image to Another

You can copy any layer, including the Background layer, from one image to another. Keep in mind that the resolution of the destination image determines how large the printed copy of the layer can be. Also, if the pixel dimensions of the two images are not the same, the copied layer may appear smaller or larger than you would expect.

To copy a layer from one image to another, steps are as follows:

(i) Open the two images you want to use.
(ii) In the Layers panel of the source image, select the layer that you want to copy.
(iii) Do one of the following:
 (a) Choose Select > All to select all of the pixels in the layer, and choose Edit > Copy. Then make the destination image active and choose Edit > Paste.
 (b) Drag the layer's name from the Layers panel of the source image into the destination image.
 (c) Use the Move tool (Select section of the toolbox), to drag the layer from the source image to the destination image.

The copied layer appears in the destination image, above the active layer in the Layers panel. If the layer you're dragging is larger than the destination image, only part of the layer is visible. You can use the Move tool to drag other sections of the layer into view.

⚠ Hold down Shift as you drag a layer to copy it to the same position it occupied in the source image (if the source and destination images have the same pixel dimensions) or to the center of the destination image (if the source and destination images have different pixel dimensions).

Duplicating Layers

You can duplicate layers within an image or into another or a new image. To do this, follow these steps:

Within an Image

(i) Select a layer or group of layers in the Layers panel.
(ii) Choose Duplicate Layer or Duplicate Group from the Layers menu or the Layers panel menu.
(iii) Enter a name for the layer or group and click OK.

In Another Image

(i) Open the source and destination images.
(ii) From the Layers panel of the source image, select one or more layers or a layer group.
(iii) Drag the layer or group from the Layers panel to the destination image.

Deleting Layers

To delete layers, steps are as follows:

(i) Select one or more layers or groups from the Layers panel.
(ii) To delete with a confirmation message, click the Delete icon. Alternatively, choose Layers> Delete> Layer or Delete Layer or Delete Group from the Layers panel menu.

Using Adjustment Layers

The Adjustment Layers in Photoshop are a group of a super useful, non-destructive image editing tools that add color and tonal adjustments to your image without permanently changing its pixels. With the adjustment layers, you can edit and discard your adjustments or restore your original image at any time.

This will make your workflow in Photoshop more flexible and efficient and is an absolute must-know. When you add an adjustment layer to your image, a new layer will appear over your image and a Properties panel specific to the type of adjustment you've selected will pop up. The Properties panel will allow you to modify your adjustment layer, which in turn will modify your image.

14.8.5 Channels and Masks

Channel Palette

Photoshop's "Channels" palette window allows you to edit, save and copy individual color channels data in either the RGB, CMYK or Lab color space. This can be useful if there is a particular problem with oversaturation in a single color channel, causing an unwanted color-cast. By modifying only one channel you are leaving intact all of the subtle shadow and highlight pixel data in the remaining channels. This technique can be used instead of the color Balance tool which can be more destructive to subtle detail at the extreme ends of the tonal range.

Showing and Hiding Channels

You can use the Channels panel to view any combination of channels in the document window.

Click in the eye column next to the channel to show or hide that channel. (Click the composite channel to view all default color channels. The composite channel is displayed whenever all the color channels are visible.)

Splitting Channels into Separate Image

You can split channels of flattened images only. Splitting channels is useful when you want to retain individual channel information in a file format that doesn't preserve channels.

(i) To split channels into separate images, choose Split Channels from the Channels panel menu.
(ii) The original file is closed and the individual channels appear in separate grayscale image windows. The title bars in the new windows show the original filename plus the channel.
(iii) You can save and edit the new images separately.

Merging Channels

You can merge channels into a single image in Photoshop. To do this, steps are follows:

(i) Open your split channel files.
(ii) Choose Merge Channels from the Channels panel menu.
(iii) In the Merge Channels dialog box, choose your desired color mode.
(iv) Enter the number of channels that you want and then click OK.
(v) Select your channels in the dialog box that will appear.
(vi) If you're merging into a multichannel image, click Next and then click OK.

Creating and Editing a Quick Mask

Quick Masks allow you to create and edit selections quickly.

To do this, steps are as follows:

(i) Open a new document and using any Selection tool, select the element that you want in your image.
(ii) Click the Edit in Quick Mask Mode button in the Tools panel (or press the Q key).
(iii) Refine the mask by using a painting or editing tool.
(iv) After you finish editing your mask, click the Edit in Standard Mode button in the Tools panel to exit the Quick Mask.

14.8.6 Painting and Editing

Brushes Palette

The Brushes palette lets you select preset brushes and design custom brushes. Displaying the Brushes palette choose Window> Brushes, or click the Palette button on the right side of the options bar if you have a painting tool, erasing tool, toning tool or focus tool selected.

Creating a Custom Brush: Edit Menu Option

If none of the preset brushes offer what you need, Photoshop allows you to create new brushes. Any image may be used to create a customized brush tip. Once you have created a brush, it is saved as a preset for use in the future. To create a custom brush, follow these steps:

(i) Select the object or image that you want to make into a brush tip.
(ii) From the Edit menu, select Define Brush Preset ... The Brush Name dialog box will appear.
(iii) In the Name text box, enter a name for your brush and click OK.

Deleting Brush

If there are many preset brush styles that you do not use, you may want to delete some of them to make finding other brush styles easier. To delete a brush, follow these steps:

(i) From the Toolbox, select the Brush Tool.
(ii) If it is not already visible, display the Brushes palette.
(iii) From the Brush Presets section, right click the brush preset you want to delete → select Delete Brush.
(iv) A confirmation dialog box will appear and click OK.

GPRS is a best effort service, implying variable throughput and latency that depends on the number of other users sharing the service concurrently, as opposed to circuit switching, where a certain Quality of Service (QoS) is guaranteed during the connection. It provides moderate speed data transfer, by using unused Time Division Multiple Access (TDMA) channels, e.g. the GSM system.

4. WLL

WLL stands for Wireless Local Loop and it is basically the use of radio to provide a telephone connection to the home. It is sometimes called **Radio In The Loop** (RITL) or **Fixed Radio Access** (FRA). When WLL connects subscribers to the **Public Switched Telephone Network** (PSTN), radio signals are used as a substitute of copper for all or part of the connection between the subscriber and the switch. WLL includes are: cordless access systems, proprietary fixed radio access and fixed cellular systems.

15.11.2 Wireless / Mobile Telecommunication Technologies

1. 1G (First Generation)

1G refers to the First Generation of wireless telephone technology, mobile telecommunications. These are the analog telecommunication standards that were introduced in the 1980s and continued until being replaced by 2G digital telecommunication. They only had voice facility available and were based on circuit switched technology. 1G mobile systems used radio towers for transmission.

2. 2G (Second Generation)

2G is short for Second Generation of wireless telephone technology. 2G cellular telecom networks were commercially launched on the GSM standard in Finland by Radiolinja (now part of Elisa Oyj) in 1991. The primary benefit of 2G network is that 2G introduced data services for mobile, starting with SMS text messages. It also provides paging, voice mail and fax services. The 2G system was based on GSM technology.

3. 3G (Third Generation)

3G is short for Third Generation of mobile telecommunications technology also called **Tri-Band 3G.**

3G telecommunication networks support services that provide information transfer rate of atleast 200 Kbps. It adds multimedia facilities that allow video, audio and graphics applications.

However, many services advertised as 3G provide higher speed than the minimum technical requirements for a 3G service. Recent 3G releases, often denoted 3.5G and 3.75G, also provide mobile broadband access of several Mbps to smartphones and mobile modems in laptop computers.

3G finds application in wireless voice telephony, mobile Internet access, fixed wireless Internet access, video calls and mobile TV.

4. 4G (Fourth Generation)

In telecommunications, 4G is the Fourth Generation of mobile phone communication standards. It is a successor of the Third Generation (3G) standard. A 4G system provides mobile ultra-broadband Internet access.

It will be based on packet switching only and these systems are projected to provide speeds up to 100 Mbps while moving and 1Gbps while stationary.

e.g. laptops with USB wireless modems, smart-phones and other mobile devices. Conceivable applications include amended mobile web access, IP telephony, gaming services, high-definition mobile TV, video conferencing, 3D television and cloud computing.

15.12 Internet Applications

There are many applications which allow us to do many things in a short while no matter how far we are or where we are. Some of them are as follows:

15.12.1 Electronic Mail

Electronic mail most commonly referred to as E-mail, is a method of exchanging digital messages from sender to one or more recipients. Modern E-mail operates across the Internet or other computer networks.

Some early E-mail systems required that the sender and the recipient both be online at the same time, in common with instant messaging. Today's E-mail systems are based on **Store-and-Forward Model**. E-mail servers accept, forward, deliver and store messages.

Neither the users nor their computers are required to be online simultaneously. They need to connect only briefly, typically to an E-mail server, for as long as it takes to send or receive messages. Interactions between E-mail servers and clients are governed by E-mail protocols.

15.12.2 Chat

Chatting is one of the wonderful things that Internet provides us. Chatting is the way of talking to other people who are using the Internet at the same time you are. Like E-mail, other people's messages appear on your screen but it happens in real time while you are connected to the Internet. Usually, chatting is just like a telephonic conversation. Like on telephone, you say something, people respond to it after hearing your talk. You can hear their responses at the same time and reply them.

Similarly, in chatting, you type a message in your chat box, which is immediately received by the recipient, then the recipient can type a message in response to your message, which is instantly received by you.

There are numerous chat programs that you can download, including Yahoo! messenger, Windows live messenger and Skype (all three of these can also do voice and video chat). In addition, there are many browser based services that do not require downloading. e.g. facebook has a built-in chat feature and gmail allows you to chat with your contacts whenever you are logged into your gmail account.

15.12.3 Video Conferencing

Video conferencing is a communication technology that integrates video and audio to connect users anywhere in the world as if they were in the same room. This term usually refers to communication between three or more users, who are in atleast two locations rather than one-on-one communication and it often includes multiple people at each location.

When you call for a conference, everyone is expected to arrive at a designated time and place to discuss an issue and resolve it. But if the people you need to speak to are in different states or countries and the cost of getting them to come is quite expensive, you have to try something else like video conferencing.

Each user or group of users who are participating in a video conference typically must have a computer, a camera, a microphone, a video screen and a sound system.

Basically, this is a system that allows you to conduct meetings or trainings in different places simultaneously. So, this technology is especially popular in the field of business. Most popular softwares used for video conferencing are TCP Cam, Ekiga and Skype for Linux.

⚠ Internet telephony is a type of communications technology that allows voice calls and other telephony services like fax, SMS and other voice messaging applications to be transmitted using the Internet as a connection medium.

15.12.4 SMS (Short Messaging Service)

SMS is a service by which a person is able to send short messages through Internet to any mobile phone irrespective of the distance. SMS is termed as the characters used in a single message are about 160 characters in standard including spaces and letters.

This service allows only one way messaging, i.e. from a computer (Internet enabled) to any mobile but it will not support mobile to computer system. There are many different private sites which allow a user to send a limited or unlimited number of messages to one or many at a time. For using these kind of site, a user may be asked to create an account to use this feature.

Some of the sites of which allows SMS are given below:

(i) way2sms.com (ii) site2sms.com
(iii) freesms.net (iv) txtweb.com
(v) 160by2.com (vi) net2mobile.com

15.12.5 Voice Mail

Voice mail is basically a voice message that stores messages electronically and which can be retrieved by the intended recipients according to their convenience. Voice mail, was developed by telephony to prevent missed calls and even to facilitate call screening.

Now-a-days, voice mails are getting integrated with Internet, which allows users to receive incoming voice message on their computers, i.e. the user or the recipient is able to receive the voice message in their mail. By this, a recipient is able to manage all his voice messages with an ease.

15.13 Terms Related to Internet

Some terms reltated to Internet are as follows:

15.13.1 HyperText Markup Language (HTML)

HTML is the main markup language for creating web pages and other information that can be displayed in a web browser.

- HTML is written in the form of HTML elements consisting of tags enclosed in angular brackets (like <html>), within the web page content. HTML tags most commonly come in pairs like <h1> and </h1>, although some tags known as **empty elements**, are unpaired, e.g. <img>.
- The <html> tag is the start tag and the </html> tag is the end tag (they are also called **opening tags** and **closing tags**). In between these tags, web designers can add text, tags, comments and other types of text based content. An HTML document has the extension .htm or .html. The purpose of a web browser is to read HTML documents and compose them into visible or audible web pages.
- The browser does not display the HTML tags, but uses the tags to interpret the content of the page.
- HTML elements form the building blocks of all websites. HTML allows images and objects to be embedded and can be used to create interactive forms.
- It provides a means to create structured documents by denoting structural semantics for text such as headings, paragraphs, lists, links, quotes and other items. It can embed scripts written in languages such as JavaScript, which affect the behaviour of HTML web pages.

There are a variety of tools to help you draw out specific sizes and shapes of selections in Photoshop.

Basic Modifications or Adjustments of Selection

The following selection options are considered basic modifications:

(i) Add to selection (hold down Shift while using the following tools: Magic Wand, Lasso tools, Marquee tools)
(ii) Subtract from selection (hold down Alt/Option while using the following tools: Magic Wand, Lasso tools, Marquee tools)
(iii) Intersect selections (hold down Alt/Option and Shift together to intersect a new selection with a previous one)
(iv) Select All (Ctrl/Cmd + A to select the whole canvas)
(v) Deselect (Ctrl/Cmd + D to deselect everything)
(vi) Reselect (Ctrl/Cmd + Shift + D to reselect previous selection)
(vii) Invert selection (Ctrl/Cmd + I to deselect what was previously selected and select what was not selected)
(viii) Move selection (hold down Space while still drawing the selection with Marquee tools to move it around)
(ix) Perfect Circle or Square (hold down Shift with Elliptical or Rectangular Marquee tools while creating them)
(x) Draw selection from the center (hold down Alt/Option with Elliptical or Rectangular Marquee tools while creating them)

Softening the Edges of a Selection

To do this, follow these steps:

(i) Create a selection.
(ii) Choose Select → Modify → Feather.
(iii) A feather dialog box apears. In this dialog box, type a value in the Feather Radius text field and then click OK.

Moving a Selection

You can move a selection elsewhere in the image or to a different photo. To do this, follow these steps:

(i) With a selection tool active, select the Move tool.
(ii) Drag the selection to a new position. You can also nudge it is a pixel at a time using the arrow keys on your keyboard. (Press Shift as you use the arrow keys to move the selection 10 pixels at a time.)

Copying a Selection

You can also copy a selection without moving it. Probably the easiest way is

(i) Choose Edit>Copy and then go where you want to copy the selection and choose Edit>Paste.
(ii) When you cut or copy a selection, it's stored in the clipboard; only one selection can be stored in the clipboard at a time.

Paste One Selection into or Outside Another

To do this, follow these steps:

(i) Cut or copy the part of the image you want to paste.
(ii) In the same image or another, select the area you want to paste into or outside.

Note If you're pasting outside, select an area smaller than the copied selection.

(iii) Do either of the following:
  (a) Choose Edit > Paste Special > Paste Into. The contents of the source selection appear within the destination selection.
  (b) Choose Edit > Paste Special > Paste Outside. The contents of the source selection appear around the destination selection.

The Paste Into or Paste Outside command adds a layer and layer mask to the image. In the Layers panel, the new layer contains a layer thumbnail for the pasted selection next to a layer mask thumbnail. The layer mask is based on the selection you pasted into: the selection is unmasked (white), the rest of the layer is masked (black). The layer and layer mask are unlinked—that is, you can move each one independently.

Select the Move tool ✥, or hold down the Ctrl (Windows) or Command (Mac OS) key to activate the Move tool. Then drag the source contents until the part you want appears through the mask.

To specify how much of the underlying image shows through, click the layer mask thumbnail in the Layers panel, select a painting tool, and edit the mask:

(i) To hide more of the image underlying the layer, paint the mask with black.
(ii) To reveal more of the underlying image, paint the mask with white.
(iii) To partially reveal the underlying image, paint the mask with gray.

If you are satisfied with your results, you can choose Layer > Merge Down to merge the new layer and layer mask with the underlying layer and make the changes permanent.

Saving a Selection

To save a selection, follow these steps:

(i) Choose Select > Save Selection.
(ii) Then choose New from the pop-up menu, name the selection and click OK.

Expanding and Reducing Selections

You can easily make that selection a few pixels larger or smaller by choosing Select > Modify. You can do this regardless of which selection tool you used to begin with.

(i) To make your selection bigger choose Select > Modify > Expand.
(ii) To make the selection smaller, choose Select > Modify > Contract.
(iii) Enter a value for the number of pixels you want to modify by. This generally works best if you Expand or Contract by only a small number of pixels at a time (i.e. 4 or 5 pixels at most). Otherwise the edges of the selection won't stay sharp and pointed at the corners, they have a tendency to turn a little roundy on you.

14.8.7 Image Tracing

Photoshop makes it easy for you do create flawless line drawings by tracing. To do this, follow these steps:

(i) Open an image you want to trace.
(ii) Open Photoshop.
(iii) There are two ways to accomplish the next step, which is to place your image on top of a plain white layer.
(iv) Try this alternate method when necessary.
(v) Click to select the layer "Original Image" and select the zoom tool (Z).
(vi) Click on the Paths tab.
(vii) Select the Pen tool (P). Use the Pen tool to trace over the key lines from the image that you want to copy and add the details.
(viii) Clean up the curves and make it unique.
(ix) Draw it out and select the Brush tool (B).
(x) Switch back to the Paths tab and Finished.

14.9 Multimedia

Any combination of text, graphic art, sound, video and animation to any individual by computer or other electronic means is known as multimedia. When the various elements of multimedia, like pictures, animations, engaging sounds, raw textual information and video clips are linked together then you can impress the thought and action centers of people's minds. Multimedia stimulates the eyes, ears and brain of the person.

Generally, multimedia is everything that you can see and hear. Some people might say that the addition of animation produces multimedia, but concurrent use of more than one presentation medium results in multimedia.

Multimedia may be any of the following:

(i) Text and sound.
(ii) Text, sound and still or animated graphic images.
(iii) Text, sound and video images.
(iv) Video and sound.
(v) Multiple display areas, images or presentations, presented concurrently.
(vi) In live situations, the use of a speaker or actors and "props" together with sound, images and motion video.

Multimedia is a very effective presentation tool. Studies indicate that if a person is stimulated with audio then retention rate would be upto 20 percent, with audiovisual. It would be upto 30 percent with interactive multimedia presentations and retention rate can be increased upto 60 percent.

Multimedia can be broadly divided into following two categories:

(i) **Linear Multimedia** This type of content generally progresses without any navigational control for the viewer, e.g. cinema presentation.
(ii) **Non-linear Multimedia** This type of content uses interactivity to control progress, e.g. a video game, hyper media.

14.9.1 Concept of Multimedia

Concept of multimedia can be understand with the following terms:

1. Images

Digital image files appear in many multimedia applications. Digital photographs can display application content or can alternatively form part of a user interface.

Interactive elements such as buttons, often use custom images created by the designers and developers involved in an application.

Digital image files use a variety of formats and file extensions. Among them, most common are JPEGs and PNGs. Both of these often appear on websites, as the formats allow developers to minimize on file size while maximizing on picture quality. Graphic design software programs such as Photoshop and Paint allow developers to create complex visual effects with digital images.

2. Audio

Audio files and streams play a major role in some multimedia systems. Audio files appear as a part of application content to aid interaction. Audio formats include MP3, WMA, Wave, MIDI and RealAudio. When developers include audio within a website, they will generally use a compressed format to minimize on download times.

Web services can also stream audio, so that users can begin playback before the entire file is downloaded.

Spam costs the sender very little to send - most of the costs are paid for by the recipient or the carriers rather than by the sender.

E-mail spam targets individual users with direct mail messages. E-mail spam lists are often created by scanning Usenet postings, stealing Internet mailing lists or searching the web for addresses.

⚠ **Phishing** is the attempt to obtain sensitive information such as usernames, passwords and credit card details, often for malicious reasons by disguising as a trustworthy entity in an electronic communication.

IP spoofing refers to connection hijacking through a fake Internet Protocol (IP) address.

15.14.2 Cookies

They are used by web developers to help users navigate their websites efficiently and perform certain functions. Due to their core role of enhancing/enabling usability or site processes, disabling cookies may prevent users from using certain websites.

Cookies are created when a user's browser loads a particular website. The website sends information to the browser, which then creates a text file. Every time the user goes back to the same website, the browser retrieves and sends this file to the website's server.

Computer cookies are created not just by the website the user is browsing but also by other websites that run ADS, widgets or other elements on the page being loaded. These cookies regulate how the ads appear or how the widgets and other elements function on the page.

15.14.3 Firewall

A system designed to prevent unauthorised access to or from a private network. Firewalls can be implemented in both hardware and software or a combination of both. Firewalls are frequently used to prevent unauthorised Internet users from accessing private networks connected to the Internet, especially Intranets. All messages entering or leaving the Intranet pass through the firewall, which examines each message and blocks those that do not meet the specified security criteria.

There are several types of firewall techniques as follows:

(i) **Packet Filter** Looks at each packet entering or leaving the network and accepts or rejects it based on user-defined rules. Packet filtering is fairly effective and transparent to users, but it is difficult to configure. In addition, it is susceptible to IP spoofing.

(ii) **Application Gateway** Applies security mechanisms to specific applications, such as FTP and Telnet servers. This is very effective, but can impose a performance degradation.

(iii) **Circuit-level Gateway** Applies security mechanisms when a TCP or UDP connection is established. Once the connection has been made packets can flow between the hosts without further checking.

(iv) **Proxy Server** Intercepts all messages entering and leaving the network. The proxy server effectively hides the true network addresses.

15.14.4 Cyber Law

Cyber law or Internet law is a term that encapsulates the legal issues related to use of the Internet. It is less a distinct field of law than intellectual property or contract law, as it is a domain covering many areas of law and regulation. Some leading topics include Internet access and usage, privacy, freedom of expression and jurisdiction.

15.14.5 Cyber Crime

Cyber crime refers to any crime that involves a computer and a network. The computer may have been used in the commission of a crime or it may be the target.

Net-crime refers to criminal exploitation of the Internet. Cyber crimes are defined as: 'Offences that are committed against individuals or groups of individuals with a criminal motive to intentionally harm the reputation of the victim or cause physical or mental harm to the victim directly or indirectly, using modern telecommunication networks such as Internet (chat rooms, E-mails, notice boards and groups) and mobile phones (SMS/MMS).

15.14.6 Crackers and Hackers

A cracker (also known as a **black hat hacker**) is an individual with extensive computer knowledge whose purpose is to breach or bypass Internet security or gain access to software without paying royalties.

Hacker (also known as **white hat hacker**) is a term used for those who have been closely associated with the development of the computer, outside of the traditional corporate structure, and the free software movement (also known as the **Open Source movement**).

The general view is that, while hackers build things, crackers break things. Cracker is the name given to hackers who break into computers for criminal gain; whereas, hackers, can also be Internet security experts hired to find vulnerabilities in systems.

The most common way crackers gain access to networks or systems is through social engineering, whereby the cracker contacts employees at a company and tricks them into divulging passwords and other information that allows a cracker to gain access.

CHAPTER PRACTICE

1. The basic components necessary for data communication in computer is a
(1) computer terminal
(2) modem
(3) communication software
(4) All of the above

2. What are the necessary criteria for an effective and efficient network?
(1) Performance (2) Reliability
(3) Security (4) All of these

3. The most important or powerful computer in a typical network is ……
(1) desktop (2) network client
(3) network server (4) network section

4. Servers are those computers which provide resources to other computer connected by
(1) network (2) mainframe
(3) super computer (4) client

5. The first network that has planted the seeds of Internet was
(1) ARPANET (2) NSFnet
(3) Vnet (4) Inet

6. The communication mode that supports data in both directions at the same time is
(1) simplex (2) half duplex
(3) full duplex (4) multiplex

7. Which of the following is a vision of what the Internet will become tomorrow?
(1) ARPANET (2) Circuit switching
(3) Interspace (4) Internet

8. …… is the transmission of data between two or more computers over communication links.
(1) Communication
(2) Networking
(3) Data communication
(4) Data networking

9. A combination of hardware and software that allows communication and electronic transfer of information between computers is a
(1) network
(2) backup system
(3) server
(4) peripheral

10. In which switching technique, the message gets broken into small data packets?
(1) Circuit switching
(2) Packet switching
(3) Message switching
(4) Data switching

11. Which of the following is the characteristic of packet switching?
(1) Each packet should contain addressing information
(2) For a best effort delivery service a connection set-up phase is not required
(3) Packets can be of arbitrary length
(4) All of the above

12. Bandwidth refers to
(1) the cost of the cable required to implement a WAN
(2) the cost of the cable required to implement a LAN
(3) the amount of information a peer-to-peer network can store
(4) the amount of information a communication medium can transfer in a given amount of time

13. What is the function of a modem?
(1) Encryption and decryption
(2) Converts data to voice
(3) Converts analog signals to digitals and *vice-versa*
(4) Serve as a hardware antivirus

14. Ethernet uses
(1) bus topology
(2) ring topology
(3) mesh topology
(4) All of the above

15. Wi-Fi uses
(1) optic fibre (2) phase line
(3) radiowaves (4) soundwaves

16. Bank's ATM facility is an example of …… .
(1) LAN
(2) WAN
(3) Mixed networking
(4) Multipurpose networking

17. Working with the WAN generally involves
(1) telephone lines (2) microwaves
(3) satellites (4) All of these

18. What is an E-mail attachment?
(1) A receipt sent by the recipient
(2) A separate document from another program sent alongwith an E-mail message
(3) A malicious parasite that feeds off your messages and destroys the contents
(4) A list of CC : or BCC: recipients

19. Passwords enables users to
(1) get into the system quickly
(2) make efficient use of time
(3) retain confidentiality of files
(4) simplify file structure

20. Viruses, trojan horses and worms are
(1) able to harm computer system
(2) unable to detect if present on computer
(3) user-friendly applications
(4) harmless applications resident on computer

21. A firewall operated by
(1) the pre-purchase phase
(2) isolating Intranet from Extranet
(3) screening packets to/from the network and provide controllable filtering of network traffic
(4) All of the above

22. What is the length of an IP address in Byte (Pre-IPU6)?
(1) 8 (2) 1 (3) 2 (4) 4

23. Which of the following represents the fastest data transmission speed?
(1) Bandwidth (2) bps
(3) gbps (4) kbps

24. In network communication, networks are categorised on the basis of
(1) size (2) distance
(3) cost (4) All of these

25. The data rate of a computer network connection is normally measured in unit of
(1) bps (2) mbps
(3) kbps (4) tbps

26. What is the meaning of bandwidth in a network?
(1) Transmission capacity of a communication channel
(2) Connected computers in a network
(3) Class of IP used in network
(4) Interconnected by communication channels

human listeners respond to the sound or gauge its perceived similarity to another sound.

Quality	Sampling Rate	Bit Depth	Channels	File Size
CD	44.1 kHz	16	Stereo	172 Kb/Sec
Radio	22.05 kHz	8	Mono	22 Kb/Sec
Telephone	11.05 kHz	8	Mono	11 Kb/Sec

Almost everyone is familiar with the most commonly used file formats - for music, mp3 and for video avi and mpeg.

14.9.9 Movie File Format

A video/movie file format is a type of file format for storing digital video data on a computer system. Video is almost always stored in compressed form to reduce the file size.

Some common movie file formats are as follows:

1. AVI

AVI stands for Audio Video Interleaved. AVI is a video and audio file format used to store audio and/or video information digitally for playback purposes. AVI format enjoys built-in support in all the Microsoft's Windows platform. AVI files have file extension .avi. Apart from Windows OS, AVI format is supported by all the major platforms.

2. MPEG

MPG allows lossy compression with little loss of quality of audio and video for easy downloading due to the less space needed for storage. This file type offers small file sizes with high quality. MPG files are also listed as MPEG-1 and MPEG-2 files. Both types of MPG files serve as container files for audio and video data to ensure the two portions remain in sync.

3. SWF

SWF is a file extension for a Shockwave Flash file format created by Macromedia and now owned by Adobe. SWF stands for Small Web Format. SWF files can contain video and vector based animations and sound are designed for efficient delivery over the web. SWF files can be viewed in a web browser using the Flash plug in.

4. MOV

A MOV file is a common multimedia container file format developed by Apple and compatible with both Macintosh and Windows platforms. It may contain multiple tracks that store different types of media data and is often used for saving movies and other video files. MOV files commonly use the MPEG-4 codec for compression.

5. DAT

The .dat file extension is associated with the Video MPEG movie file format. The .dat files are stored on VCD (Video CD) optical disks.

14.9.10 Movie Frames

In filmmaking, video production, animation and related fields, a film frame or video frame is one of the many still images which compose the complete moving picture.

Concept of Frame

A frame is uniquely defined by a combination of the image to be displayed and the time the image is to be displayed. A sequence of frames makes an animation. Each frame is displayed on the screen until the next frame overwrites it. Since, each frame remains displayed on the screen for a tiny but finite time period, you can think of an animation as frames displayed at discreet intervals of time in a continued sequence.

Frame Buffer

A framebuffer (frame buffer or sometimes framestore) is a portion of RAM containing a bitmap that is used to refresh a video display from a memory buffer containing a complete frame of data. The total amount of memory required for the framebuffer depends on the resolution of the output signal and on the color depth and palette size. Each framebuffer was connected to an RGB color output (one for red, one for green and one for blue), with a Digital Equipment Corporation PDP 11/04 minicomputer controlling the three devices as one.

Frame Rate

Frame rate, (expressed in frames per second or FPS) is the frequency (rate) at which consecutive images called frames are displayed in an animated display. The term applies equally to film and video cameras, computer graphics and motion capture systems. Frame rate may also be called the frame frequency and be expressed in hertz. There are three main frame rate standards in the TV and digital cinema business: 24p, 25p and 30p.

Authoring Tools

Authoring tools are tools by which various media components are brought together (integrated) into a structure and flow. Authoring tools usually enable you to create a final application merely by linking together objects, such as a paragraph of text, an illustration or a song. Authoring tools require less technical knowledge to master and are used exclusively for applications that present a mixture of textual, graphical and audio data.

Making Animation

To create an Animated GIF in Photoshop, follow these steps:

(i) Upload your images to Photoshop.
(ii) Open up the Timeline window.
(iii) In the Timeline window, click "Create Frame Animation."
(iv) Create a new layer for each new frame.
(v) Open the same menu icon on the right and choose "Make Frames From Layers."
(vi) Under each frame, select how long it should appear for before switching to the next frame.
(vii) At the bottom of the toolbar, select how many times you would like it to loop.
(viii) Preview your GIF by pressing the play icon.
(ix) Save your GIF to use online.

Embedding Audio/Video

To embed audio/video, follow these steps:

(i) Save your audio and video files in a new directory on your computer.
(ii) Create a new HTML file in the same directory, called index.html.
(iii) Add <audio> and <video> elements to the page; make them display the default browser controls.
(iv) Give both of them <source> elements so that browsers will find the audio format they support best and load it. These should include type attributes.
(v) Give the <video> element a poster that will be displayed before the video starts to be played. Have fun creating your own poster graphic.

Embedding Video on the Web Page by Following Code

```
<video src="foo.mp4" width="300" height="200"
controls>
  Your browser does not support the <video> element.
</video>
```

Embedding Audio on the Web Page by Following Code

```
<audio src="foo.wav" controls autoplay>
  Your browser does not support the <audio> element.
</audio>
```

14.10 Macromedia Flash

Macromedia Flash is a multimedia graphics program especially for creating moving images for use on the Web. Flash has opened up a whole new world for digital animators. You can rotoscope with it, but you can also animate directly in Flash.

14.10.1 Making of Simple Flash Movie

The basics of creating a simple animation in Macromedia Flash are as follows:

(i) Open Macromedia Flash 10.
(ii) Choose frame 1 on the timeline which is located above the canvas.
(iii) Draw whatever you want to in your first frame (e.g. a stick figure).
(iv) Choose the next frame depending upon the length of your animation.
(v) Right click on the frame and click "Insert KEYFrame".
(vi) Right click anywhere between the first and the last frame and select "Create Motion Tween".
(vii) Edit this picture in any way.
(viii) Press

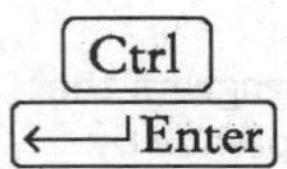

to view the animation.
(ix) Play around and experiment.

14.10.2 Setting Properties with the Properties Panel

Now it is time to apply a little of what you have learned about the Flash panels. In this project, you will use the Properties panel to set a number of different properties for various types of objects in a Flash movie.

The steps are as follows:

(i) Open the Properties panel by using the Window Properties command or pressing Ctrl + F3.
(ii) If the Properties panel is docked along the bottom of the Flash window, move it by pointing to the five dots near the upper-left corner of the panel and dragging it to a new location, as shown here. When a panel is undocked, you can place it wherever you want.
(iii) Click the Text tool to change the options available in the Properties panel, as shown next. When a text block or the Text tool is selected, you can make changes that will affect the text options.
(iv) Select different options in the Properties panel and see how these affect text that you draw.
(v) Click the Pen tool to change the options available in the Properties panel, as shown next. When a drawing tool or a drawn object is selected, you can make changes to properties such as the stroke color and width and the fill color.

88. **What is the bit rate for transmitting uncomposed 800 × 600 pixel color frame with 8 bits/pixel at 40 frames/second?**

(1) 1536 Mbps (2) 24 Mbps
(3) 15.36 Mbps (4) 153.6 Mbps

89. **A communication network which is used by large organisations over regional, national or global area is called**

(1) LAN (2) WAN
(3) MAN (4) Internet

90. **A person who uses his or her expertise to gain access to other people computers to get information illegally or do damage is a**

(1) spammer
(2) hacker
(3) instant messenger
(4) All of the above

91. **It is a self-replicating program that infects computer and spreads by inserting copies of itself into other executable code or documents.**

(1) Keylogger (2) Worm
(3) Virus (4) Cracker

92. **When a real time telephone call between people is made over the Internet using computers, it is called**

(1) a chat session
(2) an E-mail
(3) an instant message
(4) Internet telephony

93. **With an IP address of 100, you currently have 80 subnets. What subnet mask should you use to maximize the number of available hosts?**

(1) 192 (2) 224 (3) 248 (4) 252

94. **After coding a document into a digital signal, it can be sent by telephone, telex or satellite to the receiver, where the signal is decoded and an exact copy of the original documents is made. What is it called?**

(1) Telex (2) Word processor
(3) Facsimile (4) Electronic mail

95. **A .... is a computer program that continuously and rapidly explores the world wide web, voraciously reading and cataloguing every web document it can find.**

(1) directory (2) web browser
(3) search engine (4) chat room

96. **Your company has a LAN in its downtown office and has now set up a LAN in the manufacturing plant in the suburbs. To enable everyone to share data and resources between the two LANs, what type of device(s) are needed to connect them? Choose the most correct answer.**

(1) Modem (2) Cable
(3) Hub (4) Router

97. **What is the name given to an interactive business providing a centralised market where many buyers and suppliers can come together for e-commerce or commerce related activities?**

(1) Direct market place
(2) B2B
(3) B2C
(4) Electronic market place

98. **The term 'duplex' refers to the ability of the data receiving stations to echo back a confirming message to the sender. In full duplex data transmission, both the sender and the receiver**

(1) cannot talk at once
(2) can receive and send data simultaneously
(3) can send or receive data one at a time
(4) can do one way data transmission only

99. • **Long cables are required.**
• **There are dependencies on the root node.**
• **Installation and reconfiguration is very difficult.**

All above disadvantages are attached to:

(1) Mesh topology
(2) Star topology
(3) Tree topology
(4) Bus topology

100. **Match List I with List II and select the correct answer using the codes given below the lists:**

List I	List II
P. Data Link Layer	1. Ensures reliable transport of data over a physical point-to-point link.
Q. Network Layer	2. Encodes/decodes data for physical transmission.
R. Transport Layer	3. Allows end-to-end communication between two processes.
	4. Routes data from one network node to the next.

Codes

	P	Q	R		P	Q	R
(1)	1	4	3	(2)	2	3	1
(3)	2	4	1	(4)	1	3	2

ANSWER KEY

1	(4)	**2**	(4)	**3**	(3)	**4**	(1)	**5**	(1)	**6**	(3)	**7**	(3)	**8**	(3)	**9**	(1)	**10**	(2)
11	(2)	**12**	(4)	**13**	(3)	**14**	(1)	**15**	(3)	**16**	(2)	**17**	(4)	**18**	(2)	**19**	(3)	**20**	(1)
21	(3)	**22**	(4)	**23**	(3)	**24**	(4)	**25**	(1)	**26**	(1)	**27**	(2)	**28**	(4)	**29**	(4)	**30**	(3)
31	(3)	**32**	(1)	**33**	(4)	**34**	(2)	**35**	(3)	**36**	(1)	**37**	(3)	**38**	(2)	**39**	(2)	**40**	(1)
41	(1)	**42**	(3)	**43**	(2)	**44**	(1)	**45**	(1)	**46**	(3)	**47**	(4)	**48**	(3)	**49**	(2)	**50**	(2)
51	(2)	**52**	(1)	**53**	(1)	**54**	(3)	**55**	(3)	**56**	(4)	**57**	(1)	**58**	(1)	**59**	(4)	**60**	(4)
61	(1)	**62**	(1)	**63**	(4)	**64**	(3)	**65**	(1)	**66**	(3)	**67**	(2)	**68**	(2)	**69**	(4)	**70**	(2)
71	(1)	**72**	(3)	**73**	(2)	**74**	(1)	**75**	(3)	**76**	(1)	**77**	(3)	**78**	(1)	**79**	(3)	**80**	(2)
81	(2)	**82**	(4)	**83**	(1)	**84**	(4)	**85**	(1)	**86**	(2)	**87**	(1)	**88**	(4)	**89**	(2)	**90**	(2)
91	(2)	**92**	(4)	**93**	(4)	**94**	(4)	**95**	(2)	**96**	(4)	**97**	(4)	**98**	(2)	**99**	(3)	**100**	(1)

PGT

PRACTICE SETS 1-2

14.10.6 Frame

A frame represents the content of the movie at one moment of time. So far, an animation is nothing more as a succession of frames. You can control all these from the Timeline, but not all the frames have the same behaviour and can be treated equally.

Types of Frame

Not all frames are created equal; different frame types are designed for different animation tasks. Let's take a look at the various frame types that can exist on the timeline:

1. Placeholder Frames

Placeholder frames are not really frames, but rather rectangular boxes where frames can be placed. They are indicated by the grid on the timeline. Devoid of content, these frames, generated automatically by Flash, make up the majority of the timeline when you begin your Flash project.

2. Keyframes

Any time your wish your animation to undergo a visual change or you want an action to occur, you must use a keyframe at that point on the timeline. Obviously, frame-by-frame animations require numerous keyframes because you must edit each frame individually. A tweened animation, on the other hand, requires only two keyframes—one to begin the tween and one to end it. Changes that occur between the beginning and ending keyframes are mapped by Flash and thus do not require additional keyframes.

3. Regular Frames

Regular frames always follow keyframes and contain the same content as the last keyframe on the same layer.

A keyframe on the timeline denotes a change; the regular frames that follow a keyframe determine the duration of that change.

A keyframe and the span of regular frames that follow it are known as a keyframe sequence. The timeline can contain any number of keyframe sequences. If the keyframe in a sequence contains graphical content that is visible on the stage, the regular frames that follow it will appear gray. If the keyframe in a sequence contains no graphical content, the regular frames that follow it appear white.

4. Tweened Frames

Tweened frames are always part of a tween sequence consisting of two keyframes and any number of frames in between. The frames between the two keyframes represent computer-calculated graphics.

You can perform two types of tweening with Flash: motion tweening and shape tweening. You use motion tweening to alter the size, position, rotation, and other aspects of symbols, groups, or text blocks in your animation. You use shape tweening to morph one simple shape into another.

Working with Frames

Now that you're familiar with the various frame types and how to use them in creating animations, let's look at the ways you can work with them on the timeline.

Selecting frames

Before you can move, duplicate, or change a frame, you must first select it. When a frame is selected, the playhead automatically moves to that frame and the contents of its layers appear on the stage.

To Select an Individual Frame

Click a frame once to select it.

The frame will appear highlighted. The selected frame becomes the current frame, and any commands you enter pertaining to frames will affect it.

To Select a Range of Frames

Click the first frame you want to be part of the range, drag to the last frame you want included, and then release.

All selected frames will appear highlighted. You can now move, delete, and duplicate them as a whole.

To Select a Keyframe or Tween Sequence

Double-click once on any frame that is part of the sequence.

The sequence will appear highlighted. You can now move, delete, and duplicate the sequence.

Adding and Inserting Regular Frames

Adding or inserting frames at any point along a layer changes the timeline position of all frames on that layer located to the right of the added or inserted frame(s).

To Add Regular Frames to the Timeline

(i) Select a placeholder frame on the timeline.
(ii) Choose Insert > Frame.

Regular frames are added until the selected placeholder frame is reached.

To Insert Regular Frames within an Existing Range of Frames

(i) Select a single frame, range of frames, or frame sequence within an existing range of frames.
(ii) Choose Insert > Frame.

The same number of frames you selected will be inserted onto the timeline; the previously selected frames will be moved to the right of the newly inserted ones.

Adding Keyframes

When you add a keyframe to a layer, you have the choice of adding a normal or blank keyframe. When adding a normal keyframe any graphical content (instances of symbols, text elements and so on) included in the last keyframe on the same layer is automatically duplicated in the new keyframe. Adding a blank keyframe places a point on the timeline where that layer's contents are no longer visible Normal keyframes are used to signify a change in an animation while keeping the content of the animation visible. With a blank keyframe, the change is the actual removal of content.

To Add a Keyframe to the Timeline

(i) Select a placeholder or regular frame on the timeline.

(ii) Choose Insert > Keyframe or Insert > Blank Keyframe to add a keyframe. If the frame you selected is a placeholder frame, regular frames will be added up to the point of the newly created keyframe. If the selected frame is a regular frame, Flash simply converts it to a regular or blank keyframe—as you specify.

To Add a Range of Keyframes to the Timeline

(i) Select a range of frames or a frame sequence.

(ii) Choose Modify > Frames > Convert to Keyframes or Convert to Blank Keyframes.

A range of keyframes will be added.

Removing Frames

Removing frames at any point on a layer changes the timeline position of all frames on that layer located to the right of the frame(s) you remove.

To Remove Frames

(i) Select a single frame, range of frames, or frame sequence.

(ii) Choose Insert > Remove Frame.

To Reversing Frames, steps are as follows:

Reversing frames will invert the timeline order of a selected span of frames, causing the graphical content of the selected frames to play in reverse.

To Reverse Frames, steps are as follows:

(i) Select a sequence of atleast two frames.

(ii) Choose Modify > Frames > Reverse.

Adding Frame Actions

Frame actions enable your movie to perform a specified action when the timeline reaches a particular frame during playback.

To Add a Frame Action, steps are as follows:

(i) Right-click on the keyframe to which you would like to add an action, and select Actions from the menu that appears.

The Actions panel will appear next.

(ii) Click the Add Action button to add any actions to this frame, then close the Action panel.

Convert Selected Elements to a Symbol

Follow the steps to convert selected elements to a symbol:

(i) Select an element or several elements on the stage.

(ii) Select Modify> Convert To Symbol.

(iii) In the Convert To Symbol dialog box, type the name of the symbol and select the behaviour. Click in the registration grid to position the registration point for the symbol.

(iv) Click OK.

Animate adds the symbol to the library. The selection on the Stage becomes an instance of the symbol.

Once you have created a symbol, you can edit it in symbol edit mode by choosing Edit> Edit Symbols, or you can edit it in the context of the Stage by choosing Edit> Edit In Place. You can also change the registration point of a symbol.

Copying or Pasting a Frame

Do one of the following:

(i) Select the frame or sequence and select Edit> Timeline > Copy Frames. Select the frame or sequence that you want to replace and select Edit> Timeline > Paste Frames.

(ii) Alt+drag a keyframe to the location where you want to copy it.

Labels and Comments

You use frame labels in Flash to identify a particular keyframe in your movie. This is especially useful when assigning frame or button actions to certain frames in your movie. Frame comments allow you to write notes, or comments, in frames of your movie—a good way to remind yourself of the thought process that informed some portion of your movie's timeline. To add a label or comment to a keyframe, steps are as follows:

1. Click the keyframe once to select it.
2. Choose Window > Properties. The Property inspector will appear.
3. In the Frame Label box, enter the text you would like to use as a label for this keyframe. Entering two forward slashes (//) prior to entering any text creates a frame comment instead.
4. Press Return/Enter.

The label or comment will appear on the timeline.

14.10.7 Special Effects

1. Motion Tweening

A motion tween is a feature available in Adobe Flash (formerly Macromedia Flash) that allows you to easily

```
        System.out.println("ELSE");
      }
    }
}
```

(1) If a is true and b is true then the output is "A && B"
(2) If a is true and b is false then the output is "notB"
(3) If a is false and b is true then the output is "ELSE"
(4) If a is false and b is false then the output is "ELSE"

11.
```
public class While
{
  public void loop()
  {
  int x = 0;
  while( 1 ) /* Line 6 */
  {
     System.out.print("x plus one is " + (x +
     1)); /* Line 8 */
  }
  }
}
```

Which statement is true?

(1) There is a syntax error on line 1.
(2) There are syntax errors on lines 1 and 6.
(3) There are syntax errors on lines 1, 6 and 8.
(4) There is a syntax error on line 6.

12. What happens when a class with parameterised constructors and having no default constructor is used in a program and we create an object that needs a zero-argument constructor?

(1) Compile-time error
(2) Preprocessing error
(3) Runtime error
(4) Runtime exception

13. What happens when we try to compile the class definition in following code snippet?

```
class Birds {};
class Peacock : protected Birds{};
```

(1) It will not compile because class body of Birds is not defined.
(2) It will not compile because class body of Peacock is not defined.
(3) It will not compile because a class cannot be protectedly inherited from other class.
(4) It will compile successfully.

14. What does the class definitions in following code represent?

```
class Bike
{
     Engine objEng;
};
class Engine
{
      float CC;
};
```

(1) Kind of relationship
(2) Has a relationship
(3) Inheritance
(4) Polymorphism

15. The DoD model (also called the TCP/IP stack) has four layers. Which layer of the DoD model is equivalent to the network layer of the OSI model?

(1) Application
(2) Host-to-Host
(3) Internet
(4) Network access

16. Routers operate at layer .... LAN switches operate at layer .... Ethernet hubs operate at layer .... Word processing operates at layer ....

(1) 3, 3, 1, 7
(2) 3, 2, 1, none
(3) 3, 2, 1, 7
(4) 3, 3, 2, none

17. As the certkiller network administrator, you are required to have a firm understanding to the OSI model.

Why does the data communication industry use the layered OSI reference model?

(i) It divides the network communication process into smaller and simpler components, thus aiding component development, design and troubleshooting.
(ii) It enables equipment from different vendors to use the same electronic components, thus saving research and development funds.
(iii) It supports the evolution of multiple competing standards and thus provides business opportunities for equipment manufacturers.
(iv) It encourages industry standardisation by defining what functions occur at each layer of the model.

(1) Only (i)
(2) (i) and (iv)
(3) (ii) and (iii)
(4) Only (iii)

18. The OS of a computer may periodically collect all the free memory space to form contiguous block of free space. This is called

(1) concatenation
(2) garbage collection
(3) collision
(4) dynamic memory allocation

19. You have to sort a list L consisting of a sorted list followed by a few "random" elements.

Which of the following sorting methods would be especially suitable for such a task?

(1) Bubble sort
(2) Selection sort
(3) Quick sort
(4) Insertion sort

20. A binary tree in which if all its levels except possibly the last, have the maximum number of nodes and all the nodes at the last level appear as far left as possible, is known as

(1) Heap tree (2) AVL tree
(3) threaded tree (4) complete binary tree

21. Which of the following equations would accurately describe a four-input OR gate when A = 1, B = 1, C = 0, and D = 0?

(1) 1 + 1 + 0 + 0 = 01 (2) 1 + 1 + 0 + 0 = 1
(3) 1 + 1 + 0 + 0 = 0 (4) 1 + 1 + 0 + 0 = 00

22. From the truth table for a three-input NOR gate, what is the only condition of inputs A, B and C that will make the output X high?

(1) A = 1, B = 1, C = 1 (2) A = 1, B = 0, C = 0
(3) A = 0, B = 0, C = 1 (4) A = 0, B = 0, C = 0

23. Which of the following describes the operation of a positive edge triggered D flip-flop?

(1) If both inputs are HIGH, the output will toggle.
(2) The output will follow the input on the leading edge of the clock.
(3) When both inputs are LOW, an invalid state exists.
(4) The input is toggled into the flip-flop on the leading edge of the clock and is passed to the output on the trailing edge of the clock.

24. If both inputs of an SR flip-flop are LOW, what will happen when the clock goes high?

(1) No change will occur in the output.
(2) An invalid state will exist.
(3) The output will toggle.
(4) The output will reset.

25. Which of the following is an important feature of the Sum-of-Products (SOP) form of expression?

(1) All logic circuits are reduced to nothing more than simple AND and OR gates.
(2) The delay times are greatly reduced over other forms.
(3) No signal must pass through more than two gates, not including inverters.
(4) The maximum number of gates that any signal must pass through is reduced by a factor of two.

26. Parity systems are defined as either .... or .... and will add an extra .... to the digital information being transmitted.

(1) positive, negative, byte (2) odd, even, bit
(3) upper, lower, digit (4) on, off, decimal

27. Show from the truth table how an exclusive-OR gate can be used to invert the data on one input if the other input is a special control function.

(1) Using A as the control, when A = 0, X is the same as B. When A = 1, X is the same as B.
(2) Using A as the control, when A = 0, X is the same as B. When A = 1, X is the inverse of B.
(3) Using A as the control, when A = 0, X is the inverse of B. When A = 1, X is the same as B.
(4) Using A as the control, when A = 0, X is the inverse of B. When A = 1, X is the inverse of B.

28. Determine odd parity for each of the following data words:

1011101 11110111 1001101

(1) P = 1, P = 1, P = 0 (2) P = 0, P = 0, P = 0
(3) P = 1, P = 1, P = 1 (4) P = 0, P = 0, P = 1

29. The 2's-complement system is to be used to add the signed binary numbers 11110010 and 11110011. Determine, in decimal, the sign and value of each number and their sum.

(1) –113 and –114, –227 (2) –14 and –13, –27
(3) –11 and –16, –27 (4) –27 and –13, –40

30. Solve this binary problem: 01110010 – 01001000 =

(1) 00011010 (2) 00101010
(3) 01110010 (4) 00111100

31. The bit sequence 0010 is serially entered (right-most bit first) into a 4-bit parallel out shift register that is initially clear. What are the Q outputs after two clock pulses?

(1) 0000 (2) 0010 (3) 1000 (4) 1111

32. What type of register would have a complete binary number shifted in one bit at a time and have all the stored bits shifted out one at a time?

(1) parallel-in, parallel-out (2) parallel-in, serial-out
(3) serial-in, parallel-out (4) serial-in, serial-out

33. Your company has a LAN in its downtown office and has now set-up a LAN in the manufacturing plant in the suburbs. To enable everyone to share data and resources between the two LANs, what type of device(s) are needed to connect them? Choose the most correct answer.

(1) Modem (2) Cable
(3) Hub (4) Router

34. The term 'duplex' refers to the ability of the data receiving stations to echo back a confirming message to the sender. In full duplex data transmission, both the sender and the receiver

(1) cannot talk at once
(2) can receive and send data simultaneously
(3) can send or receive data one at a time
(4) can do one way data transmission only

35. In VBScript, ... loop repeats a group of statements for each item in a collection of objects or for each element of an array.

(1) For (2) Do Until
(3) For Each (4) Do While

f. **Windows Projector (.exe)** This format creates a standalone movie that is playable on any Windows-based operating system without the use of a flash player or Shockwave plug-in, but is a considerably larger file than a swf.

g. **Macintosh Projector (.hqx)** The same as the Windows projector but for Macintosh computers instead. Will create a considerably larger file than a SWF.

h. **Quicktime Movie (.mov)** This format creates a Quicktime standalone movie.

i. **Real Player (.smil)** This format will include in latest version of flash. This media player is compatible with numereous container file formats of the multimedia realm, including MP3, MP4, QuickTime File Format, Windows Media format, and the proprietary RealAudio and RealVideo formats.

An option also appears here is the **Use Default Names** checkbox. If this option is enabled, the SWF and HTML files that are about to be created will be automatically named whatever the original .fla file was labelled as.

Select any types of file depending on the future use. Here, we are select **Flash** and **HTML** formats.

3. After selecting types of file, click on **Flash** tab. In this tab, you can access various options related with the SWF generated files.

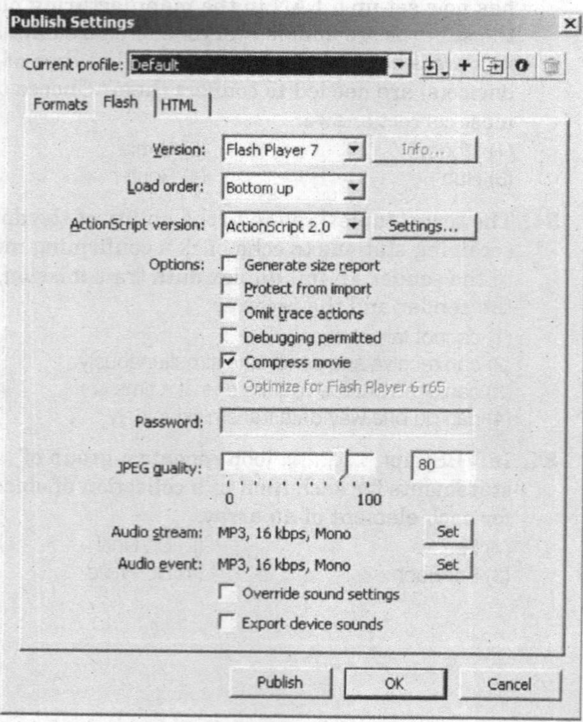

Options are as follows:

a. **Version**: If we want to publish our movie so that it is seen with previous versions of Flash, we must select here the desirable version.

b. **Load Order**: Here we indicate the order in which we want the document to be loaded.
If we select Bottom up the content of the inferior layer will be loaded firstly (from the layer 1 until the last layer that we have in the document).
By the opposite, if we select Top down first the content of the superior layer will be loaded (from the last layer that we have in the document until the first layer).

c. **ActionScript Version**: The use of ActionScript 2.0 will allow us to use the new features relative to objects, classes etc... If our movie uses only simple actions we can leave in this tab the option ActionScript 1.0

d. **Options:**
   i. **Generate size report:** If we activate it, a text file with a detailed relation of the document size will be created.
   ii. **Protect from Import**: Activating this checkbox we'll obtain that when another user wants to import it we can't or must introduce a password if some has been chosen.
   iii. **Omit trace actions**: The trace actions are used to verify the correct operation of the movie during the creation of this (during the tests).
   iv. **Debugging Permitted**: It allows that file SWF can be debugged. It also demands the introduction of a password since a permission of the creator is necessary to Import the file and debug it.
   v. **Compress movie:** Compress the movie as much as possible.

e. **JPEG Quality:** If we haven't indicated a concrete compression in the bitmap properties panel, here we can determine its compression degree that will determine the space token in memory by this type of images. The greater compression, the lesser space in memory that the image will take but its quality also will be smaller.

f. **Audio Stream or Audio Event:** This option allows us to access to the Panel "Sound Settings" from where we can set characteristics for each type of sounds.

g. **Override sound settings:** Having this the selected compression levels for each sound file of our document will be override.

Change above setting as per your requirements.

4. Finally, click on **HTML** tab. This tab allows you to set some aspects of the final HTML file. Some parameters could not be set from here, and you will need to use specific programs like Dreamweaver.

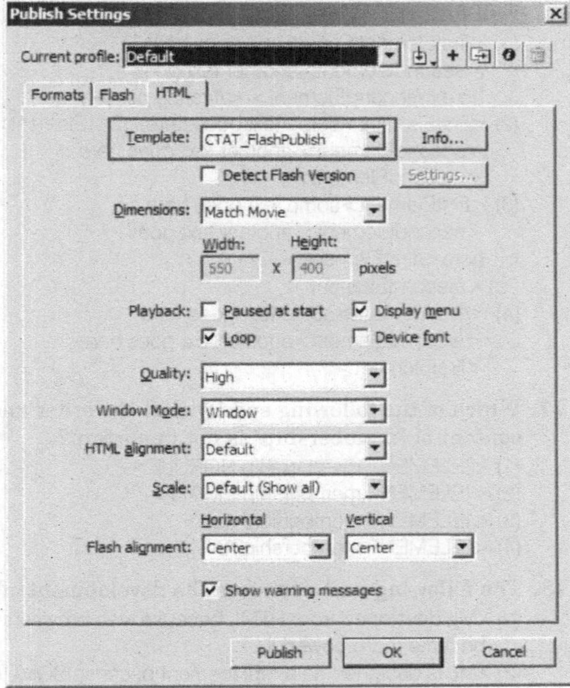

HTML tab options are as follows:

a. **Template**: In order to embed a Flash movie in an HTML document, it is necessary to write a series of program codes that are rather difficult and laborious to do manually.
In order to make this task easier Flash includes Templates that automatically create this code according to the type of publishing we want:
In the button **Info** which it is at the right of the Template option you will find very useful information on each type of template. These are the most common templates: Flash Only, Flash with FSCommand, Image Map, Pocket PC 2003, and QuickTime.

b. **Detect Flash Version**: From here we can select if we want that our movie detects the existence of the Flash plugin in the user's computer.

c. **Dimension**: It specifies the units in which we'll measure the dimensions of the Document.
Width X Height: Here we'll introduce the width and height, taking into account that sometimes an object greater than these dimensions will cause a change in them.

d. **Playback**: It allows to make certain changes in respect to the movie reproduction: Paused at Start, Loop, Display Menu, and Device Font.

e. **Quality**: Here we can modify the quality of our movie. The options are: Low, Autolow, Autohigh, High, and Best.

f. **Window Mode**: Options are applied for the playback inside of the windows of Windows: Window, Opaque Windowless, and Transparent Windowless.

g. **HTML Alignment**: It is the relative position of the movie inside of the Web HTML page. We have several options: Default, Left, Right, Top, and Bottom.

h. **Scale**: If we have specified the size in pixels or in percentage, we can indicate to Flash how to distribute the movie in the rectangle that contains it according to our decision: Default, No Border, and Exact Fit.

i. **Flash Alignment**: It becomes necessary to align the movie when this does not have the same dimensions as the specified rectangle. The options are: Horizontal Alignment and Vertical Alignment.

j. **Show warning Messages**: It allows the possible error messages of Action Script code to be shown.

5. Now you could click on Publish in order to publish your movie with the established settings.
Or you could click on OK to save these settings and publish the movie later. To publish the movie later, we will return to File menu and now finally click on Publish.

The movie will be published, and you will find in your work folder 2 files, one with the HTML code and the SWF movie.

⚠ If you want to publish Flash to only SWF: In Formats tab of Publish Settings dialog box, select a Flash (.swf) checkbox. And the Flash tab of Publish Settings dialog box creates the Flash Player file, also called an .swf file. On this tab only, you specify settings that affect the .swf file.

67. In the signal integrate phase, the differential input voltage between IN LO(input low) and IN HI(input high) pins is integrated by the internal integrator for a fixed period of

(1) 256 clock cycles (2) 1024 clock cycles
(3) 2048 clock cycles (4) 4096 clock cycles

68. Suppose that a bus has 16 data lines and requires 4 cycles of 250 nsecs each to transfer data The bandwidth of this bus would be 2 Megabytes/sec If the cycle time of the bus was reduced to 125 nsecs and the number of cycles required for transfer stayed the same what would the bandwidth of the bus?

(1) 1 Megabyte/sec (2) 4 Megabytes/sec
(3) 8 Megabytes/sec (4) 2 Megabytes/sec

69. The type of the interrupt may be passed to the interrupt structure of CPU from

(1) interrupt service routine (2) stack
(3) interrupt controller (4) register

70. If exploiting and finding parallelism, across branches require scheduling code, a substantially very difficult algorithm is

(1) Global scheduling (2) Local scheduling
(3) Pre scheduling (4) Post scheduling

71. Decimal representation of this binary $(1011)_2$ is

(1) $(9)_{10}$ (2) $(10)_{10}$ (3) $(11)_{10}$ (4) $(1)_{10}$

72. Loops when gets vectored then they do not have dependences among iterations of a loop, which are called

(1) data dependencies (2) control dependencies
(3) loop-control dependencies (4) loop-carried dependencies

73. Addressing mode which is set to index arrays, is applied to indexed addressing mode, in computers is

(1) Register addressing mode
(2) Immediate addressing mode
(3) Scaled addressing mode
(4) Register indirect addressing mode

74. Consider a set of 5 processes whose arrival time, CPU time needed and the priority are given below

Process Priority	*Arrival Time (in ms)*	*CPU Time Needed (in ms)*	*Priority*
P1	0	10	5
P2	0	5	2
P3	2	3	1
P4	5	20	4
P5	10	2	3

Note that smaller the number, higher the priority.

If the CPU scheduling policy FCFS, the average waiting time will be

(1) 12.8 ms (2) 8 ms
(3) 6 ms (4) 10 ms

75. DTD includes the specifications about the markup that can be used within the document, the specifications consists of all EXCEPT

(1) the browser name (2) the size of element name
(3) entity declarations (4) element declarations

76. Which of the following XML documents are well-formed?

(1) <firstElement>some text goes here <secondElement>another text goes here</secondElement> </firstElement>
(2) <firstElement>some text goes here</firstElement> <secondElement> another text goes here </secondElement>
(3) <firstElement>some text goes here <secondElement> another text goes here</firstElement> </secondElement>
(4) </firstElement>some text goes here </secondElement>another text goes here <firstElement>

77. Which of the following specify that the order and content of "membership" is not important?

(1) <!ELEMENT membership NORULE>
(2) <!ELEMENT membership EMPTY>
(3) <!ELEMENT membership ALL>
(4) <!ELEMENT membership ANY>

78. The following best describes the development of XML.

(1) XML developed from HTML because web browsers became more powerful.
(2) XML is designed as a replacement because SGML cannot be used for document development.
(3) XML builds on HTMLs ability to provide content to virtually any audience by adding the power of intelligent content.
(4) XML is the modern replacement for HTML and SGML, taking the good points from each, making both of those languages obsolete.

79. Web links are stored within the page itself and when you wish to "jump" to the page that is linked, we select the hotspot or anchor. This technique is called

(1) hypertext (2) hypermedia
(3) Both (1) and (2) (4) anchoring

80. C++ encourages structuring a software as a collection of components that are

(1) highly cohesive and loosely coupled
(2) not highly cohesive but loosely coupled
(3) highly cohesive and tightly coupled
(4) not highly cohesive but tightly coupled

81. The use of hardware in memory management is through segment relocation and protection is

(1) to perform address translation to reduce size of the memory
(2) to perform address translation to reduce execution time overhead
(3) to perform address translation to increase size of the memory
(4) Both (1) and (2)

82. Which of the following function of String object splits a String object into an array of strings by separating the string into substrings?

(1) slice() (2) split()
(3) replace() (4) search()

83. Which of the following is the correct way for writing JavaScript array?

(1) var salaries = new Array(1:39438, 2:39839 3:83729)
(2) var salaries = new (Array1=39438, Array 2=39839 Array 3=83729)
(3) var salaries = new Array(39438, 39839, 83729)
(4) var salaries = new Array() values = 39438, 39839 83729

84. How does JavaScript store dates in objects of Date type?

(1) The number of days since 1st, 1900
(2) The number of seconds since January 1st, 1970
(3) The number of milliseconds since January 1st, 1970
(4) The number of picoseconds since January 1st, 1970

85. Which of the following code creates an object?

(1) var book = Object(); (2) var book = new Object();
(3) var book = new OBJECT(); (4) var book = new Book();

86. Which of the following is correct about variable declared using 'Dim' in VBScript?

(1) Variables declared using 'Dim' keyword at a Procedure level are available only within the same procedure.
(2) Variables declared using 'Dim' keyword at script level are available to all the procedures within the same script.
(3) Variables declared using 'Dim' keyword at a procedure level are available within or outside the procedure.
(4) Both (1) and (2)

87. Which of the following is a correct way to assign a value to an array element in VBScript?

(1) arr(0) = "VBScript" (2) arr[0] = "VBScript"
(3) arr.set(0,"VBScript") (4) None of these

88. The statement to declare a local variable called Index that will store whole numbers is

(1) Dim Index as WHOLE (2) Dim strIndex as String
(3) Dim Index as Integer (4) Dim Integer as index

89. What is the output of this program?

```
#include <iostream.h>
int main()
{
 int i, j;
 j = 10;
 i = (j++, j + 100, 999 + j);
 cout<<i;
 return 0;
}
```

(1) 1000 (2) 11 (3) 1010 (4) 1001

90. ASP is microsoft technology and is considered to be

(1) less expensive to use because every server has asp loaded on their computer
(2) more expensive because you must purchase a host that has microsoft technology loaded on their server.
(3) the best language to learn for dynamic content
(4) worse than php

91. What's the difference between Response.Write() and Response.Output.Write()?

(1) Response.Output.Write() allows you to flush output
(2) Response.Output.Write() allows you to buffer output
(3) Response.Output.Write() allows you to write formatted output
(4) Response.Output.Write() allows you to stream output

92. ActiveX Data Objects (ADO) comes installed with ASP and allows your pages to easily connect to databases. Which two ADO objects are used to open a connection and interact with the database?

(1) Connection object, RecordingSet object
(2) Connection object, Recordset object
(3) Connect object, RecordingSet object
(4) Connect object, Recordset object

93. In your ASP web application you want to display an image that it selected from a collection of images. What approach will you use to implementing this?

(1) Use the Image Map control and randomly select a Hotspot to show or hide.
(2) Use the Image control to hold this image and a calendar control to randomly select a date for each image to be displayed
(3) Use the AdServer control and create an XML file with configuration of the control
(4) Use an ImageButton control to predict randomness of the image to be loaded based on the clicks of the control.

94. In Photoshop, when using the SAVE AS: feature, the .... file type saves my graphic design with all layers visible for changes upon opening the next time.

(1) .pdf (2) .gif
(3) .psd (4) .jpeg

95. What is the term for an individual dot of color and light that is the basic unit used to create digital images?

(1) Unit (2) Pixel
(3) Swatch (4) Dot

96. Which tool looks like a pointing finger and blends the pixels within the image creating a blurred/blended effect?

(1) Move Tool
(2) Eraser Tool
(3) Gradient Tool
(4) Smudge Tool

60. **Which of the following animation types is also known as path animation?**
(1) AVI (2) Alpha
(3) SWF (4) Vector animation

61. **Adding ...... to objects on your slides not only controls the flow of information but adds interest to your presentation.**
(1) background (2) transition
(3) animation (4) popups

62. **Twirl, ripple and spherize are examples of distortion ...... you may use to change the look of your graphic.**
(1) filters
(2) blending options
(3) image adjustments
(4) layer modes

63. **Luminosity, darken, exclusion and color dodge are examples of .... you may use to allow graphics to interact with background.**
(1) filters
(2) blending options
(3) image adjustments
(4) layer modes

64. **Clouds, motion blur, ocean ripple and plastic wrap are all examples of that can be used in your graphic design.**
(1) Transparency (2) Opacity
(3) Filter (4) Zoom

65. **...... when used appropriately, adds to the viewer's experience, making for a much richer and enjoyable activity.**
(1) Advertisements (2) Sound
(3) Commericals (4) Tweens

66. **Michelle is in the process of adding tweens to her animation. Tweens are a characteristic of what type of animation?**
(1) AVI (2) Alpha
(3) Animation (4) Vector animation

67. **Stuart is playing a video game that has a lot of depth and a very realistic appearance. What type of animation is Stuart enjoying?**
(1) 2D animation
(2) AVI
(3) 3D animation
(4) Vector animation

68. **What is the best type of animation to use for a web-based project that requires a small file size, quick loading and no pixilation?**
(1) Frames Per Second
(2) Vector
(3) MOV
(4) SWF

69. **Dave is animating a ball moving with slight changes on each frame. What type of animation is being used?**
(1) Scenes
(2) Vector
(3) Frames Per Second
(4) Frame-based animation

70. **Steve wants to export his animated movie in a native QuickTime format. What file extension should he choose?**
(1) SWF (2) MOV
(3) GIF (4) .FLA

71. **When selecting an area of pixels to delete, which of the following tools could be used? Choose all that apply. You must select non-correct possibilities.**
(1) Magic wand (2) Marquee
(3) Paint bucket (4) Lasso

72. **When using the SAVE AS: feature, the ...... file type saves my graphic design with all layers visible for changes upon opening the next time. Choose all that apply.**
(1) .pdf (2) .gif
(3) .psd (4) Both (1) and (3)

73. **The visual representation of a project that includes a table of contents as well as a chart of the logical flow of the interactive interface is often called**
(1) a master layout
(2) a navigation map
(3) a workflow diagram
(4) a prototype

74. **...... is a way to partially hide an image in the layer immediately below another layer. The 2 layers get "locked" together to produce the effect.**
(1) Morphing (2) Tweening
(3) Stacking (4) Masking

75. **Jason is defining the target audience for an animation project. This is a component of which phase in the process of producing animation?**
(1) Pre-production (2) Production
(3) Animated GIF (4) Post-production

76. **Rachel is creating an animation that consists of movement defined by computer-generated formulas. What type of animation is being used?**
(1) Animated GIF (2) Vector animation
(3) Alpha (4) Animation

77. **Any item placed on a frame that has not been converted to a graphic, button, or movie clip. This includes shapes you draw as well as images you insert/import (jpg, bitmaps etc.). Use this to do a shape tween or mask effect.**
(1) Layer (2) Vector
(3) Bitmap (4)Object

78. **The process of planning your multimedia presentation is known as**
(1) design (2) storyboard
(3) development (4) layout

ANSWER KEY

1	(3)	2	(1)	3	(4)	4	(4)	5	(1)	6	(2)	7	(1)	8	(1)	9	(1)	10	(3)
11	(1)	12	(1)	13	(2)	14	(1)	15	(4)	16	(1)	17	(2)	18	(4)	19	(4)	20	(2)
21	(2)	22	(1)	23	(4)	24	(2)	25	(3)	26	(1)	27	(2)	28	(4)	29	(4)	30	(1)
31	(2)	32	(4)	33	(4)	34	(2)	35	(2)	36	(1)	37	(3)	38	(2)	39	(4)	40	(1)
41	(2)	42	(2)	43	(2)	44	(2)	45	(2)	46	(4)	47	(1)	48	(4)	49	(4)	50	(4)
51	(2)	52	(1)	53	(2)	54	(3)	55	(3)	56	(2)	57	(3)	58	(4)	59	(1)	60	(4)
61	(3)	62	(1)	63	(4)	64	(3)	65	(2)	66	(4)	67	(3)	68	(3)	69	(4)	70	(2)
71	(3)	72	(4)	73	(2)	74	(1)	75	(1)	76	(2)	77	(3)	78	(3)				

CHAPTER

15

Communication and Network Concepts

15.1 Data Communication

Data communication is the exchange of data between two devices using some form of transmission media. It includes the transfer of data or information and the method of preservation of data during the transfer process.

This transmission of data is done between a centralised computer and remote terminals or between two or more computer centres over established communication links. Data is transferred from one place to another in the form of signals.

There are three types of signals as follows:

1. **Digital Signal** In digital signal, data is transmitted in the electronic form of data, i.e. *binary digits* (0 or 1).
2. **Analog Signal** In analog signal, data is transmitted in the form of radio waves like in telephone line.
3. **Hybrid Signal** Hybrid signals have properties of both analog signal and digital signal.

Communication Channel

The communication channel refers to the direction of signal flow between two linked devices. There are mainly three types of transmission of data as follows:

1. Simplex Channel

In this channel, the flow of data is always in one direction, with no capability to support response in other direction. This communication is unidirectional. Only one of the communicating devices transmits information and the other can only receive it. e.g. Radio, Television, Keyboard etc.

2. Half Duplex Channel

In this channel, the data can flow in both directions, but not at a same time. When one device transmits information, then other can only receive at that point of time. e.g. Walkie–Talkie

3. Full Duplex Channel

In this channel, the flow of data is in both directions at a time, i.e. both stations can transmit and receive information simultaneously. e.g. Wireless handset (mobile phone).

12. Identify the most accurate statement about the application of XML:

(1) XML must be used to produce XML and HTML output.
(2) XML cannot specify or contain presentation information.
(3) XML is used to describe hierarchically organised information.
(4) XML performs the conversion of information between different e-business applications.

13. Consider the declarations

```
char a;
const char aa = 'h';
char *na;
const char *naa;
```

Which of the following statements

Statement I: aa = a;

Statement II: na = &a;

Statement III: na = &aa;

is/are illegal?

(1) I and II
(2) II and III
(3) I and III
(4) All the three statements are illegal

14. Which of the following syntax is correct to refer an external script called "formValidation.js"?

(1) <script href = "formValidation.js">
(2) <script source = "formValidation.js">
(3) <script name = "formValidation.js">
(4) <script src = "formValidation.js">

15. Which of the following is correct about variable declared using 'Private' in VBScript?

(1) Variables that are declared as 'Private' have scope only within that script in which they are declared.
(2) When declaring a variable of type 'Private', Dim keyword is replaced by 'Private'
(3) Both of the above
(4) When declaring a variable of type, Dim keyword is not replaced by 'Private'

16. What will be the output?

```
Void main ()
{
    char *p;
    p = ''Hello'';
    printf (''%C'',*&*p);
}
```

(1) Hello
(2) H
(3) Some address will be printed
(4) None of the above

17. When an .aspx page is requested from the web server, the output will be rendered to browser in following format.

(1) HTML
(2) XML
(3) WML
(4) JSP

18. What happens when a user types in a URL that requests an ASP page?

(1) Browser requests ASP code, server returns code, browser executes code into HTML form
(2) Browser requests ASP code, server executes ASP code and returns HTML document to browser
(3) Browser requests code, server returns code, Windows executes code, since ASP is Microsoft code.
(4) None of the above

19. Some say that JavaScript is easier to use than ASP and will run regardless of whatever operating system the web server is using (Unix, Linux, Windows 2000 etc.) Then others say that ASP has advantages over JavaScript such as what?

(1) ASP does not depend upon which browser the viewer is using.
(2) ASP code does not show up in the source code; thus the code is protected
(3) ASP does not download with the page to the viewer.
(4) All of the above

20. You want to add ASP capability to your company's website. What is the first thing you would check?

(1) That all pages are saved in .asp extensions.
(2) Check that the web server has Microsoft FrontPage extensions installed
(3) Make sure the web server is capable of hosting ASP pages.
(4) Check the coding and be sure the ASP code is surrounded with <% and %>

21. .... is a way to partially hide an image in the layer immediately below another layer. Two layers get "locked" together to produce the effect.

(1) Morphing (2) Tweening (3) Stacking (4) Masking

22. Designed to be an interactive object. You create these so that action scripts can be used to control other objects or events in the movie.

(1) Layer (2) Mask (3) Button (4) Tween

23 Assembly code database is associated with

(1) assembly language version of the program which is created by the code generation phase and is input to the assembly phase.
(2) a permanent table of decision rules in the form of patterns for matching with the uniform symbol table to discover syntactic structure.
(3) consists of a full or partial list or the token's as they appear in the program. Created by Lexical analysis and used for syntax analysis and interpretation.
(4) a permanent table which lists all keywords and special symbols of the language in symbolic form.

24. In which addressing mode, the effective address of the operand is the contents of a register specified in the instruction and after accessing the operand, the contents of this register is incremented to point to the next item in the list?

(1) Index addressing
(2) Indirect addressing
(3) Auto increment
(4) Auto decrement

25. With round robin scheduling algorithm in a time shared system,
(1) using very large time slices converts it into First Come First Served scheduling algorithm.
(2) using very small time slices converts it into First Come First Served scheduling algorithm.
(3) using extremely small time slices increases performance.
(4) using very small time slices converts it into Shortest Job First algorithm.

26. To ensure no preemption, if a process is holding some resources and requests another resource that cannot be immediately allocated to it:
(1) then the process waits for the resources be allocated to it
(2) the process keeps sending requests until the resource is allocated to it
(3) the process resumes execution without the resource being allocated to it
(4) then all resources currently being held are preempted

27. Because the kernel thread management is done by the Operating System itself:
(1) kernel threads are faster to create than user threads
(2) kernel threads are slower to create than user threads
(3) kernel threads are easier to manage as well as create then user threads
(4) None of the above

28. If multiple threads are concurrently searching through a database and one thread returns the result then the remaining threads must be:
(1) continued (2) cancelled
(3) protected (4) None of these

29. Processor architectures use several levels of cache memories to reduce the effective memory access time. Which is the correct match
(i) L1 Cache (a) part of memory chip
(ii) L2 Cache (b) Cache on CPU chip
(iii) L3 Cache (c) Cache external to CPU
(1) (i)-a ii)-b iii)-c (2) (i)-b ii)-c iii)-a
(3) (i)-c ii)-b iii)-a (4) (i)-c ii)-a iii)-b

30. What is the output of this program?

```
class mainclass
{
public static void main(String args[])
{
    char a = 'A';
    a++;
    System.out.print((int) a);
}
}
```

(1) 66 (2) 67 (3) 65 (4) 64

31. With x = 0, which of the following are legal lines of Java code for changing the value of x to 1?
I. x++; II. x = x + 1;
III. x += 1; IV. x =+1;
(1) I, II and III (2) I and IV
(3) I, II, III and IV (4) III and II

32. What should be expression1 evaluate to in using ternary operator as in this line?
expression1 ? expression2 : expressions.
(1) Integer (2) Floating – point numbers
(3) Boolean (4) Object

33. SQL view is said to be updatable (that is, inserts, updates or deletes can be applied on the view) if which of the following conditions are satisfied by the query defining the view?
(1) The from clause has only one database relation.
(2) The query does not have a group by or having clause.
(3) The select clause contains only attribute names of the relation, and does not have any expressions, aggregates, or distinct specification.
(4) All of the mentioned

34. Which of the following can be addressed by enforcing a referential integrity constraint?
(1) All phone numbers must include the area code
(2) Certain fields are required (such as the email address, or phone number) before the record is accepted
(3) Information on the customer must be known before anything can be sold to that customer
(4) When entering an order quantity, the user must input a number and not some text (i.e. 12 rather than 'a dozen')

35. Consider the following action:
Transaction.....
Commit;
Rollback;
What does Rollback do?
(1) Undoes the transactions before commit
(2) Clears all transactions
(3) Redoes the transactions before commit
(4) No action

36. Empdt1(empcode, name, street, city, state pincode). For any pincode, there is only one city and state. Also, for given street, city and state, there is just one pincode. In normalisation terms, empdt1 is a relation in
(1) 1NF only
(2) 2NF and hence also in 1NF
(3) 3NF and hence also in 2NF and 1NF
(4) BCNF and hence also in 3NF, 2NF and 1NF

37. Which one of the following allows a user at one site to establish a connection to another site and then pass keystrokes from local host to remote host?
(1) HTTP (2) FTP (3) Telnet (4) POP3

38. What is the output of this program?

```
#include <iostream.h>
void main()
{
    double a = 21.09399;
    float b = 10.20;
    int c ,d;
```

transmission medium. Some of guided media are given below:

1. Ethernet Cable or Twisted Pair Cable

These are two identical 1mm thick copper wires wrapped together and twisted around each other. These are twisted in order to reduce cross-talk and electro-magnetic induction. The drain of a signal from one cable to another and which can corrupt signals and cause network errors. This form of signal interference is called **crosstalk**. There are two types of twisted pair cables as follows:

(i) **Shielded Twisted Pair** (STP) **Cable** It has shielding of the individual pair of wires, which protects it from external interference and crosstalk.

(ii) **Unshielded Twisted Pair** (UTP) **Cable** It has two unshielded wires twisted around each other. UTP cables are found in many LAN networks and telephone systems.

2. Co-axial Cable

It consists of a solid wire core surrounded by foil shields or conducting braid or wire mesh, each separated by some kind of plastic insulator. The inner solid wire core carries the signal through the network and the shield is used to provide earthing or ground.

Co-axial cable is commonly used in transporting multi-channel television signals in cities. The two most commonly used types of co-axial cable are as follows:

(i) **Thicknet** This form of co-axial cable is thicker than thinnet. The length of thicknet co-axial cable segments can be upto 500 metres long.

(ii) **Thinnet** This form of co-axial cable is thinner and it can maximum segment length of 185 metres, i.e. using this cable, nodes having maximum distance of 185 metres can be joined.

3. Optical Fibre

It consists of thin threads made up of glass or glass like material, which are capable of carrying light signals from a source at one end to another end. At the source, there are either Light Emitting Diodes (LEDs) or Laser Diodes (LDs), which modulate the data into light beam using frequency modulation techniques. At the receiver's end, the signals are demodulated. There are two types of fibre optic cables as follows:

(i) **Single Mode** It supports a segment length of upto 2 kms and bandwidth of upto 100 Mbps.

(ii) **Multi Mode** The maximum segment length of multi mode is upto 100 kms and bandwidth of 2 Gbps.

15.5.2 Unguided Media or Wireless Technologies

When the computers in a network are interconnected and data is transmitted through waves, then they are said to be connected through unguided media. Some of the unguided media are given below:

1. Bluetooth

Bluetooth is used for exchanging data over a short distance from fixed and mobile devices. This comes under Personal Area Network (PAN). The name bluetooth is derived from Harald Bluetooth, a king in Denmark.

2. Infrared

Infrared is the frequency of light that is not visible to human eye. It has a range of wavelengths, just like visible light has wavelengths from red light to violet light. Far infrared waves are thermal. This is the reason why we feel the heat from sunlight, a fire or a radiator. Shorter, near infrared waves are not hot at all infact we cannot even feel them. These shorter wavelengths are the ones used by your TV remotes.

Infrared communication requires a transreceiver (a combination of transmitter and receiver) in both devices that communicate. Infrared communication is playing an important role in wireless data communication due to the popularity of laptop computers, Personal Digital Assistants (PDAs), digital cameras, mobile phones, pagers and other devices but being a line-of-sight transmission, it is sensitive to fog and other atmospheric conditions.

3. Radiowave

When two terminals communicate by using radio frequencies, then such type of communication is known as radiowave transmission. Radiowave transmission set-up has two parts as follows:

(i) Devices which transmit signals are termed as **transmitter**.

(ii) Devices which receive signals are termed as **receiver**.

Both the transmitter and receiver use antennas to radiate and capture the radio signal.

4. Microwave

Another popular transmission medium is the microwave which permits data transmission rates of about 16 gigabits per second. This type of transmission uses high frequency radio signals to transmit data through space. Like radio waves, microwaves can pass through obstacles *viz* buildings, mountains etc. Microwaves offer a line of sight method of communication.

A transmitter and receiver of a microwave system are mounted on very high towers and both should be visible to each other (line of sight). In case of microwave transmission, curvature of the earth, mountains and other structures often block the line of sight. Hence, several repeater stations are required for long distance transmission thereby increasing the cost considerably. It is generally used for long distance telephonic communications.

5. Satellite Communication

Satellites are an essential part of telecommunication systems worldwide today. They can carry a large amount of data in addition to TV signals. When the data is transmitted using satellite then it is said to be satellite communication.

Satellite communication is a special use of microwave transmission system. A satellite is placed precisely at 36000 km above the equator where its orbit speed exactly matches the earth's rotation speed. Hence, it always stays over the same point with respect to the earth. This allows the ground station to aim its antenna at a fixed point in the sky.

The ground station consists of a satellite dish that functions as an antenna and communication equipment to transmit (called Uplink) and receive (called Downlink) data from satellites passing overhead. Such satellites can cost $60 million to build but only three of them are needed to cover the entire earth's surface. Capacity or number of channels used in satellite communications depends on the frequency used. Typical data transfer rates are 1 to 10 Mbps.

Satellites are especially used for remote locations, which are difficult to reach with wired infrastructure. Also, communication and data transfer on Internet, is only possible through satellites.

15.6 Network Devices

Network devices or communication devices are the units that mediate data in a computer network and also called **network equipments**. There are many types of network devices used in networking and some of them are described below:

1. Hub

A hub is a device, used with computer systems to connect several computers together. It acts as a centralised connection to several computers with the central node or server.

It is a multiport device, which provides access to computers. There are two types of hub as follows:

(i) **Active Hub** This acts as repeaters. It amplifies the signal as it moves from one device to another.

(ii) **Passive Hub** This simply passes the signal from one connected device to another.

2. Switch

A switch is a hardware device, which is used to connect devices or segments of the network into smaller subsets of LAN segments.

The main purpose of segmenting is to prevent the traffic overloading in a network. Switch forwards a data packet to a specific route by establishing a temporary connection between the source and the destination. After the transmission or once the conversation is done, the connection is terminated. There is a vast difference between switch and hub. A hub forward each incoming packet (data) to all the hub ports, while a switch forwards each incoming packet to the specified recipient.

3. Repeater

Repeater is a hardware device. It is used to amplify the feeble signals when they are transported over a long distance. The basic function of a repeater is to amplify the incoming signal and retransmit it, to the other device.

Repeaters are of two types as follows:

(i) **Amplifier** It amplifies or boosts the incoming signals. So, it amplifies both the signal and any concurrent noise.

(ii) **Signal Repeater** This only amplifies the signal and filters out the noise signals. So, we get only the clear signals at the receiver end.

4. Gateway

A gateway is a device, which is used to connect dissimilar networks. The gateway establishes an intelligent connection between a local network and external networks, which are completely different in structure.

5. Bridge

Bridges serve a similar function as switches. A bridge filters data traffic at a network boundary. Bridges reduce the amount of traffic on a LAN by dividing it into two segments.

Traditional bridges support one network boundary, whereas switches usually offer four or more hardware ports. Switches are sometimes called **multiport bridges**.

6. Router

Router is a hardware device, which is designed to take incoming packets, analyse the packets, moving the packets to another network, converting the packets to another network interface, dropping the packets, directing packets to the appropriate locations etc. Routers are called **hop in the series.**

60. The following statements are about three important browser objects in JavaScript.

I. window object : The highest of all objects in the client-side JavaScript object hierarchy.

II. navigator object : A collection of information about the browser. Useful in browser sniffing.

III. document object : Provides access to the document being viewed.

Which of the above statements is/are true?

(1) Only (I) (2) Only (II)
(3) Only (III) (4) All (I), (II) and (III)

61. Assume that an HTML form is designed to purchase the furniture. All the items required are being checked. After selecting the items, the payment details are entered and the submit button is pressed. From the following options which one would you prefer to send the data to the server. Assume that all the security is handled.

(1) Only POST (2) Only GET
(3) Either of GET or POST (4) Neither GET nor POST

62. Suppose that the selector in a Selelct case block is the string variable myVar. Which of the following is not a valid case clause?

(1) Case Adams
(2) Case "739"
(3) Case (myVar. Substring (0,1)
(4) Case myVar.Length

63. Suppose a variable is passed by reference to a parameter of a Sub procedure, and the parameter has its value changed inside the Sub procedure. What will the value of the variable be after the Sub procedure has executed?

(1) It will have the newly modified value from inside the Sub procedure.
(2) Its value cannot be determined without more information
(3) It will retain the value it had before the call to the Sub procedure
(4) It will have the addition of value before the call and newly modified after the call.

64. Suppose the variable myName is declared in a Dim statement in two different Sub procedures. Which statement is true?

(1) The program will malfunction when it is executed
(2) When the value of myName is changed in one Sub procedure, it will also be changed in the other Sub procedure.
(3) Visual Basic's smart editor will alert you that this is an error before the program is executed.
(4) The two variables will be local to their respective Sub procedures.

65. Which of the following access modifier specifies that one or more declared programming elements are accessible only from within their declaration context, including from within any contained types?

(1) Private (2) Protected
(3) Public (4) ReadOnly

66. In your ASP web application you want to display a list of clients on a web page. The client list displays 10 clients at a time, and you require the ability to edit the clients. Which web control is the best choice for this scenario?

(1) The DetailsView control (2) The Table control
(3) The GridView control (4) The FormView control

67. The postfix expression for * + a b-c d is?

(1) ab + cd - * (2) ab cd + - *
(3) ab + cd * - (4) ab + - cd *

68. From the truth table below, determine the standard SOP expression:

Inputs			*Output*
A	B	C	X
0	0	0	0
0	0	1	1
0	1	0	0
0	1	1	1
1	0	0	0
1	0	1	0
1	1	0	1
1	1	1	0

(1) $X = \overline{A}\,\overline{B}\,\overline{C} + ABC + A\overline{B}C$
(2) $X = ABC + ABC + ABC$
(3) $X = A\overline{B}C + \overline{A}BC + AB\overline{C}$
(4) $X + \overline{A}\overline{B}C + \overline{A}BC + AB\overline{C}$

69. In 2's complement representation, if two numbers with the same sign are added, then

(1) overflow occur if and only if the result has the opposite sign
(2) overflow occur if and only if the result has same sign
(3) overflow does not occur
(4) overflow occur but it does not depend on sign.

70. Consider the following floating point number representation

31 24	23 0
Exponent	Mantissa

The exponent is in 2's complement representation and mantissa is in the sign magnitude representation. The range of the magnitude of the normalised number in this representation is

(1) 0 to 1 (2) 0.5 to 1
(3) 2^{-23} to 0.5 (4) 0.5 to $(1 - 2^{-23})$

71. Match the following:

a. Immediate address mode	1. local variables
b. Direct address mode	2. Relocatable program
c. Indirect address mode	3. Pointers
d. Index address mode	4. Locality of references
e. Base address mode	5. Arrays
f. Relative address mode	6. Constant operands

(1) a-6, b-1, c-3, d-5, e-2, f-4 (2) a-5, b-4, c-6, d-3, e-1, f-2
(3) a-3; b-5, c-2, d-4, e-1, f-6 (4) a-6, b-5, c-2, d-3, e-1, f-4

72. Consider the following statements

S_1: 2 words with the same index in their address bus with different tag values cannot reside in cache at the same time in direct mapping strategy.

S_2: The fastest and most flexible cache organisation uses associative memory.

Which of the following is true?

(1) S_1 (2) S_2 (3) S_1 and S_2 (4) Can't say

73. In a network of LAN's connected by bridges, packets are sent from one LAN to another through intermediate bridges. Since, more than one path may exist between two LANs, packets may have to be routed through multiple bridges. Why is the spanning tree algorithm used for bridge-routing?

(1) For shortest path routing between LANs
(2) For avoiding loops in the routing paths
(3) For fault tolerance
(4) For minimizing collisions

74. Which of the following property of a table element specifies whether the browser should control the appearance of the adjacent borders that touch each other or whether each cell should maintain its style?

(1) border-collapse (2) border-spacing
(3) caption-side (4) empty-cells

75. If following tree is used for sorting, then new node labelled 8 should be placed as the

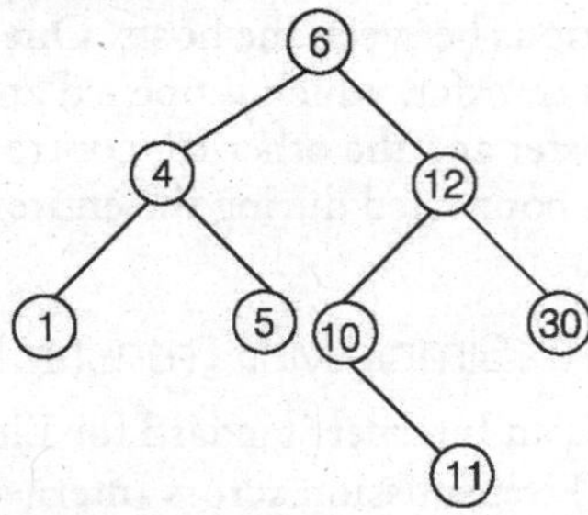

(1) left child of the node labelled 30
(2) right child of the node labelled 5
(3) right child of the node labelled 30
(4) left child of the node labelled 10

76. A sort which iteratively passes through a list to exchange the first element with any element less than it and then repeats with a new first element is called

(1) insertion sort (2) selection sort
(3) heap sort (4) quick sort

77. If the binary search algorithm determines that the search argument is in the lower half of the array, which of the following statements will, set the appropriate variable to the appropriate value?

(1) startSub = middleSub - 1; (2) startSub = middleSub + 1;
(3) stopSub = middleSub - 1; (4) stopSub = middleSub + 1;

78. Which of the following refers to dangerous programs that can be 'caught' by opening E-mail attachments and downloading software from the Internet?

(1) Spam (2) Utility
(3) Honey pot (4) Virus

79. When specifying the source of an image referenced in your HTML document, the image should

(1) either be within the same folder as the HTML page, or the complete path name should be specified.
(2) be located on the flashdrive in use
(3) be sized appropriately on the HTML page in order to fit
(4) be of a format that HTML can recognise and manipulate

80. To reference a web page called web_1.htm to be displayed in a frame which of the following tags would be used?

(1) The tag - frame src="web_1.ht"
(2) The tag - frame src="web_1.htm"
(3) The tag - frameset src="web_1.ht"
(4) The tag - frameset src="web_1.html"

81. The frameset column size value can be set in pixels (cols="200, 500"), and one of the columns can be set to use the remaining space using a wildcard asterisk * for the actual value. Which of the following would be appropriate for a 3 column using a wildcard?

(1)The tag ("3 column, 200, *, *")
(2)The tag - frameset cols="500,200,300"
(3)The tag - frameset cols= "200,*,250"
(4)The tag - frameset cols= "50%,250,*"

82. A clickable link that takes you from one document to another, or to any resource, even within the same document, with text that is highlighted in some fashion is called

(1) locator
(2) URL
(3) protocol
(4) hyperlink

83. The .... is a set of standards that defines how a dynamic web document should be written, how input data should be supplied to the program, and how the output result should be used.

(1) HyperText Transfer Protocol
(2) File Transfer Protocol
(3) HyperText Markup Language
(4) Common Gateway Interface

84. Consider the following statements:

Statement A: In duplex transmission, either node can transmit while the other node can receive data

Statement B: In half-duplex transmission, both the nodes can transmit as well as receive data at the same time.

Which of the following is true with respect to the above statements?

(1) Both statements A and B are false
(2) Statement A is false and statement B is true
(3) Both statements A and B are true
(4) Statement A is true and statement B is false

phone lines, satellite links, high speed fibre optic cables and data packet carrier services.

Wide area networking can be as simple as a modem and remote access server for employees to dial into, or it can be as complex as hundreds of branch offices globally linked using special routing protocols and filters to minimise the expense of sending data sent over vast distances.

Let us take an example of your local telephone exchange which is a part of WAN. The computers at each telephone exchange connect to other exchanges to allow you to talk to people all over the world. The Internet is the largest WAN , spanning the entire earth.

15.9 Network Protocols

Protocol refers to the set of rules applicable for a network. The protocol defines standardised format for the data packet to be transmitted through the network. Some of the commonly used protocols are as follows:

1. HTTP (HyperText Transfer Protocol)

HTTP is an application layer protocol. It is widely used protocol. This protocol is used by the world wide web. HTTP defines how messages are formatted and transmitted and what actions web servers and browsers should take in response to various commands. It is a request/response standard between a client (end-user) and a server (website).

e.g. when you enter a URL in your browser, this actually sends an HTTP command to the web server directly to fetch and transmit the requested web page. It is generic, stateless and object oriented protocol.

2. TCP/IP (Transmission Control Protocol/Internet Protocol)

TCP/IP is the communication protocol for the Internet. It defines the rules, computers must follow to communicate with each other over the Internet. The TCP/IP is a protocol used in E-mail transmission. Infact, it is a set of protocol, i.e. TCP and IP.

The TCP/IP is a protocol, which is responsible for finding path for the destination. It also splits the message into several datagrams, if it does not fit in one datagram. Therefore, these datagrams are sent through different alternate paths towards the destination. The TCP makes sure that the datagram arrives at the destination correctly. While IP is responsible for moving packet of data from source to destination. It handles the address part of each packet so that it reaches to the right destination.

3. PPP (Point-to-Point Protocol)

It is a data link layer protocol, which encapsulates other network layer protocols for transmission on synchronous and asynchronous communication lines.

The PPP is used with dial-up Internet connections including ISDN. It is a layered protocol, which is used for transmitting the IP data packets over usual telephone lines. It encapsulates packets into PPP frames and then forwards them to the server over the serial transmission lines.

PPP defines the format of frame to be exchanged between devices on one or multiple links and also defines the authenticity of the two devices.

There are three layers of PPP as follows:

(i) **LCP** (Link Control Protocol) LCP establishes the link between the source and destination.

(ii) **NCP** (Network Control Protocol) NCP controls and transports the traffic.

(iii) **IPCP** (Internet Protocol Control Protocol) IPCP permits the transformation of IP packets over the established PPP link.

4. FTP (File Transfer Protocol)

It is a standard network protocol used to transfer files from one host to another host over a TCP-based network, such as the Internet.

FTP is based on client/server principle. It establishes two connections between the hosts. One connection is used for data transfer, which is opened and closed for each file transfer and the other for control information, which remains connected during the entire interactive FTP session.

5. SMTP (Simple Mail Transfer Protocol)

SMTP is an Internet standard for Electronic mail (E-mail) transmission across Internet Protocol (IP) networks. SMTP was first defined by RFC 821 (1982) and last updated by RFC 5321 (2008), which includes the extended SMTP additions and is the protocol in widespread use today.

Most E-mail software are designed to use SMTP for communication purposes when sending E-mail. Another purpose of SMTP is to set-up communication rules between servers.

6. Remote Login (Telnet)

Telnet is a protocol used for creating a connection with a remote computer. Once your telnet client establishes a connection to the remote host, telnet client becomes a virtual terminal, allowing you to communicate with the remote host from your computer. It establishes a connection either with command line client or with a programmatic interface. Telnet provides an error free connection, which is always faster than the latest conventional modems.

15.10 OSI Model

Open System Interconnection (OSI) is a standard reference model for communication between two end users in a network. In 1983, the International Standards Organisation (ISO) published a document called *Basic Reference Model for Open System Interconnection*, which visualises network protocols as a seven layered model.

It is a layered framework for the design of network system that allows communication between all types of computer system. It is mainly consists of seven layers across a network *as shown in table*.

Seven layers of OSI model and their functions

Name of the Layer	Functions
Application Layer (User-Interface)	Retransferring files of information, login, password checking, packet filtering etc.
Presentation Layer (Data formatting)	It works as a translating layer, i.e. encryption or decryption.
Session Layer (Establish and maintain connection)	To manage and synchronise conversation between two systems . It controls logging ON and OFF, user identification, billing and session management.
Transport Layer [Transmission Control Protocol (TCP) accurate data]	It decides whether transmission should be parallel or single path, multiplexing, splitting or segmenting the data, to break data into smaller units for efficient handling, packet filtering.
Network Layer [Internet Protocol (IP) routers]	Routing of the signals, divide the outgoing message into packets, to act as network controller for routing data.
Data Link Layer [Media Access Control (MAC) switches]	Synchronisation, error detection and correction. To assemble outgoing messages into frames.
Physical Layer [Signals-cables or operated by repeater]	Make and break connections, define voltages and data rates, convert data bits into electrical signal. Decide whether transmission is simplex, half duplex or full duplex.

⚠ In OSI model, physical layer is the *lowest layer* which is implemented on both hardware and software and application layer is the *highest layer*.

15.11 Mobile Computing

Mobile computing means that the computing device is not continuously connected to the base or central network. Mobile devices include PDAs, laptop, computers and many of today's cell phones. These products may communicate with a base location with or without a wireless connection.

15.11.1 Mobile Computing Technologies

Some common mobile computing tectinologies are as follows:

1. GSM

GSM (Global System for Mobile Communication, originally Group Special Mobile) is a standard set developed by the European Telecommunications Standards Institute (ETSI) to describe protocols for second generation (2G) digital cellular networks used by mobile phones.

The GSM standard was developed as a replacement of first generation (1G) analog cellular networks and originally described a digital, circuit switched network optimised for full duplex voice telephony. This was expanded over time to include data communications, first by circuit switched transport, then packet data transport *via* GPRS (General Packet Radio Services) and EDGE (Enhanced Data rates for GSM Evolution or EGPRS).

GSM network is divided into three systems as follows:

(i) Switching System (SS)
(ii) Base Switching System (BSS)
(iii) Operation and Support System (OSS)

"GSM" is a trademark owned by the GSM Association.

2. CDMA

Code Division Multiple Access (CDMA) is a channel access method used by various radio communication technologies.

One of the concept in data communication is the idea of allowing several transmitters to send information simultaneously over a single communication channel. CDMA employs spread-spectrum technology and a special coding scheme (where each transmitter is assigned a code) to allow multiple users to be multiplexed over the same physical channel. In this, each user is allocated a unique code sequence.

On the sender's end, the data signal is encoded using the given unique code. The receiver decodes the signal according the unique code and recovers the original data. By contrast, **Time Division Multiple Access** (TDMA) divides by access time, while **Frequency Division Multiple Access** (FDMA) divides it by frequency.

3. GPRS

General Packet Radio Services (GPRS) is a packet oriented mobile data service on the 2G and 3G cellular communication system's Global System for Mobile (GSM) communication. GPRS usage is typically charged that is based on volume of data transferred, contrasting with circuit switched data, which is usually billed per minute of connection time. GPRS data may be sold either as part of a bundle (e.g. up to 5 GB per month for a fixed fee) or on a pay as you use basis.

15.13.2 **eXtensible Markup Language** (XML)

XML is a markup language that defines a set of rules for encoding documents in a format, that is both human-readable and machine-readable. It is defined in the XML 1.0 specification produced by the W3C and several other related specifications.

The design goals of XML emphasise simplicity, generality and usability over the Internet. The design of XML focuses on documents, it is widely used for the representation of arbitrary data structures.

15.13.3 **Domain Name**

A domain name is a unique name that identifies a particular website and represents the name of the server, where the web pages store. Domain names are formed by the rules and procedures of the Domain Name System (DNS). Domain names are used in various networking contexts and application specific naming and addressing purposes. In general, a domain name represents an Internet Protocol (IP) resource, such as a personal computer used to access the Internet, a server computer hosting a website or the website itself or any other service communicated *via* the Internet.

Domain Name System (DNS)

DNS stores and associates many types of information with domain names, but most importantly, it translates domain names (computers host names) to IP addresses.

15.13.4 **Uniform Resource Locator** (URL)

A URL, also known as **web address**, is a specific character string that constitutes a reference to a resource. In most web browsers, the URL of a web page is displayed on top inside an address bar. A URL is a formatted text string used by web browsers, E-mail clients and other software to identify a network resource on the Internet. Network resources are files that can be plain web pages, other text documents, graphics or programs.

URL consists of three parts as follows:

(i) Network protocol (ii) Host name or address

(iii) File or resource location.

These parts are separated by special characters as follows:

```
Protocol://host/location
```

An example of a typical URL would be:

```
"http://en.example.org/wiki/Main_Page".
```

15.13.5 **IP Address** (Internet Protocol Address)

The Internet Protocol (IP) is the method or protocol by which data is sent from one computer to another on the Internet. Each computer (known as a **host**) on the Internet has atleast one IP address that uniquely identifies it from all other computers on the Internet. When you send or receive data (e.g. an E-mail note or a web page), the message gets divided into little chunks called **packets**. Each of these packets contains both the sender's address and the receiver's address.

Any packet is sent first to a gateway computer that understands a small part of the Internet. The gateway computer reads the destination address and forwards packet to an adjacent gateway that in turn reads the destination address and so forth across the Internet until one gateway recognises the packet as belonging to a computer within its immediate neighbourhood or domain. That gateway then forwards the packet directly to the computer, whose address is specified.

15.13.6 **Web Page**

Web page is an electronic document designed using HTML. It displays information in textual or graphical form. Traversal from one web page to another web page is possible through hyperlinks. A web page can be of two types:

1. Static Web Page

A web page which displays same kind of information whenever a user visits, it is known as a static web page. A static web page generally has .htm or .html as extension.

2. Dynamic Web Page

An interactive web page is a dynamic web page. A dynamic web page uses scripting languages to display changing content on the web page. Such a page generally has .php, .asp or .jsp as extension.

15.13.7 **Website**

A website, also written as site is a set of related web pages served from a single web domain. A website is hosted on atleast one web server, accessible *via* a network such as the Internet or a private local area network through an Internet address known as a **Uniform Resource Locator** (URL). All publicly accessible websites collectively constitute the World Wide Web (WWW).

15.13.8 **Web Browser**

A web browser (commonly referred to as a **browser**) is a software application for retrieving, presenting and traversing information resources on the World Wide Web. An information resource is identified by a Uniform Resource Identifier (URI) and may be a web page, image, video or other piece of content. Hyperlinks present in resources enable users easily to navigate their browsers to related resources. Although, browsers are primarily intended to use the World Wide Web, they can also be used to access information provided by web servers in private networks or files in file systems. The major web browsers are Google Chrome, Firefox, Internet Explorer, Opera and Safari.

15.13.9 Web Server

The term web server can refer to either the hardware (the computer) or the software (the computer application) that helps to deliver web content, accessible through the Internet. The most common use of web server is to host websites, but there are other uses such as gaming, data storage or running enterprise applications.

Any computer can be turned into a web server by installing server software and connecting the machine to the Internet. There are many web server software applications including public domain software from NCSA and Apache and commercial packages from Microsoft, Netscape and others.

15.13.10 Web Hosting

A web hosting service is a type of Internet hosting service that allows individuals and organisations to make their website accessible *via* the World Wide Web.

A web host is in the business of providing server space, web services and file maintenance for websites controlled by individuals or companies that do not have their own web servers. Many ISPs, such as America Online will allow subscribers a small amount of server space to host a personal web page. Other commercial ISPs will charge the user a fee depending on the complexity of the site being hosted. Web hosting can be of four types as follows:

(i) Free hosting (ii) Virtual or shared hosting
(iii) Dedicated hosting (iv) Co-location hosting.

⚠ **E-Commerce** includes sharing business information, maintaining business relationships and conducting business transactions by means of telecommunication networks or process of trading goods over the Internet.

15.14 Network Security Concepts

Networking offers so many facilities to protect the network from unauthorised access and misuse of network resources. But, alongwith the benefits it involves certain risks as well.

15.14.1 Malware (Threats of Computer Security)

Malware includes computer viruses, computer worms, ransomware, trojan horses, keyloggers, most rootkits, spyware, dishonest adware, malicious BHOs and other malicious softwares. Some of them are described below:

1. Computer Virus

A computer virus is a software program that can replicate itself and spread from one computer to another. It is designed to infect the host program and gain control over the system without the owner's knowledge. They can spread through external media such as CDs, browsing infected Internet sites and from E-mail attachments.

⚠ The Creeper virus was first virus detected on ARPANET. Creeper was an experimental self-replicating program written by Bob Thomas at BBN Technologies in 1971.

2. Computer Worm

A computer worm is a stand-alone malware computer program that replicates itself in order to spread to other computers. It resides in active memory. It uses parts of an OS that are automatic and usually invisible to the user. Often, it uses a computer network to spread itself, relying on security failures on the target computer to access it.

Unlike a computer virus, it does not need to attach itself to an existing program. Worms almost always cause atleast some harm to the network, even if only by consuming bandwidth, whereas viruses almost always corrupt or modify files on a targeted computer.

3. Trojan Horse

A trojan horse or trojan, is a non-self replicating type of malware, which appears to perform a desirable function but instead facilitates unauthorised access to the user's computer system.

Trojans do not attempt to inject themselves into other files like a computer virus. Trojan horses may steal information or harm their host computer systems. These are actually programmed to pass the user's data or access rights to someone else.

Trojans may use drive by downloads or install *via* online games or Internet-driven applications in order to reach target computers.

The term is derived from the Tojan horse story in Greek mythology because Trojan horses employ a form of '**social engineering**,' presenting themselves as harmless, useful gifts, in order to persuade victims to install them on their computers.

4. Spam

Spam is flooding the Internet with many copies of the same message. It is an attempt to force the message on people who would not otherwise choose to receive it. Spam is commercial advertising, often for dubious products, get-rich-quick schemes or quasi legal services.